Documents in World History

VOLUME 2

DOCUMENTS IN WORLD HISTORY

Volume 2

The Modern Centuries: From 1500 to Present

THIRD EDITION

Peter N. Stearns
George Mason University

Stephen S. Gosch
University of Wisconsin, Eau Claire

Erwin P. Grieshaber
Mankato State University

Longman

New York   San Fransisco   Boston
London   Toronto   Sydney   Tokyo   Singapore   Madrid
Mexico City   Munich   Paris   Capetown   Hong Kong   Montreal

Vice President/Publisher: Priscilla McGeehon
Acquisitions Editor: Erika Gutierrez
Executive Marketing Manager: Sue Westmoreland
Production Manager: Denise Phillip
Project Coordination, Text Design, and Electronic Page Makeup: WestWords, Inc.
Cover Designer/Manager: Wendy Ann Fredericks
Cover Photos: *Frame:* © PhotoDisc; *Art:* Arrival of a Foreigner (center) in India, 17th Century. © The Granger Collection, New York.
Photo Researcher: WestWords, Inc.
Manufacturing Buyer: Al Dorsey
Printer and Binder: Hamilton Printers
Cover Printer: Coral Graphics

Library of Congress Cataloging-in-Publication Data

Documents in world history / [selected by] Peter N. Stearns, Stephen S. Gosch, Erwin P. Grieshaber.— 3rd ed.
   p. cm.
  Contents: v. 2. The Modern Centuries: From 1500 to Present.
  ISBN 0-321-10054-9
  1. World history—Sources.   I. Stearns, Peter N. II. Gosch, Stephen S. (Stephen Spencer), 1941– III. Grieshaber, Erwin P. (Erwin Peter), 1943–

D5 .D623 2002b
909—dc21

2002066112

Please visit our website at http://www.ablongman.com

ISBN 0-321-10054-9

5 6 7 8 9 10—HT—05 04 03

Contents

Geographical Contents: The Major Societies

Sub-Saharan Africa

Topical Contents

Social Structure

Women and the Family

Economic Relations

Preface

This volume focuses on the major currents in the development of the modern world—not just the American or Western world, but the wider world in which we live today. It deals with the interaction between established civilizations and new forces of change, many of them springing from intensifications of international commerce and the results of industrialization. It also deals with the impact of change on loyalties and beliefs, on social institutions and the conditions of various groups such as workers and women, and on the activities and the organization of the state.

The book examines the formation of the modern world not through an overview or through scholarly interpretation, but by presenting primary sources—that is, documents written at the time. Such an approach is inherently selective, leaving many important developments out; and it is meant to be combined with some kind of textbook coverage. But primary source materials do convey elements of the flavor and tensions of history in the making that cannot be captured by a progression of names, dates, and main events or trends. The book presents what people—great and ordinary—expressed in various societies in the modern periods, and it challenges the reader to distill the meaning of these expressions.

The various documents offered illustrate characteristic features of key civilizations in the major modern stages of world history from about 1500 C.E. to the present. These documents were not written for posterity; some were not even intended for a wide audience at the time. They are collected here to raise issues of understanding and interpretation that can enliven and enrich the study of world history.

The book covers several key facets of the human experience, again in various times and places. It deals with the organization and functions of the state. It treats philosophy and religion and, at points, literature and science. It explores contacts among civilizations, particularly the diverse impacts of Western imperialism and international commercial expansion and heightened cultural interchange in recent centuries. It also deals with families and women and with issues of social structure.

The book's organization facilitates relating it to a core textbook. Major civilizations—East Asia, the West, India, the Middle East, Eastern Europe, Africa, and Latin America—are represented with several readings. Thus a course can trace elements of change and continuity within each civilization. The readings are divided into three modern periods: 1500 to 1750, during which the rise of the West and diverse reactions to the rise formed a central thread in world history; 1750 to

1914, a century dominated by new patterns of manufacturing, new international technologies for transportation and communication, and new cultural forces such as nationalism; and the twentieth century, during which Western influence continued strong but the other major civilizations also began to find their own distinctive modern voices.

The goal of the book is not, however, maximum coverage. Many interesting and significant documents are left out, of necessity. Readings have been chosen that illustrate important features of an area or period, that raise challenging problems of interpretation, and that express some human drama. The readings also invite comparisons across cultures and over time. Chapter introductions not only identify the readings but also raise some issues that can be explored. Study Questions at the end of each chapter further facilitate an understanding of issues.

This book was prepared by three world history teachers at work in several kinds of institutions. It is meant, correspondingly, to serve the needs of different kinds of students. It is motivated by two common purposes: First, a strong belief that some perspective on the world is both desirable and possible as a key element in contemporary American education; and second, that an understanding of world history can be greatly enhanced by exposure not just to an overall factual and interpretive framework but also to the kinds of challenges and insights raised by primary materials.

Dealing with primary sources is not an easy task. Precisely because the materials are not written with American college students in mind, they require some thought. They must be related to other elements we know about a particular society; they must be given meaning; and they must be evaluated more carefully than a secondary account or textbook designed deliberately to pinpoint what should be learned. By the same token, however, gaining ease with the meaning of primary sources is a skill that carries well beyond a survey history course, into all sorts of research endeavors. Gaining such skill in the context of the civilizations that compose the world goes some distance toward understanding how our world has become what it is—which is, in essence, the central purpose of history.

Thanks go to the reviewers of this and previous editions. They are Professor Brandon H. Beck, Shenandoah University; Professor Jolane Culhane, Western New Mexico University; Professor Susan Hult, Houston Community College Central; Professor Richard Kornweibel, California State University; Professor Gary Land, Andrews University; Mary Lauranne Lifka, Lewis University; Professor Robert B. McCormick, Newman University; Professor Robert Patch, University of California; Professor William Rodner, Tidewater Community College; Professor Arthur Schmidt, Temple University; Professor Marvin Slind, Washington State University; and Professor Andrew Zimmerman, University of California-San Diego.

Peter N. Stearns
Stephen S. Gosch
Erwin P. Grieshaber

Introduction

The past five centuries have been a busy time in world history. Many Americans, accustomed to a culture that emphasizes change, believe the modern age has witnessed more fundamental shifts, coming at a more rapid pace, than any other time in the human past. Although the notion of accelerating change may be somewhat exaggerated, it is true that relationships among major areas of the world (including the gradual integration of the Americas into a wide network), basic technologies, belief systems, forms of government, and even fundamental ingredients of daily life have changed mightily, not only in the United States and Western civilization but in every major society in the world. This volume, with selected documents on a number of significant areas of change, conveys something of the flavor of the modern world in transition.

The need to study world history becomes increasingly apparent. Although the twentieth century was hailed as the "American century," it is obvious that even given the United States' claim to some world leadership, it must interact with various other societies and, in part, on their terms. As a power with worldwide military responsibilities or aspirations, the United States maintains increasingly close diplomatic contacts with all the inhabited continents. Economically, American reliance on exports and imports—once a minor footnote to this nation's industrial vigor—grows greater every year. Cultural influences from abroad are significant. Even though the United States remains a leading exporter of consumer fads and styles, we can see among the American people cultural standards imported from Europe, joined with interest in various schools of Buddhism or a fascination with Japan's gifts at social coordination. Even the composition of the U.S. population reflects growing worldwide contacts. The United States is now experiencing its highest rates of immigration ever, with new arrivals from Latin America and various parts of Asia joining earlier immigrant groups from Europe and Africa.

Enmeshed in this world, shaping it but also shaped by it, U.S. citizens need to know something of how that world has been formed and what major historical forces created its diversities and contacts. We need to know, in sum, something about world history. Study of our own past—that is, U.S. history—or even the larger history of Western civilization from which many American institutions and values spring, risks now being unduly narrow. This explains why the study of world history is receiving renewed attention.

A danger exists, however, in emphasizing the need to study world history too piously. True, growing global interdependence and communication make knowledge of past world patterns increasingly essential as the basis for interpreting policy options open to the United States or American business—or simply for grasping the daily headlines in more than a superficial manner. The mission, however, of a world history course does not rest entirely on the desire to create a more informed and mature citizenry. It can also rest directly on the intrinsic interest and the analytical challenge world history offers.

The modern centuries in particular involve a growing drama of confrontation between deeply rooted, highly valued, and often successful cultural forms and some common forces of change. Over the past 700 years, all the major civilizations have encountered growing pressures from new ideas and institutions, often initially generated in Europe or the United States—and often brute force and commercial exploitation from the West as well. During the past century (and in some cases longer) these same civilizations have tried to take into account the new technologies springing from industrialization; new ways of thinking shaped by modern science and belief systems such as nationalism and socialism; the need to reshape government functions and the contacts between government and citizens; and pressures to redefine the family to allow for children's formal education, new roles for women, and often a reduction in traditional birthrates. The modern drama, played out in different specific ways depending on region, has involved combining some of the common, worldwide pressures with retention of vital continuities from the past.

The varieties of response have been considerable because the variety of established cultures is great. Some societies, often after experimenting with other responses, copied Western technologies and organizations sufficiently to industrialize while maintaining their own identities in part. Other societies have faced greater problems in matching the West's industrial might. Some, such as Latin America, partially merged with cultural styles initially developed in the West; others have tried to remain aloof from Western art or popular culture. Some societies have widely embraced new belief systems, whereas in others—such as the Islamic Middle East—pressures to retain older religious values have maintained greater force. The point is clear: No civilization in the modern world has been able to stand pat, and all have responded to challenge in some similar ways—using nationalism, for example, or extending formal systems of education. At the same time, overall responses have been extremely varied, because of continuities from diverse pasts and diverse modern experiences. Defining the tension between common directions of change and the variety that still distinguishes the major civilizations forms one of the major analytical tasks of modern world history.

World history is challenging as well as varied. Putting the case mildly, much has happened in the history of the world; and although some developments, particularly in early societies, remain unknown for want of records, the amount that we do know is astounding—and steadily expanding. No person can master the whole, and in presenting a manageable course in world history, selectivity is essential. Fortunately, there is considerable agreement on certain developments that are significant to a study of world history. The student must gain, for example, some sense of the special political characteristics of Chinese civilization; or of the nature of Islam; or of the new world economy that Western Europe organized, to its benefit, after about 1500. This list of history basics, of course, is not uniform, and it can change with new interests and new data. The condition of women, for example, as it varied from one civilization to the next and changed over time, has become a staple of up-to-date world history teaching in ways that were unimaginable 20 years ago. Despite changes in the list, though, the idea of approaching world history in terms of basics—key civilizations, key points of change, or key factors such as technology or family—begins the process of making the vast menu of information digestible.

In practice, however, the teaching of world history has sometimes obscured the focus on basics with a stream-of-narrative textbook approach. An abundance of important and interesting facts can produce a way of teaching world history so bent on leaving nothing out (though in fact, much must be omitted in even the most ponderous tome) that little besides frenzied memorization takes place. Yet world history, although it must convey knowledge, must also stimulate thought—about why different patterns developed in key civilizations, about what impact new contacts between civilizations had, about how our present world relates to worlds past.

One way to stimulate thought—and to give a dash of the spice that particular episodes in world history offer—is to provide access to original sources. The purpose of this volume is to facilitate world history teaching by supplementing a purely textbook survey approach with the immediacy of contact that original source documents offer.

The readings in this volume are designed to illustrate several features of various civilizations at crucial points in modern world history through direct evidence. Thus the readings convey, through direct statements, some sense of how Gandhi defined Indian nationalism and its relation to the West, or what a number of twentieth-century social revolutionaries said were their goals. Because the documents were written for specific themes and audiences, they invariably require some effort of interpretation. The writers, by trying to persuade others of their beliefs or reporting what they saw at the time, did not focus on distilling the essence of a religion, a political movement, or a list of government functions for early-twenty-first century students of world history. The reader must provide such distillation, aided by the brief introduction given in each chapter before the selections, as well as by the Study Questions at the end of chapters. Analytical thinking is also encouraged and challenged by recurrent comparisons across space and time. Thus documents dealing with social or family structure in China can be compared with documents on the same subject for the Middle East, and a picture of China's world position 500 years ago begs for juxtaposition with descriptions of twentieth-century Chinese world contacts to see what changed and what persists.

Many readers of this collection will already have covered the traditional periods of world history before 1300. Volume 1 of *Documents in World History*, a companion reader organized similarly to this volume, offers source materials on important features of the traditional world and its major civilizations, including the great religious, durable political patterns, and aspects of social structure and family life. Such features should be compared with developments after 1300 C.E. to obtain a full sense of the interplay between the continuity of civilizations' traditions and the general forces shaping the modern world.

Volume 2 focuses on three basic modern periods that took shape after the fourteenth century C.E. During the first period, which began to form around 1400 and extended to the mid-eighteenth century, the rise of the West and Western sponsorship of a new world economy provided one central theme for world history, though different societies were diversely affected. Other major forces included the capacity to form new empires—the territorial agglomerations developed by the Ottomans, Russians, and Mughals—and the impacts of contact with the Americas. Specific patterns varied. Russia, for example, reached out for selective contacts with Western Europe, while East Asia opted for a policy of substantial isolation. The West itself was undergoing a fascinating series of changes that produced new political and intellectual forms. Latin America became defined, under heavy Western influence; and Africa and India encountered different degrees of Western impact. In retrospect, these early modern centuries were a time of transition, with a growing Western role but very diverse reactions, all complicated by the fact that the West itself was changing its geographical and cultural shape.

The second modern period in world history opened in the middle of the eighteenth century and extended until about 1914. After 1750, Western influence intensified, becoming more literally international; and during the nineteenth century, Western controls—through imperialism—extended over new sections of the world. The only societies that remained fully independent were those that struggled frantically to change, notably Russia and Japan. The West itself underwent the Industrial Revolution, which heightened its economic advantage over the rest of the world while ushering in radically new technological, social, and cultural forms. Western influence was furthered by the expansion of frontier societies in North America and in Australia and New Zealand, heavily influenced by European settlers, institutions, and cultures. Yet, even amid the undeniable Western preponderance and the resultant international contacts, situations continued to vary widely. Different societies reacted to change distinctively, depending in part on prior values. New forces, such as nationalism, promoted significant political and cultural adjustments while also invigorating diverse traditions.

The third chronological section of this book is reserved for the twentieth and early twenty-first centuries. In part this simply reflects the fact that twentieth-century developments such as the Russian Revolution and feminism are particularly important today because of their proximity. Readings on the twentieth century allow analysis of what has changed and what persists in the world's major societies. But the twentieth century also serves as the beginning of a new period in world history, marked by the relative decline of the West, the development of radically new forms of warfare, and the extension of at least partial industrialization and urbanization to most portions of the world. The twentieth century is not only, then, close to us by definition; it also seems to harbor an unusual number of fundamental changes in world history. These transitions—and the various efforts to resist them in the name of older values, ranging from Islamic purity to yearnings for Western supremacy—provide some of the overriding themes for the selections in the final group of readings.

Placing stress on the twentieth century is not always characteristic of courses in world history, which often focus on the fascinating passages of the world in earlier periods of time. The claim that the twentieth century is ushering in a new period of world history should be tested, not simply accepted on faith. Using the selections dealing with the most recent century, readers can assess the proposition that change is taking new forms in the world at large. They can compare twentieth-century developments with those that occurred earlier in the modern era. This book's provision of a full section on the twentieth century is meant to encourage making a connection between our time and the past, seeing how older values echo in a modern age, as well as gaining insight into some of the newer issues of world history. All three of the major periods—1500 to 1750, 1750 to 1914, and the twentieth century—must be seen through the seven major civilizations, in each of which the central modern drama of change interacts with past values to take its own particular form.

The documents presented are not randomly chosen. The selections follow certain general principles around which one can organize an approach to world history. Quite simply, these principles involve place, time, and topic.

First is the focus on major societies in organizing choice of place. The readings deal with seven parts of the world that have produced durable civilizations that still exist, at least in part. East Asia embraces China and a surrounding zone—most notably Japan—that came under partial Chinese influence. Indian civilization, which constitutes the second case, had considerable influence in other parts of southern Asia. The Middle East and North Africa, where civilization was born, form a third society to be addressed at various points in time, both before and after the advent of its major religion, Islam. Europe, although sharing some common values through Christianity, developed two partially distinct civilizations in the east (centered ultimately on Russia) and west. Both East and West European civilizations innovated as new religion, trade, and political organizations spread northward. Values and institutions from Western Europe would also help shape new settler societies in North America and in Australia and New Zealand. Sub-Saharan Africa, a vast region with great diversity, forms a sixth civilization area. Finally, civilization developed independently in South and Central America. Here, as in Africa, signs of civilizations showed early. The seven civilizations represented in the readings are not sacrosanct: They do not embrace all the world's cultures, past or present. They overlap at points, and they contain some marked internal divisions, such as the division between China and Japan in East Asia. These civilizations, however, do provide some geographic coherence for the study of world history, and they are all represented repeatedly in the selections that follow.

The second basis of our selection of places involves contact among different societies, as a result of migrations, invasions, trade, deliberate borrowing, or missionary intrusions. Here is a key, recurrent source of change, friction, and creativity. Documents on the nature and results of significant contacts complement those focused on the characteristics of major civilizations. For each period in this volume, one or more sections on global contacts highlight key interchanges among societies in different parts of the world.

The third organizing principle in the sources that follow is the topic. In dealing with major periods and civilizations, the readings convey four features inherent in human society. First, every civilization must develop some government structure and political values. Second, it must generate a culture, that is, a system of beliefs and artistic expressions that help explain how the world works. Among these, religion is often a linchpin of a society's culture, but science and art play crucial roles as well. Economic relationships—the nature of agriculture, the level of technology and openness to technological change, the position of merchants—form a third feature of a civilization. And fourth, social groupings, hierarchies, and family institutions—including gender relations—organize human relationships and provide for the training of children. Until recently, world history focused primarily on the political and cultural side of the major societies, with some bows to technology and trade. More recently, the explosion of social history—with its inquiry into popular as well as elite culture, families, and social structure—has broadened world history concerns.

Readings in this book provide a sense of all four aspects of the leading civilizations—political, cultural, economic, and social—and a feeling for how they changed under the impact of new religions or economic systems, the rise and fall of empires, or new contacts among civilizations themselves.

This book aims at providing the flavor of such topics, a sense of how people at the time lived and perceived them, and an understanding of the issues involved in interpreting and comparing diverse documents from the past. The collection is meant to help readers, themselves, breathe life into world history and grasp some of the ways that both great and ordinary people have lived, suffered, and created in various parts of the world at various points in our rich human past.

SECTION ONE

The Early Modern Period, Centuries of Dramatic Change: 1400s–1700s

The Early Modern Period focuses on developments between about 1450 and the eighteenth century. A new range of global interconnections was the most important change in the period. But new activity by Western Europe was an important component as well, and some of this was prepared by innovations in the fourteenth and fifteenth centuries.

Western Europe's emergence as an increasingly important actor on the world stage between 1300 and 1500 depended on several developments: new technologies, in part gained by previous contacts with Asia (such as explosive powders and the compass); acute international trade problems and fear of Muslim power, which prompted Europeans to seek new routes to Asia and also sources of gold that would give them greater bargaining power; and changes within European society itself, including greater rivalries among monarchs. New international positions continued the process of change within Europe, helping to promote new attitudes toward science. Western Europe's power at the same time affected other societies, particularly in the Americas, which were now open to growing European control. Elsewhere, the impact of Western contacts, higher levels of international trade, and the foodstuffs available from the Americas had diverse results, ranging from altered commercial patterns in Africa to deliberate imitation from Russia to deliberate isolation (aside from trade contacts) in East Asia. Other developments shaped the early modern centuries as well, including the formation of vigorous new empires (the Ottoman and the Mughal) in the Middle East and India, both of which extended Muslim power. Renewed political strength in China was another vital Asian development, as European influence and new global trading patterns had only selective impact on the largest continent during the early modern centuries.

I

The Italian Renaissance

The Renaissance was, above all, a significant new cultural movement that began in fourteenth-century Italy, somewhat before the early modern period in larger world history. Its innovations included new styles and a new attention to style; an increase in secular interests, as opposed to strictly religious goals; and a major revival of attention to classical Roman and Greek models in writing, art, and philosophy. The Italian Renaissance also included new political developments in competing city-states and a growing level of trade. Some scholars have identified growing delight in individualism and individual achievement as another unifying feature of the Renaissance.

As a cultural movement, the Renaissance lasted into the sixteenth century, by which time it was involving northern Europe as well. The Renaissance contrasted greatly, in religious, stylistic, and philosophical terms, with the medieval culture that had preceded it in Western Europe.

The following documents come from letters written by Francesco Petrarch, one of the leading influential figures in the Italian Renaissance. From 1304 to 1374 Petrarch lived in Florence, a major Renaissance center. Petrarch was a poet, historian, and scholar, known both for his advancement of Latin classics and for his work in Italian. He wrote a number of letters to figures in the classical past, but also to contemporary authors like Boccacio, in order to discuss some of his intellectual and personal concerns. Four letters are cited here: one simply generally entitled "To Posterity"; another to Boccacio; and two more to the long-dead Roman politician and philosopher Cicero, best known for his writing and for his talents in the field of rhetoric. The letters were written in Latin and intended for publication.

The letters raise a number of Renaissance themes. The relationship to Roman culture is one that Petrarch deals with directly, in discussing Latin and vernacular Italian. The Renaissance ultimately encouraged the rise of vernacular languages—English and French as well as Italian—in cultural life, but it also promoted esteem for good Latin. The relationship to religion is another key theme: Petrarch writes as a Christian, but suggests a rebalancing of interests between religion and other concerns in intellectual and even ethical life. Petrarch also describes a new sense of himself as an individual, and this invites definition as well, as part of figuring out what the Renaissance was all about.

Petrarch's work can be fruitfully compared with medieval intellectual life, in terms of the different cultural goals and values. It also raises deeper questions about the range of the Renaissance: how much was the Renaissance an elitist movement, and how much did it affect the wider society?

The Italian Renaissance must also be connected to world history. In one sense, it was a very self-contained cultural movement with specifically Italian features. But some scholars have found in the Renaissance a source of wider changes in culture and values that help explain new European initiatives in the world at large.

THE LETTERS OF PETRARCH

I. TO POSTERITY

Greetings. It is possible that some word of me may have come to you, though even this is doubtful, since an insignificant and obscure name will scarcely penetrate far in either time or space. If, however, you should have heard of me, you may desire to know what manner of man I was, or what was the outcome of my labours, especially those of which some description or, at any rate, the bare titles may have reached you.

To begin with myself, then, the utterances of men concerning me will differ widely, since in passing judgment almost everyone is influenced not so much by truth as by preference, and good and evil report alike know no bounds. I was, in truth, a poor mortal like yourself, neither very exalted in my origin, nor, on the other hand, of the most humble birth, but belonging, as Augustus Caesar says of himself, to an ancient family. As to my disposition, I was not naturally perverse or wanting in modesty, however the contagion of evil associations may have corrupted me. My youth was gone before I realized it; I was carried away by the strength of manhood; but a riper age brought me to my senses and taught me by experience the truth I had long before read in books, that youth and pleasure are vanity—nay, that the Author of all ages and times permits us miserable mortals, puffed up with emptiness, thus to wander about, until finally, coming to a tardy consciousness of our sins, we shall learn to know ourselves. In my prime I was blessed with a quick and active body, although not exceptionally strong; and while I do not lay claim to remarkable personal beauty, I was comely enough in my best days. I was possessed of a clear complexion, between light and dark, lively eyes, and for long years a keen vision, which however deserted me, contrary to my hopes, after I reached my sixtieth birthday, and forced me, to my great annoyance, to resort to glasses. Although I had previously enjoyed perfect health, old age brought with it the usual array of discomforts.

My parents were honourable folk, Florentine in their origin, of medium fortune, or, I may as well admit it, in a condition verging upon poverty. They had been expelled from their native city, and consequently I was born in exile. I have always possessed an extreme contempt for wealth; not that riches are not desirable in themselves, but because I hate the anxiety and care which are invariably associated

From James Harvey Robinson, *Petrarch: The First Modern Scholar and Man of Letters* (New York, G.P. Putnam's, 1914), pp. 59–65, 207–209. Copyright 1898 by G.P. Putnam's Sons, London.

with them. I certainly do not long to be able to give gorgeous banquets. So-called convivial affairs which are but vulgar bouts, sinning against sobriety and good manners, have always been repugnant to me. I have ever felt that it was irksome and profitless to invite others to such affairs, and not less so to be bidden to them myself. On the other hand, the pleasure of dining with one friends is so great that nothing has ever given me more delight than their unexpected arrival, nor have I ever willingly sat down to table without a companion. Nothing displeases me more than display, for not only is it bad in itself, and opposed to humility, but it is troublesome and distracting.

I have taken pride in others, never in myself, and however insignificant I may have been, I have always been still less important in my own judgment. My anger has very often injured myself, but never others. I have always been most desirous of honourable friendships, and have faithfully cherished them. I make this boast without fear, since I am confident that I speak truly. While I am very prone to take offence, I am equally quick to forget injuries, and have a memory tenacious of benefits. In my familiar associations with kings and princes, and in my friendship with noble personages, my good fortune has been such as to excite envy. But it is the cruel fate of those who are growing old that they can commonly only weep for friends who have passed away. The greatest kings of this age have loved and courted me. They may know why; I certainly do not. With some of them I was on such terms that they seemed in a certain sense my guests rather than I theirs; their lofty position in no way embarrassing me, but, on the contrary, bringing with it many advantages. I fled, however, from many of those to whom I was greatly attached; and such was my innate longing for liberty, that I studiously avoided those whose very name seemed incompatible with the freedom that I loved.

I possessed a well-balanced rather than a keen intellect, one prone to all kinds of good wholesome study, but especially inclined to all philosophy and the art of poetry. The latter indeed, I neglected as time went on, and took delight in sacred literature. Finding in that hidden sweetness which I had once esteemed but lightly, I came to regard the works of the poets as only amenities. Among the many subjects which interested me, I dwelt especially, upon antiquity, for our own age has always repelled me, so that, had it not been for the love of those dear to me, I should have preferred to have been born in any other period than our own. In order to forget my own times, I have continually striven to place myself in spirit in other ages, and consequently I delighted in history; not that the conflicting statements did not offend me, but when in doubt I accepted what appeared to me most probable, or yielded to the authority of the writer.

My style, as many claimed, was clear and forcible; but to me it seemed weak and obscure. In ordinary conversation with friends, or with those about me, I never gave any thought to my language, and I have always wondered that Augustus Caesar should have taken such pains in this respect. When, however, the subject itself, or the place or listener, seemed to demand it, I gave some attention to style, with what success I cannot pretend to say; let them judge in whose presence I spoke. If only I have lived well, it matters little to me how I talked. Mere elegance of language can produce at best but an empty renown.

II. TO BOCCACCIO

To be sure, the Latin, in both prose and poetry, is undoubtedly the nobler language, but for that very reason it has been so thoroughly developed by earlier writers that neither we nor anyone else may expect to add very much to it. The vernacular, on the other hand, has but recently been discovered, and, though it has been ravaged by many, it still remains uncultivated, in spite of a few earnest labourers, and still shows itself capable of much improvement and enrichment. Stimulated by this thought, and by the enterprise of youth, I began an extensive work in that language. I laid the foundations of the structure, and got together my lime and stones and wood. And then I began to consider a little more carefully the times in which we live, the fact that our age is the mother of pride and indolence, and that the ability of the vainglorious fellows who would be my judges, and their peculiar grace of delivery is such that they can hardly be said to recite the writings of others, but rather to mangle them. Hearing their performances again and again, and turning the matter over in my mind, I concluded at length that I was building upon unstable earth and shifting sand, and should simply waste my labours and see the work of my hands levelled by the common herd. Like one who finds a great serpent across his track, I stopped and changed my route—for a higher and more direct one, I hope. Although the short things I once wrote in the vulgar tongue are, as I have said, so scattered that they now belong to the public rather than to me, I shall take precautions against having my more important works torn to pieces in the same way.

And yet why should I find fault with the unenlightenment of the common people, when those who call themselves learned afford so much more just and serious a ground for complaint? Besides many other ridiculous peculiarities, these people add to their gross ignorance an exaggerated and most disgusting pride. It is this that leads them to carp at the reputation of those whose most trivial sayings they were once proud to comprehend, in even the most fragmentary fashion. O inglorious age! that scorns antiquity, its mother, to whom it owes every noble art, that dares to declare itself not only equal but superior to the glorious past. I say nothing of the vulgar, the dregs of mankind, whose sayings and opinions may raise a laugh but hardly merit serious censure.

Such are the times, my friend, upon which we have fallen; such is the period in which we live and are growing old. Such are the critics of today, as I so often have occasion to lament and complain—men who are innocent of knowledge or virtue, and yet harbour the most exalted opinion of themselves. Not content with losing the words of the ancients, they must attack their genius and their ashes. They rejoice in their ignorance, as if what they did not know were not worth knowing.

III. TO MARCUS TULLIUS CICERO

Your letters I sought for long and diligently; and finally, where I least expected it, I found them. At once I read them, over and over, with the utmost eagerness. And as I read I seemed to hear your bodily voice, O Marcus Tullius, saying many things, uttering many lamentations, ranging through many phases of thought and feeling. I long had known how excellent a guide you have proved for others; at last I was to learn what sort of guidance you gave yourself.

Now it is your turn to be the listener. Hearken, wherever you are, to the words of advice, or rather of sorrow and regret, that fall, not unaccompanied by tears, from the lips of one of your successors, who loves you faithfully and cherishes your name. . . .

But the [Roman] republic had fallen before this into irretrievable ruin, as you had yourself admitted. Still, it is possible that a lofty sense of duty, and love of liberty, constrained you to do as you did, hopeless though the effort was. That we can easily believe of so great a man. But why, then, were you so friendly with Augustus? . . . If you accept Octavius, . . . we must conclude that you are not so anxious to be rid of all tyrants as to find a tyrant who will be well-disposed toward yourself. . . . These shortcomings fill me with pity and shame. . . . What, pray, does it profit a man to teach others, and to be prating always about virtue, in high-sounding words, if he fails to give heed to his own instructions? Ah! How much better it would have been, how much more fitting for a philosopher, to have grown old peacefully in the country, meditating, as you yourself have somewhere said, upon the life that endures for ever, and not upon this poor fragment of life; to have . . . yearned for no triumphs . . . [or] All this, however, is vain. Farewell, forever, my Cicero.

Written in the land of the living; on the right bank of the Adige, in Verona, a city of Transpadane Italy; on the 16th of June, and in the year of that God whom you never knew the 1345th.

IV. TO MARCUS TULLIUS CICERO

If my earlier letter gave you offence . . . you shall listen now to words that will soothe your wounded feelings and prove that the truth need not always be hateful. For, if censure that is true angers us, true praise, on the other hand, gives us delight.

You lived then, Cicero, if I may be permitted to say it, like a mere man, but spoke like an orator, wrote like a philosopher. It was your life that I criticised; not your mind, nor your tongue; for the one fills me with admiration, the other with amazement. And even in your life I feel the lack of nothing but stability, and the love of quiet that should go with your philosophic professions, and abstention from civil war, when liberty had been extinguished and the republic buried and its dirge sung. . . .

I ridicule in you nothing at all. Your life does awaken my pity, as I have said; but your eloquence call for your talents and nothing but congratulation. O great father of Roman eloquence! not I alone but all who deck themselves with the flowers of Latin speech render thanks unto you. It is from your wellsprings that we draw the streams that water our meadows. You, we freely acknowledge, are the leader who marshals us; yours are the words of encouragement that sustain us; yours is the light that illumines the path before us. In a word, it is under your auspices that we have attained to such little skill in this art of writing as we may possess. . . .

You have heard what I think of your life and your genius. Are you hoping to hear of your books also; what fate has befallen them, how they are esteemed by the masses and among scholars? They still are in existence, glorious volumes, but we of today are too feeble a folk to read them, or even to be acquainted with their mere titles. Your fame extends far and wide; your name is mighty, and fills the ears of men; and yet those who really know you are very few, be it because the times are unfavourable, or because men's minds are slow and dull, or, as I am the more inclined to believe, because the love of money forces our thoughts in other directions. Consequently right in our own day, unless I am much mistaken, some of your books have disappeared, I fear beyond recovery. It is a great grief to me, a great disgrace to this generation, a great wrong done to posterity. The shame of failing to cultivate our own talents, thereby depriving the future of the fruits that they might have yielded, is not enough for us; we must waste and spoil, through our cruel and insufferable neglect, the fruits of your labours too, and of those of your fellows as well, for the fate that I lament in the case of your own books has befallen the works of many another illustrious man.

STUDY QUESTIONS

1. Was Petrarch highly individualistic in his presentation and assessment of himself?
2. What were Petrarch's religious views? How do these compare with more traditional Christian values? How does he define the nature and purpose of ethics?
3. What are Petrarch's attitudes toward the classical past? What does he urge his contemporaries to find in classical styles and examples? How does his love of the classics relate to his sense of his own achievements and individuality?
4. Judging by Petrarch's interests, what kinds of changes were involved in the development of Renaissance culture? How does it compare to medieval culture in Western Europe? What kinds of implications did it have for society at large?
5. How does Petrarch compare in his interests to late medieval writers in northern Europe like Chaucer?
6. Again judging by Petrarch's interests alongside major developments in world history at the time: How would you define the significance of the Renaissance in world history?

2

The Protestant Reformation

In 1517 a German monk, Martin Luther, posted 95 theses, or propositions, on a church door in Wittenberg. These theses condemned many practices of the Catholic Church. Luther particularly objected to the Church's practice of selling indulgences, or spiritual credits, by which people might gain credit toward salvation in heaven. In Luther's eyes, this practice reflected a corrupt church, headed by a venal papacy, but also a totally mistaken belief that people could gain salvation by specific practices, rather than faith and divine predestination.

Luther's attacks were met by Catholic rejection, but Luther continued his efforts, appealing to many groups in Germany for a variety for reasons. Some sincerely agreed with Luther and thought he was pointing toward a true version of Christianity. Others also saw political or social advantages in a new religion. Because Luther and his followers were protesting Catholicism, they were soon called Protestants. A permanent split had opened in Western Christendom.

Lutheranism spread widely in Germany, and also in Scandinavia. Other versions of Protestantism, which picked up Lutheran elements but added other doctrines, spread in parts of France, Switzerland, the Netherlands, England, and Scotland, and from these centers spread to North America. Protestantism, and the Catholic response, which included some key reforms within the Church, proved vital in European history not only because of the religious division and ensuing wars, but also because of the role of religious change in spurring new developments in areas as diverse as the economy and family life.

Early in his reformist career, in 1520, Luther wrote (in German, rather than Latin) a "Letter to the German Nobility," which sought to rouse their support.

In it he explained many of his objections to Catholic practices and his growing opposition to the pope. He also implied the need for major changes in church government, in family life, in leisure, and in the economy that foreshadowed important developments in Protestant regions in the decades to come.

This document is an important statement in the early Reformation, but also a challenge to analysis, in figuring out some of the wider implications of Protestantism. Luther's letter also explains some of the diverse appeals offered through this new religious movement. Finally, the letter offers insight into Luther's own motivation, in what proved to be a determined but very difficult personal crusade.

From *Works of Martin Luther*, Vol. II (Philadelphia: A.J. Holman Company and The Castle Press, 1915), pp. 108–111, 114–115, 119, 127, 129, 134, 163–164.

WORKS OF MARTIN LUTHER

I. POPE AND EMPEROR

The pope should have no authority over the emperor, except that he anoints and crowns him at the altar, just as a bishop anoints and crowns a king; and we should not henceforth yield to that devilish pride which compels the emperor to kiss the pope's feet or sit at his feet, or, as they claim, hold his stirrup or the bridle of his mule when he mounts for a ride; still less should he do homage and swear faithful allegiance to the pope, as the popes have shamelessly ventured to demand as if they possessed that right. . . .

Such extravagant, over-presumptuous, and more than wicked doings of the pope have been devised by the devil, in order that under their cover he may in time bring in Antichrist, and raise the pope above God, as many are already doing and have done. It is not proper for the pope to exalt himself above the temporal authorities, save only in spiritual offices such as preaching and absolving. . . .

Of the same sort is also that unheard-of lie about the "Donation of Constantine" [a forged document backing the power of the pope]. It must have been some special plague of God that so many people of understanding have let themselves be talked into accepting such lies as these, which are so manifest and clumsy that I should think any drunken peasant could lie more adroitly and skillfully. How can a man rule an empire and at the same time continue to preach, pray, study and care for the poor? Yet these are the duties which properly and peculiarly belong to the pope, and they were imposed by Christ in such earnest that He even forbade His disciples to take with them cloak or money, since these duties can scarcely be performed by one who has to rule even a single household. Yet the pope would rule an empire and continue to be pope! This is a device of the knaves who would like, under the pope's name, to be lords of the world, and by means of the pope and the name of Christ, to restore the Roman Empire to its former state. . . .

II. PAPAL HOMAGE

The kissing of the pope's feet should take place no more. It is an unchristian, nay, an antichristian thing for a poor sinful man to let his feet be kissed by one who is a hundred times better than himself. If it is done in honor of his authority, why does not the pope do the same to others in honor of their holiness? Compare the two—Christ and the pope! Christ washed His disciples' feet and dried them, and the disciples never washed His feet; the pope, as though he were higher than Christ, turns things around and, as a great favor, allows people to kiss his feet, though he ought properly to use all his power to prevent it . . .

[By] pilgrimages men are led away into a false conceit and a misunderstanding of the divine commandments; for they think that this going on pilgrimage is a precious, good work, and this is not true. It is a very small good work, oftentimes an evil, delusive work, for God has not commanded it. But He has commanded that a man shall care for his wife and children, and look after such other duties as belong to the married state, and besides this, to serve and help his neighbor. Now it comes to pass that a man makes a pilgrimage to Rome when no one has commanded him to do so, spends fifty or a hundred gulden, more or less, and leaves his wife and child, or at least his neighbor, at home to suffer want. Yet the foolish fellow thinks to gloss over such disobedience and contempt of the divine commandments with his self-willed pilgriming, when it is really only curiosity or devilish delusion which leads him to it. The popes have helped this along with their false, feigned, foolish, "golden years," [jubilees] by which the people are excited, stirred up, torn away from God's commandments, and drawn toward their own deluded undertakings. Thus they have accomplished the very thing they should have forbidden; but it has brought in money and strengthened false authority, therefore it has had to continue, though it is against God and the salvation of souls.

In order to destroy in simple Christians this false, seductive faith, and to restore a true understanding of good works, all pilgrimages should be given up; for there is in them nothing good—no commandment, no obedience—but, on the contrary, numberless occasions for sin and for the despising of God's commandments. Hence come the many beggars, who by this pilgriming carry on endless knaveries and learn the habit of begging when they are not in want. Hence, too, come vagabondage, and many other ills which I shall not now recount.

If any one, now, wishes to go on pilgrimage or take a pilgrim's vow, he should first show his reasons to his parish-priest or to his lord. If it turns out that he wishes to do it for the sake of the good work, the priest or lord should boldly tread the vow and good work under foot, as though it were a lure of the devil, and show him how to apply the money and labor necessary for the pilgrimage to the keeping of God's commandments and to works a thousandfold better, viz., by spending it on his own family or on his poor neighbors. . . .

So then we clearly learn from the Apostle that it should be the custom for every town to choose out of the congregation a learned and pious citizen, entrust to him the office of the ministry, and support him at the expense of the community, leaving him free choice to marry or not. He should have with him several priests or deacons, who might also be married or not, as they chose, to help him rule the people of the community by means of preaching and the sacraments, as is still the practice in the Greek Church. At a later time, when there were so many persecutions and controversies with heretics, there were many holy fathers who of their own accord abstained from matrimony, to the end that they might the better devote themselves to study and be prepared at any time for death or for controversy. Then the Roman See [papacy] interfered, out of sheer wantonness, and made a universal commandment forbidding priests to marry. This was done at the bidding of the devil . . .

All festivals should be abolished, and Sunday alone retained. If it were desired, however, to retain the festivals of Our Lady and of the greater saints, they should be transferred to Sunday, or observed only by a morning mass, after which all the rest of the day should be a working-day. The reason is this: The feast-days are now abused by drinking, gaming, idleness and all manner of sins, so that on the holy days we anger God more than on other days, and have altogether turned things around; the holy days are not holy and the working days are holy, and not only is no service done to God and His saints by the many holy days, but rather great dishonor. There are, indeed, some mad prelates who think they are doing a good work if they make a festival in honor of St. Ottilia or St. Barbara or some other saint, according to the promptings of their blind devotion; but they would be doing a far better work if they honored the saint by turning a saint's-day into a working day.

This is the place to say too that the fasts should be matters of liberty, and all sorts of food made free, as the Gospel makes them. For at Rome they themselves laugh at the fasts, making us foreigners eat the oil with which they would not grease their shoes, and afterwards selling us liberty to eat butter and all sorts of other things; yet the holy Apostle says that in all these things we already have liberty through the Gospel. But they have caught us with their canon law and stolen our rights from us, so that we may have to buy them back with money. Thus they have made our consciences so timid and shy that it is no longer easy to preach about this liberty because the common people take such great offense, thinking it a greater sin to eat butter than to lie, to swear, or even to live unchastely. Nevertheless, what men have decreed, that is the work of man; put it where you will, nothing good ever comes out of it.

One of our greatest necessities is the abolition of all begging throughout Christendom. Among Christians no one ought to go begging! It would also be easy to make a law, if only we had the courage and the serious intention, to the effect that every city should provide for its own poor, and admit no foreign beggars by whatever name they might be called, whether pilgrims or mendicant monks. Every city could support its own poor, and if it were too small, the people in the surrounding villages also should be exhorted to contribute, since in any case they have to feed so many vagabonds and knaves in the guise of mendicants. In this way, too, it could be known who were really poor and who not.

There would have to be an overseer or warden who knew all the poor and informed the city council or the priests what they needed; or some other better arrangement might be made. In my judgment there is no other business in which so much knavery and deceit are practiced as in begging, and yet it could all be easily abolished. Moreover, this free and universal begging hurts the common people. . . .

I think too that I have pitched my song in a high key, have made many propositions which will be thought impossible and have attacked many things too sharply. But what am I to do? I am in duty bound to speak. If I were able, these are the things I should wish to do. I prefer the wrath of the world to the wrath of God; they can do no more than take my life. Many times heretofore I have made overtures of peace to my opponents; but as I now see, God has through them compelled me to open my mouth wider and wider and give them enough to say, bark, shout and write, since they have nothing else to do. Ah well, I know another little song about Rome and about them! If their ears itch for it I will sing them that song too, and pitch the notes to the top of the scale. Understandest thou, dear Rome, what I mean?

I have many times offered my writings for investigation and judgment, but it has been of no use. To be sure, I know that if my cause is just, it must be condemned on earth, and approved only by Christ in heaven; for all the Scriptures show that the cause of Christians and of Christendom must be judged by God alone. Such a cause has never yet been approved by men on earth, but the opposition has always been too great and strong. It is my greatest care and fear that my cause may remain uncondemned, by which I should know for certain that it was not yet pleasing to God.

Therefore let them boldly go to work—pope, bishop, priest, monk and scholar! They are the right people to persecute the truth, as they have ever done.

God give us all a Christian mind, and especially to the Christian nobility of the German nation a right spiritual courage to do the best that can be done for the poor Church. Amen.

STUDY QUESTIONS

1. What are the main objections Luther had to Catholic practice? What kinds of change does Luther seek in the clergy, and why?
2. What aspects of the existing church-state relationship does Luther attack? What kinds of church-state relations might follow from his views?
3. Why does Luther attack pilgrimages? What are more appropriate duties of the good Christian?
4. What kinds of economic change does Luther imply? Would the spread of Protestantism affect the European economy?
5. What kinds of changes in family life does Luther imply?
6. What kinds of appeals does Luther offer, explicitly or implicitly, to the various groups in German society? What might motivate various groups to become Protestant? How does Luther relate to a sense of German identity?
7. How would you interpret Luther's own motivation? What caused him to take on one of the most powerful institutions in Western Europe?

3

Protestantism and Women

The rise of Protestantism inevitably affected discussion of women's roles. By arguing against the special sanctity of celibacy and religious orders, Protestant leaders, beginning with Luther, focused new attention on marriage. At the same time, Protestantism also encouraged a belief in the capacity of individuals to nurture their own contacts with God and the Bible, without elaborate intermediate apparatus from church and priests. This belief might apply to women as well as men. In sum: New debate about women's roles emerged as part of religious ferment, and this extended well into the seventeenth century.

There were other factors involved. Throughout Western Europe, new arguments were developing about economic roles. The rise of commerce was accompanied by greater gender differentiations, and women who had once held positions in trade and craft manufacture were now often attacked. Women's labor remained essential, but their range of activities narrowed. At the same time, growing prosperity led to more complex household activities, such as more formal evening meals, in which women could take a lead role. Here was another situation in which complex trade-offs occurred.

The following selections relate directly to the implications of Protestantism, coming from sixteenth and seventeenth century England. Protestantism generated ringing reassertions of male authority, derived among other things from close reading of parts of the Bible. But it also generated more radical sects that took quite a different view, and individual women built on this religious ferment to venture some political claims as well.

In recent decades, historians have paid increasing attention to the impact of Protestantism on the family and on women. They have come to realize that some important new issues were emerging, particularly in terms of the imagery and actual roles of women in the family.

The implications of this debate were varied. In many Protestant families, men assumed new moral authority, responsible among other things for guiding family Bible reading. But there was also new attention to the importance of happiness in marriage, which could lead to greater appreciation of women's roles, at least domestically. The idea of

---

Selection I from John Knox, *The First Blast of the Trumpet against the Monstrous Regiment of Women* (Geneva, 1558) and from William Gouge, *Of Domestical Duties* (London, 1662); Selection II from George Fox, *A Collection of Many Select and Christian Epistles;* Selection III from *The Thomason Tracts.* All selections from Julia O'Faolain and Lauro Martines, eds., *Not in God's Image: Women in 17th Century England* (New York: Harper and Row, 1973), pp. 262–269.

some political claims, though it led to no immediate change, set the context for renewed discussion of political rights beginning in the late eighteenth century.

The first selections show the gender-conservative side of Protestantism, with a statement by the Scottish Calvinist leader, John Knox, and a seventeenth century marriage text by a Protestant minister, William Gouge. The more radical side is expressed by George Fox, an English Quaker leader. Quakers argued that women could be priests, and organized women's meetings widely in 1671. A third selection shows how Protestantism could lead to political claims, as seventeenth century women asserted their rights to a voice before the English parliament in seeking the release of husbands who had been arrested for their participation in the Levelers, a radical religious/political group.

CONSERVATIVE VIEWS

I A. JOHN KNOX, *THE FIRST BLAST OF THE TRUMPET AGAINST THE MONSTROUS REGIMENT OF WOMEN*. FIRST PUBLISHED IN 1558.

The holy ghost doth manifestly [say]: I suffer not that women usurp authority over men: he sayeth not, that woman usurp authority over her husband, but he nameth man in general, taking from her all power and authority, to speak, to reason, to interpret or to teach, but principally to rule or judge in the assembly of men. So that woman by the law of God and the interpretation of the holy ghost is utterly forbidden to occupy the place of God in the offices aforesaid, which he hath assigned to man, whom he hath appointed and ordained his lieutenant in earth: secluding from that honor and dignity all women. . . . And therefore yet again I repeat that, which I have affirmed: to wit, that a woman promoted to sit in the seat of God, that is to teach, to judge or to reign above man, is a monster in nature, contumely to God, and a thing most repugnant to his will and ordinance.

I B. WILLIAM GOUGE, *OF DOMESTICAL DUTIES*, 1662.

Objection   What if a man of mean place be married to a woman of eminent place, or a servant married to a mistress, or an aged woman to a youth, must such a wife acknowledge such an husband her superior?

Answer   Yea verily: for in giving herself to be his wife, and taking him to be her husband, she advanceth him above herself, and subjecteth herself to him.

Objection   But what if a man of lewd and beastly conditions, as a drunkard, a glutton, a profane swaggerer, an impious swearer and blasphemer, be married to a wise, sober, religious matron, must she account him her superior and worthy of an husband's honor?

Answer   Surely she must. For the evil quality and disposition of his heart and life doth not deprive a man of that civil honor which God hath given unto him. Though an husband in regard of evil qualities may carry the image of the devil, yet in regard of his place and office, he beareth the Image of God: so do Magistrates in the Commonwealth, Ministers in the Church, Parents and Masters in the Family. Note for our present purpose, the exhortation of St. Peter to Christian wives which have infidel husbands, 'Be in subjection to them: let your conversation be in fear.'

If Infidels carry not the devil's image and are not, so long as they are Infidels, vassals of Satan, who are? Yet wives must be subject to them.

II.   QUAKER VIEWS, FROM GEORGE FOX, *A COLLECTION OF MANY SELECT AND CHRISTIAN EPISTLES*, 1672.

For Man and Woman were helps meet in the Image of God, and in Righteousness and Holiness, in the Dominion before they fell; but after the Fall, in the Transgression, the Man was to rule over his Wife; but in the Restoration by Christ, into the Image of God, and his Righteousness . . . they are helps meet, Man and Woman, as they were before the Fall. . . . And there are Elder Women in the Truth, as well as Elder Men in the Truth; and these Women are to be teachers of good things; so they have an Office as well as the Men, for they have a Stewardship, and must give account of their Stewardship to the Lord, as well as the Men. Deborah was a judge; Miriam and Huldah were prophetesses; old Anna was a prophetess. . . . Mary Magdalene and the other Mary were the first preachers of Christ's Resurrection to the Disciples . . . they received the Command, and being sent, preached it: So is every Woman and Man to do, that sees him risen, and have the Command and Message. . . . And if the Unbelieving Husband is sanctified by the Believing Wife, then who is the Speaker, and who is the Hearer? Surely such a Woman is permitted to speak and to work the Works of God, and to make a Member in the Church; and then as an Elder, to oversee that they walk according to the Order of the Gospel.

What, are Women Priests? Yes, Women Priests. And can Men and Women offer Sacrifice without they wear the holy Garments? No: What are the holy Garments Men and Women must wear? . . . the Priest's Surplice? Nay. . . . It is the Righteousness of Christ. . . . this is the Royal Garment of the Royal Priesthood, which everyone must put on, Men and Women.

III.   MAY 5, 1649, POLITICAL PETITION TO THE ENGLISH PARLIAMENT, SEEKING RELEASE OF FOUR LEVELER MEN WHO HAD BEEN ARRESTED.

[Parliament had earlier, on April 23, sent a message to women seeking to attend a meeting of the House of Commons, claiming that the issue they were concerned about "was of a higher concernment than they understood," that the House would communicate with their husbands, "and therefore desired them to go home, and look after their own business, and meddle with their husbandry."]

The Humble Petition of divers well-affected women of the Cities of London and Westminster, etc. Sheweth, that since we are assured of our creation in the image of God, and of an interest in Christ equal unto men, as also of a proportional share in the freedoms of this Commonwealth, we cannot but wonder and grieve that we should appear so despicable in your eyes, as to be thought unworthy to petition or represent our grievances to this honorable House.

Have we not an equal interest with the men of this Nation, in those liberties and securities contained in the Petition of Right, and the other good laws of the land? Are any of our lives, limbs, liberties or goods to be taken from us more than from men, but by due process of law and conviction of twelve sworn men of the neighborhood?

And can you imagine us to be so sottish or stupid, as not to perceive, or not to be sensible when daily those strong defenses of our peace and welfare are broken down, and trod under foot by force and arbitrary power?

Would you have us keep at home in our houses, when men of such faithfulness and integrity as the FOUR PRISONERS our friends in the Tower are fetched out of their beds, and forced from their houses by soldiers, to the affrighting and undoing of themselves, their wives, children and families? Are not our husbands, ourselves, our children and families by the same rule as liable to the like unjust cruelties as they? . . . Doth not the Petition of Right declare that no person ought to be judged by Law Martial (except in time of war) . . . ? And are we Christians and shall we sit still and keep at home, while such men as have borne continual testimony against the unjustice of all times, and unrighteousness of men, be picked out and delivered up to the slaughter . . . ?

No. . . . Let it be accounted folly, presumption . . . or whatsoever in us . . . we will never forsake them, nor ever cease to importune you . . . for justice . . . that we, our husbands, children, friends, and servants may not be liable to be thus abused, violated and butchered at men's wills and pleasures. . . .

And therefore again, we entreat you to review our last petition in behalf of our friends above mentioned, and not to slight the things therein contained because they are presented to you by the weak hand of women. . . . For we are no whit satisfied with the answer you gave unto our husbands and friends. . . . Nor shall we be . . . except you free them [the leaders] from their present extrajudicial imprisonment and . . . give them full reparation . . . and leave them to be proceeded against by due process of law. . . . Our houses being worse than prisons to us . . . until you grant our design . . . harden not your hearts against petitioners nor deny us in things so evidently just and reasonable as you would not be dishonorable to all posterity.

STUDY QUESTIONS

1. Why was there a tension in Protestantism over women's position and religious role?
2. How did conservatives base their claims? How did radicals base theirs?
3. What was the relationship between the "humble petition" to parliament and Protestant ideas? What kind of rights were the petitioners claiming, and were they revolutionary?
4. What were the implications of this running debate over women's status? How might it affect relations between men and women in early modern England?
5. How might Protestant leaders and ordinary Protestants work out some compromise between conservative and radical views about women?

4

New Tensions in the Western Political Tradition: Absolutism and Parliament

A leading historian-sociologist, Charles Tilly, has recently argued that one of the few great changes in early modern Western history was the strengthening of the state under national monarchs. Without question, many European governments in the seventeenth century completed the tasks of seizing basic political powers from the feudal nobility, developing a strong bureaucracy, and expanding the functions of the central government. New or revived ideals of government power accompanied this shift. In the first selection, Bishop Bossuet expounds the doctrine of a strong king—essential to keep order among unruly subjects, father to his people, owed respect and obedience by everyone. The result, Bossuet argued, would be far from arbitrary rule and would work to the greater benefit of the subjects—but there was no question about who was in command. Bossuet was writing in the period of Louis XIV, the model for the absolute monarch not only in France but across Europe.

Older ideals of limited government did not die, however. They revived in seventeenth-century England at the same time that France was constructing its new absolute monarchy. English civil war led to the execution of one king. In 1688, renewed unrest brought a strong statement of the rights of the parliament and of individual liberties, as King James II was forced to flee, replaced by Dutch ruler William of Orange. The so-called "Glorious Revolution" brought an unprecedented statement on the limits of royal power, as England moved from feudal practices toward parliamentary monarchy.

The diverse changes in the Western political tradition proved durable. Government functions expanded, though less in England than elsewhere until the twentieth century. Even when kings were toppled, the state continued to wield new powers—as in revolutionary France after 1789. But the idea of limiting government through individual rights and controlling it through elected bodies remained an important Western emphasis, later copied in some other parts of the world. Some historians have argued that it

Selection I from J. B. Bossuet, *Politique Tirée des Propres Paroles de l'Ecriture Sainte* (1870), translated by L. Pearce Williams, published in Brian Tierney, Donald Kagan, and L. Pearce Williams, eds., *Great Issues in Western Civilization*, Vol. I (New York: Random House, Inc., 1967), pp. 659–663. Copyright © 1967 by Random House, Inc. Reprinted by permission. Selection II from E. P. Cheyney, *Readings in English History* (New York: Ginn and Company, 1922), pp. 545–547.

was the flexibility of the Western political tradition, in contrast, say, to the purer Russian or Chinese emphasis on the state, that has fostered the development and, at times, the distinctive vigor of Western society.

The following two selections invite comparison. Were those who sought to limit the state in times of unrest—as in seventeenth-century England—talking the same language, or did goals and methods shift? How did the constitutional parliamentary ideal differ from the absolutist standards of Bossuet? Has the West managed successfully to reconcile its two modern political traditions?

DIVINE RIGHTS AND BILL OF RIGHTS

I. ABSOLUTISM: BISHOP BOSSUET'S THEORY OF DIVINE-RIGHT MONARCHY

Justice has no other support than authority and the subordination of powers.

It is this order which restrains license. When everyone does what he wishes and has only his own desires to regulate him, everything ends up in confusion. . . .

By means of government each individual becomes stronger.

The reason is that each is helped. All the forces of the nations concur in one and the sovereign magistrate has the right to reunite them. . . .

Thus the sovereign magistrate has in his hand all the forces of the nation which submits itself to obedience to him. . . .

Thus, an individual is not troubled by oppression and violence because he has an invincible defender in the person of the prince and is stronger by far than all those who attempt to oppress him.

The sovereign magistrate's own interest is to preserve by force all the individuals of a nation because if any other force than his own prevails among the people his authority and his life is in peril. . . .

The law is sacred and inviolable.

In order to understand perfectly the nature of the law it is necessary to note that all those who have spoken well on it have regarded it in its origin as a pact and a solemn treaty by which men agree together under the authority of princes to that which is necessary to form their society.

This is not say that the authority of the laws depends on the consent and acquiescence of the people; but only that the prince who, moreover by his very station has no other interest than that of the public good, is helped by the sagest heads in the nation and leans upon the experience of centuries gone by. . . .

Everybody thus begins with monarchy and almost everybody has retained it as being the most natural state.

We have also seen that it has its foundation and its model in the rule of the father, that is to say in nature itself.

All men are born subjects: and paternal authority which accustoms them to obey, accustoms them at the same time to have only one chief.

Monarchical government is the best.

If it is the most natural, it is consequently the most durable and from that it follows also the strongest.

It is also the most opposed to divisiveness, which is the worst evil of states, and the most certain cause of their ruin. . . . "Every kingdom divided against itself is brought to desolation; and every city or house divided against itself shall not stand."

We have seen that Our Lord in this sentence has followed the natural progress of government and seems to have wished to show to realms and to cities the same means of uniting themselves that nature has established in families.

Thus, it is natural that when families wish to unite to form a body of State, they will almost automatically coalesce into the government that is proper to them.

When states are formed there is the impulse to union and there is never more union than under a single leader. Also there is never greater strength because everything works in harmony. . . .

Royal authority is paternal and its proper character is goodness.

After what has been said, this truth has no need of proof.

We have seen that kings take the place of God, who is the true father of the human species. We have also seen that the first idea of power which exists among men is that of the paternal power; and that kings are modeled on fathers.

Everybody is also in accord, that the obedience which is owned to the public power can be found in the ten commandments only in the precept which obliges him to honor his parents.

Thus it follows from this that the name of king is a name for father and that goodness is the most natural character of kings. . . .

The prince must provide for the needs of the people.

It is a royal right to provide for the needs of the people. He who undertakes it at the expense of the prince undertakes royalty: this is why it has been established. The obligation to care for the people is the foundation of all the rights that sovereigns have over their subjects.

This is why, in time of great need, the people have the right to have recourse to its prince. . . .

II. THE ENGLISH BILL OF RIGHTS, 1689

Whereas the said late King James II having abdicated the government, and the throne being thereby vacant, his Highness the prince of Orange (whom it hath pleased Almighty God to make the glorious instrument of delivering this kingdom from popery and arbitrary power) did (by the advice of the lords spiritual and temporal, and diverse principal persons of the Commons [parliament]) caused letters to be written to the lords spiritual and temporal, being Protestants . . . to meet and sit at Westminster upon the two and twentieth day of January, in this year 1689, in order to such an establishment as that their religion, laws, and liberties might not again be in danger of being subverted; upon which letters elections have been accordingly made.

And thereupon the said lords spiritual and temporal and Commons, pursuant to their respective letters and elections, being now assembled in a full and free representation of this nation, taking into the most serious consideration the best means for attaining the ends aforesaid, do in the first place (as their ancestors in like case have usually done), for the vindication and assertion of their ancient rights and liberties, declare:

1. That the pretended power of suspending laws, or the execution of laws, by regal authority, without consent of parliament is illegal.
2. That the pretended power of dispensing with the laws, or the execution of law by regal authority, as it hath been assumed and exercised of late, is illegal.
3. That the commission for erecting the late court of commissioners for ecclesiastical causes, and all other commissions and courts of like nature, are illegal and pernicious.
4. That levying money for or to use of the crown by pretense of prerogative, without grant of parliament, for longer time or in other manner than the same is or shall be granted, is illegal.
5. That it is the right of the subjects to petition the king, and all commitments and prosecutions for such petitioning are illegal.
6. That the raising or keeping a standing army within the kingdom in time of peace, unless it be with consent of parliament, is against law.
7. That the subjects which are Protestants may have arms for their defense suitable to their conditions, and as allowed by law.
8. That election of members of parliament ought to be free.
9. That the freedom of speech, and debates or proceedings in parliament, ought not to be impeached or questioned in any court or place out of parliament.
10. That excessive bail ought not to be required, nor excessive fines imposed, nor cruel and unusual punishments inflicted. . . .
11. And that for redress of all grievance and for the amending, strengthening, and preserving of the laws, parliament ought to be held frequently.

And they do claim, demand, and insist upon all and singular the premises, as their undoubted rights and liberties. . . .

STUDY QUESTIONS

1. How does Bossuet define the powers of monarchy? How does he argue that these powers are essential?
2. Why did this kind of monarchy become known as "absolute"?
3. What were the key features of the "parliamentary monarchy" established in principle in Great Britain during 1688 and 1689?
4. What general rights were accorded to all Englishmen by the Bill of Rights? What freedoms were not granted to all?
5. What were the key differences between absolute and parliamentary monarchies? What caused two such different patterns to emerge?

5

The Scientific Revolution and the Enlightenment: New Intellectual Standards in the West

From the fifteenth through the eighteenth centuries, intellectual life in the West went through a dizzying series of changes, some contradictory. Renaissance thinkers and artists challenged medieval styles and standards, urging a greater focus on humanity and things of this world. The Reformation, shortly on the heels of the Renaissance, argued for a return to religious authority but also shattered the unity of Western Christendom. Ultimately—as became clear by the later seventeenth century—the cutting edge of Western intellectual life was redefined away from religion and toward the growing authority of science. By science, in turn, Western intellectuals meant a set of rational operations, including both deductive reasoning and experiment, by which scientists could discover the clear-cut laws of nature. Religious authority was not directly attacked, but it was sidestepped in favor of a belief that humans could know what they needed to know by unaided reason. Knowledge itself could progress, rather than referring constantly to faith or tradition.

The following selections, written by leading figures in the Scientific Revolution in the seventeenth century and its aftermath, the eighteenth-century Enlightenment, describe the new intellectual framework. Isaac Newton, whose great discoveries in physics and mathematics brought together more than a century of work on planetary motion and the laws of gravity, shows how science and religion could be combined—but obviously on the terms of science. John Locke, also a seventeenth-century Englishman, sketches new principles of knowledge wherein reason has the crucial role.

Locke and Enlightenment figures after him intended to apply rational principles and the idea of a harmonious, knowable nature to human society. Obviously, education had to change in order to develop the rational spark inherent in each child. Human institutions, such as criminal punishments, long based on outmoded religion and tradition, could

Selection I from Sir Isaac Newton, *Optics, or A Treatise of the Reflections, Refractions, Inflections and Colours of Light*, 4th ed. (London: 1730), p. 18. Selection II from John Locke, *An Essay Concerning Human Understanding* (Oxford: 1894), pp. 28, 37–38, 121–122, 387, 412–416, 420–421, 425–426. Selection III reprinted with permission of Macmillan Publishing Company. From Cesare Beccaria, *On Crimes and Punishments*, translated by Henry Paolucci, p. 67. Copyright © 1963 by Macmillan Publishing Company. Reprinted by permission of Prentice Hall/Pearson Education.

be rethought, again to make the best of the fundamental reason and goodness in each person. Cesare Beccaria, an Italian Enlightenment writer, took the lead here.

Science and the Enlightenment were not unchallenged in the Western world, but they did reshape previously dominant belief. Western intellectual life came to rest on assumptions radically different from those of a few centuries before. And there was more. The intellectual revolution reverberated in the wider culture of the West, as ordinary people picked up some of the same assumptions and began to challenge many traditions of popular culture. Finally, as the West spread its influence in the wider world, the baggage of the Age of Reason accompanied its journeys, challenging traditional cultures in Asia and Africa. Here, too, the intellectual revolution that started in the West is still working in the world, though with varied results.

FROM THE SCIENTIFIC REVOLUTION AND THE ENLIGHTENMENT

I. NEWTON'S VIEW OF THE WORLD (1704)

All these things considered, it seems probable to me, that God in the beginning formed matter in solid, massy, hard, impenetrable, moveable particles [atoms], of such sizes and figures, and with such other properties, and in such proportion to space, as most conduced to the end for which he formed them; and that these primitive particles, being solids, are incomparably harder than any porous bodies compounded of them; even so very hard, as never to wear or break in pieces; no ordinary power being able to divide what God himself made one in the first creation. . . .

Now by the help of these principles, all material things seem to have been composed of the hard and solid particles above-mentioned, variously associated in the first creation by the counsel of an intelligent agent. For it became him who created them to set them in order. And if he did so, it's unphilosophical to seek for any other origin of the world or to pretend that it might arise out of a chaos by the mere laws of nature; though being once formed, it may continue by those laws for many ages.

II. JOHN LOCKE ON THE POWER OF REASON (1690)

I

It is an established opinion amongst some men, that there are in the understanding certain *innate principles;* some primary notions, characters, as it were stamped upon the mind of man; which the soul receives in its very first being, and brings into the world with it. It would be sufficient to convince unprejudiced readers of the falseness of this supposition, if I should only show (as I hope I shall in the following parts of this Discourse) how men, barely by the use of their natural faculties, may attain to all the knowledge they have, without the help of any innate impressions; and may arrive at certainty, without any such original notions or principles. . . .

Let us then suppose the mind to be, as we say, white paper, void of all characters, without any ideas:—How comes it to be furnished? Whence comes it by that vast store which the busy and foundless fancy of man has painted on it with an almost endless variety? Whence has it all the *materials* of reason and knowledge? To this I answer, in one word, from EXPERIENCE. In that all our knowledge is founded; and from that it ultimately derives itself. Our observation employed either about external sensible objects, or about the internal operations of our minds perceived and reflected on by ourselves, is that which supplies our understandings with all the *materials* of thinking. These two are the fountains of knowledge, from whence all the ideas we have, or can naturally have, do spring. . . .

Sense and intuition reach but a very little way. The greatest part of our knowledge depends upon deductions and intermediate ideas: and in those cases where we are fain to substitute assent instead of knowledge, and take propositions for true, without being certain they are so, we have need to find out, examine, and compare the grounds of their probability. In both these cases, the faculty which finds out the means, and rightly applies them, to discover certainty in the one, and probability in the other, is that which we call reason. . . .

II

Assent to supposed innate truths depends on having clear and distinct ideas of what their terms mean, and not on their innateness. A child knows not that three and four are equal to seven, till he comes to be able to count seven, and has got the name and idea of equality; and then, upon explaining those words, he presently assents to, or rather perceives the truth of that proposition. But neither does he then readily assent because it is an innate truth, nor was his assent wanting till then because he wanted the use of reason; but the truth of it appears to him as soon as he has settled in his mind the clear and distinct ideas that these names stand for.

III

Faith and Reason

By what has been said of reason, we may be able to make some guess at the distinction of things, into those that are according to, above, and contrary to reason. 1. *According to reason* are such propositions whose truth we can discover by examining and tracing those ideas we have from sensation and reflection; and by natural deduction find to be true or probable. 2. *Above reason* are such propositions whose truth or probability we cannot by reason derive from those principles. 3. *Contrary to reason* are such propositions as are inconsistent with or irreconcilable to our clear and distinct ideas. Thus the existence of one God is according to reason; the existence of more than one God, contrary to reason; the resurrection of the dead, above reason. . . .

From these things thus premised, I think we may come to lay down *the measures and boundaries between faith and reason:* the want whereof may possibly have been the cause, if not of great disorders, yet at least of great disputes, and perhaps mistakes in the world. For till it be resolved how far we are to be guided by reason, and how far by faith, we shall in vain dispute, and endeavour to convince one another in matters of religion. . . .

Reason, therefore, here, as contradistinguished to *faith,* I take to be the discovery of the certainty or probability of such propositions or truths, which the mind arrives at by deduction made from such ideas, which it has got by the use of its natural faculties: viz. by sensation or reflection.

Faith, on the other side, is the assent to any proposition, not thus made out by the deductions of reason, but upon the credit of the proposer, as coming from God, in some extraordinary way of communication. This way of discovering truths to men, we call *revelation.* . . .

But yet nothing, I think, can, under that title [revelation] shake or overrule plain knowledge; or rationally prevail with any man to admit it for true, in a direct contradiction to the clear evidence of his own understanding. . . . And therefore *no proposition can be received as divine revelation . . . if it be contradictory to our clear intuitive knowledge.* Because this would be to subvert the principles and foundations of all knowledge, evidence, and assent whatsoever: and there would be left no difference between truth and falsehood, no measures of credible and incredible in the world, if doubtful propositions shall take place before self-evident; and what we certainly know give way to what we may possibly be mistaken in. In propositions therefore contrary to the clear perception of the agreement or disagreement of any of our ideas, it will be in vain to urge them as matters of faith. They cannot move our assent under that or any other title whatsoever. For faith can never convince us of anything that contradicts our knowledge. . . .

Thus far the dominion of faith reaches, and that without any violence or hindrance to reason; which is not injured or disturbed, but assisted and improved by new discoveries of truth, coming from the eternal fountain of all knowledge. Whatever God hath revealed is certainly true; no doubt can be made of it. This is the proper object of faith: but whether it be a *divine* revelation or no, reason must judge; which can never permit the mind to reject a greater evidence to embrace what is less evident, nor allow it to entertain probability in opposition to knowledge and certainty. There can be no evidence that any traditional revelation is of divine origin, in the words we receive it, and in the sense we understand it, so clear and so certain as that of the principles of reason: and therefore *Nothing that is contrary to, and inconsistent with, the clear and self-evident dictates of reason, has a right to be urged or assented to as a matter of faith, wherein reason hath nothing to do.*

III. BECCARIA APPLIES RATIONALISM TO PUNISHMENT (1764)

A. Crimes and Punishments

To examine and distinguish all the different sorts of crimes and the manner of punishing them would not be our natural task, were it not that their nature, which varies with the different circumstances of times and places, would compel us to enter upon too vast and wearisome a mass of detail. But it will suffice to indicate the most general principles and the most pernicious and common errors, in order to undeceive no less those who, from a mistaken love of liberty, would introduce anarchy, than those who would be glad to reduce their fellow men to the uniform regularity of a convent.

What will be the penalty suitable for such and such crimes?

Is death a penalty really *useful and necessary* for the security and good order of society?

Are torture and torments *just,* and do they attain the *end* which the law aims at?

What is the best way of preventing crimes?

Are the same penalties equally useful in all times?
What influence have they on customs?

These problems deserve to be solved with such geometrical precision as shall suffice to prevail over the clouds of sophistication, over seductive eloquence, or timid doubt. Had I no other merit than that of having been the first to make clearer to Italy that which other nations have dared to write and are beginning to practise, I should deem myself fortunate; but if, in maintaining the rights of men and of invincible truth, I should contribute to rescue from the spasms and agonies of death any unfortunate victim of tyranny or ignorance, both so equally fatal, the blessings and tears of single innocent man in the transports of his joy would console me for the contempt of mankind. . . .

B. *Torture*

The torture of a criminal during the course of his trial is a cruelty consecrated by custom in most nations. It is used with an intent either to make him confess his crime, or to explain some contradictions into which he had been led during his examination, or discover his accomplices, or for some kind of metaphysical and incomprehensible purgation of infamy, or, finally, in order to discover other crimes of which he is not accused, but of which he may be guilty.

No man can be judged a criminal until he be found guilty; nor can society take from him the public protection until it has been proved that he has violated the conditions on which it was granted. What right, then, but that of power, can authorize the punishment of a citizen so long as there remains any doubt of his guilt? This dilemma is frequent. Either he is guilty, or not guilty. If guilty, he should only suffer the punishment ordained by the laws, and torture becomes useless, as his confession is unnecessary. If he be innocent his crime has not been proved. Besides, it is confounding all relations to expect a man should be both the accuser and accused; and that pain should be the test of truth, as if truth resided in the muscles and fibres of a wretch in torture. By this method the robust will escape, and the feeble be condemned.

STUDY QUESTIONS

1. How did Newton seek to reconcile the idea of a scientifically discoverable nature with Christianity? What was new about his approach?
2. How did Locke alter common Christian thinking about human nature? How would his ideas lead to growing emphasis on the importance of education?
3. Would Locke and Newton have agreed about the importance of religion?
4. How did Beccaria suggest a new approach to the punishment of criminals? Did his approach suggest the scientific and philosophical ideas pioneered earlier by people like Newton and Locke?
5. Were the Scientific Revolution and Enlightenment, in fact, revolutionary compared with earlier Western culture? Would their implications be radical in the context of most other major cultures in the early modern world?

VISUAL SOURCE

The Italian artist Leonardo da Vinci (1452–1519), known for Renaissance classics such as the *Last Supper* and the *Mona Lisa*, also did a series of technological and scientific sketches. This one represents one of his anatomical sketches.

Obviously, Leonardo worked well before the Scientific Revolution. Obviously also, the Renaissance is not usually known for its strong interest in science. Issues of literary and artistic style, manners, and other preoccupations were more typical—as in the writings of Petrarch (see Chapter 1). But da Vinci's work shows how Renaissance concerns could also relate to science. His anatomical sketches resulted from his observations in medical school classrooms, and in turn furthered an interest in scientific as well as artistic inquiries about

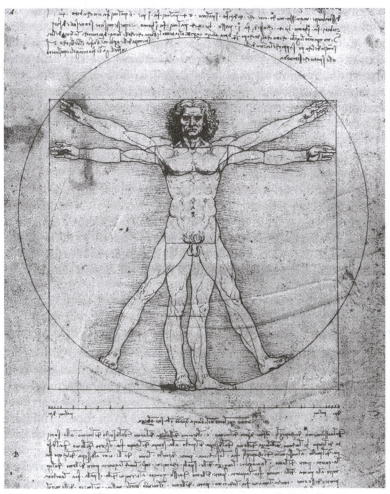

Renaissance Art Often Prefigured the Scientific Revolution.
Anatomical sketches by Leonardo da Vinci. (Alinari/Art Resource, NY)

the human body. Da Vinci was also a literal Renaissance man, in terms of the range of his interests, and this too helps explain connections with later scientific activity.

STUDY QUESTIONS

1. In what ways does this sketch reflect characteristic Renaissance interests? Can you see connections to the interests of Petrarch? Why would a Renaissance painter be drawn to this kind of representation (and why would earlier painters during the Middle Ages in Western Europe not have been so interested)?
2. In what ways does this sketch prefigure aspects of the Scientific Revolution?
3. Does this sketch suggest an important connection between the Renaissance and the Scientific Revolution, or does it simply reflect the distinctive genius of da Vinci? What other evidence would help you to answer this question?
4. How did work on anatomy and other aspects of human physiology relate to other aspects of the Scientific Revolution, such as physics?

6

Peter the Great Reforms Russia

Peter the Great ruled Russia as tsar from 1682 until 1725. A huge man, Peter pushed his government into many new directions. He brutally repressed protest, executing certain army mutineers personally. He moved vigorously in war, winning new territory in the Baltic region, where he located a new westward-looking capital he modestly called St. Petersburg. With its military success, Russia was on its way to becoming a major European power; it was already a growing empire in Central Asia.

Peter was also eager to update Russia's administration and economy, which he saw as essential for military purposes and to establish Russian prestige and position in the wider European arena. His measures were both symbolic and real: He enforced Western-style dress on his *boyars* (the nobles) and required them to cut off their Mongol-style beards. He developed a major iron industry to serve as a basis for armaments production and to avoid Russian dependence on the West in this crucial sector.

The following selections show a number of Peter's initiatives to reform Russia and bring it in line with Western patterns. In these reforms Peter sets up an administrative council to improve the direction of the state bureaucracy and expand its functions. He works to improve education, particularly of the nobility, and to facilitate manufacturing as well. These reforms, in sum, give a good picture of the directions in which the tsar was pushing his vast empire.

Peter's reforms also suggest important links with authoritarian political trends in Russia, including a willingness to regiment ordinary workers and peasants. While other European rulers at this time, such as Louis XIV in France, were claiming new powers in the name of military goals, Peter seemed unusually free to order his nobility about and command their service. He was not interested in aspects of Western politics such as parliaments that

All selections from Basil Dmytryshyn, *Imperial Russia: A Sourcebook, 1700–1917* (New York: Holt, Rinehart and Winston, Inc., 1967), pp. 14–16, 18–19, 21–22. Copyright © 1967 by Holt, Rinehart and Winston, Inc. Reprinted by permission. Duties of the Senate from *Polnoe Sobranie*, Vol. 4, No. 2321, p. 627 and No. 2330, p. 643. Compulsory Education from *Polnoe Sobranie*, Vol. 5, No. 2762, p. 78 and No. 2778, p. 86. Instructions to Students from *Pisma I Bumagi Imperatora Petra Velokogo* (Letters and Papers of Emperor Peter the Great) (St. Petersburg: 1887), Vol. 1, pp. 117–118. Right of Factories from *Polnoe Sobranie*, Vol. 6, No. 3711, pp. 311–312. Founding of the Academy from *Polnoe Sobranie*, Vol. 7, No. 4443. Reprinted by permission of Academic International Press.

stressed restraints on the monarch. Not surprisingly, then, Peter's vision of a Westernized Russia proved highly selective, as he found certain aspects of the Russian tradition eminently useful. Peter's reforms must be interpreted in terms of how much they changed, but also in terms of their confirmation of distinctive features of, the Russian state and society.

Peter the Great clearly illustrates a reform process from the top down. How do you think Russians at various levels would have reacted? From what you can judge by these documents, was Peter moving Russia in a useful direction?

PETER THE GREAT

I. DECREES ON THE DUTIES OF THE SENATE

This *ukaz* [decree] should be made known. We have decreed that during our absence administration of the country is to be [in the hands of] the Governing Senate [Peter then names its new members].

. . .

Each *gubernia* [region] is to send two officials to advise the Senate on judicial and legislative matters. . . .

In our absence the Senate is charged by this *ukaz* with the following:

1. To establish a just court, to deprive unjust judges of their offices and of all their property, and to administer the same treatment to all slanderers.
2. To supervise governmental expenditures throughout the country and cancel unnecessary and, above all, useless things.
3. To collect as much money as possible because money is the artery of war.
4. To recruit young noblemen for officer training, especially those who try to evade it; also to select about 1000 educated *boyars* for the same purpose.
5. To reform letters of exchange and keep these in one place.
6. To take inventory of goods leased to offices or *gubernias*.
7. To farm out the salt trade in an effort to receive some profit [for the state].
8. To organize a good company and assign to it the China trade.
9. To increase trade with Persia and by all possible means to attract in great numbers Armenians [to that trade]. To organize inspectors and inform them of their responsibilities.

II. DECREES ON COMPULSORY EDUCATION OF THE RUSSIAN NOBILITY (JANUARY 12 AND FEBRUARY 28, 1714)

Send to every *gubernia* [region] some persons from mathematical schools to teach the children of the nobility—except those of freeholders and government clerks—mathematics and geometry; as a penalty [for evasion] establish a rule that no one will be allowed to marry unless he learns these [subjects]. Inform all prelates to issue no marriage certificates to those who are ordered to go to schools. . . .

The Great Sovereign has decreed: in all *gubernias* children between the ages of ten and fifteen of the nobility, of government clerks, and of lesser officials, except those of freeholders, must be taught mathematics and some geometry. Toward that end, students should be sent from mathematical schools [as teachers], several into each *gubernia,* to prelates and to renowned monasteries to establish schools. During their instruction these teachers should be given food and financial remuneration of three *altyns* and two *dengas* per day from *gubernia* revenues set aside for that purpose by personal orders of His Imperial Majesty. No fees should be collected from students. When they have mastered the material, they should then be given certificates written in their own handwriting. When the students are released they ought to pay one ruble each for their training. Without these certificates they should not be allowed to marry nor receive marriage certificates.

III. AN INSTRUCTION TO RUSSIAN STUDENTS ABROAD STUDYING NAVIGATION

1. Learn [how to draw] plans and charts and how to use the compass and other naval indicators.
2. [Learn] how to navigate a vessel in battle as well as in a simple maneuver, and learn how to use all appropriate tools and instruments; namely, sails, ropes, and oars, and the like matters, on row boats and other vessels.
3. Discover as much as possible how to put ships to sea during a naval battle. Those who cannot succeed in this effort must diligently ascertain what action should be taken by the vessels that do and those that do not put to sea during such a situation [naval battle]. Obtain from [foreign] naval officers written statements, bearing their signatures and seals, of how adequately you [Russian students] are prepared for [naval] duties.
4. If, upon his return, anyone wishes to receive [from the Tsar] greater favors for himself, he should learn, in addition to the above enumerated instructions, how to construct those vessels aboard which he would like to demonstrate his skills.
5. Upon his return to Moscow, every [foreign-trained Russian] should bring with him at his own expense, for which he will later be reimbursed, at least two experienced masters of naval science. They [the returnees] will be assigned soldiers, one soldier per returnee, to teach them [what they have learned abroad]. And if they do not wish to accept soldiers they may teach their acquaintances or their own people. The treasury will pay for transportation and maintenance of soldiers. And if anyone other than soldiers learns [the art of navigation] the treasury will pay 100 rubles for the maintenance of every such individual. . . .

IV. A DECREE ON THE RIGHT OF FACTORIES TO BUY VILLAGES (JANUARY 18, 1721)

Previous decrees have denied merchants the right to obtain villages. This prohibition was instituted because those people, outside their business, did not have any establishments that could be of any use to the state. Nowadays, thanks to Our decrees, as every one can see, many merchants have companies and many have succeeded in establishing new enterprises for the benefit of the state; namely: silver, copper, iron, coal and the like, as well as silk, linen, and woolen industries, many of which have begun operations. As a result, by this Our *ukaz* aimed at the increase of factories. We permit the nobility as well as merchants to freely purchase villages for these factories, with the sanction of the Mining and Manufacturing College, under one condition: that these villages be always integral parts of these factories. Consequently, neither the nobility nor merchants may sell or mortgage these villages without the factories . . . and should someone decide to sell these villages with the factories because of pressing needs, it must be done with the permission of the Mining and Manufacturing College. And whoever violates this procedure will have his possessions confiscated.

And should someone try to establish a small factory for the sake of appearance in order to purchase a village, such an entrepreneur should not be allowed to purchase anything. The Mining and Manufacturing College should adhere to this rule very strictly. Should such a thing happen, those responsible for it should be deprived of all their movable and immovable property.

V. A DECREE ON THE FOUNDING OF THE ACADEMY (JANUARY 28, 1724)

His Imperial Majesty decreed the establishment of an academy, wherein languages as well as other sciences and important arts could be taught, and where books could be translated. On January 22 [1724], during his stay in the Winter Palace, His Majesty approved the project for the Academy, and with his own hand signed a decree that stipulates that the Academy's budget of 24,912 rubles annually should come from revenues from custom dues and export-import license fees collecting in the following cities: Narva, Dorpat, Pernov and Arensburg. . . .

Usually two kinds of institutions are used in organizing arts and sciences. One is known as a University; the other as an Academy or society of arts and sciences.

1. A University is an association of learned individuals who teach the young people the development of such distinguished sciences as theology and jurisprudence (the legal skill), and medicine and philosophy. An Academy, on the other hand, is an association of learned and skilled people who not only know their subjects to the same degree [as their counterparts in the University] but who, in addition, improve and develop them through research and inventions. They have no obligation to teach others.

2. While the Academy consists of the same scientific disciplines and has the same members as the University, these two institutions, in other states, have no connection between themselves in training many other well-qualified people who could organize different societies. This is done to prevent interference into the activity of the Academy, whose sole task is to improve arts and sciences through theoretical research that would benefit professors as well as students of universities. Freed from the pressure of research, universities can concentrate on educating the young people.

3. Now that an institution aimed at the cultivation of arts and sciences is to be chartered in Russia, there is no need to follow the practice that is accepted in other states. It is essential to take into account the existing circumstances of this state [Russia], consider [the quality of Russian] teachers and students, and organize such an institution that would not only immediately increase the glory of this [Russian] state through the

development of sciences, but would also, through teaching and dissemination [of knowledge], benefit the people [of Russia] in the future.

4. These two aims will not be realized if the Academy of Sciences alone is chartered, because while the Academy may try to promote and disseminate arts and sciences, these will not spread among the people. The establishment of a university will do even less, simply because there are no elementary schools, gymnasia or seminaries [in Russia] where young people could learn the fundamentals before studying more advanced subjects [at the University] to make themselves useful. It is therefore inconceivable that under these circumstances a university would be of some value [to Russia].

5. Consequently what is needed most [in Russia] is the establishment of an institution that would consist of the most learned people, who, in turn, would be willing: (a) to promote and perfect the sciences while at the same time, wherever possible, be willing (b) to give public instruction to young people (if they feel the latter are qualified) and (c) instruct some people individually so that they in turn could train young people [of Russia] in the fundamental principles of all sciences.

STUDY QUESTIONS

1. What were the main purposes of Peter's reforms?
2. What relationship between tsar and nobility did the reforms suggest?
3. What kind of economy was Peter seeking to build? For what reasons?
4. How did Peter's moves relate to changes occurring in Western European politics and culture around 1700? What major trends did Peter ignore?
5. Did Peter's reforms make Russian society more or less like that of Western Europe at the time?

7

Peasant Revolt

Conditions for Russian peasants worsened steadily during the eighteenth century. Landlords increased their efforts to exploit peasant labor, particularly to take advantage of opportunities to export grain to Western Europe. Government decrees stepped up landlord rights to discipline and punish their serfs, even to kill them or exile them to Siberia.

Peasant discontent increased in this context. In 1773 a major revolt broke out under the leadership of Emel'ian Pugachev (1726–1775), a Don Cossack and former Russian soldier. (Cossacks were a minority group of ex-peasants who began to form military bands on Russia's frontiers in the fifteenth century. The government used many of them for fighting, but also attempted to bring them under greater control.) The Pugachev rising was one of the great episodes in Russian history, rousing support from many groups before being crushed by Catherine the Great's forces. Pugachev was arrested and beheaded, and his head publicly displayed to demonstrate the folly of revolt.

The following documents come first from the "decrees" of Pugachev himself, in 1773–1774. Pugachev adopted an old protest tradition by saying that he was the legitimate tsar, Peter III. His decrees appealed not just to peasants but to a variety of aggrieved groups. It is important to sort out the various grievances he was trying to capture, to get a picture of the strains that had opened up in early modern Russian society. A second set of documents involves reports by Pugachev's officials.

A third document comes from a serf who was being interrogated by government officials about the uprising. The serf, Vasilii Chernov, renounced his belief in Pugachev as tsar only under extreme torture.

A fourth set of documents emanates from government officials commenting on the uprising. And finally, a fifth document is a decree by Catherine after the rising had been suppressed.

Peasant protest dropped after this great rising, but it would increase once more in the nineteenth century, as the peasant problem became one of the fundamental issues in Russian society. This set of documents allows analysis of peasant and other grievances, and also raises the question of what kind of sources to believe in a protest situation—the sources from the protest leaders, from the government, or from other quarters. What, in your opinion, did ordinary protesters believe and want?

All selections from George Vernadsky, Ralph Fisher, Alan Ferguson, Andrew Lossky, and Sergei Pushkarev, eds., *A Source Book for Russian History from Early Times to 1917* (New Haven, Conn.: Yale University Press, 1972), pp. 454–459.

PROCLAMATIONS AND DECREES DURING THE PUGACHEV REVOLT, 1773–1774

I. PUGACHEV'S DECREES

[Decree of September 17, 1773, complete text:]

From the autocratic emperor, our great sovereign Petr Feodorovich of all Russia, etcetera, etcetera, etcetera.

Through this, my sovereign decree, be it expressed to the Iaik (Ural) Cossacks: Just as you, my friends, and your grandfathers and fathers served former tsars to the last drop of blood, now should you serve me, the great sovereign and emperor Petr Feodorovich, for the good of your fatherland. For as you stand up for your fatherland, your Cossack glory and that of your children shall not pass away now or ever. And I, the great sovereign, shall bestow my bounty upon you: Cossacks and Kalmyks and Tatars. As for those of you who have been at fault before me, the sovereign and imperial majesty Petr Feodorovich, I, the sovereign Petr Feodorovich, forgive you these faults and confer upon you: the [Iaik, renamed "Ural" as an aftermath of the rebellion] river from its source to its mouth, and land, and meadows, and a monetary wage, and lead, and powder, and grain provisions.

I, the great sovereign and emperor Petr Feodorovich, bestow my bounty upon you.

The seventeenth day of September 1773.

[Decree of October 1773, complete text:]

From our autocratic emperor, the great sovereign of all Russia Petr Feodorovich, etcetera, etcetera, etcetera.

Through this, my sovereign decree, I issue this command to my regular army:

As you, my faithful slaves, soldiers of the regular army, both privates and officers, have in the past served me and my ancestors, the great sovereigns and emperors of all Russia, faithfully and invariably, now likewise must you serve me, your lawful great sovereign Petr Feodorovich, to the last drop of your blood. Cast off the obedience you were forced to show your false commanders, who corrupt you and deprive you, along with themselves, of my good graces; and come to me in obedience and, placing your weapons beneath my banners, display the loyalty of faithful subjects to me, the great sovereign. For this I shall reward you and bestow upon you wages in money and grain and confer ranks upon you; and you and your descendants shall be granted the greatest privileges in my state and shall be enlisted in glorious service, attached to my own person. But if anyone should forget his duty to his hereditary [*prirodnyi,* natural] sovereign Petr Feodorovich, should dare to disobey this, my sovereign decree, and by force of arms should fall into the hands of my faithful army, he shall feel my righteous wrath upon himself and then suffer the death penalty.

The great sovereign emperor of all Russia Petr Feodorovich.

["Manifesto" of Pugachev, July 31, 1774, complete text:]

By the grace of God, we, Petr III, emperor and autocrat of all Russia, etcetera, etcetera, etcetera, announce the following tidings to all the world:

Through this sovereign decree we declare, in our monarchical and fatherly mercy, that all who were formerly peasants and subjected landowners shall be faithful subjects and slaves of our own crown; we grant you your ancient cross and prayers [referring to the Old Believers], your heads and your beards, and bestow upon you freedom and liberty and the eternal rights of Cossacks, including freedom from recruiting levies, the soul tax, and other monetary taxes; we confer likewise the ownership of lands, forests, hayfields, fisheries, and salt lakes without purchase or rent; and we free the peasants and all the people from the taxes and oppression formerly imposed by villainous nobles and the venal city judges. And we desire salvation of your souls and a peaceful life on this earth, for which we have tasted and endured many wanderings and many hardships from the above-mentioned villainous nobles. But since our name now flourishes in Russia by the power of Almighty God, we therefore command through this, our sovereign decree: those who formerly were nobles on their estates and patrimonies, opposing our power, disturbing the empire, and despoiling the peasantry shall be caught, executed, and hanged, and treated just in the same fashion as they, lacking any Christian feeling, dealt with you, the peasants. After the extermination of which enemies and villainous nobles, every man may experience peace and a tranquil life, which shall forever endure.

Given the thirty-first day of July 1774.

Petr

[Decree to the Don Cossacks, August, 1774:]

By the grace of God we, Peter III, emperor and autocrat of all Russia, etcetera, etcetera, etcetera.

A proclamation to the ataman of the Berezov *stanitsa* [Cossack settlement] and to all the Don Cossacks living in it, and to all the world.

Long enough has Russia been filled with the credible rumor of our concealment from the villains (chief senators and nobles); nor was this unknown to foreign states. This resulted from nothing other than the fact that during our reign we beheld that the Christian faith as laid down by the ancient traditions of the holy fathers had been entirely violated and dishonored by the said villainous nobles; instead they introduced into Russia another faith of pernicious invention taken from German customs, and introduced likewise the most godless shaving of beards, and they have done violence to the Christian faith in the cross and in other matters. . . . Looking upon all that has been described above with fatherly compassion, we took pity and intended to free you from their villainous tyranny and to establish liberty throughout Russia.

II. CORRESPONDENCE WITHIN PUGACHEV'S "GOVERNMENT," 1774

Something of the operational methods of Pugachev's army, which at one time numbered perhaps more than twenty thousand troops, is seen in excerpts from instructions and reports such as these.
Reference: Tsentrarhkiv, Pugachevshchina, 1:82, 207.

[Instructions of "Count Chernyshev," the head of Pugachev's State Military Collegium, to Ataman Semen Volkov, February 13, 1774:]

From His Most Exalted Serenity Count Ivan Nikiforovich Chernyshev to Ataman Semen Volkov and *Esaul* [captain] Vasilii Zav'ialov.

Instructions

From a signed letter sent to me by the communal men [*mirskie liudi*] of the Rozh[d]estvenskii factory and the villages of Pristanichnaia and Zobachevka, I have perceived that with the consent of the commune you, Volkov and Zav'ialov, have been elected: you, Volkov, as ataman, and Zav'ialov as esaul. It is therefore incumbent upon you to maintain your detachment in good order and to permit no insubordination and plundering; and if someone shows himself an enemy of His Imperial Majesty and disobedient to you, it is your duty to inflict corporal punishment upon him according to your will and the guilt involved. On the contrary, you must not risk any bad conduct yourselves, and at all times you must heed the manifestos and decrees of His Majesty and execute them immediately, for which you may receive special praise for yourselves. But do not inflict any wrongs, extortions, and desolation upon your detachment, and touch not bribes, being mindful of the inescapable death penalty for any such delinquency. And furthermore, direct your efforts to the immediate execution of the orders and other instructions I send you.

[Report of "Colonel" Bakhtiar Kankeev, July 14, 1774:]

To the most serene and regal emperor Petr Feodorovich, the great autocrat of all Russia, our all-merciful sovereign.

From Colonel Bakhtiar Kankeev to the State Military Collegium [Gosudarstvennaia Voennaia Kollegiia]—a most humble report.

At present, during my march along this side of the Kama and Viatka rivers in the Kazan' region, [I find that] people of all callings, young and old alike, wholeheartedly and very willingly desire to serve Your Imperial Majesty and make haste to come to me; from every Russian and Tatar settlement they come out a verst ahead to meet us, and besides offering us bread and salt weep tears of joy that God has elevated you as tsar; they rejoice in Your Majesty and pray that God grant you a long life, so that they may obtain relief from heavy factory labor and taxes. At present we have more than six hundred people, Russians and Tatars, in our military force; each day more people eagerly hasten with promises to serve, and some who are eager to serve come without horses and without weapons. I most humbly beg you to issue to me your imperial decree as to where they can get horses and weapons; for there are noble estates along my route which have horses left in them and these we can seize for the crown and give to the people.

III. SERF TESTIMONY: VASILII CHERNOV

And therefore on the twentieth day of the month [of July 1774], by order of the *sotskii* [elected peasant police official] Andrei Anan'in . . . all the peasants and factory workers assembled at a meeting, at which meeting . . . all shouted unanimously that they would leave their master and become the subjects of the said impostor and scoundrel [*zlodei*] Pugachev, considering him to be their sovereign Peter III; and all who were at the meeting, the peasant deputy [*vybornyi*], the starosta, and the sotskii Urusov, together with the peasants and factory workers, were asked to agree to this. And on their advice all consented to seize and put in chains and confine in the master's house the manager [of the estate and factory], Aleksei Teteev, his wife, Natas'ia Nikolaevna, his brother Ivan Teteev, his nephew Vasilii Ivanov, a Frenchman, a German, and the Vorotynets peasant Andrei Kireev, with this intention: if the scoundrel Pugachev or someone sent by him should come to their village, they would hand the prisoners over to him, so that he might order them to be hanged for the wrongs they had perpetrated. . . .

Therefore, on the morning of the following day, that is, the twenty-third day of July, the priests Ivan Fedorov and Grigorii Timofeev and their sextons, holding icons in their hands, and the peasants with the sotskii and *desiatskii* [assistant to the sotskii], as well as the peasant deputy Stepanov and the elder Chuev . . . and the factory workers, all gathered together with bread and salt, and waited for the said so-called colonel; nor did the priests make them any admonishment; and they all greeted him together when he rode into the settlement. And upon his arrival this so-called colonel went into the tavern, where the factory worker Aleksei . . . had brought the manager's brother Ivan Teteev and his son Vasilii. And the said so-called colonel, inquiring only of their position, ordered them to be hanged on the peasants' gates as had been done with the manager and the others. This was carried out by the peasants Nikita Denisov, Grigorii Krivenkov, and who else hanged them I don't remember any more. After all this had taken place, this so-called colonel first called forth those willing to enter the service of the scoundrel Pugachev, with the announcement that each man who wished to come with him would receive a wage of twenty rubles a month; seduced by this promise, the peasants of Vorotynets along with the sotskii Andrei Anan'in and the factory workers agreed. Then they performed still further villainies, until finally the factory workers were stirred up and, by the order of that so-called colonel and accompanied also by the peasants living in the village of Vorotynets, destroyed the entire linen factory, leaving nothing standing, and divided the cloth up among themselves; they burned the tannery and wrecked the master's house; the belongings of those who were hanged were locked up and sealed in a closet by the elder.

IV. REPORTS BY OFFICIALS

On August 21 of this year a villainous mob of three hundred mounted men and a thousand of the rabble [*chern'*] arrived at the crown village [*dvortsovoe selo*] Raskazovo. Calling together the rabble they gave them wine to drink and themselves drank the health of Petr Feodorovich. The crown peasants met them with bread and salt and helped these scoundrels in their assault on the factories of the manufacturers Tulinov and Olisov: they carried cannon and set fire to the factories. . . .

Along the rivers Vorona and Khoper there are many such villainous parties organized in various bands and totaling two thousand people; and they all agree they should join forces. These same scoundrels testify that in the course of the looting many nobles and other people, the common people excepted, were barbarously tortured and hanged.

The twenty-third day of August 1774.

[Testimony of Second Major (*sekund-maior*) Andrei, son of Mikhail Salmanov, who had been taken prisoner by Pugachev's men and had served with them, September 26, 1774:]

On the march from Saratov to Tsaritsyn, not only did the settlements along the road itself willingly submit to [Pugachev's] will, but from all sides as well priests came forth with the peasants to greet him with bread and salt; they knelt and bowed to the ground, and begged his protection as the sovereign, which people he dismissed to their homes; while his bands raided and despoiled everyone alike. In the town of Dmitrievsk [Kamyshin], which is on the Kamyshenka [River], a certain defense was effected, but soon the firing ceased: the landless Little Russian peasants met them and the soldiers were taken prisoner; Sergeant Abyzov was selected from their number and on the following day was appointed colonel and given a detachment. From the Kamyshenka they went through the territory of the Volga Cossacks, through four of their towns; in each place they were greeted with crosses and joyful congratulations by a large gathering which included priests; and in their chief town of Dubovka even by a whole assembly, elders and Cossacks, all dressed in their best garments, carrying banners and presenting a joyful appearance.

[Testimony of Pugachev's "colonel" Ivan, son of Aleksandr Tvorogov, October 27, 1774:]

I considered the scoundrel to be the true sovereign Peter III because, first, the Iaik Cossacks accepted and considered him as such; second, the old soldiers as well as the people of other classes who through various circumstances happened to be with us made assurances that the scoundrel was the true sovereign; and third, all the rabble, namely the factory and landowners' peasants, bowed down before him joyfully, and zealously furnished us with men and all else that might be demanded of them, without protest.

V. CATHERINE'S MANIFESTO "CONCERNING THE CRIMES OF THE COSSACK PUGACHEV," DEC. 19, 1774

Realizing that our sole aspiration is to bring the empire to the highest degree of prosperity . . . who can help but feel righteous indignation at these internal foes of the tranquillity of the fatherland: these men who, casting aside all manner of obedience, have first dared to raise arms against the legal authority and join that notorious rebel and imposter, the Don Cossack of the Zimoveisk stanitsa Emel'ka [contemptuous form for Emel'ian] Pugachev, and have then for a whole year perpetrated together with him the most ferocious barbarities in the Orenburg, Kazan' [regions], Nizhnii-Novgorod, and Astrakhan' guberniias; who set aflame the churches of God, towns, and settlements, who have pillaged the holy places [*sviatye mesta*, i.e. churches and monasteries] and every sort of property, who with the sword and with various tortures they have devised have smitten and put to death clergymen and persons of high and low estate and of both sexes, including even innocent children. . . .

· · ·

And his own accomplices and favorites, the Iletsk Cossack Tvorogov and the Iaik Cossacks Chumakov and Fedulev, repenting of the villainies in which they had participated, and learning of the pardon promised by the manifestos of Her Imperial Majesty to all those who exhibit sincere repentance, agreed among themselves to put Emel'ka Pugachev in chains and bring him to Iaitskii Gorodok [later renamed Ural'sk]; they induced some other Cossacks, about twenty-five in number, to aid them in this deed and carried it out.

STUDY QUESTIONS

1. What were the main grievances Pugachev tried to represent and exploit? What was the relationship of this protest to Peter the Great's reforms?

2. Why did many protesters accept Pugachev's claims that he was the legitimate tsar? What was the purpose of these claims, and what do they suggest about peasant political attitudes?
3. Who were the main targets in this revolt?
4. How did the government portray the revolt? Was the government picture persuasive?
5. How do you think ordinary peasants would react to the revolt and its suppression? As a historian, given this kind of evidence, how would you interpret the Pugachev rising?

8

Suleiman the Lawgiver and Ottoman Military Power

In 1300 the Ottoman Turks were one of many groups of Muslim warriors living on the frontier of the Byzantine Empire in western Anatolia. As the power of the Byzantine emperors weakened, the Ottoman *gazis* (warriors fighting on behalf of Islam) began to conquer nearby regions. During the 1350s Turkish armies crossed the Dardenelles (or Hellespont), the narrow strait separating Anatolia from the Balkan Peninsula, and began to establish their power in southeast Europe. By 1400 the Ottomans controlled most of the Balkan Peninsula. The Turks' most dramatic victory came in 1453. In the spring of that year they broke through the massive walls surrounding Constantinople—the capital of the Byzantine Empire and the center of Orthodox Christianity—and captured the city (now known as Istanbul). It had taken only 150 years for the former frontier *gazis* to establish one of the most powerful empires in the world.

Ottoman power continued to expand for about another century or so following the capture of Constantinople. For much of this period the Turkish state was led by Suleiman, the greatest of the Turkish sultans, who reigned from 1520 to 1556 and was known to his subjects as *Kanuni,* the "Lawgiver." Under Suleiman's leadership the Ottoman system of governance reached a high level of efficiency and the Ottoman army and navy continued to be formidable fighting forces.

Ottoman strength rested, in part, on a form of slavery. Christian children in the Balkans were regularly conscripted by the Turks, a practice known to the Turks as the *devshirme* (collection), and taken to Constantinople, where they were trained to be palace officials, governmental administrators, or members of the elite Janissary corps in the army. This distinctive way of "recruiting" effective administrators and soldiers was

From Halil Inalcik, *The Ottoman Empire: The Classical Age, 1300–1600,* translated by Norman Itzkowitz and Colin Imber (New Rochelle, N.Y.: Aristide D. Caratzas, 1989), p. 41; and *The Turkish Letters of Ogier Ghiselin de Busbecq,* translated by Edward Seymour Foster (Oxford: The Clarendon Press, 1968), pp. 67–68, 109–114, 135–137.

already flourishing when Suleiman came to power and continued to work well for a couple of generations after his death.

The following two selections provide us with clues to the reasons for the success of the Ottomans during the reign of Suleiman. In the first selection, Suleiman describes his power in an inscription from a citadel built by the Turks at Bender in the northern Balkans in 1538. The second selection is a series of excerpts from letters written by Ogier Ghiselin de Busbecq, the ambassador from the Holy Roman Empire to the Ottoman Empire from 1554 to 1562. During Busbecq's time as ambassador to Constantinople there was much concern among Europeans about the military power of the Ottomans. In 1529 the Turks had surrounded Vienna, the capital of the Holy Roman Empire, and nearly captured it. The memory of this near-disaster and the continuing military threat posed by the Turks form part of the subtext of Busbecq's letters.

THE REIGN OF SULEIMAN

I. SULEIMAN THE LAWGIVER DESCRIBES HIS POWER

I am God's slave and sultan of this world. By the grace of God I am head of Muhammad's community. God's might and Muhammad's miracles are my companions. I am Süleymân, in whose name the *hutbe* [sermon] is read in Mecca and Medina. In Baghdad I am the shah, in Byzantine realms the Caesar, and in Egypt the sultan; who sends his fleets to the seas of Europe, the Maghrib and India. I am the sultan who took the crown and throne of Hungary and granted them to a humble slave. The voivoda Petru raised his head in revolt, but my horse's hoofs ground him into the dust, and I conquered the land of Moldavia.

II. FROM BUSBECQ'S LETTERS

A. *The Turkish Army (1560)*

The Sultan, when he sets out on a campaign, takes as many as 40,000 camels with him, and almost as many baggage-mules, most of whom, if his destination is Persia, are loaded with cereals of every kind, especially rice. Mules and camels are also employed to carry tents and arms and warlike machines and implements of every kind. The territories called Persia which are ruled by the Sophi, as we call him (the Turkish name being Kizilbash), are much less fertile than our country; and, further, it is the custom of the inhabitants, when their land is invaded, to lay waste and burn everything, and so force the enemy to retire through lack of food. The latter, therefore, are faced with serious peril, unless they bring an abundance of food with them. They are careful, however, to avoid touching the supplies which they carry with them as long as they are marching against their foes, but reserve them, as far as possible, for their return journey, when the moment for retirement comes and they are forced to retrace their steps through regions which the enemy has laid waste, or which the immense multitude of men and baggage animals has, as it were, scraped bare, like a swarm of locusts. It is only then that the Sultan's store of provisions is opened, and just enough food to sustain life is weighed out each day to the Janissaries and the other troops in attendance upon him. The other soldiers are badly off, if they have not provided food for their own use; most of them, having often experienced such difficulties during their campaigns—and this is particularly true of the cavalry—take a horse on a leading-rein loaded with many of the necessities of life. These include a small piece of canvas to use as a tent, which may protect them from the sun or a shower of rain, also some clothing and bedding and a private store of provisions, consisting of a leather sack or two of the finest flour, a small jar of butter, and some spices and salt; on these they support life when they are reduced to the extremes of hunger. They take a few spoonfuls of flour and place them in water, adding a little butter, and then flavour the mixture with salt and spices. This, when it is put on the fire, boils and swells up so as to fill a large bowl. They eat of it once or twice a day, according to the quantity, without any bread, unless they have with them some toasted bread or biscuit. They thus contrive to live on short rations for a month or even longer, if necessary. Some soldiers take with them a little sack full of beef dried and reduced to a powder, which they employ in the same manner as the flour, and which is of great benefit as a more solid form of nourishment. Sometimes, too, they have recourse to horseflesh; for in a great army a large number of horses necessarily dies, and any that die in good condition furnish a welcome meal to men who are starving. I may add that men whose horses have died, when the Sultan moves his camp, stand in a long row on the road by which he is to pass with their harness or saddles on their heads, as a sign that they have lost their horses, and implore his help to purchase others. The Sultan then assists them with whatever gift he thinks fit. . . .

I mentioned that baggage animals are employed on campaign to carry the arms and tents, which mainly belong to the Janissaries. The Turks take the utmost care to keep their soldiers in good health and protected from the inclemency of the weather; against the foe they must protect themselves, but their health is a matter for which the State must provide. Hence one sees the Turk better clothed than armed. He is particularly afraid of the cold, against which, even in the summer, he guards himself by wearing three garments, of which the innermost—call it shirt or what you will—is woven of coarse thread and provides much warmth. As a further protection against cold and rain tents are always carried, in which each man is given just enough space to lie down, so that one tent holds twenty-five or thirty Janissaries. The material for the garments to which I have referred is provided at the public expense. To prevent any disputes or suspicion of favour, it is distributed in the following manner. The soldiers are summoned by companies in the darkness to a place chosen for the purpose—the balloting station or whatever name you like to give it—where are laid out ready as many portions of cloth as there are soldiers in the company; they enter and take whatever chance offers them in the darkness, and they can only ascribe it to chance whether they get a good or a bad piece of cloth. For the same reason their pay is not counted out to them but weighed, so that no one can complain that he has received light or chipped coins. Also their pay is given them not on the day on which it falls due but on the day previous.

The armour which is carried is chiefly for the use of the household cavalry, for the Janissaries are lightly armed and do not usually fight at close quarters, but use muskets. When the enemy is at hand and a battle is expected, the armour is brought out, but it consists mostly of old pieces picked up in various battlefields, the spoil of former victories. These are distributed to the household cavalry, who are otherwise protected by only a light shield. You can image how badly the armour, thus hurriedly given out, fits its wearers. One man's breastplate is too small, another's helmet is too large, another's coat of mail is too heavy for him to bear. There is something wrong everywhere; but they bear it with equanimity and think that only a coward finds fault with his arms, and vow to distinguish themselves in the fight, whatever their equipment may be; such is the confidence inspired by repeated victories and constant experience of warfare. Hence also they do not hesitate to re-enlist a veteran infantryman in the cavalry, though he has never fought on horseback, since they are convinced that one who has warlike experience and long service will acquit himself well in any kind of fighting. . . .

B. Bows and Arrows and Other Matters (1560)

In many streets of Constantinople and at cross-roads there are shooting-grounds where not only boys and young men but even men of more advanced years congregate. An official is put in charge of the target and looks after it, watering the butt every day, since otherwise it would dry up and the arrows would not stick in it; for in the shooting-grounds they only use blunt arrows. The custodian of the target is always present and extracts the arrows from the earth, and after cleaning them throws them back to the archers. This entitles him to a fixed payment from every one, which provides him with a livelihood. The front of the target looks like a small door, which may perhaps have given rise to the proverb about 'shooting against the door,' which the Greeks applied to any one who altogether missed the target. For I believe that the Greeks formerly used the same kind of target, and that the Turks adopted it from them. I know, of course, that the use of the bow by the Turks is very ancient, but there is no reason why, when they came as conquerors to the Greek cities, they should not have continued the use of the target and butt which they found there. For no nation has shown less reluctance to adopt the useful inventions of others; for example, they have appropriated to their own use large and small cannons and many other of our discoveries. They have, however, never been able to bring themselves to print books and set up public clocks. They hold that their scriptures, that is, their sacred books, would no longer be scriptures if they were printed; and if they established public clocks, they think that the authority of their muezzins and their ancient rites would suffer diminution. In other matters they pay great respect to the time-honoured customs of foreign nations, even to the detriment of their own religious scruples. This, however, is only true of the lower classes. Every one knows how far they are from sympathizing with the rites of the Christian Church. The Greek priests, however, have a custom of, as it were, opening the closed sea by blessing the waters at a fixed date in the spring, before which the sailors do not readily entrust themselves to the waves. This ceremony the Turks do not altogether disregard. And so, when their preparations for a voyage have been made, they come to the Greeks and ask whether the waters have been blessed; and if they say that they have not been blessed, they put off the sailing, but, if they are told that the ceremony has been performed, they embark and set sail. . . .

There is one point about Turkish military manœuvres which I must not omit, namely, the old custom which goes back to the Parthians of pretending to flee on horseback and then shooting with their arms at the enemy when he rashly pursues.

They practise the rapid execution of this device in the following manner. They fix a brazen ball on the top of a very high pole, or mast, erected on level ground, and urge their horses at full speed towards the mast; and then, when they have almost passed it, they suddenly turn round and, leaning back, discharge an arrow at the ball, while the horse continues its course. By frequent practice they become able without any difficulty to hit their enemy unawares by shooting backwards as they fly. . . .

C. Christian Slaves (1555)

After remaining about a fortnight at Constantinople in order to regain my strength, I started on my journey to Vienna, the beginning of which may be said to have been ill omened. Just as we were leaving the city, we were met by wagon-loads of boys and girls who were being brought from Hungary to be sold in Constantinople. There is no commoner kind of merchandise than this in Turkey; and, just as on the roads out of Antwerp one meets loads of various kinds of goods, so from time to time we were met by gangs of wretched Christian slaves of every kind who were being led to horrible servitude. Youths and men of advanced years were driven along in herds or else were tied together with chains, as horses with us are taken to market, and trailed along in a long line. At the sight I could scarcely restrain my tears in pity for the wretched plight of the Christian population. . . .

STUDY QUESTIONS

1. What does Suleiman reveal about his religious convictions in the inscription? How does Suleiman describe the extent of his power?
2. According to Busbecq, in what ways did the Ottomans attempt to ensure the effectiveness of their army? In what ways did the Turkish army combine the use of new technologies with very old approaches to warfare?
3. What does Busbecq observe about the openness of the Turks to borrowing from other cultures? What technologies that were important to the Europeans did the Turks choose not to borrow? Why?
4. What is Busbecq's reaction to the *devshirme*?
5. Do you detect any bias in Busbecq's observations? Are there hints of exaggeration in Busbecq's letters? Why might he have wanted to overplay Ottoman military strength?
6. How did slavery in the Ottoman Empire compare with slavery in other parts of the world, for example, the Americas and Africa?
7. What are the advantages and disadvantages of using travelers' reports like that of Busbecq as sources of historical evidence?

VISUAL SOURCE

Ottoman Mosques

After the Ottomans conquered Constantinople in 1453 they converted the famed Church of the Holy Wisdom (Hagia Sophia) into a mosque and then launched a major program of building additional mosques in their new capital. To coordinate the construction program the sultans established a palace department of buildings. At the beginning of Suleiman's reign this agency employed 13 architects, all of whom were Muslim. Soon, however, the Turks discovered talented building designers among the Christians they recruited in the *devshirme* system. In 1538, Sinan, who came from a Christian family and was brought into the Janissary corps via the *devshirme* system, became chief court architect. For the next 50 years, until his death in 1588, Sinan designed and oversaw the construction of numerous mosques and imperial tombs in Istanbul and elsewhere. Scholars regard his buildings as the highpoint of Ottoman architectural design.

The New Mosque (*Yeni Cami*) pictured here was designed by a former apprentice of Sinan and is the last of the great mosques built during the classical period of Ottoman architecture. It was begun in the 1590s under the sponsorship of the Valide Sultan Safiye, the

The New Mosque (*Yeni Cami*) on the Golden Horn in Present-day Istanbul. Completed in 1663. (Photo by Stephen S. Gosch)

mother of Sultan Mehmet III. When Mehmet III died in 1603, construction was halted. After the unfinished mosque was destroyed by fire in 1660, it was rebuilt under the sponsorship of Valide Turhan Hadice, the mother of Sultan Mehmet IV.

The completed *Yeni Cami,* like the other imperial mosques in Istanbul, was part of a larger complex of religious and philanthropic institutions that included a hospital, a primary school, a mausoleum, two fountains, a public bath and a market. Revenues raised from the bath and the market helped support the rest of the complex.

STUDY QUESTIONS

1. How does the design of the mosque combine Islamic and Byzantine styles of religious architecture?
2. What features of the mosque suggest connections between religious and political authority?
3. How does the shape of the Istanbul skyline provide clues to the history of this city?

9

Babur and the Establishment of Mughal Rule in India

In 1000 C.E. Muslim nomads from the region of present-day Afghanistan began to conduct raids against the predominantly Hindu princes and peasants of India. Gradually, the Central Asian nomads were able to gain control over much of northern India and to establish a capital at Delhi. From 1206 to 1526 the Islamic sultans in Delhi struggled, with intermittent success, against both rival Muslim and native Hindu military leaders to make their rule effective.

Around 1500 a powerful new Muslim military leader of Turkish and Mongol descent, Zahiruddin Muhammad Babur (1483–1530), emerged on the arid plains northwest of India. Babur captured Kabul, made this city his capital, and then began a series of raids on the Muslim and Hindu warlords south of Khyber Pass. After winning a major victory at Panipat in 1526, he captured Delhi and took charge of much of northern India.

Babur's seizure of Delhi was a major turning point in the history of India. Although he died only a few years later, his brief period of rule was the beginning of the Mughal dynasty (1526–1858). The Mughal emperors brought political unity to most of the Indian subcontinent for the first time since the fall of the Gupta empire a thousand years earlier. From the reign of Babur's grandson Akbar (reigned 1556–1605) to that of Aurangzeb (reigned 1658–1707) the Mughal emperors were among the greatest rulers of the early modern world. The splendid palaces, fortresses, and tombs they built in Delhi, Agra (the home of the Taj Mahal), Fatehpur Sikri, and Lahore testify to their vast wealth and enormous power.

Babur, the founder of the Mughal dynasty, was a fierce warrior who also loved Persian poetry and elaborate gardens. He seem to have spent much of his life on horseback, but nonetheless found the time to write a fascinating account of his own life. His memoir, known as the *Baburnama,* is remarkably revealing about personal matters and provides scholars with valuable information regarding the process of state-building in sixteenth-century South Asia. In the selections from the *Baburnama* we can follow Babur and his soldiers as they enter India for the first time in 1505, win the Battle of Panipat, and begin the process of establishing the new regime.

From *The Baburnama: Memoirs of Babur, Prince and Emperor,* translated, edited, and annotated by Wheeler M. Thackston (New York: Oxford University Press, 1996). Translation copyright © 1996 by Smithsonian Institution. Used by permission of Oxford University Press, Inc., pp. 185, 323–327, 363, 415.

SELECTIONS FROM THE *BABURNAMA*

First Incursion into Hindustan

In the month of Sha'ban [January 1505] when the sun was in the sign of Aquarius we rode out of Kabul for Hindustan. Stopping six times overnight on the Badam Chashma and Jagdalak road, we came to Adinapur. I had never seen a hot climate or any of Hindustan before. When we reached Nangarhar, a new world came into view—different plants, different trees, different animals and birds, different tribes and people, different manners and customs. It was astonishing, truly astonishing. . . .

· · ·

Preparation for Battle [1526]

We marched from there, arrayed the right and left wings and center, and had a *dim* [a count of the soldiers]. We had fewer men than we had estimated. I ordered the whole army, in accordance with rank, to bring carts, which numbered about seven hundred altogether. Master Ali-Quli was told to tie them together with ox-harness ropes instead of chains, after the Anatolian manner, keeping a distance of six to seven large shields between every two carts. The matchlockmen could then stand behind the fortification to fire their guns. Five or six days were spent arranging it, and when it was ready I summoned to general council all the begs and great warriors who knew what they were talking about. We discussed the following: Panipat was a town with lots of suburbs and houses. The suburbs and houses would protect one side, but it was necessary to fortify our other sides with the carts and shields and to station matchlockmen and foot soldiers behind them. This having been decided, we marched, bivouacked, and then came to Panipat on Wednesday the last day of Jumada II [April 12].

To our right were the town and suburbs. Directly before us were the arranged shields. To the left and elsewhere were trenches and pylons. At every distance of an arrow shot, space was left for 100 to 150 cavalrymen to emerge. Some of the soldiers were hesitant, but their trepidation was baseless, for only what God has decreed from all eternity will happen. They cannot be blamed, however, for being afraid, even if God was on their side. They had traveled for two or three months from their homeland, and had had to deal with an unfamiliar people whose language we did not know and who did not know ours. . . .

Sultan Ibrahim's army was estimated at one hundred thousand. He and his commanders were said to have nearly a thousand elephants. Moreover, he possessed the treasury left over from two generations of his fathers. The custom in Hindustan is to hire liege men for money before major battles. Such people are called *badhandi*. If Sultan Ibrahim had had a mind to, he could have hired one hundred thousand to two hundred thousand troops. Thank God he was able neither to satisfy his warriors nor to part with his treasury. How was he to please his men when his nature was so overwhelmingly dominated by miserliness? He himself was an inexperienced young man who craved beyond all things the acquisition of money—neither his oncoming nor his stand was calculated to have a good end, and neither his march nor his fighting was energetic. . . .

The Battle of Panipat [1526]

On Friday the eighth of Rajab [April 20] news came at dawn from the scouts that the enemy was coming in battle array. We put on our armor, armed ourselves, and got to horse.

The enemy's troops appeared, headed toward the left wing. For this reason Abdul-Aziz, who had been assigned to the reserve, was dispatched as reinforcement to the left wing. Sultan Ibrahim's army could be seen nearby, coming quickly without stopping. However, as they came farther forward and our troops became visible to them, they broke the ranks they had maintained and, as though undecided whether to stand or proceed, were able to do neither.

The order was given for the men who had been assigned to the flank assault to circle around to the enemy's rear from left and right, shoot their arrows, and begin to fight, and for the right and left wings to advance and engage the enemy. The flank assaulters circled around and began to shoot. From the left wing Mahdi Khwaja had already reached the enemy; advancing upon him was a contingent with an elephant, but by shooting many arrows he drove them back.

Master Ali-Quli got off a few good gunshots from in front of the center. Mustafa the artilleryman also fired some good shots from the mortars mounted on carts to the left of the center. Right wing, left wing, center, and flank assault shot arrows into the enemy from all sides and fought in all seriousness. Once or twice the enemy tried half-hearted assaults in the direction of our right and left wings, but our men pushed them into their own center by shooting. The enemy's right and left flanks were so crowded into one spot that they were not able to go forward or to find a way to escape.

The sun was one lance high when battle was enjoined. The fighting continued until midday. At noon the enemy was overcome and vanquished to the delight of our friends. By God's grace and generosity such a difficult action was made easy for us, and such a numerous army was ground into the dust in half a day. Five or six thousand men were killed in one place near Ibrahim. All told, the dead of this battle were estimated at between fifteen and sixteen thousand. Later, when we came to Agra, we learned from reports by the people of Hindustan that forty to fifty thousand men had died in the battle. With the enemy defeated and felled, we proceeded. Along the way the men began to capture the fallen commanders and Afghans and bring them in. Droves of elephants were caught and presented by the elephant keepers. Thinking that Ibrahim may have escaped, we assigned Qïsïmtay Mirza, Baba Chuhra, and Böchkä's troops from the royal tabin to pursue him behind the enemy lines and move with all speed to Agra. Crossing through the midst of Ibrahim's camp, we inspected the tents and pavilions and then camped beside a still river. It was midafternoon when Tahir the Axman, Khalifa's brother-in-law, discovered Sultan Ibrahim's body amidst many corpses and brought in his head.

That very day we assigned Humayun Mirza, Khwaja Kalan, Muhammadi, Shah-Mansur Barlas, Yunus Ali, Abdullah, and Wali Khazin to proceed swiftly and unencumbered, get hold of Agra, and confiscate the treasury. We appointed Mahdi Khwaja, Muhammad-Sultan Mirza, Adil Sultan, Sultan-Junayd Barlas, and Qutlugh-Qadam to separate themselves from the baggage and ride fast, enter the Delhi fortress, and guard the treasuries. The next morning we proceeded for a league and then, for the sake of the horses, camped beside the Jumna.

Babur Enters Delhi

On Tuesday, after two bivouacs, I circumambulated Shaykh Nizam Awliya's tomb and camped beside the Jumna directly opposite Delhi. That evening I toured the Delhi fortress, where I spent the night; the next morning, Wednesday, I circumambulated Khwaja Qutbuddin's tomb and toured Sultan Ghiyasuddin Balban's and Sultan Aluddin Khalji's tombs, buildings, and minaret, the Shamsi pool, the Khass pool, and Sultan Bahlul's and Sultan Iskandar's tombs and gardens. After the tour I returned to the camp, got on a boat, and drank spirits.

I made Wali Qïzïl the provost of Delhi; I made Dost the divan of the province of Delhi; and I had the treasuries there sealed and turned them over to them for safekeeping.

On Thursday we marched out and camped beside the Jumna directly opposite Tughluqabad.

On Friday we stayed in camp. Mawlana Mahmud, Shaykh Zayn, and some others went to perform the Friday prayer in Delhi and read the proclamation in my name. Having distributed some money to the poor and unfortunate, they returned to camp.

On Saturday the army proceeded by forced march toward Agra. I went for a tour of Tughluqabad and returned to camp.

On Friday the twenty-second of Rajab [May 4] we stopped in Sulayman Farmuli's quarters in the suburbs of Agra. Since this site was far from the fortress, we moved the next morning to Jalal Khan Jighat's palace. Humayun had gone on ahead, but the men inside the fortress made excuses to keep him out. When they noticed how unruly the people were, they maintained watch over the exit, afraid someone might pilfer the treasury, until we should get there. . . .

• • •

Ali-Qulï Casts a Mortar

Master Ali-Qulï was ordered to cast a large mortar to be used on Bayana and some of the other fortresses that had not yet entered our domain. When he had the smelting furnace and all the implements ready, he sent someone to inform me. On Monday the fifteenth of Muharram [October 22, 1526] we went to watch Master Ali-Qulï cast the mortar. Around the place where it was to be cast he had constructed eight smelting furnaces and had already melted the metal. From the bottom of each furnace he had made a channel straight to the mortar mold. Just as we got there he was opening the holes in the furnaces. The molten metal was pouring like water into the mold, but after a while, before the mold was filled, one by one the streams of molten metal coming from the furnaces stopped. There was some flaw either in the furnace or in the metal. Master Ali-Qulï went into a strange depression and was about to throw himself into the mold of molten bronze, but I soothed him, gave him a robe of honor, and got him out of his black mood. A day or two later, when the mold had cooled, they opened it, and Master Ali-Qulï sent someone to announce with glee that the shaft was flawless. It was then easy to attach the powder chamber. He took out the shaft and assigned some men to fix it, and got to work connecting the chamber.

• • •

Post System Established between Agra and Kabul

On Thursday the fourth of Rabi' II [December 17, 1528], it was decided that Chaqmaq Beg with Shahi Tamghachī as recorder should measure by cord the distance from Agra to Kabul. Every nine kos they were to raise a tower twelve yards high with a chardara on top. Every eighteen kos six post horses were to be kept, and maintenance for the post riders, grooms, and feed for the horses were to be assigned. It was ordered that if the place where the post horses were kept was a royal demesne, the above-mentioned items were to be taken care of therefrom. Otherwise, they were to make it the responsibility of the beg on whose estate it was. Chaqmaq and Shahi left Agra that same day. . . .

STUDY QUESTIONS

1. What was Babur's first reaction to India?
2. What measures did he take to prepare for the battle of Panipat?
3. How did he compare his army with that of Sultan Ibrahim?
4. How did he explain his victory at Panipat? In Babur's judgment, which was more important, his own preparations for the battle or God's "grace and generosity"?
5. What measures did Babur take to consolidate his power and establish a new regime after his victory at Panipat?
6. What weapons seem to have been most important to Babur? Where did he obtain them?
7. To what extent did Babur's Muslim beliefs shape his actions? Did he disregard some Muslim tenets? Did he think of himself as leading a *jihad*? Why did he invade India?
8. How did Babur's army compare with that of his contemporary, Suleiman, the Ottoman sultan? (See Chapter 8.)
9. In what ways were the political systems in the Ottoman empire, Mughal India, and Ming China similar and different?

VISUAL SOURCE

Mughal Painting

Babur spent his early years on the grasslands north of present-day Afghanistan, where at a very young age he was swept into the fighting between rival tribes of nomads. In 1504, at age 21, he led his army in the capture of Kabul. For the rest of his life Babur seems to have regarded this great walled caravan city, then a leading center of long-distance trade and cross-cultural interchange, as his base. While in Kabul, he launched numerous military expeditions into Central Asia and northern India, indulged his passion for gardening, wrote poetry, and fathered four sons.

Babur at Court in Kabul, 1508. From the *Baburnama*, ca. 1590.
(Victoria & Albert Museum/Art Resource, NY)

In this painting Babur is at court in Kabul, receiving gifts to celebrate the birth of his eldest son Humayun, his successor as Mughal emperor. Dating from the 1590s, the painting is one of many illustrations done for the sumptuous hand-copied edition of the *Babur-nama* sponsored by Babur's grandson Emperor Akbar (reigned 1556–1605), under whose leadership the power and wealth of the Mughal dynasty reached its highpoint.

Although Akbar could not read, he enjoyed being read to daily and established a huge palace workshop—which included calligraphers, illustrators, and bookbinders—for the production of fine books. The illustrators worked in teams and created a distinctive tradition of Mughal art by fusing Persian, Indian, and European styles of painting.

STUDY QUESTIONS

1. What aspects of Babur's court are illustrated in the painting?
2. How does the construction of Babur's throne recall his early life on the plains of Central Asia?
3. What does the painting suggest about gender relations at Babur's court?
4. How might this painting, and the book in which it appeared, be viewed as attempts by Akbar to strengthen the authority of the Mughal dynasty?

10

Confucian Ideals in Ming China: A Set of Family Instructions

For the past 2,000 years the ideas of Confucius, the sixth-century B.C.E. philosopher, have been enormously influential in China. As early as the Han dynasty (206 B.C.E.–220 C.E.) Chinese emperors promoted the study of Confucianism and made mastery of Confucian texts a means of obtaining an appointment to the government. By the time of the Song dynasty (960–1279) every candidate for a position in the Chinese government had to spend many years preparing for rigorous civil service examinations based on the teachings of Confucius; there was now no other way to become an official.

The conquest of China by the Mongols, who ruled China from 1279 to 1368, was a setback for Confucianism. But the restoration of native Chinese rule by the Ming emperors starting in 1368 marked the beginning of a revival of Confucian teachings. Chinese emperors during the Ming (1368–1644) and succeeding Qing (1644–1912) dynasties gave strong support to the examination system and to the diffusion of Confucian teachings throughout their realm.

In this selection, dating from the late Ming period, Confucian ideals are illustrated in a set of instructions issued by the leaders of a lineage group in southern China. Lineage groups, also known as clans or common-descent groups, were alliances of extended families who joined together for mutual support. The members of lineages met regularly to celebrate the memory of their ancestors and to manage their common interests, which often included the joint ownership of land. Lineages were important social institutions in China from the Ming period onward, especially in the south.

How do the instructions illustrate the power of Confucianism at the local level? Why did emperors and lineage heads encourage adherence to Confucian teachings?

CONFUCIAN TEACHINGS

Work Hard at One of the Principal Occupations

1. To be filial to one's parents, to be loving to one's brothers, to be diligent and frugal—these are the first tenets of a person of good character. They must be thoroughly understood and faithfully carried out.

From *Chinese Civilization: A Sourcebook,* 2nd ed., by Patricia Buckley Ebrey (New York: The Free Press, 1993), pp. 238–244. Copyright © 1993 by Patricia Buckley Ebrey. Reprinted with the permission of The Free Press, a Division of Simon & Schuster, Inc.

One's conscience should be followed like a strict teacher and insight should be sought through introspection. One should study the words and deeds of the ancients to find out their ultimate meanings. One should always remember the principles followed by the ancients, and should not become overwhelmed by current customs. For if one gives in to cruelty, pride, or extravagance, all virtues will be undermined, and nothing will be achieved.

Parents have special responsibilities. The *Book of Changes* says: "The members of a family have strict sovereigns." These "sovereigns" are the parents. Their position in a family is one of unique authority, and they should utilize their authority to dictate matters to maintain order, and to inspire respect, so that the members of the family will all be obedient. If the parents are lenient and indulgent, there will be many troubles which in turn will give rise to even more troubles. Who is to blame for all this? The elders in a family must demand discipline of themselves, following all rules and regulations to the letter, so that the younger members emulate their good behavior and exhort each other to abide by the teachings of the ancient sages. Only in this way can the family hope to last for generations. . . .

2. Those youngsters who have taken Confucian scholarship as their hereditary occupation should be sincere and hard-working, and try to achieve learning naturally while studying under a teacher. Confucianism is the only thing to follow if they wish to bring glory to their family. Those who know how to keep what they have but do not study are as useless as puppets made of clay or wood. Those who study, even if they do not succeed in the examinations, can hope to become teachers or to gain personal benefit. However, there are people who study not for learning's sake, but as a vulgar means of gaining profit. These people are better off doing nothing.

Youngsters who are incapable of concentrating on studying should devote themselves to farming; they should personally grasp the ploughs and eat the fruit of their own labor. In this way they will be able to support their families. If they fold their hands and do nothing, they will soon have to worry about hunger and cold. If, however, they realize that their forefathers also worked hard and that farming is a difficult way of life, they will not be inferior to anyone. In earlier dynasties, officials were all selected because they were filial sons, loving brothers, and diligent farmers. This was to set an example for all people to devote themselves to their professions, and to ensure that the officials were familiar with the hardships of the common people, thereby preventing them from exploiting the commoners for their own profit.

3. Farmers should personally attend to the inspection, measurement, and management of the fields, noting the soil as well as the terrain. The early harvest as well as the grain taxes and the labor service obligations should be carefully calculated. Anyone who indulges in indolence and entrusts these matters to others will not be able to distinguish one kind of crop from another and will certainly be cheated by others. I do not believe such a person could escape bankruptcy.

4. The usual occupations of the people are farming and commerce. If one tries by every possible means to make a great profit from these occupations, it usually leads to loss of capital. Therefore it is more profitable to put one's energy into farming the land; only when the fields are too far away to be tilled by oneself should they be leased to others. One should solicit advice from old farmers as to one's own capacity in farming.

Those who do not follow the usual occupations of farming or business should be taught a skill. Being an artisan is a good way of life and will also shelter a person from hunger and cold. All in all, it is important to remember that one should work hard when young, for when youth expires one can no longer achieve anything. Many people learn this lesson only after it is too late. We should guard against this mistake. . . .

5. Housewives should take full charge of the kitchen. They should make sure that the store of firewood is sufficient, so that even if it rains several days in succession, they will not be forced to use silver or rice to pay for firewood, thereby impoverishing the family. Housewives should also closely calculate the daily grocery expenses, and make sure there is no undue extravagance. Those who simply sit and wait to be fed not only are treating themselves like pigs and dogs, but also are leading their whole households to ruin. . . .

Observe the Rituals and Proprieties

1. Capping and wedding ceremonies should be carried out according to one's means. Funerals and burials, being important matters, should be more elaborate, but one should still be mindful of financial considerations. Any other petty formalities not found in the *Book of Rites* should be abolished.

2. Marriage arrangements should not be made final by the presenting of betrothal gifts until the boy and girl have both reached thirteen; otherwise, time might bring about changes which cause regrets.

3. For the seasonal sacrifices, the ancestral temple should be prepared in advance and the ceremonies performed at dawn in accordance with [Zhu Xi's] *Family Rituals* and our own ancestral temple regulations.

4. For burials one should make an effort to acquire solid and long-lasting objects to be placed in the coffin; but one need not worry as much about the tomb itself, which can be constructed according to one's means. The ancients entrusted their bodies to the hills and mountains, indifferent to whether their names would be remembered by posterity; their thinking was indeed profound.

5. Sacrifices at the graves should be made on Tomb Sweeping Day and at the Autumn Festival. Because the distances to different mountains vary, it is difficult to reach every grave on those days. Therefore, all branch families should be notified in advance of the order of priority: first, the founding father of our lineage; then ancestors earlier than great-great-grandfather; next, ancestors down to each person's grandfather. Established customs should be followed in deciding how much wine and meat should be used, how many different kinds of sacrificial offerings should be presented, and how much of the yearly budget should be spent on the sacrifices. All of these should be recorded in a special "sacrifice book" in order to set standards.

6. Not celebrating one's birthday has since ancient times been regarded as an exemplary virtue. An exception is the birthdays of those who are beyond their sixty-first year, which should be celebrated by their sons and grandsons drinking to their health. But under no circumstances should birthdays become pretexts for heavy drinking. If either of one's parents has died, it is an especially unfilial act to forget him or her and indulge in drinking and feasting. Furthermore, to drink until dead-drunk not only affects one's mind but also harms one's health. The numbers of people who have been ruined by drinking should serve as a warning.

7. On reaching five, a boy should be taught to recite the primers and not be allowed to show arrogance or laziness. On reaching six, a girl should be taught [Ban Zhao's] *Admonitions for Women* and not be allowed to venture out of her chamber. If children are frequently given snacks and playfully entertained, their nature will be spoiled and they will grow up to be unruly and bad. This can be prevented if caught at an early age.

8. When inviting guests to dinner, one should serve not more than five dishes or more than two soups. Wine and rice should also be served in the right proportion.

9. When attending a funeral service, one should bring only incense and paper money, never hand towels, fruit, or wine, and should stay for only one cup of tea.

10. Gifts presented to us on the occasion of ancestor worship are to be properly compensated for by cash. If the gift box contains a pig's head, the corresponding return would be one-tenth of a tael [ounce] of silver; for two geese and wine it would be three-tenths of a tael; for a lamb and wine, half a tael; a pig and wine, one tael. In addition, two-hundredths of a tael [ounce] should be placed in an envelope and presented as a token compensation for fruit and wine. Whether or not these are accepted, and whether or not another present is given in return, depends on the other party. For ceremonies held in our own village, each person should contribute two-hundredths of a tael of silver, and four people should share one table. Those who have contributed yet fail to attend the banquet will get their money back in the original envelope. This is to be stated in the village agreements and to be practiced by all.

Prohibit Extravagance

1. All our young people should wear cotton clothes and eat vegetables. Only on special occasions such as ancestor worship or dinner parties are they to be allowed to drink wine, eat meat, and temporarily put on new clothes. They are fortunate enough to be sheltered from hunger and cold; how dare they feel ashamed of their coarse clothing and coarse food! Also, they should do physical labor. As long as they are capable of carrying loads with their hands and on their backs, they have no need to hire servants. They are fortunate enough not to be ordered around by others; how dare they order other people around! They should learn to cherish every inch of cloth and every half-penny, thereby escaping poverty.

2. Among relatives, presents should not be exchanged more than twice a year, and the gifts should not cost more than one-tenth of a tael of silver. Relatives should agree to abide by the principle of frugality and refuse any gift exceeding this limit. This rule, however, does not include celebrations and funerals, for which custom should be followed. . . .

Exercise Restraint

1. Our young people should know their place and observe correct manners. They are not permitted to gamble, to fight, to engage in lawsuits, or to deal in salt privately. Such unlawful acts will only lead to their own downfall.

2. If land or property is not obtained by righteous means, descendants will not be able to enjoy it. When the ancients invented characters, they put gold next

to two spears to mean "money," indicating that the danger of plunder or robbery is associated with it. If money is not accumulated by good means, it will disperse like overflowing water; how could it be put to any good? The result is misfortune for oneself as well as for one's posterity. This is the meaning of the saying: "The way of Heaven detests fullness, and only the humble gain." Therefore, accumulation of great wealth inevitably leads to great loss. How true are the words of Laozi!

A person's fortune and rank are predestined. One can only do one's best according to propriety and one's own ability; the rest is up to Heaven. If one is easily contented, then a diet of vegetables and soups provides a lifetime of joy. If one does not know one's limitations and tries to accumulate wealth by immoral and dishonest means, how can one avoid disaster? To be able to support oneself through life and not leave one's sons and grandsons in hunger and cold is enough; why should one toil so much?

3. Pride is a dangerous trait. Those who pride themselves on wealth, rank, or learning are inviting evil consequences. Even if one's accomplishments are indeed unique, there is no need to press them on anyone else. "The way of Heaven detests fullness, and only the humble gain." I have seen the truth of this saying many times.

4. Taking concubines in order to beget heirs should be a last resort, for the sons of the legal wife and the sons of the concubine are never of one mind, causing innumerable conflicts between half brothers. If the parents are in the least partial, problems will multiply, creating misfortune in later generations. Since families have been ruined because of this, it should not be taken lightly.

5. Just as diseases are caused by what goes into one's mouth, misfortunes are caused by what comes out of one's mouth. Those who are immoderate in eating and unrestrained in speaking have no one else to blame for their own ruin.

6. Most men lack resolve and listen to what their women say. As a result, blood relatives become estranged and competitiveness, suspicion, and distance arise between them. Therefore, when a wife first comes into a family, it should be made clear to her that such things are prohibited. "Start teaching one's son when he is a baby; start teaching one's daughter-in-law when she first arrives." That is to say, preventive measures should be taken early.

7. "A family's fortune can be foretold from whether its members are early risers" is a maxim of our ancient sages. Everyone, male and female, should rise before dawn and should not go to bed until after the first drum. Never should they indulge themselves in a false sense of security and leisure, for such behavior will eventually lead them to poverty.

8. Young family members who deliberately violate family regulations should be taken to the family temple, have their offenses reported to the ancestors, and be severely punished. They should then be taught to improve themselves. Those who do not accept punishment or persist in their wrongdoings will bring harm to themselves.

9. As a preventive measure against the unpredictable, the gates should be closed at dusk, and no one should be allowed to go out. Even when there are visitors, dinner parties should end early, so that there will be no need for lighting lamps and candles. On very hot or very cold days, one should be especially considerate of the kitchen servants.

10. For generations this family has dwelt in the country, and everyone has had a set profession; therefore, our descendants should not be allowed to change their place of residence. After living in the city for three years, a person forgets everything about farming; after ten years, he does not even know his lineage. Extravagance and leisure transform people, and it is hard for anyone to remain unaffected. I once remarked that the only legitimate excuse to live in a city temporarily is to flee from bandits.

11. The inner and outer rooms, halls, doorways, and furniture should be swept and dusted every morning at dawn. Dirty doorways and courtyards and haphazardly placed furniture are sure signs of a declining family. Therefore, a schedule should be followed for cleaning them, with no excuses allowed.

12. Those in charge of cooking and kitchen work should make sure that breakfast is served before nine o'clock in the morning and dinner before five o'clock in the afternoon. Every evening the iron wok and other utensils should be washed and put away, so that the next morning, after rising at dawn, one can expect tea and breakfast to be prepared immediately and served on time. In the kitchen no lamps are allowed in the morning or at night. This is not only to save the expense, but also to avoid harmful contamination of food. Although this is a small matter, it has a great effect on health. Furthermore, since all members of the family have their regular work to do, letting them toil all day without giving them meals at regular hours is no way to provide comfort and relief for them. If these rules are deliberately violated, the person in charge will be punished as an example to the rest.

13. On the tenth and twenty-fifth days of every month, all the members of this branch, from the honored aged members to the youngsters, should gather at dusk for a meeting. Each will give an account of what he has learned, by either calling attention to examples of good and evil, or encouraging diligence, or expounding his obligations, or pointing out tasks to be completed. Each member will take turns presenting his own opinions and listening attentively to others. He should examine himself in the matters being discussed and make efforts to improve himself. The purpose of these meetings is to encourage one another in virtue and to correct each other's mistakes.

The members of the family will take turns being the chairman of these meetings, according to schedule. If someone is unable to chair a meeting on a certain day, he should ask the next person in line to take his place. The chairman should provide tea, but never wine. The meetings may be canceled on days of ancestor worship, parties, or other such occasions, or if the weather is severe. Those who are absent from these meetings for no reason are only doing themselves harm.

There are no set rules for where the meeting should be held, but the place should be convenient for group discussions. The time of the meeting should always be early evening, for this is when people have free time. As a general precaution the meeting should never last until late at night.

14. Women from lower-class families who stop at our houses tend to gossip, create conflicts, peek into the kitchens, or induce our women to believe in prayer and fortune-telling, thereby cheating them out of their money and possessions. Consequently, one should question these women often and punish those who come for no reason, so as to put a stop to the traffic.

15. Blood relatives are as close as the branches of a tree, yet their relationships can still be differentiated according to importance and priority: Parents should be considered before brothers, and brothers should be considered before

wives and children. Each person should fulfill his own duties and share with others profit and loss, joy and sorrow, life and death. In this way, the family will get along well and be blessed by Heaven. Should family members fight over property or end up treating each other like enemies, then when death or misfortune strikes they will be of even less use than strangers. If our ancestors have consciousness, they will not tolerate these unprincipled descendants who are but animals in man's clothing. Heaven responds to human vices with punishments as surely as an echo follows a sound. I hope my sons and grandsons take my words seriously.

16. To get along with patrilinear relatives, fellow villagers, and relatives through marriage, one should be gentle in speech and mild in manners. When one is opposed by others, one may remonstrate with them; but when others fall short because of their limitations, one should be tolerant. If one's youngsters or servants get into fights with others, one should look into oneself to find the blame. It is better to be wronged than to wrong others. Those who take affront and become enraged, who conceal their own shortcomings and seek to defeat others, are courting immediate misfortune. Even if the other party is unbearably unreasonable, one should contemplate the fact that the ancient sages had to endure much more. If one remains tolerant and forgiving, one will be able to curb the other party's violence.

Preserve the Family Property

1. The houses, fields, and ponds that have been accumulated by the family should not be divided or sold. Violators of this rule will be severely admonished and barred from the ancestral temple. . . .

STUDY QUESTIONS

1. According to the *Family Instructions,* what are the attributes of someone with "good character"?
2. What roles are prescribed in the *Instructions* for parents, young people, and women?
3. What procedures does the lineage have for enforcing these prescriptions?
4. What do we learn from the *Instructions* about the importance of ritual and ancestor worship in Chinese culture?
5. What do the *Instructions* reveal about the Chinese economy?
6. What can you infer about the likely age, sex, and social class of the author of the *Instructions*?
7. What are the strengths and weaknesses of Confucianism as a means of providing for social order?
8. Why did Confucianism spread to Korea, Japan, and Vietnam, but not elsewhere?
9. How did lineages in China resemble and differ from castes in India?
10. In what ways would the ideas in the *Family Instructions* promote or discourage the development of a modern industrial society? How does Confucianism compare with Islam and Christianity in this regard?
11. What explains the strength of Confucian teachings among present-day Chinese?
12. Are social hierarchies inevitable in large-scale societies?

VISUAL SOURCE

Confucian Architecture

One of the most influential books in China, ca. 1200–1900, was Zhu Xi's *Family Rituals,* a work first published around 1170 and frequently reprinted in later centuries. Zhu Xi was the leading Confucian philosopher of the Song dynasty (960–1279). He wrote the *Family Rituals* to provide commoners with instructions regarding the correct way to practice the Confucian rites required at births, weddings, funerals, and other ceremonial occasions.

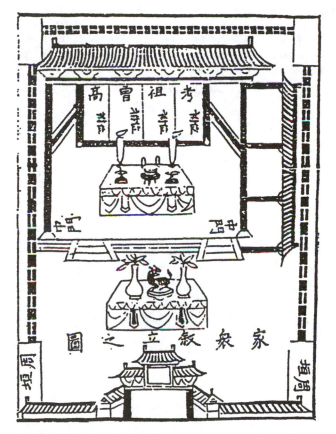

Family Offering Hall, China. Woodblock print, 1602.
(Francesca Bray, Technology and Gender: Fabrics of Power in Late Imperial China, 1997, p. 97.)

The first chapter of *Family Rituals* focuses on the importance of the offering hall, the ritual center in the ideal Chinese home. In the offering hall the family worshipped the spirits of its ancestors from the past four generations. (The spirits of earlier forebears were worshipped in communal offering halls.) Small wooden tablets that bore the names of the deceased—arranged according to generation and sex—stood on the shrine in the center of the hall.

Although no ancestor tablets appear in the woodcut shown here, many of the features of a typical offering hall are clearly illustrated. The hall, which was to face south whenever possible, is located at the rear of a walled courtyard, to which a large and decorative gate gives access. Two small stairways lead from the courtyard to the shrine, one on the east for the eldest male and one on the west for the eldest female. Behind the shrine, the characters on a four-part screen indicate the order in which the ancestral tablets are to be arranged.

Illustrated guidebooks on the proprieties of ancestor worship circulated widely during the Ming and Qing periods.

STUDY QUESTIONS

1. How does the print illustrate the importance of Confucian teachings?
2. What does the publication of guidebooks imply about the extent of literacy in China during the Ming and Qing dynasties?

11

Early Modern Japan

From 1600 to 1868 Japan was under the rule of the Tokugawa shoguns, a dynasty of military leaders. The new regime was founded by Tokugawa Ieyasu, a member of the new class of landowning warriors called *daimyō*. Ieyasu triumphed over his key rivals at the Battle of Sekigahara in 1600 and then pressured the emperor, who was effectively powerless but was the official head of state, to appoint him as shogun (supreme military leader). During the following half-century Ieyasu and his first two successors as shogun established the main features of the new system of rule.

From their immense palace complex at Edo (present-day Tokyo), which Ieyasu established as the Tokugawa capital, the shoguns issued a steady stream of decrees designed to control the conduct of their subjects in the most thorough way. In order to make the system of controls effective, the shoguns adopted a policy of isolating Japan from foreign influences. They suppressed Christianity—which had spread widely in southern Japan since the 1550s—and also expelled European merchants, banned most overseas commerce, and prohibited Japanese who were living abroad from returning home. To obtain some knowledge of developments abroad, the shoguns allowed trade with China to continue and also permitted an annual visit to Nagasaki harbor by Dutch merchants. The overall effect of the policies of the shoguns was to isolate Japan from the wider world for about 250 years.

Within Japan, the shoguns balanced their harsh system of rules with a measure of genuine autonomy for the 250 or so *daimyō* whose large rice-producing domains (estates) were scattered throughout the Japanese countryside. The *daimyō* were feudal lords whose domains resembled small states. Each of the domains was strictly administered by thousands of sword-bearing samurai officials for whom, given the Tokugawa system, literacy and numeracy rather than military prowess were increasingly important.

The system of shared authority between the shoguns and the *daimyō* rested squarely on the strong backs of the Japanese peasants. The peasants produced all the rice, soybeans, cotton, hemp, and silk consumed in Japan during the Tokugawa period. About one-third of the peasants lived on lands directly administered by the shoguns. The rest of the cultivators resided on the domains of the *daimyō*.

Selections I–IV from David John Lu, *Sources of Japanese History*, Vol. 1 (New York: McGraw-Hill, 1974), pp. 201–203, 205–209, 215, 225–227, 248–250. Selection V from E. S. Crawcour, "Some Observations on Merchants: A Translation of Mitsui Takafusa's *Chonin Koken Roku*," *Transactions of the Asiatic Society of Japan*, 3rd series, Vol. 8 (1962), pp. 31–32, 38–39, 114–116, 120–122.

Despite the policy of isolation and the extraordinarily strict laws to which the population was subjected, there was much vibrancy in Japanese economic, social, and cultural life during the Tokugawa period. Commerce flourished in rice, *sake*, soy sauce, silk, cotton, and tea. A prosperous merchant class developed, especially in the cities of Edo, Osaka, and Kyoto, all of which became major population centers by 1750. Performances of colorful *kabuki* plays before huge crowds of urban commoners and the production of beautiful woodblock prints of leading actors and *geisha* courtesans signaled the emergence of a lively popular culture. Schools that taught at least the basics of literacy were widespread. Indeed, recent research suggests that by 1800 literacy and certain aspects of material life in Japan (diet, housing, clothing, and standards of hygiene) were quite high by world standards.

How do the following documents illustrate policies of the shoguns and the *daimyō*, and also hint at some of the dynamism in early modern Japan?

SHOGUN AND *DAIMYŌ* POLICIES

I. LAWS FOR THE WARRIOR CLASS (1615)

[Shortly before his death, Tokugawa Ieyasu issued the following decree to the members of the warrior class (daimyō, lesser lords, and samurai).]

1. The study of literature and the practice of the military arts, including archery and horsemanship, must be cultivated diligently.

"On the left hand literature, on the right hand use of arms" was the rule of the ancients. Both must be pursued concurrently. Archery and horsemanship are essential skills for military men. It is said that war is a curse. However, it is resorted to only when it is inevitable. In time of peace, do not forget the possibility of disturbances. Train yourselves and be prepared.

2. Avoid group drinking and wild parties.

The existing codes strictly forbid these matters. Especially when one indulges in licentious sex, or becomes addicted to gambling, it creates a cause for the destruction of one's own domain.

3. Anyone who violates the law must not be harbored in any domain. Law is the foundation of social order. Reason may be violated in the name of law, but law may not be violated in the name of reason. Anyone who violates the law must be severely punished.

4. The *daimyō*, the lesser lords (*shōmyō*), and those who hold land under them (*kyunin*) must at once expel from their domains any of their own retainers or soldiers who are charged with treason or murder.

Anyone who entertains a treasonous design can become an instrument for destroying the nation and a deadly sword to annihilate the people. How can this be tolerated?

5. Hereafter, do not allow people from other domains to mingle or reside in your own domain. This ban does not apply to people from your own domain.

Each domain has its own customs different from others. If someone wishes to divulge his own domain's secrets to people of another domain, or to report the secrets of another domain to people of his own domain, he is showing a sign of his intent to curry favors.

6. The castles in various domains may be repaired, provided the matter is reported without fail. New construction of any kind is strictly forbidden.

A castle with a parapet exceeding ten feet in height and 3,000 feet in length is injurious to the domain. Steep breastworks and deep moats are causes of a great rebellion.

7. If innovations are being made or factions are being formed in a neighboring domain, it must be reported immediately.

Men have a proclivity toward forming factions, but seldom do they attain their goals. There are some who [on account of their factions] disobey their masters and fathers, and feud with their neighboring villages. Why must one engage in [meaningless] innovations, instead of obeying old examples?

8. Marriage must not be contracted in private [without approval from the *bakufu* (shogunate)].

Marriage is the union symbolizing the harmony of *yin* and *yang*, and it cannot be entered into lightly. The thirty-eighth hexagram *kui* [in the *Book of Changes*], says "Marriage is not to be contracted to create disturbance. Let the longing of male and female for each other be satisfied. If disturbance is to take hold, then the proper time will slip by." The "Peach young" poem of the *Book of Odes* says "When men and women observe what is correct, and marry at the proper time, there will be no unattached women in the land." To form a factional alliance through marriage is the root of treason.

9. The *daimyō*'s visits (*sankin*) to Edo [which became compulsory in alternate years after 1635] must follow the following regulations:

The *Shoku Nihongi* (*Chronicles of Japan, Continued*) contains a regulation saying that "Unless entrusted with some official duty, no one is permitted to assemble his clansmen at his own pleasure. Furthermore no one is to have more than twenty horseman as his escort within the limits of the capital. . . ." Hence it is not permissible to be accompanied by a large force of soldiers. For the *daimyō* whose revenues range from 1,000,000 *koku* [1 *koku* = 5 bushels] down to 200,000 *koku* of rice, not more than twenty horseman may accompany them. For those whose revenues are 100,000 *koku* or less, the number is to be proportionate to their incomes. On official business, however, the number of persons accompanying him can be proportionate to the rank of each *daimyō*.

10. The regulations with regard to dress materials must not be breached.

Lords and vassals, superiors and inferiors, must observe what is proper within their positions in life. Without authorization, no retainer may indiscriminately wear fine white damask, white wadded silk garments, purple silk kimono, purple silk linings, and kimono sleeves which bear no family crest. Lately retainers and soldiers have taken to wearing rich damask and silk brocade. This was not sanctioned by the old laws, and must now be kept within bounds.

11. Persons without rank are not to ride in palanquins.

Traditionally there have been certain families entitled to ride palanquins without permission, and there have been others receiving such permission. Lately ordinary retainers and soldiers have taken to riding in palanquins, which is a wanton act. Hereafter, the *daimyō* of various domains, their close relatives, and their distinguished officials may ride palanquins without special permission. In addition, briefly, doctors and astrologers, persons over sixty years of age, and those who are sick or invalid may ride palanquins after securing necessary permission. If retainers and soldiers wantonly ride palanquins, their masters shall be held responsible. The above restrictions do not apply to court nobles, Buddhist prelates, and those who have taken the tonsure.

12. The samurai of all domains must practice frugality. When the rich proudly display their wealth, the poor are ashamed of not being on a par with them. There is nothing which will corrupt public morality more than this, and therefore it must be severely restricted.

13. The lords of the domains must select as their officials men of administrative ability.

The way of governing a country is to get the right men. If the lord clearly discerns between the merits and faults of his retainers, he can administer due rewards and punishments. If the domain has good men, it flourishes more than ever. If it has no good men, it is doomed to perish. This is an admonition which the wise men of old bequeathed to us.

Take heed and observe the purport of the foregoing rules.
First year of Genna [1615], seventh month.

II. INSTRUCTIONS FOR PEASANTS (ca. 1619)

[The following instructions applied to the peasants on a domain north of Edo. Similar rules were enforced on the other domains.]

1. Consider the Lord of your domain the sun and the moon. Respect your fief holder (*jitō*) or magistrate (*daikan*) as the patron deity (*uji gami*) of your place. Treat your village head (*kimoiri*) as if he were your own father.

2. During the first five days of the new year, pay respect to those around you in accordance with your position. Within the first fifteen days, make more than enough ropes needed to perform your major and minor public services (corvée labor for the year). After the first fifteen days, when mountains and fields are covered with snow, accumulate all the firewood needed for the year. Use a sleigh to pull nightsoil on the fields. At night make sandals for horses. Daughters and wives must sew and weave China-grass to make clothing for their menfolk. If there is a housewife who makes an excessive amount of tea to entertain others, visits around in the absence [of menfolk] and gossips, then she must have a hidden lover. Even if a man has a child with her, that kind of woman must be sent away. . . .

5. During the fourth month, men must work in the fields from dawn to dusk and make furrows as deep as the hoe can penetrate. Wives and daughters must make meals three times, put on red headbands and take the meals to the fields. Old and young alike must put the meals in front of the men who are soiled from their work. By seeing the wives attired in red, men, old and young alike, can be so encouraged . . . to the extent of forgetting their fatigue. Once men are home after dusk, give them bath water, and let them wash their feet. Sisters-in-law and female cousins must put the chapped feet of the man on the stomach of his wife and massage them. Let him forget the toil of the day.

Near the end of the fourth month, put a harrow on the horse and rake the fields. Cut miscanthus grass from the nearby mountains and put them on the China-grass field. If the field is located near a house, always check how the wind is blowing before burning the miscanthus grass. If time is appropriate, sew millet, barley and wheat seeds. . . .

13. During the twelfth month, if there is a notification from the fief holder or magistrate about a tax overdue, quickly make the payment. For this favor he renders you, send a bowl of loach fish soup accompanied by a dish of fried sardines. Although, according to the regulations, all that is expected of a farmer on such an occasion is a bowl of soup and a dish of vegetables, the ones [just suggested] are more appropriate. If no tax is paid after the due notice, you can have your precious wife taken away from you as security. Do not forget that in your master's house there are many young minor officials and middlemen who may steal your wife. To make sure that kind of thing never happens to you, pay all your taxes before the end of the eleventh month. Take heed that this advice is adhered to. You are known as a man of lowly origin. But even so, you do not wish to see your precious wife exposed to wild winds (misfortunes), being taken away from you and stolen by younger men. In this fashion you may lose the support of the way of heaven, come to the end of the rope, be scorned by your lowly peer groups, and regret the incident forever. Always remember that such a misfortune can befall you, and be diligent in delivering your annual tax rice and in doing work for the magistrate. Once all the annual taxes are paid, prepare for the coming of the new year. Make the remaining rice into rice cake (*mochi*), brew some *sake*, buy some salted fish, and add another year to your life happily.

New Year is the time you must be able to chant along with others: I set sail on this journey of longevity. May the moon also accompany me!

III. THE GROUP OF FIVE (1632)

[These regulations, issued by the lord of Echizen domain, were typical of those in place throughout Japan during the Tokugawa period. Organizing families into groups of five for purposes of surveillance and control was introduced in China by the First Emperor (reigned 221–210 B.C.E.).]

1. If there is anyone in the group of five who is given to malfeasance, that fact must be reported without concealing anything.

2. If there is anyone in the group of five who fails to pay his annual taxes or perform the services required, other members of the group must quickly rectify the situation.

3. If there is anyone in the group of five who runs away, those who are remaining must quickly search and return him [to the original domicile]. If the return of the runaway cannot be secured, the group of five will be rendered culpable.

4. No one in the group of five may ask to work outside of the domain, or to work in a mine elsewhere. Even if he wishes to work within the domain at places such as Maruoka, Oné . . . he must secure permission from the authorities ahead of time.

5. If there is anyone in the group of five who is exceptionally strong, that fact must be reported.

6. Members of the group of five must not permit anyone who absconds, or any stranger who is not beyond suspicion regardless of being man or woman, to

lodge in his house. Nor can they provide lodging for any single person. However, if the stranger is an express messenger, lodging may be provided after his letter box is examined.

If there is anyone who violates any of the provisions above, that fact must be reported to the office of the village head (*shōya*) without delay. The village head must report the same to the *tedai's* (minor magistrate's) office immediately. If there is any violation of the above rules, we [as members of the group of five] shall be deemed culpable, and at that time we shall bear no grudges.

In witness whereof, we have jointly affixed our seals for the group of five.

IV. RULES FOR BUDDHIST TEMPLES (1665)

[Beginning in 1640 all Japanese were required to register at their local Buddhist temple. The temples were required to observe the following rules.]

1. The doctrines and rituals established for different sects must not be mixed and disarranged. If there is anyone who does not behave in accordance with this injunction, an appropriate measure must be taken expeditiously.

2. No one who does not understand the basic doctrines or rituals of a given sect is permitted to become the chief priest of a temple. Addendum: If a new rite is established, it must not preach strange doctrines.

3. The regulations which govern the relationships between the main temple and branch temples must not be violated. However, even the main temple cannot take measures against branch temples in an unreasonable manner.

4. Parishioners of the temples can choose to which temple they wish to belong and make contributions. Therefore priests must not compete against one another for parishioners.

5. Priests are enjoined from engaging in activities unbecoming of priests, such as forming groups or planning to fight one another.

6. If there is anyone who has violated the law of the land, and that fact is communicated to you, he must be turned away without question.

7. When making repairs to a temple or a monastery, do not make them ostentatiously. Addendum: Temples must be kept clean without fail.

8. The estate belonging to a temple is not subject to sale, nor can it be mortgaged.

9. Do not allow anyone who has expressed a desire to become a disciple but is not of good lineage to enter the priesthood freely. If there is a particular candidate who has an improper and questionable background, the judgment of the domanial lord or magistrate of his domicile must be sought and then act accordingly.

The above articles must be strictly observed by all the sects. . . .

Fifth year of Kanbun [1665], seventh month, 11th day.

V. ADVICE TO MERCHANTS (CA. 1730)

[The author of the following selection, Mitsui Takahira (1653–1737), was one of the wealthiest merchant-financiers of his day. He was the son of the founder of the vast Mitsui business dynasty.]

The world is divided into four classes—samurai, farmers, artisans and merchants. Each man works at his calling, and his descendants carry on the business and establish the family. Merchants in particular, although divided into various lines of business, are all concerned primarily with the profit to be earned on money. In rural areas, merchants pay deference to their respective provincial lords and squires. When they look at their superiors, they see no great splendor and so do not get carried away. Thus most of them work at their business generation after generation. As for the merchants of Kyoto, Edo and Osaka, the founder of the firm, starting either in a country area or as someone's clerk, gradually works his way up, extends his business and, with the idea of leaving a fortune to his descendants, lives frugally all his life, paying no heed to anything but his family business. After he has built up a record of difficulties and sufferings, his son inherits the family business. Having learned from observation of his father's frugality and having passed his formative years while the house was still not so prosperous, he just manages to keep things intact during his lifetime. When it comes to the grandchildren's time, however, having been brought up after the family had already become rich and knowing nothing of physical hardships or of the value of money, they unconsciously pick up the ways of the world, get big ideas, leave their family business to others and pass their time in idleness. With their personal expenses mounting, they gradually grow older. Even if they pay any attention to their business affairs, they do not know how to run them. While letting their expenses rise, they borrow ready money from other people. The usual thing is for them gradually to become saddled with interest payments and to end by ruining their houses. We know from our own observation that notable merchant houses of Kyoto generally are ruined in the second or third generation and disappear from the scene. The old sayings "Some begin well, but few end well" and "When you are in safety, do not forget dangers" are applicable to one who in his own generation sets up a family business and gains wealth. How much more do they apply to one who receives his father's savings by inheritance and has had wealth from his upbringing. . . .

He [Futamura Juan] too was a retainer of the Echigo family but became a ronin [masterless warrior] in the time of Lord Ippaku and lived at Shimodachiuri, Muromachi. The mansion of Ryōgaeya Zenroku was originally this Juan's residence. He was related to the Takayas, and he too advanced large sums of money to Hosokawa, Satsuma and other daimyō and was ruined at the same time as Ishiko. His fortune, in fact, was lost in one generation.

This business of lending to daimyō is like gambling. Instead of being cut in the first place while they are small, losses become a kind of bait. Using the argument that if further loans are made the original ones will be reactivated, the officials and financial agents of daimyō who raise loans decoy the lenders with specious talk. This is like setting fried bean curd for mice, as the saying has it, and finally they are caught in the trap. They thus incur heavier losses than before. Such being the case, one should give up making loans of this sort. However, no gambler places a bet with expectations from the beginning that he will lose. If you lend to townspeople, moreover, it is very difficult to keep large sums of money actively employed. When townspeople get into financial difficulties, one collects only a small bankruptcy dividend, and the other party vanishes without trace. It is therefore very hard to do anything with one's money. If in lending to daimyō the dealings go according to contract, certainly there is no better business. It does not require a large staff. With one account book and one pair of scales, the thing is settled. This really is genuinely making money while you sleep. As the classical saying goes, however, "for every profit there is a loss." Such a fine business as this is liable to turn out very badly in the end. Consider well that you should never rely on lending to daimyō. . . .

The above is what I was told about Kyoto only, and I have written it down briefly here. Apart from that, in Osaka and such places, people make profits by buying up for later sale as a speculation, but, as they have not accumulated merit though meeting difficulties, they think that good times are here to stay and live up to the limit of their resources. When finally they incur losses, they crash without hope of recovery. In Edo also, some take on building for the government or other speculative ventures and make a fortune at one mighty bound, but they only go to prove the common adage that "he who lives by the river drowns in the river." It is like a gambler's money, which, as everyone knows, finally is lost in the way in which it was made.

Things ought to be the same as if an ancestor has worked well at his family calling and provided ditches for the field divisions for his descendants and his descendants clean out the ditches from time to time, carefully have water flow through them, weed the fields and cultivate them. In business bargaining, you should concentrate on following the opportunities of the times, and, in observing the times, you should consider how they might change. If you do not give some thought to your business from time to time, it is the same as failing to clean out the ditches or weed the fields. Your shop's business finally will fall off, and you will lose a good patrimony. Never waste your attention on matters which have nothing to do with your work. Merchants who ape samurai or think that Shinto, Confucianism or Buddhism will preserve their inner hearts will find that they will only ruin their houses if they become too deeply engrossed in them. How much more true is this of other [sic] arts and entertainments! Remember that it is the family business which must not be neglected for a moment.

In this connection, there was a man in Edo called Fushimiya Shirōbei. His father was a timber merchant who made the most of his opportunities. When Shirōbei took over, he was very much the type who has to keep up with the neighbors and was extremely fond of ostentation. He frequently came up to Kyoto. Mitsui Jōtei II betrothed his son Saburozaemon to Shirōbei's daughter, but when he heard about Shirōbei's behavior, even Jōtei, who himself knew little about business, considered the future and broke off the engagement.

Later, Shirōbei sought permission for an exchange of goods at Nagasaki to the value of five thousand *kamme*. His request was granted on payment of a contribution, and he proceeded down to Nagasaki for two years. He distributed large sums to the people of that place and to the local temples and shrines. He built a Hall of the Great Teacher, an Inari shrine and also a hall for continuous Buddhist prayers for the Shinnyodō temple in Rakutō. However, just when he was astonishing everyone with his luxury, a petition was put in by Takagi Hikoemon, a town elder of Nagasaki, offering a bigger contribution than that paid by Fushimiya. As a result, Fushimiya had his license revoked, and Takagi got the concession. Shirōbei's position was therefore hopeless, and after twenty years he eventually ran out of food and died of starvation. . . .

Isoda, Iguchi, Isuichi, Horiuchi, Higuchi, the Fushimiya crowd, Kurata and Kinokuniya, merchants famous in Edo at that time, have all crashed or, if still carrying on, might as well not be. Merchants always have been in the position of having no fixed stipends, and so they grow rich through having a time of good fortune.

However much wealth their children inherit, it is as though they were, thanks to their fathers' labors, holding in trust for a time money which is common currency. Thus, when the trustees fail to look after it properly, it immediately is dispersed.

In recent years, after their fathers die, young persons seclude themselves on the pretext of illness and behave as though in retirement. As they give themselves over to idleness, their behavior naturally deteriorates. Having no regard for reputation or appearances, they lose their sense of responsibility towards other people and carry on just as they please. By acting in this way, they start the decline of their families. They are not acting as human beings should. It is the law of nature that birds and beasts and in fact all things which dwell between heaven and earth—and, above all, human beings—should seek their sustenance by working at their callings. This being so, such behavior on the part of people far from being in their dotage displays ignorance of the will of heaven.

A Buddhist priest aims to spend his old age as head of a great temple and pass on his understanding of the Law to the congregation. *A fortiori,* anyone born a layman who prefers pleasures from an early age is doing nothing else but preferring hardships later. To make one's own house prosperous, to nurture one's family properly, to have a long life and to pass away with a clear conscience would be to be a living Buddha. On the other hand, to love pleasure when young, to have one's house decline in old age and not to be at ease at the end, is this not to go straight to eternal hell? There is no one who does not like long life and wealth. Everyone dislikes the hardships of sickness and poverty. Nevertheless, it is hard to keep things the way one would like them to be. Everything changes in various ways, depending on where the heart is. Is it not true that things turn out as they do because people do not think highly of their calling or family?

STUDY QUESTIONS

1. How do the "laws for the warrior class" illustrate Ieyasu's political goals? What problems was he trying to solve? What were his solutions? Was he a Confucian?
2. What aspects of the peasants' lives did the *daimyō* seek to control? How did they try to accomplish this?
3. What do the documents suggest about the economic lives of the peasants? About gender relations?
4. What specific goals did the shoguns have regarding the Buddhist temples? What do the regulations for temples suggest about the importance of Buddhism in Japan?
5. Do you see any evidence of peasant protest in these documents?
6. How does Matsui's book provide us with evidence of the spread of commerce during the Tokugawa period?
7. According to Matsui, why did merchant enterprises fail? What did Matsui think were the characteristics of a good merchant? Was Matsui a Confucian? Was he a Buddhist? Were his ideas compatible with the thinking of the shoguns and the *daimyō*?
8. How might Matsui's ideas compare with those of a merchant in England in 1700?
9. What similarities and differences do you see between the Tokugawa shoguns and other rulers of the early modern period?

VISUAL SOURCE

The Art of the "Floating World"

Japanese gave the name "floating world" to the lively popular culture that emerged in eighteenth century cities such as Edo, Osaka, and Kyoto. By 1700 each of these great urban centers had a large entertainment district that featured popular theater (performed by both male actors and marionettes), *sumo* wrestling matches, and numerous *geisha* houses. Prosperous merchants were the great patrons of the new entertainment districts. While enjoying their "night on the town," the merchants rubbed shoulders with artisans, apprentices, unskilled workers, peddlers, and even an occasional (and furtive) member of the samurai class.

***Geisha* with Stringed Instrument (*Shamisen*) and text.** Woodblock print by Kitagawa Utamaro (1754–1806). (V&A Picture Library)

In the floating world, talent, wealth, beauty, and emotional expressiveness trumped the unusually repressive version of Confucianism promoted by the shoguns. Indeed, the floating world may have been the birthplace of the modern celebrity entertainer, a development at complete odds with the values of the Tokugawa rulers. "Stardom" for *kabuki* actors, *sumo* wrestlers and *geisha* was a result, in part, of their depiction in colorful woodblock prints produced in the entertainment districts. The prints sold for no more than the price of a bowl of noodles.

Woodblock prints were the result of a collaboration between four types of people—publishers, artists, woodcarvers, and printers. The artists were especially careful in depicting the material culture of the entertainment districts. Although the woodblock method of printing was an import from China, the style of the prints of the floating world was a major departure by Japanese artists from the traditions of Chinese painting.

STUDY QUESTIONS

1. What aspects of the culture of the floating world are illustrated in the print?
2. How does the print suggest the preparation (education and training) involved in becoming a *geisha*?
3. What is beauty?

12

Economy and Society in Latin America

On settling in the Americas, Spanish and Portuguese colonists created new economic systems that tied the New World to European capitalism. By the middle of the sixteenth century, Spaniards discovered large veins of silver north of Mexico City at Zacatecas and in the southern Andes at Potosí. As the great wealth of these discoveries became apparent, Spaniards shaped the other sectors of the American economy to support silver. Colonists formed large estates (*haciendas*) and textile mills (*obrajes*) to supply animals, food, and clothing to mining centers and to growing cities that served as administrative centers as well as commercial and transportation hubs. Although most of the silver was exported to Europe and Asia, either going into the king's treasury or paying for luxury goods, enough minted money stayed in the New World to monetize the economy. In this process money exchange replaced tribute as the means by which producers transferred goods to consumers. In Portuguese America a similar process took place, except that the product was sugar, not silver. Sugar plantations, particularly in northeastern Brazil, forged a direct economic link to Europe, spurred the development of ranches and farms, and monetized the economy. Despite boom and bust periods, the economic ties between Europe and America became stronger, and the monetary economy spread ever more widely.

The formation of haciendas, plantations, mills, and mines had dramatic social consequences. To solve their labor needs, Spaniards and Portuguese recruited Native Americans and African blacks. The unequal exploitative relationship between European owner and colored worker, whether Indian, black, or mixed, became the chief characteristic of society. The two passages describing work in the silver mine at Potosí and in a textile mill in Puebla, Mexico, were written by a Carmelite monk who traveled throughout Spanish

Selection I from "The Potosí Mine and Indian Forced Labor in Peru," in Antonio Vásquez de Espinosa. *Compendium and Description of the West Indies,* translated by C. U. Clark (Washington, D.C.: The Smithsonian Institution, 1942), pp. 623–625. Selection II from "A Mexican Textile Factory," in Espinosa. *Compendium,* pp. 133–134. Selection III from L. F. Tollenare, *Notas dominicaes tomadas durante una residencia em Portugal e no Brasil no annos de 1816, 1817 e 1818. Parte relativa a Pernmabuco* (Recife: Empreza do Jornal de Recife, 1905), pp. 78–87, 93–96 excerpted and translated by Robert Edgar Conrad in *Children of God's Fire, A Documentary History of Black Slavery in Brazil* (Princeton, NJ: Princeton University Press, 1983), pp. 63–71.

America between 1612 and 1620. The third passage describing social conditions on a Brazilian sugar plantation was written by a French cotton merchant who resided in Brazil between 1816 and 1818.

LATIN AMERICAN WORKING CONDITIONS

I. THE POTOSÍ MINE AND INDIAN LABOR IN PERU

Continuing to Describe the Magnificence of the Potosí Range; and of the Indians There under Forced Labor (Mita) in Its Operations.

1652. According to his Majesty's warrant, the mine owners on this massive range have a right to the mita of 13,300 Indians in working and exploitation of the mines, both those which have been discovered, those now discovered, and those which shall be discovered. It is the duty of the Corregidor [colonial local official] of Potosí to have them rounded up and to see that they come in from all provinces between Cuzco over the whole of El Collao and as far as the frontiers of Tarija and Tomina; this Potosí Corregidor has power and authority over all the Corregidors in those provinces mentioned; for if they do not fill the Indian mita allotment assigned each one of them in accordance with the capacity of their provinces as indicated to them, he can send them, and does, salaried inspectors to report upon it, and when the remissness is great or remarkable, he can suspend them, notifying the Viceroy of the fact.

These Indians are sent out every year under a captain whom they choose in each village or tribe, for him to take them and oversee them for the year each has to serve; every year they have a new election, for as some go out, others come in. This works out very badly, with great losses and gaps in the quotas of Indians, the villages being depopulated; and this gives rise to great extortions and abuses on the part of the inspectors toward the poor Indians, ruining them and thus depriving the caciques and chief Indians of their property and carrying them off in chains because they do not fill out the mita assignment, which they cannot do, for the reasons given and for others which I do not bring forward.

1653. These 13,330 are divided up every 4 months into 3 mitas, each consisting of 4,433 Indians, to work in the mines on the range and in the 120 smelters in the Potosí and Tarapaya areas; it is a good league between the two. These mita Indians earn each day, or there is paid each one for his labor, 4 reals. Besides these there are others not under obligation, who are mingados or hire themselves out voluntarily: these each get from 12 to 16 reals, and some up to 24, according to their reputation of wielding the pick and knowing how to get the ore out. These mingados will be over 4,000 in number. They and the mita Indians go up every Monday morning to the locality of Guayna Potosí which is at the foot of the range; the Corregidor arrives with all the provincial captains or chiefs who have charge of the Indians assigned them, and he there checks off and reports to each mine and smelter owner the number of Indians assigned him for his mine or smelter; that keeps him busy till 1 p.m., by which time the Indians are already turned over to these mine and smelter owners.

After each has eaten his ration, they climb up the hill, each to his mine, and go in, staying there from that hour until Saturday evening without coming out of the mine; their wives bring them food, but they stay constantly underground, excavating and carrying out the ore from which they get the silver. They all have tallow candles, lighted day and night; that is the light they work with, for as they are underground, they have need of it all the time. The mere cost of these candles used in the mines on this range will amount every year to more than 300,000 pesos, even though tallow is cheap in that country, being abundant; but this is a very great expense, and it is almost incredible, how much is spent for candles in the operation of breaking down and getting out the ore.

These Indians have different functions in the handling of the silver ore; some break it up with bar or pick, and dig down in, following the vein in the mind; others bring it up; others up above keep separating the good and the poor in piles; others are occupied in taking it down from the range to the mills on herds of llamas; every day they bring up more than 8,000 of these native beasts of burden for this task. These teamsters who carry the metal do not belong to the mita, but are mingados—hired.

II. A MEXICAN TEXTILE FACTORY

Continuing the Description of the Features of This City and Diocese, and of Other Cities.

There are in this city [Puebla] large woolen mills in which they weave quantities of fine cloth, serge, and grogram, from which they make handsome profits, this being an important business in this country; and those who run these mills are still heathen (gentiles) in their Christianity. To keep their mills supplied with labor for the production of cloth and grograms they maintain individuals who are engaged and hired to ensnare poor innocents; seeing some Indian who is a stranger to the town, with some trickery or pretext, such as hiring him to carry something, like a porter, and paying him cash, they get him into the mill: once inside, they drop the deception, and the poor fellow never again gets outside that prison until he dies and they carry him out for burial. In this way they have gathered in and duped many married Indians with families, who have passed into oblivion here for 20 years, or longer, or their whole lives, without their wives and children knowing anything about them; for even if they want to get out, they cannot, thanks to the great watchfulness with which the doormen guard the exits. These Indians are occupied in carding, spinning, weaving, and the other operations of making cloth and grograms; and thus the owners make their profits by these unjust and unlawful means.

And although the Royal Council of the Indies, with the holy zeal which animates it for the service of God our Lord, of His Majesty, and of the Indians' welfare, has tried to remedy this evil with warrants and ordinances, which it constantly has sent and keeps sending, for the proper administration and amelioration of this great hardship and enslavement of the Indians, and the Viceroy of New Spain appoints mill inspectors to visit them and remedy such matters, nevertheless, since most of those who set out on such commissions, aim rather at their own enrichment, however much it may weigh upon their consciences, than at the relief of the Indians, and since the mill owners pay them well, they leave the wretched Indians in the same slavery; and even if some of them are fired with holy zeal to remedy such abuses when they visit the mills, the mill owners keep places provided in the mills in which they hide the wretched Indians against their will, so that they do not see or find them, and the poor fellows cannot complain about their wrongs. This is the usual state of affairs in all the mills of this city and jurisdiction, and that of Mexico City; the mill owners and those who have the mills under their supervision, do this without scruple, as if it were not a most serious mortal sin.

III. A BRAZILIAN SUGAR PLANTATION, PERNAMBUCO, LATE COLONIAL ERA: 1816–1818

I will divide the inhabitants of these regions into three classes (I am not speaking of the slaves, who are nothing but cattle). These three classes are:

1. The owners of sugar mills [*senhores de engenho*], the great landowners.
2. The *lavradores,* a type of tenant farmer.
3. The *moradores,* squatters or small cultivators.

The sugar-mill owners are those who early received land grants from the crown, by donation or transfer. These subdivided grants constitute considerable properties even today, as can be seen from the expanses of 7,000 and 10,000 acres of which I spoke earlier; the crown does not have more lands to grant; foreigners should be made aware of this.

There are some sugar-mill owners who interest themselves in the theoretical aspects of agriculture and who make some effort to improve the methods of cultivation and production. I was conscious of their existence, at least, because of the derision of which they were the object. I visited six mills and encountered few notable men.

With bare legs, clad in a shirt and drawers or a dressing gown of printed calico, the sugar-mill owner, armed with a whip and visiting the dependencies of his estate, is a king who has only animals about him: his blacks; his squatters or *moradores,* slaves whom he mistreats; and some hostile vassals who are his tenants or *lavradores.*

The great distances and lack of security on the roads do not encourage contacts with neighbors. Not even in the church are there opportunities to meet, because each mill either has its own chapel, or, what is more frequently the case, there isn't any church and no religious worship is carried on at all.

When a sugar-mill owner visits another one, the ladies do not make their appearance. I spent two days in the house of one of them, a very charming man who overwhelmed me with kindness, and I did not see his family either in the living room or at the dinner table. On a different occasion I arrived unexpectedly after supper at the house of another of them, the splendor of which promised better taste; I noticed on the floor a piece of embroidery which seemed to have been tossed there suddenly. I asked for a glass of water in order to have a chance to go into the next room, but they made me wait for a long time. The lady of the house prepared a choice meal, but I did not see her. Furthermore, the same thing happened to me in a country house near Recife that belonged to a native of Lisbon.

In these houses, where the owners reside for the whole year, one does not observe anything fashioned to make them comfortable; one does not even find the avenue which among [the French] adorn both the simple property and the sumptuous chateau, neither parks, nor gardens, nor walks, nor pavillions. Living in the midst of forests, the inhabitants seem to fear shadows; or more precisely stated, up to the edge of the forest around the mill everything is denuded and scorched to a distance of a quarter of a league. I witnessed at Salgado [a sugar plantation near the town of Cabo] the cutting down for firewood of orange groves which the previous owner had planted near the house, either for his pleasure or his profit.

Generally the residences are elevated on pillars; the cellar serves as a stable or as a dwelling place for the blacks; a long stairway provides access to the main floor, and it is on this level, or terrace, where one can enjoy the cool air. The rooms do not have ceilings; instead the timberwork of the roof is exposed and, between its extremities and the walls that hold it up, there is a free space of five inches to increase the air currents. The interior divisions are made with simple lath partitions measuring nine to ten feet in height, so that all the rooms have the roof as a common ceiling.

Luxury consists of a great variety of silverware. When a foreigner is entertained, in order to wash himself he is given splendid vessels made of this metal, of which also the coffee trays used at table, the bridles and stirrups for the horses, and knife hilts are made. Some sugar-mill owners showed me luxurious and expensive English firearms, and I also saw porcelain tea sets from England of the most beautiful type.

I ought to say a few words about meals. Supper consists of an abundant and thick soup, in which garlic abounds, or some other plant of a very pronounced and disagreeable taste which I did not recognize. The first plate is boiled meat which is not very succulent, the tastelessness of which they try to conceal with bacon, which is always a little rancid, and with manioc flour, which each serves himself with his fingers. For a second plate they serve a chicken ragout and rice with pepper. Bread is not seen, although it is much appreciated; they could manufacture it from foreign flour, which Recife is well supplied with, but it is not the custom. The black men or mulatto women (I saw many of the latter serving at table) fill the glasses with wine as soon as they are emptied, but people do not persist in drinking; liqueurs are not served with dessert. . . .

The sugar-mill owners are the only landholders. The only exceptions I know of are some chapels erected 100 or 150 years ago by the piety of the Portuguese and endowed with 50 to 60 uncultivated acres. . . . The extension of the lands owned by the mills is therefore immense, and the capital invested in them is much less considerable than it was in the French [Caribbean] islands. Only the most important establishments have 140 or 150 blacks. One could estimate the importance of the mills by the number of slaves, if it were not for the existence of the *lavradores*.

The *lavradores* are tenants without leases. They plant cane, but do not own mills. They send the harvested cane to the mill that they are dependent upon, where it is transformed into sugar. Half of it belongs to the *lavrador* and half to the the sugar-mill owner. The latter keeps the molasses, but furnishes the cases for the sugar. Each one pays his tithe separately. The *lavradores* normally possess from six to ten blacks and themselves wield the hoe. They are Brazilians of European descent, little mixed with mulattoes. I counted from two to three *lavradores* per mill.

This class is truly worthy of interest since it possesses some capital and performs some labor. Nevertheless, the law protects it less than it does the mill owners. Since they do not make contracts, once a piece of land becomes productive, the mill owner has the right to expel them without paying compensation. It should be recognized that leases of only a year are not very favorable to agriculture. The *lavrador* builds only a miserable hut, does not try to improve the soil, and makes only temporary fences, because from one year to the next he can be expelled, and then all his labor is lost. He invests his capital in slaves and cattle, which he can always take with him. . . .

If I estimate an average of eight blacks for each *lavrador,* and sugar production at fifty *arrobas* per slave, which is not too much considering the vigilance and labor of the master himself, I can calculate the annual income of each *lavrador* at four hundred *arrobas* of sugar [about 12,800 pounds], which six or seven years ago was sold for about 3,000 francs. Now, this income is clear, since the *lavrador* does not buy anything at all to feed his blacks, and he lives very frugally from the manioc he plants.

I was witness to a rich mill owner's expulsion from his property of *all* the *lavradores* and squatters whom his less wealthy predecessors had allowed to establish themselves there. The number of exiles reached almost 600 persons, the property measuring two square leagues in size [about thirty square miles]. . . .

The *lavradores* are quite proud to receive on a basis of equality the foreigner who comes to visit them. Under the pretext of seeking shelter, I entered the houses of several to speak with them. The women disappeared as in the homes of ladies, though I was always offered sweets. I never managed to get them to accept the little presents of cheap jewelry which I had supplied myself with for the trip. This noble pride caused me to respect the hard-working *lavradores,* a class intermediate between the haughty mill owner and the lazy, subservient, and humble squatter. The *lavrador* has a miserable house, for the reasons I have already mentioned. However, when he abandons the hoe to go to Serinhaem [a nearby town] or to church, he dresses himself up like a city man, rides a good horse, and has stirrups and spurs made of silver.

The *moradores* or squatters are small settlers to whom the sugar-mill owners grant permission to erect a hut in the middle of the forest and to farm a small piece of land. The rent they pay is very small, worth at the most a tenth part of their gross product, without an obligation to pay the royal tithe. Like the *lavradores,* they do not have a contract, and the master can send them away whenever he wishes. As a general rule they are a mixture of mulattoes [mixed-race], free blacks, and Indians, but Indians and pure blacks are rarely encountered among them. This free class comprises the true Brazilian population, an impoverished people because they perform little labor. It would seem logical that from this class a number of salaried workers would emerge, but this does not happen. The squatter refuses work, he plants a little manioc, and lives in idleness. His wife has a small income because, if the manioc crop is good, she can sell a bit of it and buy some clothing. This comprises their entire expense, because their furniture consists of only a few mats and clay pots. Not even a manioc scraper is found in all their houses.

The squatters live isolated, far from civil and religious authority, without comprehending, so to speak, the value of property. They replaced the Brazilian savages but have less value, since the latter at least had some political and national affiliation. The squatters know only their surroundings, and look upon all outsiders practically as enemies. The sugar-mill owners court their women for their pleasure; they flatter them greatly, but from these seductions acts of vengeance as well as stabbings result. Generally speaking, this class is hated and feared. Because they pay them little or badly and often rob them, the sugar-mill owners who have the right to dismiss the squatters fear taking this dangerous step in a country that lacks police. Assassinations are common, but do not result in any pursuit whatsoever. I knew a certain mill owner who did not travel alone a quarter of a league from his house, because of the hostility and treachery of his squatters. He had incurred their wrath, and I had similar reasons to fear them when I entered their huts. . . .

I promised to make a quick survey of the black population. I am not in possession, however, of enough information about the laws that govern them to be able to deal with the matter adequately. Here is what I can say at the moment in respect to them.

The Salgado mill contains about 130 to 140 slaves, including those of all ages, but there is no written list of them. Deducting the children, the sick, and the people employed in domestic service and in the infirmary, there remain only about a hundred people who are fit for agricultural labor. During the four or five months that the sugar harvest lasts, the toil of the mill blacks is most violent; they alternate so as to be able to stay on their feet for eighteen hours. I said earlier that they received for food a pound of manioc flour and seven ounces of meat. Here it is distributed already cooked. There are few properties on which slaves are allowed to plant something for themselves. Passing through the forests I sometimes came upon small clearings where the blacks had come secretly to plant a little manioc. These were certainly not the lazy ones. Nevertheless, Gonçalo [a slave] told me not to speak about it to their master, because this could expose them to punishment.

Upon arrival from Africa, the blacks who have not been baptized in Angola, Mozambique, or another place where there are Portuguese governors, receive baptism upon disembarking; this is nothing but a pointless formality, because they are not given any instruction whatsoever. At certain mills I saw the blacks being married by the priest, but in others they are united only by their whims or inclinations. In either case the master may sell separately the husband and the wife and the children to another buyer, regardless of how young they may be. A black baby is worth 200 francs at birth. Some masters make their slaves hear mass, but others save the cost of a chaplain, claiming that the sacrifice of the mass is a matter too grand for such people. Finally, there are mill owners who are more or less formalistic in matters of religion, and more or less able to appreciate its influence upon the conduct and habits of their slaves. It seems to me that it is in the interest of the masters to maintain family ties.

At the Salgado mill I saw only good slave quarters; everywhere, for that matter, they are of stone and lime and well roofed. Those of Salgado are ten feet wide and fifteen feet in depth, with a small interior division forming almost two rooms. It has a door which can be locked with a key, and a round opening toward the field to provide ventilation. The brick floor is two feet above the level of the adjacent ground, which makes such houses much more healthful than those of many French peasants. Each black is supposed to have his own private room, but love and friendship generally prevent them from living alone.

A mat, a clay cup or a gourd, sometimes a few claypots, and some tatters and rags make up the furnishings of the home of a black couple. All have permission to light a fire in their rooms and they take advantage of it. Their food is furnished to them already prepared, so that they have no need to cook. However the fire is a distraction for them and serves for preparing fish or other food which they manage to acquire, lawfully or not. I observed that they were very careful to lock their doors and that when they were barred inside their houses they opened them with great reluctance. Although I was rather friendly with them in Salgado, I had some difficulty in satisfying my curiosity regarding the interior of their huts. I also saw some of the latter that were made of mud and covered with cocoa leaves. . . .

The blacks employed in domestic service, or close to their masters, dress with less elegance and more in the European manner. They take care of their breeches and shirts and sometimes even possess a waistcoat. Gonçalo had an embroidered shirt, and when he wore his lace hat and small trinkets which I had given him his pride was greater than that of any dandy; but when we went out hunting, his greatest pleasure was to leave at home both his necessary and unnecessary items of clothing.

STUDY QUESTIONS

1. How were *mita* laborers recruited? Describe the difference between a *mingado* laborer and a *mita* laborer. What does this difference suggest about the formation of a new society in Peru?
2. How were workers for *obrajes* recruited? What was the result of government intervention to improve workers' conditions?
3. Describe the relations among the various social groups on the sugar plantation.
4. Summarize the French merchant's view of the Brazilian sugar mill owner's lifestyle.
5. How did the French merchant view the living conditions of the slaves? What was his reference point?
6. How did conditions of *mita* laborers in Peru, textile workers in Puebla, Mexico, and workers on the sugar plantation of Brazil compare with those of Russian serfs?
7. What are the advantages and disadvantages of traveler's accounts in getting at Latin American social conditions?

13

Political Styles in Latin America: Colonial Bureaucracy

After the overthrow of Indian states, the first governments in Latin America were colonial administrations set up by Spain and Portugal. This selection deals with important aspects of their political style. Many historians argue that the nature of colonial administration helped shape later political values and institutions in Latin America—even when colonial controls themselves were thrown off.

In theory, Spanish and Portuguese governmental systems concentrated power in the hands of their monarchs. Once a decision was made, it was supposedly executed by a hierarchy of officials descending from the king and his advisers in Europe to a vice-king, or viceroy, in the New World to local officials, or corregidores. Since local officials often lived far from centers of administration, they had the opportunity to exercise much freedom in the application of the law. But more than distance, the social and economic positions of local officials influenced the execution of their duties. Being often poor relatives of high churchmen or top governmental officials, they came to the New World to gain wealth and elevate their status. Furthermore, since the few lucrative jobs in mining and merchant activity were long ago occupied, and since manual labor, whether agricultural or artisan, was performed by the colored majority, Spanish newcomers sought government positions as a way of entering the economy in a favorable capacity. Few alternatives for upward mobility existed, a condition that remained endemic and persists today. Local officeholding became a means of enrichment.

Just as the owners of haciendas and mines exploited the labor of Indians and blacks, so the corregidores extorted money from Indian communities. They manipulated the tribute tax, which since 1650 was a head tax on adult male Indians paid in money. The selection describes the activities of a corregidor in the viceroyalty of Peru in the 1740s. The account was written by two agents of the king sent specifically to find corruption. Potential exaggeration on the part of the king's "spies" is lessened by the structure of the system. Since the corregidores had to pay a "surety bond" before collecting the money, they were forced to make up what they already had pledged. The system invited extortion.

From Don Jorge Juan and Don Antonio De Ulloa, *Discourse and Political Reflections on the Kingdom of Peru,* edited by John J. TePaske, translated by John J. TePaske and Bessie A. Clement (Norman, Okla.: University of Oklahoma Press, 1978), pp. 70–72. Copyright © 1978 by University of Oklahoma Press. Reprinted by permission.

TRIBUTE COLLECTION IN PERU

Corregidores use many methods to enrich themselves at the expense of the Indians, and we shall start with the collection of tribute. In this matter they institute severe treatment, ignore justice, forget charity, and totally disregard the fear of God. Tribute is one revenue that corregidores count as profit or personal gain from their corregimiento. Clearly if they made collections honestly, they would not profit personally from the tribute, would do no harm to the Indians, and would not defraud the king; but all three result from their corrupt conduct. Their insatiable greed seeks nothing but its own satisfaction; overwhelmed by avarice, corregidores satisfy it by any means possible. They keep accounts in such a way that when they have completed their term in office and the accounts are examined as part of their *residencia* [judicial review after completion of office], they are absolved of all guilt simply by payment of a bribe to the judge making the investigation.

Tribute paid by the Indians to Your Majesty is a perquisite of the corregimientos. If corregidores initially find some reason for not assuming the obligation to collect tribute, they discover their own revenues are so small that they are obliged to do so in order to enjoy their full salaries and enrich themselves. Royal treasury officials of the corregimiento confer the right to collect tribute on corregidores after requiring payment of a surety bond as security for the money collected. Since bonds must be paid to these royal officials, they appoint functionaries satisfactory to them. While they have no obligation to name the corregidor, this is usually the case in order to avoid conflicts that might arise if someone else were named.

In the province of Quito [Ecuador] collections are made in two ways—one for the king's account and another for the corregidores'. Using the first method, the corregidor submits to the royal treasury officials an account of the total amount collected, checked against a census of the Indians in the corregimiento based on the baptismal and death records for each parish. Using the second method, royal officials auction off the right to collect tribute to the highest bidder. In this case the corregidor gets preference, if he wishes to take this privilege for the highest amount bid. Although an official account is drawn up, the Indians are told only whom they should pay. The corregidor is obligated to send to the royal treasury only the total amount of tribute bid. He is not required to give detailed accounts. In the province of Quito they began to use the first method at the order of the Viceroy of Peru, the Marqués de Villagarcía, as a result of our visit with him. This occurred because of the great amount of fraud perpetrated by the corregidores to the detriment of the royal treasury. Corregidores included in their accounts only the number of Indians they wished to mention, a group much smaller than those from whom they actually collected tribute. The remainder were listed as absent, disabled, or unable to pay. Another reason for the change in method was delay in payment to the royal treasury. Corregidores used tribute monies for their own trade and personal profit. Thus, besides the losses, the royal treasury suffered greatly from delays, so long in some instances that eight to ten years passed without closing the accounts. Ultimately, the new method was a way of protecting corregidores from the extortions of royal treasury officials, which often resulted in complete loss of the tribute.

STUDY QUESTIONS

1. By what mechanisms did the corregidor profit from his office?
2. What device did the king institute to detect fraud? How did the corregidor avoid censure and punishment?
3. What kind of political heritage is suggested by this report on Peru for later Latin American rulers and also for the ruled?

14

Baroque Culture in Latin America

The intellectual, cultural, and religious life of Latin America during its formative period was largely Iberian, but contained important indigenous and African elements as well. Peninsular Iberians living in the New World, as well as their American-born descendants (creoles), copied forms from Spain and Portugal whether in architecture, poetry, or Catholic ritual. The varieties of Iberian regional practices gave way in America to one broadly adopted style that spread throughout the region. By the late seventeenth century the evolving cultural and intellectual forms were designated as Baroque. In church architecture, builders constructed elaborate, ornate facades and altars. Literature included obscure theological debates in which form counted more than substance. Poetry focused on a profusion of detail and vivid contrasts that revealed the multiple dimensions of a theme and showed the skill of the writer with words.

No person was more influential in this effort than the Jeronymite nun Sister Juana Inez de la Cruz (1651–1695). Like other Baroque poets, she mastered the intricate rules of Baroque style and became adept at wordplay that often obscured meaning. Her cleverness failed to hide a troubled soul. In several poems she confronted problems encountered by women intellectuals in a male-dominated society. Born to a unmarried mother in a small village outside Mexico City, in her poetry she rebuked the double standard in sexual relations. Attracted by experimentation to establish truth, she ridiculed the scholastics of the Catholic Church who manipulated biblical texts and the writings of Church fathers to prove anything they wished. Such views conflicted with her status as a woman and a nun. Having vowed obedience to the Church and her religious order, she became increasingly tormented by the jealousy and criticism of her superiors, male and female. Four years before she died, Sister Juana stopped writing, sold all her books to charity, and submitted totally to serving members of her order, many of whom had fallen ill during the pestilence of 1691. One of Sister Juana's poems directly exposed the arrogance and stupidity of men in their relations with women.

Although Baroque culture in Mexico tormented independent thinkers such as Sister Juana, its popular side attracted ordinary people. Commoners could not write but

Selection I from Robert Graves, "Juana Inez de la Cruz" in *Encounter*, vol. 1, no. 3 (December 1953) pp. 10–12. Selection II from Carlos de Siguenza y Góngora, *Glorias de Querétaro en la Nueva Congregación Eclesiastica de Maria Santisima de Guadalupe* (Mexico City, 1680, reprinted 1945); translated by Irving A. Leonard, in *Baroque Times in Old Mexico* (Ann Abor: University of Michigan Press, 1959), pp. 125–128. Copyright © 1959 by the University of Michigan Press. Reprinted by permission.

they could dress up. To contribute to religious celebrations, Indians organized costume parades, or *máscaras*. As described by Carlos de Siguenza y Góngara in 1680, the natives of Querétaro, a grain-producing area north of Mexico City, dedicated their *máscara* to the Virgin of Guadalupe, for whom they had recently built a new church that was officially opened on the day of the parade. The description of the *máscara* shows that the Indians remembered their separate cultural inheritance. It also shows that the Spaniards provided a place for the Indians in society by encouraging cultural blending.

SAMPLING OF BAROQUE CULTURE IN LATIN AMERICA

I. SELECTION OF SISTER JUANA INEZ DE LA CRUZ'S POETRY

Ah stupid men, unreasonable
   In blaming woman's nature,
Oblivious that your acts incite
   The very faults you censure.

If, of unparalleled desire,
   At her disdain you batter
With provocation of the flesh,
   What should her virtue matter?

Yet once you wear resistance down
   You reprimand her, showing
That what you diligently devised
   Was all her wanton doing.

With love you feign to be distraught
   (How gallant is your lying!
Like children, masked with coconuts.
   Their own selves terrifying).

And idiotically would seek
   In the same woman's carriage
A Thais for the sport of love,
   And a Lucrece for marriage.

What sight more comic than the man,
   All decent counsel loathing,
Who breathes upon a mirror's face
   Then mourns: "I can see nothing."

Whether rejected or indulged,
   You all have the same patter:
Complaining in the former case,
   But mocking in the latter.

No woman your esteem can earn,
   Though cautious and mistrustful;

You call her cruel, if denied,
   And if accepted, lustful.

Inconsequent and variable
   Your reason must be reckoned:
You charge the first girl with disdain;
   With lickerishness, the second.

How can the lady of your choice
   Temper her disposition,
When to be stubborn vexes you,
   But you detest submission?

So, what with all the rage and pain
   Caused by your greedy nature,
She would be wise who never loved
   And hastened her departure.

Let loved ones cage their liberties
   Like any captive bird; you
Will violate them none the less,
   Apostrophising virtue.

Which has the greater sin when burned
   By the same lawless fever:
She who is amorously deceived,
   Or he, the sly deceiver?

Or which deserves the sterner blame,
   Though each will be a sinner:
She who becomes a whore for pay,
   Or he who pays to win her?

Are you surrounded at your faults,
   Which could not well be direr?
Then love what you have made her be,
   Or, make as you desire her.

I warn you: trouble her no more,
   But earn the right to visit
Your righteous wrath on any jade
   Who might your lust solicit.

This arrogance of men in truth
   Comes armored with all evil—
Sworn promise, please of urgency—
   O world, O flesh, O devil!

II. VIRGIN OF GUADALUPE PARADE

If I could present this *máscara* to the ears as it delighted the eyes, I doubt not that I could achieve with my words what the Indians accomplished in it with their adornments. I shall do all that I can, though I know that I shall expose myself to the censure of incredulity. . . .

At three o'clock in the afternoon the masquerade in four sections started to make its appearance on the city streets. The first part was not especially noteworthy as it consisted of a disorganized band of wild Chichimeca Indians who swarmed about the thoroughfares garbed in the very minimum that decency allows. They had daubed their bodies with clay paints of many hues, and their disheveled hair was made even more unsightly by filthy feathers thrust into it in no particular pattern. Like imaginary satyrs and demoniacal furies they whooped, yelled, and howled, waved clubs, and flourished bows and arrows in such a realistic imitation of their warlike practices, that spectators were quite startled and terrified.

More enthusiastic applause greeted the second section, a company of infantrymen formed by one hundred and eight youths marching six abreast, each one bedecked in finest Spanish regalia, with bright-colored plumes fluttering from the crest of helmets and multihued ribbons streaming in the breeze from their shoulders. They presented a noble and inspiring appearance, but nothing amazed me quite as much as the superb precision and perfect rhythm with which they marched, with no other practice or training than that acquired in festive parades and on like occasions. Veterans could not have kept their ranks more evenly, or shown greater dexterity in firing and reloading, or manoeuvered their squads more expertly . . . This indicates very clearly . . . that these American-born youths are not incapable of discipline should it be necessary to make professional soldiers of them. The rapidity and skill with which the company leader flourished his pike astonished everyone.

Next came four buglers, mounted on well-trained horses barely visible under scarlet trappings and silver trimmings. The clear, shrill notes of their instruments heralded the approach of the most important section of this brilliant *máscara*. This was the part representing the nobility and lords of aboriginal aristocracy which, even though it was pagan and heathenish, must be reckoned as majestic and august inasmuch as it held sway over a vast northern empire in the New World. In taking part in these festivities it is quite unthinkable that these Indians should put on tableaux borrowed from an alien culture when they have such an abundance of themes and subjects for pageantry in the lives of their kings and emperors and in annals of their history. So it was that, on this occasion, they appeared in ancient garbs of their people as portrayed in their hieroglyphic paintings and as still preserved in tribal memory. All were dressed alike with an amazing array of adornments. . . .

Bringing up the rear of this colorful section was a figure representing the august person of the most valiant Emperor Charles V of Spain and the Holy Roman Empire, whose dominions extended from Germany in the north to the western hemisphere of America. He was arrayed in full armor, burnished black and engraved in gold. Like the Indian monarchs preceding him in the procession, he rode behind airy steeds that pranced with grace and stately rhythm as if fully aware of the sublime majesty of the ruler who held the reins. Indeed, these gallant horses, with the rhythmic swaying of plumes and the even gait of their hooves and the carriage gliding like Apollo's chariot across the heavens, made them seem so like Pegasus that onlookers burst into enthusiastic applause. In short, the elegance and splendor of the trappings harmonized completely with the august majesty of the figure represented.

Then came the triumphal float, lovelier than the starry firmament and its twinkling constellations. The base, supported by wheels, was six yards long, about half that width, and from the ground it was raised about a yard and a half. On this ample space rested the form of a large ship plowing through imitation waves of silver and bluish white gauze. The sides covering the underparts of the float bore complex designs of involved spirals, ornate capitals, and decorative emblems, imbuing the whole with an aura of brilliance and splendor. From a large figurehead at the bow of the ship ribbons of scarlet taffeta fell away, intertwined so intricately with the harness traces that they actually seemed to be drawing the conveyance. Above the stern of the simulated vessel rose two exceedingly graceful arches, forming a throne, in the middle of which reposed a large, curved shell, supported from behind by a pair of Persian caryatids [draped female figures supporting an entablature]. Within it was an image of the Virgin of Guadalupe, and from her canopied throne descended a staircase with silken mats. Further embellishing this lovely ensemble were varicolored taffeta streamers, and a plethora of bouquets of many hues. Like an ambulant springtime, it appeared, dedicated to the immortal Queen of the heavenly paradise, and far exceeding in beauty the Hanging Gardens of Babylon which, in their time, were dedicated to Semiramis. At appropriate intervals stood six graceful angels, symbolizing some of the attributes of the most Holy Virgin. Kneeling on the first step of the throne was a lovely child garbed in the native raiment of the Indians, who thus represented the whole of America, particularly this northern part which, in pagan days, was known as Anahuac. One hand held a heart while the other supported an incensor diffusing perfumes and delicate aromas. All about this triumphal float the Indians were dancing one of the famous, royal *toncontines* of the ancient Mexicans. If their costumes in such ceremonial festivities were lavishly colorful in the days of their monarchs, how much more they would be on so auspicious an occasion as this one!

STUDY QUESTIONS

1. In what ways did Sister Juana challenge authority? What did her poetry reveal about a woman's place in colonial Latin American society? Compare Sister Juana with women in earlier Asian and European societies, discussed in Chapters 8, 14, and 37 Volume 1. How did they challenge traditional authority?
2. Referring to the parade for the Virgin of Guadalupe, indicate the ways Indians remembered their pre-Columbian past. In what ways did the Indians incorporate Spanish beliefs and practices? How did the public celebrations, such as the parade, shape a culture different from Indian traditions and European models?
3. How would such parades and the celebrations of popular Christianity likely influence the rural and urban workers such as peasants on *haciendas*, mine workers, and textile laborers?
4. Given the various cultural currents in early modern Latin America, discuss the relationship between Latin America and the Western European intellectual and religious life.

VISUAL SOURCE

The Catholic Church in Latin America amassed wealth not only via regular tithe levies but also through donations of land, payments for prayers for deceased relatives, and rents from urban and rural properties. Church officials poured much of this wealth into construction of holy buildings. During the seventeenth and early eighteenth centuries, architects attempted to outdo one another in decoration of church buildings. This church, dedicated to the Virgin Mother, is located in the village of Tonantzintla, which in Náhuatl signified "place of our mother." Church leaders clearly attempted to use indigenous traditions to promote reverence for the cult of the virgin.

Exterior   Interior

Exterior and Interior of Baroque Church Santa María de Tonantzintla, near Cholula, Mexico. Photos found in Joseph Armstrong Baird, Jr., *The Churches of Mexico 1530–1810*. (Photos by Manuel Aguilar)

STUDY QUESTIONS

1. Describe the distinctive features of the church.
2. In what ways does the church resemble the poetry of Sister Juana or the parade dedicated to the Virgin of Guadalupe?

15

Africa and the European Slave Trade

Many developments took place in sub-Saharan Africa from the fifteenth through the eighteenth centuries. Major regional kingdoms were established in several sectors. Bantu immigration to the south persisted, spreading agriculture. Conversions to Islam increased in the area below the Sahara, particularly in the eighteenth century, and European adventurers and traders made their first contacts with the vast African subcontinent.

Because many African societies lacked writing and instead expressed their values and history through art and oral traditions, during this period many key political and cultural developments were not recorded using conventional historical records. Documentation focuses on the European impact, which was not the only major current of the period; and it focuses on European, not African, perceptions. This poses unusual dangers for the student of early modern African history in terms of incompleteness and distortion.

The European arrival, however, was a major new ingredient in African history. Because most Europeans worked through local traders and set up only small outposts of their own, their cultural impact before 1800 was limited. Even their political impact was highly localized, except in a few regions such as the Dutch-held Cape region in the south. African rulers used European funds and armaments in their own political rivalries, and while Westerners were often on the stage, they did not yet write the script. Direct penetration into the interior was rare. However, Europe's vast appetite for slaves, intended for use in the Americas, did have huge consequences for many regions, reducing population and economic vitality despite the collaboration of many African rulers and traders in the process.

The following three selections range from the fifteenth to the eighteenth century and suggest aspects of European-African interaction. They are taken from the east coast, where European activity was less intense than in parts of the west. Coastal settlements along the Indian Ocean already participated in an extensive trading network dominated

All selections from G.S.P. Freeman-Greenville, *The East African Coast* (Oxford: Clarendon Press, 1962), pp. 47–48, 191, 196–197. Copyright © 1962 by Oxford University Press. Reprinted by permission. Selection I from *An Arabic History of Kilwa Kisiwani* (1520). Selection II from Monsieur Morice, *A Slaving Treaty with the Sultan of Kilwa* (1776). Selection III from J. Crassons de Medeuil, *The French Slave Trade in Kilwa* (1784–1785).

by Arabs. The Islamic religion had won many adherents, and Swahili, a written language, had developed well before the eighteenth century.

The first document, written around 1520 in Arabic, offers an unusual opportunity to glimpse directly African reactions to the first Portuguese explorers, colored of course by the Muslim author's hostility to Christianity. The second document, drawn from the same region on the coast around the port city of Kilwa Kisiwani, is a characteristic slave-trade treaty drawn up between a French adventurer and the Sultan of Kilwa. Around the same period a French ship's captain in the slave trade offered a businessman's approach to human trade, in which the view of slaves as profit-and-loss commodities comes through clearly.

While the documents sketch European activities in the period, they also allow some evaluation of diverse African reactions and the reasons why some Africans believed they profited from Western ventures.

AFRICAN AND WESTERN INTERACTION

I. REACTIONS TO THE FIRST PORTUGUESE ARRIVALS IN EAST AFRICA (1520)

During al-Fudail's reign there came news from the land of Mozambique that men had come from the land of the Franks. They had three ships, and the name of their captain was al-Mirati [Dom Vasco da Gama]. After a few days there came word that the ships had passed Kilwa and had gone on to Mafia. The lord of Mafia rejoined, for they thought they [the Franks] were good and honest men. But those who knew the truth confirmed that they were corrupt and dishonest persons who had only come to spy out the land in order to seize it. And they determined to cut the anchors of their ships so that they should drift ashore and be wrecked by the Muslims. The Franks learnt of this and went on to Malindi. When the people of Malindi saw them, they knew they were bringers of war and corruption, and were troubled with very great fear. They gave them all they asked, water, food, firewood, and everything else. And the Franks asked for a pilot to guide them to India, and after that back to their own land—God curse it!

Then in the [next] year . . . there came al-Kabitan Bidharis [Dom Pedro Alvarez Cabral] with a fleet of ships. He asked the people of Kilwa to send water and firewood and desired that the sultan or his son should go on board to converse with him. The amir and the people of the land decided it best to send him an important citizen. So they sent Sayyid Luqman ibn al-Malik al-Adil. They dressed him in royal robes and sent him over.

Then they wanted water, and the Kilwa people drew it in a number of water-skins, and the porters carried it to the shore. Then they called out to the Portuguese to come ashore and take it. As they were coming, one of the principal slaves of the Amir Hajj Ibrahim, who was surnamed Hajj Kiteta, ordered the water carriers [of Kilwa] to carry the water away. So they did so. When the Christians disembarked on shore to fetch water, they saw neither much nor little water, but none at all. So they went back to their ships in anger. They set off again—God curse them!—to Malindi, and received everything they wanted in the way of water, firewood and food. When the Franks went to their own land, they left seven convert

Christians at Malindi. They told the people that two should remain there, and four were to be sent to Gujarat to Sultan Mahmud and one to Kilwa. Then the Portuguese left, and the four men went to India and were circumcised and became Muslims.

II. A SLAVE-TRADE AGREEMENT (1776)

A copy of M. Morice's Treaty with the King of Kilwa written in Arabic on the reverse side, with two identical octagonal seals inscribed in white in Arabic. On the front was the translation in these terms:

We the King of Kilwa, Sultan Hasan son of Sultan Ibrahim son of Sultan Yusuf the Shirazi of Kilwa, give our word to M. Morice, a French national, that we will give him a thousand slaves annually at twenty *piastres* each and that he [M. Morice] shall give the King a present of two *piastres* for each slave. No other but he shall be allowed to trade for slaves, whether French, Dutch, Portuguese, &c. [etc.], until he shall have received his slaves and has no wish for more. This contract is made for one hundred years between him and us. To guarantee our word we give him the fortress in which he may put as many cannon as he likes and his Flag. The French, the Moors and the King of Kilwa will henceforth be one. Those who attack one of us we shall both attack. Made under our signs and seals the 14th X. 1776 signed Morice.

And further down is written:

We the undersigned Captain and Officer of the ship *Abyssinie,* commissioned by M. Morice, certify to all whom it may concern that the present treaty was made in our presence at Kilwa on the 14th X. 1776 signed Pichard, Pigné,—Bririard.

III. REPORT OF A FRENCH SLAVE-TRADER (1784–1785)

The country is superb and pleasing once one has extricated oneself from the forests of half submerged trees called Mangroves. Judging from the ruins of stone-built houses, which can be seen not only on the island of Kilwa but also on the southern side of the pass, it appears that this was once a very important town and that it must have had a big trade; at Kilwa one can see the whole of a big mosque built in stone whose arches are very well constructed. Within the last three years a pagoda which stood at the southern extremity, and which was very curious looking, fell. Finally, this country produces millet, indigo, superb cotton, silkier even than the cotton produced on the Ile de Bourbon, sugar cane, gums in abundance, brown cowries of the second sort which are currency at Jiddah and in Dahomey, besides elephant ivory which is very common, as are elephants, and lastly negroes—superb specimens if they are selected with care. This selection we cannot make ourselves, being at the discretion of the traders, who are now aware of our needs and who know that it is absolutely essential for us to sail at a given season in order to round the Cape of Good Hope. In addition to competition amongst ourselves the expeditions have never been properly thought out and always left to chance, and so it happens that three or four ships find themselves in the same place and crowd each other out. This would not happen if there were a properly organized body and the expeditions were planned to fit in with the seasons and the quantity of cargo and the means of using up surplus also planned, since it is not the business of seamen to concern themselves with correspondence and administration. To my knowledge, the trading that has been done in this port for the last three years, without counting traders not personally known to me, is as follows:

La Pintade	Capt. . . .		600	blacks	
La Victoire	"	La Touche	224	"	1st Voyage
Les bons amis	"	Beguet	336	"	
La Samaritaine	"	Herpin	254	"	
La Créolle	"	Crassons	176	"	
La Victoire	"	La Touche			In his three
		3rd voyage 230	690	"	voyages
[omitted]	"	Berton	233	"	
La Grande Victoire	"	Michel	289	"	
La Thémis	"	Bertau	450	"	
La Grande Victoire	"	Michel	289	"	
La Créolle	"	Crassons	211	"	
La Thémis 2nd voyage	"	Bertau	480	"	
La Gde. Victoire	"	Rouillard	250	"	
				"	
			4,193	"	

A total, to my knowledge, of 4,193, and certainly there must have been more in three years.

It is clear that if this number of captives, i.e. 4,193, who were traded for at least in this period of three years, cost forty *piastres* each, this represents a sum of 167,720 *piastres,* raised for the most part from [French colonies] or from France direct. It is therefore important not only to safeguard this trade but also to find a way of spending rather fewer *piastres,* which would be quite possible if one considers that the *piastres* which we give them for their captives do not remain long in their hands and that they almost immediately give them to the Moors and Arabs who provide them with their needs which are rice, millet, lambs, tunics, shirts, carpets, needles, swords, shoes, and silk materials for dresses and linings. The Arabs obtain most of these things from Surat, and why should we not get them direct from there ourselves? We should make the profit they make, and we should employ men and ships and we should keep a good number of our *piastres* which would remain in the Ile de France and in Bourbon; more certainly still, if privately owned ships from Europe or these islands could not go to the coast of Mozambique and if ships belonging to a private company sent out from Europe could participate in this trade only by means of *piastres* taken to Kilwa, it can be estimated how much we have paid into the hands of the Portuguese at Mozambique, Kerimba and . . . [omitted: Ibo] where they make us pay fifty or sixty *piastres* each for them. This does not include presents and tiresome vexations. What need is there to give our money to the Portuguese, when we have the means to operate among ourselves and when we can use our own industry and keep our money? I have heard for a long time talk of establishing a settlement or trading post in Madagascar. Truly, seeing the number of idle hands we have and the great number of poor and needy and foundlings in our almshouses it is surprising that we have not yet considered this plan, at least as far as that part of the island which we have most visited over a long period is concerned, and also, in certain ports which are particularly well situated, trading posts could be established without straining the resources of the state.

STUDY QUESTIONS

1. Why might African reactions to Europeans vary? What probable causes differentiated the 1520 Arabic account from the King of Kilwa's response to European demands?
2. What were the dominant motives of the French slave trader? What problems did he report and how did he suggest they be resolved? Based on this account, what were the main features of early European colonialism in Africa?
3. What do the documents suggest about the impact of the slave trade on Africa and Africans in the early modern period?

16

The Columbian Exchange in the Early Modern Period

Disseminated most widely by Alfred Crosby in *The Columbian Exchange: Biological and Cultural Consequences of 1492*, the term *Columbian exchange* refers to the worldwide transfer of pathogens, plants, and animals resulting from the expanded and intensified contact among civilizations after 1492. To America, Europeans brought diseases (smallpox and measles), animals (cattle, horses, sheep, and pigs), and plants (grapes, sugar, wheat, barley, and oats). From America, traders carried away not only precious metals but also corn (maize), potatoes, and sweet potatoes. These transfers contributed significantly to the formation of new civilizations in the Americas and altered the civilizations of Europe, Asia, and Africa.

In the Americas smallpox and measles reduced the indigenous population of the Caribbean Islands almost to the vanishing point by 1540. In Central Mexico, the Indian population declined from about 18 million at the time of contact to approximately 1 million in 1605. Peru's native-American population declined from 11 million to about 700,000 by the early eighteenth century. Throughout the Americas, the indigenous population declined by about 90 percent.

In place of people, European animals claimed the land. This was especially true where open grasslands were available. To cite one example, in the Mesquital Valley north of Mexico City, sheep increased from 39,000 in 1539 to 4.4 million in 1589. As the number of sheep increased, the former corn-producing valley became scrub land. In other

Selection I from Bernardino de Sahagún, *Florentine Codex: General History of the Things of New Spain,* 2nd ed., translated by Arthur J. O. Anderson and Charles E. Dibble (Santa Fe, N.M.: The School of American Research and the University of Utah, 1975), part 13, p. 83. Reprinted courtesy of the University of Utah Press. Selection II from Antonio Vázquez de Espinosa, *Description of the Indies* (ca. 1620) (originally published as *Compendium and Description of the West Indies* in 1942), translated by Charles Upson Clark, (Washington, D.C.: Smithsonian Institution Press, 1968), pp. 170–171, 173–175, 190–191, 731–733. Selection III from John Locke, *Locke's Travels in France, 1675–1679 as Related in His Journals, Correspondence and Other Papers,* edited by John Lough (Cambridge, Mass.: Cambridge University Press, 1953), p. 236. Selection IVA from remarks by Robert Boyle in *Royal Society, 1662. Miscellaneous Papers of the Council,* etc., 20 March; Selection IVB from the gardener of Robert Boyle to Robert Boyle, *Royal Society Letter Book* (1663), Vol. 1, p. 83. The two quotes may be found in Redcliffe N. Salaman, *The History and Social Influence of the Potato* (Cambridge, Mass.: Cambridge University Press, 1949), pp. 228 and 238, respectively. Selection V from Adam Smith, *An Inquiry into the Nature and Causes of the Wealth of Nations,* edited by Edwin Caanan (New York: Random House, 1937) pp. 160–161. Selection VI from *Studies on the Population of China* by Ping-Ti Ho (Cambridge, Mass.: Harvard University Press, 1959), pp. 142–143, 146–147, 149–151. Copyright © 1959 by the President and Fellows of Harvard College. Reprinted by permission.

zones, now virtually empty of Indian farmers because of population loss, new crops of wheat, barley, and sugar became predominant.

In Europe and Asia, maize and potatoes became staple foods for the poor, and in both areas contributed to population increases. Between 1650 and 1750, the population of Europe, including Asiatic Russia, increased from 103 million to 144 million; the population of Asia, excluding Russia, increased from 327 million to 475 million. As one of many factors, new crops bore a direct relationship to the population rise. Maize and potatoes increased the total food supply because they allowed previously uncultivated land to be used, including fallow land.

The first selection describes a smallpox epidemic in the Aztec capital of Tenochtitlan, just months prior to the Spanish siege in August 1521. Written originally in Náhuatal, the Aztec language, in 1555 by native informants, the document was translated into Spanish in 1557 by Bernadino de Sahagūn, a member of the Franciscan order. The selections on the spread of European plants and animals in Mexico and Chile were written in 1620 by a Carmelite friar, Antonio Vázquez de Espinoza. He not only identified the plants and animals but also described the native-Americans' adjustments to their spread. Information on maize and potatoes in China came from local histories in the 18th and 19th centuries. European Enlightenment intellectuals wrote about maize and potatoes in Europe. As well, European artists depicted the social consequences of the new crops. Vincent Van Gogh's *The Potato Eaters* (1885) depicts the social and psychological circumstances of people who became dependent on potatoes.

THE MIGRATION OF FOOD AND DISEASES

I. DISEASE IN MEXICO

Twenty-ninth Chapter, in which it is told how there came a plague, of which the natives died. Its name was smallpox. It was at the time that the Spaniards set forth from Mexico.

But before the Spaniards had risen against us, first there came to be prevalent a great sickness, a plague. It was in Tepeilhuitl that it originated, that there spread over the people a great destruction of men. Some it indeed covered [with pustules]; they were spread everywhere, on one's face, on one's head, on one's breast, etc. There was indeed perishing; many indeed died of it. No longer could they walk; they only lay in their abodes, in their beds. No longer could they move, no longer could they bestir themselves, no longer could they raise themselves, no longer could they stretch themselves out on their sides, no longer could they stretch themselves out face down, no longer could they stretch themselves out on their backs. And when they bestirred themselves, much did they cry out. There was much perishing. Like a covering, covering-like, were the pustules. Indeed many people died of them, and many just died of hunger. There was death from hunger; there was no one to take care of another; there was no one to attend to another.

And on some, each pustule was placed on them only far apart; they did not cause much suffering, neither did many die of them. And many people were harmed by them on their faces; their faces were roughened. Of some, the eyes were injured; they were blinded.

At this time this plague prevailed indeed sixty days—sixty day-signs—when it ended, when it diminished; when it was realized, when there was reviving, the plague was already going toward Chalco.

II. EUROPEAN PLANTS AND ANIMALS IN MEXICO AND CHILE

Mexico: Mexico City

Of Other Features of the Archdiocese of Mexico, and of the Fruit Growing There.

- In the provinces of this district of the Archdiocese of Mexico described in the preceding chapters, there are over 250 Indian villages, with many cities among them; 100 [of them] are county seats (cabezas de partido). In these, and on over 6,000 establishments—corn and wheat farms, sugar plantations, cattle, sheep, and hog ranches—there are over 500,000 Indians paying tribute, and more than 150 convents of the Dominican, Franciscan, and Augustinian orders, and many curacies under priests, not to speak of the [many] Spanish towns in the district of the Archiodicese, and especially all the silver-mining towns, which are Spanish settlements.

- The city of Mexico is luxuriously provided with fruit, both of Spanish and native varieties: they all yield abundantly. There are excellent olive groves from which they gather quantities of eating olives. Grapes are brought in from Querétaro, and there are a few vines in the city, as well as peaches large and small, pippins, quinces, pomegranates, oranges, limes, grapefruit, citrons, and lemons; the gardens produce in abundance all varieties of Spanish garden stuff and vegetables; the lake provides delicious fish of different sorts, and the streams, bobos, which is an excellent fish, and others.

Mexico: Michoacán

The province has varieties of climate—cold, hot, and springlike—and famous valleys and meadowlands, with streams of crystal-clear water running through them; hot baths very beneficial for invalids; fertile fields which yield abundance of corn, wheat, and other cereals, both native and Spanish; there is plenty of pastureland, and in consequence large cattle ranches with constantly increasing product; sheep from Castile, from whose wool they weave in the mills fine and coarse woolen cloth, blankets, sombreros, etc.; they raise also many hogs.

At these villages they get two abundant harvests of wheat and corn each year, one in the rainy season and the other by irrigation; from them they supply many cities and towns in New Galicia, and San Luís de Potosí.

- In the northern part of this diocese, along their frontier with the Indian tribe of the Chichimecas, they gather wild cochineal, very fine when worked up; there are large cattle, sheep, and hog ranches: they raise excellent horses and mules.

Mexico: Michoacán

- The town of La Concepción de Celaya was founded by the Viceroy Don Martin Enríquez in the year 1570 on the Zacatecas King's Highway to New Galicia and New Vizcaya, as a frontier post against the Chichimeca Indians. It has a springlike climate and fertile fields with wealth of pastureland, for which reason there are large cattle, sheep, and hog ranches, with good mules and horses; they harvest abundance of corn, wheat, and other cereals, (Marg.: for which there are large irrigation ditches); they raise many kinds of native fruit and all the Spanish ones. The town will contain 400 Spanish residents, with a parish church, Franciscan, Augustinian, and Barefoot Carmelite convents, with other hospitals, churches, and shrines; there are many Indian villages in the district. In this region there are other Spanish settlements with many farms full of cattle, (which I do not enumerate because it would be almost impossible). Celaya belongs to the Marqués de Villamayor.

Mexico: New Vizcaya

- The Diocese and State of New Vizcaya begins at the mines of Fresnillo, 12 leagues distant from Zacatecas; there will be 100 Spanish residents here, with a Franciscan convent; it has rich silver mines and veins. Twelve leagues farther on, as one travels toward Guadiana, like the mines of Los Plateros and Sombrerete and others, with rich silver veins and ore beds, and some establishments in which they smelt the metal. All this country has a good climate and is provided with plenty of supplies, for it is very fertile; they raise quantities of wheat, corn, and other cereals, with abundance of native and Spanish fruit and grapes, and much cattle, sheep, swine, mules, and horses.

Chile: City of Santiago

In the district of the city of Santiago there are 48 small Indian villages, assigned to 30 encomenderos. In the 48 villages in the year 1614 when they were inspected by Licentiate Machado, Justice of that Circuit Court, there were 2,345 Indians, 331 old people, etc. Tribute payers in the villages were 696; the others were away, some out on their work, others in the service of their encomenderos. In these villages of the district of this city and Diocese, and on the farms, there are 23 curacies, 21 administered by clerics and 2 by friars.

- At the above date there were 72 Indian men and 85 Indian women (?) slaves captured in the war after the slavery proclamation. There were likewise 501 Huarpes Indians from the Province of Cuyo residing in the country, of those who had come in for their mita, and 225 from Peru and Tucumán. There were likewise 481 of the Beliches tribe from these villages, who were artisans: Carpenters, 124; tanners, 100; tailors, 33; shoemakers, 81; silk weavers, 3; ropemakers for rigging, 2; masons, 30; blacksmiths, 7; water-jar makers, 19; stonecutters, 6; house painters, 4; they all lived and resided in the outer wards of the city of Santiago; the artisans alone numbered 409.

  Round about the city there were 102 chacras, of wheat, corn, chickpeas, lentils, kidney beans, and other cereals and vegetables; there were some carts (carretas) which brought wood into the city and transported merchandise from the port and did all else necessary in the city service. In the city and on the chacras and ranches there are 41 tanneries in which every year they tan over 30,000 pieces of cordovan leather, and some hides for soles. On the river bank and on the chacras and ranches of the district there are 39 gristmills for wheat, and 3 woolen mills in which they work up and turn out every year over 14,000 varas of coarse cloth and grograms and more than 500 blankets.

Chapter IV

Continuing the Description of the Preceding Subject.

- Besides the above there were 354 farms—cattle ranches, corn, wheat, and other cereals; on them there were some Beliches Indians and 2,162 Yana-conas—part of them from the upcountry cities abandoned because of the re-bellion of the Indians in that Kingdom, and others from elsewhere. These In-dians are civilized (Ladinos); because their villages and natural surroundings are uncongenial, or because they are escaping from troubles they might have at home, or because they are wanderers, they bring themselves to enter the Spaniards' service. They are assigned (repartidos) to these farms, with their wives and children, 4, 6, or more to each, just as they would naturally settle: normally they live there and cultivate their own gardens and fields for their necessities, in addition to what the masters they serve give them in clothing, cash, or food.

  On the majority of the farms there are superintendents (mayor-domos), Spanish soldiers or mestizos, the sons of Spaniards and Indian women, or mu-lattoes or free Negroes. These keep track of the figures for the sowing and the harvest, and see that the people work and do all else necessary. On all the farms and ranches in the Indies, of any importance, they are to be found and have excellent salaries, according to the size of the establishment. In this Kingdom most are paid one-fourth of the products of the soil and of the stock bred; some are paid less, for there is every sort of system.

- In this Kingdom there are very large rivers, swollen in winter with water from the rains and in summer from the great freshets from the snow melting under the sun up on the Cordillera Nevada. These all run from E. to W., to the Pa-cific; with them they irrigate their property and fields. They are utilized for a distance of about 40 leagues, in which irrigation produces large amounts of wheat, corn, barley chickpeas, lentils, peas (porotos), and other cereals and vegetables, which yield abundantly; they raise a few potatoes. The fanega of wheat is usually worth 8 reals; they normally ship large amounts to Lima when they need it there, and it is also taken for His Majesty's camp and army, for the soldiers' sustenance.

  There are quantities of vineyards around Santiago and on the farms; every year they get more than 200,000 jugs of wine from them; that was the figure in the year 1614, when they made the inspection of that Kingdom. In the 3 preceding years they had planted 498,500 vines, and many more have been set out since then; the land is very fertile and the vine grows thick, strong, and sturdy; they treat it with gypsum and ferment (cocido) as is done in many places. It is all consumed within the country; some is taken for His Majesty's army to the city of La Concepción.

- The residents of Santiago possessed in the district of the city 39,250 cattle, the yearly increase of which was 13,500; quantities are slaughtered every year for tal-low; they raise oxen for plowing and for their carts. Every young steer is worth

4 8-real pesos; an ox broken to work, 8; when a herd is sold, it is at the rate of 12 reals a head. There were on the ranches in the district 4,278 mares, and their annual increase, 1,200; each is worth 4 reals. Riding horses are worth from 16 to 20 8-real pesos; sumpter horses, 8 to 10; choice fine steeds, from 100 to 200 pesos.

They had in the district 323,956 goats, whose annual increase was 94,764; they slaughter quantities of gelded males and of females, and get over 2,500 quintals of tallow from them annually, worth 13 8-real pesos a quintal, and 25,100 pieces of cordovan leather, which they ship to Callao for Lima, since it is the best in the Kingdom. Before tanning, each sells for 16 reals; tanning each piece comes to $3\frac{1}{2}$ reals. There were 623,825 sheep, whose annual increase was 223,944; they slaughter great numbers of them and get on the average 7,650 quintals of tallow from them every year. The usual price of a sheep is 2 reals, and a dressed mutton (carnero) the same, and in the city, 4. They are large, fat, and very good.

III. JOHN LOCKE ON MAIZE IN FRANCE

"MOND. SEPT. 12 from Petit Niort to Blay 6 (leagues). The country between Xantes & Blay is a mixture of corne, wine, wood, meadow, champaine inclosure, wall nuts & chestnuts, but that which I observd particularly in it was plots of Maize in severall parts, which the country people call bled d'Espagne, &, as they told me, serves poor people for bred. That which makes them sow it, is not only the great increase, but the convenience also which the blade & green about the stalke yeilds them, it being good nourishment for their cattle."

IV. POTATOES IN IRELAND AND ENGLAND

A. Robert Boyle on Potatoes in Ireland (1662)

[H]e knew that in a time of famine in Ireland, there were kept from starving, thousands of poor people by potatoes; and that this root would make good bread, mixed with wheaten meale; that it will yield good drink too, but of no long duration; that it feeds poultry and other animals well; that any refuse will keep them from frost; that the very stalks of them thrown into the ground, will produce good roots; that the planning of them doth not hinder poor people from other employment.

B. Robert Boyle's Gardener (1663)

I have according to your desire sent a box of Potato rootes; my care hath been to make choice of such, that are fit to set without cutting; for many, that have not small ones enough, are constrained to cut the great ones; but I doe not approve of that husbandry, neither doe I make use of it, because when they are cut, the wormes doe feed on them, and so devouring the substance, the branch groweth the weaker, and the roote small: the ground which they thrive best in is a light sandy soyle, where ferns or briars do naturally grow. Their nature is not to grow fruitful in a rich soyle because they will spring forth many branches, and so encumber the ground, that they will have but small roots. You may cause them to be set a foot apart or something better, whole as they are, and there will be great encrease, and the branch will bring forth fruit which we call the Potato-apple, they are very good to pickle for winter and sallets, and also to preserve; I have tasted of many sorts of fruit, and have not eaten the like of that, they are to be gathered in September, before the first frost doth take them. If you are minded to have great store of small rootes which are fittest to set, you may cause them to lay down the branches; in the month before named, and cover them with earth three or four inches thick, and the branch of every joint will bring forth small rootes in so great number that the increase of one yard of ground will set twenty the next season, and it must be the care of the gardner to cover the ground where the rootes are with fearns or straw, halfe a foote thick and better at the beginning of the winter, otherwise the frost will destroy the rootes; and as they have occasion to dig out the great rootes, they may uncover the ground, and leave the small ones in the earth, and cover them as before and preserve the seed.

Now the season to dig the ground is April or May, but I hold it best the latter end of April, and when they dig the ground let them pick out as many as they can find small and great, and yet there will be enough for the next crop left; let the covering which they are covered withall be burried in the ground, and that is all the improvement that I doe bestow. I could speak in praise of the roote, what a good and profitable thing it is, and might be to a commonwealth, could it be generally experienced; as the inhabitants of your towne can manifest the truth of it, but I will be silent in speaking in the praise of them, knowing you are not ignorant of it.

V. ADAM SMITH ON POTATOES

[A]n acre of potatoes will still produce . . . three times the quanity [of food] produced by the acre of wheat . . . [and] is cultivated with less expence than an acre of wheat; the fallow, which generally precedes the sowing of wheat, more than compensating the hoeing and other extraordinary culture which is always given to potatoes. Should this root ever become in any part of Europe, like rice is in some rice countries, the common and favourite vegetable food of the people, so as to occupy the same proportion of the lands in tillage which wheat and other sorts of grain for human food do at present, the same quanity of cultivated land would maintain a much greater number of people, and the labourers being generally fed with potatoes, a greater surplus would remain after replacing all the stock and maintaining all the labour employed in cultivation. A greater share of this surplus too would belong to the landlord. Population would increase, and rents would rise much beyond what they are at present. . . .

It is difficult to preserve potatoes through the year, and impossible to store them like corn [refers to traditional grain crops such as wheat, oats, and barley; corn does not refer to maize] for two or three years together. The fear of not being able to sell them before they rot, discourages their cultivation, and is perhaps, the chief obstacle to their ever becoming in any great country, like bread, the principal vegetable food of all the different ranks of the people.

VI. AMERICAN CROPS IN CHINA

Szechwan

[1814 history of San-t'ai county referring to immigrants and new products, which were identified as maize and sweet potatoes.]

Our soil is not poor and our people are not lazy. The innumerable immigrants have brought with them every conceivable food plant or product, all of which have been extensively propagated here. Many things that were unknown in the past are now our staple products. Our locality is so full of life and vigor that prosperity surpasses that of any previous period.

West-Central Kiangsi, Bordering Hunan (Yangtze Highlands)

[1760 edition of history of Yüan-chou prefecture.]

Formerly this prefecture abounded in idle land. On account of rapid population increase more land was cultivated but it was still confined to level areas. Since the influx of immigrants from Fukien and Kwangtung, their men and womenfolk have systematically cultivated high hills and even steep mountains.

[1873 local history of Kiangsi.]

The leading crop of hills and mountains is maize . . . which provides half a year's food for the mountain dwellers. . . . In general maize is grown on the sunny side of the hills, sweet potatoes on the shady side.

[1745 testimony of resident of Wu-ning county in Kiangsi.]

The shack people usually dig the mountain soil five or six inches deep. The loosened soil at first yielded ten times as large a crop (as when shallow planting was practiced). But from time to time there were torrential rains which washed down the soil and choked rivers and streams. After consecutive planting for more than ten years none of the fertile topsoil was left and the soil was utterly exhausted. Now in such places . . . mountains are reduced to bare rocks. Unless land is rested for several decades there is no hope of renewed cultivation.

Han River Drainge Area (Tributary of Yangtze)

[1864 edition of the history of I-ch'ang prefecture.]

Maize . . . had originally been grown only in Szechwan. Since our area became a prefecture (in 1735), the natives have opened up mountains and grown maize to an ever increasing extent until now it is grown everywhere.

[1866 edition of Fang-hsien prefecture.]

After several consecutive bumper crops from 1752 on, maize has become the mountain farmers' very source of sustenance and has been grown by every household.

[1866 edition of Fang-hsien prefecture (introduction of "Irish" potato after 1800).]

The Irish potato is mostly grown in the southwestern mountains. In the level area in the vicinity of the walled city rice is usually grown. In the comparatively shallow hills and mountains maize predominates. In the lofty mountains where maize cannot be successfully grown the only source of food is the Irish potato. . . . Some local people of means buy Irish potatoes, which are ground into flour, and occasionally make a fortune of it.

[1837–1838 testimony of Lin Tse-Hsü, governor-general of Hupei and Hunan.]

Formerly the bed of the Hsiang River (a tributary of the Han River that runs through southwestern Honan and Northern Hupei) was several tens of feet deep. Ever since the systematic deforestation consequent upon maize growing the topsoil has been washed down by torrential rains and silted up (the Hsiang River). Between Han-yang (where the Han River joins the Yangtze) and Hsiang-yang (the junction of the Hsiang and Han rivers) the further upstream one goes, the shallower the river bed becomes. Small wonder that from 1821 to the present there has hardly been a single year in which the Hsiang river did not flood.

STUDY QUESTIONS

1. Description of smallpox epidemic in Tenochtitlán: What statements in the document indicate that community cohesiveness broke down as a result of the disease? What are the military implications of such a breakdown?

2. Spread of animals and plants in Mexico and Chile: Identify the plants and animals introduced from Europe. Review numbers of animals compared with people. Indians who survived the epidemics were forced to adjust to new conditions. How did they adjust? What jobs did they perform? How were the jobs related to the new plants and animals? Who controlled the conditions under which they worked? What are the implications for social relations?

3. American crops in France, England, and Ireland: Who were Locke, Boyle, and Smith? In what way did they represent Enlightenment ideas? Why were they optimistic about cultivation of maize and potatoes? What were the advantages of cultivating these crops?

4. American crops in China: What types of sources were used to describe the cultivation of maize and potatoes in China? Who were the cultivators of maize and potatoes? In what kind of terrain did they cultivate these crops? What was the environmental result?

VISUAL SOURCE

Dutch artist Vincent Van Gogh (1853–1890) began painting approximately 10 years prior to his suicide at age 37. His short life was marked by strong humanitarian impulses toward the poor, especially miners, weavers, and peasants. Despite his intentions, the poor often ridiculed his efforts. Failures in his personal life and sickness led to dispair. Unable to support himself regularly, he lived off his younger brother Theo. Bouts of epilepsy worsened his depression. Although tragic, these experiences enabled Van Gogh to depict the social circumstances and psychological moods of the people who interested him.

***The Potato Eaters* by Vincent Van Gogh, 1885.** Photo found in Carol Zemel, *Van Gogh's Progress: Utopia, Modernity, and Late-Nineteenth-Century Art* (Copyright Erich Lessing/Art Resource, NY)

STUDY QUESTIONS

1. What features of the painting reveal the social circumstances of the people who became dependent on potatoes as their staple food? How do their circumstances compare with the views of thinkers who had earlier praised the potato?
2. How does the painting suggest the inner mood of the individuals depicted? How might Van Gogh define the purpose of this kind of art in industrial Europe?

SECTION TWO

The Long Nineteenth Century: 1750–1914

The framework for world history from the late eighteenth to the early twentieth centuries was increasingly shaped by growing European power. This power was based on previous gains in international trade and key colonies planted in India, Indonesia, and elsewhere. It was increased by European population growth and by a more explicit imperialist spirit, eager to seek new gains and conquests in the wider world. It was greatly furthered by Europe's growing industrial strength. Industrialization, beginning in the late eighteenth century, generated new goods to sell, new modes of international transportation that facilitated wider market contacts, and new and more lethal weaponry that enhanced Europe's military advantage. Yet the long nineteenth century was by no means shaped by European activities alone. Most societies could resist European penetration to at least some degree, and several undertook active reform programs designed to enhance independence and the preservation of important values. Latin America freed itself from direct European control early in the nineteenth century, although its economic subordination in many ways intensified. The development of new institutions and social patterns in the United States, Canada, and Australia, although they reflected Western European strength, added another important source of complexity to modern world history. Finally, the emergence of various kinds of nationalisms and other cultural responses, in many otherwise different societies, reflected the capacity to define distinctive identities combined with the pressing need to innovate. By 1900 reform developments, independence movements, and nationalism were beginning to limit Western European hegemony, although the full reaction would begin to take shape only after 1914.

17

The French Revolution

The French Revolution burst forth in the summer of 1789. It lasted for 10 years, and was followed by consolidations and conquests under Napoleon's Empire. Napoleon's defeat in 1815 led to a rollback of some of the revolutionary measures, but most of these would return during the political changes of the nineteenth century. The Revolution, in sum, was something of a blueprint for the constitutions of the modern state.

The Revolution was guided by many of the philosophical ideas developed in the eighteenth-century Enlightenment. The American Revolution and the constitutions it engendered were direct inspirations as well. The Revolution was also a massive social protest, as peasants and workers articulated the grievances they had developed during the Old Regime.

The Revolution was French, but it had European and, soon, world impact. French conquests spread many of the principles of the Revolution to most of Western Europe. Wars of independence in Latin America were inspired in part by French revolutionary principles. So was liberal-nationalist agitation in Eastern Europe, for example in the Balkans against the Ottoman Empire. Revolutionary ideas would show up in other revolutions in the twentieth century, and in proclamations of human rights such as the United Nations charter.

There were vital disagreements within the Revolution, as in all complex events—quite apart from the outright resistance the Revolution generated among conservatives. The first three years of the Revolution emphasized liberal principles, but then the Revolution turned more radical, for example instituting universal suffrage for all adult males for the first time, although briefly.

The following three documents are classics from the Revolution. The first two emerged quickly in August 1789, as the revolutionary legislature attempted to define basic political and social principles. The third document, the first two verses of *La Marseillaise* (the French national anthem), represent the more radical phase, when revolutionary leaders were guiding armies to fight opposition at home and abroad.

Selections I and II from James Harvey Robinson, ed., *Readings in European History,* Vol. II (New York: Ginn and Company, 1906), pp. 405–411; Selection III from http://www.elysee.fr/ang/in-stit/symb1.htm (Website of the Republic of France). No permissions needed.

The Declaration of Rights of Man and the Citizen was a fundamental statement of human rights, inspired in part by American revolutionary documents. It was intended to guide the new political constitution the revolutionary legislature decided was essential. The Declaration invites analysis to determine what its main principles were and why. In the context of the old regime, they were revolutionary. Note that not all the principles were fully followed up by the liberal constitution of 1791, which most notably did not establish universal suffrage. Women were not accorded the same rights as men.

The second document, enacted on August 11, 1789, details the abolition of the feudal and manorial system in France. This act, spurred by peasant revolts against their noble landlords in many parts of the country, was the basic social measure of the Revolution, and it was never really reversed. Here, analysis should focus again on what the main principles were—including the relationship to the Declaration of Rights of Man and the Citizen. Equally important were the wider implications: Given what was now abolished, what new systems would result? The document had massive implications for an extension of government services, for new conflicts between the state and the Catholic Church, and for the control of landed property.

Finally, *La Marseillaise* reflects the Revolution at war. It was composed in April 1792, on the French front against German and Austrian forces, and it spread quickly as a battle song. *La Marseillaise* was, essentially, the first national anthem ever written, adopted as a "national song" in 1795 and then as an anthem in 1879. The anthem was written by Claude-Joseph Rouget de Lisle (1760–1836), an army captain and, otherwise, a fairly mediocre musical composer.

CLASSIC REVOLUTION DOCUMENTS

I. DECLARATION OF THE RIGHTS OF MAN AND OF THE CITIZEN

The representatives of the French people, organized as a National Assembly, believing that the ignorance, neglect, or contempt of the rights of man are the sole cause of public calamities and of the corruption of governments, have determined to set forth in a solemn declaration the natural, inalienable, and sacred rights of man, in order that this declaration, being constantly before all the members of the social body, shall remind them continually of their rights and duties; in order that the acts of the legislative power, as well as those of the executive power, may be compared at any moment with the objects and purposes of all political institutions and may thus be more respected; and, lastly, in order that the grievances of the citizens, based hereafter upon simple and incontestable principles, shall tend to the maintenance of the constitution and redound to the happiness of all. Therefore the National Assembly recognizes and proclaims, in the presence and under the auspices of the Supreme Being, the following rights of man and of the citizen:

Article 1. Men are born and remain free and equal in rights. Social distinctions may be founded only upon the general good.

2. The aim of all political association is the preservation of the natural and imprescriptible rights of man. These rights are liberty, property, security, and resistance to oppression.

3. The principle of all sovereignty resides essentially in the nation. No body nor individual may exercise any authority which does not proceed directly from the nation.

4. Liberty consists in the freedom to do everything which injures no one else; hence the exercise of the natural rights of each man has no limits except those which assure to the other members of the society the enjoyment of the same rights. These limits can only be determined by law.

5. Law can only prohibit such actions as are hurtful to society. Nothing may be prevented which is not forbidden by law, and no one may be forced to do anything not provided for by law.

6. Law is the expression of the general will. Every citizen has a right to participate personally, or through his representative, in its formation. It must be the same for all, whether it protects or punishes . All citizens, being equal in the eyes of the law, are equally eligible to all dignities and to all public positions and occupations, according to their abilities, and without distinction except that of their virtues and talents.

7. No person shall be accused, arrested, or imprisoned except in the cases and according to the forms prescribed by law. Any one soliciting, transmitting, executing, or causing to be executed, any arbitrary order, shall be punished. But any citizen summoned or arrested in virtue of the law shall submit without delay, as resistance constitutes an offense.

8. The law shall provide for such punishments only as are strictly and obviously necessary, and no one shall suffer punishment except it be legally inflicted in virtue of a law passed and promulgated before the commission of the offense.

9. As all persons are held innocent until they shall have been declared guilty, if arrest shall be deemed indispensable, all harshness not essential to the securing of the prisoner's person shall be severely repressed by law.

10. No one shall be disquieted on account of his opinions, including his religious views, provided their manifestation does not disturb the public order established by law.

11. The free communication of ideas and opinions is one of the most precious of the rights of man. Every citizen may, accordingly, speak, write, and print with freedom, but shall be responsible for such abuses of this freedom as shall be defined by law.

12. The security of the rights of man and of the citizen requires public military forces. These forces are, therefore, established for the good of all and not for the personal advantage of those to whom they shall be intrusted.

13. A common contribution is essential for the maintenance of the public forces and for the cost of administration. This should be equitably distributed among all the citizens in proportion to their means.

14. All the citizens have a right to decide, either personally or by their representatives, as to the necessity of the public contribution; to grant this freely; to know to what uses it is put; and to fix the proportion, the mode of assessment and of collection and the duration of the taxes.

15. Society has the right to require of every public agent an account of his administration.

16. A society in which the observance of the law is not assured, nor the separation of powers defined, has no constitution at all.

17. Since property is an inviolable and sacred right, no one shall be deprived thereof except where public necessity, legally determined, shall clearly demand it, and then only on condition that the owner shall have been previously and equitably indemnified.

II. THE DECREE ABOLISHING THE FEUDAL SYSTEM

Article I. The National Assembly hereby completely abolishes the feudal system. It decrees that, among the existing rights and dues, . . . all those originating in or representing real or personal serfdom shall be abolished without indemnification. All other dues are declared redeemable, the terms and mode of redemption to be fixed by the National Assembly. Those of the said dues which are not extinguished by this decree shall continue to be collected until indemnification shall take place.

II. The exclusive right to maintain pigeon houses and dovecotes is abolished. The pigeons shall be confined during the seasons fixed by the community. During such periods they shall be looked upon as game, and every one shall have the right to kill them upon his own land.

III. The exclusive right to hunt and to maintain uninclosed warrens is likewise abolished, and every landowner shall have the right to kill, or to have destroyed on his own land, all kinds of game, observing, however, such police regulations as may be established with a view to the safety of the public.

All hunting [preserves] including the royal forests, and all hunting rights under whatever denomination, are likewise abolished. Provision shall be made, however, in a manner compatible with the regard due to property and liberty, for maintaining the personal pleasures of the king.

The president of the Assembly shall be commissioned to ask of the king the recall of those sent to the galleys or exiled, simply for violations of the hunting regulations, as well as for the release of those at present imprisoned for offenses of this kind, and the dismissal of such cases as are now pending.

IV. All manorial courts are hereby suppressed without indemnification. But the magistrates of these courts shall continue to perform their functions until such time as the National Assembly shall provide for the establishment of a new judicial system.

V. Tithes of every description, as well as the dues which have been substituted for them, under whatever denomination they are known or collected (even when compounded for), possessed by secular or regular congregations, . . . are abolished, on condition, however, that some other method be devised to provide for the expenses of divine worship, the support of the officiating clergy, for the assistance of the poor, for repairs and rebuilding of churches and parsonages, and for the maintenance of all institutions, seminaries, schools, academies, asylums, and organizations to which the present funds are devoted. Until such provision shall be made and the former possessors shall enter upon the enjoyment of an income on the new system, the National Assembly decrees that the said tithes shall continue to be collected according to the law and in the customary manner. . . .

VI. All perpetual ground rents, payable either in money or in kind, of whatever nature they may be, whatever their origin and to whomsoever they may be due, . . . shall be redeemable at a rate fixed by the Assembly. No due shall in the future be created which is not redeemable.

VII. The sale of judicial and municipal offices shall be abolished forthwith. Justice shall be dispensed *gratis*. Nevertheless the magistrates at present holding such offices shall continue to exercise their functions and to receive their emoluments until the Assembly shall have made provision for indemnifying them. . . .

IX. Pecuniary privileges, personal or real, in the payment of taxes are abolished forever. Taxes shall be collected from all the citizens, and from all property, in the same manner and in the same form. Plans shall be considered by which the taxes shall be paid proportionally by all, even for the last six months of the current year.

X. Inasmuch as a national constitution and public liberty are of more advantage to the provinces than the privileges which some of these enjoy, and inasmuch as the surrender of such privileges is essential to the intimate union of all parts of the realm, it is decreed that all the peculiar privileges, pecuniary or otherwise, of the provinces, principalities, districts, cantons, cities, and communes, are once for all abolished and are absorbed into the law common to all Frenchmen.

XI. All citizens, without distinction of birth, are eligible to any office or dignity, whether ecclesiastical, civil, or military; and no profession shall imply any derogation. . . .

XVII. The National Assembly solemnly proclaims the king, Louis XVI, the *Restorer of French Liberty*.

XVIII. The National Assembly shall present itself in a body before the king, in order to submit to him the decrees which have just been passed, to tender to him the tokens of its most respectful gratitude, and to pray him to permit the Te Deum to be chanted in his chapel, and to be present himself at this service. . . .

III. *LA MARSEILLAISE*

La Marseillaise, the French national anthem, was composed in one night during the French Revolution (April 24, 1792) by Claude-Joseph Rouget de Lisle, a captain of the engineers and amateur musician stationed in Strasbourg in 1792. It was played at a patriotic banquet at Marseilles, and printed copies were given to the revolutionary forces then marching on Paris. They entered Paris singing this song, and to it they marched to the Tuileries on August 10th.

Ironically, Rouget de Lisle was himself a royalist and refused to take the oath of allegiance to the new constitution. He was imprisoned and barely escaped the guillotine. Originally entitled *Chant de guerre de l'armeé du Rhin* (War Song of the Army of the Rhine), the anthem became called La Marseillaise because of its popularity with volunteer army units from Marseilles.

The Convention accepted it as the French national anthem in a decree passed July 14, 1795. *La Marseillaise* was banned by Napoleon during the Empire, and by Louis XVIII on the Second Restoration (1815), because of its revolutionary associations. Authorized after the July Revolution of 1830, it was again banned by Napoleon III and not reinstated until 1879.

The text here consists of only the first two verses (out of seven).

1. Allons enfants de la Patrie
Le jour de gloire est arrivé.
Contre nous, de la tyrannie,

1. Arise you children of our motherland,
Oh now is here our glorious day!
Over us the bloodstained banner

L'étandard sanglant est levé,
l'étandard sanglant est levé,
Entendez-vous, dans la compagnes.
Mugir ces farouches soldats
Ils viennent jusque dans nos bras
Egorger vos fils,
vos compagnes.
> *Aux armes citoyens!*
> *Formez vos bataillons,*
> *Marchons, marchons!*
> *Qu'un sang impur*
> *Abreuve nos sillons.*

Of tyranny holds sway!
Of tyranny holds sway!
Oh, do you hear there in our fields
The roar of those fierce fighting men?
Who came right here into our midst
To slaughter sons, wives and kin.
Your country
> *To arms, oh citizens!*
> *Form up in serried ranks!*
> *March on, march on!*
> *And drench our fields*
> *With their tainted blood!*

2. Amour sacré de la Patrie,
Conduis, soutiens nos bras vengeurs,
Liberté, liberté cherie,
Combats avec tes défénseurs;
Combats avec tes défénseurs.
Sous drapeaux, que la victoire
Acoure à tes mâles accents;
Que tes ennemis expirants
Voient ton triomphe et notre gloire!
> *Aux armes citoyens!*
> *Formez vos bataillons,*
> *Marchons, marchons!*
> *Qu'un sang impur*
> *Abreuve nos sillons.*

2. Supreme devotion to our Motherland,
Guides and sustains avenging hands
Liberty, oh dearest Liberty,
Come fight with your shielding bands,
Come fight with your shielding bands!
Beneath our banner come, oh Victory,
Run at your soul-stirring cry.
Oh come, come see your foes now die,
Witness your pride and our glory.
> *To arms, oh citizens!*
> *Form up in serried ranks!*
> *March on, march on!*
> *And drench our fields*
> *With their tainted blood!*

STUDY QUESTIONS

1. What are the main principles of the Declaration of the Rights of Man and the abolition of feudalism? Are the two documents entirely consistent? What was revolutionary about each of the documents?

2. What were the implications of the abolition of feudalism for relations with the king? What were the implications for property rights?

3. In what ways did the abolition of feudalism imply an expansion of government functions?

4. What were the implications of both the Declaration and the abolition of feudalism for relations with the Catholic Church?

5. What were the implications of both documents for the lives of ordinary people? Would their lives be "revolutionized"?

6. What were the main themes of *La Marseillaise* verses? What new elements in the Revolution do they suggest? How does *La Marseillaise* suggest the radicalization of the Revolution?

7. Taking the three documents together, what did the Revolution suggest about the nature and meaning of citizenship in a modern state?

18

Conservative Reaction in Europe

Napoleon's defeat by the combined forces of Austria, Prussia, England, and Russia in 1815 opened up an intensely conservative period in European history. The Treaty of Vienna that ended the war was not reactionary, nor was it unduly punitive to France. But the leaders of the victorious powers, headed by Prince Metternich, the chief minister in Austria, were vowed to provide renewed support to monarchy, aristocracy, and church. They sincerely believed that stability with at most very gradual change was best for the people of Europe, and certainly for the institutions and social classes they most cherished.

But various groups in Europe continued to be interested in the revolutionary cause, advocating nationalism—particularly strong in Italy and Germany, which bothered Metternich greatly—liberalism, or even more radical ideas. Conservatives struggled to find laws and police apparatus that would allow them to hold the line.

Already in the treaty of Vienna, the four monarchs pledged alliance in favor of the status quo. The first document repeats article VI of a secret treaty signed in conjunction with the peace conference in 1815.

In 1819, as revolutionary agitation increased and after the political assassination of a journalist, Metternich managed to cajole the separate German states into passing the Carlsbad decrees, which were aimed at direct repression of students and the press.

While conservatism predominated in most countries for several decades, this particular version was not ultimately victorious. The revolutions of 1848, which among other things chased Metternich from Austria, convinced conservatives that they needed to add to their arsenal if basic conservative principles were to be preserved. The repressive element did not disappear, but it became enmeshed in a more flexible approach.

Nevertheless, the emergence of formal conservatism, for which Metternich was long the leading advocate, was an important result of the French revolution. Determining the core interests of this conservatism allows comparison with later versions in European history, and with conservatism elsewhere—for example, in Russia or in the United States.

Selections I and II from James Harvey Robinson, *Readings in European History,* Vol. II (New York: Ginn and Company, 1906), pp. 547–551. No permission needed.

CONSERVATIVE PRINCIPLES

I. ARTICLE VI OF THE SECRET TREATY OF 1815 AMONG AUSTRIA, RUSSIA, PRUSSIA, AND ENGLAND

To facilitate and secure the execution of the present treaty and to strengthen the bonds which at the present moment so closely unite the four sovereigns for the happiness of the world, the high contracting parties have agreed to renew their meetings at fixed periods, either under the immediate auspices of the sovereigns themselves or by their respective ministers, for the purpose of consulting upon their common interests and for the consideration of the measures which, at each of these periods, shall be considered the most salutary for the repose and prosperity of nations and for the peace of Europe.

II. THE CARLSBAD DECREES

1. A special representative of the ruler of each state shall be appointed for each university, with appropriate instructions and extended powers, and shall reside in the place where the university is situated. This office may devolve upon the existing curator or upon any other individual whom the government may deem qualified.

The function of this agent shall be to see to the strictest enforcement of existing laws and disciplinary regulations; to observe carefully the spirit which is shown by the instructors in the university in their public lectures and regular courses, and, without directly interfering in scientific matters or in the methods of teaching, to give a salutary direction to the instruction, having in view the future attitude of the students. Lastly, he shall devote unceasing attention to everything that may promote morality, good order, and outward propriety among the students. . . .

2. The confederated governments mutually pledge themselves to remove from the universities or other public educational institutions all teachers who, by obvious deviation from their duty, or by exceeding the limits of their functions, or by the abuse of their legitimate influence over the youthful minds, or by propagating harmful doctrines hostile to public order or subversive of existing governmental institutions, shall have unmistakably proved their unfitness for the important office intrusted to them. . . .

No teacher who shall have been removed in this manner shall be again appointed to a position in any public institution of learning in another state of the union.

3. Those laws which have for a long period been directed against secret and unauthorized societies in the universities shall be strictly enforced. These laws apply especially to that association established some years since under the name Universal Students' Union (*Allgemeine Burschenschaft*), since the very conception of the society implies the utterly unallowable plan of permanent fellowship and constant communication between the various universities. The duty of especial watchfulness in this matter should be impressed upon the special agents of the government.

The governments mutually agree that such persons as shall hereafter be shown to have remained in secret or unauthorized associations, or shall have entered such associations, shall not be admitted to any public office.

4. No student who shall be expelled from a university by a decision of the university senate which was ratified or prompted by the agent of the government, or who shall have left the institution in order to escape expulsion, shall be received in any other university. . . .

. . .

1. So long as this decree shall remain in force no publication which appears in the form of daily issues, or as a serial not exceeding twenty sheets of printed matter, shall go to press in any state of the union without the previous knowledge and approval of the state officials.

Writings which do not belong to one of the above-mentioned classes shall be treated according to the laws now in force, or which may be enacted, in the individual states of the union. . . .

4. Each state of the union is responsible, not only to the state against which the offense is directly committed, but to the whole Confederation, for every publication appearing under its supervision in which the honor or security of other states is infringed or their constitution or administration attacked. . . .

6. The Diet [Assembly] shall have the right, moreover, to suppress on its own authority, without being petitioned, such writings included in Article 1, in whatever German state they may appear, as, in the opinion of a commission appointed by it, are inimical to the honor of the union, the safety of individual states, or the maintenance of peace and quiet in Germany. There shall be no appeal from such decisions, and the governments involved are bound to see that they are put into execution. . . .

7. When a newspaper or periodical is suppressed by a decision of the Diet, the editor thereof may not within a period of five years edit a similar publication in any state of the union.

. . .

1. Within a fortnight, reckoned from the passage of this decree, there shall convene, under the auspices of the Confederation, in the city and federal fortress of Mayence, an extraordinary commission of investigation to consist of seven members, including the chairman.

2. The object of the commission shall be a joint investigation, as thorough and extensive as possible, of the facts relating to the origin and manifold ramifications of the revolutionary plots and demagogical associations directed against the existing constitution and the internal peace both of the union and of the individual states; of the existence of which plots more or less clelar evidence is to be had already, or may be produced in the course of the investigation. . . .

10. The central investigating commision is to furnish the Diet from time to time with a report of the results of the investigation, which is to be carried out as speedily as possible. . . .

STUDY QUESTIONS

1. The language of Article VI of the Secret Treaty of 1815 is fairly general. What do you think it meant, in the context of post-Napoleonic Europe? What interests did these four powers have in common?

2. What were the main targets of the Carlsbad decrees? What methods were urged to prevent unrest? How would conservatives like Metternich justify these measures?

3. What were the main principles of the French revolution that the conservatives opposed, and why?

4. How does this early nineteenth-century version of conservatism compare to later European conservatism, and to conservative movements in other parts of the world? What would be added to conservatism to make it more attractive? What principles and methods would be retained?

19

Work and Workers in the Industrial Revolution

The Industrial Revolution was one of the great changes in Western and ultimately world history. Taking shape toward the end of the eighteenth century in Great Britain, industrialization dominated the nineteenth century in Western Europe and North America. Based on radically new technologies, including the use of fossil fuels for power, industrialization revolutionized the production and transportation of goods. It sustained rapid population growth in the West and created growing material abundance as well. This industrialization transformed a social structure once based on the land into divisions based on urban wealth and property. It fostered large organizations and a growing state capable of using new technologies of communication and marshaling large amounts of capital and large numbers of goods and people. It challenged family life by taking work out of the home and redefining the roles of many women and children. It was, in sum, as basic a change in human history as had occurred since the advent of settled agriculture.

One of the many areas altered by industrialization was the nature of work, particularly for those people who labored in the proliferating mines and factories. Some features of industrialization benefited work: Machines could lighten labor, factories could provide social stimulation, and some jobs that demanded new technical expertise became unusually interesting. But many workers found industrial working conditions a strain because they challenged a number of traditional values and habits. Certainly, changes in work provide one way of measuring the human impact of the vast industrialization process—some would say, of measuring human degradation.

The selections focus on three aspects of industrial work during the nineteenth century. The first document comes from a parliamentary inquiry on child labor, conducted in Britain in the early 1830s and ultimately the source of laws restricting children's work. Child labor was not in fact new, so one question to ask is what aspects of the factory system made it seem newly shocking. A second, related feature of industrial work—and one

Selection I from *British Sessional Papers, 1831–1832,* House of Commons, Vol. XV, pp. 17–19. Selection II from *The Archives du Haut Rhin* IM123C1, translated by Peter N. Stearns. Selection III from Adolf Levenstein, *Aus Der Tief, Arbeiterbriefe,* translated by Gabriela Wettbert (Berlin: 1905), pp. 48, 57, 60.

that persisted far longer than child labor—was the attempt to bring new discipline to the labor force. In the second document, shop rules—in this case, from a French factory in the late 1840s—did battle with a number of customary impulses in an effort to make work more predictable, less casual. Finally, new working conditions provoked direct comment by workers through protest and individual statements. The comment offered in the third document, by an unusually sensitive German miner around 1900—among other things, an ardent socialist—is not typical, but it does express some widely shared grievances. All three documents suggest the tensions that changes in work could bring. A basic feature of Western life in the nineteenth century, this strain spread with industrialization to other societies later. How could workers modify or adapt to new work habits? How might changes in work affect other aspects of their lives, in the family, politics, or culture?

INDUSTRIAL REVOLUTION DOCUMENTS

I. BRITISH CHILD LABOR INQUIRY (1831–1832)

Mr. Abraham Whitehead

431. What is your business?—A clothier.

432. Where do you reside?—At Scholes, near Holmfirth.

433. Is not that in the centre of very considerable woollen mills? Yes, for a space of three or four miles; I live nearly in the centre of thirty or forty woollen mills. . . .

436. Are there children and young persons of both sexes employed in these mills?—Yes.

437. At how early an age are children employed?—The youngest age at which children are employed is never under five, but some are employed between five and six in woollen mills at piecing.

438. How early have you observed these young children going to their work, speaking for the present in the summer time?—In the summer time I have frequently seen them going to work between five and six in the morning, and I know the general practice is for them to go as early to all the mills. . . .

439. How late in the evening have you seen them at work, or remarked them returning to their homes?—I have seen them at work in the summer season between nine and ten in the evening; they continue to work as long as they can see, and they can see to work in these mills as long as you could see to read. . . .

441. You say that on your own personal knowledge?—I live near to parents who have been sending their children to mills for a great number of years, and I know positively that these children are every morning in the winter seasons called out of bed between five and six, and in some instances between four and five.

442. Your business as a clothier has often led you into these mills?—Frequently. . . .

. . .

460. What has been the treatment which you have observed that these children received at the mills, to keep them attentive for so many hours at such early ages?—They are generally cruelly treated; so cruelly treated, that they dare not hardly for their lives be too late at their work in a morning. . . . My heart has been ready to bleed for them when I have seen them so fatigued, for they appear in such a state of apathy and insensibility as really not to know whether they are doing their work or not. . . .

461. Do they frequently fall into errors and mistakes in piecing when thus fatigued?—Yes; the errors they make when thus fatigued are, that instead of placing the cording in this way [describing it], they are apt to place them obliquely, and that causes a flying, which makes bad yarn; and when the billy-spinner sees that, he takes his strap or the billy-roller, and says, "Damn thee, close it, little devil, close it," and they smite the child with the strap or the billy-roller. . . .

510. You say that the morals of the children are very bad when confined in these mills; what do you consider to be the situation of children who have nothing to do, and are running about such towns as Leeds, with no employment to keep them out of mischief?—Children that are not employed in mills are generally more moral and better behaved than children who are employed in mills.

511. Those in perfect idleness are better behaved than those that are employed?—That is not a common thing; they either employ them in some kind of business at home, or send them to school.

512. Are there no day-schools to which these factory children go?—They have no opportunity of going to school when they are thus employed at the mill.

II. RULES FOR WORKERS IN THE FACTORY OF BENCK AND CO. IN BÜHL, ALSACE (1842)

Article 1. Every worker who accepts employment in any work-site is obligated to read these rules and to submit to them. No one should be unfamiliar with them. If the rules are violated in any work-site, the offenders must pay fines according to the disorder or damage they have caused.

Art. 2. All workers without exception are obligated, after they have worked in the factory for fourteen days, to give a month's notice when they wish to quit. This provision can be waived only for important reasons.

Art. 3. The work day will consist of twelve hours, without counting rest periods. Children under twelve are excepted; they have to work only eight hours a day.

Art. 4. The bell denotes the hours of entry and departure in the factory when it first rings. At the second ring every worker should be at his work. At quitting time the bell will also be sounded when each worker should clean his workplace and his machine (if he has one). It is forbidden under penalty of fines to abandon the workplace before the bell indicates that the work-site is closed.

Art. 5. It is forbidden to smoke tobacco inside the factory. Whoever violates this prohibition is subjected to a heavy fine and can be dismissed. It is also forbidden under penalty of fines to bring beer or brandy into the factory. Any worker who comes to the factory drunk will be sent away and fined.

Art. 6. The porter, whoever he may be, is forbidden to admit anyone after the workday begins. If someone asks for a worker he will make him wait and have the worker called. All workers are forbidden to bring anyone into the factory and the porter is forbidden to admit anyone. The porter is also forbidden to let any workers in or out without the foreman's permission during the hours of work.

Art. 7. Any worker who misses a day without the Director's permission must pay a fine of two francs. The fine is doubled for a second offense. Any worker who is absent several times is dismissed, and if he is a weaver he is not paid for any piece he may have begun unless he can prove he missed work because of illness and should therefore be paid for work he has already done.

Art. 8. All workers in the factory are obligated to be members of the Sickness Fund, to pay their dues, and conduct themselves according to its statutes.

Art. 9. The foreman and the porter are empowered to retain any worker leaving the factory and to search him, as often as the interests of the Director may require. It is also recommended to the foreman to close the work-site himself, give the key to the porter, and to allow no worker inside during meal periods.

Art. 10. Workers should only go in and out of doors where a porter resides, else they will be fined, brought under suspicion, and dismissed. They cannot refuse to surrender any of their belongings at work, for which they will be reimbursed according to the valuation of the Director and the foreman. Workers are also ordered to be obedient to the foreman, who is fully empowered by the Director. Any disobedience will be punished by fines according to the importance of the case. Any offender is responsible for the consequences of his action. It is also forbidden for any worker to seek work in any of the company's work-sites other than the one in which he is employed; anyone encountered in another work-site will be punished.

Art. 11. Every worker is personally responsible for the objects entrusted to him. Any object that cannot be produced at the first request must be paid for. Weavers are obligated to pay careful attention to their cloth when they dry it. They will be fined and held responsible for any damage.

Art. 12. In return for the protection and care which all workers can expect from the Director, they pledge to him loyalty and attachment. They promise immediately to call to his attention anything that threatens good order or the Director's interests. Workers are also put on notice that any unfortunate who commits a theft, however small it may be, will be taken to court and abandoned to his fate.

III. MAX LOTZ, A GERMAN MINER, DESCRIBES HIS WORK (CA. 1900)

A trembling of the pupils forms in the eyes of many miners. At first it is not noticeable but it gradually becomes stronger. Where this eye ailment reaches a certain stage the stricken person becomes unable to work in the pit any longer. The stricken man becomes unsure of his grip, he often misses the desired object by one foot. He has particular difficulties in directing his glance upward. If he fixes but barely on an object his eyes begin to tremble immediately. But this calamity only appears in the mine or in artificial light. Above ground and in daylight it is never present. I know a laborer working quite close to me who takes a quart of liquor daily into the shaft. As soon as the trembling begins he takes a sip and the pupil becomes calm for a short while—so he states. Thus one can become a habitual drunk, too.

But this is not all. Almost all miners are anemic. I do not know what causes this pathological diminution of blood corpuscles in miners, whether this results from a general lack of protein in the blood. I suppose that it is caused mainly by the long, daily stay in bad air combined with the absence of sun or day light. I reason that if one places a potted plant in a warm but dark cellar for a long time it will grow significantly more pale and sickly than her beautifully scenting sisters in the rose-colored sunlight. It must be like this for the drudges down there. Anemia renders the miner characteristically pale. . . .

Let's go, shouted Prüfer, who had already picked up a shovel. Four more wagons have to fall. It is almost 12:30 [p.m.] now. All right, I agreed, and we swung the shovels.

Away it goes, commanded Bittner when the wagons were fully loaded. Jump to it, there is plenty of coal. Well, if I were a pickman, mumbled the chief pickman then I'd have myself a drink. And he breathed heavily behind the wagon.

Let's set up the planking until Rheinhold comes back so that things don't look so scruffy, I said to Bittner even though we would rather have stretched out on the pile of coal because we were so tired.

He replied: I don't care, but first I want to wring out my trousers. And standing there naked he started to squeeze the water from the garment. I followed his example. When we had finished, it looked around us as though a bucket full of water had been spilled. I do not exaggerate. In other locations where it was warmer yet, the workers were forced to undergo this procedure several times during their working hours. But let us remain here.

We put our undergarments back on and did not pay attention to the unpleasant feeling which we had doing so. We placed the wooden planks and cleared aside the debris in order to establish good working conditions for the other third which usually did not do the same for us—because they were too fatigued.

The work is becoming increasingly mechanical. No more incentive, no more haste, we muddle along wearily, we are worn out and mindless. There was sufficient coal, Rheinhold could come at any time. My forehead burned like fire. As a consequence of the anemia from which I suffer I occasionally experience a slight dizzy spell. Bittner does not know about it. But in my head it rages and paralyzes me beyond control or without my being able to think. When it becomes unbearable I stop my slow, phlegmatic and energyless working. I then sit on the side wall of the mountain in order to slurp the last remaining coffee. . . .

This is a brief description of one shift in the pit. And this torture, this inhuman haste repeats itself day after day [so] that the various states of exhaustion express themselves mildly or very pronouncedly in the physical state of the individuals. And that is not all; the spirit, too, the conscience of the individual degenerates. And one drudge, grown vacuous through his work, is put beside another one, and another one and finally this "modern" circle has closed in on the entire working force. And he who says that primarily the professional group of the miners is the rudest, least educated and spiritually lowest class of men does not lie. Of course, there are exceptions here, too. But these exceptions are supposed to validate the rule according to a simple type of logic. In any event, it truly takes spiritual magnitude to occupy still oneself with belletristic, scientific and thought-provoking materials after a completed shift. When I come home in that condition I still have to cope with other necessary heavy work around the house. And finally there only remains the evening hours for the writing tasks which I deem noble.

STUDY QUESTIONS

1. What features of child labor seemed newly objectionable in the context of factory industry?
2. What were the main goals of factory work rules? What problems did they address? What innovations did they particularly suggest, compared with more traditional work patterns?
3. What does Max Lotz see as the primary problems of mine work? Were work conditions getting better or worse by 1900 in highly industrialized societies like Germany? Why might some workers disagree with Lotz's assessment?
4. Do problems of work in nineteenth-century Europe suggest that industrialization deteriorated the quality of human life? What other factors need to be taken into account? How did workers and others deal with the issues identified in these documents?

20

The Expansion of Frontier Societies

One of the crucial developments in nineteenth-century world history involved developments in relatively new nations like the United States and Australia, where expanding frontiers created space for massive immigration and economic growth. These new nations, which also included New Zealand and Canada, shared several characteristics. They contained aboriginal populations, such as Native Americans, which were steadily pushed back by the combined forces of disease, military force, and seizures of property. Expanding frontiers (facilitated by rapid railroad development) created conditions for extensive farming and stock-raising, which in turn—particularly after further developments in shipping, around 1870—provided massive grain and meat exports to European markets. Mining resources added to this export thrust. New immigrants flocked to the frontier societies, although they filled cities as well as farmlands and mining territories. Most of them came from Europe. Finally, European, particularly British, institutions and cultural values were extensively imported.

The result was a set of societies closely tied to Western European civilization, but also colored by distinctive racial combinations, frontiers, and export economics. There were, of course, important differences among these new societies. The United States was larger than the others in population, and it industrialized more quickly, which added to its world power. It also had the distinctive experience and then legacy of extensive slavery. Finally, it had won independence through military action, whereas the other societies evolved toward increasingly autonomous political expression within the British Empire. Australia, for example, gained independence within the British Commonwealth only in 1900. But all the societies were marked by their combination of frontier and Western European characteristics. They all moved relatively quickly to leadership in the development of democratic political reforms, including, by 1900, pressure to provide voting rights for women. They all gained growing economic importance and potential military-diplomatic importance in world affairs during the nineteenth century—in trends that would continue through the twentieth century as well.

Selection I from *Twenty Years on the Pacific Slope: Letters of Henry Eno from California and Nevada, 1848–1871,* edited by E. Turentine Jackson (New Haven, Conn.: Yale University Press, 1965), pp. 97–99. Selection II from *Discourses of Brigham Young,* edited by John A. Widtsoe (Salt Lake City: Deseret Book Co., 1925), pp. 738–741. Selection III from David Fitzpatrick, *Oceans of Consolation: Personal Accounts of Irish Migration to Australia* (Ithaca, N.Y.: Cornell University Press, 1994). Reprinted by permission of the Public Record Office of Northern Ireland.

The selections offer personal reactions to the nineteenth-century frontier, all by people of European origin. In the first document, Henry Eno talks about prospects and prospecting in Nevada, as he writes to his brother William on August 21, 1869. Eno was one of many pioneers bent on gaining wealth in the Western territories. Miners were first to arrive, moving back east from California when the California gold rush of 1849 subsided. In Nevada, prospectors like Eno looked for gold but more often found silver; 1869 was the height of Nevada's fame as a mining territory.

In the second document, also from the American West, Brigham Young, leader of the movement of thousands of members of the Church of Jesus Christ of Latter-day Saints (Mormons) to Utah in 1847, writes of the gains he saw in his new home. The Latter-day Saints had launched their religious movement in upstate New York, claiming divine inspiration for a new Christian community. Encountering persecution in several places, they finally settled in Utah, where their community took deep roots.

The third document comes from a Protestant Irish immigrant to Australia. John McCance came from County Down in 1853 with his wife and family, settling in the gold-fields of the province of Victoria. He came after the first big gold rushes and never managed to become wealthy, although he earned enough to support his family. Here he writes in 1858 to an Irish former neighbor, William Orr, a wealthier man, whom Mc-Cance had charged with looking after his elderly parents.

THE WILD FRONTIER

I. A NEVADA SILVER MINER, HENRY ENO (1869)

Dear Brother:

Yours of the 11th August was received yesterday. Have now been here since 3rd of July. I came here expecting to find a rich mineral country, also to find much such a population as California had in 1849 and 1850. The great mineral wealth of eastern Nevada has not been exaggerated. In fact I did not expect to find so rich or so many silver mines. There is not so much wild reckless extravagance among the people of the towns and the miners as in the early days of California. There are not as many homicides according to the numbers, but there is perhaps more highway robberies committed. We have here, as twenty years ago, numbers too lazy to work but not too lazy to steal, and some too proud to work and not afraid to steal. The laws of Nevada license gambling, and here at Hamilton, in Treasure City, and Sher-mantown are some ten or twelve licensed gambling tables. The next session of the legislature may perhaps license highway robbery.

There are two banking establishments, two express offices. Wells Fargo and Union Express, some ten or twelve assay offices, and a small army of lawyers. The District Court has been in session ever since I arrived. A trial often occupies ten or twelve days. A very few lawyers are doing well. From what I can discover I believe that lawyers depend more upon perjury and subornation of perjury than upon principles of law or precedents. Experts in mining do a thriving business as witnesses.

There are, I judge, nearly 200 paying mines within four miles square. There ought to be a dozen more quartz mills erected and would find full employment.

The price of crushing and working ores is too high for low grade ores. The common price is $30 per ton. Under ordinary circumstances free ores yielding $15 per ton can be worked at a fair profit. There are very many mining districts within 80 and 100 miles that are now attracting attention of miners and capitalists. The merchants of Chicago are turning their attention to this silver country and will enter into competition with San Francisco, and I should not be surprised if they succeed in establishing and building up a heavy business and a profitable one. The money market in California as well as in Nevada is very stringent. There is much financial distress. Very many men reputed to be worth their many thousands last spring are now reputed worthless. But in no country that I have ever seen (not even in California) do I believe that well-directed industry and judiciously invested capital would meet with richer rewards.

It will never be considered a good grain country, but as a pastoral country it is unquestionably a good one. Millions of sheep can be kept here and without cutting hay for winter. It is also a good dairy country. There is a great scarcity of water, it is true, but artesian wells can supply it. It is also a healthy country: no fever and ague. At this high elevation, persons of weak lungs are subject to pneumonia, but a little care will prevent it. It is *no money,* not *pneumonia,* that I am troubled about and am afraid it will become chronic.

I went out a few days ago with a young fellow on a prospecting trip, about four or five miles from here. Went over as rough a country as I ever traveled over. Stiping Mountain is but a molehill compared with ours. On our return, struck a silver lode. Brought home some specimens and had them assayed. Sent you the assay, so that you may see how we manage here. Intend to prospect it further.

Have made up my mind to go to Iowa and St. Louis, if I can possibly raise the means, the forepart of October and return in the spring. I made the acquaintance of Judge G. C. Bates of Chicago who was here a short time since. I formerly knew him in Sacramento. He tells me I can make money by lecturing, advises me to make my debut at Chicago, and that he will introduce me. And also at Detroit. Am now busily engaged in preparing several lectures, but I labor under many disadvantages. Still hope to overcome them. If I can but put my foot on the lower round of fortune's ladder and grasp with my hand another, I have faith to believe I can yet climb it.

Was pleased to hear about your farming operations. Reapers, mowing machines, gang plows, and the threshers have found their way to the Pacific Coast. Between Elko and Hamilton there are several mowing machines at work. Almost all the wheat of California is harvested by machines. Last year a Mr. Mitchell on the San Joaquin plains raised 14,000 acres of wheat, and that year Bidwell of the Sacramento Valley, candidate for governor last year, raised 27,000 acres of wheat. Last year, in June I was in San Francisco. A farmer living near Sacramento River told me that he had 1,500 acres of wheat which would yield on an average, 30 bushels to the acre. He said he could harvest it, thrash it, put in sacks and store it in a warehouse in San Francisco within a fortnight's time. There have been fifty-six harvesting machines employed this year on the Salinas Plains. I crossed them in 1850, and there was not a furrow turned.

Our markets here are well supplied with everything man wants to sustain life and some of the luxuries. Flour, $8 per hundredweight; beef and mutton, 15 to 20 cents per lb.; sugar, 3 lbs. for $1; bacon, 40 cents per lb.; apples, peaches, apricots, nectarines, and grapes from California in abundance, all about 25 cents per lb.; potatoes, 10 cents per lb.; beans the same; and rice, $12\frac{1}{2}$ cents a bucket; $7 a day for a horseride—I find it cheaper to go afoot for wood, $6 per cord. Rents all the way from $40 to $400 per month for one or two rooms. Plenty of good air but of rather light quality, nothing.

I think you would like a trip to wild country and to the more civilized portion of California. It would give materials for thought and reflection and would in all probability enable you to enjoy with a greater zest the comforts of a quiet home. As for me, I feel as if I had no country and no home, but try to make the best of wherever I am.

II. BRIGHAM YOUNG AND THE MORMONS IN UTAH (1847)

Seven years ago tomorrow, about 11 o'clock, I crossed the Mississippi River with my brethren for this place, not knowing, at the time, whither we were going, but firmly believing that the Lord had in reserve for us a good place in the mountains, and that He would lead us directly to it. . . .

The most of the people called Latter-day Saints have been taken from the rural and manufacturing districts of this and the old countries, and they belonged to the poorest of the poor. Many of them, I may say the great majority, never had anything around them to make life very desirable; they have been acquainted with poverty and wretchedness, hence it cannot be expected that they should manifest that refinement and culture prevalent among the rich. Many and many a man here, who is now able to ride in his wagon and perhaps in his carriage, for years before he started for Zion never saw daylight. His days were spent in the coal mines, and his daily toil would commence before light in the morning and continue until after dark at night.

Now, what can be expected from a community, so many of whose members have been brought up like this, or, if not just like this, still under circumstances of poverty and privation? Certainly not what we might expect from those reared under more favorable circumstances. But I will tell you what we have in our mind's eye with regard to these very people and what we are trying to make of them.

We take the poorest we can find on earth who will receive the truth, and we are trying to make ladies and gentlemen of them. We are trying to educate them, to school their children, and to so train them that they may be able to gather around them the comforts of life that they may pass their lives as the human family should do—that their days, weeks, and months may be pleasant to them. We prove that this is our design, for the result, to some extent, is already before us.

Talk about these rich valleys, why there is not another people on the earth that could have come here and lived. We prayed over the land and dedicated it and the water, air, and everything pertaining to them unto the Lord; and the smiles of Heaven rested on the land, and it become productive and today yields us the best of grain, fruit, and vegetables.

There never has been a land, from the Days of Adam until now, that has been blessed more than this land has been blessed by our Father in Heaven; and it will still be blessed more and more, if we are faithful and humble and thankful to God for the wheat and the corn, the oats, the fruit, the vegetables, the cattle, and everything He bestows upon us, and try to use them for the building up of His kingdom on the earth. . . .

When water is brought to the termination of the canal, which we can accomplish in a few days, I presume that the reservoirs on the line of the work and those portions which are excavated in full will contain water enough to allow the people to irrigate when necessary and thus do away with the practice of watering only two hours a week on a city lot, and much of that to be done in the night. And that is not all, for by the time the water is fairly on a lot it is taken to the next person whose right it is to use it. And lots which have had thousands of dollars expended on them, and which would yield more than a thousand dollars' worth of fruit and vegetables, could they be properly irrigated, are only allowed a small stream of water for two hours once a week, and at the same time an adjoining lot planted with corn, the hills six feet apart and one stalk in a hill, comparatively speaking, the balance of the ground being covered with weeds, is allotted the same time and amount of water as the one on which the fruit trees and other choice vegetation are worth thousands of dollars. . . .

Until the Latter-day Saints came here, not a person among all the mountaineers and those who had traveled here, so far as we could learn, believed that an ear of corn would ripen in these valleys. We know that corn and wheat produce abundantly here, and we know that we have an excellent region wherein to raise cattle, horses, and every other kind of domestic animal that we need. . . .

III. AN IMMIGRANT MINER IN AUSTRALIA: JOHN McCANCE (1858)

Chewton Forest Creek
June 7th/58.

Dear Sir

(a) I would wish to write a few more lines to you but realy I scarcely do Know what to write to you as there is very little new here that I do Know or remember as this does leave us in our useual health Praise the Lord for His continued merceys to us as we are very unworthy of the least of His notice yet still He spares our very unworthy lives and bestows on us a good measure of hea[l]th and strength and a good many of His bountys and we trust that this will find you all as a family in good health also and now what shall I say.

(b) If I was to tell you of our own township how it is growing as if it were by m[a]gic and also our market town Castlemaine you would not feel much interest in them. But realy they astonish me. As to our digging there is little new but likely I will send you a newspaper which will give you all the information of these Things. I sent you one by the last mail of the 15th may. I hope you may have got it. Our great railway is now all the talk but is not begun yet. It was to have begun on the first of June but oweing to the severe illness of a great ireish man a Mr Duffy it is put off till the tenth of June. There is a great many goldmining compenys starting up about this place I beleive five or six some of them so large as 2000 shares. It is causing work to get more plenty for those who is willing to work for wages and if our great railway was started I think there need not be many idle. But I think that wages will never be high again as there is still a goodly number waiting in hops of the same perhaps more Than will work when they get the chance. But now what shall I say more.

(c) I wish I could Know what you would wish to Know but I will begin with our season. This is now the month of June and our white frosts are now set in. I have washed my face in icey water this last week. We have it nearly one eighth of an inch thick betimes but allways followed by a most beautifull day. We have a good deal of our garden seed sowen and above the ground such as the frost will not Kill. That is onions leeks parsnips carrotts lettuces cress Redish parsley celery and peas which are fit for stakeing at this time. Cabbage curley Kale culiflowers and all such like I have had sowen and all grew very well even the seeds which I kindly received from you. But alas this blight with which we are sorly perplexed pays no respect to seeds or where they come from. As soon as the plant gets its second or third leaf the blight lays hold on them and in spite of all our care it has Killed the most of them but still I have preserved a few of all sorts yet espeicly the curley Kale. I have also a little of all the flower seeds sowen which you sent but the are not up yet. But I intend to protect them from the frost by means of a square of calico and four posts which will furle up every morning and spread out every eve[n]ing.

(d) Now sir supose I would turn to nature a little but realy I scarsley dare as I am no naturlist. But perhaps you might wonder what sort of things we may have here and I think I have hinted at our trublesome things. Our venomous Reptiles are very numerous. We have a great variety of birds more than I could now inform you of and some of most beautifull plumbage. If you would give me a hint of your desire to hear of them I would take a list of them. We have some very nice butterflys of almos every hue except white as I have never saw a white one yet. I have seen no bees as yet either tame or wild although I beleive that there is some in this colney [colony]. Our bat is the very same as the are with you. They fly about very thick every eveining. Our swallow is much the same also. They remain with us all winter but there is more in summer. Now I must tell you that we have lots of mice here although I think they are not natives and we have plenty of rats in severl places although I have not seen any on the diggings as yet. They have plenty in Castlemaine and they are awefull numerious in Melbourne a perfect plague. They are not natives either but indeed I could scarcely tell you what is natives. I have seen the Kangaroo and the opossum the Kangaroorat about the size of a rabbit. The native cat is a prety thing. It is not so large as our cat is all spotted like a laopord withe spots about the size of buttons. I have never saw a native dog but I beleive they are very pretty also rather like a fox. Now I have told you what I have seen & must refer you to natural history for the others. I have never seen a hare but there [are] plenty of tame Rabbits and I belive there is some wild ones which has been let loose. I have never seen either pheasent or patridge. We have plenty of Quales and native pidgeons. But perhaps this will wearie you but what shall I say next.

(e) I would ask you a very important Questin and that is as I Know that my father is not very plenty of ready Change if you would be so Kind (as I cannot doubt your Kindness) as to give him a half or whole Quire of letter paper ink pens &c. and every letter that he would bring in to you if you would back it and stamp it that is with postage stamps. By so doeing you would certinly very much oblidge me and it may be that I may get an oppertunity of some one returning home by which I may recomepence you. If not sooner I shall have a chance when Thomas Brooks des go and if I do not get any I shall not forget to pay you with intresst.

(f) Now as I have named T. B. I must tell you that he is in good health and I have heard good accounts of his hole by Mrs John McMillin who is up with us at this time to stop a week or so. Thomas still lives with them. John Regan is in good health also and works in the same hole with Thomas. Mrs Boyce and all her family are well also. I supose you will have heard that her doughter Eliza is got married since they came. Hamilton lives up here now close to our garden fence. James McMillin still works at the work with me as I still work at the companys work yet but we have had no word from Nathaniel yet. Thomas & Alexander are still out in the bush at stations. I have never had the chance of seeing any aquentance of yous and may be I never shall unless they make themselves Known to me.

(g) I still hold the Boomarang yet. I have just been showing it to Mrs McMillin and another young woman a Mrs McAnally from Bellfast who is up with her. She would wish that you would let her father & Mother Know that they are all well also but there is nothing new with them. They are still working at thair deep hole also that is Mrs John McMillin.

(h) Now I do not Know what news to ask of you but you may let me Know of any deaths that may occour in the old neighbourhood with any perticular news that you may think right. When you write you may direct to myself John McCance Chewton forest Creek by Castlemaine Victoria Australia. So I conclude with your friend & wellwisher

John McCance

STUDY QUESTIONS

1. What criteria does Eno use to evaluate Nevada? How do his criteria compare with those of Brigham Young?
2. What is Brigham Young's religious interpretation of the Mormon settlement in Utah? How does he combine his faith with insistence on human effort? How was Mormon Utah different from Nevada as a result of religion?
3. What pulled McCance to Australia? How did he assess the frontier?
4. How do McCance and Eno suggest possible failures on the frontier?
5. What does "civilization" mean to former Europeans on the frontiers?
6. Did settlers of European origin on the frontiers feel that the frontier had changed them? Were immigrants, like McCance, more or less likely than simple migrants to feel the results of a new environment?
7. What kinds of values for the building societies of Australia and the United States do these documents suggest? How do they compare?

Russia

21

Russian Peasants: Serfdom and Emancipation

More than most Eurasian societies, Russia long remained a land of small cities with limited manufacturing. Not only a majority, but a vast majority of its people were peasants well into the nineteenth century. Numbers alone, however, do not account for the omnipresence of peasant issues in Russian history. From a once-held position of substantial freedom and control of village lands, Russian peasants had been subjected to increasingly rigorous serfdom—by the state or by noble landlords—from the fifteenth century onward. Their trend thus reversed that of Western Europe, where serfdom on the whole became lighter over time. The Russian economy relied on agricultural exports forced from peasant labor on the large estates, and Russian politics and society, which traded noble control over their peasants for docility to the Russian tsar, relied heavily on the subjection of the serfs.

Yet the peasants' condition created increasingly visible problems. It violated standards of justice felt keenly by many Russians, including those open to Western ideas during the eighteenth and nineteenth centuries. Serfs rioted frequently, for peasants were quite aware of their own servitude (See Chapter 7). Furthermore, tight control of peasant labor limited Russia's economic flexibility, making it hard to recruit urban labor and, at least in the eyes of some observers, reducing productivity on the land as well. Finally, prodded by its loss in the Crimean War, the Russian government took the step of emancipation, ending serfdom while trying to preserve the noble-dominated social hierarchy. This move redefined the peasant question but did not remove it.

The following selections stem from two sources. The first document is an account by an early Russian intellectual, Alexander Radishchev (1749–1802), who wrote about

Selection I from Alexander Radishchev, *A Journey from St. Petersburg to Moscow* (Cambridge, Mass.: Harvard University Press, 1958), pp. 158–160. Copyright © 1958 by the President and Fellows of Harvard College. Reprinted by permission. Selection II from Basil Dmytryshyn, *Imperial Russia: A Sourcebook, 1700–1917* (New York: Holt, Rinehart and Winston, Inc., 1967), pp. 221–223, 225. Copyright © 1967 by Holt, Rinehart and Winston, Inc. Reprinted by permission. Manifesto from *Polnoe Sobranie Zakonov Russkoi Imperii* (Complete Collection of the Laws of the Russian Empire), 2nd series, Vol. 36, No. 36,490, pp. 130–134.

the peasants' condition in the book *A Journey from St. Petersburg to Moscow* (1790), which was repressed by the government until 1905. His account reveals peasants' suffering and reactions and also the reformist zeal of a segment of the educated upper class. The second document presents excerpts from the emancipation decree of 1861. They reveal how a new tsar, Alexander II, tried to juggle reform interests with noble resistance. The document invites appraisal in terms of how much was changed and why peasants were so widely disappointed with the results.

RUSSIAN DOCUMENTS

I. RADISHCHEV'S JOURNEY (1790)

I suppose it is all the same to you whether I traveled in winter or in summer. Maybe both in winter and in summer. It is not unusual for travelers to set out in sleighs and to return in carriages. The corduroy road tortured my body; I climbed out of the carriage and went on foot. While I had been lying back in the carriage, my thoughts had turned to the immeasurable vastness of the world. By spiritually leaving the earth I thought I might more easily bear the jolting of the carriage. But spiritual exercises do not always distract us from our physical selves; and so, to save my body, I got out and walked. A few steps from the road I saw a peasant ploughing a field. The weather was hot. I looked at my watch. It was twenty minutes before one. I had set out on Saturday. It was now Sunday. The ploughing peasant, of course, belonged to a landed proprietor, who would not let him pay a commutation tax [*obrok*]. The peasant was ploughing very carefully. The field, of course, was not part of his master's land. He turned the plough with astonishing ease.

"God help you," I said, walking up to the ploughman, who, without stopping, was finishing the furrow he had started. "God help you," I repeated.

"Thank you, sir," the ploughman said to me, shaking the earth off the ploughshare and transferring it to a new furrow.

"You must be a Dissenter, since you plough on a Sunday."

"No, sir, I make the true sign of the cross," he said, showing me the three fingers together. "And God is merciful and does not bid us starve to death, so long as we have strength and a family."

"Have you no time to work during the week, then, and can you not have any rest on Sundays, in the hottest part of the day, at that?"

"In a week, sir, there are six days, and we go six times a week to work on the master's fields; in the evening, if the weather is good, we haul to the master's house the hay that is left in the woods; and on holidays the women and girls go walking in the woods, looking for mushrooms and berries. God grant," he continued, making the sign of the cross, "that it rains this evening. If you have peasants of your own, sir, they are praying to God for the same thing."

"My friend, I have no peasants, and so nobody curses me. Do you have a large family?"

"Three sons and three daughters. The eldest is nine years old."

"But how do you manage to get food enough, if you have only the holidays free?"

"Not only the holidays: the nights are ours, too. If a fellow isn't lazy, he won't starve to death. You see, one horse is resting; and when this one gets tired, I'll take the other; so the work gets done."

"Do you work the same way for your master?"

"No, Sir, it would be a sin to work the same way. On his fields there are a hundred hands for one mouth, while I have two for seven mouths: you can figure it out for yourself. No matter how hard you work for the master, no one will thank you for it. The master will not pay our head tax; but, though he doesn't pay it, he doesn't demand one sheep, one hen, or any linen or butter the less. The peasants are much better off where the landlord lets them pay a commutation tax without the interference of the steward. It is true that sometimes even good masters take more than three rubles a man; but even that's better than having to work on the master's fields. Nowadays it's getting to be the custom to let villages to tenants, as they call it. But we call it putting our heads in a noose. A landless tenant skins us peasants alive; even the best ones don't leave us any time for ourselves. In the winter he won't let us do any carting of goods and won't let us go into town to work; all our work has to be for him, because he pays our head tax. It is an invention of the Devil to turn your peasants over to work for a stranger. You can make a complaint against a bad steward, but to whom can you complain against a bad tenant?"

"My friend, you are mistaken; the laws forbid them to torture people."

"Torture? That's true; but all the same, sir, you would not want to be in my hide." Meanwhile the ploughman hitched up the other horse to the plough and bade me goodbye as he began a new furrow.

The words of this peasant awakened in me a multitude of thoughts. I thought especially of the inequality of treatment within the peasant class. I compared the crown peasants with the manorial peasants. They both live in villages; but the former pay a fixed sum, while the latter must be prepared to pay whatever their master demands. The former are judged by their equals; the latter are dead to the law, except, perhaps, in criminal cases. A member of society becomes known to the government protecting him, only when he breaks the social bonds, when he becomes a criminal! This thought made my blood boil.

Tremble, cruelhearted landlord! on the brow of each of your peasants I see your condemnation written.

II. THE EMANCIPATION MANIFESTO (1861)

By the Grace of God We, Alexander II, Emperor and Autocrat of All Russia, King of Poland, Grand Duke of Finland, etc., make known to all Our faithful subjects:

Called by Divine Providence and by the sacred right of inheritance to the throne of Our Russian ancestors, We vowed in Our heart to respond to the mission which is entrusted to Us and to surround with Our affection and Our Imperial solicitude all Our faithful subjects of every rank and condition, from the soldier who nobly defends the country to the humble artisan who works in industry; from the career official of the state to the plowman who tills the soil.

Examining the condition of classes and professions comprising the state, We became convinced that the present state legislation favors the upper and middle classes, defines their obligations, rights, and privileges, but does not equally favor the serfs, so designated because in part from old laws and in part from custom they have been hereditarily subjected to the authority of landowners, who in turn were obligated to provide for their well being. Rights of nobles have been hitherto very broad and legally ill defined, because they stem from tradition, custom, and the good will of the noblemen. In most cases this has led to the establishment of good patriarchal relations based on the sincere, just concern and benevolence on the part of the nobles, and on affectionate submission on the part of the peasants. Because of the decline of the simplicity of morals, because of an increase in the diversity of relations, because of the weakening of the direct paternal attitude of nobles toward the peasants, and because noble rights fell sometimes into the hands of people exclusively concerned with their personal interests, good relations weakened. The way was opened for an arbitrariness burdensome for the peasants and detrimental to their welfare, causing them to be indifferent to the improvement of their own existence.

These facts had already attracted the attention of Our predecessors of glorious memory, and they had adopted measures aimed at improving the conditions of the peasants; but these measures were ineffective, partly because they depended on the free, generous action of nobles, and partly because they affected only some localities, by virtue of special circumstances or as an experiment. Thus Alexander I issued a decree on free agriculturists, and the late Emperor Nicholas, Our beloved father, promulgated one dealing with the serfs. In the Western *gubernias,* inventory regulations determine the peasant land allotments and their obligations. But decrees on free agriculturists and serfs have been carried out on a limited scale only.

We thus became convinced that the problem of improving the condition of serfs was a sacred inheritance bequeathed to Us by Our predecessors, a mission which, in the course of events, Divine Providence has called upon Us to fulfill.

We have begun this task by expressing Our confidence toward the Russian nobility, which has proven on so many occasions its devotion to the Throne, and its readiness to make sacrifices for the welfare of the country.

We have left to the nobles themselves, in accordance with their own wishes, the task of preparing proposals for the new organization of peasant life—proposals that would limit their rights over the peasants, and the realization of which would inflict on them [the nobles] some material losses. Our confidence was justified. Through members of the *gubernia* committees, who had the trust of the nobles' associations, the nobility voluntarily renounced its right to own serfs. These committees, after collecting the necessary data, have formulated proposals on a new arrangement for serfs and their relationship with the nobles.

These proposals were diverse, because of the nature of the problem. They have been compared, collated, systematized, rectified and finalized in the main committee instituted for that purpose; and these new arrangements dealing with the peasants and domestics of the nobility have been examined in the Governing Council.

Having invoked Divine assistance, We have resolved to execute this task.

On the basis of the above mentioned new arrangements, the serfs will receive in time the full rights of free rural inhabitants.

The nobles, while retaining their property rights on all the lands belonging to them, grant the peasants perpetual use of their domicile in return for a specified obligation; and, to assure their livelihood as well as to guarantee fulfillment of their obligations toward the government, [the nobles] grant them a portion of arable land fixed by the said arrangements, as well as other property.

While enjoying these land allotments, the peasants are obliged, in return, to fulfill obligations to the noblemen fixed by the same arrangements. In this state, which is temporary, the peasants are temporarily bound.

At the same time, they are granted the right to purchase the domicile, and, with the consent of the nobles, they may acquire in full ownership the arable lands and other properties which are allotted them for permanent use. Following such acquisition of full ownership of land, the peasants will be freed from their obligations to the nobles for the land thus purchased and will become free peasant landowners. . . .

We leave it to the nobles to reach a friendly understanding with the peasants and to reach agreements on the extent of the land allotment and the obligations stemming from it, observing, at the same time, the established rules to guarantee the inviolability of such agreements. . . .

What legally belongs to nobles cannot be taken away from them without adequate compensation, or through their voluntary concession; it would be contrary to all justice to use the land of the nobles without assuming responsibility for it.

And now We confidently expect that the freed serfs, on the eve of a new future which is opening to them, will appreciate and recognize the considerable sacrifices which the nobility has made on their behalf.

STUDY QUESTIONS

1. What are Radishchev's main arguments against serfdom? Where did he derive his criteria for judgment? What kind of society would he find preferable to Russia's?
2. What aspects of serfdom persisted from earlier decades (Chapter 7)?
3. Was the emancipation of the serfs a radical move? Why did it provoke renewed discontent among the peasants? How did the arguments and implementation relate to earlier critiques by Westernizers like Radishchev?
4. What does the emancipation document suggest about the flexibility of Russia's authoritarian political structure?
5. Do these two documents provide clues as to why Russia encountered less social protest than Western Europe did during the first half of the nineteenth century, but more fundamental protest movements by the century's end?

22

Russian Conservatism

The emergence of an anti-Western conservatism in Russia during the nineteenth century was an important development for two reasons. First, conservatives usually dominated the Russian government (the main exception was the Reform Era of 1861–1881) and opposed significant political or social reform. Their strength helps explain why the course of Russian politics remained distinctive and why pressures for revolution built up by the end of the nineteenth century. The second significance attached to Russian conservatism was its articulation of criticisms of key features of Western society at a time when Western world influence was growing steadily. Here, Russian conservatives mounted some arguments that other opponents of the West, in Russia and elsewhere, would develop as well. Russian communists, for example, in power after 1917, disagreed with conservative political prescriptions, but they shared a distrust of Western individualism and capitalism.

The following two selections come from leading Russian conservatives, both writing after the Emancipation of the Serfs in 1861. In an 1869 book Danilevsky shows the growing strength of Russian nationalism and its opposition to further change. Russian conservatives gained ascendancy again after the terrorist assassination of tsar Alexander II in 1881. Pobyedonostsev (1827–1907), a leading statesman, reflected this tougher conservatism. Although they did not oppose all change (industrialization continued), late-nineteenth-century conservatives resisted any further alterations to the political and social structure. Their obstinacy helped develop an atmosphere of inflexibility and repression that led to the revolutions of 1905 and 1917.

Russian conservatism was not single-minded. Conservatives disagreed about how much of the existing system had to be preserved. They did not, after 1861, argue for a return to serfdom, though they rarely wanted many more concessions to the aggrieved peasantry. While conservative nationalists argued against Western values, some of them recognized that some aspects of the West had to be imitated if Russia was to gain power. Here again, there was room for dispute.

There is a final complexity. Russian conservatives offered some arguments against Western institutions that were clearly tied to their own time and their own politics. This was particularly true in the attacks on Western political instability and political radicalism,

Selection I is from Nikolai Danilevsky, "Russia and Europe," in *The Mind of Modern Russia,* ed. Hans Kohn (New Brunswick, N.J.: Rutgers University Press, 1955), pp. 200–211; Selection II is from Konstantin P. Pobyedonostsev, *Reflections of a Russian Statesman,* trans. Robert Crozieer Long (London: Grant Richard, 1898) pp. 23–30, 32–46, 53–54, 62–74.

which must be understood in the specific context of the later nineteenth century. Other arguments were not so time-bound. Criticisms of Western society or the parliamentary system, and praise for the real or imagined qualities of a Russian or Slavic "soul" could appeal to other Russians at other times, including communists in the twentieth century and post-communists in the early twenty-first century. It is important to try to understand what aspects of the West seemed open to attack and why.

CONSERVATIVE IDEAS

I. DANILEVSKY

And now let us turn to the Slav world, and chiefly to Russia, its only independent representative, in order to examine the results and the promises of this world, a world still only at the beginning of its cultural-historical life. We must examine it from the viewpoint of the above four foci of reference: religion, culture, politics, and socio-economic structure, in order to elucidate what we rightfully expect as well as hope from the Slav cultural-historical type.

Religion constituted the most essential element of ancient Russian life, and at the present time, the overwhelming spiritual interest of the ordinary Russian is also involved in it; in truth, one cannot but wonder at the ignorance and the impertinence of those people who could insist (to gratify their fantasies) on the religious indifference of the Russian people.

From an objective, factual viewpoint, the Russian and the majority of Slav peoples became, with the Greeks, the chief guardians of the living tradition of religious truth, Orthodoxy, and in this way they continued the high calling, which was the destiny of Israel and Byzantium: to be the chosen people. . . .

. . . The religious aspect of the cultural activity belongs to the Slav cultural type and to Russia in particular; it is its inalienable achievement, founded on the psychology of its people and on its guardianship of religious truth. . . .

Whatever the future may bring we are entitled, on the evidence of the past alone, to consider the Slavs among the most gifted families of the human race in political ability. Here we may turn our attention to the special character of this political ability and show how it manifested itself during the growth of the Russian state. The Russians do not send out colonists to create new political societies, as the Greeks did in antiquity or the English in modern times. Russia does not have colonial possessions, like Rome or like England. The Russian state from early Muscovite times on has been Russia herself, gradually, irresistibly spreading on all sides, settling neighboring nonsettled territories, and assimilating into herself and into her national boundaries foreign populations. This basic character of Russian expansion was misunderstood because of the distortion of the original Russian point of view through Europeanization, the origin of every evil in Russia. . . .

But the expansion of the state, its attainment of stability, strength, and power, constitutes only one aspect of political activity. It has still another one, consisting of the establishment of equal relationships between the citizens themselves and between them and the state, i.e., in the establishment of civil and political freedom.

A people not endowed with this freedom cannot be said to possess a healthy political sense. Is the Russian people capable of freedom?

Naturally our "well-wishers" give a negative answer: some regard slavery as a natural element of the Russians, and others are afraid, or pretend to be afraid, that freedom in Russian hands must lead to all sorts of excesses and abuses. But on the basis of Russian history and with knowledge of the views and traits of the Russian people, one can only form an opinion diametrically opposed to this view—namely, that there hardly ever has existed or exists a people so capable of enduring such a large share of freedom as the Russians and so little inclined to abuse it, due to their ability and habit to obey, their respect and trust in the authorities, their lack of love for power, and their loathing of interference in matters where they do not consider themselves competent. If we look into the causes of all political troubles, we shall find their root not in the striving after freedom, but in the love for power and the vain cravings of human beings to interfere in affairs that are beyond their comprehension. . . .

This nature of the Russian people is the true reason why Russia is the only state which never had (and in all probability never will have) a political revolution, i.e., a revolution having as its aim the limitation of the power of the ruler. . . .

With legality in the succession of the throne secured . . . and finally with the liberation of the peasants, all the reasons which in former times had agitated the people disappeared; and even an ordinary rebellion, going beyond the limits of a regrettable misunderstanding, has become impossible in Russia so long as the moral character of the Russian people does not change. . . .

. . . Thus we may conclude that the Russian people, by their attitude towards the power of the state, by their ability to sacrifice to it their won personal interests, and by their attitude towards the use of political and civil freedom, are gifted with wonderful political sense.

In the socio-economic sphere, Russia is the only large state which has solid ground under its feet, in which there are no landless masses, and in which, consequently, the social edifice does not rest on the misery of the majority of the citizens and on the insecurity of their situation. In Russia only there cannot and does not exist any contradiction between political and economic ideals. This contradiction threatens disaster to European life, a life which has embarked on its historical voyage in the dangerous seas between the Charybdis of Caesarism or military despotism and the Scylla of social revolution. The factors that give such superiority to the Russian social structure over the European, and give it an unshakable stability, are the peasant's land and its common ownership. On this health of Russia's socio-economic structure we found our hope for the great socio-economic significance of the Slav cultural-historical type. This type has been able for the first time to create a just and normal system of human activity, which embraces not only human relations in the moral and political sphere, but also man's mastery of nature, which is a means of satisfying human needs and requirements. Thus it establishes not only formal equality in the relations between citizens, but a real and concrete equality.

However, as regards the prominent place of the Slav cultural-historical type in the field of culture proper, one must admit that so far the Russian and other Slav achievements in the sciences and in the arts are insignificant in comparison with the accomplishments of the two great cultural types, the Greek and the European. . . .

Scientific and artistic activity can thrive only under conditions of leisure, of an overflow of forces that remain free from daily toil. Could much leisure be left over among Russians and Slavs? . . . All these considerations fully answer, it seems to me, the question why until now Russia and the other Slav countries could not occupy a respected position in purely cultural activities. . . . But indications of these aptitudes, of these spiritual forces, which are necessary for brilliant achievements in the fields of science and art are now indisputably present among the Slav peoples in spite of all the unfavorable conditions of their life; and, consequently, we are justified in expecting that with a change in these conditions, these peoples will bring forth remarkable creations. . . .

The Slav cultural type has already produced enough examples of artistic and, to a lesser degree, scientific achievements to allow us to conclude that it has attained a significant degree of development in these fields. The relative youth of the race and the concentration of all its forces upon other, more urgent types of activity have not, until now, given the Slavs the opportunity of acquiring cultural significance, in the exact meaning of the phrase. This should not embarrass us; rather, it points to the right path in our development. As long as there is no strong foundation, we cannot and we must not think of the erection of a durable edifice; we can only set up temporary buildings, which cannot be expected to display the talents of the builder in every respect. The political independence of the race is the indispensable foundation of culture, and consequently all the Slav forces must be directed towards this goal. Independence is indispensable . . . [for] without the consciousness of Slav racial unity, as distinct from other races, an independent culture is impossible. . . .

The requisite preliminary achievement of political independence has still another importance in the cultural as well as in all other spheres: the struggle against the Germano-Roman world (without which Slav independence is impossible) will help to eradicate the cancer of imitativeness and the servile attitude towards the West, which through unfavorable conditions has eaten its way into the Slav body and soul.

II. POBYEDONOSTSEV

What is this freedom by which so many minds are agitated, which inspires so many insensate actions, so may wild speeches, which leads the people so often to misfortune? In the democratic sense of the word, freedom is the right of political power, or, to express it otherwise, the right to participate in the government of the State. This universal aspiration for a share in the government has no constant limitations, and seeks no definite issue, but incessantly extends . . . Forever extending its base, the new Democracy now aspires to universal suffrage—a fatal error, and one of the most remarkable in the history of mankind. By this means, the political power so passionately demanded by Democracy would be shattered into a number of infinitesimal bits, of which each citizen acquires a single one. What will he do with it, then? How will he employ it? In the result it has undoubtedly been shown that in the attainment of this aim Democracy violates its sacred formula of "Freedom indissolubly joined with Equality." It is shown that this apparently equal distribution of "freedom" among all involves the total destruction of equality. Each vote, representing an inconsiderable fragment of power, by itself signifies nothing; an aggregation of votes alone has a relative value. The result may be likened to the general meetings of shareholders in public companies. By themselves individuals are ineffective, but he who controls a number of these fragmentary forces is master of all power, and directs all decisions and dispositions. We may well ask in what consists the superiority of Democracy. Everywhere the strongest man becomes master of the State; sometimes a fortunate and resolute general, sometimes a monarch or administrator with knowledge, dexterity, a clear plan of action, and a determined will; in a Democracy, the real rulers are the dexterous manipulators of votes, with their placemen, the mechanics who so skillfully operate the hidden springs which move the puppets in the arena of democratic elections. Men of this kind are ever ready with loud speeches lauding equality; in reality, they rule the people as any despot or military dictator might rule it. The extension of the right to participate in elections is regarded as progress and as the conquest of freedom by democratic theorists, who hold that the more numerous the participants in political rights, the greater is the probability that all will employ this right in the interests of the public welfare, and for the increase of the freedom of the people. Experience proves a very different thing. The history of mankind bears witness that the most necessary and fruitful reforms—the most durable measures—emanated from the supreme will of statesmen, or from a minority enlightened by lofty ideas and deep knowledge, and that, on the contrary, the extension of the representative principle is accompanied by an abasement of political ideas and the vulgarization of opinions in the mass of the electors. . . .

In what does the theory of Parliamentarism consist? It is supposed that the people in its assemblies make their own laws, and elect responsible officers to execute their will. Such is the ideal conception. Its immediate realization is impossible. The historical development of society necessitates that local communities increase in numbers and complexity; that separate races be assimilated, or, retaining their polities and languages, unite under a single flag, that territory extend indefinitely. Under such conditions direct government by the people is impracticable. The people must, therefore, delegate its right of power to its representatives, and invest them with administrative autonomy. These representatives in turn cannot govern immediately, but are compelled to elect a still smaller number of trustworthy persons—ministers—to whom they entrust the preparation and execution of the laws, the appointment and collection of taxes, the appointment of subordinate officials, and the disposition of the militant forces.

In the abstract this mechanism is quite symmetrical; for its proper operation many conditions are essential. The working of the political machine is based on impersonal forces constantly acting and completely balanced. It may act successfully only when the delegates of the people abdicate their personalities; when on the benches of Parliament sit mechanical fullfillers of the people's behests; when the ministers of State remain impersonal, absolute executors of the will of the majority; when the elected representatives of the people are capable of understanding precisely, and executing conscientiously the programme of activity, mathematically expressed, which has been delivered to them. Given such conditions the machine would work exactly, and would accomplish its purpose. The law would actually embody the will of the people; administrative measures would actually emanate from Parliament; the pillars of the State would rest actually on the elective assemblies, and each citizen would directly and consciously participate in the management of public affairs.

Such is the theory. Let us look at the practice. Even in the classic countries of Parliamentarism it would satisfy not one of the conditions enumerated. The elections in no way express the will of the electors. The popular representatives are in no way restricted by the opinions of their constituents, but are guided by their own views and considerations, modified by the tactics of their opponents. In reality, ministers are autocratic, and they rule, rather than are ruled by Parliament. They attain power, and lose power, not by virtue of the will of the people, but through immense influence . . . and they fear no censure while they enjoy the support in Parliament of a majority which they maintain by the distribution of bounties from the rich tables which the State has put at their disposal. In reality, the ministers are as irresponsible as the representatives of the people. Mistakes, abuse of power, and arbitrary acts, are of daily occurrence, yet how often do we hear of the grave responsibility of a minister? It may be once in fifty years a minister is tried for his crimes, with a result contemptible when compared with the celebrity gained by the solemn procedure. . . .

Such is the complicated mechanism of the Parliamentary farce; such is the great political lie which dominates our age. By the theory of Parliamentarism, the rational majority must rule; in practice the party is ruled by five or six of its leaders who exercise all power. In theory, decisions are controlled by clear arguments in the course of Parliamentary debates; in practice, they in no wise depend from debates, but are determined by the wills of the leaders and the promptings of personal interest. In theory, the representatives of the people consider only the public welfare; in practice, their first consideration is their own advancement, and the interests of their friends. In theory, they must be the best citizens; in practice, they are the most ambitious and impudent. In theory, the elector gives his vote for his candidate because he knows him and trusts him; in practice the elector gives his vote for a man whom he seldom knows, but who has been forced on him by the speeches of an interested party. In theory, Parliamentary business is directed by experience, good sense, and unselfishness; in practice, the chief motive powers are a firm will, egoism, and eloquence.

Such is the Parliamentary institution, exalted as the summit and crown of the edifice of State. It is sad to think that even in Russia there are men who aspire to the establishment of this falsehood among us; that our professors glorify to their young pupils representative government as the ideal of political science; that our newspapers pursue it . . . , under the name of justice and order, without troubling to examine without prejudice the working of the parliamentary machine. Yet even where centuries have sanctified its existence, faith already decays; the Liberal intelligence exalts it, but the people groans under its despotism, and recognizes its falsehood. We may not see, but our children and grandchildren assuredly will see, the overthrow of this idol, which contemporary thought in its vanity continues still to worship. . . .

The prevalent doctrine of the perfection of Democracy and of democratic government stands on the same delusive foundation. This doctrine presupposes the capacity of the people to understand subtleties of political science which have a clear and substantial existence in the minds of its apostles only. Precision of knowledge is attainable only by the few minds which constitute the aristocracy of intellect; the mass, always and everywhere, is *vulgus,* and its conceptions of necessity are vulgar.

Democracy is the most complicated and the most burdensome system of government recorded in the history of humanity. For this reason it has never appeared save as a transitory manifestation, with few exceptions giving place before long to other systems. It is in no way surprising. The duty of the State is to act and to ordain: its dispositions are manifestations of a single will; without this, government is inconceivable. But how can a multitude of men, or a popular assembly act with a single will? . . . Such conditions inevitably lead to anarchy, from which society can be saved alone by dictatorship—that is, by the rehabilitation of autocracy in the government of the world.

STUDY QUESTIONS

1. How did Danilevsky define Russian superiority? What, in his view, were Russia's key strengths?
2. What did Danilvesky mean by freedom? What recent reforms did he defend? What few aspects of the West did he admire?
3. In what sense was Pobedonostsev more deeply conservative than Danilevsky? How was Russian conservatism changing by the late nineteenth century? Did the two agree on the qualities of a strong state? On the nature of the Russian common people?
4. How did Russian conservatism compare with the European conservatism of the earlier nineteenth century, around the time of Metternich (see Chapter 18)? What were the consistent qualities of nineteenth-century conservatism? What were the distinctive Russian or late-nineteenth century features?
5. What aspects of Western society and politics did Russian conservatives criticize? Are any of these Western features still criticized by skeptical foreign observers today?
6. What is conservative nationalism? How does it compare to liberal or radical nationalism, of the sort, for example, that emerged during the French Revolution?

Asia

23

China and the West: The Opium War

During most of the Ming dynasty (1368–1644) and during the first half of the Qing dynasty (1644–1912) Chinese emperors presided over an orderly and prosperous society. Jesuit missionaries to the Qing court, who had little success in winning converts, nonetheless sent letters to their colleagues in Europe that were strongly positive about what they observed in China. Leaders of the European Enlightenment such as Voltaire (1694–1778), based their views of China on the Jesuit reports and praised the Chinese political system for its stability and reasonableness.

Around 1800, however, much began to go wrong in China. By this date the Chinese population, which had been growing rapidly for the past three centuries, began to press hard against the available food supply. In the past, the Chinese had been among the world's most innovative people with regard to technology, but for reasons that are poorly understood, this was no longer the case. In consequence, living standards in China, which scholars think were roughly comparable to those in Europe up to 1800, began to decline. In addition, Chinese emperors in the nineteenth century were less competent than those who had reigned during the first half of the Qing period.

The emperors' problems were exacerbated by the actions of the British East India Company and other Western traders who began to ship huge quantities of opium to China around 1800. Attempts by the Qing authorities to halt the trade in opium (which was grown in British-controlled India) proved ineffective; addiction to the drug began to spread. In response, the emperor Daoguang (reigned 1821–1850) dispatched one of his most highly regarded officials, Lin Zexu, to Canton (present-day Guangzhou) in 1839 to find a remedy. In these circumstances Lin addressed his famous letter to Queen Victoria (1837–1901), reprinted here. Lin also blockaded Canton harbor and had a large quantity of opium seized and destroyed. The British responded by attacking Canton and several other Chinese ports. Overwhelmed, the Chinese surrendered in 1842. By the terms of

From *China's Response to the West: A Documentary Survey, 1839–1923*, edited by Ssu-Yu Teng and John King Fairbank (Cambridge, Mass: Harvard University Press), pp. 24–27. Copyright 1952 and renewed 1980 by Alfred A. Knopf Inc. Reprinted by permission of the publisher.

the subsequent Treaty of Nanjing the Chinese were forced to open several ports to trade, to cede the island of Hong Kong, and to make other significant concessions to the British (concessions that were soon extended to other Western governments). For the West, the door to China was now open. For the Chinese, the downward slide accelerated.

How does Lin's letter illustrate the thinking of Chinese leaders in the early nineteenth century, and suggest reasons why the Chinese were quickly defeated by the British?

CHINESE-ENGLISH RELATIONS

A communication: magnificently our great Emperor soothes and pacifies China and the foreign countries, regarding all with the same kindness. If there is profit, then he shares it with the peoples of the world; if there is harm, then he removes it on behalf of the world. This is because he takes the mind of heaven and earth as his mind.

The kings of your honorable country by a tradition handed down from generation to generation have always been noted for their politeness and submissiveness. We have read your successive tributary memorials saying, "In general our countrymen who go to trade in China have always received His Majesty the Emperor's gracious treatment and equal justice," and so on. Privately we are delighted with the way in which the honorable rulers of your country deeply understand the grand principles and are grateful for the Celestial grace. For this reason the Celestial Court in soothing those from afar has redoubled its polite and kind treatment. The profit from trade has been enjoyed by them continuously for two hundred years. This is the source from which your country has become known for its wealth.

But after a long period of commercial intercourse, there appear among the crowd of barbarians both good persons and bad, unevenly. Consequently there are those who smuggle opium to seduce the Chinese people and so cause the spread of the poison to all provinces. Such persons who only care to profit themselves, and disregard their harm to others, are not tolerated by the laws of heaven and are unanimously hated by human beings. His Majesty the Emperor, upon hearing of this, is in a towering rage. He has especially sent me, his commissioner, to come to Guangdong, and together with the governor-general and governor jointly to investigate and settle this matter.

All those people in China who sell opium or smoke opium should receive the death penalty. If we trace the crime of those barbarians who through the years have been selling opium, then the deep harm they have wrought and the great profit they have usurped should fundamentally justify their execution according to law. We take into consideration, however, the fact that the various barbarians have still known how to repent their crimes and return to their allegiance to us by taking the 20,183 chests of opium from their storeships and petitioning us, through their consular officer [superintendent of trade], Elliot, to receive it. It has been entirely destroyed and this has been faithfully reported to the Throne in several memorials by this commissioner and his colleagues.

Fortunately we have received a specially extended favor from His Majesty the Emperor, who considers that for those who voluntarily surrender there are still some circumstances to palliate their crime, and so for the time being he has magnanimously excused them from punishment. But as for those who again violate the opium prohibition, it is difficult for the law to pardon them repeatedly. Having established new regulations, we presume that the ruler of your honorable country, who takes delight in our culture and whose disposition is inclined towards us, must be able to instruct the various barbarians to observe the law with care. It is only necessary to explain to them the advantages and disadvantages and then they will know that the legal code of the Celestial Court must be absolutely obeyed with awe.

We find that your country is sixty or seventy thousand *li* [three *li* make one mile, ordinarily] from China. Yet there are barbarian ships that strive to come here for trade for the purpose of making a great profit. The wealth of China is used to profit the barbarians. That is to say, the great profit made by barbarians is all taken from the rightful share of China. By what right do they then in return use the poisonous drug to injure the Chinese people? Even though the barbarians may not necessarily intend to do us harm, yet in coveting profit to an extreme, they have no regard for injuring others. Let us ask, where is your conscience? I have heard that the smoking of opium is very strictly forbidden by your country; that is because the harm caused by opium is clearly understood. Since it is not permitted to do harm to your own country, then even less should you let it be passed on to the harm of other countries—how much less to China! Of all that China exports to foreign countries, there is not a single thing which is not beneficial to people: they are of benefit when eaten, or of benefit when used, or of benefit when resold: all are beneficial. Is there a single article from China which has done any harm to foreign countries? Take tea and rhubarb, for example; the foreign countries cannot get along for a single day without them. If China cuts off these benefits with no sympathy for those who are to suffer, then what can the barbarians rely upon to keep themselves alive? Moreover the woolens, camlets, and longells [textiles] of foreign countries cannot be woven unless they obtain Chinese silk. If China, again, cuts off this beneficial export, what profit can the barbarians expect to make? As for other foodstuffs, beginning with candy, ginger, cinnamon, and so forth, and articles for use, beginning with silk, satin, chinaware, and so on, all the things that must be had by foreign countries are innumerable. On the other hand, articles coming from the outside to China can only be used as toys. We can take them or get along without them. Since they are not needed by China, what difficulty would there be if we closed the frontier and stopped the trade? Nevertheless our Celestial Court lets tea, silk, and other goods be shipped without limit and circulated everywhere without begrudging it in the slightest. This is for no other reason but to share the benefit with the people of the whole world.

The goods from China carried away by your country not only supply your own consumption and use, but also can be divided up and sold to other countries, producing a triple profit. Even if you do not sell opium, you still have this threefold profit. How can you bear to go further, selling products injurious to others in order to fulfill your insatiable desire?

Suppose there were people from another country who carried opium for sale to England and seduced your people into buying and smoking it; certainly your honorable ruler would deeply hate it and be bitterly aroused. We have heard heretofore that your honorable ruler is kind and benevolent. Naturally you would not wish to give unto others what you yourself do not want. We have also heard that the ships coming to Canton have all had regulations promulgated and given to them in which it is stated that it is not permitted to carry contraband goods. This indicates that the administrative orders of your honorable rule have been originally strict and clear. Only because the trading ships are numerous, heretofore perhaps they have not been examined with care. Now after this communication has been dispatched and you have clearly understood the strictness of the prohibitory laws of the Celestial Court, certainly you will not let your subjects dare again to violate the law.

We have further learned that in London, the capital of your honorable rule, and in Scotland, Ireland, and other places, originally no opium has been produced. Only in several places of India under your control such as Bengal, Madras, Bombay, Patna, Benares, and Malwa has opium been planted from hill to hill, and ponds have been opened for its manufacture. For months and years work is continued in order to accumulate the poison. The obnoxious odor ascends, irritating heaven and frightening the spirits. Indeed you, O King, can eradicate the opium plant in these places, hoe over the fields entirely, and sow in its stead the five grains [millet, barley, wheat, etc.]. Anyone who dares again attempt to plant and manufacture opium should be severely punished. This will really be a great, benevolent government policy that will increase the common weal and get rid of evil. For this, Heaven must support you and the spirits must bring you good fortune, prolonging your old age and extending your descendants. All will depend on this act.

As for the barbarian merchants who come to China, their food and drink and habitation are all received by the gracious favor of our Celestial Court. Their accumulated wealth is all benefit given with pleasure by our Celestial Court. They spend rather few days in their own country but more time in Canton. To digest clearly the legal penalties as an aid to instruction has been a valid principle in all ages. Suppose a man of another country comes to England to trade, he still has to obey the English laws; how much more should he obey in China the laws of the Celestial Dynasty?

Now we have set up regulations governing the Chinese people. He who sells opium shall receive the death penalty and he who smokes it also the death penalty. Now consider this: if the barbarians do not bring opium, then how can the Chinese people resell it, and how can they smoke it? The fact is that the wicked barbarians beguile the Chinese people into a death trap. How then can we grant life only to these barbarians? He who takes the life of even one person still has to atone for it with his own life; yet is the harm done by opium limited to the taking of one life only? Therefore in the new regulations, in regard to those barbarians who bring opium to China, the penalty is fixed at decapitation or strangulation. This is what is called getting rid of a harmful thing on behalf of mankind.

Moreover we have found that in the middle of the second month of this year [April 9] Consul [Superintendent] Elliot of your nation, because the opium prohibition law was very stern and severe, petitioned for an extension of the time limit. He requested a limit of five months for India and adjacent harbors and related territories, and ten months for England proper, after which they would act in conformity with the new regulations. Now we, the commissioner and others, have memorialized and have received the extraordinary Celestial grace of His Majesty the Emperor, who has redoubled his consideration and compassion. All those who within the period of the coming one year (from England) or six months (from India) bring opium to China by mistake, but who voluntarily confess and completely surrender their opium, shall be exempt from their punishment. After this limit of time, if there are still those who bring opium to China then they will plainly have committed a willful violation and shall at once be executed according to law, with absolutely no clemency or pardon. This may be called the height of kindness and the perfection of justice.

Our Celestial Dynasty rules over and supervises the myriad states, and surely possesses unfathomable spiritual dignity. Yet the Emperor cannot bear to execute people without having first tried to reform them by instruction. Therefore he especially promulgates these fixed regulations. The barbarian merchants of your country, if they wish to do business for a prolonged period, are required to obey our statutes respectfully and to cut off permanently the source of opium. They must by no means try to test the effectiveness of the law with their lives. May you, O King, check your wicked and sift your vicious people before they come to China, in order to guarantee the peace of your nation, to show further the sincerity of your politeness and submissiveness, and to let the two countries enjoy together the blessings of peace. How fortunate, how fortunate indeed! After receiving this dispatch will you immediately give us a prompt reply regarding the details and circumstances of your cutting off the opium traffic. Be sure not to put this off. The above is what has to be communicated. This is appropriately worded and quite comprehensive.

STUDY QUESTIONS

1. What were Lin's objections to the opium trade? What was his solution to the problem of opium consumption in China? Why did his policies fail?
2. Was Lin well informed about England and about Chinese relations with England? Did his actions make war inevitable?
3. What does Lin's letter suggest about the traditional goals of China's leaders in international relations? What changes in the nineteenth-century world made the attainment of these aims more difficult?
4. What does the letter suggest about the characteristics of the Chinese political system in the early nineteenth century? What is implied about the role of the emperor? How important was Confucianism in Lin's thinking?
5. Was Lin a nationalist?
6. Why did the use of opium spread widely in China during the nineteenth century?
7. Why was it more difficult for the leaders of China to respond to the rise of the West than it was for the leaders of Japan?
8. Was Lin loyal to Confucian ideals (see Chapter 10)?
9. How did Chinese responses to European power compare with those of Russia (Chapter 6) or Japan (Chapter 25)?

VISUAL SOURCE

LIN ZEXU

Lin Zexu's career illustrates how the long-standing strengths of the Chinese system of governance proved inadequate to the new challenges of the nineteenth century. The son of a schoolteacher, Lin was born in the tea-growing coastal province of Fujian in 1785. He was a brilliant and hard-working student of the Confucian classics and passed the first level of the rigorous imperial civil service examinations at age 19. For the next five years, while studying for the highest level of examinations, Lin served on the staff of the governor of Fujian province.

Woodblock Print of Lin Zexu, ca. 1850.
(Jonathan Spence, The Search for Modern China, 1992, pp. 132–133)

In 1811, at age 24, Lin passed the palace examinations, obtaining the esteemed *jinshi* degree, the approximate Chinese equivalent of a Ph.D. in the humanities. An appointment to the Hanlin Academy, the government's prestigious Confucian "think tank" in Beijing, soon followed. Over the course of the next three decades Lin accumulated much administrative experience from a variety of increasingly important postings in the provinces, his rectitude earning him the nickname "Lin the Clear Sky." Emulating many of his predecessors in Chinese officialdom, Lin was also a poet and Confucian scholar of considerable achievement.

In September of 1840, having failed to halt the flow of opium into China, Lin was removed as imperial commissioner in Canton, reduced in rank, and posted to the remote region of Ili in far northwestern China. After serving his "sentence," he was recalled from Ili in 1845 and appointed to several high administrative positions during the remaining years of his life.

STUDY QUESTIONS

1. How does the depiction of Lin's costume, hairstyle, and posture illustrate the continuing importance of Confucianism in nineteenth-century China?
2. In what ways might the memory of Lin's career both strengthen and undermine nationalism in present-day China?

24

Chinese Reform Movements

During the half-century following the Opium War the emperors of the Qing dynasty (1644–1912) faced a series of increasingly grave challenges. In the 1850s and 1860s several huge peasant uprisings convulsed much of the country. The largest of these upheavals, the Taiping Rebellion (1850–1864), was inspired by a convert to Christianity who preached a doctrine of communal egalitarianism and believed he was the brother of Jesus. Qing authorities were successful in suppressing the Taipings and the other rebels, but the fighting caused more than 20 million deaths. No other country in the nineteenth-century world experienced a comparable catastrophe (although the severe famines in India during the late nineteenth century came close).

Chinese emperors also had to cope with relentless pressures from Western Europeans, Russians, and Americans, all of whom sought increased commercial advantages in China. From the 1840s onward the growing disparity between the power of the Western states and China forced the emperors to agree to a steady increase in the number of "treaty ports," i.e. Chinese cities largely controlled by western diplomats and merchants. In the treaty ports, whose very existence was deeply offensive to China's Confucian officials, conflict between arrogant Westerners and Chinese was endemic.

In 1894–1895, as living standards for many Chinese spiraled downward and as opium addiction continued to spread, China's leaders confronted a new source of humiliation when the military leadership in Meiji Japan seized upon political unrest in Korea, a longtime vassal state of China, as a pretext for imperialist expansion. A brief war between China and Japan ensued. Well-led, well-trained, and well-equipped Japanese soldiers quickly defeated their Chinese adversaries. The Chinese surrendered and agreed to the terms of the Treaty of Shimonoseki, which gave control of Korea to Japan and also ceded the island of Formosa to the Japanese. In addition, the Chinese were forced to pay a huge indemnity in silver and provide access to four new treaty ports for the Japanese.

Buffeted by these repeated shocks, the Chinese scrambled for an effective response. In the aftermath of the Opium War some officials had recommended that Chinese scholars begin to study western science and technology and that the government

Selection IA from Ssu-Yu Keng and John K. Fairbank, eds., *China's Response to the West: A Documentary Survey* (New York: Atheneum, 1975), pp. 152–153. Selections IB, II and III from Wm. Theodore de Bary and Richard Lufrano, eds., *Sources of Chinese Tradition*, 2nd ed., Vol. II (New York: Columbia University Press, 2000), pp. 269–270, 285–287, 289–292.

take the lead in establishing arsenals for the manufacture of Western-style weapons. Policies along these lines were subsequently implemented, but there was no basic reform of the Chinese government, and no Chinese counterpart to the reforms introduced by the leaders of the Meiji Restoration in Japan. However, following China's defeat by Japan in 1894–1895, pleas by officials for thorough reform increased sharply.

The following documents come from the period of deep crisis triggered by the signing of the Treaty of Shimonoseki, a crisis that culminated in the collapse of the Qing dynasty in 1911–1912. The selections include excerpts from the writings of Kang Yuwei (1858–1927) and Liang Qichao (1873–1929), two of the most influential reformers. The third selection contains key passages from the 1901 reform decree issued by the Empress Dowager Cixi, the *de facto* head of state for most of the period from the 1860s to 1908.

How did Chinese leaders respond to the problems they faced at the end of the nineteenth century? Why did they fail?

CHINESE CRISIS

I. FROM KANG YUWEI

[Kang Yuwei was the learned Confucian scholar who led the reform movement in the 1890s.]

A. Statement For The "Society For The Study Of Self-Strengthening" (1895)

The Russians are spying on us in the north and the English are peeping at us on the west; the French are staring at us in the south and the Japanese are watching us in the east. Living in the midst of these four strong neighbors, and being the Middle Kingdom, China is in imminent peril. How much more so will it be when there are more than ten nations who are sharpening their teeth and watering at the mouth, desiring to share the surplus? The Liaodong peninsula and Formosa are in confusion, the Mohammedan rebellion is disturbing us, the popular mind is perturbed and the situation seems hardly supportable.

Formerly, India was a celebrated nation in Asia, but she preserved her traditions without changing and so during the time of Qianlong [1736–1795] the British people organized a company with one hundred and twenty thousand gold as capital to carry on a trade with her and subjugated the five parts of India. Formerly, Turkey was a large Moslem nation. Her territory extended over three continents, Asia, Europe, and Africa, but she was conservative and made no changes; so her government was seized by six nations, her territory was partitioned, and her ruler was banished. Of others, such as Annam, Burma, Korea, Liugiu, Siam, Persia, Afghanistan and Baluchistan, as well as those established in Africa and on the islands of the Pacific Ocean, the general number may be estimated at several hundred or one thousand. Actually the (territories of these conservative states) have been either reduced or annexed, and among all the conservative nations on the globe there is probably not a single one which has been kept intact.

Our enfeebled China has been lying in the midst of a group of strong powers and soundly sleeping on the top of a pile of kindling. In administration she cares only to prevent evils but does not care to develop sources of profit. Her officials know only how to be law-abiding, but do not know how to judge the trends of the time. Her scholars specialize in the study of antiquity, not in the understanding of the present. Her people can defend their immediate surroundings but cannot go far afield. Mencius said, "A state must first smite itself, and then others will smite it." The defense of the Mongolian leagues, Fengtien, Kirin, Qinghai, Xinjiang, Tibet, the native tribes and the frontier guards is all a defense of alien waste land. The fertile soil of Guizhou, Shandong, Fujian, Zhejiang, Anhui, Hunan, Hubei, Guangdong, Sichuan, Guizhou, Yunnan and Guangxi has become entirely a bandits' granary. It will not be long until we become Turks and Negroes.

Westerners are very strict about races and they look upon other races as enemies. When the French obtained Annam, the way for the Annamese to become rich and ennobled through civil service examinations was cut off, and the former prominent officials have now become silk merchants. England conquered India more than a hundred years ago, but it was not until 1889 that an Indian was elected a member of Parliament. Other native peoples are treated like cattle and horses. If we do not plan in advance, but suddenly are divided among ourselves . . . then, alas, the fate of our sacred race will be unspeakable, utterly unspeakable!

For China, on the great earth, has had a ceaseless succession of sacred emperors and the country has been very famous. Her principles, institutions, and culture are the most elevated in the world. The vastness of her territory is ranked third among myriads of states, the number of her people is rated the first; her climate is in the temperate zone, her people are intelligent and accomplished, and her soil is rich and productive. Among all countries on earth none is her equal. Only because her customs are unenlightened and because of a dearth of men of ability, she is passively taking aggression and insult. Formerly Zeng Guofan discussed academic problems with wise scholars like Woren and others in Beijing, and he deliberated on the method of militia training with various eminent officials like Jiang Zhongyuan and Luo Zenan in Hunan; eventually he achieved the merit of suppressing the Taiping Rebellion. In Prussia there was a society established to make the nation strong [*giangguo zhi hui*] and then she was revenged on her enemy France. In Japan there were people who advocated respect for the Emperor and the rejection of the barbarians and hence they accomplished their reforms. Generally, knowledge can be achieved by means of discussion, and men of ability can be produced by encouragement. When the talent and power of many people are combined, then it is easy to assemble the books; and when the minds and thinking of many people are combined, then it is easy to exchange information. The *Book of Changes* says, "Superior men discuss problems with friends." The *Analects of Confucius* say, "Mechanics have their shops to dwell in, in order to accomplish their work. The superior man learns, in order to reach the utmost of his principles." The water in the ocean is bubbling and boiling. In our ears and in our dreams the noise of artillery is roaring. All you gentlemen, how can you avoid the grief of being ruined and (becoming) subject to the rule of a different race? Are we trying to avoid slander? O you closed-door scholars, are some of you coming to the point of speaking about respecting the emperor and rejecting the barbarians? If you do, not only the teachings of the sacred Qing dynasty, the two emperors, the three kings, and Confucius, but also the four hundred millions of the people will have something to rely upon.

B. Memorial to the Emperor (January 1898)

[*This memorial (or memorandum) from Kang Yuwei helped persuade the reigning emperor, known as the Guangxu emperor, to sponsor the abortive "Hundred Days' Reforms" in the summer of 1898. During the reform period Kang was the emperor's key adviser. The reforms were halted and undone by the emperor's aunt, the Empress Dowager Cixi.*]

A survey of all states in the world will show that those states that undertook reforms became strong while those states that clung to the past perished. The consequences of clinging to the past and the effects of opening up new ways are thus obvious. If Your Majesty, with your discerning brilliance, observes the trends in other countries, you will see that if we can change, we can preserve ourselves; but if we cannot change, we shall perish. Indeed if we can make a complete change, we shall become strong, but if we only make limited changes, we shall still perish. If Your Majesty and his ministers investigate the source of the disease, you will know that this is the right prescription.

Our present trouble lies in our clinging to old institutions without knowing how to change. In an age of competition between states, to put into effect methods appropriate to an era of universal unification and laissez-faire is like wearing heavy furs in summer or riding a high carriage across a river. This can only result in having a fever or getting oneself drowned. . . .

It is a principle of things that the new is strong but the old weak; that new things are fresh but old things rotten; that new things are active but old things static. If the institutions are old, defects will develop. Therefore there are no institutions that should remain unchanged for a hundred years. Moreover, our present institutions are but unworthy vestiges of the Han, Tang, Yuan, and Ming dynasties; they are not even the institutions of the [Manchu] ancestors. In fact, they are the products of the fancy writing and corrupt dealing of petty officials rather than the original ideas of the ancestors. To say that they are the ancestral institutions is an insult to the ancestors. Furthermore, institutions are for the purpose of preserving one's territories. Now that the ancestral territory cannot be preserved, what good is it to maintain the ancestral institutions? . . .

Although there is a desire to reform, yet if the national policy is not fixed and public opinion not united, it will be impossible for us to give up the old and adopt the new. The national policy is to the state just as the rudder is to the boat or the pointer is to the compass. It determines the direction of the state and shapes the public opinion of the country.

Nowadays the court has been undertaking some reforms, but the action of the emperor is obstructed by the ministers, and the recommendations of the able scholars are attacked by old-fashioined bureaucrats. If the charge is not "using barbarian ways to change China" then it is "upsetting the ancestral institutions." Rumors and scandals are rampant, and people fight each other like fire and water. To reform in this way is as ineffective as attempting a forward march by walking backward. It will inevitably result in failure. Your Majesty knows that under the present circumstances reforms are imperative and old institutions must be abolished. I beg Your Majesty to make up your mind and to decide on the national policy. After the fundamental policy is determined, the methods of implementation must vary according to what is primary and what is secondary, what is imporant and what is insignificant, what is strong and what is weak, what is urgent and what can wait. . . . If anything goes wrong, no success can be achieved.

After studying ancient and modern institutions, Chinese and foreign, I have found that the institutions of the sage kings and Three dynasties [of Xia, Shang, and Zhou] were excellent, but that ancient times were different from today. I hope Your Majesty will daily read Mencius and follow his example of loving the people. The development of the Han, Tang, Song, and Ming dynasties may be learned, but it should be remembered that the age of universal unification is different from that of sovereign nations. I wish Your Majesty would study *Guanzi* and follow his idea of managing the country. As to the republican governments of the United States and France and the constitutional governments of Britain and Germany, these countries are far away and their customs are different from ours. Their changes occurred a long time ago and can no longer be traced. Consequently I beg Your Majesty to adopt the purpose of Peter the Great of Russia as our purpose and to take the Meiji Reform of Japan as the model for our reform. The time and place of Japan's reform are not remote and her religion and customs are somewhat similar to ours. Her success is manifest; her example can be easily followed.

II. REFORM EDICT OF JANUARY 1901

[The Boxer Uprising (1898–1901) intensified the crisis in China and impelled the Empress Dowager to issue her own reform decree.]

Certain principles of morality (*changjing*) are immutable, whereas methods of governance (*zhifa*) have always been mutable. The *Classic of Changes* states that "when a measure has lost effective force, the time has come to change it." And the *Analects* states that "the Shang and Zhou dynasties took away from and added to the regulations of their predecessors, as can readily be known."

Now, the Three Mainstays (Bonds) [ruler/minister, parent/child, and husband/wife] and the Five Constant Virtues [humaneness, rightness, ritual decorum, wisdom, and trustworthiness] remain forever fixed and unchanging, just as the sun and the stars shine steadfastly upon the earth. . . .

Throughout the ages, successive generations have introduced new ways and abolished the obsolete. Our own august ancestors set up new systems to meet the requirements of the day. . . . Laws and methods (*fa*) become obsolete and, once obsolete, require revision in order to serve their intended purpose of strengthening the state and benefiting the people. . . .

It is well known that the new laws propounded by the Kang rebels were less reform laws (*bianfa*) than lawlessness (*luanfa*). These rebels took advantage of the court's weakened condition to plot sedition. It was only by an appeal to the Empress Dowager to resume the reins of power that the court was saved from immediate peril and the evil rooted out in a single day. How can anyone say that in suppressing this insurrectionary movement the Empress Dowager declined to sanction anything new? Or that in taking away from and adding to the laws of our ancestors, we advocated a complete abolition of the old? We sought to steer a middle course between the two extremes and to follow a path to good administration. Officials and the people alike must know that mother and son [the Empress Dowager and the Guangxu emperor] were activated by one and the same motive.

We have now received Her Majesty's decree to devote ourselves fully to China's revitalization, to suppress vigorously the use of the terms *new* and *old,* and to blend together the best of what is Chinese and what is foreign. The root of China's weakness lies in harmful habits too firmly entrenched, in rules and regulations too minutely drawn, in the overabundance of inept and mediocre officials and in the paucity of truly outstanding ones, in petty bureaucrats who hide behind the written word and in clerks and yamen runners who use the written words as talismans to acquire personal fortunes, in the mountains of correspondence between government offices that have no relationship to reality, and in the seniority system and associated practices that block the way of men of real talent. The curse of our country lies in the one word *si,* or "private advantage"; the ruin of our realm lies in the one word *li,* or "narrow precedent."

Those who have studied Western methods up to now have confined themselves to the spoken and written languages and to weapons and machinery. These are but surface elements of the West and have nothing to do with the essentials of Western learning. Our Chinese counterparts to the fundamental principles upon which Western wealth and power are based are the following precepts, handed down by our ancestors: "to hold high office and show generosity to others," "to exercise liberal forbearance over subordinates," "to speak with sincerity," and "to carry out one's purpose with diligence." But China has neglected such deeper dimensions of the West and contents itself with learning a word here and a phrase there, a skill here and a craft there, meanwhile hanging on to old corrupt practices of currying favor to benefit oneself. If China disregards the essentials of Western learning and merely confines its studies to surface elements that themselves are not even mastered, how can it possibly achieve wealth and power?

To sum up, administrative methods and regulations must be revised and abuses eradicated. If regeneration is truly desired, there must be quiet and reasoned deliberation.

We therefore call upon the members of the Grand Council, the Grand Secretaries, the Six Boards and Nine Ministries, our ministers abroad, and the governor-general and governors of the provinces to reflect carefully on our present sad state of affairs and to scrutinize Chinese and Western governmental systems with regard to all dynastic regulations, state administration, and official affairs, matters related to people's livelihood (*minsheng*), modern schools, systems of examination, military organization, and financial administration. Duly weigh what should be kept and what abolished, what new methods should be adopted and what old ones retained. By every available means of knowledge and observation, seek out how to renew our national strength, how to produce men of real talent, how to expand state revenues and how to revitalize the military. . . .

The first essential, even more important than devising new systems of governance (*zhifa*), is to secure men who govern well (*zhi ren*). Without new systems, the corrupted old system cannot be salvaged; without men of ability, even good systems cannot be made to succeed . . . Once the appropriate reforms are introduced to clear away abuses, it will be more than ever necessary to select upright and capable men to discharge the functions of the office. Everone, high and low: take heed!

The Empress Dowager and we have long pondered these matters. Now things are at a crisis point where change must occur, to transform weakness into strength. Everything depends upon how the change is effected.

III. FROM LIANG QICHAO

[When the 1898 "Hundred Days' Reforms" collapsed, Liang Qichao fled to Tokyo where there was a large community of Chinese students. In books, pamphlets, and newsapapers that made a deep impact on Chinese living abroad and those at home, Liang Qichao argued that the problems in China could only be solved by "renewing the people."]

The term *renewing the people* does not mean that our people must give up entirely what is old in order to follow others. There are two meanings of *renewing*. One is to improve what is original in the people and so renew it; the other is to adopt what is originally lacking in the people and so make a new people. Without both of these, there will be no success. . . .

When a nation can stand up in the world its citizens must have a unique character. From morality and laws to customs, habits, literature, and the arts, these all possess a certain unique spirit. Then the ancestors pass them down and their descendants receive them. The group becomes unified and a nation is formed. This is truly the wellspring of nationalism. Our people have been established as a nation on the Asian continent for several thousand years, and we must have some special characteristics that are grand, noble, and perfect, and distinctly different from those of other races. We should preserve these characteristics and not let them be lost. What is called preserving, however, is not simply to let them exist and grow by themselves and then blithely say, "I am preserving them, I am preserving them." It is like a tree: unless some new buds come out every year, its withering may soon be expected. Or like a well: unless there is always some new spring bubbling, its exhaustion is not far away.

Is it enough merely to develop what we already have? No, it is not. The world of today is not the world of yesterday. In ancient times, we Chinese were people of villages instead of citizens. This is not because we were unable to form a citizenry but due to circumstances. Since China majestically used to be the predominant power in the East, surrounded as we were by small barbarian groups and lacking any contact with other large states, we Chinese generally considered our state to encompass the whole world. All the messages we received, all that influenced our minds, all the instructions of our sages, and all that our ancestors passed down qualified us to be individuals on our own, family members, members of localities and clans, and members of the world. But they did not qualify us to be citizens of a state. Although the qualifications of citizenship are not necessarily much superior to these other characteristics, in an age of struggle among nations for the survival of the fittest while the weak perish, if the qualities of citizens are wanting, then the nation cannnot stand up independently between Heaven and earth.

If we wish to make our nation strong, we must investigate extensively the methods followed by other nations in becoming independent. We should select their superior points and appropriate them to make up for our own shortcomings.

Now with regard to politics, academic learning, and technology, our critics know how to take the superior points of others to make up for our own weakness; but they do not know that the people's virture, the people's wisdom, and the people's vitality are the great basis of politics, academic learning, and techniques. If they do not take the former but adopt the latter, neglect the roots but tend the branches, it will be no different from seeking the luxuriant growth of another tree and wishing to graft its branches onto our withered trunk, or seeing the bubbling flow of another well and wishing to draw its water to fill our dry well. Thus, how to adopt and make up for what we originally lacked so that our people may be renewed should be deeply and carefully considered.

All phenonmena in the world are governed by no more than two principles: the conservative and the progressive. Those who are applying these two principles are inclined either to the one or to the other. Sometimes the two arise simultaneously and conflict with each other; sometimes the two exist simultaneously and compromise with each other. No one can exist if he is inclined only to one. Where there is conflict, there must be compromise. Conflict is the forerunner of compromise.

Those who excel at making compromises become a great people, such as the Anglo-Saxons, who, in a manner of speaking, make their way with one foot on the ground and one foot going forward, or who hold fast to things with one hand and pick up things with another. Thus, what I mean by "renewing the people" does not refer to those who are infatuated with Western ways and, in order to keep company with others, throw away our morals, learning, and customs of several thousand years' standing. Nor does it refer to those who stick to old paper and say that merely embracing the morals, learning, and customs of these thousands of years will be sufficient to enable us to stand upon the great earth. . . .

Generally, those who talk about "renewal" may be divided into two groups. The lower group consists of those who pick up others' trite expressions and assume a bold look in order to climb up the official hierarchy. Their Western learning is stale stuff, their diplomacy relies on bribes, and their travels are moving in the dark. These people, of course are not worth mentioning. The higher group consists of those who are worried about the situation and try hard to develop the nation and to promote well-being. But when asked about their methods, they would begin with diplomacy, training of troops, purchase of arms, and manufature of instruments; then they would proceed to commerce, mining, and railways; and finally they would come, as they did recently, to officers' training, police, and education. Are these not the most important and necessary things for modern civilized nations? Yes. But can we attain the level of modern civilization and place our nation in an invincible postion by adopting a little of this and that, or taking a small step now and then? I know we cannot.

Let me illustrate this by commerce. Economic competition is one of the big problems of the world today. It is the method whereby the powers attempt to conquer us. It is also the method whereby we should fight for our existence. The importance of improving our foreign trade has been recognized by all. But in order to promote foreign trade, it is necessary to protect the rights of our domestic trade and industry, and in order to protect these rights, it is necessary to issue a set of commercial laws. Commerical laws, however, cannot stand by themselves, and so it is necessary to complement them with other laws. A law that is not carried out is tantamount to no law; it is therefore necessary to define the powers of the judiciary. Bad legislation is worse than no legislation, and so it is necessary to decide where the legislative power should belong. If those who violate the law are not punished, laws will become void as soon as they are proclaimed; therefore, the duties of the judiciary must be defined. When all these are carried to the logical conclusion, it will be seen that foreign trade cannot be promoted without a constitution, a parliament, and a responsble government. Those who talk about foreign trade today blithely say, "I am promoting it, I am promoting it," and nothing more. I do not know how they are going to promote it. The above is one illustration, but it is true with all other cases. Thus I know why the so-called new methods nowadays are ineffectual. Why? Because without destruction there can be no construction. . . . What, then, is the way to effect our salvation and to achieve progress? The answer is that we must shatter at a blow the despotic and confused govermental system of some thousands of years; we must sweep away the corrupt and sycophantic learning of these thousands of years.

STUDY QUESTIONS

1. What problems was the founding of the "Society for the Study of Self-Strengthening" intended to solve? How were these problems to be solved? To whom was this appeal directed?

2. In his memorial to the emperor, what was Kang Yuwei's rationale for reform? What foreign models did he reject? What foreign models did he think were appropriate for China?

3. According to the Empress Dowager's edict, what was the source of China's weakness? Where had earlier attempts at reform gone wrong? What was the solution to China's problems? How were reforms to be implemented?

4. What did Liang Qichao mean by "renewing the people"? In what ways did this idea represent a new trend in the reform movement? How did "renewing the people" compare with "self-strengthening? How do you explain the change? Was Liang Qichao more of a reformer or a revolutionary?

5. How do you explain the power of Confucian teachings in China around 1900, 2,500 years after they had first been articulated?

6. Why did the attempts to reform and preserve the Qing dynasty fail?

7. Why was there no Meiji Restoration in China (see Chapter 25)?

25

The Meiji Restoration in Japan

Far-reaching changes transformed the lives of the Japanese people during the second half of the nineteenth century. In 1853–1854 ships from the United States appeared in Edo harbor and forced the Tokugawa shoguns to end the policy of isolation from the wider world they had enforced for more than two centuries. For the next 15 years the country was racked by political turmoil and economic crisis, the latter development a result of Japan's sudden plunge into the global economy. Finally, in 1867–1868, the *daimyo* from two of the largest domains, Satsuma and Choshu, joined forces to overthrow the rule of the shoguns in the name of "restoring" the full authority of the emperor.

The emperor, who had just come to the throne and was only 15 years old, chose the name Meiji (Enlightened Rule) for his reign, which lasted until 1912, but he was much too young to lead. Instead, a coalition of innovative younger samurai, many of who came from Satsuma and Choshu, quickly grasped the levers of power and began to rule on behalf of the "restored" Meiji emperor. In an astonishing turnabout, the new leaders of the country dismantled the essentials of the Tokugawa system— ending the privileges of the *daimyo* and the samurai—and launched Japan on a course of modernization.

Learning much from study missions to the United States, Western Europe, and Russia, the Meiji oligarchs established a modern system of banking, constructed a railway system, organized a national army and navy, founded a modern system of education, and in 1889 put in place a system of constitutional rule. Two brief and victorious wars, against China in 1894–1895, and against Russia 10 years later, demonstrated that Japan was now a major force in international relations. No other country outside the West experienced such changes in the nineteenth century.

How do the following documents illuminate important aspects of Meiji Restoration?

Selections, I, II, V and VI from Ryusaku Tsunoda, Wm. Theodore de Bary, and Donald Keene, eds., *Sources of Japanese Tradition*, Vol. II (New York: Columbia University Press, 1958), pp. 103, 137, 169–172, 206–209. Selections III and IV from David J. Lu, *Sources of Japanese History*, Vol. 2 (New York: McGraw-Hill, 1974), pp. 48–50.

THE MEIJI RESTORATION

I. A GENTLEMAN'S FIVE PLEASURES

[Sakuma Shozan (1811–1864) was a samurai from a domain (fief) in the north of Japan who argued for an end to the Tokugawa policy of isolation, for which he spent eight years in prison. Shortly after his release in 1862, Sakuma wrote the book from which the following excerpt comes. He was assassinated in 1864 by "isolationist" samuari.]

The gentleman has five pleasures, but wealth and rank are not among them. That his house understands decorum and righteousness and remains free from family rifts—this is one pleasure. That exercising care in giving to and taking from others, he provides for himself honestly, free, internally, from shame before his wife and children, and externally, from disgrace before the public—this is the second pleasure. That he expounds and glorifies the learning of the sages, knows in his heart the great Way, and in all situations contents himself with his duty, in adversity as well as in prosperity—this is the third pleasure. That he is born after the opening of the vistas of science by the Westerners, and can therefore understand principles not known to the sages and wise men of old—this is the fourth pleasure. That he employs the ethics of the East and the scientific technique fo the West, neglecting neither the spiritual nor material aspects of life, combining subjective and objective, and thus bringing benefit to the people and serving the nation—this is the fifth pleasure.

II. THE CHARTER OATH, 1868

[On April 8, 1868, the Meiji emperor issued the following statement of principles, which were drawn up by the samurai who led the overthrow of the Tokugawa regime.]

By this oath we set up as our aim the establishment of the national weal on a broad basis and the framing of a constitution and laws.

1. Deliberative assemblies shall be widely etablished and all matters decided by public discussion.

2. All classes, high and low, shall unite in vigorously carrying out the administration of affairs of state.

3. The common people, no less than civil and military officials, shall each be allowed to pursue his own calling so that there may be no discontent.

4. Evil customs of the past shall be broken off and everything based upon the just laws of Nature.

5. Knowledge shall be sought throughout the world so as to strengthen the foundations of imperial rule.

III. ON THE NEED FOR A NEW SYSTEM OF EDUCATION, 1872

[Oki Takato, the minister of education in 1872, is the author of the following selection.]

As your subject reflects on the matter of education, he discovers that behind the wealth, power, security and well-being of a nation there lies invariably an advance in the talents of a civilized people. Therefore it is necessary to build schools and establish educational methods which enable us to attain similar goals. It is recom-

mended that educational laws and regulations be uniformly established to eliminate useless miscellaneous studies. In their place there shall be created an educational system consisting of universities, middle schools and primary schools, and a
trend toward the development of arts shall be introduced. To attain these goals, we
shall adopt the best educational law in the world, and take into account the facilities available in and out of the country. The country shall be divided into seven or
eight educational regions which will be formulated on the basis of population and
land area. In each of these regions, there shall be a university, and a number of
middle schools and grade schools. Furthermore there shall be established a detailed system of inspection to make it certain that the standards will not be violated.
As to the admission, the wealthy and the poor shall be differentiated, and there
shall be no indiscriminate acceptance of pupils and students. As to the order of implementation, all the existing educational systems shall be abolished, and a new law
and regulations be established. New textbooks shall be issued, and new educational
materials be supplied. The method of teaching as well as the regulations governing
those who receive instruction shall be newly formulated. Once the above described
regulations come into effect, even village schools and private schools shall be governed by their provisions. Detailed recommendations will be submitted at a later
date. . . .

February 12, 1872
Minister of Education, Ōki Takatō

IV. OKUBO TOSHIMICHI: ON THE ROLE OF THE STATE IN INDUSTRIALIZATION, 1874

*[Okubo Toshimichi (1830–1878) was a samurai from Satsuma domain. He was one of the
three most important leaders of the early Meiji government. Okubo was assassinated in 1878
by advocates of accelerated political reform.]*

Generally speaking, the strength or weakness of a country is dependent on the
wealth or poverty of is people, and the people's wealth or poverty derives from
the amount of available products. The diligence of the people is a major factor in
determining the amount of products available, but in the final analysis, it can all
be traced to the guidance and encouragement given by the government and its
officials. . . .

We have come to a point where all the internal conflicts have ceased, and the
people can now enjoy peace and can securely engage in their respective callings.
This is the most opportune time for the government and its officials to adopt a protective policy which has as its goal the enhancement of people's livelihood. . . .

Anyone who is responsible for a nation or its people must give careful consideration to the matters which enhance the livelihood of the people, including the
benefits to be gained from industrial production and the convenience derived
from maritime and land transportation. He must set up a system suitable to the
country's natural features and convention, taking into account the characteristics
and intelligence of its people. Once that system is established it must be made the
pivot of the country's administrative policies. Those industries which are already
developed must be preserved, and those which are not in existence must be
brought into being.

An example can be found in England which is a very small country. However, she is an island nation and has excellent harbors. She is also richly endowed with mineral resources. Her government and its officials have considered it the greatest fulfillment of their duties when they have made full use of their natural advantages, and have brought about maximum [industrial] development. In this endeavor the Queen and her subjects have put together their ingenuity and created an unprecedented maritime law in order to monopolize the maritime transportation of the world and to enhance her national industries. . . .

In this way her industries have prospered, and there has always been a surplus after providing the necessary commodities to her people. . . .

It is true that time, location, natural features and convention are not the same for each country, and one must not always be dazzled by the accomplishments of England and seek to imitate her blindly. . . .

However, our topography and natural conditions show similarities to those of England. What differs most is the feebleness in the temperament of our people. It is the responsibility of those who are in the administrative positions in the government to guide and importune those who are weak in spirit to work diligently in the industries and to endure them. Your subject respectfully recommends that a clear-cut plan be established to find the natural advantages we enjoy, to measure the amount by which production can be increased, and to determine the priorities under which industries may be encouraged [subsidized]. It is further recommended that the characteristics of our people and degree of their intelligence may be taken into account in establishing legislation aimed at encouraging development of industries. Let there not be a person who is derelict in performing his work. Let there not be a fear of anyone unable to have his occupation. If these goals can be attained the people can reach a position of adequate wealth. If the people are adequately wealthy, it follows naturally that the country will become strong and wealthy. . . . If so, it will not be difficult for us to compete effectively against major powers. This has always been your subject's sincere desire. He is even more convinced of the necessity of its implementation today, and is therefore submitting humbly his recommendations for Your Majesty's august decision.

V. ITO HIROBUMI: A SPEECH ON CONSTITUTIONAL GOVERNMENT, 1899

[Ito Hirobumi (1841–1909) was one of the key leaders of the Meiji government during the 1880s and 1890s. He oversaw the drafting of the Meiji constitution promulgated by the emperor on February 11, 1889, the supposed anniversary of the founding of the Japanese state in 600 B.C.E. Ito was much influenced by constitutional ideas in Germany and Austria, countries to which he had led a study mission in 1882.]

When our enlightened emperor decided to accept the open-door principle as an imperial policy. . . . it became a matter of urgent necessity to develop the intellectual faculties of our people and to increase their business activities. This led to the abolition of the feudal system and made it possible for the Japanese people to live in a new political environment and to have diverse freedoms. . . . The first of these freedoms was the freedom of movement, followed by the freedom to pursue an occupation of one's own choosing. Moreover, the freedom to study at any place of one's choosing was given to all. There was also granted freedom of speech in political affairs. Thus, the Japanese today enjoy freedom, each according to his own desires, within the limits of the law. These rights belong to people who live in a civilized government. If these rights are withheld and their enjoyment refused, a people cannot develop. And if the people cannot develop the nation's wealth and the nation's strength cannot develop. . . . But the fact is that because of the imperial policy of the open-door, we have established a government which is civilized. And as we have advanced to such a position, it has become necessary to establish a fixed definition of the fundamental laws. This, in short, is the reason for the establishment of constitutional government.

A constitutional government makes a clear distinction between the realms of the ruler and the ruled, and thereby defines what the people and the sovereign should do; that is, the rights which the sovereign should exercise and the rights which the people should enjoy, followed by the procedure for the management of the government. According to the Constitution the people have the right to participate in government, but this right is at once an important obligation as well as a right. Government is a prerogative of the emperor. As you will be participating in government—which is the emperor's prerogative—your must regard this right as the responsibility of the people, the honor of the people, and the glory of the people. It is therefore a matter of the greatest importance.

In this connection what all Japanese must bear in mind is Japan's national polity [*kokutai*]. It is history which defines the national polity; thus the Japanese people have a duty to know their history. . . . The national polity of the various countries differs one from another, but it is the testimony of the history of Japan to this day that the unification of the country was achieved around the Imperial House. So I say that the understanding of the national polity of Japan is the first important duty of our people.

In the next place we must know the aims and the policies of our country. Political parties may have their arguments, and others may have their views about the government, but they must be kept within the bounds of the aims and policies of the government. What then is the aim of the nation? It is the imperial aim decided upon at the time of the Restoration of imperial rule. . . . The aim of our country has been from the very beginning, to attain among the nations of the world the status of a civilized nation and to become a member of the comity of European and American nations which occupy the position of civilized countries. To join this comity of nations means to become one of them, but in this connection, we must consider the rights and duties attendant upon membership. Among fellow men of civilized nations there is a thing called common justice. To become a member of this comity of nations it is necessary to respect this common justice. Generally speaking, all Oriental countries—China and Japan included—have the habit of holding foreign countries in contempt and of holding their own country in esteem. But in carrying on relations according to civilized standards of common justice, it is done according to a procedure of mutual equality without contempt for the other and esteem for oneself, or vice versa. . . .

From the standpoint of the sovereign power, that is, the emperor's prerogative to rule the country, the people are one and equal under the constitutional government. They are all direct subjects of the emperor. The so-called "indirect subjects" no longer exist. This means that the Japanese people have been able to raise their status and to achieve for themselves a great honor. They now have the right to share in legislative rights, which come from the emperor's sovereign powers, and to elect and send representatives. Having the right to send representatives they can, indirectly, voice their opinions on the advisability and the faults of their country's administration. Thus, every member of the nation—be he a farmer, craftsman, or merchant—must become familiar beforehand with the merits and demerits of questions of government. Not only on questions of government, but also on matters concerning his own occupation, the citizen must give due thought and become prosperous. When every man becomes wealthy, the village, the county, and the prefecture in turn become wealthy, and the accumulated total of that wealth becomes the wealth of Japan. The expansion of military strength and the promotion of national prestige depend upon the power of the individual members of the country. Therefore, in order to promote the development of military strength and national prestige, it is only proper and necessary to diffuse education so that the people can understand the changes and improvements with respect to their government and their society. In a constitutional government the occasions for secrecy are few—except for laws not yet proclaimed—in contradistinction to a despotic government. The principle of keeping the people uninformed in order to make them obedient has no place here. To inform them well so that they will serve well is the way of constitutional government. . . .

Since government is concerned with the administration of the country as a whole it does not follow that its acts are always favorable to all individuals. The nation's affairs, of their own nature, are not personal and concerned with the individual. They must be carried out according to the nation's aims, the nation's prestige, and the nation's honor. It is for this reason that the people have an obligation to understand the nation's aims. They must regard the nation as their own, meet the military obligation to defend it and pay for the cost of defending it. And what happens when this cost is paid? In the past the people remitted their payments to the authorities above, beyond which they were no longer concerned. It is not so today. Government is conducted today so that one may know clearly how the money is spent and what relation the payments have to the state of the nation. If one believes that an expenditure is unwise, he may readily avail himself of the freedom of speech which he possesses as a citizen and raise his voice in objection. To resolve a situation in which the opinions of the people are so diverse as to seem impossible of reaching a decision we have established a parliament to make the decision on the basis of majority rule of its members. If you do not send representatives who are well informed on matters of government, the rights which you have earned by great effort will prove ineffective in practice.

VI. YAMAGATA ARITOMO: A LETTER ON JAPANESE FOREIGN POLICY, AUGUST 1914

[Yamagata Aritomo (1838–1922) was a samurai from Choshu domain who had a long career as a military and political leader during the Meiji era. An admirer of Bismark's Germany, Yamagata oversaw the founding of a modern army, police force, and system of local government in Japan. In the following letter, written to the Japanese prime minister at the beginning of World War I, Yamagata addresses key foreign policy issues.]

There are people in our country who rely excessively on the military prowess of our empire and who believe that against China the application of force alone will suffice to gain our objectives. But the problems of life are not so simple as to permit of their solution by the use of force alone. The principal aim of our plan today should be to improve Sino-Japanese relations and to instill in China a sense of abiding trust in us. . . .

The recent international situation points to an increasing intensity in racial rivalry from year to year. It is a striking fact that the Turkish and Balkan wars of former years and the Austro-Serbian and the Russo-German wars of today all had their inception in racial rivalry and hatred. The anti-Japanese movement in the state of California in the United States, and the discrimination against Hindus in British Africa are also manifestations of the same racial problem. Thus, the possibility of the rivalry between the white and colored races henceforth growing in intensity and leading eventually to a clash between them cannot be ruled out entirely. When the present great conflict in Europe is over and when the political and economic order are restored, the various countries will again focus their attention on the Far East and the benefits and rights they might derive from this region. When that day comes, the rivalry between the white and the non-white races will become violent, and who can say that the white races will not unite with one another to oppose the colored peoples?

Now among the colored peoples of the Orient, Japan and China are the only two countries that have the semblance of an independent state. True, India compares favorably with China in its expansive territory and teeming population, but she has long since lost her independence, and there seems to be no reason today to believe that she will recover it. Thus, if the colored races of the Orient hope to compete with the so-called culturally advanced white races and maintain friendly relations with them while retaining their own cultural identity and independence, China and Japan, which are culturally and racially alike, must become friendly and promote each other's interests. China in the past has been invaded by other races and even subjugated by them. Thus, it is not difficult to understand why China, in the rivalry with white races, is not as deeply sensitive as Japan is in this regard. But the Chinese ought to know that China in her four thousand years of history has never been under the yoke of the white man. And thus, if she is approached with reason it will not be entirely hopeless to make her change her attitude and to instill in her the feeling of trust and reliance in our empire.

In the formulation and execution of our Chinese policy, an indispensable consideration is our American policy. America is rich, and of late she is giving great attention to the commerce, industry, and trade of China. Moreover, the great European war has not deterred her in the least. On the contrary, America enjoys, because of the war, the full advantages of the proverbial fisherman [who makes off with the catch while birds quarrel over it]. And the government of China, suspicious of the true motives of our empire, and as a means of restraining our activities in China, has been turning to America. If we fail to dissipate China's suspicion of us, she will rapidly turn against us and instead turn more and more to America. America herself will take advantage of such a situation and will increasingly extend her influence over China.

The immigration problem in California has made for an unhappy situation in the relations between the empire and America. It is regrettable that this problem still awaits settlement. But the empire has never regarded America as a foe. Therefore, it is advisable, for the realization of our China policy, not to aggravate America's feelings toward us nor needlessly to arouse her suspicions over our actions. For the maintenance of peace in the Orient in the future, and the promotion of China's independence, I deem it a matter of utmost importance to negotiate in a frank and open manner with America.

I have explained above the prevailing trend of racial problems and my premonitions of a bitter clash in the future between the white and colored peoples. However, I consider it more prudent, as far as China is concerned, not to raise the issue of a league of colored peoples. Our empire is now in alliance with England; it has agreements with Russia and France; and we are mutually striving to promote both the peace of the Orient and the independence of China. But we must also realize the need to negotiate with America. Our politicians must be sternly warned against raising the issue of racialism which would hurt the feelings of other countries and impair their friendship for us. The crux of the matter is that China must be won over by hints and suggestions, and only gradually, before we can realize our plans in the future.

STUDY QUESTIONS

1. How does the excerpt from Sakuma Shozan illustrate leading ideas of the Meiji Restoration?
2. In what ways did the Charter Oath break with Tokugawa tradition (Chapter 11)? Do you see any continuities?
3. What was Oki's rationale for establishing a new system of education? What were to be its key characteristics?
4. Why did Okubo favor the development of modern industries? What did he think should be the role of the state in stimulating the process of industrialization? What similarities and differences did Okubo see between Japan and England?
5. According to Ito, what are the main features of constitutional government? What should a constitutional government do? What rights should citizens have? What limitations should there be on a government, or on the citizens?
6. What foreign policy issues did Yamagata think were most important? What were Japan's objectives regarding China and the United States? How does Yamagata's letter suggest some of the causes of World War II?
7. What characteristics of Japanese life during the Tokugawa period may have contributed to the success of the Meiji Restoration?
8. How do the results of the Meiji Restoration compare to those of the French Revolution (Chapter 17)?
9. Why was there not a process similar to the Meiji Restoration in nineteenth-century China (Chapter 24)?
10. Why was Japan the only country outside the West to experience modernization in the nineteenth century?

26

Rammohun Roy, the British East India Company, and the Abolition of *Sati*

Beginning in the 1750s the British East India Company rapidly enlarged the boundaries of its authority in India, partly by means of victories on the battlefield and partly by forming alliances with regional princes. In exchange for promises of local autonomy, many of India's princes agreed to submit to overall rule by the Company. The Mughal emperors, whose regime had spiraled downward in the eighteenth century, were in no position to offer serious opposition to the British. As a result, by 1800 the East India Company's military and diplomatic successes had created a most unusual situation: A private corporation, jointly controlled by its major stockholders and the government in London, had become the *de facto* ruler of most of the Indian subcontinent. Company governance of India lasted until 1858.

Was the century of rule by the East India Company a "good thing" for India? This simple question raises immensely complex issues and has long been a subject of debate among scholars. In this chapter we will consider one of the many changes introduced into India by the Company—the abolition of *sati* in 1829. *Sati* was the practice of cremating upper caste widows on the funeral pyres of their deceased husbands. Supporters of *sati* argued that in joining her dead husband in the flames, a widow demonstrated her devotion to him. (The original meaning of the Sanskrit word *"sati"* is "virtuous wife.") When this ghastly custom began is something of a mystery, but there are reports of its practice as early as the fourth century B.C.E. It is also unclear how often *sati* was carried out. Travelers to India from Marco Polo onward reported that they witnessed the cremation of widows, but they may have exaggerated the frequency of incidents in order to shock their readers back home.

Although in the late eighteenth century the officials of the East India Company moved aggressively to assert their authority in Indian political and economic life, they were hesitant to interfere with the practice of *sati*. Company officials saw the practice as a religious issue best left in the hands of the Hindu community. However, as criticism of *sati* spread among the British in India and at home, the Company was forced to act. In 1813 it issued a circular stating that *sati* was lawful if it was the voluntary act of a widow

From *The English Works of Raja Rammohun Roy,* Part III, edited by Kalidas Nag and Debajyoti Burman (Calcutta: Sadharan Brahmo Samaj, 1947), pp. 124–127.

who was at least 16 years of age. The circular also provided that records were to be kept of each future incident. During the following decade Company officials and missionaries recorded hundreds of cases each year. Chilling eyewitness accounts of the practice were published in British newspapers in Calcutta. Responding to mounting public pressure for its abolition, Lord William Bentinck, the governor-general, outlawed *sati* in Bengal in 1829. Somewhat later the ban was extended to all of India.

One of the most fascinating aspects of the public discussion of *sati* in the 1820s was the role that Indian writers played in it. The leading Indian opponent of the practice was Rammohun Roy (1772–1833), a learned Bengali *brahman* and prolific writer on religious issues who had once been an employee of the East India Company. Roy was fluent in at least 10 languages, including English, and may have been one of the most broadly educated people in the early-nineteenth-century world. In two influential pamphlets on *sati*, published in both Bengali and English in 1818 and 1820, Roy staged a debate between "an advocate for, and an opponent of, the practice of burning widows alive." The selection that follows comes from the conclusion of his second pamphlet, which he dedicated to the Marchioness of Hastings, the wife of the current governor-general.

DEBATING *SATI*

Advocate. I alluded, in page 18, line 18, to the real reason for our anxiety to persuade widows to follow their husbands, and for our endeavors to burn them pressed down with ropes: *viz.*, that women are by nature of inferior understanding, without resolution, unworthy of trust, subject to passions, and void of virtuous knowledge; they, according to the precepts of the Sastra [ancient teachings], are not allowed to marry again after the demise of their husbands, and consequently despair at once of all worldly pleasure; hence it is evident, that death to these unfortunate widows is preferable to existence; for the great difficulty which a widow may experience by living a purely ascetic life, as prescribed by the Sastras, is obvious; therefore, if she do not perform Concremation, it is probable that she may be guilty of such acts as may bring disgrace upon her paternal and maternal relations, and those that may be connected with her husband. Under these circumstances, we instruct them from their early life in the idea of Concremation, holding out to them heavenly enjoyments in company with their husbands, as well as the beatitude of their relations, both by birth and marriage, and their reputation in this world. . . . From this many of them, on the death of their husbands, become desirous of accompanying them; but to remove every chance of their trying to escape from the blazing fire, in burning them we first tie them down to the pile.

Opponent. The reason you have now assigned for burning widows alive is indeed your true motive, as we are well aware; but the faults which you have imputed to women are not planted in their constitution by nature; it would be, therefore, grossly criminal to condemn that sex to death merely from precaution. By ascribing to them all sorts of improper conduct, you have indeed successfully persuaded the Hindu community to look down upon them as contemptible and mischievous creatures, whence they have been subjected to constant miseries. I have, therefore, to offer a few remarks on this head.

Women are in general inferior to men in bodily strength and energy; consequently the male part of the community, taking advantage of their corporeal weakness, have denied to them those excellent merits that they are entitled to by nature, and afterwards they are apt to say that women are naturally incapable of acquiring those merits. But if we give the subject consideration, we may easily ascertain whether or not your accusation against them is consistent with justice. As to their inferiority in point of understanding, when did you ever afford them a fair opportunity of exhibiting their natural capacity? How then can you accuse them of want of understanding? If, after instruction in knowledge and wisdom, a person cannot comprehend or retain what has been taught him, we may consider him as deficient; but as you keep women generally void of education and acquirements, you cannot, therefore, in justice pronounce on their inferiority. On the contrary, Lilavati, Bhanumati, the wife of the prince of Karnat, and that of Kalidasa, are celebrated for their thorough knowledge of all the Sastras: moreover in the Vrihadaranyaka Upanishad of the Yajur Veda it is clearly stated that Yajnavalkya imparted divine knowledge of the most difficult nature to his wife Maitreyi, who was able to follow and completely attain it!

Secondly. You charge them with want of resolution, at which I feel exceedingly surprised: for we constantly perceive, in a country where the name of death makes the male shudder, that the female, from her firmness of mind, offers to burn with the corpse of her deceased husband; and yet you accuse these women in deficiency in point of resolution.

Thirdly. With regard to their trustworthiness, let us look minutely into the conduct of both sexes, and we may be enabled to ascertain which of them is the most frequently guilty of betraying friends. If we enumerate such women in each village or town as have been deceived by men, and such men as have been betrayed by women, I presume that the number of the deceived women would be found ten times greater than that of the betrayed men. Men are, in general, able to read and write, and manage public affairs, by which means they easily promulgate such faults as women occasionally commit, but never consider as criminal the misconduct of men towards women. One fault they have, it must be acknowledged, which is, by considering others equally void of duplicity as themselves, to give their confidence too readily, from which they suffer much misery, even so far that some of them are misled to suffer themselves to be burnt to death.

In the fourth place, with respect to their subjection to the passions, this may be judged of by the custom of marriage as to the respective sexes; for one man may marry two or three, sometimes even ten wives and upwards; while a woman, who marries but one husband, desires at his death to follow him, forsaking all worldly enjoyments, or to remain leading the austere life of an ascetic.

Fifthly. The accusation of the want of virtuous knowledge is an injustice. Observe what pain, what slighting, what contempt, and what afflictions their virtue enables them to support! How many Kulin Brahmans are there who marry ten or fifteen wives for the sake of money, that never see the greater number of them after the day of marriage, and visit others only three or four times in the course of their life. Still, amongst those women, most, even without seeing or receiving any support from their husbands, living dependent on their fathers or brothers, and suffering much distress, continue to preserve their virtue; and when Brahmans, or those of other tribes, bring their wives to live with them, what misery do the women not suffer? At marriage the wife is recognized as half of her husband, but in after-conduct they are treated worse than inferior animals. For the woman is employed to do the work of a slave in the house, such as, in her turn, to clean the place very early in the morning, whether cold or wet, to scour the dishes, to wash the floor, to cook night and day, to prepare and serve food for her husband, father, mother-in-law, sisters-in-law, brothers-in-law, and friends and connections! (for amongst Hindus more than in other tribes relations long reside together, and on this account quarrels are more common amongst brothers respecting their worldly affairs). If in the preparation or serving up of the victuals they commit the smallest fault, what insult do they not receive from their husband, their mother-in-law, and the younger brothers of their husband? After all the male part of the family have satisfied themselves, the women content themselves with what may be left, whether sufficient in quantity or not. Where Brahmans or Kayasthas are not wealthy, their women are obliged to attend to their cows, and to prepare the cow-dung for firing. In the afternoon they fetch water from the river or tank, and at night perform the office of menial servants in making the beds. In case of any fault or omission in the performance of those labours they receive injurious treatment. Should the husband acquire wealth, he indulges in criminal amours to her perfect knowledge and almost under her eyes, and does not see her perhaps once a month. As long as the husband is poor, she suffers every kind of trouble, and when he becomes rich, she is altogether heart-broken. All this pain and affliction their virtue alone enables them to support. Where a husband takes two or three wives to live with him, they are subjected to mental miseries and constant quarrels. Even this distressed situation they virtuously endure. Sometimes it happens that the husband, from a preference for one of his wives, behaves cruelly to another. Amongst the lower classes, and those even of the better class who have not associated with good company, the wife, on the slightest fault, or even on bare suspicion of her misconduct, is chastised as a thief. Respect to virtue and their reputation generally makes them forgive even this treatment. If unable to bear such cruel usage, a wife leaves her husband's house to live separately from him, then the influence of the husband with the magisterial authority is generally sufficient to place her again in his hands; when, in revenge for her quitting him, he seizes every pretext to torment her in various ways, and sometimes even puts her privately to death. These are facts occurring every day, and not to be denied. What I lament is, that, seeing the women thus dependent and exposed to every misery, you feel for them no compassion, that might exempt them from being tied down and burnt to death.

STUDY QUESTIONS

1. What arguments did Roy present on behalf of *sati*?
2. What reasons did he give for opposing *sati*? Did Roy think *sati* was voluntary?
3. What basic problems did Roy see in Hindu gender relations? What was the reason for the problems? Was Roy a feminist?
4. What attitude toward Hinduism is implied in the pamphlet?
5. To whom was Roy appealing? Why did he publish in English? What was he calling upon his readers to do?

6. Was it a "good thing" for India that the British abolished the practice of *sati*? How might the banning of *sati* have strengthened the British claim that they had a moral right to rule India?
7. Can colonial rule ever be just?
8. Why did patriarchy take such an extreme form in India?

VISUAL SOURCE

RAMMOHUN ROY

Rammohun Roy came from a prosperous Hindu landowning family in Bengal, the first region of India to come under the authority of the British East India Company. Roy's extraordinarily rich education began at home, where as a young child he was tutored in Bengali. At about age 10 Roy's father sent him to Patna, a leading center of Muslim learning in India, to obtain fluency in Arabic and Persian, the two languages of India's Mughal rulers. Following his studies in Patna, Roy moved on to Benares, the home of India's greatest *brahman* scholars, where he mastered Sanskrit and became learned in the ancient Hindu classics. Having completed his formal studies, Roy returned to Bengal and

Portrait of Rammohun Roy by an Unknown British Artist. In James Cowles Prichard, *Researches into the Physical History of Mankind,* 3rd ed. (London, 1844). In Bruce Carlisle Robertson, *Raja Rammohan Roy: The Father of Modern India* (Delhi: Oxford University Press, 1995), frontispiece.

settled in Calcutta, the rapidly growing base of the East India Company. In Calcutta he learned English while serving as secretary to a leading Company official.

During the 1810s and 1820s Roy's public activities made him Asia's first "modern" intellectual. Roy's opposition to *sati* was part of his broader campaign to rid Hinduism of practices he thought had no basis in the ancient texts. He also engaged Christian missionaries in debate on the doctrine of the Trinity, which he regarded as a form of polytheism. To promote his views, Roy made new translations of classic Hindu writings and used the printing press to disseminate them. In addition, he founded an English-language magazine and two of India's earliest newspapers (in Bengali). Leading Hindu reformers met regularly at his home, which functioned as a kind of "salon."

Roy spent the last three years of his life in England, where he pushed for the reform of British rule in India and met with leading thinkers such as Jeremy Bentham and Robert Owen. He died in Bristol in 1833.

STUDY QUESTIONS

1. How do Roy's costume and hairstyle illustrate his Indian identity?
2. What aspect of Roy's character do you think the artist was trying to emphasize?
3. In what ways does the protrait indicate cultural contacts between India and the British in the nineteenth century?
4. What similarities and differences do you see in the portraits of Roy and Lin Zexu?

27

The 1857 "Mutiny": Rebel Goals

In May of 1857 Indian soldiers, who were known as *sepoys*, rose in rebellion against their British officers at a garrison near Delhi, the Mughal dynasty capital. Some of the mutineers were Hindus, others were Muslim. The uprising was triggered by the distribution of new cartridges, which the troops believed were packed in a mixture of beef and pork fat. Handling beef fat was deeply offensive to Hindus and pork was proscribed for Muslims. When about 90 of the soldiers refused to accept the new bullets, they were immediately court-martialed and sentenced to long terms in prison. The day after the trial the entire garrison rose in rebellion and marched toward Delhi, the home of the aged and powerless Mughal emperor, Bahadur Shah.

India's real rulers, the officials of the British East India Company, were surprised and initially confused by the uprising of formerly loyal soldiers. The rebels were able to gain control of Delhi and the movement spread to other garrisons and cities in northern India. Disaffected princes, whose lands had been seized by the East India Company, joined the soldiers against the British. The *rani* (princess) of Jhansi also led her army into the fray on the side of the rebels. In the summer of 1857 Company officials feared they might be driven out of northern India permanently.

But the rebels were an extremely heterogeneous force and were not able to produce a unified leadership. Religious affiliation, caste loyalty, and regional ties trumped any sense of national identity among the people of India in the mid-nineteenth century. Perhaps the small but growing number of British-educated Indians could have provided the leaders necessary to prevail over the British in 1857, but this group chose not to join the uprising.

Seizing on the rebels' lack of unity and drawing on loyal *sepoys*, the British retook northern India in fighting that lasted until the summer of 1858. As they recovered their authority, the British introduced major reforms in their system of rule. The Mughal emperor was deposed, ending the dynasty that had been founded by Babur in the 1520s, and the East India Company, the *de facto* ruler of India since about 1800, was also dissolved. India now came under the direct authority of the government in London, becoming the brightest jewel in Queen Victoria's imperial crown. The British government remained in charge in India until 1947.

From Ainslie T. Embree, ed., *India in 1857: Mutiny or War of Independence?* (Boston: D.C. Heath, 1963), pp. 3–7.

The following selection is excerpted from a proclamation issued by a grandson of the Mughal emperor on behalf of the rebels who gained control of the north Indian garrison town of Azamgarh in the summer of 1857. How does the proclamation illustrate the goals of the rebels and suggest reasons why the uprising failed?

PROCLAMATION BY INDIAN REBELS

25th. August, 1857.

It is well known to all, that in this age the people of Hindoostan, both Hindoos and Mohammedans, are being ruined under the tyranny and oppression of the infidel and treacherous English. It is therefore the bounden duty of all the wealthy people of India, especially of those who have any sort of connection with any of the Mohammedan royal families, and are considered the pastors and masters of their people, to stake their lives and property for the well being of the public. With the view of effecting this general good, several princes belonging to the royal family of Delhi, have dispersed themselves in the different parts of India, Iran, Turan, and Afghanistan, and have been long since taking measures to compass their favourite end; and it is to accomplish this charitable object that one of the aforesaid princes has, at the head of an army of Afghanistan &c., made his appearance in India: and I, who am the grandson of Abul Muzuffer Serajuddin Bahadur Shah Ghazee, King of India, having in the course of circuit come here to extirpate the infidels residing in the eastern part of the country, and to liberate and protect the poor helpless people now groaning under their iron rule, have, by the aid of the *Majahdeens* [religious warriors], erected the standard of Mohammed, and persuaded the orthodox Hindoos who had been subject to my ancestors, and have been and are still accessories in the destruction of the English, to raise the standard of Mahavir.

Several of the Hindoo and Mussalman chiefs, who have long since quitted their homes for the preservation of their religion, and have been trying their best to root out the English in India, have presented themselves to me, and taken part in the reigning Indian crusade, and it is more than probable that I shall very shortly receive succours from the West. Therefore, for the information of the public, the present *Ishtahar,* consisting of several sections, is put in circulation, and it is the imperative duty of all to take it into their careful consideration, and abide by it. Parties anxious to participate in the common cause, but having no means to provide for themselves, shall receive their daily subsistence from me; and be it known to all, that the ancient works, both of the Hindoos and the Mohammedans, the writings of the miracle-workers and the calculations of the astrologers, pundits, and rammals, all agree in asserting that the English will no longer have any footing in India or elsewhere. Therefore it is incumbent on all to give up the hope of the continuation of the British sway, side with me, and deserve the consideration of the Badshahi, or imperial Government, by their individual exertion in promoting the common good, and thus attain their respective ends; otherwise if this golden opportunity slips away, they will have to repent of their folly, as it is very aptly said by a poet in two fine couplets, the drift whereof is "Never let a favourable opportunity slip, for in the field of opportunity you are to meet with the ball of fortune; but if you do not avail yourself of the opportunity that offers itself, you will have to bite your finger through grief."

No person, at the misrepresentation of the well-wishers of the British Government, ought to conclude from the present slight inconveniences usually attendant on revolutions, that similar inconveniences and troubles should continue when the Badshahi Government is established on a firm basis: and parties badly dealt with by any sepoy or plunderer, should come up and represent their grievances to me, and receive redress at my hands; and for whatever property they may lose in the reigning disorder, they will be recompensed from the public treasury when the Badshahi Government is well fixed.

Section I—Regarding Zemindars [land holders]. It is evident, that the British Government in making zemindary settlements have imposed exorbitant *Jumas* [taxes], and have disgraced and ruined several zemindars, by putting up their estates to public auction for arrears of rent, in so much, that on the institution of a suit by a common Ryot, a maid servant, or a slave, the respectable zemindars are summoned into court, arrested, put in gaol and disgraced. In litigations regarding zemindaries, the immense value of stamps, and other unnecessary expenses of the civil courts, which are pregnant with all sorts of crooked dealings, and the practice of allowing a case to hang on for years, are all calculated to impoverish the litigants. Besides this, the coffers of the zemindars are annually taxed with subscription for schools, hospitals, roads, etc. Such extortions will have no manner of existence in the Badshahi Government; but on the contrary, the *Jumas* will be light, the dignity and honour of the zemindars safe, and every zemindar will have absolute rule in his own zemindary . . .

Section II—Regarding Merchants. It is plain that the infidel and treacherous British Government have monopolized the trade of all the fine and valuable merchandise, such as indigo, cloth, and other articles of shipping, leaving only the trade of trifles to the people, and even in this they are not without their share of the profits, which they secure by means of customs and stamp fees, &c. in money suits, so that the people have merely a trade in name. Besides this, the profits of the traders are taxed, with postages, tolls, and subscriptions for schools, &c. Notwithstanding all these concessions, the merchants are liable to imprisonment and disgrace at the instance or complaint of a worthless man. When the Badshahi Government is established, all these aforesaid fraudulent practices shall be dispensed with, and the trade of every article, without exception, both by land and water, shall be open to the native merchants of India, who will have the benefit of the Government steam-vessels and steam-carriages for the conveyance of their merchandise gratis; and merchants having no capital of their own shall be assisted from the public treasury. It is therefore the duty of every merchant to take part in the war, and aid the Badshahi Government with his men and money, either secretly or openly, as may be consistent with his position or interest, and forswear his allegiance to the British Government.

Section III—Regarding Public Servants. It is not a secret thing that under the British Government, natives employed in the civil and military services, have little respect, low pay, and no manner of influence; and all the posts of dignity and emolument in both the departments, are exclusively bestowed on Englishmen for natives in the military service, after having devoted the greater part of their lives, attain to the post of soobadar (the very height of their hopes) with a salary of 60r. [rupees]

or 70r. per mensem [month]; and those in the civil service obtain the post of Sudder Ala, with a salary of 500r. a month, but no influence. . . .

Therefore, all the natives in the British service ought to be alive to their religion and interest, and, abjuring their loyalty to the English, side with the Badshahi Government, and obtain salaries of 200 or 300 rupees per month for the present, and be entitled to high posts in future. If they, for any reason, cannot at present declare openly against the English, they can heartily wish ill to their cause, and remain passive spectators of passing events, without taking any active share therein. But at the same time they should indirectly assist the Badshahi Government, and try their best to drive the English out of the country. . . .

Section IV—Regarding Artisans. It is evident that the Europeans, by the introduction of English articles into India, have thrown the weavers, the cotton dressers, the carpenters, the blacksmiths, and the shoemakers, &c., out of employ, and have engrossed their occupations, so that every description of native artisan has been reduced to beggary. But under the Badshahi Government the native artisan will exclusively be employed in the services of the kings, the rajahs, and the rich; and this will no doubt ensure their prosperity. Therefore these artisans ought to renounce the English services, and assist the *Majahdeens,* engaged in the war, and thus be entitled both to secular and eternal happiness.

Section V—Regarding Pundits, Fakirs and other learned persons. The pundits and fakirs being the guardians of the Hindoo and Mohammedan religions respectively, and the Europeans being the enemies of both the religions, and as at present a war is raging against the English on account of religion, the pundits and fakirs are bound to present themselves to me, and take their share in the holy war. . . .

Lastly, be it known to all, that whoever, out of the above named classes, shall after the circulation of this Ishtabar, still cling to the British Government, all his estates shall be confiscated, and his property plundered, and he himself, with his whole family, shall be imprisoned, and ultimately put to death.

STUDY QUESTIONS

1. What was the basic goal of the Azamgarh rebels?
2. To whom was the proclamation addressed? Which groups in society did the rebels regard as most important to the success of their uprising? What did they offer to potential allies? What groups were ignored by the proclamation?
3. As stated in the proclamation, what seem to have been the major objections to British rule in India?
4. If Rammohun Roy had been alive in 1857, would he have been a likely supporter of the rebels?
5. In what sense did the goals of the 1857 rebels fall short of being revolutionary?
6. Was India a nation in 1857?
7. Were there movements in other countries in the nineteenth century that resembled the 1857 rebellion in India?

28

The Economy of India Under British Rule: The Views of an Indian Nationalist

When the British East India Company first began to take possession of the Indian subcontinent in the 1750s, the Indian economy was strong. Agricultural output and the size of the population had been growing since 1500. Commerce and banking had expanded widely on the subcontinent over the same period. Mid-eighteenth century India was a world leader in the production of hand woven textiles, especially cotton and silk. Finally, the export of textiles, rice, diamonds, and pepper from Indian ports during the early modern period made many South Asian merchants and shippers major participants in international trade.

By 1900 India's economic circumstances had changed significantly. The selection that follows, excerpted from a book first published in 1902 by Romesh Chunder Dutt (1848–1909), discusses the long downturn that seems to have begun in the late eighteenth century. Dutt wrote the book shortly after retiring from a distinguished career in the Indian Civil Service (ICS), where he had been one of the very few Indians permitted by the British to rise to a position of responsibility. During his childhood and years in the ICS, Dutt had many opportunities to observe conditions in India's villages. A good part of his book was based on these observations. For the earlier period of Company rule, Dutt relied heavily on the surveys of Indian rural life conducted from 1800 to 1814 by East India Company official Francis Buchanan. Modern scholars regard Buchanan's volumes, if used carefully, as valuable sources of evidence on Indian life in the early nineteenth century.

Dutt was a leader of the Indian nationalist movement and was elected president of the Indian National Congress in 1899, factors that surely do not invalidate his writing on the Indian economy but which should be kept in mind when reading the selection. According to Dutt, why was the Indian economy so troubled in 1900?

From Romesh Dutt, *The Economic History of India under Early British Rule,* Vol. I: *From the Rise of the British Power in 1757 to the Accession of Queen Victoria in 1837* (London: Kegan Paul, Trench, Trubner, 1902; reprint edition, New York: Augustus M. Kelly, 1969), pp. ix–xi, xxiii–xxiv.

INDIAN ECONOMICS

Englishmen can look back on their work in India, if not with unalloyed satisfaction, at least with some legitimate pride. They have conferred on the people of India what is the greatest human blessing—Peace. They have introduced Western Education, bringing an ancient and civilised nation in touch with modern thought, modern sciences, modern institutions and life. They have built up an Administration which, though it requires reform with the progress of the times, is yet strong and efficacious. They have framed wise laws, and have established Courts of Justice, the purity of which is as absolute as in any country on the face of the earth. These are results which no honest critic of British work in India regards without high admiration.

On the other hand, no open-minded Englishman contemplates the material condition of the people of India under British rule with equal satisfaction. The poverty of the Indian population at the present day is unparalleled in any civilised country; the famines which have desolated India within the last quarter of the nineteenth century are unexampled in their extent and intensity in the history of ancient or modern times. By a moderate calculation, the famines of 1877 and 1878, of 1889 and 1892, of 1897 and 1900, have carried off fifteen millions of people. The population of the fair-sized European country has been swept away from India within twenty-five years. A population equal to half of that of England has perished in India within a period which men and women, still in middle age, can remember.

What are the causes of this intense poverty and these repeated famines in India? Superficial explanations have been offered one after another, and have been rejected on close examination. It was said that the population increased rapidly in India and that such increase must necessarily lead to famines; it is found on inquiry that the population has never increased in India at the rate of England, and that during the last ten years it has altogether ceased to increase. It was said that the Indian cultivators were careless and improvident, and that those who did not know how to save when there was plenty, must perish when there was want; but it is known to men who have lived all their lives among these cultivators, that there is not a more abstemious, a more thrifty, a more frugal race of peasantry on earth. It was said that the Indian money-lender was the bane of India, and by his fraud and extortion kept the tillers of the soil in a chronic state of indebtedness; but the inquiries of the latest Famine Commission have revealed that the cultivators of India are forced under the thraldom of money-lenders by the rigidity of the Government revenue demand. It was said that in a country where the people depended almost entirely on their crops, they must starve when their crops failed in years of drought; but the crops in India, as a whole, have never failed, there has never been a single year when the food supply of the country was insufficient for the people, and there must be something wrong, when failure in a single province brings on a famine, and the people are unable to buy their supplies from neighboring provinces rich in harvests.

Deep down under all these superficial explanations we must seek for the true causes of Indian poverty and Indian famines. The economic laws which operate in India are the same as in other countries of the world; the causes which lead to wealth among other nations lead to prosperity in India; the causes which impoverish other nations impoverish the people of India. Therefore, the line of inquiry which the economist will pursue in respect of India is the same which he adopts in inquiring into the wealth or poverty of other nations. Does agriculture flourish? Are industries and manufactures in a prosperous condition? Are the finances properly administered, so as to bring back to the people an adequate return for the taxes paid by them? Are the sources of national wealth widened by a Government anxious for the material welfare of the people? These are questions which the average Englishman asks himself when inquiring into the economic condition of any country in the world; these are questions which he will ask himself in order to ascertain the truth about India.

It is, unfortunately, a fact which no well-informed Indian official will ignore, that, in many ways, the sources of national wealth in India have been narrowed under British rule. India in the eighteenth century was a great manufacturing as well as a great agricultural country, and the products of the Indian loom supplied the markets of Asia and of Europe. It is, unfortunately, true that the East Indian Company and the British Parliament, following the selfish commercial policy of a hundred years ago, discouraged Indian manufacturers in the early years of British rule in order to encourage the rising manufactures of England. Their fixed policy, pursued during the last decades of the eighteenth century and the first decades of the nineteenth, was to make India subservient to the industries of Great Britain, and to make the Indian people grow raw produce only, in order to supply material for looms and manufactories of Great Britain. This policy was pursued with unwavering resolution and with fatal success; orders were sent out, to force Indian artisans to work in the Company's factories; commercial residents were legally vested with extensive powers over villages and communities of Indian weavers; prohibitive tariffs excluded Indian silk and cotton goods from England; English goods were admitted into India free of duty or on payment of a nominal duty.

The British manufacturer, in the words of the historian, H. H. Wilson, "employed the arm of political injustice to keep down and ultimately strangle a competitor with whom he could not have contended on equal terms;" millions of Indian artisans lost their earnings; the population of India lost one great source of their wealth. It is a painful episode in the history of British rule in India; but it is a story which has to be told to explain the economic condition of Indian people, and their present helpless dependence on agriculture. The invention of the power-loom in Europe completed the decline of the Indian industries; and when in recent years the power-loom was set up in India, England once more acted towards India with unfair jealousy. An excise duty has been imposed on the production of cotton fabrics in India which disables the Indian manufacturer from competing with the manufacturer of Japan and China, and which stifles the new steam-mills of India. . . .

The dawn of a new century finds India deeper in distress and discontent than any preceding period of history. A famine, wider in the extent of country affected than any previous famine, has desolated the country. In parts of India, not affected by this famine, large classes of people attest to semi-starvation by their poor physique; numbers of them suffer from daily insufficiency of food; and the poorer classes are trained by life-long hunger to live on less food than is needed for proper nourishment. In the presence of facts like these, party controversy is silenced; and every Englishman and every Indian, experienced in administration and faithful to the British Empire, feel it their duty to suggest methods for the removal of the gravest danger which has ever threatened the Empire of India.

STUDY QUESTIONS

1. What did Dutt think were the benefits of British rule in India?
2. What did he think was the cause of poverty in India?
3. How did Dutt think that Indian poverty could be alleviated? Was he opposed to British rule in India?
4. How did Dutt's thinking compare with that of China's Confucian reformers (Chapter 24)?
5. Did the process of "deindustrialization" described by Dutt occur elsewhere in the nineteenth-century world? Could it have been avoided in India?
6. Did the British become wealthy by impoverishing India?
7. Why is there so much poverty in present-day India? Is it a legacy of British policy, or are there other causes?
8. Is there a relationship between the policies of the British in India and present-day globalization?

29

The *Tanzimat* Reforms in the Ottoman Empire

At the end of the seventeenth century European and Russian armies inflicted a series of major defeats on the Ottoman Turks. Troubled by the gap that had opened up between the effectiveness of their forces and those of their long-time Christian adversaries, the Ottoman sultans began to seek advice from European military experts. They also began to send diplomants to cities such as Paris, Berlin, Madrid, and Vienna. As the sultans and their advisers digested the reports on life in the West filed by these envoys, they began to consider the possibility that upgrading their armies might require broader changes—in education, the economy, and in the administration of their empire.

Selim III (reigned 1789–1807) was the first of several sultans who had ambitious plans for reform. He tried to introduce changes in the military and the system of administration, but could not overcome resistance by powerful vested interests, especially the now-corrupt Janissary corps. Selim's nephew and successor, Mahmud II (reigned 1808–1839) continued the reform effort and was able to make some progress. He abolished the Janissaries, established a small number of secular schools, and reduced the role of Muslim judges (*qadis*) in the judicial system.

Under the leadership of Mahmud's two sons, Abdul Mejid (reigned 1839–1861) and Abdul Aziz (reigned (1861–1876), the movement for reform, now known as *Tanzimat* ("restructuring" or "reorganization"), became more sweeping. The Ottoman leaders expanded the number of secular schools, issued new law codes, and sponsored the construction of factories, railways, and steamships. When Sultan Abdul Hamid II (reigned 1876–1909) agreed to a constitution providing for a parliament, the reform movement seemed to be entering a new stage, one that might include the establishment of liberal political institutions.

But Abdul Hamid II dismissed the parliament soon after it convened, having become fearful that the process of change was going too far. The sultan then set aside the new constitution, allied himself with the conservative *ulema* [Islamic scholars], and governed autocratically during the remaining years of his long reign. Although reform did not end entirely, the era of the *Tanzimat* movement was now over. One of the most significant efforts

Selections I and II from E. Hertslet, *The Map of Europe by Treaty*, 4 vols. (London: Butterworths, 1875–1891), Vol. II, pp. 1,002–1,005, 1,243–1,249.

at reform undertaken by a non-Western elite in the nineteenth century had fallen short of its goal of full modernization. The continued survival of the Ottoman empire was now in question.

The basic ideas of the *Tanzimat* movement are illustrated in two imperial rescripts (decrees) issued by Sultan Abdul Mejid, in 1839 and 1856. How do the decrees illustrate the challenges facing the Ottoman reformers?

TANZIMAT DOCUMENTS

I. IMPERIAL RESCRIPT OF NOVEMBER 3, 1839

All the world knows that in the first days of the Ottoman Monarchy, the glorious precepts of the Koran and the Laws of the Empire were always honoured. The Empire in consequence increased in strength and greatness, and all her Subjects, without exception, had risen in the highest degree to ease and prosperity. In the last 150 years a succession of accidents and divers[e] causes have arisen which have brought about a disregard for the sacred code of Laws, and the Regulations flowing therefrom, and the former strength and prosperity have changed into weakness and poverty; an Empire in fact loses all its stability as soon as it ceases to observe its Laws.

The considerations are ever present to our mind, and, ever since the day of our advent to the Throne, the thought of the public weal, of the improvement of the state of the Provinces, and relief of to the peoples, has not ceased to engage it. If, therefore, the geographical position of the Ottoman Provinces, the fertility of the soil, the aptitude and intelligence of the inhabitants are considered, the conviction will remain that, by striving to find efficacious means, the result, which by the help of God we hope to attain, can be obtained within a few years. Full of confidence, therefore, in the help of the Most High, assisted by the intercession of our Prophet, we deem it right to seek by new institutions to give to the Provinces composing the Ottoman Empire the benefit of a good Administration.

These institutions must be principally carried out under three heads, which are: 1. The guarantees insuring to our subjects perfect security for life, honour, and fortune. 2. A regular system of assessing and levying Taxes. 3. An equally regular system for the levy of Troops and the duration of their service. . . .

From henceforth, therefore, the cause of every accused person shall be publicly judged in accordance with our Divine Law, after enquiry and examination, and so long as a regular judgment shall not have been pronounced, no one can, secretly or publicly, put another to death by poison or in any other manner.

No one shall be allowed to attack the honour of any other person whatever.

Each one shall possess his Property of every kind, and shall dispose of it in all freedom, without let or hindrance from any person whatever; thus, for example, the innocent Heirs of a Criminal shall not be deprived of their legal rights, and the Property of the Criminal shall not be confiscated.

These Imperial concessions shall extend to all our subjects, of whatever Religion or sect they may be; they shall enjoy them without exceptions. We therefore grant perfect security to the inhabitants of our Empire, in their lives, their honour, and their fortunes, as they are secured to them by the sacred text of our Law. . . .

As all the Public Servants of the Empire receive a suitable salary, and that the salaries of those whose duties have not, up to the present time, been sufficiently remunerated, are to be fixed, a rigorous Law shall be passed against the traffic of favouritism and of appointments (*richvet*), which the Divine Law reprobates, and which is one of the principal causes of the decay of the Empire.

II. IMPERIAL RESCRIPT OF FEBRUARY 18, 1856

Let it be done as herein set forth.

To you, my Grand Vizier, Mehemed Emin Ali Pasha, decorated with my Imperial Order of the Medjidiyé of the first class, and with the Order of Personal Merit; may God grant to you greatness, and increase your power! . . .

It being now my desire to renew and enlarge still more the new Institutions ordained with the view of establishing a state of things conformable with the dignity of my Empire and— . . . by the kind and friendly assistance of the Great Powers, my noble Allies, . . . the guarantees promised on our part by the Hatti-Humaïoun of Gülhané, and in conformity with the Tanzimat, . . . are today confirmed and consolidated, and efficacious measures shall be taken in order that they may have their full and entire effect.

All the Privileges and Spiritual Immunities granted by my ancestors *ab antiquo* [in former times], and at subsequent dates, to all Christian communities or other non-Mussulman persuasions established in my Empire under my protection, shall be confirmed and maintained.

Every Christian or other non-Mussulman community shall be bound within a fixed period, and with the concurrence of a Commission composed *ad hoc* of members of its own body, to proceed with my high approbation and under the inspection of my Sublime Porte, to examine into its actual Immunities and Privileges, and to discuss and submit to my Sublime Porte the Reforms required by the progress of civilization and of the age. The powers conceded to the Christian Patriarchs and Bishops by the Sultan Mahomet II and his successors, shall be made to harmonize with the new position which my generous and beneficent intentions insure to these communities. . . . The principles of nominating the Patriarchs for life, after the revision of the rules of election now in force, shall be exactly carried out, conformably to the tenor of the Firmans of Investiture. . . . The ecclesiastical dues, of whatever sort or nature they be, shall be abolished and replaced by fixed revenues of the Patriarchs and heads of communities. . . . In the towns, small boroughs, and villages, where the whole population is of the same Religion, no obstacle shall be offered to the repair, according to their original plan, of buildings set apart for Religious Worship, for Schools, for Hospitals, and for Cemeteries. . . .

Every distinction or designation tending to make any class whatever of the subjects of my Empire inferior to another class, on account of their Religion, Language, or Race, shall be for ever effaced from the Administrative Protocol. The laws shall be put in force against the use of any injurious or offensive term, either among private individuals or on the part of the authorities.

As all forms of Religion are and shall be freely professed in my dominions, no subject of my Empire shall be hindered in the exercise of the Religion that he professes. . . . No one shall be compelled to change their Religion . . . and . . . all the subjects of my Empire, without distinction, nationality, shall be admissable to public employments. . . . All the subjects of my Empire, without distinction, shall be received into the Civil and Military Schools of the Government. . . . Moreover, every community is authorized to establish Public Schools of Science, Art, and Industry. . . .

All Commercial, Correctional, and Criminal Suits between Mussulmans and Christian or other non-Mussulman subjects, or between Christians or other non-Mussulmans of different sects, shall be referred to Mixed Tribunals. The proceedings of these Tribunals shall be public: the parties shall be confronted, and shall produce their witnesses, whose testimony shall be received, without distinction, upon oath taken according to the religious law of each sect. . . .

Penal, Correctional, and Commercial Laws, and Rules of Procedure for the Mixed Tribunals, shall be drawn up as soon as possible, and formed into a code. . . . Proceedings shall be taken, for the reform of the Penitentiary System. . . .

The organization of the Police . . . shall be revised in such a manner as to give to all the peaceable subjects of my Empire the strongest guarantees for the safety both of their persons and property. . . . Christian subjects, and those of other non-Mussulman sects, . . . shall, as well as Mussulmans, be subject to the obligations of the Law of Recruitment. The principle of obtaining substitutes, or of purchasing exemption, shall be admitted.

Proceedings shall be taken for a Reform in the Constitution of the Provincial and Communal Councils, in order to ensure fairness in the choice of the Deputies of the Mussulman, Christian, and other communities, and freedom of voting in the Councils. . . .

As the Laws regulating the purchase, sale, and disposal of Real Property are common to all the subjects of my Empire, it shall be lawful for Foreigners to possess Landed Property in my dominions. . . .

The Taxes are to be levied under the same denomination from all the subjects of my Empire, without distinction of class or of Religion. The most prompt and energetic means for remedying the abuses in collecting the Taxes, and especially the Tithes, shall be considered. The system of direct collection shall gradually, and as soon as possible, be substituted for the plan of Farming, in all the branches of the Revenues of the State.

A special Law having been already passed, which declared that the Budget of the Revenue and Expenditure of the State shall be drawn up and made known every year, the said law shall be most scrupulously observed. . . .

The heads of each Community and a Delegate, designated by my Sublime Porte, shall be summoned to take part in the deliberations of the Supreme Council of Justice on all occasions which might interest the generality of the subjects of my Empire. . . .

Steps shall be taken for the formation of Banks and other similar institutions, so as to effect a reform in the monetary and financial system, as well as to create Funds to be employed in augmenting the sources of the material wealth of my Empire.

Steps shall also be taken for the formation of Roads and Canals to increase the facilities of communication and increase the sources of the wealth of the country. Everything that can impede commerce or agriculture shall be abolished. . . .

Such being my wishes and my commands, you, who are my Grand Vizier, will, according to custom, cause this Imperial Firman [edict] to be published in my capital and in all parts of my Empire; and will watch attentively, and take all the necessary measures that all the orders which it contains be henceforth carried out with the most rigorous punctuality.

STUDY QUESTIONS

1. According to the 1839 rescript, why had the Ottoman empire declined? What did the decree describe as the strengths of the Ottoman state?
2. What remedies for Ottoman problems were proposed in the two decrees?
3. What problems seem to have been most worrisome to the Ottoman authorities—political, economic, or religious?
4. Which groups would likely have welcomed the reforms? What groups would have probably opposed the innovations?
5. How might the European states, including Russia, have influenced the course of the Ottoman reforms?
6. What implications did the *Tanzimat* movement have for the role of Islam in the Ottoman lands?
7. How did the Ottoman attempts at reform compare with similar efforts in Russia, China, and Japan (Chapters 6, 24 and 25)? What circumstances made the Ottoman situation unique?
8. Why did the *Tanzimat* movement fail?
9. Is there a conflict between the teachings of Islam and the desire to be modern?
10. Are "modern" and "Western" synonymous?

ATLANTIC OCEAN

San
Antonio

BAHAMA IS.
(Br.)

Gulf of
Mexico

HAITI 1804

**MEXICO
1821**

CUBA
(Sp.)

PUERTO RICO
(Sp.)

Mexico
City

Veracruz

**BR.
HONDURAS**

Caribbean Sea

TRINIDAD (Br.)

GUIANA

**UNITED PROVINCES OF
CENTRAL AMERICA
1823–1839**

Panama

Caracas

DUTCH GUIANA

FRENCH GUIANA

**GRAN COLOMBIA
1819-1830**

Bogotá

Quito

GALÁPAGOS IS.

**EMPIRE
OF BRAZIL
1822**

Indefinite

Boundary

**PERU
1821**

Lima

Bahia

**BOLIVIA
1825**

Sucre

PACIFIC OCEAN

**PARAGUAY
1811**

Rio de Janeiro

Asunción

**CHILE
1817**

**UNITED
PROVINCES OF
LA PLATA
1826**

Santiago

**URUGUAY
1828**

Montevideo

Buenos Aires

0	500	1000 Miles
0		1000 Kilometers

Latin America at Independence

30

Independence and Consolidation of New States (1810–1914)

Creoles, or American-born descendants of Spaniards and Portuguese, achieved independence from their former colonial masters between 1810 and 1825. Fifty years later, new political leaders, also from the creole class, overcame a long period of internal fighting and consolidated national governments in the last quarter of the nineteenth century.

Creoles were elitists who considered themselves far superior to their *mestizo,* Indian, and black working classes. Owning the principal means of production and trade—that is, mines, *haciendas,* and merchant businesses—creoles employed and paternally controlled the racially different lower classes. By the end of the eighteenth century, creoles amounted to about 20 percent of the total population. Seeking freedom from colonial restrictions and a more autonomous role in government, creoles ridiculed the weaknesses of their mother country in Europe. When Napoleon invaded the Iberian Peninsula in 1808, the creoles in Latin America seized the initiative. After a number of military failures, creole armies in Spanish America gathered sufficient strength to expel Spain's expeditionary forces by 1825. In Brazil, where the king of Portugal resided after he escaped from Napoleon in 1808, the king's son, Pedro I, at the urging of the Brazilian creole elite, declared independence in 1822 after his father returned to Portugal in 1820.

Once free, the creoles fought among themselves to determine control of an economy devastated by the wars of independence. A 50-year period of extreme political instability and civil war followed. Local *caudillos* (military leaders with a personal following) pillaged the treasury, ruled by extortion, and toppled one another in an endless succession of coups and countercoups. By the 1870s, new leaders from the creole class emerged.

Selection I from Simón Bolívar to the Congress of Angostura in 1819, in Vicente Lecuna and Harold A. Bierck, Jr., eds., *Selected Writings of Bolivar* (New York: Colonial Press, 1951), pp. 175–176, 183, 185–190. Selection II from Gabino Barreda's speech, September 16, 1867, in Carlos B. Gil, ed., *The Age of Porfirio Diaz: Selected Readings* (Albuquerque: University of New Mexico Press, 1977), pp. 35–36. Selection III from Porfirio Diaz interview, 1908, Carlos B. Gill, ed., *The Age of Porfirio Diaz: Selected Readings* (Albuquerque: University of New Mexico Press, 1977), pp. 78–81.

Well educated and wealthy (through exports of raw materials to the industrialized world), this new oligarchy ended *caudillo* rule.

Simón Bolivar, the liberator of northern South America, Peru, and Bolivia, came from this creole class. His political ideas clearly expressed the biases of his social origins. He mistrusted the lower classes and advocated elite-run governments. In the first section these prejudices are clearly shown in Bolivar's advice to the legislators gathered at Angostura in 1819 to discuss the proposed constitution for the new state of Venezuela.

In Mexico Porfirio Diaz ruled with an iron hand from 1876 to 1910. Although he was a rough *mestizo* military leader, Diaz enjoyed the support of the Mexican oligarchy and their articulate spokesmen. With the oligarchy's help, he ended 50 years of civil war. Through concessions to foreign investors, particularly in mining, railroads, and oil, Diaz presided over an impressive economic boom in exports to the United States. To maintain economic growth, the oligarchy sought stability, and Diaz provided it. In the second selection this call for order is expressed in a speech by Gabino Barreda, a Mexican intellectual who had just returned from France, where he studied under the positivist August Comte. Presented on September 16, 1867, the first Independence Day celebration after the French-installed European monarch, Maximilian, had been defeated by the Liberal General Benito Juarez, the speech called for an end to violent revolution and a new respect for order. The third selection is from an interview given by Porfirio Diaz in 1908 to the American reporter James Creelman. Diaz candidly revealed how he achieved order.

SOUTH AMERICAN INDEPENDENCE

I. SIMON BOLIVAR'S ADVICE TO THE CONGRESS OF ANGOSTURA (1819)

We are not Europeans; we are not Indians; we are but a mixed species of aborigines and Spaniards. Americans by birth and Europeans by law, we find ourselves engaged in a dual conflict: we are disputing with the natives for titles of ownership, and at the same time we are struggling to maintain ourselves in the country that gave us birth against the opposition of the invaders.

Subject to the threefold yoke of ignorance, tyranny, and vice, the American people have been unable to acquire knowledge, power, or [civic] virtue. The lessons we received and the models we studied, as pupils of such pernicious teachers, were most destructive. We have been ruled more by deceit than by force, and we have been degraded more by vice than by superstition.

Venezuela had, has, and should have a republican government. Its principles should be the sovereignty of the people, division of powers, civil liberty, proscription of slavery, and the abolition of monarchy and privileges. We need equality to recast, so to speak, into a unified nation, the classes of men, political opinions, and public customs.

Like the North Americans, we have divided national representation into two chambers: that of Representatives and the Senate. The first is very wisely constituted. It enjoys all its proper functions, and it requires no essential revision, because the Constitution, in creating it, gave it the form and powers which the people deemed necessary in order that they might be legally and properly represented. If the Senate were hereditary rather than elective, it would, in my opinion, be the basis, the tie, the very soul of our republic. In political storms this body would arrest the thunderbolts of the government and would repel any violent popular reaction. Devoted to the government because of a natural interest in its own preservation, a hereditary senate would always oppose any attempt on the part of the people to infringe upon the jurisdiction and authority of their magistrates. It must be confessed that most men are unaware of their best interests and that they constantly endeavor to assail them in the hands of their custodians—the individual clashes with the mass, and the mass with authority. It is necessary, therefore, that in all governments there be a neutral body to protect the injured and disarm the offender. To be neutral, this body must not owe its origin to appointment by the government or to election by the people, if it is to enjoy a full measure of independence which neither fears nor expects anything from these two sources of authority. The hereditary senate, as a part of the people, shares its interests, its sentiments, and its spirit. For this reason it should not be presumed that a hereditary senate would ignore the interests of the people or forget its legislative duties. The senators in Rome and in the House of Lords in London have been the strongest pillars upon which the edifice of political and civil liberty has rested.

At the outset, these senators should be elected by Congress. The successors to this Senate must command the initial attention of the government, which should educate them in a *colegio* designed especially to train these guardians and future legislators of the nation. They ought to learn the arts, sciences, and letters that enrich the mind of a public figure. From childhood they should understand the career for which they have been destined by Providence, and from earliest youth they should prepare their minds for the dignity that awaits them.

The creation of a hereditary senate would in no way be a violation of political equality. I do not solicit the establishment of a nobility, for, as a celebrated republican has said, that would simultaneously destroy equality and liberty. What I propose is an office for which the candidates must prepare themselves, an office that demands great knowledge and the ability to acquire such knowledge. All should not be left to chance and the outcome of elections. The people are more easily deceived than is Nature perfected by art; and, although these senators, it is true, would not be bred in an environment that is all virtue, it is equally true that they would be raised in an atmosphere of enlightened education. Furthermore, the liberators of Venezuela are entitled to occupy forever a high rank in the Republic that they have brought into existence. I believe that posterity would view with regret the effacement of the illustrious names of its first benefactors. I say, moreover, that it is a matter of public interest and national honor, of gratitude on Venezuela's part, to honor gloriously, until the end of time, a race of virtuous, prudent, and persevering men who, overcoming every obstacle, have founded the Republic at the price of the most heroic sacrifices. And if the people of Venezuela do not applaud the elevation of their benefactors, then they are unworthy to be free, and they will never be free.

A hereditary senate, I repeat, will be the fundamental basis of the legislative power, and therefor the foundation of the entire government. It will also serve as a counterweight to both government and people; and as a neutral power it will weaken the mutual attacks of these two eternally rival powers. In all conflicts the calm reasoning of a third party will serve as the means of reconciliation. Thus the Venezuelan senate will give strength to this delicate political structure, so sensitive to violent repercussions; it will be the mediator that will lull the storms and it will maintain harmony between the head and the other parts of this political body.

No inducement could corrupt a legislative body invested with the highest honors, dependent only upon itself, having no fear of the people, independent of the government, and dedicated solely to the repression of all evil principles and to the advancement of every good principle—a legislative body that would be deeply concerned with the maintenance of a society, for it would share the consequences, be they honorable or disastrous. It has rightly been said that the upper house in England is invaluable to that nation because it provides a bulwark of liberty; and I would add that the Senate of Venezuela would be not only a bulwark of liberty but a bastion of defense, rendering the Republic eternal.

The British executive power possesses all the authority properly appertaining to a sovereign, but he is surrounded by a triple line of dams, barriers, and stockades. He is the head of the government, but his ministers and subordinates rely more upon law than upon his authority, as they are personally responsible, and not even decrees of royal authority can excempt them from this responsibility. The executive is commander in chief of the army and navy; he makes peace and declares war; but Parliament annually determines what sums are to be paid to these military forces. While the courts and judges are dependent on the executive power, the laws originate in and are made by Parliament. To neutralize the power of the King, his person is declared inviolable and sacred; but, while his head is left untouched, his hands are tied. The sovereign of England has three formidable rivals: his Cabinet, which is responsible to the people and to Parliament; the Senate, which, representing the nobility of which it is composed, defends the interests of the people; and the House of Commons, which serves as the representative body of the British people and provides them with a place in which to express their opinions. Moreover, as the judges are responsible for the enforcement of the laws, they do not depart from them; and the administrations of the exchequer, being subject to prosecution not only for personal infractions but also for those of the government, take care to prevent any misuse of public funds. No matter how closely we study the composition of the English executive power, we can find nothing to prevent its being judged as the most perfect model for a kingdom, for an aristocracy, or for a democracy. Give Venezuela such an executive power in the person of a president chosen by the people or their representatives, and you will have taken a great step toward national happiness.

No matter what citizen occupies this office, he will be aided by the Constitution, and therein being authorized to do good, he can do no harm, because his ministers will cooperate with him only insofar as he abides by the law. If he attempts to infringe upon the law, his own ministers will desert him, thereby isolating him from the Republic, and they will even bring charges against him in the Senate. The ministers, being responsible for any transgressions committed, will actually govern, since they must account for their actions. The obligation which this system places upon the officials closest to the executive power, that is, to take a most interested and active part in the governmental deliberations and to regard this department as their own, is not the smallest advantage of the system. Should the president be a man of no great talent or virtue, yet, notwithstanding his lack of these essential qualities, he will be able to discharge his duties satisfactorily, for in such a case the ministry, managing everything by itself, will carry the burdens of the state.

Although the authority of the executive power in England may appear to be extreme, it would, perhaps, not be excessive in the Republic of Venezuela. Here the Congress has tied the hands and even the heads of its men of state. This deliberative assembly has assumed a part of the executive functions, contrary to the maxim of Montesquieu, to wit: A representative assembly should exercise no active function. It should only make laws and determine whether or not those laws are enforced. Nothing is as disturbing to harmony among the powers of government as their intermixture. Nothing is more dangerous with respect to the people than a weak executive; and if a kingdom has deemed it necessary to grant the executive so many powers, then in a republic these powers are infinitely more indispensable.

The people of Venezuela already enjoy the rights that they may legitimately and easily exercise. Let us now, therefore, restrain the growth of immoderate pretensions which, perhaps, a form of government unsuited to our people might excite. Let us abandon the federal forms of government unsuited to us; let us put aside the triumvirate which holds the executive power and center it in a president. We must grant him sufficient authority to enable him to continue the struggle against the obstacles inherent in our recent situation, our present state of war, and every variety of foe, foreign and domestic, whom we must battle for some time to come. Let the legislature relinquish the powers that rightly belong to the executive; let it acquire, however, a new consistency, a new influence in the balance of authority. Let the courts be strengthened by increasing the stability and independence of the judges and by the establishment of juries and civil and criminal codes dictated, not by antiquity nor by conquering kings, but by the voice of Nature, the cry of Justice, and the genius of Wisdom.

II. GABINO BARREDA'S SPEECH (SEPTEMBER 16, 1867)

Fellow citizens: we have taken giant strides in summarizing Mexico's emancipation; we have brought to mind all of the struggles and painful crises through which our country has traversed beginning with those that brought separation from Spain to the others that restored its emancipation from foreign tutelage under which it was subjected. We have seen that none of those struggles or crises have helped eliminate the harmful elements from our social constitution [that is, the promonarchists and other conservatives]. We have likewise seen that, as a result of those painful but necessary crises, our full emancipation has gradually occurred too; that the assertion, made blindly or perversely by villainous politicians who deny to those conflicts signs of progress and incessant evolution, is wicked as it is irrational. Such politicians far too simply judge those conflicts as products of criminal aberrations or inexplicable delirium.

We have seen that two entire generations have sacrificed themselves to the present task of renovation and to the indispensable preparation of the materials necessary for reconstruction.

Moreover, the job is done; all the necessary elements for social reconstruction are gathered; all of the obstacles are razed; all of the moral, intellectual, or political forces that must offer their cooperation are at hand.

The foundation for the edifice is implanted. We have the Laws of the Reform which have placed us on the road to civilization farther ahead than any other people. We have a Constitution that has been a beacon which, amidst the tempestuous sea of invasion, everyone has sighted and taken as a source of consolation and as a guide, particularly for all the patriots who fought isolated and dispersed; it is a Constitution which, opening the gates to those innovations which experience may indicate as necessary, closes them to constitutional reform through revolution which is useless and imprudent, not to say criminal.

Now peace and order, maintained for an undefined period of time, will bring about everything that remains undone.

Fellow citizens: in the future let our motto be Liberty, Order, and Progress; Liberty as a means; Order as a base, and Progress as an end; it is a triple motto represented by the tricolor on our beautiful flag, that same flag which became in 1821 a blessed emblem of our independence in the hands of Guerrero and Iturbide; the emblem which, in the clutches of Zaragoza on May 5, 1862, assured the future of America and of the world by rescuing republican institutions.

In the future, may a complete freedom of conscience and an absolute freedom of expression permitting all ideas and inspirations, concede an enlightenment everywhere and make all disturbance not spiritual and all revolution which is not merely intellectual, unnecessary and impossible. May the physical order, conserved and maintained by all governors and respected by the governed, be a sure guarantor and the best way to walk forever along the florid path of progress and civilization.

III. INTERVIEW WITH PORFIRIO DIAZ (1908)

. . . I received this Government from the hands of a victorious army at a time when the people were divided and unprepared for the exercise of the extreme principles of democratic government. To have thrown upon the masses the whole responsibility of government at once would have produced conditions that might have discredited the cause of free government.

Yet, although I got power at first from the army, an election was held as soon as possible and then my authority came from the people. I have tried to leave the Presidency several times, but it has been pressed upon me and I remained in office for the sake of the nation which trusted me. The fact that the price of Mexican securities dropped eleven points when I was ill in Cuernavaca indicates the kind of evidence that persuaded me to overcome my personal inclination to retire from private life.

We preserved the republican and democratic form of government. We defended the theory and kept it intact. Yet we adopted a patriarchal policy in the administration of the nation's affairs, guiding the restraining popular tendencies, with full faith that an enforced peace would allow education, industry and commerce to develop elements of stability and unity in a naturally intelligent, gentle and affectionate people.

I have waited patiently for the day when the people of the Mexican Republic would be prepared to choose and change their government at every election without danger of armed revolutions and without injury to the national credit or interference with national progress. I believe the day has come.

. . .

. . . The principles of democracy have not been planted very deeply in our people, I fear. But the nation has grown and it loves liberty. Our difficulty has been that the people do not concern themselves enough about public matters for a democracy. The individual Mexican as a rule thinks much about his own rights and is always ready to assert them. But he does not think so much about the rights of others. He thinks of his privileges, but not of his duties. Capacity for self-restraint is the basis of democratic government, and self-restraint is possible only to those who recognize the rights of their neighbors.

The Indians, who are more than half of our population, care little for politics. They are accustomed to looking to those in authority for leadership instead of thinking for themselves. That is a tendency they inherited from the Spanish, who taught them to refrain from meddling in public affairs and rely on the Government for guidance.

Yet I firmly believe that the principles of democracy have grown and will grow in Mexico.

. . .

It is enough for me that I have seen Mexico rise among the peaceful and useful nations. I have no desire to continue in the Presidency. This nation is ready for her ultimate life of freedom. At the age of seventy-seven years I am satisfied with robust health. That is one thing which neither law nor force can create. I would not exchange it for all the millions of your American oil king.

. . .

The railway has played a great part in the peace of Mexico. . . . When I became President at first there were only two small lines, one connecting the capital with Vera Cruz, the other connecting it with Querétaro. Now we have more than 19,000 miles of railways. Then we had a slow and costly mail service, carried on by stage coaches, and the mail coach between the capital and Puebla would be stopped by highwaymen two or three times in a trip, the last robbers to attack it generally finding nothing left to steal. Now we have a cheap, safe and fairly rapid mail service throughout the country with more than twenty-two hundred post offices. Telegraphing was a difficult thing in those times. Today we have more than forty-five thousand miles of telegraph wires in operation.

We began by making robbery punishable by death and compelling the execution of offenders within a few hours after they were caught and condemned. We ordered that wherever telegraph wires were cut and the chief officer of the district did not catch the criminal, *he should himself suffer;* and in the case the cutting occurred on a plantation *the proprietor* who failed *to prevent it should be hanged* to the nearest telegraph pole [emphasis added]. These were military orders, remember.

We were harsh. Sometimes we were harsh to the point of cruelty. But it was all necessary then to the life and progress of the nation. If there was cruelty, results have justified it.

. . .

It was better that a little blood should be shed that much blood should be saved. The blood that was shed was bad blood; the blood that was saved was good blood.

Peace was necessary, even an enforced peace, that the nation might have time to think and work. Education and industry have carried on the task begun by the army.

. . .

. . . I want to see education throughout the Republic carried on by the national Government. I hope to see it before I die. It is important that all citizens of a republic should receive the same training, so that their ideals and methods may be harmonized and the national unity intensified. When men read alike and think alike they are more likely to act alike.

STUDY QUESTIONS

1. What is Bolivar's view of the common people of Venezuela?
2. What types of institutions does he recommend to rule these people? What type of legislature? What type of executive? Why are these types needed?
3. Who does Bolivar have in mind as the rightful rulers of Venezuela?
4. In Gabino Barreda's Independence Day speech he contrasts Mexico's past experiences and its future goals. How does he characterize Mexico's past? What are his goals for the future?
5. In what way did Porfirio Diaz, as ruler of Mexico, fulfill the ideas of Bolivar and Barreda? How did Diaz view the common people? What kind of government did he establish? How were his policies related to the economy? What was Diaz's goal for education?
6. Using these documents together: What were some of the key issues in Latin American politics in the nineteenth century?

31

Economy and Society of Latin America: Plantation Life in Cuba and Yucatan

During the period 1870–1914, many regions of Latin America became fully integrated into the world economy. Exports of raw materials, including minerals, oil, food products, and fibers, bound Latin America to the industrialized nations. Latin American nations became dependent on the industrial world's manufactured goods, markets for the export of raw materials, transportation, and credit.

The development of these economies altered patterns of work in the areas they affected. In Cuba sugar plantations expanded production to supply the growing populations of Europe and North America. Although processing and transportation became mechanized, sugar planting and harvesting remained handwork. The first selection, taken from the transcription of an oral history of a runaway slave, reveals the social conditions among the workers on the Cuban sugar plantations after abolition of slavery in 1886. The Spanish government granted abolition after a violent upheaval in Cuba known as the Ten Years War from 1868–1878, followed by intense pressure from foreign powers, especially Great Britain and the United States.

The second selection describes conditions on the henequen plantations of Yucatan. In contrast to sugar, the demand for henequen (a cactus-like plant) fibers was directly related to the Industrial Revolution in the United States. After a new knotting mechanism for grain binding had been invented for harvesting machines in 1878, the search for acceptable binder twine led directly to henequen in Yucatan. Cyrus McCormick, the developer of the mechanical reaper, imported hundreds of thousands of tons of henequen during the late nineteenth century. Exports from Yucatan increased from 40,000 bales in 1875 to 600,000 in 1910. In 1902, the same year that McCormick merged with other harvesting machine companies to form International Harvester, he also secretly negotiated with the governor of Yucatan to lower prices of henequen in return for steady purchases from the governor's export companies. With that agreement, International Harvester established its "informal empire" in Yucatan. The company neither needed to own its own land nor produce henequen directly.

Selection I from Esteban Montejo, *The Autobiography of a Runaway Slave,* edited by Miguel Barnet and translated from the Spanish by Jocasta Innes (New York: Random House, 1968), pp. 63–75, 96–97, 101–105. Selection II from Channing Arnold and Fredrick J. Tabor Frost, *American Egypt: A Record of Travel in Yucatan* (London: Hutchinson and Co., 1909), pp. 324–325, 361, 365–367.

Production was left in the hands of local landowners and merchants, who became fabulously wealthy and who also controlled the Yucatecan state government.

The expansion of henequen production also affected land tenure and labor relations. When henequen became king, new plantations absorbed Indian communal land and imposed on their workers a much stricter regime of work. Seedlings and young plants required constant attention until they matured in seven years and harvesting the leaves was done by hand. The need for labor on henequen left little time for traditional cultivation of the Mayan workers' plots of corn (*milpas*). Labor shortages also resulted in the importation of Yaqui Indians captured in Northern Mexico and Puerto Rican and Korean workers. But most of all, owners relied on the local Mayan *campesinos,* whether they wanted to work on the plantation or not.

PLANTATION LIFE IN CUBA AND YUCATAN

I. FORMER SLAVE'S LIFE ON A SUGAR PLANTATION AFTER ABOLITION: CUBA 1880'S

After all this time in the forest I had become half savage. I didn't want to work anywhere, and I was afraid they would shut me up again. I knew quite well that slavery had not ended completely. A lot of people asked me what I was doing and where I came from. Sometimes I told them, 'My name is Stephen and I was a runaway slave.' Other times I said I had been working on a certain plantation and could not find my relations. I must have been about twenty at the time. This was before I came across my relations. That happened later.

Since I did not know anyone I walked from village to village for several months. I did not suffer from hunger because people gave me food. You only had to say you were out of work and someone would always help you out. But you can't carry on like that for ever. I began to realise that work had to be done in order to sleep in a barracoon [slave quarter] at least. By the time I decided to cut cane, I had already covered quite a bit of ground. I know all the part north of Las Villas well. It is the prettiest part of Cuba. That was where I started work.

The first plantation I worked on was called Purio. I turned up there one day in the rags I stood in and a hat I had collected on the way. I went in and asked the overseer if there was work for me. He said yes. I remember he was Spanish, with moustaches, and his name was Pepe. There were overseers in these parts until quite recently, the difference being that they didn't lay about them as they used to do under slavery. But they were men of the same breed, harsh, overbearing. There were still barracoons after Abolition, the same as before. Many of them were newly built of masonry, the old ones having collapsed under the rain and storms. The barracoon at Purio was strong and looked as if it had been recently completed. They told me to go and live there. I soon made myself at home, for it wasn't too bad. They had taken the bolts off the doors and the workers themselves had cut holes in the walls for ventilation. They no longer had to worry about escapes or anything like that, for the Negroes were free now, or so they said. But I could not help noticing that bad things still went on. There were bosses who still believed that the blacks were created for locks and bolts and whips, and treated them as before. It struck me that many Negroes did not know that things had changed, because they went on saying, 'Give me your blessing, my master.'

Those ones never left the plantation at all. I was different in that I disliked having anything to do with the whites. They believed they were the lords of creation. At Purio I lived alone most of the time. I might have a concubine from Easter to San Juan's day; but women have always been selfish, and there wasn't a Christian soul alive who could support a black woman in those days. Though I do say that women are the greatest thing there is. I was never short of a black woman to say, 'I want to live with you.'

The work was exhausting. You spent hours in the fields and it seemed as if the work would never end. It went on and on until you were worn out. The overseers were always bothering you. Any worker who knocked off for long was taken off the job. I worked from six in the morning. The early hour did not bother me since in the forest it had been impossible to sleep late because of the cocks crowing. There was a break at eleven for lunch, which had to be eaten in the workers' canteen, usually standing because of the crowd of people squashed in. At one everyone went back to the fields. This was the worst and hottest time. Work ended at six in the afternoon. Then I would take myself off to the river, bathe for a while and go back to get something to eat. I had to hurry because the kitchen did not work at night.

Food cost around six pesos a month. They gave good portions, but it never varied: rice with black or white beans, or chick peas and jerked beef.

The Negroes who worked at Purio had almost all been slaves; they were so used to the life in the barracoon they did not even go out to eat. When lunch-time came they shut themselves up in their rooms to eat and the same with dinner. They did not go out at night. They were afraid of people, and they said they would get lost if they did, they were convinced of this. I wasn't like that—if I got lost I always found myself again. When I think of the times I got lost in the forest and couldn't find a river!

On Sundays all the workers who wanted to could work overtime. This meant that instead of resting you went to the fields and cleared, cleaned or cut cane. Or if not that, you stayed in, cleaning out the troughs or scraping the boilers. This would only be in the morning. As there was nothing special to do that day, all the workers used to go and earn themselves extra money. Money is a very evil thing. A person who gets used to earning a lot is on the road to ruination. I earned the same as the rest. The pay worked out at around twenty-four pesos, including food. Some plantations paid twenty-five.

There were still plenty of taverns around to spend one's cash in. There were two or three at Purio. I used to go into them for a drink now and then, and I also went there if I wanted to buy something. To tell the truth, the taverns weren't very nice places. Almost every day fights would break out because of rivalries or jealousy over women. At night there were fiestas, and anyone who wanted could go. They were held in the mill compound. There was enough room to dance, and the Negroes themselves sang the rumbas. The fun was in dancing and shouting and drinking.

In those days you could get either permanent or temporary work on the plantations. Those employed on a permanent basis had to keep to a time-table. This way they would live in the barracoons and did not need to leave the plantations for anything. I preferred being a permanent worker myself, because the other life was too troublesome. A man who decided to freelance would simply go along to a cane-field and, according to the amount of cane there, agree on a price . . . Those freelance workers were very sharp. They could rest whenever they felt like it, get a drink of water, and even took their women along to the cane-fields to lie with them. . . . Then the overseer came back and, if he was satisfied, they would go off with their money to the towns to wait till the cane grew again. If their money ran out quickly, they would find some way of getting work on another plantation. They lived like tramps, bedding in the smaller rooms of the barracoons. They hardly ever took their women to their rooms, but used to see them at night because they were allowed out after a day's work.

With us fixed-rate workers things were different. We couldn't go out at night because at nine o'clock we had to be ready for the silence bell.

The barracoons were a bit damp, but all the same they were safer than the forest. There were no snakes and all the workers slept in hammocks which were very comfortable, and one could wrap up well in the cold. Many of the barracoons were made of sacking. The one tiresome thing about them was the fleas; they didn't hurt, but you had to be up all night scaring them off with Spanish broom, which gets rid of fleas and ticks.

At Purio, as on all plantations, there were Africans of various countries, but the Congolese were in the majority. It's not for nothing they call all the region in the north of Las Villas 'the Congo'. At that time there were Filipinos, Chinese, Canary Islanders, and an increasing number of Creoles there as well. They all worked on the cane, clearing the ground with spades and machetes and earthing up. Earthing up means ploughing with a bullock and a tree-trunk on a chain to turn over the soil, just as under slavery.

Relations between the groups remained unchanged. The Filipinos were as criminal as before. The Canary Islanders did not speak; the only thing that existed for them was work, and they were as arrogant as ever. They took against me because I wouldn't make friends with them. One had to be careful of the Islanders, because they knew a lot of magic and they would do anyone a bad turn. I think they earned more than the Negroes, although they always used to say that everyone earned the same amount.

[Relations with Women and Children]

I felt better then than I do now. I had my youth. Now I still have my concubine from time to time, but it is not the same. A woman is a wonderful thing. Women, to tell the truth, are what I have got most pleasure from in my life. In the old days, when I was at Purio, I used to get up and go to the village on Sundays, always in the afternoons so as not to miss the morning's overtime, and sometimes I found myself a woman before even reaching the village.

This thing of going to the cane-fields to screw was a common practice, the people made use of the wagon track between the mill and the cane-fields. In those days you grabbed any woman and took her into the cane. There wasn't all the courtship there is now. If a woman went with a man she knew she would have to get down on her back. . . .

Casual relationships were more convenient. The women were free and they didn't have to get along with their parents. They worked in the fields, helping in the hoeing and sowing, and they went with a man when they felt like it. The easy-going fellows always went in for this kind of arrangement, one woman one day, another woman the next. I think this is the better way myself. I stayed free and didn't marry till I was old; I was a bachelor in many places. I knew women of all colours, proud women and kind ones.

If I count up all the women I had it seems that I must have had any number of children, but the strange thing is that I never knew of a single one. At least, none of the women who lived with me in the barracoon ever had any. The others, the women I took into the woods, used to come and say 'This boy is yours,' but how could you ever be certain with them? Besides, children were a big problem in those days. You couldn't educate them because there weren't any schools like there are now.

Little boys . . . were brought up wild and uneducated. The only thing they were taught was raising vegetables and hoeing; but no learning. They were often beaten, and if they went on being naughty they were made to kneel on grains of rice or corn. A whipping was the most common punishment. The parents came and then the boy was beaten with a birch or piece of braided rope until the blood ran. The cane was a green switch which never broke even when it was wielded violently enough to flay the skin. I believe I had sons, maybe many or maybe not, but I don't think I would ever have punished them like that.

Children were always playing truant. They would come scavenging round the houses to get out of work, and they often used to hide to escape from punishments their parents threatened them with.

II. WORK ON THE HENEQUEN PLANTATIONS OF YUCATAN

The Yucatecans have a cruel proverb, *"Los Indios no oigan sino por las nalgas"* ("The Indians can hear only with their backs"). The Spanish half-breeds have taken a race once noble enough and broken them on the wheel of tyranny so brutal that the heart of them is dead. The relations between the two peoples is ostensibly that of master and servant; but Yucatan is rotten with a foul slavery—the fouler and blacker because of its hypocrisy and pretence.

The peonage system of Spanish America, as specious and treacherous a plan as was ever devised for race-degradation, is that by which a farm labourer is legally bound to work for the land-owner, if in debt to him, until that debt is paid. Nothing could sound fairer: nothing could lend itself better to the blackest abuse. In Yucatan every Indian peon is in debt to his Yucatecan master. Why? Because every Indian is a spendthrift? Not at all; but because the master's interest is to get him and keep him in debt. This is done in two ways. The plantation-slave must buy the necessaries of his humble life at the plantation store, where care is taken to charge such prices as are beyond his humble earnings of sixpence a day. Thus he is always in debt to the farm; and if an Indian is discovered to be scraping together the few dollars he owes, the books of the hacienda are "cooked"—yes, deliberately "cooked"—and when he presents himself before the magistrate to pay his debt, say, of twenty dollars (£2) the haciendado can show scored against him a debt of fifty dollars. The Indian pleads he does not owe it. The haciendado-court smiles. The word of an Indian cannot prevail against the Señor's books, it murmurs sweetly, and back to his slave-work the miserable peon must go, first to be cruelly flogged to teach him that freedom is not for such as he, and that struggle as he may he will never escape the cruel master who under law as at present administered in Yucatan has as complete a disposal of his body as one of the pigs which root around in the hacienda yard.

Henequen (Spanish *jeniquen* or *geniquen*) is a fibre commercially known as Sisal hemp, from the fact that it is obtained from a species of cactus, the *Agave Sisalensis,* first cultivated around the tiny port of Sisal in the Yucatan. The older Indian name for the plant is *Agave Ixtli.* From its fleshy leaves is crushed out a fine fibre which, from the fact that it resists damp better than ordinary hemp, is valuable for making ships' cables, but the real wealth-producing use of which is so bizarre that no one in a hundred guesses would hit on it. It is used in the myriad corn-binding machines in America and Canada. They cannot use wire, and cheap string is too easily broken. Henequen is at once strong enough and cheap enough. Hence the piles of money heaping up to the credit of Yutatecans in the banks of Merida. . . .

[At the mill] three or four Indians set to work to arrange the leaves so that their black-pointed ends are all in one direction. Next these thorny points are severed by a machete and in small bundles of six or eight the leaves are handed to men who are feeding a sliding belt-like platform about a yard wide, and on this they are conveyed to the machine. Before they enter its great blunt-toothed, gaping jaws, they are finally arranged, as the sliding belt goes its unending round, so that they do not enter more than one at a time. Woe betide the Indian who has the misfortune to get his fingers in these revolving jaws of the gigantic crusher, and many indeed are there fingerless, handless, and armless from this cause. . . .

For there is money for everyone who touches the magic fibre except the miserable Indian, by whose never-ending labours the purse-proud monopolists of the Peninsula are enabled to be ever adding to their ill-gotten gold. There are in Yucatan to-day some 400 henequen plantations of from 25 to 20,000 acres, making the total acreage under cultivation some 140,000 acres. The cost of production, including shipping expenses, export duties, etc., is now about 7 pesos (14s.) per 100 kilogrammes. The average market price of henequen is 28 pesos per 100 kilogrammes, so the planter gets a return of 400 per cent. All this is obviously only possible as long as he can get slave-labour and the hideous truth about the exploitation of the Mayans is kept dark. The Indian gets a wage of 50 centavos for cutting a thousand leaves, and if he is to earn this in a day he must work ten hours. Near the big towns, 75 centavos are paid, but practically, on many haciendas, it is so managed that the labour is paid for by his bare keep.

STUDY QUESTIONS

1. How did the plantation workers' conditions change (or stay the same) after the abolition of slavery in 1886?
2. Identify the different types of workers on the sugar plantation. What were the relations among them?

3. What do the narrator's attitudes toward women and children suggest about family life on the plantation?
4. What are the ties that bound the peon to the henequen hacienda in Yucatan?
5. When and why did henequen become valuable?
6. What conditions contributed to the profitability of henequen exportation?
7. Describe the moral tone expressed by the Englishmen who wrote the document on Yucatan. What does this suggest about their attitudes toward Latin American cvilization in general?

32

Literature and Cultural Values: Civilization and Barbarism

Latin American intellectuals in the middle of the nineteenth century despaired about their new nations' turmoil and lack of progress. Examining their traditions, inherited partly from Iberian and partly from native American sources, they concluded that their societies lagged far behind Europe. To catch up, they strove for rapid Europeanization of their population and culture. They sought not only immigrants from England, France, and Germany but also adoption of their political and economic forms.

An exaggerated example of this type of literature is *Life in the Argentine Republic in the Days of the Tyrants; or, Civilization and Barbarism* by Domingo F. Sarmiento. Published in 1868, the same year that Sarmiento became president of Argentina, the book describes the long struggle (1816–1862) between nativist, tyrannical forces, represented in the book by Facundo Quiroga, the *caudillo* of La Rioja province, and the liberal, urban politicians of Buenos Aires. Sarmiento belonged to the Europeanizers. He joined a liberal faction opposing another of the tyrants, Juan Manuel de Rosas, the *caudillo* of Buenos Aires province, who ruled the city and the province with extreme brutality from 1829 to 1852. Exiled to Chile in 1833, Sarmiento conspired with opponents of Rosas until he was overthrown in 1852. Ten years of civil war followed Rosas's fall. Bartolomé Mitre, the leader of a new army from Buenos Aires, allied with certain interior chieftains and finally defeated the worst of the old-style *caudillos* in 1862. In the 1860s Mitre and Sarmiento began the institutionalization of stable government, based on North American and European forms, and also opened Argentina to European immigrants.

ARGENTINA

Description of Lower Classes

In these long journeys, the lower classes of the Argentine population acquire the habit of living far from society, of struggling single-handed with nature, of disregarding privation, and of depending for protection against the dangers ever imminent upon no other resources than personal strength and skill.

From Domingo F. Sarmiento, *Life in the Argentine Republic in the Days of the Tyrants: or, Civilization and Barbarism* (New York: Hafner Publishing Co., 1960), pp. 10–11, 112, 122–123, 126–127, 161–162, 250. Reprinted by permission of Simon and Schuster, Inc.

The people who inhabit these extensive districts, belong to two different races, the Spanish and the native; the combinations of which form a series of imperceptible gradations. The pure Spanish race predominates in the rural districts of Cordova and San Luis, where it is common to meet young shepherdesses fair and rosy, and as beautiful as the belles of a capital could wish to be. In Santiago del Estero, the bulk of the rural population still speaks the Quichua dialect, which plainly shows its Indian origin. The country people of Corrientes use a very pretty Spanish dialect. "Dame, general, una chiripà," said his soldiers to Lavalle. The Andalusian soldier may still be recognized in the rural districts of Buenos Ayres; and in the city foreign surnames are the most numerous. The negro race, by this time nearly extinct (except in Buenos Ayres), has left, in its zambos and mulattoes, a link which connects civilized man with the denizen of the woods. This race mostly inhabiting cities, has a tendency to become civilized, and possesses talent and the finest instincts of progress.

With these reservations, a homogeneous whole has resulted from the fusion of the three above-named families. It is characterized by love of idleness and incapacity for industry, except when education and the exigencies of a social position succeed in spurring it out of its customary pace. To a great extent, this unfortunate result is owing to the incorporation of the native tribes, effected by the process of colonization. The American aborigines live in idleness, and show themselves incapable, even under compulsion, of hard and protracted labor. This suggested the idea of introducing negroes into America, which has produced such fatal results. But the Spanish race has not shown itself more energetic than the aborigines, when it has been left to its own instincts in the wilds of America. Pity and shame are excited by the comparison of one of the German or Scotch colonies in the southern part of Buenos Ayres and some towns of the interior of the Argentine Republic; in the former the cottages are painted, the front-yards always neatly kept and adorned with flowers and pretty shrubs; the furniture simple but complete; copper or tin utensils always bright and clean; nicely curtained beds; and the occupants of the dwelling are always industriously at work. Some such families have retired to enjoy the conveniences of city life, with great fortunes gained by their previous labors in milking their cows, and making butter and cheese. The town inhabited by natives of the country, presents a picture entirely the reverse. There, dirty and ragged children live, with a menagerie of dogs; there, men lie about in utter idleness; neglect and poverty prevail everywhere; a table and some baskets are the only furniture of wretched huts remarkable for their general aspect of barbarism and carelessness.

On Buenos Aires

In 1777, Buenos Ayres had already become very conspicuous, so much so, indeed, that it was necessary to remould the administrative geography of the colonies, and to make Buenos Ayres the chief section. A viceroyal government was expressly created for it.

In 1806, the attention of English speculators was turned to South America, and especially attracted to Buenos Ayres by its river, and its probable future. In 1810, Buenos Ayres was filled with partisans of the revolution, bitterly hostile to anything originating in Spain or any part of Europe. A germ of progress, then, was still alive west of the La Plata. The Spanish colonies cared nothing for commerce or navigation. The Rio de la Plata was of small importance to them. The Spanish disdained it and its banks. As time went on, the river proved to have deposited its sediment of wealth upon those banks, but very little of Spanish spirit or Spanish modes of government. Commercial activity had brought thither the spirit and the general ideas of Europe; the vessels which frequented the waters of the port brought books from all quarters, and news of all the political events of the world. It is to be observed that Spain had no other commercial city upon the Atlantic coast. The war with England hastened the emancipation of men's minds and awakened among them a sense of their own importance as a state. Buenos Ayres was like a child, which, having conquered a giant, fondly deems itself a hero, and is ready to undertake greater adventures. The *Social Contract* flew from hand to hand. Mably and Raynal were the oracles of the press; Robespierre and the Convention the approved models. Buenos Ayres thought itself a continuation of Europe, and if it did not frankly confess that its spirit and tendencies were French and North American, it denied its Spanish origin on the ground that the Spanish Government had patronized it only after it was full grown. The revolution brought with it armies and glory, triumphs and reverses, revolts and seditions. But Buenos Ayres, amidst all these fluctuations, displayed the revolutionary energy with which it is endowed. . . .

Communication with all the European nations was ever, even from the outset, more complete here than in any other part of Spanish America; and now, in ten years' time (but only, be it understood, in Buenos Ayres), there comes to pass a radical replacement of the Spanish by the European spirit. We have only to take a list of the residents in and about Buenos Ayres to see how many natives of the country bear English, French, German, or Italian surnames.

Difference between Bernadino Rivadavia, Liberal President of Argentina (1826–1827),
and Juan Manuel de Rosas, dictator of Buenos Aires Province (1829–1852)

Thus elevated, and hitherto flattered by fortune, Buenos Ayres set about making a constitution for itself and the Republic, just as it had undertaken to liberate itself and all South America: that is, eagerly, uncompromisingly, and without regard to obstacles. Rivadavia was the personification of this poetical, utopian spirit which prevailed. He therefore continued the work of Las Heras upon the large scale necessary for a great American State—a republic. He brought over from Europe men of learning or the press and for the professor's chair, colonies for the deserts, ships for the rivers, freedom for all creeds, credit and the national bank to encourage trade, and all the great social theories of the day for the formation of his government. In a word, he brought a second Europe, which was to be established in America, and to accomplish in ten years what elsewhere had required centuries. Nor was this project altogether chimerical; all his administrative creations still exist, except those which the barbarism of Rosas found in its way. Freedom of conscience, advocated by the chief clergy of Buenos Ayres, has not been repressed; the European population is scattered on farms throughout the country, and takes arms of its own accord to resist the only obstacle in the way of the wealth offered by the soil. The rivers only need to be freed from governmental restrictions to become navigable, and the national bank, then firmly established, has saved the people from the poverty to which the tyrant would have brought them. And, above all, however fanciful and impracticable that great system of government may have been, it was at least easy and endurable for the people; and, notwithstanding the assertions of misinformed men,

Rivadavia never shed a drop of blood, nor destroyed the property of any one; but voluntarily descended from the Presidency to poverty and exile. Rosas, by whom he was so calumniated, might easily have been drowned in the blood of his own victims; and the forty millions of dollars from the national treasury, with the fifty millions from private fortunes which were consumed in ten years of the long war provoked by his brutalities, would have been employed by the "*fool*—the *dreamer*—Rivadavia," in building canals, cities, and useful public buildings. Then let this man, who died for his country, have the glory of representing the highest aspirations of European civilization, and leave to his adversaries that of displaying South American barbarism in its most odious light. For Rosas and Rivadavia are the two extremes of the Argentine Republic, connecting it with savages through the pampas, and with Europe through the River La Plata.

Description of Tyrant Facundo Quiroga

Facundo is now in possession of La Rioja, its umpire and absolute master; no other voice is heard there, no other interest than his exists there. As there is no literature, there are no opposing opinions. La Rioja is a military machine. . . .

Facundo, ignorant, barbarous, for the greater part of his life an outlaw, and famous only for his acts of desperation; brave to rashness, endowed with herculean strength, always upon his horse, which he managed skillfully through terror and violence, knowing no other power than that of brute force, had no faith but in his horse, and depended for success upon bravery, the lance, and the terrible charges of his cavalry. In all the Argentine Republic there was not a more perfect specimen of the "*gaucho malo.*"

"When the Ignorant Rule"

Obscure men who rise to power through the chances of social revolutions, never fail to persecute in others the intelligence and knowledge which they have not themselves; when the ignorant rule, civilization is brought down to their own level, and woe to those who rise above it, be it ever so little. In France, in 1793, the sovereign people guillotined those who could read and write as aristocrats; in the Argentine Republic, men of culture were called *savages*, and had their throats cut, and though the name seems mere irony, it is something more when applied by the assassin, knife in hand. The Caudillos of the interior rid their provinces of all lawyers, doctors, and men of letters; and Rosas pursued them even within the walls of the university and private schools. Those who were allowed to remain were such persons as could be useful in getting up a repetition of the government of Philip II of Spain, and of the Inquisition.

STUDY QUESTIONS

1. What types of people, including rulers, are described positively? Negatively? What was Sarmiento's basis for judgment?
2. What cultural balues are expressed in Sarmiento's views of the people of Argentina? How might these views shape the development of Latin American civilization?

33

The Decades of Imperialism in Africa

The four selections in this chapter all date from the period 1880 to 1910. This was the great age of European imperialism in Africa, when virtually all available territory was swept up by the British, French, Germans, or Belgians. African political and economic life was transformed by the inescapable European presence.

The first document comes from German southwest Africa. It is unusual because it was written in Swahili by an African trader. A prosaic account of theft on a trip to an inland tribal village, the statement shows how some Africans and their new rulers could interact to apparent mutual benefit.

The second document briefly describes the new work system the Europeans brought. It uses the derogatory term *kaffir,* taken from the Arab word for pagan, to describe labor in the British-controlled mines in South Africa, while at the same time it claims great benefits from the jobs. The vantage point is that of an owner and Westerner. What might the workers have thought of this system?

The third document, also from British-controlled southern Africa, describes a characteristic legal arrangement used to deprive African chiefs of their land. It was carried through by agents of Cecil Rhodes. By granting full powers to the concession holders, this land-use agreement made later incorporation into the British Empire possible.

The fourth document, from French-held Mali in the region below the Sahara, was issued in 1890 by a French military commander who let no African stand in his way. The arrangement described was meant to regularize a local government, in part by playing different groups against each other, while disclaiming French power. What roles were reserved for the imperialist forces?

Selection I from "The Uses of Colonial Government," in *Swahili Prose Texts: A Selection from the Material Collected by Carl Velten from 1893 to 1896,* edited and translated by Lyndon Harries (Oxford: Oxford University Press, 1965), pp. 243–244. Copyright © 1965 by Oxford University Press. Reprinted by permission. Selection II from John Noble, *Official Handbook: History, Production, and the Resources of the Cape of Good Hope,* 2nd ed. (Cape Town, 1886), pp. 194–195. Selection III from Sir Lewis Michell, *The Life of the Right Honourable Cecil John Rhodes,* Vol. I (London: 1910), pp. 244–245. Selection IV from John D. Hargreaves, ed., *France and West Africa* (London: St. Martin's Press, Inc., 1969), pp. 198–199. Copyright © 1969 by St. Martin's Press, Inc. Reprinted by permission.

Collectively, the documents on the imperialist impact raise a number of basic questions. How did the Europeans view Africans at this point? How did imperialist penetration and controls compare with earlier colonial outposts described in Chapter 15? What accounts for the change? Finally, how would Africans perceive the new imperialism, and how might their reactions differ?

Imperialism is recent in African history. Understanding its impact, its limitations, and the responses it provoked is vital to a grasp of African patterns even after imperialism subsided.

AFRICAN IMPERIALISM

I. AN AFRICAN ACCOUNT: THE USES OF COLONIAL GOVERNMENT

We consulted together, saying, "Brothers, hadn't we better get going? We talk, and this pagan does not hear. Perhaps he will change his mind and seek to kill us? Our property is lost, and shall not our souls be lost?" Some said, "Shall we not go to Karema and inform the European, because Chata has robbed us? Now when shall we get out of here? It is no good leaving in the daytime, for perhaps the tribesmen will follow us to get us on the way and kill us; we had better go to the Chief and tell him, We agree to what you say, keep our property safe, and we are going to look for Matumla."

We agreed and went to the Chief and told him what we intended, and he said, "Isn't that just what I wanted? Very well, take a hut and go to rest, do not be afraid; sleep until morning, let us take proper leave of one another, and I will give you food for the way [enough] until you arrive at your place [your destination]." And we sat disconsolately, being sorry for our property which was lost and for our brethren who were dead. It was without any proper reason.

In the morning we reached Karema, and we found the European still in bed. . . . So when the Bwana came, we told him, "Bwana, we have been attacked." And he asked, "Who has attacked you?" We replied, "Chata." And he said to us, "But haven't I said that all traders should first come to me! What did you go to do at the pagan's? But never mind, I will send soldiers to make enquiry why you traders have been robbed. And you provide one person from among you to go along with my soldier, so that he can listen to what my soldier says with Chata, and so that you yourselves may hear about it."

So they set off for Chata's place. The soldiers said to him, "You Chata, so now you have become a man who robs people of their property? Aren't you afraid of government rule?" And he said, "I did not attack them for nothing; I attacked them because of Matumla taking my property, twenty pieces of ivory." The soldiers told him, "Oh no, we don't agree, bring the traders' property, that is what the District Officer told us [you must do]." When he saw their superior strength he took out the stuff and gave it to the soldiers, and they brought it to Karema, all that was left of our goods.

When they reached Karema, the European called us [saying], "You traders, come here, come and look at your property, is this what Chata took?" We looked at it and told him, "Yes, Bwana, some more was lost in the fire." And he said, "Never mind, take this which is left."

II. AFRICAN WORK IN SOUTH AFRICA'S DIAMOND MINES

Kaffir labour is mainly employed in all the less responsible operations of the mines: in drilling holes for the dynamite cartridges, in picking and breaking up the ground in the claims and *trucking* it away from the depositing boxes and the margin on the mine and tipping it on the depositing floors, where it undergoes a variety of processes before it is ready for washing, and is again filled into trucks and driven to the machines. For every three truckloads of ground daily hauled out of the mine there is on an average one Kaffir labourer employed, and to every five Kaffirs there is one white overseer or artizan. In 1882 the number of native labourers at Kimberley mine was 4,000; but in 1884, owing to the serious stoppage of works, they had sunk to 1,500. These labourers are recruited from 16 or 20 different native tribes from various part of the Colony and the Interior, the proportion of the several tribes at any time on the Fields varying greatly according to the internal state, whether of peace or war, of the district whence they hail. Out of 20,000 natives arriving in search of work in the first half of 1882, 8,000 were Secocoeni's Basutos, 6,000 Shangaans, 1,500 British Basutos, and 1,000 Zulus, the balance consisting of representatives of no less than 16 other different tribes and races. The market afforded for the employment of native labour and the consequent development of native trade is not the least of the incidental benefits conferred on South Africa by the discovery of the Diamond Fields.

III. AN IMPERIALIST CONTRACT: AN ECONOMIC PACT WITH A REGIONAL KING

Know all men by these presents, that whereas Charles Dunell Rudd, of Kimberley; Rochfort Maguire, of London; and Francis Robert Thompson, of Kimberley, hereinafter called the grantees, have covenanted and agreed, and do hereby covenant and agree, to pay to me, my heirs and successors, the sum of one hundred pounds sterling, British currency, on the first day of every lunar month; and, further, to deliver at my royal kraal one thousand Martini-Henry breech-loading rifles, together with one hundred thousand rounds of suitable ball cartridge, five hundred of the said rifles and fifty thousand of the said cartridges to be ordered from England forthwith and delivered with reasonable dispatch, and the remainder of the said rifles and cartridges to be delivered as soon as the said grantees shall have commenced to work mining machinery within my territory; and further, to deliver on the Zambesi River a steamboat with guns suitable for defensive purposes upon the said river, or in lieu of the said steamboat, should I so elect to pay to me the sum of five hundred pounds sterling, British currency. On the execution of these presents, I, Lo Bengula, King of Matabeleland, Mashonaland, and other adjoining territories, in exercise of my council of indunas, do hereby grant and assign unto the said grantees, their heirs, representatives, and assigns, jointly and severally, the complete and exclusive charge over all metals and minerals situated and contained in my kingdoms, principalities, and dominions, together with full power to do all things that they may deem necessary to win and procure the same, and to hold, collect, and enjoy the profits and revenues, if any, derivable from the said metals and minerals, subject to the aforesaid payment; and whereas I have been much molested [of] late by diverse persons seeking and desiring to obtain grants and concessions of land and mining rights in my territories, I do hereby authorise the said grantees, their heirs, representatives, and assigns, to take all necessary and lawful steps to exclude from my kingdom, principalities, and dominions all persons seeking land, metals, minerals, or mining rights therein, and I do hereby undertake to render them all such needful assistance as they may from time to time require for the exclusion of such persons, and to grant no concessions of land or mining rights from and after this date without their consent and concurrence; provided that, if at any time the said monthly payment of one hundred pounds shall cease [the agreement's end dates from] the last-made payment.

IV. THE FRENCH ARRANGE LOCAL GOVERNMENT

I have had you brought here to explain to you the French way of doing things. The French have not come to Ségou to take the country and govern it themselves, but with the intention of restoring it to the Bambaras, from whom it was stolen by the Tukolors. . . .

I am going to give Ségou to the son of your ancient kings. As from today your *Fama* will be Mari-Diara; but on certain conditions which will provide us with guarantees that the welfare of the country will be assured, that trade will be free, and that the Bambaras of the right bank will not be pillaged as were those of the left bank, where Mari-Diara was recently living.

To ensure this, the Commandant Supérieur will firstly station a white officer here, with troops. This Resident will reside in the *dionfoutou* of Ahmadu. Part of the fort will be demolished so that the Resident can have a private gate leading out of the village, and a view over the Niger.

The French Resident will not concern himself with administrative problems between the *Fama* and his villages. The *Fama* will exercise all his rights, will appoint or change chiefs as he thinks fit, but the Resident will have the right to be kept fully informed on all matters and to know everything that takes place.

He may help the *Fama* maintain order in the country by giving him military support, with his troops. . . . But the *Fama* will not have the right to make war or undertake negotiations in neighbouring countries without authorisation from the Resident. If such actions should be undertaken without the Resident's approval, the *Fama* would have to meet all the costs, and accept all the consequences. The Resident would not help him, but would report to the Commandant Supérieur, who is to decide whether the *Fama* has acted wisely or must be reprimanded. . . .

The Tukolors must leave the country within three days after the departure of the Commandant Supérieur; Major Colonna de Giovellina will protect their convoy. After that date the Bambaras may massacre those who remain behind.

STUDY QUESTIONS

1. What gains did Europeans think they were bringing to Africa through imperialism?
2. How did Europeans treat local rulers?

3. Why did Europeans find it appropriate to relegate Africans to low-level, dangerous, and low-paying jobs? What is the evidence on this subject in the Kimberley mines document?
4. What do these imperialist documents suggest about the effects of European conquest on Africa and Africans at the end of the nineteenth century?

Comparisons

34

The Spread of Mass Education: Sources and Comparisons

One of the most striking developments in Western European and North American society in the nineteenth century was the unprecedented proliferation of education for the children of almost all social classes, both boys and girls. Education spread for several reasons: Enlightenment ideals, now influencing other political movements such as liberalism, argued that education would lead to progress, as children were open vessels that could be filled with knowledge. The advance of scientific discoveries led to a new belief in the importance of providing at least some groups with training in science and technology. The same held true, if a bit more vaguely, for the social sciences and history. Growing commitment to more democratic voting systems generated concern for training children to be good citizens; many people hoped that education would keep the lower classes away from dangerous doctrines such as socialism. The Industrial Revolution, although it actively involved child labor in its early stages, ultimately contributed to a redefinition of childhood: Simpler work processes were increasingly accomplished by machines, making child labor less necessary, while humanitarian concerns also prompted movements to withdraw young children from the labor force. Schools, here, could serve as an alternative source of supervision for children.

Many countries began to expand school systems in the early decades of the nineteenth century. By the 1830s, some American states, such as Massachusetts, were making primary education obligatory, at least in principle. American schools had the additional function of teaching immigrant children "American ways"—including the English language. School attendance and literacy began to increase rapidly.

Selection I from Horace Mann, *On the Education of Free Men* (New York: Columbia University Press, 1987), pp. 49–59. Selection II from Noah Webster, *The American Spelling Book* (Lexington, Ky.: W.W. Worsley, 1831), pp. 53–57. Selection III from *The Autobiography of Yukichi Fukuzawa*, translated by Eüchi Kiyooka (New York: Columbia University Press, 1966), pp. 214–217. Selection IV from *Sources of Japanese Tradition II*, edited by Ryusaku Tsunoda, W. T. de Bary, and Donald Keene (New York: Columbia University Press, 1958), pp. 139–140, 189–191.

Western educational systems were an obvious exemplar for leaders in other societies who wanted to set the basis for industrial development and political change. Many Latin American liberals, for example, pushed for extensions of school systems by the later nineteenth century. One of the most important instances of educational change occurred in Japan. As the Japanese began to discuss the need for significant reform, in the wake of Western pressure to open Japan to international trade after 1853, education provided a key target. Japanese visitors to the West quickly seized on the importance of schools in providing the basis for new technical skills. Japan already had an extensive Confucian school system and considerable literacy, which helped highlight both the importance and the feasibility of further educational development. In 1872 the nation enacted a compulsory primary school system, and although it took almost 20 years to translate law into reality, educational expansion, and with it mass literacy, occurred very rapidly.

With all this, debates over the purposes of actual educational systems were intense, and often inconsistent. These selections suggest the flavor of nineteenth-century discussions about education in the United States and Japan, during crucial decades in which mass primary schools were being established (1830s to 1840s in the United States, 1870s to 1890s in Japan). Discussions in each country revealed far more concern about using education as a means of controlling and indoctrinating children than might be imagined from resounding invocations of education for democracy or for the advance of scientific understanding.

Both Japanese and American educators sought to instill moral guidance, using schools to supplement or replace older sources of authority. Divisions occurred between reformers and more conservative moralists—although contradictions might emerge even within a single reform statement. At the same time, Japanese and American debates were not identical. What Americans meant by moralization and control differed from what Japanese conservatives intended.

Two documents from each country follow. Horace Mann (1796–1859) was a reform leader in Massachusetts; the following passages are taken from reports he issued as head of the state Board of Education between 1839 and 1846. The second American document is a passage from Noah Webster's spelling book in 1831. Yukichi Fukuzawa (1834–1904) was Japan's leading educational reformer, and traveled widely in the West beginning in 1860. His ideas had a profound effect on Japanese schools, and he describes his principles in his *Autobiography,* published in 1899. But reform currents and Western guidance provoked a reaction from conservatives in the government beginning in 1878; the second document reflects an anti-Western current, in the Imperial Rescript of 1890.

AMERICAN AND JAPANESE EDUCATION

I. HORACE MANN, *THE GOALS OF EDUCATION*

The preservation of order, together with the proper despatch of business requires a mean, between the too much and the too little, in all the evolutions of the school, which it is difficult to hit. When classes leave their seats for the recitation-stand, and return to them again, or when the different sexes have a recess, or the hour of intermission arrives;—if there be not some order and succession of movement, the school will be temporarily converted into a promiscuous rabble, giving both the temptation and the opportunity for committing every species of indecorum and aggression. In order to prevent confusion, on the other hand, the operations of the school may be conducted with such military formality and procrastination:—the second scholar not being allowed to leave his seat, until the first has reached the door, or the place of recitation, and each being made to walk on tiptoe to secure silence,—that a substantial part of every school session will be wasted, in the wearisome pursuit of an object worth nothing when obtained.

When we reflect, how many things are to be done each half day, and how short a time is allotted for their performance, the necessity of system in regard to all the operations of the school, will be apparent. System compacts labor; and when the hand is to be turned to an almost endless variety of particulars, if system does not preside over the whole series of movements, the time allotted to each will be spent in getting ready to perform it. With lessons to set; with so many classes to hear; with difficulties to explain; with the studious to be assisted; the idle to be spurred; the transgressors to be admonished or corrected; with the goers and comers to observe; —with all these things to be done, no considerable progress can be made, if one part of the wheel is not coming up to the work, while another is going down. And if order do not pervade the school, as a whole, and in all its parts, all is lost; and this is a very difficult thing;—for it seems as though the school were only a point, rescued out of a chaos that still encompasses it, and is ready, on the first opportunity, to break in and reoccupy its ancient possession. As it is utterly impracticable for any committee to prepare a code of regulations coextensive with all the details, which belong to the management of a school, it must be left with the teacher; and hence the necessity of skill in this item of the long list of his qualifications.

The government and discipline of a school demands [*sic*] qualities still more rare, because the consequences of error, in these, are still more disastrous. What caution, wisdom, uprightness, and sometimes, even intrepidity, are necessary in the administration of punishment. After all other means have been tried, and tried in vain, the chastisement of pupils found to be otherwise incorrigible, is still upheld by law, and sanctioned by public opinion. . . . The discipline of former times was inexorably stern and severe, and even if it were wished, it is impossible now to return to it. The question is, what can be substituted, which, without its severity, shall have its efficiency.

In the contemplation of the law, the school committee are sentinels stationed at the door of every schoolhouse in the State, to see that no teacher ever crosses its threshold, who is not clothed, from the crown of his head to the sole of his foot, in garments of virtue; and they are the enemies of the human race,—not of contemporaries only, but of posterity,—who, from any private or sinister motive, strive to put these sentinels to sleep, in order that one, who is profane, or intemperate, or addicted to low associations, or branded with the stigma of any vice, may elude the vigilance of the watchmen, and be installed over the pure minds of the young, as their guide and exemplar. If none but teachers of pure tastes, of good manners, of exemplary morals, had ever gained admission into our schools, neither the school rooms, nor their appurtenances would have been polluted, as some of them now are, with such ribald inscriptions, and with the carvings of such obscene emblems, as would make a heathen blush. Every person, therefore, who endorses another's character, as one befitting a school teacher, stands before the public as his moral bondsman and sponsor, and should be held to a rigid accountability. . . .

One of the highest and most valuable objects, to which the influences of a school can be made conducive, consists in training our children to self-government. . . . So tremendous, too, are the evils of anarchy and lawlessness, that a government by mere force, however, arbitrary and cruel, has been held preferable to no-government. But self-government, self-control, a voluntary compliance with the laws of reason and duty, have been justly considered as the highest point of excellence attainable by a human being. No one, however, can consciously obey the laws of reason and duty, until he understands them. Hence the preliminary necessity of their being clearly explained, of their being made to stand out, broad, lofty, and as conspicuous as a mountain against a clear sky. There may be blind obedience without a knowledge of the law, but only of the will of the lawgiver; but the first step towards rational obedience is a knowledge of the rule to be obeyed, and of the reasons on which it is founded.

The above doctrine acquires extraordinary force, in view of our political institutions,—founded, as they are, upon the great idea of the capacity of man for self-government,—an idea so long denounced by the state as treasonable, and by the church as heretical. In order that men may be prepared for self-government, their apprenticeship must commence in childhood. The great moral attribute of self-government cannot be born and matured in a day; and if school children are not trained to it, we only prepare ourselves for disappointment, if we expect it from grown men. Everybody acknowledges the justness of the declaration, that a foreign people, born and bred and dwarfed under the despotisms of the Old World, cannot be transformed into the full stature of American citizens, merely by a voyage across the Atlantic, or by subscribing the oath of naturalization. If they retain the servility in which they have been trained, some self-appointed lord or priest, on this side of the water, will succeed to the authority of the master they have left behind them. If, on the other hand, they identify liberty with an absence from restraint, and an immunity from punishment, then they are liable to become intoxicated and delirious with the highly stimulating properties of the air of freedom; and thus, in either case, they remain unfitted, until they have been morally acclimated to our institutions, to exercise the rights of a freeman. But can it make any substantial difference, whether a man is suddenly translated into all the independence and prerogatives of an American citizen, from the bondage of an Irish lord or an English manufacturer, or from the equally rigorous bondage of a parent, guardian, or school teacher? He who has been a serf until the day before he is twenty-one years of age, cannot be an independent citizen the day after; and it makes no difference whether he has been a serf in Austria or in America. As the fitting apprenticeship for despotism consists in being trained to despotism, so the fitting apprenticeship for self-government consists in being trained to self-government; and liberty and self-imposed law are as appropriate a preparation for the subjects of an arbitrary power, as the law of force and authority is for developing and maturing those sentiments of self-respect, of honor, and of dignity, which belong to a truly republican citizen. . . . Now, for the high purpose of training an American child to become an American citizen,—a constituent part of a self-governing people,—is it not obvious that, in all cases, the law by which he is to be bound should be made intelligible to him; and, as soon as his capacity will permit, that the reasons on which it is founded, should be made as intelligible as the law itself?

II. NOAH WEBSTER, *THE AMERICAN SPELLING BOOK*

Additional Lessons. Domestic Economy, Or, the History of Thrifty and Unthrifty

There is a great difference among men, in their ability to gain property; but a still greater difference in their power of using it to advantage. Two men may acquire the same amount of money, in a given time; yet one will prove to be a poor man, while the other becomes rich. A chief and essential difference in the management of property, is, that one man spends only the *interest* of his money, while another spends the *principal.* I know a farmer by the name of *Thrifty,* who manages his affairs in this manner: He rises early in the morning, looks to the condition of his house, barn, homelot, and stock—sees that his cattle, horses, and hogs are fed; examines the tools to see whether they are all in good order for the workmen—takes care that breakfast is ready in due season, and begins work in the cool of the day—When in the field, he keeps steadily at work, though not so violently as to fatigue and exhaust the body—nor does he stop to tell or hear long stories—When the labor of the day is past, he takes refreshment, and goes to rest at an early hour—In this manner he earns and gains money.

When *Thrifty* has acquired a little property, he does not spend it or let it slip from him, without use or benefit. He pays his taxes and debts when due or called for, so that he has not officers' fees to pay, nor expenses of court. He does not frequent the tavern, and drink up all his earnings in liquor that does him no good. He puts his money to use, that is, he buys more land, or stock, or lends his money at interest—in short, he makes his money produce some profit or income. These savings and profits, though small by themselves, amount in a year to a considerable sum, and in a few years they swell to an estate—*Thrifty* becomes a wealthy farmer, with several hundred acres of land, and a hundred head of cattle.

Very different is the management of *unthrifty:* He lies in bed till a late hour in the morning—then rises, and goes to the bottle for a dram, or to the tavern for a glass of bitters—Thus he spends six cents before breakfast late, when he ought to be at work. When he supposes he is ready to begin the work of the day, he finds he has not the necessary tools, or some of them are out of order,—the plow-share is to be sent half a mile to a blacksmith to be mended; a tooth or two in a rake or the handle of a hoe is broke; or a sythe or an ax is to be ground.—Now, he is in a great hurry, he bustles about to make preparation for work—and what is done in a hurry is ill done—he loses a part of the day in getting ready—and perhaps the time of his workmen. At ten or eleven o'clock, he is ready to go to work—then comes a boy and tells him, the sheep have escaped from the pasture—or the cows have got among his corn—or the hogs into the garden—He frets and storms, and runs to drive them out—a half hour or more time is lost in driving the cattle from mischief, and repairing a poor old broken fence—a fence that answers no purpose but to lull him into security, and teach his horses and cattle to be unruly—After all this bustle, the fatigue of which is worse than common labor, *Unthrifty* is ready to begin a day's work at twelve o'clock.—Thus half his time is lost in supplying defects, which proceed from want of foresight and good management. His small crops are damaged or destroyed by unruly cattle.—His barn is open and leaky, and what little he gathers, is injured by the rain and snow.—His house is in a like condition—the shingles and clapboards fall off and let in the water, which causes the timber, floors, and furniture to decay—and exposed to inclemencies of weather, his wife and children fall sick—their time is lost, and the mischief closes with a ruinous train of expenses for medicines and physicians.—After dragging out some years of disappointment, misery, and poverty, the lawyer and the sheriff sweep away the scanty remains of his estate. This is the history of *unthrifty*—his principal is spent—he has no interest.

Not unlike this, is the history of the Grog-drinker. This man wonders why he does not thrive in the world; he cannot see the reason why his neighbor *Temperance* should be more prosperous than himself—but in truth, he makes no calculations. Ten cents a day for grog is a small sum, he thinks, which can hurt no man! But let us make an estimate—arithmetic is very useful for a man who ventures to spend small sums every day. Ten cents a day amounts in a year to thirty-six dollars and a half—a sum sufficient to buy a good farm-horse! This surely is no small sum for a farmer or mechanic—But in ten years, this sum amounts to three hundred and sixty-five dollars, besides interest in the mean time! What an amount is this for drams and bitters in ten years! It is money enough to build a small house! But look at the amount in thirty years!—One thousand and ninety-five dollars!—What a vast sum to run down one man's throat. . . .

III. YUKICHI FUKUZAWA, *AUTOBIOGRAPHY*

In my interpretation of education, I try to be guided by the laws of nature and I try to coordinate all the physical actions of human beings by the very simple laws of "number and reason." In spiritual or moral training, I regard the human being as the most sacred and responsible of all orders, unable in reason to do anything base. Therefore, in self-respect, a man cannot change his sense of humanity, his justice, his loyalty, or anything belonging to his manhood even when driven by circumstances to do so. In short, my creed is that a man should find his faith in independence and self-respect.

From my own observations in both Occidental and Oriental civilizations, I find that each has certain strong points and weak points bound up in its moral teachings and scientific theories. But when I compare the two in a general way as to wealth, armament, and the greatest happiness for the greatest number, I have to put the Orient below the Occident. Granted that a nation's destiny depends upon the education of its people, there must be some fundamental differences in the education of Western and Eastern peoples.

In the education of the East, so often saturated with Confucian teaching, I find two things lacking; that is to say, a lack of studies in number and reason in material culture, and a lack of the idea of independence in spiritual culture. But in the West I think I see why their statesmen are successful in managing their national affairs, and the businessmen in theirs, and the people generally ardent in their patriotism and happy in their family circles.

I regret that in our country I have to acknowledge that people are not formed on these two principles, though I believe no one can escape the laws of number and reason, nor can anyone depend on anything but the doctrine of independence as long as nations are to exist and mankind is to thrive. Japan could not assert herself among the great nations of the world without full recognition and practice of these two principles. And I reasoned that Chinese philosophy as the root of education was responsible for our obvious shortcomings.

With this as the fundamental theory of education, I began and, though it was impossible to institute specialized courses because of lack of funds, I did what I could in organizing the instructions on the principles of number and reason. And I took every opportunity in public speech, in writing, and in casual conversations, to advocate my doctrine of independence. Also I tried in many ways to demonstrate the theory in my actual life. During my endeavor I came to believe less than ever in the old Chinese teachings. . . .

The true reason of my opposing the Chinese teaching with such vigor is my belief that in this age of transition, if this retrogressive doctrine remains at all in our young men's minds, the new civilization cannot give its full benefit to this country. In my determination to save our coming generation, I was prepared even to face single-handed the Chinese scholars of the country as a whole.

Gradually the new education was showing its results among the younger generation; yet men of middle age or past, who held responsible positions, were for the most part uninformed as to the true spirit of Western culture, and whenever they had to make decisions, they turned invariably to their Chinese sources for guidance. And so, again and again I had to rise up and denounce the all-important Chinese influence before this weighty opposition. It was not altogether a safe road for my reckless spirit to follow.

IV. IMPERIAL RESCRIPT ON EDUCATION 1890

Know ye, Our subjects:

Our Imperial Ancestors have founded Our Empire on a basis broad and everlasting, and have deeply and firmly implanted virtue; Our subjects ever united in loyalty and filial piety have from generation to generation illustrated the beauty thereof. This is the glory of the fundamental character of Our Empire, and herein also lies the source of Our education. Ye, Our subjects, be filial to your parents, affectionate to your brothers and sisters; as husbands and wives be harmonious, as friends true; bear yourselves in modesty and moderation; extend your benevolence to all; pursue learning and cultivate arts, and thereby develop intellectual faculties and perfect moral powers; furthermore advance public good and promote common interests; always respect the Constitution and observe the laws; should emergency arise, offer yourselves courageously to the State; and thus guard and maintain the prosperity of Our Imperial Throne coeval with heaven and earth. So shall ye not only be Our good and faithful subjects, but render illustrious the best traditions of your forefathers.

The Way here set forth is indeed the teaching bequeathed by Our Imperial Ancestors, to be observed alike by Their Descendants and the subjects, infallible for all ages and true in all places. It is Our wish to lay it to heart in all reverence, in common with you, Our subjects, that we may all attain to the same virtue.

STUDY QUESTIONS

1. What did Horace Mann see as the primary purposes of education and the relationship between moral and intellectual training? Were there inconsistencies within his views about the best ways to raise free citizens—for example, in the relationship between discipline and individualism?

2. What kind of moralism did Noah Webster's reader seek to instill? How did it compare with Mann's approach?

3. Why did Fukuzawa attack Confucianism? What did he see as the main purposes of modern education? How did his approach relate to other Meiji reforms (Chapter 25)?

4. How did the Imperial Rescript seek to modify Fukuzawa's approach?

5. How did Japanese and American views about moralism through education compare? What would a Japanese educational conservative think about Webster's moral principles? How did Fukuzawa and Mann compare as educational reformers?

6. Based on the documents, which pattern is more striking: the similarities in basic modern educational concerns and principles in the United States and Japan in the nineteenth century, or the ability to express different cultural goals through modern education?

7. Are nineteenth-century debates about the principles of education still reflected in Japanese and American school systems, and in the differences between them?

VISUAL SOURCE

This cartoon, from the late nineteenth century, was from a series entitled "Yokohama Prints to Acquaint People in the Far East with Western Civilization." The cartoon portrays a French inventor, Bernard Palissy, who introduced new techniques for producing enameled pottery, viciously breaking a chair as fuel for his furnace, while a woman and child cower in fear. Industrial methods of pottery production were of great interest to traditional manufacturing sectors, as in Japan, where pottery had long been important as a commercial item and as a field for artistic expression.

Japan and the West in Cartoons. (Corbis/Bettmann)

Japan had a long tradition of woodcut cartoons. With the abrupt confrontation with the West after 1853, many artists sought to capture new fears and anxieties about this distant but clearly powerful civilization. This artistic effort should be compared with text statements about the West, for example in the area of education. Cartoons invite some careful analysis because they are based on cultural assumptions that in this case, for most American readers, are not only from the past but from a very different kind of society.

The Japanese cartoon tradition has continued, even as adjustments to the West have greatly changed. Japanese animation forms one of the nation's major contributions to global culture in the early twenty-first century.

STUDY QUESTIONS

1. In what ways is this cartoon supposed to be frightening? What is the symbolism involved?
2. What aspects of the West are being highlighted?
3. How would reformers like Fukuzawa react to a cartoon of this sort?
4. What kind of impact would a cartoon like this have on Japanese viewers? Would it increase fear of the West or, by allowing the expression of anxiety, make adjustments easier?

35

European Imperialism

The spread of European imperialism throughout Africa and much of Southeast Asia and the Pacific was the most important development in world history during the late nineteenth century. It was fueled by Europe's great advantages in weaponry and industrial productivity. Imperialism brought new domination, new exposure to European-dominated world markets, and new cultural contacts to the colonies involved, plus new needs for resistance and definitions of regional identity. For the Europeans, imperialism brought new economic opportunities but also additional responsibilities, and it unquestionably heightened militarism and nationalist rivalry.

Analysis of the motives of European imperialists is not the only question imperialism raises—the interactions with conquered peoples are even more complex and important—but it is intriguing. Motivations require assessment of conditions within Europe, on the part of governments, imperialist adventurers, and even ordinary people, many of whom supported imperialism enthusiastically. They built on beliefs about economic and military needs, but also intellectual developments such as the rise of social Darwinism with its arguments about racial competition. The result of the various sources of imperialist rhetoric was an array of justifications, not all of which were consistent; here is an obvious challenge to historical interpretation.

Analysis of the causes of imperialism also provides a partial entry into discussions about impact. Imperialists presented several different faces to the people in the colonies, from rank exploitation to humanitarian concern. It is important to consider the policy implications of the various arguments for imperialism, and the potential reactions of Africans or Asians to these policies.

Selection I from F.D. Lugard, *The Rise of Our East African Empire* (Edinborough, 1983; reproduced in the Internet Modern History Sourcebook, copyright Paul Halsall, July, 1988. Selection II from Jules Ferry, *Discours et Opinions de Jules Ferry,* ed. Paul Robiquet (Paris: Armand Coli, 1897). Translated by Ruth Kleinman. Reproduced in the Internet Modern History Sourcebook, copyright Paul Halsall, July, 1998. Selection III from Rudyard Kipling, "The White Man's Burden," *McClure's Magazine* XII #4 (Feb., 1899), pp. 290–291.

The first of the documents that follow is from a book by a British soldier, F.D. Lugard, published in 1893, defending the expansion of the empire in East Africa. The second excerpt is from a speech by Jules Ferry, French prime minister, in 1884. Finally, the third document is the famous poem by British author Rudyard Kipling, first published in *McClure's Magazine* in February 1899.

EUROPEAN IMPERIALISM

I. CAPT. F. D. LUGARD: THE RISE OF OUR EAST AFRICAN EMPIRE

It is sufficient to reiterate here that, as long as our policy is one of free trade, we are compelled to seek new markets; for old ones are being closed to us by hostile tariffs, and our great dependencies, which formerly were the consumers of our goods, are now becoming our commercial rivals. It is inherent in a great colonial and commercial empire like ours that we go forward or go backward. To allow other nations to develop new fields, and to refuse to do so ourselves, is to go backward; and this is the more deplorable, seeing that we have proved ourselves notably capable of dealing with native races and of developing new countries at a less expense than other nations. We owe to the instincts of colonial expansion of our ancestors those vast and noble dependencies which are our pride and the outlets of our trade today; and we are accountable to posterity that opportunities which now present themselves of extending the sphere of our industrial enterprise are not neglected, for the opportunities now offered will never recur again. Lord Rosebery [British prime minister] in his speech at the Royal Colonial Institute expressed this in emphatic language: "We are engaged in 'pegging out claims' for the future. We have to consider, not what we want now, but what we shall want in the future. We have to consider what countries must be developed either by ourselves or some other nation. . . . Remember that the task of the statesman is not merely with the present, but with the future. We have to look forward beyond the chatter of platforms, and the passions of party, to the future of the race of which we are at present the trustees, and we should, in my opinion, grossly fail in the task that has been laid upon us did we shrink from responsibilities, and decline to take our share in a partition of the world which we have not forced on, but which has been forced upon us."

If some initial expense is incurred, is it not justified by the ultimate gain? I have already pointed out what other nations are doing in the way of railway extension. The government is not asked to provide the capital of the railway, but only a guarantee on the subscribed capital. . . . Independently of money spent on railways, the conquest of Algeria alone cost France £150,000,000, and it is estimated that her West Coast colonies cost her half a million yearly. . . . Belgium, besides her heavy expenses for the Congo railway, the capital of which she has advanced without interest, guarantees £80,000 per annum to the Congo state, and is altering her constitution in order to allow her to take over that state as a colonial possession. Germany has spent over a million sterling in East Africa, besides her expenditure on the west and southwest colonies. The parallel is here complete, for the German company failed, and government stepped in to carry out the pledges and obligations incurred. Even Portugal who is content to support a yearly deficit on each of her African possessions, gives heavy subsidies to the mail steamers, and £10,000 per annum to the cable. All these nations are content to incur this yearly cost in the present, confident that in the future these possessions will repay the outlay. . . .

The Zanzibar Gazette, which is in a good position to judge, since the imports and exports from German East Africa can be fairly assessed there, speaking of "the comparatively large sums from the national resources" invested in this country, says, "We think it is only a question of time for such investments, with a careful management of the territory, to show highly profitable returns." Such a view from those on the spot and possessing local knowledge, should be a strong testimony in favor of the far richer British sphere. . . .

A word as to missions in Africa. Beyond doubt I think the most useful missions are the medical and the industrial, in the initial stages of savage development. A combination of the two is, in my opinion, an ideal mission. Such is the work of the Scotch Free Church on Lake Nyasa. The medical missionary begins work with every advantage. Throughout Africa the ideas of the cure of the body and of the soul are closely allied. The "medicine man" is credited, not only with a knowledge of the simples and drugs which may avert or cure disease, but owing to the superstitions of the people, he is also supposed to have a knowledge of the charms and *dawa* which will invoke the aid of the Deity or appease His wrath, and of the witchcraft and magic (*ulu*) by which success in war, immunity from danger, or a supply of rain may be obtained. As the skill of the European in medicine asserts its superiority over the crude methods of the medicine man, so does he in proportion gain an influence in his teaching of the great truths of Christianity. He teaches the savage where knowledge and art cease, how far natural remedies produce their effects, independent of charms or supernatural agencies, and where divine power overrules all human efforts. Such demonstration from a medicine man, whose skill they cannot fail to recognize as superior to their own, has naturally more weight than any mere preaching. A mere preacher is discounted and his zeal is not understood. The medical missionary, moreover, gains an admission to the houses and homes of the natives by virtue of his art, which would not be so readily accorded to another. He becomes their adviser and referee, and his counsels are substituted for the magic and witchcraft which retard development.

The value of the industrial mission, on the other hand, depends, of course, largely on the nature of the tribes among whom it is located. Its value can hardly be overestimated among such people as the Waganda, both on account of their natural aptitude and their eager desire to learn. But even the less advanced and more primitive tribes may be equally benefited, if not only mechanical and artisan work, such as the carpenter's and blacksmith's craft, but also the simpler expedients of agriculture are taught. The sinking of wells, the system of irrigation, the introduction and planting of useful trees, the use of manure, and of domestic animals for agricultural purposes, the improvement of his implements by the introduction of the primitive Indian plough, etc.—all of these, while improving the status of the native, will render his land more productive, and hence, by increasing his surplus products, will enable him to purchase from the trader the cloth which shall add to his decency, and the implements and household utensils which shall produce greater results for his labor and greater comforts in his social life.

In my view, moreover, instruction (religious or secular) is largely wasted upon adults, who are wedded to custom and prejudice. It is the rising generation who should be educated to a higher plane, by the establishment of schools for children. They, in turn, will send their children for instruction; and so a progressive advancement is instituted, which may produce really great results. [Mission] schools were literally thronged with thousands of children, and chiefs of neighboring tribes were eagerly offering to erect schools in their own villages at their own cost. . . .

Just as the mission houses and plantations were themselves an object lesson to the natives of Africa, so the little colony became itself a model. The spotless clothes of the children, the neatness, and order, and discipline enforced, were like nothing I have ever seen elsewhere in Africa. The children in the schools were boarders; native chiefs from surrounding tribes sent their sons to live in Blantyre, and be taught in the schools; neighboring chiefs came to the white man of Blantyre, as arbitrator in disputes; his intervention on more than one occasion prevented war. . . .

One word as regards missionaries themselves. The essential point in dealing with Africans is to establish a respect for the European. Upon this—the prestige of the white man—depends his influence, often his very existence, in Africa. If he shows by his surroundings, by his assumption of superiority, that he is far above the native, he will be respected, and his influence will be proportionate to the superiority he assumes and bears out by his higher accomplishments and mode of life. In my opinion—at any rate with reference to Africa—it is the greatest possible mistake to suppose that a European can acquire a greater influence by adopting the mode of the life of the natives. In effect, it is to lower himself to their plane, instead of elevating them to his. The sacrifice involved is wholly unappreciated, and the motive would be held by the savage to be poverty and lack of social status in his own country. The whole influence of the European in Africa is gained by this assertion of a superiority which commands the respect and excites the emulation of the savage. To forego this vantage ground is to lose influence for good. I may add, that the loss of prestige consequent on what I should term the humiliation of the European affects not merely the missionary himself, but is subversive of all efforts for secular administration, and may even invite insult, which may lead to disaster and bloodshed. To maintain it a missionary must, above all things, be a gentleman; for no one is more quick to recognize a real gentleman than the African savage. He must at all times assert himself, and repel an insolent familiarity, which is a thing entirely apart from friendship born of respect and affection. His dwelling house should be as superior to those of the natives as he is himself superior to them. And this, while adding to his prestige and influence, will simultaneously promote his own health and energy, and so save money spent on invalidings [sick leaves] to England, and replacements due to sickness or death. . . .

I am convinced that the indiscriminate application of such precepts as those contained in the words to turn the other cheek also to the smiter, and to be the servant of all men, is to wholly misunderstand and misapply the teaching of Christ. The African holds the position of a late-born child in the family of nations, and must as yet be schooled in the discipline of the nursery. He is neither the intelligent ideal crying out for instruction, and capable of appreciating the subtle beauties of Christian forbearance and self-sacrifice, which some well-meaning missionary literature would lead us to suppose, nor yet, on the other hand, is he universally a rampant cannibal, predestined by Providence to the yoke of the slave, and fitted for nothing better, as I have elsewhere seen him depicted. . . .

[T]here is in him, like the rest of us, both good and bad, and that the innate good is capable of being developed by culture.

II. JULES FERRY (1832–1893): ON FRENCH COLONIAL EXPANSION

The policy of colonial expansion is a political and economic system . . . that can be connected to three sets of ideas: economic ideas; the most far-reaching ideas of civilization; and ideas of a political and patriotic sort.

In the area of economics, I am placing before you, with the support of some statistics, the considerations that justify the policy of colonial expansion, as seen from the perspective of a need, felt more and more urgently by the industrialized population of Europe and especially the people of our rich and hardworking country of France: the need for outlets [for exports]. Is this a fantasy? Is this a concern [that can wait] for the future? Or is this not a pressing need, one may say a crying need, of our industrial population? I merely express in a general way what each one of you can see for himself in the various parts of France. Yes, what our major industries [textiles, etc.] . . . lack more and more are outlets. Why? Because next door Germany is setting up trade barriers; because across the ocean the United States of America have become protectionists, and extreme protectionists at that; because not only are these great markets . . . shrinking, becoming more and more difficult of access, but these great states are beginning to pour into our own markets products not seen there before. This is true not only for our agriculture, which has been so sorely tried . . . and for which competition is no longer limited to the circle of large European states . . . Today, as you know, competition, the law of supply and demand, freedom of trade, the effects of speculation, all radiate in a circle that reaches to the ends of the earth. . . . That is a great complication, a great economic difficulty; . . . an extremely serious problem. It is so serious, gentlemen, so acute, that the least informed persons must already glimpse, foresee, and take precautions against the time when the great South American market that has, in a manner of speaking, belonged to us forever will be disputed and perhaps taken away from us by North American products. Nothing is more serious; there can be no graver social problem; and these matters are linked intimately to colonial policy.

Gentlemen, we must speak more loudly and more honestly! We must say openly that indeed the higher races have a right over the lower races. . . .

I repeat, that the superior races have a right because they have a duty. They have the duty to civilize the inferior races. . . . In the history of earlier centuries these duties, gentlemen, have often been misunderstood; and certainly when the Spanish soldiers and explorers introduced slavery into Central America, they did not fulfill their duty as men of a higher race. . . . But, in our time, I maintain that European nations acquit themselves with generosity, with grandeur, and with sincerity of this superior civilizing duty.

I say that French colonial policy, the policy of colonial expansion, the policy that has taken us under the Empire [the Second Empire, of Napoleon III, to Saigon, to Indochina [Vietnam]], that has led us to Tunisia, to Madagascar—I say that this policy of colonial expansion was inspired by . . . the fact that a navy such as ours cannot do without safe harbors, defenses, supply centers on the high seas . . . Are you unaware of this? Look at a map of the world.

Gentlemen, these are considerations that merit the full attention of patriots. The conditions of naval warfare have greatly changed. . . . At present, as you know, a warship, however perfect its design, cannot carry more than two weeks' supply of coal; and a vessel without coal is a wreck on the high seas, abandoned to the first occupier. Hence the need to have places of supply, shelters, ports for defense and provisioning. . . . And that is why we needed Tunisia; that is why we needed Saigon and Indochina; that is why we need Madagascar . . . and why we shall never leave them! . . . Gentlemen, in Europe such as it is today, in this competition of the many rivals we see rising up around us, some by military or naval improvements, others by the prodigious development of a constantly growing population; in a Europe, or rather in a universe thus constituted, a policy of withdrawal or abstention is simply the high road to decadence! In our time nations are great only through the activity they deploy; it is not by spreading the peaceable light of their institutions . . . that they are great, in the present day.

Spreading light without acting, without taking part in the affairs of the world, keeping out of all European alliances and seeing as a trap, an adventure, all expansion into Africa or the Orient—for a great nation to live this way, believe me, is to abdicate and, in less time than you may think, to sink from the first rank to the third and fourth.

III. KIPLING'S *THE WHITE MAN'S BURDEN*

Take up the White Man's burden—
  Send forth the best ye breed—
Go, bind your sons to exile
  To serve your captive's need;
To wait, in heavy harness,
  On fluttered folk and wild—
Your new-caught sullen peoples,
  Half devil and half child.

Take up the White Man's burden—
  In patience to abide,
To veil the treat of terror
  And check the show of pride;
By open speech and simple,
  An hundred times made plain,
To seek another's profit
  And work another's gain.

Take up the White Man's burden—
  The savage wars of peace—
Fill full the mouth of Famine,
  And bid the sickness cease;
And when your goal is nearest

(The end for others sought)
Watch sloth and heathen folly
    Bring all your hopes to nought.

Take up the White Man's burden—
    No iron rule of kings,
But toil of serf and sweeper—
    The tale of common things.
The ports ye shall not enter,
    The roads ye shall not tread,
Go, make them with your living
    And mark them with your dead.

Take up the White Man's burden,
    And reap his old reward—
The blame of those ye better
    The hate of those ye guard—
The cry of those ye humor
    (Ah, slowly!) toward the light:—
"Why brought ye us from bondage,
    Our loved Egyptian night?"

Take up the White Man's burden—
    Ye dare not stoop to less—
Nor call too loud on Freedom
    To cloak your weariness.
By all ye will or whisper,
    By all ye leave or do,
The silent sullen peoples
    Shall weigh your God and you.

Take up the White Man's burden!
    Have done with childish days—
The lightly-proffered laurel,
    The easy ungrudged praise:
Comes now, to search your manhood
    Through all the thankless years,
Cold, edged with dear-bought wisdom,
    The judgment of your peers.

STUDY QUESTIONS

1. What are Lugard's main arguments for imperialism? Are the arguments entirely consistent? Would they lead to harmonious policies?
2. How do Lugard's arguments compare with those of Jules Ferry? Where do they overlap, and where do they differ?
3. What aspects of the European and world economy in the nineteenth century helped provoke imperialism? Was imperialism economically beneficial to the European powers?

4. How do Kipling's arguments compare with those of Lugard and Ferry? What was the "white man's burden"?

5. How important were religious and humanitarian arguments in actually causing imperialism? How important were they in shaping how imperialism worked out in Africa?

6. What kinds of arguments for imperialism would be most popular in Europe itself, and why?

7. What attitudes toward Africans are suggested in the three documents? Are they entirely consistent?

8. What do the arguments for imperialism suggest about potential African reaction?

9. What kind of future did the imperialists envisage for Africa? How do their implicit forecasts compare with what actually happened in Africa in the twentieth century?

36

Nineteenth-Century Sports

One unexpected but powerful result of growing trade connections and cultural interchange in the nineteenth century was the beginning of a globalization of athletics—a process that has continued vigorously to the present day. The sports involved were Western in origin, soccer football heading the list. Their dissemination was a function of Western power and prestige. Western businessmen and diplomats played their familiar games on foreign soil—colonies and noncolonies alike—and gradually local residents sought to emulate what seemed to be part of a superior, or at least very attractive, way of life.

Sports history in nineteenth-century Western Europe and the United States was itself a vital development. At the beginning of the century few organized sports existed. Village games and individual athletic pastimes abounded, but overall patterns were haphazard. Industrialization spurred a set of changes in sports. First, many urban people began to see the need to exercise to make up for sedentary jobs, and they also valued the social contact sports provided. Middle-class and working-class teams developed on this basis. Schools seized on sports as a diversion but also as building character: Upper-class schools first trumpeted the glories of sports, but lower-class education soon followed their lead. In this context, by the 1850s and 1860s, entrepreneurs saw new ways to make money from sports. There was new equipment to sell, much of it based on the vulcanization of rubber. There were commercial teams to organize, to draw spectators into new stadiums (which would be reached by equally novel tramways). Initial professional teams emerged in English soccer and American baseball. All these developments gave sports an unprecedented importance in modern life. They also changed sports: Athletics became more regulated, with standardized rules of play enforced by a new monitor, the official; consciousness of speed and recordkeeping increased; specialization affected sports, with different team members assigned distinct responsibilities.

The internationalization of sports brought some of the same qualities occurring in the West to a variety of other societies—starting with tremendous enthusiasm among young athletes and a wide range of spectators. Teams built by imitation and contact included a range of Latin American soccer groups, formed initially on the example of local British players. The first Buenos Aires football club, copied from British residents in the

Selection I from Pierre de Coubertin, "The Olympic Games of 1896," *The Century Magazine,* November 1896, pp. 35, 42, 46–48, 50, 53. Selection IIA. from *Buenos Aires Herald,* June 27, 1904; Selection IIB from Anstol Rosenfeld, "O futebol no Brasil," *Revista Argumento,* Vol. 4 (1979).

city, was founded in 1867, and a national network of teams had fanned out by the 1890s. Argentine soccer style was more exuberant and individualistic than the European version, showing a kind of cultural fusion even as imitation occurred. Japanese students began playing baseball by the 1890s and in 1896 proudly defeated a team of American sailors. At the same time, not all sports spread equally wide. The United States remained addicted to some parochial interests, like American football, not widely shared elsewhere. South Asians were interested in more individual sports, such as badminton and tennis, rather than team sports, with the exception of polo and cricket. Nevertheless, the rapid dissemination of sports as international currency constitutes a major development in world history.

The first selection picks up a formal aspect of sports internationalization: the revival of the Olympics in the 1890s, under the leadership of a French nobleman, Baron de Coubertin (1863–1937). An educational reformer, Coubertin had seen the importance of sports in American and British schools. He formed an International Olympic Congress in 1894 to push for a revival of the old Greek games, but now on an international basis: His hope was that sports would transcend national conflicts. On his death he ordered that his heart be sent to Greece and buried on Mt. Olympus. His comments in the following document reflect on the first modern games, held in Athens in 1896. Obviously, the movement he launched has become a major reflection of and spur to sports internationalism, although some of the initial reliance on amateurism and avoidance of nationalistic rivalries has not proved durable. At the same time some of the limitations in Coubertin's vision have lifted as well: His statement reflects a transition in sports internationalism that hardly embraced most of the world directly. Progressively in the twentieth century, but particularly after World War II, the Olympics would do steadily better as a genuinely global assemblage.

The second selection—a pair of documents—conveys the initial atmosphere of the introduction of soccer into Latin America. One document describes the setting for one of the first matches in which Latin Americans were confident enough to invite a British team to play against them; elite Buenos Aires society turned out, including General Julio Roca, the president of the Republic (football had just been introduced into the Argentine army). The British team, Southampton, savaged the Argentine team and several others during their visit. The other document is from a poem by Ana Amélia (entitled "The Leap") to the goalie of the Brazilian team, Fluminense, around 1910, again suggesting the early days of Latin American soccer in which young men from good families displayed their masculine qualities to admiring young women of the same class. The subject of her poem, Marcos de Mendonça, played for the Brazilian national team in 1919 and also became a prominent banker and industrialist; he married Ana Amélia.

SPORTS ACCOUNTS

I. THE OLYMPICS

The Olympic games which recently took place in Athens were modern in character, not alone because of their programs, which substituted bicycle for chariot races, and fencing for the brutalities of pugilism, but because in their origin and regulations they were international and universal, and consequently adapted to the conditions in which athletics have developed at the present day. The ancient games had an exclusively Hellenic character; they were always held in the same place, and Greek blood was a necessary condition of admission to them. It is true that strangers were in time tolerated; but their presence at Olympia was rather a tribute paid to the superiority of Greek civilization than a right exercised in the name of racial equality. With the modern games it is quite otherwise. Their creation is the work of "barbarians." It is due to the delegates of the athletic associations of all countries assembled in congress at Paris in 1894. It was there agreed that every country should celebrate the Olympic games in turn. The first place belonged by right to Greece; it was accorded by unanimous vote; and in order to emphasize the permanence of the institution, its wide bearings, and its essentially cosmopolitan character, an international committee was appointed, the members of which were to represent the various nations, European and American, with whom athletics are held in honor. The presidency of this committee falls to the country in which the next games are to be held. A Greek, M. Bikelas, has presided for the last two years. A Frenchman now presides, and will continue to do so until 1900, since the next games are to take place at Paris during the Exposition. Where will those of 1904 take place? Perhaps at New York, perhaps at Berlin, or at Stockholm. The question is soon to be decided. . . .

While the Hellenic Committee . . . labored over the scenic requirements, the international committee and the national committees were occupied in recruiting competitors. The matter was not as easy as one might think. Not only had indifference and distrust to be overcome, but the revival of the Olympic games had aroused a certain hostility. Although the Paris Congress had been careful to decree that every form of physical exercise practised in the world should have its place on the program, the gymnasts took offense. They considered that they had not been given sufficient prominence. The greater part of the gymnastic associations of Germany, France, and Belgium are animated by a rigorously exclusive spirit; they are not inclined to tolerate the presence of those forms of athletics which they themselves do not practise; what they disdainfully designate as "English sports" have become, because of their popularity, especially odious to them. These associations were not satisfied with declining the invitation sent them to repair to Athens. The Belgian federation wrote to the other federations, suggesting a concerted stand against the work of the Paris Congress. These incidents confirmed the opinions of the pessimists who had been foretelling the failure of the fêtes, or their probable postponement. Athens is far away, the journey is expensive, and the Easter vacations are short. The contestants were not willing to undertake the voyage unless they could be sure that the occasion would be worth the effort. The different associations were not willing to send representatives unless they could be informed of the amount of interest which the contests would create. An unfortunate occurrence took place almost at the last moment. The German press, commenting on an article which had appeared in a Paris newspaper, declared that it was an exclusively Franco-Greek affair; that attempts were made to shut out other nations; and furthermore, that the German associations had been intentionally kept aloof from the Paris Congress of 1894. The assertion was acknowledged to be incorrect, and was powerless to check the efforts of the German committee under

Dr. Gebhardt. M. Kémény in Hungary, Major Balck in Sweden, General de Boutonski in Russia, Professor W. M. Sloane in the United States, Lord Ampthill in England, Dr. Jiri Guth in Bohemia, were, meantime, doing their best to awaken interest in the event, and to reassure the doubting. They did not always succeed. Many people took a sarcastic view, and the newspapers indulged in much pleasantry on the subject of the Olympic games. . . .

Needless to say that the various contests were held under amateur regulations. An exception was made for the fencing-matches, since in several countries professors of military fencing hold the rank of officers. For them a special contest was arranged. To all other branches of the athletic sports only amateurs were admitted. It is impossible to conceive the Olympic games with money prizes. But these rules, which seem simple enough, are a good deal complicated in their practical application by the fact that definitions of what constitutes an amateur differ from one country to another, sometimes even from one club to another. Several definitions are current in England; the Italians and the Dutch admit one which appears too rigid at one point, too loose at another. How to conciliate these divergent or contradictory utterances? The Paris Congress made an attempt in that direction, but its decisions are not accepted everywhere as law, nor is its definition of amateurship everywhere adopted as the best. The rules and regulations, properly so called, are not any more uniform. This and that are forbidden in one country, authorized in another. All that one can do, until there shall be an Olympic code formulated in accordance with the ideas and the usages of the majority of athletes, is to choose among the codes now existing. It was decided, therefore, that the foot-races should be under the rules of the Union Française des Sports Athlétiques; jumping, putting the shot, etc., under those of the Amateur Athletic Association of England; the bicycle-races under those of the International Cyclists' Association, etc. This had appeared to us the best way out of the difficulty; but we should have had many disputes if the judges (to whom had been given the Greek name of ephors) had not been headed by Prince George, who acted as final referee. His presence gave weight and authority to the decisions of the ephors, among whom there were, naturally, representatives of different countries. The prince took his duties seriously, and fulfilled them conscientiously. He was always on the track, personally supervising every detail, an easily recognizable figure, owing to his height and athletic build. It will be remembered that Prince George, while traveling in Japan with his cousin, the czarevitch (now Emperor Nicholas II), felled with his fist the ruffian who had tried to assassinate the latter. During the weight-lifting in the Stadion, Prince George lifted with ease an enormous dumb-bell, and tossed it out of the way. The audience broke into applause, as if it would have liked to make him the victor in the event. . . .

Many banquets were given. The mayor of Athens gave one at Cephissia, a little shaded village at the foot of Pentelicus. M. Bikelas, the retiring president of the international committee, gave another at Phalerum. The king himself entertained all the competitors, and the members of the committees, three hundred guests in all, at luncheon in the ball-room of the palace. The outside of this edifice, which was built by King Otho, is heavy and graceless; but the center of the interior is occupied by a suite of large rooms with very high ceilings, opening one into another through colonnades. The decorations are simple and imposing. The tables were set in the largest of these rooms. At the table of honor sat the king, the princes, and the ministers, and here also were the members of the committees. The competitors were seated at the other tables according to their nationality. The king, at dessert, thanked and congratulated his guests, first in French, afterward in Greek. The Americans cried "Hurrah!" the Germans, "*Hoch!*" the Hungarians, "*Eljen!*" the Greeks, "*Zito!*" the French, "*Vive le Roi!*" After the repast the king and his sons chatted long and amicably with the athletes. It was a really charming scene, the republican simplicity of which was a matter of wonderment particularly to the Austrians and the Russians, little used as they are to the spectacle of monarchy thus meeting democracy on an equal footing.

Then there were nocturnal festivities on the Acropolis, where the Parthenon was illuminated with colored lights, and at the Piræus, where the vessels were hung with Japanese lanterns. Unluckily, the weather changed, and the sea was so high on the day appointed for the boat-races, which were to have taken place in the roadstead of Phalerum, that the project was abandoned. The distribution of prizes was likewise postponed for twenty-four hours. It came off with much solemnity, on the morning of April 15, in the Stadion. The sun shone again, and sparkled on the officers' uniforms. When the roll of the victors was called, it became evident, after all, that the international character of the institution was well guarded by the results of the contests. America had won nine prizes for athletic sports alone (flat races for 100 and 400 meters; 110-meter hurdle-race; high jump; broad jump; pole-vault; hop, step, and jump; putting the shot; throwing the discus), and two prizes for shooting (revolver, 25 and 30 meters); but France had the prizes for foil-fencing and for four bicycle-races; England scored highest in the one-handed weight-lifting contest, and in single lawn-tennis; Greece won the run from Marathon, two gymnastic contests (rings, climbing the smooth rope), three prizes for shooting (carbine, 200 and 300 meters; pistol, 25 meters), a prize for fencing with sabers, and a bicycle-race; Germany won in wrestling, in gymnastics (parallel bars, fixed bar, horse-leaping), and in double lawn-tennis; Australia, the 800-meter and 1500-meter foot-races on the flat; Hungary, swimming-matches of 100 and 1200 meters; Austria, the 500-meter swimming-match and the 12-hour bicycle-race; Switzerland, a gymnastic prize; Denmark, the two-handed weight-lifting contest. . . .

It is interesting to ask oneself what are likely to be the results of the Olympic games of 1896, as regards both Greece and the rest of the world. In the case of Greece, the games will be found to have had a double effect, one athletic, the other political. It is a well-known fact that the Greeks had lost completely, during their centuries of oppression, the taste for physical sports. There were good walkers among the mountaineers, and good swimmers in the scattered villages along the coast. It was a matter of pride with the young *palikar* to wrestle and to dance well, but that was because bravery and a gallant bearing were admired by those about him. Greek dances are far from athletic, and the wrestling-matches of peasants have none of the characteristics of true sports. The men of the towns had come to know no diversion beyond reading the newspapers, and violently discussing politics about the tables of the cafés. The Greek race, however, is free from the natural indolence of the Oriental, and it was manifest that the athletic habit would, if the opportunity offered, easily take root again among its men.

Indeed, several gymnastic associations had been formed in recent years at Athens and Patras, and a rowing-club at Piræus, and the public was showing a growing interest in their feats. It was therefore a favorable moment to speak the words "Olympic games." No sooner had it been made clear that Athens was to aid in the revival of the Olympiads than a perfect fever of muscular activity broke out all over the kingdom. And this was nothing to what followed the games. I have seen, in little villages far from the capital, small boys, scarcely out of long clothes, throwing big stones, or jumping improvised hurdles, and two urchins never met in the streets of Athens without running races. . . .

When one realizes the influence that the practice of physical exercises may have on the future of a country, and on the force of a whole race, one is tempted to wonder whether Greece is not likely to date a new era from the year 1896. . . .

So much for Greece. On the world at large the Olympic games have, of course, exerted no influence as yet; but I am profoundly convinced that they will do so. May I be permitted to say that this was my reason for founding them? Modern athletics need to be *unified* and *purified*. Those who have followed the renaissance of physical sports in this century know that discord reigns supreme from one end of them to the other. Every country has its own rules; it is not possible even to come to an agreement as to who is an amateur, and who is not. All over the world there is one perpetual dispute, which is further fed by innumerable weekly, and even daily, newspapers. In this deplorable state of things professionalism tends to grow apace. Men give up their whole existence to one particular sport, grow rich by practising it, and thus deprive it of all nobility, and destroy the just equilibrium of man by making the muscles preponderate over the mind. It is my belief that no education, particularly in democratic times, can be good and complete without the aid of athletics; but athletics, in order to play their proper educational rôle, must be based on perfect disinterestedness and the sentiment of honor.

If we are to guard them against these threatening evils, we must put an end to the quarrels of amateurs, that they may be united among themselves, and willing to measure their skill in frequent international encounters. But what country is to impose its rules and its habits on the others? The Swedes will not yield to the Germans, nor the French to the English. Nothing better than the international Olympic games could therefore be devised. Each country will take its turn in organizing them. When they come to meet every four years in these contests, further ennobled by the memories of the past, athletes all over the world will learn to know one another better, to make mutual concessions, and to seek no other reward in the competition than the honor of the victory. One may be filled with desire to see the colors of one's club or college triumph in a national meeting; but how much stronger is the feeling when the colors of one's country are at stake! I am well assured that the victors in the Stadion at Athens wished for no other recompense when they heard the people cheer the flag of their country in honor of their achievement.

It was with these thoughts in mind that I sought to revive the Olympic games. I have succeeded after many efforts. Should the institution prosper,—as I am persuaded, all civilized nations aiding, that it will,—it may be a potent, if indirect, factor in securing universal peace. Wars break out because nations misunderstand each other. We shall not have peace until the prejudices which now separate the different races shall have been outlived. To attain this end, what better means than to bring the youth of all countries periodically together for amicable trials of muscular strength and agility? The Olympic games, with the ancients, controlled athletics and promoted peace. It is not visionary to look to them for similar benefactions in the future.

II. LATIN AMERICA TAKES ON FOOTBALL

A. From the Buenos Aires Herald (1904)

The football field proper was fenced in with a strong and neat wire fence at the back of which was a space of about five yards in width, followed by a continuous row of stands on all sides of the field with the lowest row of benches well raised, so that their occupants could easily see over the heads of those using the standing room in front. Opposite the centre of the field on each side were the reserved seats, and on the south west side was a break in the stands, occupied by the box for the use of the President and the official guests. The seats to the north of the President's box being reserved for members of the Hippic club and their families. Long before 2 o'clock the seats were well filled, and at five minutes past two, the band of the 3rd Battalion of the line struck up 'Hail to the Chief' and the carriage of General Roca was seen to be approaching. . . . Great applause greeted his appearance, which he gracefully acknowledged.

. . .

It is not clear why Southampton was chosen. It was, at the time, one of the leading professional teams in the Southern League and had twice been losing finalists in the FA Cup, in 1900 and 1902. The team swept through their five matches in Buenos Aires and one in Montevideo like an irresistible force. The day after they got off the boat they beat Alumni 3–0. A team of Britishers was savaged 10–0, Belgrano destroyed 6–1: much was made of the first goal to be scored against 'foreigners' by Arthur Forester in that game. An Argentine eleven was then beaten 8–0 and a team representative of the league in Buenos Aires lost 5–3 to the triumphant visitors. On the way home a Uruguayan combination was similarly despatched 8–1 in Montevideo.

B. Ana W. Amélia

When I saw you today, executing your relaxed, daring and vigorous leap like a figure from the *Iliad* I trembled in the most intimate part of my being, swept by a frenetic impulse as if I was before a Greek, the hero of an Olympiad. Shaken like Dryad before Apollo, I measure his magnificent figure. Against the incomparable background of a pale twilight you threw yourself into space, tensed all your muscles, enrapt by the roar of the crowd's enthusiastic applause. Like an agile God that graciously came down from Olympus, you touched the ground, glorious, fervent, and fearless, perfect in the beauty of the classic Greek sculpture.

STUDY QUESTIONS

1. What was Coubertin's idea of internationalism? What problems did he encounter in trying to internationalize sports, and how did he handle them?

THE SPREAD OF FOOTBALL 1863–1985

Country	National Organization Set Up	Affiliation to FIFA*	National League	Professionalism Introduced	First International Match
England	1863	1905–20 1924–28 1946	1888	1885	v. Scotland 30 Nov 1872
Scotland	1873	1910–20 1924–28 1946	1890	1893	v. England
Denmark	1889	1904	1913	1978	v. France 19 Oct 1908
Argentina	1893	1912	1967	1931	v. Uruguay 16 May 1901
Switzerland	1895	1904	1934	1933	v. France 12 Feb 1905
Belgium	1895	1904	1896	1972	v. France 1 May 1904
Chile	1895	1912	1933	1933	v. Argentina 27 May 1910
Italy	1898	1905	1930	1929	v. France 13 May 1920
Netherlands	1899	1904	1957	1954	v. Belgium 30 April 1905
Germany	1900	1904–46 1950	1963 (WG†)		v. Switzerland 5 April 1908
Uruguay	1900	1923	1900	1932	v. Argentina 16 May 1901
Czechoslovakia (Bohemia pre-1918)	1901	1906	1925	1925	v. Hungary 5 April 1903
Hungary	1901	1906	1901	1926	v. Austria 12 Oct 1902
Norway	1902	1908	1961		v. Sweden 12 July 1908
Austria	1904	1905	1911	1924–38	v. Hungary 12 Oct 1902
Sweden	1904	1904	1925	1967	v. Norway 12 July 1908
Paraguay	1906	1921	1906	1935	v. Argentina 11 May 1919
Romania	1908	1930	1910		v. Yugoslavia 8 June 1922
Spain	1913	1904	1929	1929	v. Denmark 28 Aug 1920
United States	1913	1913	1967–84		v. Canada 28 Nov 1885
Brazil	1914	1923	1971	1933	v. Argentina 20 Sept 1914
Portugal	1914	1926	1935		v. Spain 18 Dec 1921
France	1918	1904	1932	1932	v. Belgium 1 May 1904
Yugoslavia	1919	1919	1923		v. Czechoslovakia 28 Aug 1920
Poland	1919	1923	1927		v. Hungary 18 Dec 1921
USSR (Soviet Union)	1922	1946	1936		v. Turkey 16 Nov 1924
Turkey	1923	1923	1959	1951	v. Romania 26 Oct 1923
Bulgaria	1923	1924	1949		v. Austria 21 May 1924
Greece	1926	1927	1960	1979	v. Sweden 28 Aug 1920
Colombia	1924	1936	1948	1948	v. Mexico 10 Feb 1938
Mexico	1927	1929	1948	1931	v. Spain 30 May 1928
Peru	1922	1924	1966	1931	v. Uruguay 1 Nov 1927
Egypt	1921	1923	1949		
New Zealand	1938	1963	1970		
Morocco	1955	1956	1916		
Tunisia	1956	1960	1921		
Algeria	1962	1963	1963		v. West Germany 1 Jan 1964

*FIFA, International Federation of Football Associations.

†WG, West Germany

THE SPREAD OF FOOTBALL 1863–1985 (continued)

Country	National Organization Set Up	Affiliation to FIFA*	National League	Professionalism Introduced	First International Match
South Africa	1892	1952–76 (suspended 1964–76) 1992	1971		
Zaire	1919	1964	1958		
Zambia	1929	1964	1962		
Nigeria	1945	1959	1972		
Zimbabwe	1950	1965	1963		
Ghana	1957	1958	1957		
Côte d'Ivoire	1950	1960	1960		
Cameroon	1960	1962	1961		
Iran	1920	1948	1974		
Japan	1921	1929–45 1950	1993		
China	1924	1931–58 1979	1953		
South Korea	1928	1948	1983	1983	v. Mexico 2 Aug 1948
North Korea	1945	1958			
Iraq	1948	1951	1974		
Saudi Arabia	1959	1959	1979		
Australia	1961	1963	1977		

*FIFA, International Federation of Football Associations.

2. What "world" was represented at the first Olympics? Why might a European find the representation an impressive demonstration of internationalism, in the context of the 1890s?

3. How did Coubertin suggest a belief that sports might be a particularly European strength?

4. What did Coubertin think the results of international sports might be in Greece? What does his approach suggest about belief in the larger meaning of modern sports?

5. Why were British sports popular in Argentina? What kinds of Argentinians were first interested, and why? Are there any connections with the motivations involved in the revival of the Olympics?

6. Can the chronology of the international spread of football organizations be explained in terms of patterns of European influence?

7. Why have sports become such an important part of modern global culture?

VISUAL SOURCE

This sketch appeared in newspaper accounts of the Games. Along with Pierre de Coubertin's account of the first Games, it helps determine what the organizers of the Games sought to convey about the purposes of the new international competition. The parade is headed by a *Greek evzone,* a soldier dressed in traditional (though not ancient Greek) garb.

The Parade of the Winners at the First Modern Olympic Games, Athens, 1896. (The Granger Collection, NY)

The sketch also invites comparisons with the way Olympic games have evolved over the ensuing century-plus. Some aspects of the Games have remained remarkably constant, but many others have changed greatly. You might want to search out a website picture of a more recent Olympic parade (the 2000 Games were held in Sydney, Australia, the 2002 Winter Games in Salt Lake City, Utah), for comparison.

STUDY QUESTIONS

1. Is this sketch meant to favor or criticize the first modern Olympics? How can you tell?
2. How does the representation compare with de Coubertin's glowing description?
3. How did the Games conceive of internationalism?
4. What does this sketch suggest about the social characteristics of the first Games?
5. How did the first Games compare with contemporary Olympic meets? What are the main differences? Are there any continuities?

37

Racism in World History: W.E.B. Du Bois and the "Problem of the Color Line"

In 1903 the African-American writer W.E.B. Du Bois (1868–1963) published *The Souls of Black Folk,* one of the most prescient books of the early twentieth century. Du Bois's book was a path-breaking study of the history and culture of African-Americans, a subject about which he was superbly qualified to write. After a brilliant undergraduate career at Fisk University in Nashville, Tennessee, Du Bois (pronounced *Due Boyss*) became the first African-American to receive a Ph.D. from Harvard. His Harvard dissertation and first book, *The Suppression of the African Slave Trade to the United States of America, 1838–1870* (1896) was for many years the outstanding work on the subject. A few years later, while teaching in Philadelphia, Du Bois published a second major book, *The Philadelphia Negro* (1899), the first empirically based sociological study of black Americans in an urban setting. Many more important books, essays, and newspaper articles followed from his pen in succeeding decades.

Du Bois was both a scholar of high achievement and a leading political activist on behalf of racial equality. His political career began in London in 1900 at the meetings of the first Pan African Congress. Having spent two years studying at the University of Berlin in the 1890s, Du Bois's horizons were already wide by the time he reached London. At the Pan African Congress he first declared that, "The problem of the twentieth century is the problem of the color line," thus connecting the struggle for racial justice in the United States to the broader issue of Western colonial rule in Africa and Asia.

Returning to the United States, Du Bois continued his scholarly work and political activism for the next decade while based at Atlanta University. In 1910 he helped found the National Association for the Advancement of Colored People (NAACP) and became the first editor of its newspaper, *The Crisis.* During the remainder of his long life Du Bois campaigned for racial justice in the United States and for the end of European colonial rule in Africa. Gradually moving leftward in his politics, he eventually joined the Communist Party and emigrated to Ghana, where he died in 1963.

In the excerpts from *The Souls of Black Folk* that follow, Du Bois introduces the main themes of the book, makes note of his disagreements with the conservative African-American leader, Booker T. Washington, and recalls his childhood in the western Massachusetts town of Great Barrington.

From The Oxford W.E.B. Du Bois Reader, edited by Eric J. Sundquist (1996). Reprinted by permission of Oxford University Press.

Du Bois's concerns focus, of course, on the United States, which has had a distinctive racial history. But thinking in racial categories was widespread around the world at the end of the long nineteenth century. Even as institutions like slavery were disappearing, racial labeling seemed to be gaining ground, strongly influencing the nature of global contacts. Racism obviously related to imperialism, well into the twentieth century. How much would it continue to affect national and international policies, even after imperialism itself began to decline?

RACIAL PERCEPTIONS

The Forethought

Herein lie buried many things which if read with patience may show the strange meaning of being black here in the dawning of the Twentieth Century. This meaning is not without interest to you, Gentle Reader; for the problem of the Twentieth Century is the problem of the color-line.

I pray you, then, receive my little book in all charity, studying my words with me, forgiving mistake and foible for sake of the faith and passion that is in me, and seeking the grain of truth hidden there.

I have sought here to sketch, in vague, uncertain outline, the spiritual world in which ten thousand thousand Americans live and strive. First, in two chapters I have tried to show what Emancipation meant to them, and what was its aftermath. In a third chapter I have pointed out the slow rise of personal leadership, and criticised candidly the leader who bears the chief burden of his race to-day [Booker T. Washington]. Then, in two other chapters I have sketched in swift outline the two worlds within and without the Veil, and thus have come to the central problem of training men for life. Venturing now into deeper detail, I have in two chapters studied the struggles of the massed millions of the black peasantry, and in another have sought to make clear the present relations of the sons of master and man.

Leaving, then, the world of the white man, I have stepped within the Veil, raising it that you may view faintly its deeper recesses,—the meaning of its religion, the passion of its human sorrow, and the struggle of its greater souls. All this I have ended with a tale twice told but seldom written.

Some of these thoughts of mine have seen the light before in other guise. For kindly consenting to their republication here, in altered and extended form, I must thank the publishers of *The Atlantic Monthly, The World's Work, The Dial, The New World,* and the *Annals of the American Academy of Political and Social Science.*

Before each chapter, as now printed, stands a bar of the Sorrow Songs,— some echo of haunting melody from the only American music which welled up from black souls in the dark past. And, finally, need I add that I who speak here am bone of the bone and flesh of the flesh of them that live within the Veil?

Of Our Spiritual Strivings

O water, voice of my heart, crying in the sand,
　　All night long crying with a mournful cry,

As I lie and listen, and cannot understand
    The voice of my heart in my side or the voice of the sea,
  O water, crying for rest, is it I, is it I?
    All night long the water is crying to me.

Unresting water, there shall never be rest
  Till the last moon droop and the last tide fail,
And the fire of the end begin to burn in the west;
    And the heart shall be weary and wonder and cry like the sea,
  All life long crying without avail,
    As the water all night long is crying to me.

Arthur Symons

    Between me and the other world there is ever an unasked question: unasked by some through feelings of delicacy; by others through the difficulty of rightly framing it. All, nevertheless, flutter round it. They approach me in a half-hesitant sort of way, eye me curiously or compassionately, and then, instead of saying directly, How does it feel to be a problem? they say, I know an excellent colored man in my town; or, I fought at Mechanicsville; or, Do not these Southern outrages make your blood boil? At these I smile, or am interested, or reduce the boiling to a simmer, as the occasion may require. To the real question, How does it feel to be a problem? I answer seldom a word.

    And yet, being a problem is a strange experience,—peculiar even for one who has never been anything else, save perhaps in babyhood and in Europe. It is in the early days of rollicking boyhood that the revelation first bursts upon one, all in a day, as it were. I remember well when the shadow swept across me. I was a little thing, away up in the hills of New England, where the dark Housatonic winds between Hoosac and Taghkanic to the sea. In a wee wooden schoolhouse, something put it into the boys' and girls' heads to buy gorgeous visiting-cards—ten cents a package—and exchange. The exchange was merry, till one girl, a tall newcomer, refused my card,—refused it peremptorily, with a glance. Then it dawned upon me with a certain suddenness that I was different from the others; or like, mayhap, in heart and life and longing, but shut out from their world by a vast veil. I had thereafter no desire to tear down that veil, to creep through; I held all beyond it in common contempt, and lived above it in a region of blue sky and great wandering shadows. That sky was bluest when I could beat my mates at examination-time, or beat them at a foot-race, or even beat their stringy heads. Alas, with the years all this fine contempt began to fade; for the worlds I longed for, and all their dazzling opportunities, were theirs, not mine. But they should not keep these prizes, I said; some, all, I would wrest from them. Just how I would do it I could never decide: by reading law, by healing the sick, by telling the wonderful tales that swam in my head,—some way. With other black boys the strife was not so fiercely sunny: their youth shrunk into tasteless sycophancy, or into silent hatred of the pale world about them and mocking distrust of everything white; or wasted itself in a bitter cry, Why did God make me an outcast and a stranger in mine own house? The shades of the prison-house closed round about us all: walls strait and stubborn to the whitest, but relentlessly narrow, tall, and unscalable to sons of night who must plod darkly on in resignation, or beat unavailing palms against the stone, or steadily, half hopelessly, watch the streak of blue above.

After the Egyptian and Indian, the Greek and Roman, the Teuton and Mongolian, the Negro is a sort of seventh son, born with a veil, and gifted with second-sight in this American world,—a world which yields him no true self-consciousness, but only lets him see himself through the revelation of the other world. It is a peculiar sensation, this double-consciousness, this sense of always looking at one's self through the eyes of others, of measuring one's soul by the tape of a world that looks on in amused contempt and pity. One ever feels his twoness,—an American, a Negro; two souls, two thoughts, two unreconciled strivings; two warring ideals in one dark body, whose dogged strength alone keeps it from being torn asunder.

The history of the American Negro is the history of this strife—this longing to attain self-conscious manhood, to merge his double self into a better and truer self. In this merging he wishes neither of the older selves to be lost. He would not Africanize America, for America has too much to teach the world and Africa. He would not bleach his Negro soul in a flood of white Americanism, for he knows that Negro blood has a message for the world. He simply wishes to make it possible for a man to be both a Negro and an American, without being cursed and spit upon by his fellows, without having the doors of Opportunity closed roughly in his face.

This, then, is the end of his striving: to be a co-worker in the kingdom of culture, to escape both death and isolation, to husband and use his best powers and his latent genius. These powers of body and mind have in the past been strangely wasted, dispersed, or forgotten. The shadow of a mighty Negro past flits through the tale of Ethiopia the Shadowy and of Egypt the Sphinx. Throughout history, the powers of single black men flash here and there like falling stars, and die sometimes before the world has rightly gauged their brightness. Here in America, in the few days since Emancipation, the black man's turning hither and thither in hesitant and doubtful striving has often made his very strength to lose effectiveness, to seem like absence of power, like weakness. And yet it is not weakness—it is the contradiction of double aims. The double-aimed struggle of the black artisan—on the one hand to escape white contempt for a nation of mere hewers of wood and drawers of water, and on the other hand to plough and nail and dig for a poverty-stricken horde—could only result in making him a poor craftsman, for he had but half a heart in either cause. By the poverty and ignorance of his people, the Negro minister or doctor was tempted toward quackery and demagogy; and by the criticism of the other world, toward ideals that made him ashamed of his lowly tasks. The would-be black *savant* was confronted by the paradox that the knowledge his people needed was a twice-told tale to his white neighbors, while the knowledge which would teach the white world was Greek to his own flesh and blood. The innate love of harmony and beauty that set the ruder souls of his people a-dancing and a-singing raised but confusion and doubt in the soul of the black artist; for the beauty revealed to him was the soul-beauty of a race which his larger audience despised, and he could not articulate the message of another people. This waste of double aims, this seeking to satisfy two unreconciled ideals, has wrought sad havoc with the courage and faith and deeds of ten thousand thousand people,—has sent them often wooing false gods and invoking false means of salvation, and at times has even seemed about to make them ashamed of themselves.

Away back in the days of bondage they thought to see in one divine event the end of all doubt and disappointment; few men ever worshipped Freedom with half such unquestioning faith as did the American Negro for two centuries. To him, so far as he thought and dreamed, slavery was indeed the sum of all villainies, the cause of all sorrow, the root of all prejudice; Emancipation was the key to a promised land of sweeter beauty than ever stretched before the eyes of wearied Israelites. In song and exhortation swelled one refrain—Liberty; in his tears and curses the God he implored had Freedom in his right hand. At last it came,—suddenly, fearfully, like a dream. With one wild carnival of blood and passion came the message in his own plaintive cadences:—

"Shout, O children!
Shout, you're free!
For God has bought your liberty!"

Years have passed away since then,—ten, twenty, forty; forty years of national life, forty years of renewal and development, and yet the swarthy spectre sits in its accustomed seat at the Nation's feast. In vain do we cry to this our vastest social problem:—

"Take any shape but that, and my firm nerves
Shall never tremble!"

The Nation has not yet found peace from its sins; the freedman has not yet found in freedom his promised land. Whatever of good may have come in these years of change, the shadow of a deep disappointment rests upon the Negro people,—a disappointment all the more bitter because the unattained ideal was unbounded save by the simple ignorance of a lowly people. . . .

STUDY QUESTIONS

1. What did Du Bois mean by the "the Veil"?
2. What did he mean by "twoness"?
3. How did Du Bois describe the aims of black Americans?
4. In what way did he think that the freeing of slaves in the United States had fallen short of justice? What dilemmas faced black Americans?
5. To what extent was Du Bois correct about the importance of race in the twentieth-century world?
6. What is a race?
7. What was the relationship between racial thinking in the United States around 1900, and the Western discussions of imperialism (Chapter 35)?

SECTION THREE

The Twentieth Century

Growing challenges to Western world dominance, sparked by growing nationalism and by divisions within the West, produced new expressions of diversity in the major world civilizations. At the same time, international contacts increased in many ways. New technologies speeded exchange; so did heightened trade, new alliance systems, and worldwide conflicts, and multinational companies spreading production and products literally around the globe. Much of twentieth-century world history involves oscillating tensions between interchange and a growing desire and capacity to define separate systems and identities.

Within this general framework, a number of more specific changes occurred, also reflecting the twentieth century's role as a transition toward a new, but not fully defined, period of world history. Religion declined in some societies but was reasserted in others. Political structures varied from liberal-democratic to authoritarian to communist, as new nations or revolutions yielded different patterns in different parts of the globe. But amid renewed diversity, including widely varying levels of economic well-being, were some common themes. Many civilizations sought ways to modify earlier political traditions—very few regimes in place in 1914 still survived by the early twenty-first century. Changes in the outlook and conditions of women marked fundamental social and personal upheaval. Hardly uniform, the twentieth-century world also shared a need to come to terms with some basic forces of innovation in the areas of technology, ideas, and social forms.

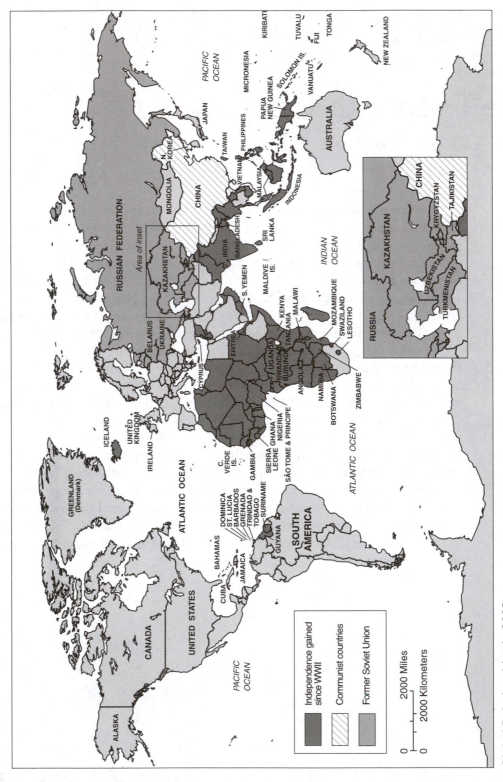

Global Relationships in 2002

38

The Experience of World War I

World War I (1914–1918) was an unprecedented conflict in many ways. It involved much of the globe, though the centers of major fighting were in Europe and the Middle East. It showed the power of industrial technology and organization to deepen conflict, causing immense casualties and also extensive economic and political disruption. And it was an agonizing human experience.

The next two sets of documents deal with the military experience in the trenches shared by all the combatants. The first set, from a memoir by the Austrian musician Fritz Kreisler, offers an overview of the early stages, suggesting initial excitement, followed by deadening conflict. Kreisler also notes the confusing impact on memory itself.

The second set of passages is from the war's most famous novel, *All Quiet on the Western Front,* by Erich Maria Remarque. Remarque had served in the German army. He wrote vividly about the nature of trench warfare and the physical and mental burdens it imposed.

The war permanently changed Europe's position in the world and greatly affected European politics—leading, for example, to the rise of fascism and Nazism. It also colored the life of a whole generation that found their expectations and rhythms totally shattered. The analytical challenge is to recapture this experience, at least in part, and discuss how it related to the larger changes the war produced.

FOUR WEEKS IN THE TRENCHES

I. FRITZ KREISLER

In trying to recall my impressions during my short war duty as an officer in the Austrian Army, I find that my recollections of this period are very uneven and confused. . . . This curious indifference of the memory to values of time and space

Selection I from Fritz Kreisler, *Four Wheels in the Trenches* (Boston; Houghton Mifflin, 1915), pp. 2, 6–8, 65–66, 69; Selection II from Erich Maria Remarque, *All Quiet on the Western Front*, A.W. Wheen, tr. (Boston: Little, Brown and Company, 1929), pp. 90–93, 109–110, 113–114. Copyright Erich Maria Remarque 1958.

may be due to the extraordinary physical and mental stress under which the impressions I am trying to chronicle were received. The same state of mind I find is rather characteristic of most people I have met who were in the war. It should not be forgotten, too, that the gigantic upheaval which changed the fundamental condition of life overnight and threatened the very existence of nations naturally dwarfed the individual into nothingness, and the existing interest in the common welfare left practically no room for personal considerations. Then again, at the front, the extreme uncertainty of the morrow tended to lessen the interest in the details of to-day; consequently I may have missed a great many interesting happenings alongside of me which I would have wanted to note under other circumstances. One gets into a strange psychological, almost hypnotic, state of mind while on the firing line which probably prevents the mind's eye from observing and noticing things in a normal way. This accounts, perhaps, for some blank spaces in my memory. . . .

I saw the crowds stop officers of high rank and well-known members of the aristocracy and clergy, also state officials and court functionaries of high rank, in quest of information, which was imparted cheerfully and patiently. The imperial princes could frequently be seen on the Ring Strasse [in Vienna] surrounded by cheering crowds or mingling with the public unceremoniously at the cafes, talking to everybody. Of course, the army was idolized. Wherever the troops marched the public broke into cheers and every uniform was the center of an ovation.

While coming from the station I saw two young reservists, to all appearances brothers, as they hurried to the barracks, carrying their small belongings in a valise. Along with them walked a little old lady crying, presumably their mother. They passed a general in full uniform. Up went their hands to their caps in military salute, whereupon the old general threw his arms wide open and embraced them both, saying: "Go on, my boys, do your duty bravely and stand firm for your emperor and your country. God willing, you will come back to your old mother." The old lady smiled through her tears. A shout went up, and the crowds surrounding the general cheered him. Long after I had left I could hear them shouting.

A few streets farther on I saw in an open cafe a young couple, a reservist in field uniform and a young girl, his bride or sweetheart. They sat there, hands linked, utterly oblivious of their surroundings and of the world at large. When somebody in the crowd espied them, a great shout went up, the public rushing to the table and surrounding them, then breaking into applause and waving hats and handkerchiefs. At first the young couple seemed to be utterly taken aback and only slowly did they realize that the ovation was meant for them. They seemed confused, the young girl blushing and hiding her face in her hands, the young man rising to his feet, saluting and bowing. More cheers and applause. He opened his mouth as if wanting to speak. There was a sudden silence. He was vainly struggling for expression, but then his face lit up as if by inspiration. Standing erect, hand at his cap, in a pose of military salute, he intoned the Austrian national hymn. In a second every head in that throng was bared. All traffic suddenly stopped, everybody, passengers as well as conductors of the cars, joining in the anthem. The neighboring windows soon filled with people, and soon it was a chorus of thousands of voices. The volume of tone and the intensity of feeling seemed to raise the inspiring anthem to the uttermost heights of sublime majesty. We were then on our way to the station, and long afterwards we could hear the singing, swelling like a human organ. . . .

We were all looking like shaggy, lean wolves, from the necessity of subsisting on next to nothing. I remember having gone for more than three days at a time without any food whatsoever, and many a time we had to lick the dew from the grass for want of water. A certain fierceness arises in you, an absolute indifference to anything the world holds except your duty of fighting. You are eating a crust of bread, and a man is shot dead in the trench next to you. You look calmly at him for a moment, and then go on eating your bread. Why not? There is nothing to be done. In the end you talk of your own death with as little excitement as you would of a luncheon engagement. There is nothing left in your mind but the fact that hordes of men to whom you belong are fighting against other hordes, and your side must win. . . .

It was there and then that I made a curious observation. After the second day we had almost grown to know each other. The Russians would laughingly call over to us, and the Austrians would answer. The salient feature of these three days' fighting was the extraordinary lack of hatred. In fact, it is astonishing how little actual hatred exists between fighting men. One fights fiercely and passionately, mass against mass, but as soon as the mass crystallizes itself into human individuals whose features one actually can recognize, hatred almost ceases. Of course, fighting continues, but somehow it loses its fierceness and takes more the form of a sport, each side being eager to get the best of the other. One still shoots at his opponent, but almost regrets when he sees him drop. . . .

ALL QUIET ON THE WESTERN FRONT

II. ERICH MARIA REMARQUE

We must look out for our bread. The rats have become much more numerous lately because the trenches are no longer in good condition. Detering says it is a sure sign of a coming bombardment.

The rats here are particularly repulsive, they are so fat—the kind we call corpse-rats. They have shocking, evil, naked faces, and it is nauseating to see their long, nude tails.

They seem to be mighty hungry. Almost every man has had his bread gnawed. Kropp wrapped his in his waterproof sheet and put it under his head, but he cannot sleep because they run over his face to get it. Detering meant to outwit them: he fastened a thin wire to the roof and suspended his bread from it. During the night when he switched on his pocket-torch he saw the wire swing to and fro. On the bread was riding a fat rat.

At last we put a stop to it. We cannot afford to throw the bread away, because then we should have nothing left to eat in the morning, so we carefully cut off the bits of bread that the animals have gnawed.

The slices we cut off are heaped together in the middle of the floor. Each man takes out his spade and lies down prepared to strike. Detering, Kropp, and Kat hold their pocket-torches ready.

After a few minutes we hear the first shuffling and tugging. It grows, now it is the sound of many little feet. Then the torches switch on and every man strikes at the heap, which scatters with a rush. The result is good. We toss the bits of rat over the parapet and again lie in wait.

Several times we repeat the process. At last the beasts get wise to it, or perhaps have scented the blood. They return no more. Nevertheless, before morning the remainder of the bread on the floor has been carried off.

In the adjoining sector they attacked two large cats and a dog, bit them to death and devoured them.

Next day there was an issue of Edamer cheese. Each man gets almost a quarter of a cheese. In one way that is all to the good, for Edamer is tasty—but in another way it is vile, because the fat red balls have long been a sign of a bad time coming. Our forebodings increase as rum is served out. We drink it of course; but are not greatly comforted. . . .

At night they send over gas. We expect the attack to follow and lie with our masks on, ready to tear them off as soon as the first shadow appears.

Dawn approaches without anything happening—only the everlasting, nerve-wracking roll behind the enemy lines, trains, trains, lorries [trucks], lorries; but what are they concentrating? Our artillery fires on it continually, but still it does not cease.

We have tired faces and avoid each other's eyes. "It will be like the Somme," says Kat gloomily. "There we were shelled steadily for seven days and nights." Kat has lost all his fun since we have been here, which is bad, for Kat is an old front-hog, and can smell what is coming. Only Tjaden seems pleased with the good rations and the rum; he thinks we might even go back to rest without anything happening at all.

It almost looks like it. Day after day passes. At night I squat in the listening-post. Above me the rockets and parachute-lights shoot up and float down again. I am cautious and tense, my heart thumps. My eyes turn again and again to the luminous dial of my watch; the hands will not budge. Sleep hangs on my eyelids, I work my toes in my boots in order to keep awake. Nothing happens till I am relieved;—only the everlasting rolling over there. Gradually we grow calmer and play skat and poker continually. Perhaps we will be lucky.

All day the sky is hung with observation balloons. There is a rumour that the enemy are going to put tanks over and use low-flying planes for the attack. But that interests us less than what we hear of the new flame-throwers.

We wake up in the middle of the night. The earth booms. Heavy fire is falling on us. We crouch into corners. We distinguish shells of every calibre.

Each man lays hold of his things and looks again every minute to reassure himself that they are still there. The dug-out heaves, the night roars and flashes. We look at each other in the momentary flashes of light, and with pale faces and pressed lips shake our heads. . . .

The days go by and the incredible hours follow one another as a matter of course. Attacks alternate with counter-attacks and slowly the dead pile up in the field of craters between the trenches. We are able to bring in most of the wounded that do not lie too far off. But many have long to wait and we listen to them dying.

For one of them we search two days in vain. He must be lying on his belly and unable to turn over. Otherwise it is hard to understand why we cannot find him; for it is only when a man has his mouth close to the ground that it is impossible to gauge the direction of his cry.

He must have been badly hit—one of those nasty wounds neither so severe that they exhaust the body at once and a man dreams on in a half-swoon, nor so light that a man endures the pain in the hope of becoming well again. Kat thinks he has either a broken pelvis or a shot through the spine. His chest cannot have been injured otherwise he would not have such strength to cry out. And if it were any other kind of wound it would be possible to see him moving.

He grows gradually hoarser. The voice is so strangely pitched that it seems to be everywhere. The first night some of our fellows go out three times to look for him. But when they think they have located him and crawl across, next time they hear the voice it seems to come from somewhere else altogether.

We search in vain until dawn. We scrutinized the field all day with glasses, but discover nothing. On the second day the calls are fainter; that will be because his lips and mouth have become dry.

Our Company Commander has promised next turn of leave with three days extra to anyone who finds him. That is a powerful inducement, but we would do all that is possible without that for his cry is terrible. Kat and Kropp even go out in the afternoon, and Albert gets the lobe of his ear shot off in consequence. It is to no purpose, they come back without him.

It is easy to understand what he cries. At first he called only for help—the second night he must have had some delirium, he talked to his wife and his children, we often detected the name Elise. Today he merely weeps. By evening the voice dwindles to a croaking. But it persists still through the whole night. We hear it so distinctly because the wind blows toward our line. In the morning when we suppose he must already have long gone to his rest, there comes across to us one last gurgling rattle.

The days are hot and the dead lie unburied. We cannot fetch them all in, if we did we should not know what to do with them. The shells will bury them. Many have their bellies swollen up like balloons. They hiss, belch, and make movements. The gases in them make noises.

The sky is blue and without clouds. In the evening it grows sultry and the heat rises from the earth. When the wind blows toward us it brings the smell of blood, which is very heavy and sweet. This deathly exhalation from the shell-holes seems to be a mixture of chloroform and putrefaction, and fills us with nausea and retching. . . .

· · ·

Suddenly the shelling begins to pound again. Soon we are sitting up once more with the rigid tenseness of blank anticipation.

Attack, counter-attack, charge, repulse—these are words, but what things they signify! We have lost a good many men, mostly recruits. Reinforcements have again been sent up to our sector. They are one of the new regiments, composed almost entirely of young fellows just called up. They have had hardly any training, and are sent into the field with only a theoretical knowledge. They do know what a hand-grenade is, it is true, but they have very little idea of cover, and what is most important of all, have no eye for it. A fold in the ground has to be quite eighteen inches high before they can see it.

Although we need reinforcement, the recruits give us almost more trouble than they are worth. They are helpless in this grim fighting area, they fall like flies. Modern trench-warfare demands knowledge and experience; a man must have a feeling for the contours of the ground, an ear for the sound and character of the shells, must be able to decide beforehand where they will drop, how they will burst, and how to shelter from them.

The young recruits of course know none of these things. They get killed simply because they hardly can tell shrapnel from high-explosive, they are mown down because they are listening anxiously to the roar of the big coal-boxes falling in the rear, and miss the light, piping whistle of the low spreading daisy-cutters. They flock together like sheep instead of scattering, and even the wounded are shot down like hares by the airmen.

Their pale turnip faces, their pitiful clenched hands, the fine courage of these poor devils, the desperate charges and attacks made by the poor brave wretches, who are so terrified that they dare not cry out loudly, but with battered chests, with torn bellies, arms and legs only whimper softly for their mothers and cease as soon as one looks at them.

Their sharp, downy, dead faces have the awful expressionlessness of dead children.

It brings a lump into the throat to see how they go over, and run and fall. A man would like to spank them, they are so stupid, and to take them by the arm and lead them away from here where they have no business to be. They wear grey coats and trousers and boots, but for most of them the uniform is far too big, it hangs on their limbs, their shoulders are too narrow, their bodies too slight; no uniform was ever made to these childish measurements.

Between five and ten recruits fall to every old hand.

A surprise gas-attack carries off a lot of them. They have not yet learned what to do. We found one dug-out full of them, with blue heads and black lips. Some of them in a shell hole took off their masks too soon; they did not know that the gas lies longest in the hollows; when they saw others on top without masks they pulled theirs off too and swallowed enough to scorch their lungs. Their condition is hopeless, they choke to death with haemorrhages and suffocation. . . .

STUDY QUESTIONS

1. What was the mood at the outset of the war, and what caused it?
2. What were the main features of trench warfare for the troops involved? What would happen to people who managed to live through this experience?
3. What makes Remarque's writing so powerful? Why would people want to read a war novel of this sort?
4. What was new about warfare as Remarque and Kreisler describe it?
5. What were the wider implications of the fighting, for example for the political values of veterans after the war had ended? Can you see connections with some of the new political and cultural movements of the 1920s?

39

The Western State

One of the key new trends in Western society during the twentieth century involved changes in the role of the state. Government powers expanded and contacts between state and ordinary citizens increased. Whether the form of government was democratic or not, voting was used to link individual and the state. New ideologies and technologies alike expanded state activities. The growth of the Western state built on earlier trends, such as absolutism, and on the needs and capacities of industrial society. Nevertheless, it was a new creature.

The growth of this state power could take vitally different forms, however. Tensions in the Western political tradition, visible in the seventeenth and eighteenth centuries, emerged anew, focusing on the extent of government power as well as constitutional structure. Between the world wars, the most striking political development in the West was the rise of fascist or Nazi totalitarianism. The totalitarian state did not emerge everywhere in the West, but rather in nations where liberal traditions were relatively weak and the shocks of World War I particularly great. Hitler, the Nazi leader, defines the fascist worship of the state in his tract *Mein Kampf,* written in 1924.

The second main version of governmental growth was the welfare state, which became the common Western form after World War II. Britain, converting from liberal suspicion of government to a desire for new social responsibility, clearly illustrated welfare-state principles. The British welfare-state concept was sketched in a vital wartime planning document, the Beveridge Report, which was put into practice after 1945.

Both the *Mein Kampf* and the Beveridge Report selections require some interpretation, for neither Hitler nor the Beveridge Commission spelled out a full definition of state functions in a tidy way. Hitler's writings were vague in most respects, featuring strong emotions more than careful programs. The Beveridge Report was a pragmatic planning exercise, not a statement of basic theory. A first task, then, is to figure out how state goals are defined and justified in each case—what Hitler means by state reliance on "personality"; what the welfare planners mean by state responsibility.

Selection I from *Mein Kampf* by Adolf Hitler, translated by Ralph Manheim, pp. 443, 449–451. Copyright 1943 and copyright © renewed 1971 by Houghton Mifflin Company of Boston. Reprinted by permission of Houghton Mifflin Company. Selection II from "Report by Sir William Beveridge," *Social Insurance and Allied Services* (Cmd 6404), London, Her Majesty's Stationery Office, 1942, pp. 6–8, 13, 158–159. British Crown copyright. Reproduced by the permission of the Controller of Her Britannic Majesty's Stationery Office.

Nazi and welfare-state definitions obviously invite comparison. How did they differ in political ideals? How did each relate to earlier Western political standards? Why did the different state forms arise amid the crises conditions of world wars and economic depression in the West, and how would each affect ordinary citizens? But also, in what ways did Nazi and welfare states reflect some similar trends and principles?

The Nazi version of the state seems to have been confined, in the West, to the special conditions of the 1920s and 1930s. Might these reemerge? Is the welfare state a more durable Western form? If so, why? Compared with contemporary political structures elsewhere in the world, has the twentieth-century Western state remained particularly distinctive?

TWO INNOVATIONS: NAZISM AND THE WELFARE STATE

I. HITLER DEFINES THE STATE (1924)

Anyone who believes today that a folkish National Socialist state must distinguish itself from other states only in a purely mechanical sense, by a superior construction of its economic life—that is, by a better balance between rich and poor, or giving broad sections of the population more right to influence the economic process, or by fairer wages by elimination of excessive wage differentials—has not gone beyond the most superficial aspects of the matter and has not the faintest idea of what we call a philosophy. All the things we have just mentioned offer not the slightest guaranty of continued existence, far less of any claim to greatness. A people which did not go beyond these really superficial reforms would not obtain the least guaranty of victory in the general struggle of nations. A movement which finds the content of its mission only in such a general leveling, assuredly just as it may be, will truly bring about no great and profound, hence real, reform of existing conditions, since its entire activity does not, in the last analysis, go beyond externals, and does not give the people that inner armament which enables it, with almost inevitable certainty I might say, to overcome in the end those weaknesses from which we suffer today. . . .

The folkish state must care for the welfare of its citizens by recognizing in all and everything the importance of the value of personality, thus in all fields preparing the way for that highest measure of productive performance which grants to the individual the highest measure of participation.

And accordingly, the folkish state must free all leadership and especially the highest—that is, the political leadership—entirely from the parliamentary principle of majority rule—in other words, mass rule—and instead absolutely guarantee the right of the personality.

From this the following realization results:

The best state constitution and state form is that which, with the most unquestioned certainty, raises the best minds in the national community to leading position and leading influence.

But as, in economic life, the able men cannot be appointed from above, but must struggle through for themselves, and just as here the endless schooling, ranging from the smallest business to the largest enterprise, occurs spontaneously, with life alone giving the examinations, obviously political minds cannot be "discovered." Extraordinary geniuses permit of no consideration for normal mankind.

From the smallest community cell to the highest leadership of the entire Reich, the state must have the personality principle anchored in its organization.

There must be no majority decisions, but only responsible persons, and the word "council" must be restored to its original meaning. Surely every man will have advisers by his side, but *the decision will be made by one man.*

The principle which made the Prussian army in its time into the most wonderful instrument of the German people must some day, in a transferred sense, become the principle of the construction of our whole state conception: *authority of every leader downward and responsibility upward.*

Even then it will not be possible to dispense with those corporations which today we designate as parliaments. But their councillors will then actually give counsel; responsibility, however, can and may be borne only by *one* man, and therefore only he alone may possess the authority and right to command.

Parliaments as such are necessary, because in them, above all, personalities to which special responsible tasks can later be entrusted have an opportunity gradually to rise up.

This gives the following picture:

The folkish state, from the township up to the Reich leadership, has no representative body which decides anything by the majority, but only *advisory bodies* which stand at the side of the elected leader, receiving their share of work from him, and in turn if necessary assuming unlimited responsibility in certain fields, just as on a larger scale the leader or chairman of the various corporations himself possesses.

As a matter of principle, the folkish state does not tolerate asking advice or opinions in special matters—say, of an economic nature—of men who, on the basis of their education and activity, can understand nothing of the subject. It, therefore, divides its representative bodies from the start into *political and professional chambers.*

In order to guarantee a profitable cooperation between the two, a special *senate* of the élite always stands above them.

In no chamber and in no senate does a vote ever take place. They are working institutions and not voting machines. The individual member has an advisory, but never a determining, voice. The latter is the exclusive privilege of the responsible chairman.

This principle—absolute responsibility unconditionally combined with absolute authority—will gradually breed an élite of leaders such as today, in this era of irresponsible parliamentarianism, is utterly inconceivable.

Thus, the political form of the nation will be brought into agreement with that law to which it owes its greatness in the cultural and economic field.

· · ·

As regards the possibility of putting these ideas into practice, I beg you not to forget that the parliamentary principle of democratic majority rule has by no means always dominated mankind, but on the contrary is to be found only in brief periods of history, which are always epochs of the decay of peoples and states.

But it should not be believed that such a transformation can be accomplished by purely theoretical measures from above, since logically it may not even stop at the state constitution, but must permeate all other legislation, and indeed all civil life. Such a fundamental change can and will only take place through a movement which is itself constructed in the spirit of these ideas and hence bears the future state within itself.

Hence the National Socialist movement should today adapt itself entirely to these ideas and carry them to practical fruition within its own organization, so that some day it may not only show the state these same guiding principles, but can also place the completed body of its own state at its disposal.

II. GREAT BRITAIN PLANS THE WELFARE STATE (1942)

In proceeding from this first comprehensive survey of social insurance to the next task—of making recommendations—three guiding principles may be laid down at the outset.

The first principle is that any proposals for the future, while they should use to the full the experience gathered in the past, should not be restricted by consideration of sectional interests established in the obtaining of that experience. Now, when the war is abolishing landmarks of every kind, is the opportunity for using experience in a clear field. A revolutionary movement in the world's history is a time for revolutions, not for patching.

The second principle is that organisation of social insurance should be treated as one part only of a comprehensive policy of social progress. Social insurance fully developed may provide income security; it is an attack upon Want. But Want is one only of five giants on the road of reconstruction and in some ways the easiest to attack. The others are Disease, Ignorance, Squalor and Idleness.

The third principle is that social security must be achieved by co-operation between the State and the individual. The State should offer security for service and contribution. The State in organising security should not stifle incentive, opportunity, responsibility; in establishing a national minimum, it should leave room and encouragement for voluntary action by each individual to provide more than that minimum for himself and his family. . . .

Abolition of want requires, first, improvement of State insurance, that is to say provision against interruption and loss of earning power. All the principal causes of interruption or loss of earnings are now the subject of schemes of social insurance. If, in spite of these schemes, so many persons unemployed or sick or old or widowed are found to be without adequate income for subsistence according to the standards adopted in the social surveys, this means that the benefits amount to less than subsistence by those standards or do not last as long as the need, and that the assistance which supplements insurance is either insufficient in amount or available only on terms which make men unwilling to have recourse to it. None of the insurance benefits provided before the war were in fact designed with reference to the standards of the social surveys. Though unemployment benefit was not altogether out of relation to those standards, sickness and disablement benefit, old age pensions and widows' pensions were far below them, while workmen's compensation was below subsistence level for anyone who had family responsibilities or whose earnings in work were less than twice the amount needed for subsistence. To prevent interruption or destruction of earning power from leading to want, it is necessary to improve the present schemes of social insurance in three directions: by extension of scope to cover persons now excluded, by extension of purposes to cover risks now excluded, and by raising the rates of benefit.

Abolition of want requires, second, adjustment of incomes, in periods of earning as well as interruption of earning, to family needs, that is to say in one form or another it requires allowances for children. Without such allowances as part of benefit or added to it, to make provision for large families, no social insurance against interruption of earnings can be adequate. But if children's allowances are given only when earnings are interrupted and are not given during earning also, two evils are unavoidable. First, a substantial measure of acute want will remain among the lower paid workers as the accompaniment of large families. Second, in all such cases, income will be greater during unemployment or other interruptions of work than during work.

. . .

There is here an issue of principle and practice on which strong arguments can be advanced on each side by reasonable men. But the general tendency of public opinion seems clear. After trial of a different principle, it has been found to accord best with the sentiments of the British people that in insurance organised by the community by use of compulsory powers each individual should stand in on the same terms; none should claim to pay less because he is healthier or has more regular employment. In accord with that view, the proposals of the Report mark another step forward to the development of State insurance as a new type of human institution, differing both from the former methods of preventing or alleviating distress and from voluntary insurance. The term "social insurance" to describe this institution implies both that it is compulsory and that men stand together with their fellows. The term implies a pooling of risks except so far as separation of risks serves a social purpose. There may be reasons of social policy for adjusting premiums to risks, in order to give a stimulus for avoidance of danger, as in the case of industrial accident and disease. There is no longer an admitted claim of the individual citizen to share in national insurance and yet to stand outside it, keeping the advantage of his individual lower risk whether of unemployment or of disease or accident. . . .

A comprehensive national health service will ensure that for every citizen there is available whatever medical treatment he requires, in whatever form he requires it, domiciliary or institutional, general, specialist or consultant, and will ensure also the provision of dental, ophthalmic and surgical appliances, nursing and midwifery and rehabilitation after accidents. Whether or not payment towards the cost of the health service is included in the social insurance contribution, the service itself should

(i) be organized, not by the Ministry concerned with social insurance, but by Departments responsible for the health of the people and for positive and preventive as well as curative measures;

(ii) be provided where needed without contribution conditions in any individual case.

Restoration of a sick person to health is a duty of the State and the sick person, prior to any other consideration. The assumption made here is in accord with the definition of the objects of medical service as proposed in the Draft Interim Report of the Medical Planning Commission of the British Medical Association:

"(a) to provide a system of medical service directed towards the achievement of positive health, of the prevention of disease, and the relief of sickness;

(b) to render available to every individual all necessary medical services, both general and specialist, and both domiciliary and institutional."

STUDY QUESTIONS

1. What did Hitler mean by the personality principle?
2. Why might Hitler's ideas appeal to Germans who had experienced World War I?
3. What kind of state, with what purposes, did the Nazis seek?
4. What changes in state functions did the Beveridge Report advocate?
5. What were the main differences between Nazi and welfare-state political definitions?
6. Why did the twentieth century see a growth in state claims, albeit under various systems, in Western society?

40

Consumerism

Modern consumerism began in Western Europe in the eighteenth century. It involved a growing emphasis on acquiring material goods and shopping on the part of a wide range of social groups, and not just the elite. Many historians argue that, as consumerism spread and solidified, it represented one of the most profound changes in human values experienced in modern world history. Ultimately, consumerism spread well beyond the West, to affect almost all parts of the globe.

Consumerism was not an event, and it is not easy to document its ascent. Changes in distribution—like the rise of the department store, from the 1830s onward—and the development of modern advertising can be traced fairly readily. But how did ordinary people redefine their lives around consumerism? What were the impacts on other cultural values, including religion and politics?

The following documents involve comments on consumerism in Germany in the 1920s, under the Weimar republic. This was a shaky time in German history, after the defeat of World War I. Not surprisingly there were many concerns about consumerism as a distraction from proper values. But consumerism gained ground nevertheless. These selections suggest some aspects of what consumerism entailed, and why it prompted criticism.

The main concept to explore is consumerism itself. Important aspects, like claims of special involvements of women, were not unique to Germany, but were common throughout Western society. But there are some specific German features addressed, including some of the political implications. Consumerism would become one of the targets of Nazi attacks, in the name of German nationalism and subordination of individual interests to the state.

The first document was a call for a boycott of French fashions during the French occupation of the Ruhr in 1923—part of the postwar tension between the two nations. A second criticism was more general, from a Berlin newspaper in 1925. But the third document, from 1926, appeared in a more professional journal for advertisers, urging embrace of consumerism with an eye to manipulation and sales. The final selection is from the first issue of a new car magazine in 1928.

Selection I from "Boykott franzoesicher Modewaren," *Sty1. Blaetter des Verbandes der deutschen Modeindutrie* 2 #1 (Feb. 1923), pp. 52–53; Selection II from "Nun aber genug! Gegen die Vermaennlichung der Frau," *Berliner Illustrierte Zeitschrift des Verbandes deutscher Reklamefachleute* (July 1926), pp. 649–650; Selection IV from "Zum Geleit," *Auto-magazin,* no. 1 (Jan. 1928), p. 1 All from Anton Kaes, Martin Jay, and Edward Dimendberg, eds., *The Weimar Republic Sourcebook* (Berkeley: University of California Press, 1994), pp. 658–662, 667. Copyright Regents of the University of California.

CONSUMERISM

I. BOYCOTT OF FRENCH FASHION GOODS

The daily and professional press has made it widely known that the German fashion industry has decided to speak out for a boycott of French fashion goods. This decision is frequently misunderstood, and it is therefore best that a few words be said about it.

We in fashion are fully aware of our dependence on Paris to provide us with the taste of worldwide fashion. It is better to say these things directly than to talk around the issue. We also know that we harm ourselves in multiple ways if we do not travel to Paris. The exporting businesses clearly suffer disadvantages from this step; likewise the fashion salons with foreign retail customers will have to sacrifice this or that sale, for among their customers quite a few specifically want to see patterns from Paris.

In order not to increase damage to ourselves, the Association has no objection if someone wants to travel to Holland, Switzerland, or Vienna to view fashion developments and perhaps purchase copies from houses that were in Paris so that we might supplement our collections with what we would otherwise have lacked. It should be noted here that in these countries too the purchase of original patterns from Paris or any sort of fashion goods originally from France is not permitted.

It was not easy for the men whose inspiration it was to recommend this resolution. It has been seriously and amply considered. Political circumstances were more powerful than any more reasonable considerations and, as so often happens these days, action must be taken under the force of these circumstances.

It is not a question of advantage and disadvantage, not a question of the interests, greater or smaller, of individuals, and not in this case a question of the interests of the industry involved. Rather this time it is a question of the whole, a matter of life and death. We took this step aware that it will put us at a disadvantage, thus we have made a willing sacrifice. We would have found it abominable if fashion representatives had traveled to Paris and made purchases there in a moment when our countrymen in the Ruhr valley, from the simplest workers to the largest industrialists and highest officials, are being harassed and mistreated to the point of bloodshed. It was no longer possible for us to turn our eyes from the fact that the French are doing absolutely everything conceivable to ruin us. In such a moment it is not a question of business, but for everyone who still possesses a spark of national feeling or a spark of the feeling of self-respect there is something natural in self-defense against such humiliation. Those who have no feeling for this have relinquished their right to demand to be respected as a German inside the country or out; neither can they have retained any self-respect, for they betray their national and personal honor for the sake of material interest. . . .

Let us make no secret of our position. Let us say openly to our customers in and outside of Germany: we were not in Paris; have a look at our things and judge whether they are good or bad. And we will see that our customers will also understand us. Most countries possess enough national feeling of their own that they will respect those who say they were not in Paris.

Inside Germany everyone must help us to put the resolution completely and thoroughly into practice and lend to the spirit of the resolution their most emphatic support.

II. ENOUGH IS ENOUGH! AGAINST THE MASCULINIZATION OF WOMEN

What started as a playful game in women's fashion is gradually becoming a distressing aberration. At first it was like a charming novelty: that gently, delicate women cut their long tresses and bobbed their hair; that the dresses they wore hung down in an almost perfectly straight line, denying the contours of the female body, the curve of the hips; that they shortened their skirts, exposing their slender legs up to calf level. Even the most traditional of men were not scandalized by this. A creature like this could have been warmly greeted with the now obsolete pet name *my angel*—for angels are asexual, yet they have always been represented in a pre-adolescent female form, even the archangel Gabriel. But the male sensibility began to take offense at this as the fashion that was so becoming to young girls and their delicate figures was adopted by all women. It did an aesthetic disservice to stately and full-figured women. But the trend went even further; women no longer wanted to appear asexual; rather fashion was increasingly calculated to make women's outward appearance more masculine. The practice of wearing men's nightclothes became increasingly widespread among women, even to the point of wearing them whenever possible for daytime lounging.

And we observe more often now that the bobbed haircut with its curls is disappearing, to be replaced by the modern, masculine hairstyle: sleek and brushed straight back. The new fashion in women's coats is also decidedly masculine: it would scarcely be noticed this spring if a woman absentmindedly put on her husband's coat. Fashion is like a pendulum swinging back and forth. With the hoop skirt the dictates of fashion brought the accentuation of the female form to an extreme, and now things are moving in the completely opposite direction. It is high time that sound male judgment take a stand against these odious fashions, the excesses of which have been transplanted here from America. In the theater we might enjoy, one time, seeing an actress playing a man's part if she is suitable for the role; but not every woman should venture to display herself in pants or shorts, be it on stage or at sporting events. And the masculinization of the female face replaces its natural allure with, at best, an unnatural one: the look of a sickeningly sweet boy is detested by every real boy or man.

III. WOMEN AS SHOPPERS

Seventy-five percent of all things are bought by women. Women buy for themselves, for their children, for their homes, and also very often for their husbands. Most money spent passes through the hands of women. For this reason you should check carefully whether your goods are not also purchased by women. The tie that a man buys because his wife likes it has in reality been purchased by her.

Women tend to think in strongly personal terms. Nevertheless they are easy to influence. Their first question will always be: is there a use or advantage in it for me? They relate everything directly to their appearance, their happiness, their sympathies. General facts, logical reasons, abstract considerations, and technical details do not say much to them. Statistics and politics leave them cold in the moment of a purchase. They demand instead that their smaller desires be understood. They are pleased by easily understood explanations of the use of an item or about the reasons it is better.

Women love a simple and personal language, however modern they might be in their professions and progressive in their opinions. With things that touch them personally, they are first of all women. And, once again, that is the reason they perceive everything personally.

Only in the rarest of cases will women analyze their feelings or actions. Their sensations, decisions, affections, and rejections are thoroughly emotional and irrevocable.

The majority of marketers find it very difficult to write advertisements for women. They think in terms that are too complicated, too masculine. The love they have for the products they sell is colored by their own perspective. They frequently use expressions that mean something entirely different to women, that lead to misunderstandings, indeed, that often offend them. An idea that is good in itself is often spoiled by an incorrect expression.

Consider the fact that women love their homes, be they ever so simple, and that they are proud of certain pieces of furniture and keepsakes. Do not insult them with sarcastic disparagement. Never use ridicule in your texts and never be skeptical. You might cause a few to laugh, but many will be irritated.

Shopping is a serious matter for all people, but most especially for women. Do not attempt to make advertisements humorous, for firstly there are only a few really humorous ads and secondly to women humor is neither generally understood, nor congenial, nor persuasive.

Women regard life as a shockingly serious business which must be endured if necessary with clenched teeth. They wash, they iron, they sweep, they cook, they sew, they attend to the children, they make the beds . . . a woman's work is never done. Not only do they have their own language in which they think and discuss these things, but they also have a whole set of very particular feelings for them, which an advertiser must know and may never overlook.

Consider the fact that women are experienced in the care and treatment of children. If you give them advice in this area, then do so in a way thay does not offend the views they learned from their mothers. Women are generally conservative. They find sudden innovations unpleasant—with the exception of those in fashion. Their education in new thoughts must proceed slowly and carefully. Convince the women that your offerings represent an easily understood advantage for them or their children and half the battle is already won.

Speak to housewives of the "small amenities of the item," of the work it saves. Give her suggestions on how to procure and prepare meals with less trouble. Speak with her new methods for simplifying housework. Inform mothers of new advances in the area of hygiene and nutrition.

Do not speak of slavery but offer the woman a hand to gain more time for herself. She will be grateful to you.

The woman with a profession, unburdened by crude household worries and in possession of more money that she can dispose of freely, wants simply to be a woman in her leisure time. She does not think so much of the price if you convince her that your goods will make her life easier, more pleasant, and nicer. Like the housewife her first question in regard to a fashion advertisement is: does it become me? And like the former, she is interested only in the one pictured, and not in the dozen presented in the text. She strives for new knowledge in order to advance herself, but learning by being entertained is most congenial to her. Women politicians and parliamentarians are captivated by a pretty and skillful speech, even if the calculation is wrong, even if the statistical figures do not add up and even if after the third word all the men are already shaking their heads. In, short, having a profession has not changed her in her heart of hearts. She remains a woman.

You see that it is not easy for men to write texts for women. It is even harder to illustrate such texts. Give your drafts, pictures, and texts to women to evaluate—not your wife or your daughter or a lady who knows what is at issue but a complete outsider. A woman's judgment is quickly influenced when she knows why she is supposed to give it.

Everything that has been said already applies to an even greater extent to illustrations. If a good picture is worth a thousand words, then ten thousand good words will not induce any woman to look at an ugly or false picture. The effect of the ad stands and falls with the picture. They look first of all at the picture, and if it appeals to them, they read the text. Something incorrect in fashion, a badly arranged kitchen, or a false step in the care of the children, everything that is ridiculous, impossible, or horrible to women occasions them to pass over the ad immediately in scorn and irritation.

Without a doubt the majority of women would rather look at a pretty, appetizing girl than an ugly one. But the ever-cheerful "sweet girl" performing the dirty chores in the public toilet wearing elegant evening gloves is even more ridiculous for women than for men.

Pure text ads, be they ever so clear and aesthetically pleasing, do not interest women. Mere text is too cold and structural for them. Not even trimmings and borders help matters. On the other hand, many women, out of curiosity and the desire for sensation, read the personal ads and the announcements of weddings and engagements, carefully. A clever ad in close proximity to these generally succeeds.

Let us summarize: ads for women must be as personal as possible. They must take into account the typical female characteristic: to agree without reservation, or to repudiate absolutely. Women see things with their eyes—nothing can move them to read an ad that, for some reason or other, does not appeal to them on first sight.

The young women of the postwar period distinguish themselves in some things very clearly from their sisters of 1914. Their bodies, freed from the corset, reasonably dressed, and athletically trained, have become more natural and prettier. Their minds, steeled by need and the worries of war and sharpened by the business of work, are freer and clearer. Their demeanor, although more tomboyish, is easier and less forced than it was in the times when it was thought that the solution to the problem of the erotic was solved by hushing it up. The fellowship of young men and women, often slandered and abused, has become a fact in many parts of Europe.

A new race of women is growing up in Europe, consciously demanding the rights from which they have been barred by the slavery to convention of earlier times.

IV. AUTO-MAGAZIN (A CAR MAGAZINE)

Editorial Statement

With the enormous upswing that automobilism in Germany has experienced in recent years, the desire for a magazine devoted, alongside the technical periodicals, to the automobile grew as well. There is scarcely any industry that is faster growing than the automobile industry. The young people of today already possess an educational background in automobile technology. Girls and women understand something about the automobile, and fathers are able in the long run to ignore the expertise their families have acquired just as little as they can escape the slow but sure arrival of the day when they purchase an automobile. In Germany today there are approximately three-quarters of a million automobiles on the streets. In just a few years this number will have doubled, so the need for an automobile magazine is obvious. Our task is to report about the automobile here at home and abroad, to illustrate innovations, to report on sporting events, to show automobile fashions just as much as to publish the latest photographs of automobile races, to convey data, ideas, and expert advice, to depict automobile travel, and to collect automotive caricatures from all over the world—in short, to unreel month by month the entire repertoire conjured by the magical word *automobile.*

The *Auto-Magazin* will do justice to all of these desires. Every month in these pages interest in the automobile will be reinvigorated in amusing form, and soon there will not be a single automobilist who can do without the *Auto-Magazine.* This, in a few brief words, is the goal we have set ourselves. To achieve it we need the cooperation of our readers—in particular we should like to receive abundant photographic material.

STUDY QUESTIONS

1. What were some of the objections to consumerism? What kinds of objections were particular to 1920s Germany, and what were more common as consumerism spread?

2. Does consumerism involve a special role for women? How did German men perceive women's interests? How did discussions of consumerism build on gender stereotypes? Has that relationship changed in contemporary society?

3. What was the relationship between consumerism and nationalism? Has that relationship changed in contemporary society?

4. On the basis of these documents, how can consumerism best be defined? What is the relationship between consumerism and fads/fashions?

5. What was the role of advertisement in spreading consumerism? Did advertisers shape tastes, or did they simply use tastes that had already developed?

41

Lenin and the Russian Revolution

The year 1917 brought momentous change to Russia. Mass upheaval in the cities and the countryside, derived in part from suffering associated with World War I, led to the destruction of key elements of the old order: The Romanov dynasty and the landlord class, each of which had deep roots in Russian history, were swept away forever. These changes alone are important enough to place the Russian Revolution in the same category as the French Revolution. But the events of 1917 had an added significance, for the victorious Bolshevik revolutionaries did not seek to establish a Western-style middle-class society. Instead, they proclaimed socialism and communism as their goals.

If the meaning and legacy of the Russian Revolution have engendered much controversy, there is, nevertheless, widespread agreement on the central role played by Lenin (Valdimir Ilych Ulyanov, 1870–1924), the indefatigable leader of the Bolshevik party and the first head of the new Soviet regime. Lenin's leading role in the Russian Revolution is traceable to the force of his ideas and his organizing ability, illustrated in the following selections from his works. In reading the following excerpts from Lenin's writings, note the way in which his thoughts embrace various tensions. Do you see elements of realism as well as utopianism in Lenin? Does his commitment to class struggle mesh with his desire to modernize Russia? Can Lenin's desire for democracy be reconciled with his belief in the necessity of authoritarian rule?

LENIN'S WRITINGS

Our Programme (1899)

We take our stand entirely on the Marxist theoretical position: Marxism was the first to transform socialism from a utopia into a science, to lay a firm foundation for this science, and to indicate the path that must be followed in further developing

From *The Lenin Anthology* by Robert C. Tucker. Copyright © 1975 by W. W. Norton & Company, Inc., of New York. Reprinted by permission of W. W. Norton & Company, Inc.

and elaborating it in all its parts. It disclosed the nature of modern capitalist economy by explaining how the hire of the labourer, the purchase of labour power, conceals the enslavement of millions of propertyless people by a handful of capitalists, the owners of the land, factories, mines, and so forth. It showed that all modern capitalist development displays the tendency of large-scale production to eliminate petty production and creates conditions that make a socialist system of society possible and necessary. It taught us how to discern, beneath the pall of rooted customs, political intrigues, abstruse laws, and intricate doctrines—the *class struggle,* the struggle between the propertied classes in all their variety and the propertyless mass, the *proletariat,* which is at the head of all the propertyless. It made clear the real task of a revolutionary socialist party: not to draw up plans for refashioning society, not to preach to the capitalists and their hangers-on about improving the lot of the workers, not to hatch conspiracies, *but to organise the class struggle of the proletariat and to lead this struggle, the ultimate aim of which is the conquest of political power by the proletariat and the organization of a socialist society.* . . .

Leading a Revolutionary Movement (1902)

I assert that it is far more difficult to unearth a dozen wise men than a hundred fools. This position I will defend, no matter how much you instigate the masses against me for my "anti-democratic" views, etc. As I have stated repeatedly, by "wise men," in connection with organisation, I mean *professional revolutionaries,* irrespective of whether they have developed from among students or working men. I assert: (1) that no revolutionary movement can endure without a stable organisation of leaders maintaining continuity; (2) that the broader the popular mass drawn spontaneously into the struggle, which forms the basis of the movement and participates in it, the more urgent the need for such an organisation, and the more solid this organisation must be (for it is much easier for all sorts of demagogues to side-track the more backward sections of the masses); (3) that such an organisation must consist chiefly of people professionally engaged in revolutionary activity; (4) that in an autocratic state, the more we *confine* the membership of such an organisation to people who are professionally engaged in revolutionary activity and who have been professionally trained in the art of combating the political police, the more difficult will it be to unearth the organisation; and (5) the *greater* will be the number of people from the working class and from the other social classes who will be able to join the movement and perform active work in it. . . .

Proclaiming the New Soviet Government (November 1917)

Comrades, the workers' and peasants' revolution, the need of which the Bolsheviks have emphasized many times, has come to pass.

What is the significance of this revolution? Its significance is, in the first place, that we shall have a soviet government, without the participation of bourgeoisie of any kind. The oppressed masses will of themselves form a government. The old state machinery will be smashed into bits and in its place will be created a new machinery of government by the soviet organizations. From now on there is a new page in the history of Russia, and the present, third Russian revolution shall in its final result lead to the victory of Socialism.

One of our immediate tasks is to put an end to the war [World War I] at once. But in order to end the war, which is closely bound up with the present capitalistic system, it is necessary to overthrow capitalism itself. In this work we shall have the aid of the world labor movement, which has already begun to develop in Italy, England, and Germany.

A just and immediate offer of peace by us to the international democracy will find everywhere a warm response among the international proletariat masses. In order to secure the confidence of the proletariat, it is necessary to publish at once all secret treaties.

In the interior of Russia a very large part of the peasantry has said: Enough playing with the capitalists; we will go with the workers. We shall secure the confidence of the peasants by one decree, which will wipe out the private property of the landowners. The peasants will understand that their own salvation is in union with the workers.

We will establish a real labor control on production.

We have now learned to work together in a friendly manner, as is evident from this revolution. We have the force of mass organization which has conquered all and which will lead the proletariat to world revolution.

We should now occupy ourselves in Russia in building up a proletarian socialist state.

Long live the world-wide socialistic revolution.

Modernizing Russia (1920)

The essential feature of the present political situation is that we are now passing through a crucial period of transition, something of a zigzag transition from war to economic development. This has occurred before, but not on such a wide scale. This should constantly remind us of what the general political tasks of the Soviet government are, and what constitutes the particular feature of this transition. The dictatorship of the proletariat has been successful because it has been able to combine compulsion with persuasion. The dictatorship of the proletariat does not fear any resort to compulsion and to the most severe, decisive and ruthless forms of coercion by the state. The advanced class, the class most oppressed by capitalism, is entitled to use compulsion, because it is doing so in the interests of the working and exploited people, and because it possesses means of compulsion and persuasion such as no former classes ever possessed, although they had incomparably greater material facilities for propaganda and agitation than we have.

. . .

We have, no doubt, learnt politics; here we stand as firm as a rock. But things are bad as far as economic matters are concerned. Henceforth, less politics will be the best politics. Bring more engineers and agronomists to the fore, learn from them, keep an eye on their work, and turn our congresses and conferences, not into propaganda meetings but into bodies that will verify our economic achievements, bodies in which we can really learn the business of economic development.

. . .

While we live in a small-peasant country, there is a firmer economic basis for capitalism in Russia than for communism. That must be borne in mind. Anyone who has carefully observed life in the countryside, as compared with life in the cities, knows that we have not torn up the roots of capitalism and have not undermined the foundation, the basis, of the internal enemy. The latter depends on small-scale production, and there is only one way of undermining it, namely, to place the economy of the country, including agriculture, on a new technical basis, that of modern large-scale production. Only electricity provides that basis.

Communism is Soviet power plus the electrification of the whole country. Otherwise the country will remain a small-peasant country, and we must clearly realise that. We are weaker than capitalism, not only on the world scale, but also within the country. That is common knowledge. We have realised it, and we shall see to it that the economic basis is transformed from a small-peasant basis into a large-scale industrial basis. Only when the country has been electrified, and industry, agriculture and transport have been placed on the technical basis of modern large-scale industry, only then shall we be fully victorious.

• • •

I recently had occasion to attend a peasant festival held in Volokolamsk Uyezd, a remote part of Moscow Gubernia, where the peasants have electric lighting. A meeting was arranged in the street, and one of the peasants came forward and began to make a speech welcoming this new event in the lives of the peasants. "We peasants were unenlightened," he said, "and now light has appeared among us, an 'unnatural light, which will light up our peasant darkness.'" For my part, these words did not surprise me. Of course, to the non-Party peasant masses electric light is an "unnatural" light; but what we consider unnatural is that the peasants and workers should have lived for hundreds and thousands of years in such backwardness, poverty and oppression under the yoke of the landowners and the capitalists. You cannot emerge from this darkness very rapidly. What we must now try is to convert every electric power station we build into a stronghold of enlightenment to be used to make the masses electricity-conscious, so to speak.

• • •

We must see to it that every factory and every electric power station becomes a centre of enlightenment; if Russia is covered with a dense network of electric power stations and powerful technical installations, our communist economic development will become a model for a future socialist Europe and Asia.

Last Reflections (1923)

The general feature of our present life is the following: we have destroyed capitalist industry and have done our best to raze to the ground the medieval institutions and landed proprietorship, and thus created a very small peasantry, which is following the lead of the proletariat because it believes in the results of its revolutionary work. It is not easy for us, however, to keep going until the socialist revolution is victorious in more developed countries merely with the aid of this confidence, because economic necessity . . . keeps the productivity of labour of the small and very small peasants at an extremely low level. Moreover, the international situation, too, threw Russia back and, by and large, reduced the labour productivity of the people to a level considerably below pre-war. The West-European capitalist powers, partly deliberately and partly unconsciously, did everything they could to throw us back, to utilise the elements of the Civil War in Russia in order to spread as much ruin in the country as possible. It was precisely this way out of the imperialist war that seemed to have many advantages. They argued somewhat as follows: "If we fail to overthrow the revolutionary system in Russia, we shall, at all events, hinder its progress towards socialism." And from their point of view they could argue in no other way. In the end, their problem was half-solved. They failed to overthrow the new system created by the revolution, but they did prevent it from at once taking the step forward that would have justified the forecasts of the socialists, that would have enabled the latter to develop the productive forces with enormous speed, to develop all the potentialities which, taken together, would have produced social-ism; socialists would thus have proved to all and sundry that socialism contains within itself gigantic forces and that mankind had now entered into a new stage of development of extraordinarily brilliant prospects. . . .

STUDY QUESTIONS

1. According to Lenin, what were the main features of Marxism? Why was it a po-tent revolutionary doctrine?
2. What were Lenin's organizational contributions to revolutionary Marxism?
3. What specific issues did Lenin face as leader of communist Russia? How did they relate to Marxist goals? How and why did Lenin approach the task of in-dustrial and technological development?
4. What was Lenin's view of the place of Russia's revolution in the larger interna-tional context? What did he think needed to happen internationally to secure revolutionary gains?
5. Do these documents provide evidence about Lenin's individual qualities as a leader? Do they help explain why he played such a decisive role in Russian history?

42

Stalin and the Soviet Union during the 1930s: Progress and Terror

Lenin's death in 1924 left a huge void at the head of the Soviet government. Gradually, however, over the next several years Joseph V. Stalin (1879–1953) emerged as the dominant force in the revolutionary regime. By the late 1920s Stalin was firmly in charge. The result was a "second revolution" during the following decade.

The key to Stalin's "revolution from above" was the all-out drive to industrialize the economy and to make agriculture a collective process. These policies were accompanied by a massive expansion of schools and healthcare facilities. While the net effect of these policies was to move Soviet society rapidly along the road to modernization, the human cost was enormous. Living standards in the 1930s were quite low; approximately several million peasants died from starvation in 1932 and 1933. In addition, political repression reached an unparalleled peak. Between 1936 and 1938, 7 to 8 million Soviet citizens—many of them dedicated communists—were arrested and imprisoned or executed. Yet industrial growth advanced rapidly, an extraordinary achievement given the lack of outside assistance. Russia proudly avoided the economic depression that slowed the capitalist world at this time, and built a solid structure of factory industry undergirded if not by high living standards at least by various welfare benefits to workers.

The two selections illustrate important aspects of Stalin's policies and their consequences. The first document is from a speech he made in 1931 at a conference of Soviet business executives. What is his basic point? How do his ideas compare with Lenin's? How might the leader of a Third World country today react to this speech? The second excerpt comes from the autobiography of Yevgeny Yevtushenko, the most famous poet in the last decades of the Soviet Union. How does Yevtushenko help us understand post-Stalinist Soviet attitudes toward Stalin and the 1930s?

Selection I from J. V. Stalin, *Works,* Vol. XIII (Moscow: Foreign Languages Publishing House, 1955), pp. 38–51, 43–44. Selection II from Yevgeny Yevtushenko, *A Precocious Autobiography,* translated by Andrew R. MacAndrew. Copyright © 1963 by Yevgeny Yevtushenko, renewed 1991 by Yevgeny Yevtushenko. Translation copyright © 1963 by E. P. Dutton, renewed 1991 by Penguin USA of New York. Used by permission of Dutton, a division of Penguin Putnam Inc.

STALIN AND A BITTER LEGACY

I. STALIN SPEAKS IN 1931

About ten years ago a slogan was issued: "Since Communists do not yet properly understand the technique of production, since they have yet to learn the art of management, let the old technicians and engineers—the experts—carry on production, and you, Communists, do not interfere with the technique of the business; but, while not interfering, study technique, study the art of management tirelessly, in order later, on, together with the experts who are loyal to us, to become true managers of production, true masters of the business." Such was the slogan. But what actually happened? The second part of this formula was cast aside, for it is harder to study than to sign papers; and the first part of the formula was vulgarised: non-interference was interpreted to mean refraining from studying the technique of production. The result has been nonsense, harmful and dangerous nonsense, which the sooner we discard the better. . . .

It is time, high time that we turned towards technique. It is time to discard the old slogan, the obsolete slogan of non-interference in technique, and ourselves become specialists, experts, complete masters of our economic affairs. . . .

This, of course, is no easy matter; but it can certainly be accomplished. Science, technical experience, knowledge, are all things that can be acquired. We may not have them today, but tomorrow we shall. The main thing is to have the passionate Bolshevik desire to master technique, to master the science of production. Everything can be achieved, everything can be overcome, if there is a passionate desire for it.

It is sometimes asked whether it is not possible to slow down the tempo somewhat, to put a check on the movement. No, comrades, it is not possible! The tempo must not be reduced! On the contrary, we must increase it as much as is within our powers and possibilities. . . .

To slacken the tempo would mean falling behind. And those who fall behind get beaten. But we do not want to be beaten. No, we refuse to be beaten! One feature of the history of old Russia was the continual beatings she suffered because of her backwardness. She was beaten by the Mongol khans. She was beaten by the Turkish beys. She was beaten by the Swedish feudal lords. She was beaten by the Polish and Lithuanian gentry. She was beaten by the British and French capitalists. She was beaten by the Japanese barons. All beat her—because of her backwardness, because of her military backwardness, cultural backwardness, political backwardness, industrial backwardness, agricultural backwardness. They beat her because to do so was profitable and could be done with impunity. You remember the words of the pre-revolutionary poet: "You are poor and abundant, mighty and impotent, Mother Russia." Those gentlemen were quite familiar with the verses of the old poet. They beat her, saying: "You are abundant," so one can enrich oneself at your expense. They beat her, saying: "You are poor and impotent," so you can be beaten and plundered with impunity. Such is the law of the exploiters—to beat the backward and the weak. It is the jungle law of capitalism. You are backward, you are weak—therefore you are wrong; hence you can be beaten and enslaved. You are mighty—therefore you are right; hence we must be wary of you.

That is why we must no longer lag behind.

In the past we had no fatherland, nor could we have had one. But now that we have overthrown capitalism and power is in our hands, in the hands of the people, we have a fatherland, and we will uphold its independence. Do you want our socialist fatherland to be beaten and to lose its independence? If you do not want this, you must put an end to its backwardness in the shortest possible time and develop a genuine Bolshevik tempo in building up its socialist economy. There is no other way. That is why Lenin said on the eve of the October Revolution: "Either perish, or overtake and outstrip the advanced capitalist countries."

We are fifty or a hundred years behind the advanced countries. We must make good this distance in ten years. Either we do it, or we shall go under. . . .

It is said that it is hard to master technique. That is not true! There are no fortresses that Bolsheviks cannot capture. We have solved a number of most difficult problems. We have overthrown capitalism. We have assumed power. We have built up a huge socialist industry. We have transferred the middle peasants on to the path of socialism. We have already accomplished what is most important from the point of view of construction. What remains to be done is not so much: to study technique, to master science. And when we have done that we shall develop a tempo of which we dare not even dream at present.

And we shall do it if we really want to.

II. YEVGENY YEVTUSHENKO REMEMBERS HIS CHILDHOOD

I was born on July 18, 1933, in Siberia, at Zima Junction, a small place near Lake Baikal. My surname, Yevtushenko, is Ukrainian.

Long ago, at the end of the last century, my great-grandfather, a peasant from the Zhitomir Province, was deported to Siberia for having "let out the red rooster" in his landlord's house. This is the Russian peasant way of saying that he had set fire to his house. That's probably the origin of my inclination to reach for that red rooster whenever I meet anyone with a landlord's mentality.

No one in our family uttered the word "Revolution" as if he were making a speech. It was uttered quietly, gently, a shade austerely. Revolution was the religion of our family.

My grandfather, Yermolay Yevtushenko, a soldier who could barely read, was one of the organizers of the peasant movement in the Urals and in eastern Siberia. Later, under the Soviet regime he studied at a military academy, became a brigade commander, and held the important post of deputy commander of artillery in the Russian Republican Army. But even in his commander's uniform he remained the peasant he had always been and kept his religious faith in Revolution.

I last saw him in 1938. I was five then. I remember our conversation very well.

My grandfather came into my room. I had already undressed and was lying in bed. He sat down on the edge of my bed. He had in his hands a box of liqueur-filled chocolates. His eyes, usually mischievous and smiling, that night looked at me from under his gray prickly crew-cut with a tired and sad expression. He offered me the box of chocolates and then pulled a bottle of vodka out of the pocket of his cavalry breeches.

"I want us to have a drink together," he said. "You have the candy and I'll have the vodka."

He slapped the bottom of the bottle with the flat of his hand and the cork shot out. I fished a chocolate out of the box.

"What shall we drink to?" I asked, trying hard to sound grown-up.

"To the Revolution," my grandfather said with grim simplicity.

We touched glasses—that is, my candy touched his bottle—and we drank.

"Now go to sleep," Grandfather said.

He switched off the light but remained sitting on my bed.

It was too dark for me to see his face but I felt that he was looking at me.

Then he began to sing softly. He sang the melancholy songs of the chain gangs, the songs of the strikers and the demonstrators, the songs of the Civil War.

And listening to them I went to sleep. . . .

I never saw my grandfather again. My mother told me he had gone away for a long trip. I didn't know that on that very night he had been arrested on a charge of high treason. I didn't know that my mother stood night after night in that street with the beautiful name, Marine Silence Street, among thousands of other women who were also trying to find out whether their fathers, husbands, brothers, sons were still alive. I was to learn all this later.

Later I also found out what had happened to my other grandfather, who similarly had vanished. He was Rudolph Gangnus, a round-shouldered gray-bearded mathematician of Latvian origin, whose textbooks were used to teach geometry in Soviet schools. He was arrested on a charge of spying for Latvia.

But at this time I knew nothing.

I went with my father and mother to watch the holiday parades, organized workers' demonstrations, and I would beg my father to lift me up a little higher.

I wanted to catch sight of Stalin.

And as I waved my small red flag, riding high in my father's arms about that sea of heads, I had the feeling that Stalin was looking right at me.

I was filled with a terrible envy of those children my age lucky enough to be chosen to hand bouquets of flowers to Stalin and whom he gently patted on the head, smiling his famous smile into his famous moustache.

To explain away the cult of Stalin's personality by saying simply that it was imposed by force is, to say the least, rather naive. There is no doubt that Stalin exercised a sort of hypnotic charm.

Many genuine Bolsheviks who were arrested at that time utterly refused to believe that this had happened with his knowledge, still less on his personal instructions. Some of them, after being tortured, traced the words "Long live Stalin" in their own blood on the walls of their prison.

Did the Russian people understand what was really happening?

I think the broad masses did not. They sensed intuitively that something was wrong, but no one wanted to believe what he guessed at in his heart. It would have been too terrible.

The Russian people preferred to work rather than to think and to analyze. With a heroic, stubborn self-sacrifice unprecedented in history they built power station after power station, factory after factory. They worked in a furious desperation, drowning with the thunder of machines, tractors, and bulldozers the cries that might have reached them across the barbed wire of Siberian concentration camps.

STUDY QUESTIONS

1. What were Stalin's main goals? What do they have to do with Marxism? What other ideologies did he reflect?
2. How did Stalin's goals for a revolutionary Russia compare with Lenin's? What are the main similarities and differences?
3. Why was Stalin so insistent on communist mastery of technique and science? What problems was he addressing? What results did this approach have in the actual framework for Soviet industrialization and research?
4. What did Stalinism come to mean to Yevtushenko? How did this Stalinism compare with the approach outlined in Stalin's speech—were there any connections?
5. How does Yevtushenko explain the lack of resistance to political oppression?

43

The Collapse of the Soviet Union

The Soviet system collapsed between 1985 and 1991, and part of the even older Russian empire fell apart as well. This was one of the signal developments of the late twentieth century. It had repercussions that will almost surely persist for decades in terms of the future political and economic systems of Russia and other successor states and world diplomatic alignments given the end of Soviet–United States Cold War rivalries.

Change began when Mikhail Gorbachev was named to the top leadership position in the Soviet Union, as first secretary of the Communist Party. Gorbachev was the first leader selected of his generation, and he had a different vantage point from older Bolsheviks. More important, he faced a number of crucial economic problems, after several post-World War II decades in which Soviet industrial growth had seemed quite strong. Workers' motivation was weakening, in part because of the absence of satisfactory consumer goods. Growing alcoholism and massive environmental problems were damaging health. Military expenditures, part of the Cold War competition, were consuming up to a third of the total national product, limiting other kinds of investment and output. Gorbachev was firmly wedded to a socialist vision, but he argued that the Soviet version of this vision required massive transformation. Greater freedom for criticism and commentary was essential—what Gorbachev called *glasnost*—along with a restructuring of management to provide greater flexibility and motivation (*perestroika*), including more participation in the international economy.

Gorbachev's reforms unleashed a massive process of change, although political results accelerated more rapidly than economic shifts. New parties began to compete in elections. Eastern European countries in the Soviet empire began to insist on greater autonomy and then, by 1989, on abolition of the communist system. Hungary and Poland installed noncommunist governments in 1988, and other countries followed. Then in 1990 and 1991 regions within the Soviet Union began to press for independence, led by the Baltic states—Latvia, Lithuania, and Estonia—which headed a parade that soon included key areas in Central Asia as well.

Many Soviet leaders were appalled at this process, and in August 1991, several organized a coup that imprisoned Gorbachev in his summer home. Led by a self-styled leader of democracy, Boris Yeltsin, the coup was thwarted; but Gorbachev resigned his position, now as president under a new constitution, at the end of the year. The process of change continued, both in Russia and in the newly independent nations.

All selections from *The Soviet System: From Crisis to Collapse,* edited by Alexander Dallin and Gail W. Lapidus (Boulder, Colo.: Westview Press, 1994), pp. 284–287, 569–573, 644–646.

Market economies gained ground, although often with considerable disruption and hardship, against the old state-run operations. Efforts to revise international relations and internal political arrangements continued as well, with many uncertainties about ultimate outcomes.

Three selections illustrate key aspects of the Soviet crisis. In the first document, from 1986, Gorbachev explains his initial reform policies to a regional Communist Party meeting in the Asian city of Khabarovsk. In the second document, Vladimir Kryuchov, head of the KGB (the secret police), outlines pressing concerns about Soviet stability in a secret memo to Gorbachev in 1991, as the Soviet Union had already begun to break apart. Kryuchov was at this point a communist conservative, hoping to stem the tide of reform; he would later be a leader of the anti-Gorbachev coup and was arrested and expelled from the KGB after the plot failed. Finally, the third document stems from Gorbachev's resignation speech on December 25, 1991. Following his resignation the heads of the component Soviet Republics voted to dissolve the USSR and form the much looser Commonwealth of Independent States in its stead, and Boris Yeltsin assumed the leadership of the new Russian state.

The end of the Soviet system was as dramatic as its beginning in the 1917 revolution, and as significant in terms of larger world history. Seldom does a structure seemingly so well-established unravel so completely. Documents provide crucial insight into how reforms turned into collapse, and why the tide could not be turned back.

RUSSIAN DOCUMENTS: THE END OF AN ERA

I. GORBACHEV AND REFORM (1986)

. . . None of us can continue living in the old way. This is obvious. In this sense, we can say that a definite step toward acceleration has been made.

However, there is a danger that the first step will be taken as success, that we will assume that the whole situation has been taken in hand. I said this in Vladivostok. I want to say it again in Khabarovsk. If we were to draw this conclusion, we would be making a big mistake, an error. What has been achieved cannot yet satisfy us in any way. In general, one should never flatter oneself with what has been accomplished. All of us must learn this well. Such are the lessons of the past decades—the last two, at least. And now this is especially dangerous.

No profound qualitative changes that would reinforce the trend toward accelerated growth have taken place as yet. In general, comrades, important and intensive work lies ahead of us. To put it bluntly, the main thing is still to come. Our country's Party, the entire Party, should understand this well. . . .

We should learn as we go along, accomplishing new tasks. And we must not be afraid of advancing boldly, of doing things on the march, in the course of the active accomplishment of economic and social tasks. . . .

Restructuring is a capacious word. I would equate the word restructuring with the word revolution. Our transformations, the reforms mapped out in the decisions of the April plenary session of the Party Central Committee and the 27th CPSU (Communist Party of the Soviet Union) Congress, are a genuine revolution in the entire system of relations in society, in the minds and hearts of people, in the psychology and understanding of the present period and, above all, in the tasks engendered by rapid scientific and technical progress.

There is a common understanding in the CPSU and in the country as a whole—we should look for answers to the questions raised by life not outside of socialism but within the framework of our system, disclosing the potential of a planned economy, socialist democracy and culture and the human factor, and relying on the people's vital creativity.

Some people in the West do not like this. There everyone lies in wait for something that would mean a deviation from socialism, for us to go hat in hand to capitalism, for us to borrow its methods. We are receiving a great deal of "advice" from abroad as to how and where we should proceed. Various kinds of provocative broadcasts are made, and articles are published, aimed at casting aspersions on the changes taking place in our country and at driving a wedge between the Party leadership and the people. Such improper attempts are doomed to failure. The interests of the Party and the people are inseparable, and our choice and political course are firm and unshakable. On this main point, the people and the Party are united.

But we also cannot allow ingrained dogmas to cloud our eyes, to impede our progress and keep us from creatively elaborating theory and applying it in practice, in the given, concrete historical stage through which our society is passing. We cannot allow this, either.

I am saying this also because among us there are still, of course, people who have difficulty in accepting the world "restructuring" [*perestroika*] and who even sometimes can pronounce it only with difficulty. In this process of renewal, they often see not what it in fact contains but all but a shaking of foundations, all but a renunciation of our principles. Our political line is aimed at fully disclosing the potential and advantages of the socialist system, removing all barriers and all obstructions to our progress, and creating scope for factors of social progress.

I want to say something else. The further we advance into restructuring, the more the complexity of this task is revealed, and the more fully the enormous scale and volume of the forthcoming work are brought out. It is becoming clearer to what extent many notions about the economy and management, social questions, statehood and democracy, upbringing and education and moral demands still lag behind today's requirements and tasks, especially the tasks of further development.

We will have to remove layer by layer, the accumulated problems in all spheres of the life of society, freeing ourselves of what has outlived its time and boldly making creative decisions. . . .

Sometimes people ask: Well, just what is this odd business, restructuring? How do you understand it, "what do you eat it with," this restructuring? Yes, we're all for it, some say, but we don't know what to do. Many say this straight out. . . .

Restructuring proposes the creation of an atmosphere in society that will impel people to overcome accumulated inertia and indifference, to rid themselves, in work and in life, of everything that does not correspond to the principles of socialism, to our world views and way of life. Frankly, there is some work to be done here. But in this instance everyone must look first of all at himself, comrades—in the Politburo, in the primary Party organizations—and everyone must make a specific attempt to take himself in hand. In past years, we got used to some things in an atmosphere of insufficient criticism, openness and responsibility, things that do not all correspond to the principles of socialism. I apply this both to rank-and-file personnel and to officials. . . .

In general, comrades, we must change our style of work. It should be permeated with respect for the people and their opinions, with real, unfeigned closeness to them. We must actually go to people, listen to them, meet with them, inform them. And the more difficult things are, the more often we must meet with them and be with them when some task or other is being accomplished. In our country, people are responsive; they are a wonderful people, you can't find another people like them. Our people have the greatest endurance. Our people have the greatest political activeness. And now it is growing. This must be welcomed and encouraged in every way. Let us consider that we have come to an agreement on this in the Khabarovsk Party organization (*Applause*).

In this connection, some words about public openness [*glasnost*]. It is sometimes said: Well, why has the Central Committee launched criticism, self-criticism and openness on such a broad scale? I can tell you that so far we have lost nothing, we have only gained. The people have felt an influx of energy; they have become bolder and more active, both at work and in public life. Furthermore, you know that all those who had been trying to circumvent our laws immediately began to quiet down. Because there is nothing stronger than the force of public opinion, when it can be put into effect. And it can be put into effect only in conditions of criticism, self-criticism and broad public openness. . . .

Incidentally, it looks as if many local newspapers in cities and provinces are keeping quiet. The central newspapers are speaking out in full voice, supporting everything good and criticizing blunders and shortcomings. But the local papers are silent. When a group of editors assembled in the Central Committee's offices, they said bluntly: "Well, you tell this to our secretaries in the city and district Party committees." And indeed, why shouldn't people know what is going on the district or the city? Why shouldn't they make a judgment on it and, if need be, express their opinion? This is what a socialism is, comrades. Are there any editors present? (*A voice:* Yes, we're here.)

I hope that the secretaries of the city and district Party committees will take our talk into account. They are the managers. These are their newspapers. We must not be afraid of openness, comrades. We are strong, and the people are in favor of socialism, the Party's policy, changes and restructuring. In general, it is impermissible to approach openness with the yardsticks of traditional short-term campaigns. Public openness is not a one-shot measure but a norm of present-day Soviet life, a continuous, uninterrupted process during which some tasks are accomplished and new tasks—as a rule, still more complicated ones—arise. (*Applause*).

I could say the same thing about criticism and self-criticism. If we do not criticize and analyze ourselves, what will happen? For us, this is a direct requirement, a vital necessity for purposes of the normal functioning of the Party and of society. . . .

II. A SECRET POLICE REPORT (1991)

On the Political Situation in the Country

The acute political crisis which has enveloped our country threatens the fate of *perestroika,* the processes of democratization, the renewal of society. The possibility of the collapse of the unity of the USSR, the destruction of the sociopolitical and economic system has become real. Provoked by the decisions of a number of Union republics, the "war of sovereignties" has practically nullified efforts to stabilize the economy and has greatly complicated conditions for the signing of a new Union treaty. Under the influence of well-known decisions of the Congress of People's Deputies and the Supreme Soviet, the confrontations between the Center and the Union republics have received a powerful impetus. The head of the Russian parliament, together with certain forces, circles of shady business, have clearly declared their intention to create a "second Center" as a counterweight to the state political leadership of the USSR. Practically all opposition parties and movements have not failed to make use of it to strengthen their positions. National chauvinistic and separatist tendencies have increased in many regions of the country.

Events have confirmed our evaluation that the policy of appeasing the aggressive wing of the "democratic movement" is not able to forestall the spread of destructive processes and, in fact, allows the pseudo-democrats to realize unhindered their plans concerning the usurpation of power and changing the nature of the social system.

The danger of this tendency is further aggravated by the numerical growth and increasing power of illegal militarized formations. Today they have at their disposal state-of-the-art weapons, from automatic weapons and machine guns down to reactive shells. Taking into consideration this factor, social and national conflicts may assume a new character, turning into numerous hotbeds of civil war.

The outcome of the political battle in the coming months will depend on who wins the support of the bulk of the toiling population. In turn, active support of the leadership of the country, it would seem, hinges decisively on the extent of its success in averting a drastic decline in the living standard of the population. It is impossible not to take into account the fact that large social groups are poorly protected and are frequently impoverished. There exists no real possibility of improving their well-being at this time.

Taking into consideration the peculiarities of the economic structure of the USSR as well as the misapprehension by a significant portion of the population of even primitive forms of market relations, every step in the transition to a market economy demands circumspection, caution, and verification. The commitment to a forced introduction of market relations might turn out to exact an exorbitantly high price from the country. . . .

Public opinion reacts negatively to the way in which shady businessmen exploit the unfolding situation. The intensifying property stratification evokes an increase in social tensions. The process of enrichment, by its internal logic, draws shady business into the battle for political influence, so that within the framework of privatization it may further broaden the scope for property accumulation. That inevitably leads to the creation of a category of "new bourgeoisie" with all that it entails. . . .

The reality is such that the United States is working towards the collapse of the USSR as a superpower. In political circles of the United States the predominant opinion is that the weakening of the Soviet Union—down to the secession of a series of republics, above all the Baltics—is in the American national interest. The departure of Lithuania, for example, would in turn make the prospect of losing the Kaliningrad oblast quite real.

Taking into account this situation, we can scarcely count on significant financial and economic help from the United States. According to reliable information, the United States is putting pressure on Japan and Western Europe to limit the possible scale of their cooperation with the USSR. One should also be aware of the fact that even extensive help from the West would not, in itself, be sufficient to extricate this country from its economic crisis. . . .

The anticonstitutional forces, acting according to a scenario worked out with the participation of Western experts, view the present moment as favorable for the organization of a frontal attack on the existing governmental and social structures of the Soviet state. The leading role in this belongs to the organizationally formed block of opposition forces "Democratic Russia" (DR), whose political precepts the leadership of the Supreme Soviet of the [Russian Federation] [Boris Yeltsin] is trying to realize.

With the formation of the governing organs of DR, the task of "transforming the soviets on all levels into instruments of the opposition" has moved into the realm of practicality, as is the imminent winning to its side of the vast majority of the population. Measures are being taken for the creation of the cells of DR in industrial enterprises, in state institutions, and colleges. The attention "Democrats" pay to engineering and technical personnel, as well as to the working class as a whole, is growing, inasmuch as expectations of an "elite coup" by the humanitarian [cultural] intelligentsia have not been fulfilled. Opposition leaders have embarked on the formation of a party built on the foundation of DR that would be capable of pushing the CPSU out of the political area. It is assumed that it will be headed by the most prominent leaders among the "Democrats" and will become de facto the leading force in the alignment of political forces both in the Supreme Soviet of the RSFSR and in the soviets of a number of large republican centers. . . .

Supporters of the "Democrats" are taking persistent measures to extend their influence in the army, striving to neutralize it as one of the guarantors of the unity of the USSR and the integrity of the constitutional system. On the other hand, the recent events in the Baltic republics have had a very negative effect on the morale of the troops and have strengthened, especially among the officer corps, doubts about the ability of the country's leadership to keep the situation under control.

The escalation of the propaganda war that is being waged by the anticommunists against their own people, and the increased material means at their disposal (including the drawing in of shady capital), are devastating for the unity of the USSR and for Soviet society. The conquest of one propaganda organ after another is under way, and when that fails, they create new ones. Within just the last month in Russia, more specifically in Moscow, four substantial new publications have begun to appear and two radio stations have begun to broadcast. Western specialists are drawn into the activity in the sphere of psychological warfare (Radio Liberty, the NTS publishing company "Posev," etc.).

Official Soviet propaganda unjustifiably delays the unfolding of a powerful propaganda offensive. The question of preparing for the all-Union referendum on the preservation of the USSR reveals most graphically the imbalance in the propaganda war: While the "democratic press" decided to disparage the referendum as soon as it was announced, the central and party-controlled mass media have carried virtually no serious features on its behalf.

The interests of the Soviet constitutional system insistently dictate essential state control over the mass media and the inadmissibility of watering down its personnel, much less its transformation into a mouthpiece for antisocialist forces.

An analysis of the unfolding situation demands serious and critical comprehension of the extent to which the concepts of democratization and *glasnost* formulated six years ago have currently been implemented in practice. It is impossible not to see that antisocialist circles have, at a given stage, succeeded in replacing their contents, imposing upon society a vision of *perestroika,* not as the renewal of socialism but as the inexorable return into the "mainstream of world civilization"—capitalism. The thesis of the "illegality of the October Revolution" [of 1917] is being promoted. Democratization and *glasnost* come to be seen as the elimination of any limitations on political insinuations and unbridled slander under the flag of "freedom of speech." The cynical manipulation of public opinion shows with particular clarity in the firmly established "double standards," in accordance with which even the criminal actions of "democratic leaders" (down to the use of bloody coercion in Lithuania, Latvia, and Georgia) are unconditionally justified or hushed up, whereas the actions of the authorities in restoring order and constitutional norms are decried wholesale as illegal and dictatorial.

According to incoming information, an understanding of the dire consequences that the lingering crisis in the CPSU will have for the country is growing among the population. It is clear that the weakening of ideological work in defense of the socialist ideal cannot be made up by any other political force. Although the opposition is able to appeal to the personal interests of the average person, Party propaganda is still fumbling about for ways to conduct mass agitational work.

The failures of a series of recent provocative actions of the opposition—in the first place, the so-called all-Union political strike—demonstrate that it does not yet have enough reliable support among wide strata of the population. The political timidity of the "silent majority" preserves for the Party the possibility of using its indispensable advantages over the opposition, such as its extensive organizations, the propaganda apparatus, and its high intellectual potential.

With all its drama, the current situation can still be turned around, considering the unused arsenal of constructive measures. There is not a great deal of room in which to maneuver, but there is some. One must not fail to consider that, as is everywhere noted, people are tired of the hardships, stress, and social collisions and are losing their faith in the ability of the leadership to restore order. The danger arises that people will follow those who take it upon themselves to restore order.

The Supreme Soviet and the Congress of People's Deputies of the USSR, as the most constructive political institutions, can and must play an essential role in the search for a way out of the unfolding crisis. This requires protecting these organs of popular government from attacks and activating and strengthening their creative potential.

At the same time, considering the depth of the crisis and the probability of a dramatic worsening of circumstances, one cannot exclude the possibility of forming, at the appropriate moment, temporary bodies within the framework of extraordinary measures to be introduced by the President of the Supreme Soviet of the USSR.

Such a step would require powerful propaganda support, a direct address to the nation with an appeal to unity for the preservation of the USSR and the defense of the public order.

III. GORBACHEV'S RESIGNATION SPEECH (1991)

Dear compatriots! Fellow citizens! Due to the situation that has taken shape as a result of the formation of the Commonwealth of Independent States, I am ceasing my activity in the post of President of the USSR. I am making this decision out of considerations of principle.

I have firmly advocated the independence of peoples and the sovereignty of republics. But at the same time I have favored the preservation of the Union state and the integrity of the country.

Events have taken a different path. A policy line aimed at dismembering the country and disuniting the state has prevailed, something that I cannot agree with. . . .

Speaking to you for the last time as President of the USSR, I consider it necessary to express my assessment of the path traversed since 1985. Especially since there are a good many contradictory, superficial and unobjective opinions on this score.

Fate ordained that when I became head of state it was already clear that things were not going well in the country. We have a great deal of everything—land, petroleum, gas and other natural resources—and God has endowed us with intelligence and talent, too, but we live much worse than people in the developed countries do, and we are lagging further and further behind them.

The reason was evident—society was suffocating in the grip of the command-bureaucratic system. Doomed to serve ideology and to bear the terrible burden of the arms race, it had been pushed to the limit of what was possible.

All attempts at partial reforms—and there were a good many of them—failed, one after the other. The country had lost direction. It was impossible to go on living that way. Everything had to be changed fundamentally.

That is why I have never once regretted that I did not take advantage of the position of General Secretary just to "reign" for a few years. I would have considered that irresponsible and immoral.

I realized that to begin reforms on such a scale and in such a society as ours was an extremely difficult and even risky endeavor. But even today I am convinced of the historical correctness of the democratic reforms that were begun in the spring of 1985.

The process of renewing the country and of fundamental changes in the world community proved to be much more complex than could have been surmised. However, what has been accomplished should be appraised on its merits.

Society has received freedom and has been emancipated politically and spiritually. This is the most important gain, one that we have not yet become fully aware of, and for this reason we have not yet learned to make use of freedom.

Nevertheless, work of historic significance has been done:

—The totalitarian system, which for a long time deprived the country of the opportunity to become prosperous and flourishing, has been eliminated.

—A breakthrough has been achieved in the area of democratic transformations. Free elections, freedom of the press, religious freedoms, representative bodies of power and a multiparty system have become a reality. Human rights have been recognized as the highest principle.

—Movement toward a mixed economy has begun, and the equality of all forms of ownership is being established. Within the framework of a land reform, the peasantry has begun to revive, private farming has appeared, and millions of hectares of land are being given to rural and urban people. The economic freedom of the producer has been legalized, and entrepreneurship, the formation of joint-stock companies and privatization have begun to gather momentum.

—In turning the economy toward a market, it is important to remember that this is being done for the sake of human beings. In this difficult time, everything possible must be done for their social protection, and this applies especially to old people and children.

We are living in a new world:

—An end has been put to the cold war, and the arms race and the insane militarization of the country, which disfigured our economy and the public consciousness and morals, have been halted. The threat of a world war has been removed.

I want to emphasize once again that, for my part, during the transitional period I did everything I could to preserve reliable control over nuclear weapons.

—We opened up to the world and renounced interference in the affairs of others and the use of troops outside the country's borders. And in response we received trust, solidarity and respect.

—We have become one of the main bulwarks in the reorganization of present-day civilization on peaceful, democratic principles.

—Peoples and nations have received real freedom in choosing the path of their self-determination. Searches for democratic reforms in the multinational state led us to the threshold of concluding a new Union Treaty.

All these changes required enormous effort and took place in an acute struggle, with mounting resistance from old, obsolete and reactionary forces—both the former Party-state structures and the economic apparatus—and also from our habits, ideological prejudices, and a leveling and parasitic mentality. The changes ran up against our intolerance, low level of political sophistication and fear of change.

For this reason, we lost a great deal of time. The old system collapsed before a new one had time to start working. And the crisis in society became even more exacerbated.

I know about the dissatisfaction with the present grave situation and about the sharp criticism that is being made of the authorities at all levels, and of my personal activity. But I would like to emphasize once again: Fundamental changes in such an enormous country, and one with such a legacy, could not proceed painlessly or without difficulties and upheavals. . . .

It seems vitally important to me to preserve the democratic gains of the past few years. They were achieved through suffering throughout our history and our tragic experience. Under no circumstances and on no pretext can they be given up. Otherwise, all hopes for something better will be buried. . . .

I am grateful to state, political and public figures and the millions of people abroad who understood our plans, supported them, met us halfway, and embarked on sincere cooperation with us.

I am leaving my post with a feeling of anxiety. But also with hope and with faith in you, in your wisdom and strength of spirit. We are the heirs to a great civilization, and its rebirth into a new, up-to-date and fitting life now depends on each and every one of us.

I want to thank from the bottom of my heart those who during these years stood with me for a right and good cause. Certainly some mistakes could have been avoided, and many things could have been done better. But I am sure that sooner or later our common efforts will bear fruit and our peoples will live in a prosperous and democratic society.

I wish all of you the very best.

STUDY QUESTIONS

1. What kinds of reforms did Gorbachev envision in 1986? What problems was he trying to address? What did he mean by "restructuring" and "public openness"?

2. What kinds of threats did the Secret Police highlight in 1991? How does the view of Soviet society implied here compare with Gorbachev's reform intentions? Does the report suggest the basis for Kryuchov's later attempted coup? What kind of state and society does Kryuchov seem to want?

3. What does Gorbachev say caused him to resign? What, by 1991, were his goals for Russian society, and how did they compare with the goals of 1986? How had his outlook toward the West changed?

4. From these documents, how much can be determined about the nature of and reasons for the collapse of the Soviet system? What kinds of disagreements persisted into the 1990s about the appropriate directions for Russian political and economic systems?

44

Ziya Gokalp: Turkish Nationalism and Western Civilization

The establishment of new nation states by Balkan Christians after 1800 and the failure of attempts to reform the Ottoman empire led, almost inevitably, to the birth of Turkish nationalism. The new movement began among young Turkish writers living as political exiles in London and Paris during the last quarter of the nineteenth century. These writers began to consider what it meant to be a Turk (as opposed to an Ottoman) and to examine the relationships between Turkish culture, Islam, and the West. Soon they became known as the "Young Turks." In 1908 a mutiny of reform-minded military officers who were loosely associated with the Young Turk movement succeeded in ending the autocratic regime of Sultan Abdul Hamid II (reigned 1876–1909).

For most of the next, and final, decade of the Ottoman empire Young Turks from the army controlled the government in Istanbul. In 1914 they took the Ottoman state into World War I on the side of the Central Powers (Germany and Austria-Hungary), a policy that led to military defeat and economic catastrophe. By 1918 the once-vast Ottoman empire was no more; it had shrunk to little more than the borders of the Anatolian Peninsula. Moreover, because of fiercely contested territorial disputes with the Greeks, the fighting did not end for the Turks until 1922.

In 1923 Turkey was proclaimed a republic under the presidency of Mustapha Kemal Ataturk, a general who had been active in the nationalist movement since 1905 and who had led the postwar expulsion of Greeks from Anatolia. Ataturk was an authoritarian modernizer who in some ways resembled the *Tanzimat* reformers of the nineteenth century (Chapter 29). He was both intolerant of political opposition and determined to bring about major economic, social, and cultural changes in Turkey. Under his leadership

From *Turkish Nationalism and Western Civilization: Selected Essays of Ziya Gokalp,* translated and edited by Niyazi Berkes (New York: Columbia University Press, 1959), pp. 259–262, 276–277, 310–311. Reprinted by permission.

a program of industrialization was launched, the *shari'a* (the traditional Muslim legal code) was replaced by a secular system of laws, numerous rights were extended to women, the Arabic alphabet gave way to the Roman script, and the fez was outlawed. At Ataturk's death in 1938 the new Turkish nation-state seemed to be emerging as a successful model of modernity for the peoples of the Middle East.

The following selections come from the writings of Ziya Gokalp (1876–1924), the most creative thinker of the late Ottoman/early republican period. Gokalp wrote mainly for newspapers and other periodicals. His ideas, especially his pleas for the Westernization of Turkey, were widely discussed by his contemporaries and were quite influential in the shaping of public policy during the Ataturk years. These passages are from essays written by Gokalp in 1923. How does Gokalp's writing capture the dilemmas facing the Turkish people following the collapse of the Ottoman empire?

GOKALP'S ESSAYS

I. ON TURKISM

One of the fundamental principles of Turkism is the drive towards 'going to the people'. . . . What is meant by going to the people? Who are to go to these people?

The intellectuals and the thinkers of a nation constitute its élite. The members of the élite are separated from the masses by their higher education and learning. It is they who ought to go to the people. But why? Some would answer: in order to carry culture to the masses. But, as we have shown elsewhere, culture is something which is alive only among the people themselves. The élite are those who lack it. Then, how can the élite, lacking culture, carry culture to the common people who are a living embodiment of culture?

To answer the question, let us first answer the following questions: what do the élite and the people have? The élite are the carriers of civilization and the people the holders of culture. Therefore, the élite's approach to the people should only have the following two purposes: to receive a training in culture from the people and to carry civilization to them. Yes, it is only with these two purposes that the élite should go to the people. The élite will find culture only there and nowhere else. . . .

The élite do acquire national culture through education from childhood. The schools in which they study are not the people's schools or national schools. Our élite get their education without acquiring national culture. Their education merely serves to denationalize them. They need to compensate the shortcoming by mixing with the people, by living with them, by learning their language, by observing the way they use their vernacular, by listening to their proverbs, their traditional wit and wisdom, by noting their mode of thinking and their style of feeling, by listening to their poetry and music, by seeing their plays and dances, by penetrating into their religiosity and morality, by tasting beauty in the simplicity of their clothes, their architecture, and their furniture. They should learn the folk-tales, anecdotes, epics, and beliefs, which are survivals from the ancient *töre* [pre-Islamic Turkish customary law]. . . . They have to find the old coffee-houses of the people where epics are being read, experience the nights of the holy month, the Friday communal feast gatherings, the religious holidays to which children look forward with so much enthusiasm. They have to build national museums in which works of art of the people will be exhibited.

It is only this way, only through such a contact with the national folk culture, and only by saturating their souls with the Turkish culture that the élite of the Turkish nation will nationalize themselves. It was through such a national education that Pushkin became the national poet of the Russians. Men like Dante, Petrarch, Rousseau, Goethe, Schiller, D'Annunzio became great creators of art and literature only because they had received their inspirations from the people.

As sociology has shown, genius is hidden in the people. An artist becomes a genius only because he becomes a manifestation of the aesthetic taste of the people. The reason why we lack great artists is that our men of art do not receive their aesthetic inspirations from the living museum of the people. No one, so far, has valued the art of the people. The old Ottoman élite scorned the peasant as 'stupid Turk'; the people of Anatolia were ridiculed as 'outsiders'; the title given to the people was 'vulgar.' The 'refined' were the Ottoman élite, who were the slaves of the court. As they had despised the people, nothing in language, poetry, literature, music, philosophy, ethics, politics, and economics has survived from the heritage of this ancient élite. The Turkish people have to start again from ABC. They did not even have a name as a nation until recently. The *Tanzimatists* said to them: 'You are Ottomans. Don't claim a national existence distinct from other nations. If you do, you will cause the destruction of the Ottoman Empire.' The poor Turk, scared to lose his fatherland, had to say: 'By God, I am not a Turk, I am nothing but an Ottoman.'

But the Ottomanists could not see that in spite of whatever they did, foreign [non-Turkish] nations would do their best to secede from the Ottoman Commonwealth because such artificial commonwealths composed of several nations could no longer survive. Each nation would be independent and would have its own homogeneous, genuine, natural social life. This trend of social evolution, which had started in Western Europe five centuries earlier, certainly would start in Eastern Europe too. The downfall of the Austro-Hungarian, Russian, and Ottoman Empires after the World War has shown that this is very near. What would be the fate of the Turks once they faced this catastrophe without a realization that they themselves were a nation, that they too had their own home and their rights in the Ottoman Empire? Were they to say: 'As the Ottoman Empire fell, we do not have national hope, or political aspiration any more?' When the Wilsonian points were known, certain conscientious Ottomanists, who until then had remained indifferent to Turkism, began to say: 'What would be our state today if Turkism had not taught many of us that we had a national home ethnographically drawn, a national existence independent of the Ottoman Empire, a national right to rule in this home in complete independence?' It was only one word, that sacred word Turk, which showed us the right path to be followed amidst anarchy.

Turkists not only taught the élite the name of the nation, but also the beautiful language of the nation. As the name they gave to the nation was taken from the people, this language also was taken from the people, because both had existed only among the people. The élite had been living the life of somnambulists [sleep walkers] until then. They, like somnambulists, had a dual personality. Their real personality was the Turk, but they thought themselves Ottomans under the delusions of their somnambulism. While their real language was Turkish, they talked an artificial language in their delirium. In poetry, they put aside their own metre and sang in artificial metres copied from the Persians.

Turkists, like a psychiatrist, tried to cure this split personality by making them believe that they were not Ottomans but Turks, that their language was Turkish, and that their poetry was the people's; they even demonstrated these scientifically. It was only then that the élite were cured from this abnormal state of somnambulism and began to think as normal men.

We must confess, however, that so far these men have taken only one step forward towards the people. To reach the people in a real sense, they must live amongst the people and get the national culture from the people. The only way to do this is for the nationalist youth to go to villages as schoolteachers. Those who are not young should at least go to the towns in inner Anatolia. The Ottoman élite will become a national élite only by completely assimilating the folk culture.

The second aim of going towards the people is to carry civilization to the people. The people lack civilization and the élite have its keys. But the civilization that they should carry to the people as a precious contribution will not be Oriental civilization or its offshoot, Ottoman civilization, but Western civilization, as we shall show below.

II. TOWARD WESTERN CIVILIZATION

There is only one road to salvation: To advance in order to reach—that is, in order to be equal to—Europeans in the sciences and industry as well as in military and judicial institutions. And there is only one means to achieve this: to adapt ourselves to Western civilization completely!

In the past, the makers of *Tanzimat* recognized this and set about to introduce European civilization. However, whatever they wanted to take from Europe, they always took not fully but by half. They created, for example, neither a real university nor a uniform judicial organization. Before they took measures to modernize national production, they wanted to change the habits of consuming, clothing, eating, building, and furniture. On the other hand, not even a nucleus of industry on European standards was built because the policy makers of *Tanzimat* attempted their reforms without studying conditions and without putting forth definite aims and plans. They were always taking only half-measures in whatever they attempted to do.

Another great mistake committed by the leaders of *Tanzimat* was their attempt to create a mental amalgam made up of a mixture of East and West. They failed to see that the two, with their diametrically opposed principles, could not be reconciled. The still existing dichotomy in our political structure, the dual court system, the two types of schools, the two systems of taxation, two budgets, the two sets of laws, are all products of this mistake. The dichotomies are almost endless. Religious and secular schools were not only two different institutions of education, but within each there was again the same dichotomy. Only in military and medical schools was education carried out exclusively along European lines. We owe to these institutions the generals and doctors who today save the life of the nation and the lives of the citizens. The training of specialists within these fields, in a way equal to their European colleagues, was made possible only because of the immunity of these two institutions from dichotomy. If the methods of warfare of the Janissaries or the medical practices of the old-fashioned surgeons were mixed into these modern institutions, we would not have our celebrated generals and doctors today. These two institutions of learning must be models for the educational revolution that has to materialize. Any attempt to reconcile East and West means carrying medieval conditions to the modern age and trying to keep them alive. Just as it was impossible to reconcile Janissary methods with a modern military system, just as it was futile to synchronize old-fashioned medicine with scientific medicine, so it is hopeless to carry the old and the new conceptions of law, the modern and the traditional conceptions of science, the old and the new standards of ethics, side by side. Unfortunately, only in the military arts and medicine was Janissary-ism abolished. It is still surviving in other professions as a ghost of medievalism. A few months ago, a new society was founded in Istanbul in order to bring Turkey into the League of Nations. What will be the use of it as long as Turkey does not enter definitely into European civilization? A nation condemned to every political interference by Capitulations is meant to be a nation outside of European civilization. Japan is accepted as a European power, but we are still regarded as an Asiatic nation. This is due to nothing but our non-acceptance of European civilization in a true sense. The Japanese have been able to take the Western civilization without losing their religion and national identity; they have been able to reach the level of Europeans in every respect. Did they lose their religion and national culture? Not at all! Why, then, should we still hesitate? Can't we accept Western civilization definitely and still be Turks and Muslims? . . .

III. ON THE NEED FOR A NATIONAL INDUSTRY

The modern state is based on large-scale industry. New Turkey, to be a modern state, must, above all, develop a national industry. What should we do to realize this?

The New Turkey, which has to introduce the latest and most developed techniques of Europe, cannot afford to wait for the spontaneous rise of the spirit of enterprise among individuals in order to industrialize. As we have done in the field of military techniques, we have to reach European levels in industry through a national effort. We have to start by utilizing the latest developments in European techniques, without necessarily following the stages of gradual evolution. The starting-point, for example, should be electrification. We must utilize the hydraulic power of the country and put it into an electric network. The people of Turkey, who have been able to adopt European military techniques in all their details, can learn and master the most modern industrial inventions and discoveries. Military techniques, however, were not introduced by the private initiative of individuals. This was accomplished through the state. Our medicine, which is equally advanced, was also initiated through state action. Therefore, only the state can achieve the task of introducing large-scale industry in every field. The Turkish state has the power to be an independent [national] state. Turks are temperamentally *étatists*. They expect the state to take the initiative in everything new and progressive. Even social changes are introduced through the state in Turkey, and it has been the state which has safeguarded social changes against the force of reaction.

In order that the state itself may become competent in economic enterprises, it must become an economic state. The statesmen and government employees should have economic experience and knowledge. The modern state, selecting its personnel with this point in view, is like a big business concern. . . . By following the same line, our state will, at the same time, perform a moral service because the rise of a new class of speculators will be prevented. The ambitions manifested in the Peace Conference clearly showed what a criminal people these capitalists, as they are called in Europe, are! Present-day European imperialism is based on private capitalism. If we accept the system of state capitalism, we will be able to prevent the rise of those insatiable and predatory capitalists in our country. . . .

STUDY QUESTIONS

1. According to Gokalp, what could the Turkish intellectuals learn from the Turkish people? What could the intellectuals teach the people?
2. How did Gokalp define Turkish culture?
3. What reasons did Gokalp give for his criticism of the old Ottoman elite?
4. Why did Gokalp think that the Turks must adapt themselves to Western civilization?
5. What was Gokalp's view of the *Tanzimat* reforms? (See Chapter 29.)
6. How do Gokalp's ideas compare with those of his contemporaries such as Lenin, Stalin, Sun Yatsen, and Gandhi? (See Chapters 41, 42, 47 and 51.)
7. Must societies industrialize in order to achieve well-being?
8. What is a nation?
9. Why did Ataturk-type reforms become less attractive to the people of the Middle East during the late twentieth century? (See Chapter 46.)

45

Middle Eastern Dreams in Conflict: The Views of an Early Zionist and a Palestinian Refugee

The Israeli-Palestinian conflict that has embittered the people of the Middle East and elsewhere for the past half-century is rooted in two powerful and contradictory claims to the same "homeland." Each of the two parties invokes history and love of the land in defense of its claims. Beginning in the 1890s European Jews, responding to an upsurge of anti-Semitic prejudice, organized the Zionist movement in order to establish a "national home" in Palestine. At that time Palestine was a part of the Ottoman empire and was inhabited largely by Arab Muslims. In the years following World War I, when the British ruled Palestine as a League of Nations Mandate, European Jews began to migrate to Palestine in large numbers, a process that greatly accelerated during and after World War II due to the Holocaust. The withdrawal of the British from Palestine and the proclamation of the independent state of Israel in 1948 made the Zionist dream a reality.

Palestine, however, had been a part of the Arab Muslim world since the seventh century. Palestinians resented the coming of the Jewish colonists and they opposed the founding of the new Israeli state, as did most other Arabs in the region. Hundreds of thousands of Palestinians were forced into exile in the late 1940s, victims of the conflicts surrounding the establishment of the Israeli state. Subsequent wars between Israel and neighboring Arab states in 1967, 1973, and 1982 increased the amount of territory and the number of Palestinians subject to Israeli authority, most notably in the region west of the Jordan River known as the West Bank, and in the Gaza Strip.

Determined to regain their homeland and to establish an independent Palestinian state (sentiments that constitute a kind of "Zionism in reverse"), in 1964 the leading Palestinian political organizations founded the Palestine Liberation Organization. The PLO was intially popular among ordinary Palestinians and is still the leading Palestinian political organization. However, since the late 1980s Hamas (the Islamic Resistance Movement) has emerged as a

Selection I from Nahum Goldman, *The Autobiography of Nahum Goldman: Sixty Years of a Jewish Life* (New York: Holt, Rinehart and Winston, 1969), pp. 38–42, 44. Copyright © 1969 by Holt, Rinehart and Winston. Reprinted by permission. Selection II from Fawaz Turki, *The Disinherited: Journal of a Palestinian Exile* (New York: Monthly Review Press, 1972), pp. 43–45, 47–48, 54. Copyright © 1972 by Monthly Review Press. Reprinted by permission.

serious rival of the PLO for the leadership of the Palestinian cause. Like the Muslim Brother-hood in Egypt, Hamas has created a huge network of educational and social welfare institutions in the interest of creating an independent Palestine based on Islamic law (*shari'a*).

Hamas has also played a leading role in carrying out a variety of violent actions, including suicide bombings, aimed at ending Isreali rule over the West Bank and the Gaza Strip. Viewers of television news reports are well aware of the harsh repression carried out by the Israeli military forces against the Palestinian *intifada* (literally, a "shaking off") in recent years. Each side sees its use of violence as justified by the wrongs committed by the other.

The documents in this chapter provide insights into the thinking of the founders of modern Israel and first generation of Palestinian exiles. In the first selection Nahum Gold-man, an early Zionist from Germany, discusses his initial impressions of Palestine. The selection that follows contains Fawaz Turki's remembrance of his family's flight from Palestine in 1948 and his childhood as an exile. Two maps that help to clarify the major territorial changes from the 1940s through the 1980s conclude the chapter. How do the documents and the maps shed light on the conflict between the Israelis and the Palestinians?

THE AUTOBIOGRAPHY OF NAHUM GOLDMAN

I. NAHUM GOLDMAN

As I have said, I was not a very diligent student and spent a lot of time during the academic year with my parents in Frankfurt and in excursions to the Odenwald or the Neckar Valley. All in all my relationship to the university was not very close, and when the chance of going to Palestine was offered to me in 1913, I jumped at it. A group of students was going there on a visit organized and led by Theodor Zlocisti, one of the oldest German Zionists in Berlin, a physician by profession and a man of literary interests. I was asked if I would like to go along; my expenses would be paid by a wealthy friend of the family. The trip was supposed to last four weeks, but I stayed five months and skipped a whole semester at Heidelberg. . . .

I left the group, which was returning to Germany shortly in any case, and decided really to get to know the country. Although I have been in Palestine probably more than a hundred times since then, I have never again had the opportunity to discover it at such a leisurely yet intensive pace. Free of the group's daily hikes, receptions, and ceremonies and having decided to stay several months, I could dispose of my time as I pleased.

I spent several weeks in Tel Aviv, which then consisted of only a few streets, several more in Rishon le-Zion and Rehovot, and a week in Rosh Pina in Galilee. But most of the time I spent in Jerusalem, where I rented, in what was then the Russian apartment-house complex, a romantic attic with a balcony. I used to sleep on the balcony when the weather got warm.

A detailed account of [Jewish] colonization in those days is beyond the scope of this book, but it was all in quite a primitive stage, except for a few old-established settlements such as Petah Tiqva, Rishon le-Zion, and one or two others. I was especially impressed by kibbutzim, such as Deganyah and Kinneret, and by the type of young *halutz*, or pioneer, Zionists I encountered for the first time. In Jerusalem I tried to get to know the old *yishuv*, the pre-Zionist Orthodox Jewish community, as well as the new one and had some very impressive encounters with kabbalists and mystics in the Meah Sherim quarter of Jerusalem. . . .

I often used to take long moonlight rides with friends and once, on our way back, we were surrounded by a Bedouin band. They would certainly have robbed us and left us naked on the road if one of my companions, who was familiar with the country, had not advised us to act naturally, to sing and occasionally pat our hip pockets as if we were carrying guns. Apparently this produced the desired effect. After riding along with us for about ten minutes, the Bedouin suddenly scattered. Another time I found myself in a precarious situation when my Arab guide in Jericho arranged for me to be a hidden spectator at an Arab wedding and at the bride's dancing—something forbidden to foreigners under Bedouin law. I had already watched several dances, unforgettable in their wild passion, when my guide rushed up to me, pale with fear, and said that one of the bride's relatives had noticed something and was looking for me. We disappeared as fast as we could and got back to the hotel before it was too late. . . .

But even more than the people and the early achievements of Jewish colonization, the country itself impressed me. Never again was Palestine to have such an impact upon me. For one thing I was younger and more sensitive to such impressions and less distracted by other responsibilities than I was during later visits. The exceptional quality of this curious little territory, which has acquired a unique significance in human history not to be explained by its natural resources or geopolitical situation—what I would like to call its mystical meaning—was brought home to me then as never again. Later it became much more difficult to sense that special aura; one was too distracted by what was happening in and to the country. But at that time Palestine was still untouched. You felt the presence of the mountains without having to think about the settlements that would be established on them. You rode across the plains unmarred by buildings and highways. You traveled very slowly; there were no cars and only a few trains; you usually rode on horseback or in a cart. It took two days to get from Haifa to Jerusalem. One saw the country clearly as if emerging from thousands of years of enchantment. The clearness of the air, the brilliance of the starry sky, the mystery of the austere mountains, made it seem as though its history had grown out of the landscape. In those days it was an extraordinarily peaceful, idealistic country, absorbed in a reverie of its own unique past. In the atmosphere lingered something of the prophets and the great Talmudists, of Jesus and the Apostles, of the Safed kabbalists, and the singers of bygone centuries. . . .

When I left Palestine my Zionism had been enriched by a momentous factor, the country itself. Until then Zionism had been an abstract idea to me, and I had no real conception of what the return of the Jews meant in any concrete sense. My visit gave me that feeling for the soil without which Zionism is bound to remain quite unsubstantial. From then on I began to understand what it means, not merely negatively in terms of leaving the Diaspora behind, but also positively, as a new beginning in a Jewish homeland.

II. FAWAZ TURKI

A breeze began to blow as we moved slowly along the coast road, heading to the Lebanese border—my mother and father, my two sisters, my brother and I. Behind us lay the city of Haifa, long the scene of bombing, sniper fire, ambushes, raids, and bitter fighting between Palestinians and Zionists. Before us lay the city of Sidon and indefinite exile. Around us the waters of the Mediterranean sparkled in the sun.

Above us eternity moved on unconcerned, as if God in his heavens watched the agonies of men, as they walked on crutches, and smiled. And our world had burst, like a bubble, a bubble that had engulfed us within its warmth. From then on I would know only crazy sorrow and watch the glazed eyes of my fellow Palestinians burdened by loss and devastated by pain.

April 1948. And so it was the cruelest month of the year; but there were crueler months, then years. . . .

After a few months in Sidon, we moved again, a Palestinian family of six heading to a refugee camp in Beirut, impotent with hunger, frustration, and incomprehension. But there we encountered other families equally helpless, equally baffled, who like us never had enough to eat, never enough to offer books and education to their children, never enough to face an imminent winter. In later years, when we left the camp and found better housing and a better life outside and grew up into our early teens, we would complain about not having this or that and would be told by our mothers: "You are well off, boy! Think of those still living there in the camps. Just think of them and stop making demands." We would look out the window and see the rain falling and hear the thunder. And we would remember. We would understand. We would relent as we thought "of those still living there."

Man adapts. We adapted, the first few months, to life in a refugee camp. In the adaptation we were also reduced as men, as women, as children, as human beings. At times we dreamed. Reduced dreams. Distorted ambitions. One day, we hoped, our parents would succeed in buying two beds for me and my sister to save us the agonies of asthma, intensified from sleeping on blankets on the cold floor. One day, we hoped, there would be enough to buy a few pounds of pears or apples as we had done on those special occasions when we fought and sulked and complained because one of us was given a smaller piece of fruit than the others. One day soon, we hoped, it would be the end of the month when the UNRWA rations arrived and there was enough to eat for a week. One day soon, we argued, we would be back in our homeland.

The days stretched into months and those into a year and yet another. Kids would play in the mud of the winters and the dust of the summers, while "our problem" was debated at the UN and moths died around the kerosene lamps. A job had been found for me in a factory not far from the camp, where I worked for six months. I felt pride in the fact that I was a bread earner and was thus eligible to throw my weight around the house, legitimately demand an extra spoonful of sugar in my tea, and have my own money to spend on comic books and an occasional orange on the side. I had even started saving to buy my own bed, but I was fired soon after that.

A kid at work had called me a two-bit Palestinian and a fist fight ensued. The supervisor, an obese man with three chins and a green stubble that covered most of his face and reached under his eyes, came over to stop the fight. He decided I had started it all, slapped me hard twice, deducted three lira from my wages for causing trouble (I earned seven lira a week), paid me the rest, called me a two-bit Palestinian, and, pointing to my blond hair, suggested I had a whore mother and shoved me out the door.

I went to the river and sat on the grass to eat my lunch. I was shaken more by the two-bit Palestinian epithet than by the plight of being unemployed. At home and around the camp, we had unconsciously learned to be proud of where we came from and to continue remembering that we were Palestinians. If this was stigmatic outside, there it was an identity to be known, perpetuated, embraced. My father, reproaching us for an ignoble offense of some kind, would say: "You are a Palestinian." He would mean: as a Palestinian one is not expected to stoop that low and betray his tradition. If we came home affecting a Lebanese accent, our mother would say: "Hey, what's wrong with your own accent? You're too good for your own people or something? You want to sound like a foreigner when we return to Haifa? What's wrong with you, hey?"

• • •

Our Palestinian consciousness, instead of dissipating, was enhanced and acquired a subtle nuance and a new dimension. It was buoyed by two concepts: the preservation of our memory of Palestine and our acquisition of education. We persisted in refusing the houses and monetary compensation offered by the UN to settle us in our host countries. We wanted nothing short of returning to our homeland. And from Syria, Lebanon, and Jordan, we would see, a few miles, a few yards, across the border, a land where we had been born, where we had lived, and where we felt the earth. "This is my land," we would shout, or cry, or sing, or plead, or reason. And to that land a people had come, a foreign community of colonizers, aided by a Western world in a hurry to rid itself of guilt and shame, demanding independence from history, from heaven, and from us.

STUDY QUESTIONS

1. Why did Nahum Goldman decide to go to Palestine in 1913 and to remain there after his friends returned home to Germany?
2. What kinds of contacts did Goldman have with Palestinian Arabs?
3. What did Goldman's first visit to Palestine mean to him?
4. What does Fawaz Turki reveal about the standard of living in the Palestinian refugee camps?
5. What attitudes did Turki encounter among the Arabs in the host countries where the refugee camps were located?
6. According to Turki, what explains the growing strength of Palestinian nationalism? What do you think of his view that the Western world is partly responsible for the conflicts in the Middle East?
7. What is the relationship between Israeli and Palestinian nationalism and nationalism in other parts of the world? (See Chapter 44 on Turkey, Chapter 47 on China, Chapter 51 on India, Chapter 53 on Latin America, and Chapter 56 on Africa.)
8. What has been the trend since the beginning of the twentieth century regarding conflicts between people of different nationalities and religions? Have the conflicts increased, stayed the same, or decreased? How do you explain this?

VISUAL SOURCE

THE CARTOGRAPHY OF CONFLICT

The two maps may be studied for the information they provide on the conflicts between Israel and the Palestinians since the 1940s. Figure 1 illustrates the 1947 proposal of the United Nations for creation of a Jewish and a Palestinian state from the British Palestine Mandate. This plan was a casualty of the fighting that erupted from 1947 to 1949 when the Palestinians and the Arab states attempted to block the establishment of the state of Israel. Triumphant in these conflicts, the Israelis took control of lands well beyond those called for in the UN proposal. The West Bank went to Jordan and the Gaza Strip went to Egypt. As for the Palestinians, approximately 700,000 of them fled their homes in the former Mandate for refugee camps in the West Bank, Gaza, and neighboring Arab states.

The next major turning point in the conflict occured in 1967. In a brief war waged in June of that year Israel decisively defeated Egypt, Jordan and Syria. This victory gave the Israelis control of two key regions of Palestinian settlement, the West Bank and Gaza (as well as other territories from which they later withdrew). When the Israelis subsequently began to establish settler communities in the occupied territories, Palestinian opposition was intense and often included acts of terror directed against Israeli citizens. Despite repeated Palestinian protests, the Israeli policy of encouraging settlements in the occupied territories has continued. Figure 2 illustrates the present-day borders of Israel, as well as the areas of the West Bank and Gaza controlled by the Israelis and the Palestinians.

STUDY QUESTIONS

1. What do the maps suggest about the reasons for the intensity of the present-day conflict between the Palestinians and the Israelis?
2. How might the maps be used to propose a resolution of the conflict?

From the UN Plan of 1947 to the Territorial Situation in 2002.

46

The Resurgence of Islam

One of the most important trends in recent world history has been the renaissance of faith among Muslims. Often referred to as the "resurgence of Islam," this development began in the Middle East and North Africa and quickly spread in all directions, reaching countries such as Indonesia and Nigeria as well as numerous cities in Europe and the Americas. For the past quarter-century or so mosque attendance has been increasing, traditional Islamic dress for women has been in favor, Muslim men have been growing their beards long, and the appeal of Islamic grassroots organizations (including those located at universities) has surged.

Muslims have also had a dramatic impact on political life. In 1979 Shiite clerics in Iran rode to power on a massive wave of popular discontent and replaced the rule of the secularist Pahlavi shahs (reigned 1925–1979) with a republican regime based on Islamic law (*shari'a*). Two years later Muslim extremists in the Egyptian army assassinated Anwar el-Sadat, the Egyptian leader who had earlier normalized relations with Israel. During the 1980s and 1990s in Sudan, the largest country in Africa, a series of authoritarian governments led by Sunni Muslims imposed the *shari'a*. In 1996 the Taliban, an insurgent army of fundamentalist Muslims, seized control of Kabul and began enforcing their harsh version of Islamic teachings in Afghanistan.

In many other Muslim countries nongovernmental Islamic organizations that sponsor schools and social services have become increasingly popular. Such organizations are descendants of the Muslim Brotherhood, the fraternal order founded in 1928 by Egyptian schoolteacher Hasan al-Banna (1906–1949). Banna believed that by establishing Islamic schools, nurseries, summer camps, and low-cost health clinics, the Brotherhood would gradually persuade Muslims to incorporate the *shari'a* into their daily lives. He thought once people had absorbed Islamic teachings, political change would naturally follow. Despite Banna's assassination in 1949 and harsh governmental repression of the Brotherhood, the organization became increasingly influential in Egyptian life from the 1950s onward. In present-day Egypt the Brotherhood's vast network of schools, social service agencies, and professional associations makes it the most serious rival of the government of Hosni Mubarak. Somewhat similar organizations flourish in Lebanon, Turkey, Pakistan, the Palestinian Territories, and other Muslim countries.

In the first selection Banna explains the thinking of the Muslim Brotherhood during its formative period and enables us to see how the Islamic resurgence was initially shaped by developments during the 1930s and 1940s. The second document, written by Ayatullah Murtada Mutahhari, provides insight into the ideas of one of the leaders of the 1979 Iranian revolution, the pivotal political event in the Islamic resurgence. Three decrees issued by the Taliban shortly after it gained control of Kabul make up the third selection. A photograph suggesting the importance of the pilgrimage to Mecca concludes the chapter. How do the documents and the visual evidence help us to put the resurgence of Islam into historical context?

ISLAMIC RESURGENCE

I. HASAN AL-BANNA (1949)

When we observe the evolution in the political, social, and moral spheres of the lives of nations and peoples, we note that the Islamic world—and, naturally, in the forefront, the Arab world—gives to its rebirth an Islamic flavor. This trend is ever-increasing. Until recently, writers, intellectuals, scholars, and governments glorified the principles of European civilization, gave themselves a Western tint, and adopted a European style and manner; today, on the contrary, the wind has changed, and reserve and distrust have taken their place. Voices are raised proclaiming the necessity for a return to the principles, teachings, and ways of Islam, and, taking into account the situation, for initiating the reconciliation of modern life with these principles, as a prelude to a final "Islamization."

This development worries a good number of governments and Arab powers, which, having lived during the past generations in a state of mind that had retained from Islam only lessons of fanaticism and inertia, regarded the Muslims only as weak drudges or as nations easily exploitable by colonialism. In trying to understand the new movement . . . these governments have produced all sorts of possible interpretations: "It is the result," said some, "of the growth of extremist organizations and fanatical groups." Others explained that it was a reaction to present-day political and economic pressures, of which the Islamic nations had become aware. Finally, others said, "It is only a means whereby those seeking government or other honors may achieve renown and position."

Now all these reasons are, in our opinion, as far as possible from the truth; for this new movement can only be the result of the following three factors, which we will now examine.

The first of the three is the failure of the social principles on which the civilization of the Western nations has been built. The Western way of life—bounded in effect on practical and technical knowledge, discovery, invention, and the flooding of world markets with mechanical products—has remained incapable of offering to men's minds a flicker of light, a ray of hope, a grain of faith, or of providing anxious persons the smallest path toward rest and tranquillity. Man is not simply an instrument among others. Naturally, he has become tired of purely materialistic conditions and desires some spiritual comfort. But the materialistic life of the West could only offer him as reassurance a new materialism of sin, passion, drink, women, noisy gatherings, and showy attractions which he had come to enjoy. Man's hunger grows from day to day: he wants to free his spirit, to destroy this materialist prison and find space to breathe the air of faith and consolation.

The second factor—the decisive factor in the circumstances—is the discovery by Islamic thinkers of the noble, honorable, moral, and perfect content of the principles and rules of this religion, which is infinitely more accomplished, more pure, more glorious, more complete, and more beautiful than all that has been discovered up till now by social theorists and reformers. For a long time, Muslims neglected all this, but once God had enlightened their thinkers and they had compared the social rules of their religion with what they had been told by the greatest sociologists and the cleverest leading theorists, they noted the wide gap and the great distance between a heritage of immense value on one side and the conditions experienced on the other. Then, Muslims could not but do justice to the spirit and the history of their people, proclaiming the value of this heritage and inviting all peoples—nonpracticing Muslims or non-Muslims—to follow the sacred path that God had traced for them and to hold to a straight course.

The third factor is the development of social conditions between the two murderous world wars (which involved all the world powers and monopolized the minds of regimes, nations, and individuals) which resulted in a set of principles of reform and social organization that certain powers, in deciding to put them into practice, have taken as an instructional basis. . . .

Thus, German Nazism and Italian Fascism rose to the fore; Mussolini and Hitler led their two peoples to unity, order, recovery, power, and glory. In record time, they ensured internal order at home and, through force, made themselves feared abroad. These regimes gave real hope, and also gave rise to thoughts of steadfastness and perseverance and the reuniting of different, divided men around the words "chief" and "order." In their resolutions and speeches, the Führer and the Duce began to frighten the world and to upset their epoch. . . .

The star of socialism and Communism, symbol of success and victory, shone with an increasing brilliance; Soviet Russia was at the head of the collectivist camp. She launched her message and, in the eyes of the world, demonstrated a system which had been modified several times in thirty years. The democratic powers—or, to use a more precise expression, the colonialist powers, the old ones worn out, the new ones full of greed—took up a position to stem the current. The struggle intensified, in some places openly, in others under cover, and nations and peoples, perplexed, hesitated at the crossroads, not knowing which was best; among them were the nations of Islam and the peoples of the Qur'an; the future, whatever the circumstances, is in the hands of God, the decision with history, and immortality with the most worthy.

This social evolution and violent, hard struggle stirred the minds of Muslim thinkers; the parallels and the prescribed comparisons led to a healthy conclusion:

to free themselves from the existing state of affairs, to allow the necessary return of the nations and peoples to Islam.

II. AYATULLAH MURTADA MUTAHHARI (1979)

Scholars and knowledgeable persons in contemporary history concede that in the second half of our century in almost all or at least in a large number of Islamic countries Islamic movements have been in ascent openly or secretly. These are practically directed against despotism, capitalist colonialism or materialist ideologies subscribing to colonialism in its new shape. Experts on political affairs acknowledge that after having passed through a period of mental crisis the Muslims are once again struggling to reestablish their "Islamic identity" against the challenges of the capitalist West and the communist East. But in no Islamic country has this type of movement gained as much of depth and extent as in Iran since the year 1960. Nor is there a parallel to the proportions which the Iranian movement has obtained. It, therefore, becomes necessary to analyze this remarkably significant event of history.

Like all natural occurrences, social and political events also tend to differ from one another in their behaviours. All historical movements cannot be considered identical in their nature. The nature of the Islamic movement is in no case similar to the French revolution or to the great October revolution of Russia.

The current Iranian movement is not restricted to any particular class or trade union. It is not only a labour, an agrarian, a student, an intellectual or a bourgeois movement. Within its scope fall one and all in Iran, the rich and the poor, the man and the woman, the school boy and the scholar, the warehouse man and the factory labourer, the artisan and the peasant, the clergy and the teacher, the literate and the illiterate, one and all. An announcement made by the preceptor of the highest station guiding the movement is received in the length and breadth of the country with equal enthusiasm by all classes of the people. . . .

This movement is one of the glaring historical proofs which falsifies the concept of materialistic interpretation of history and that of the dialectics of materialism according to which economy is recognised as the cornerstone of social structure and a social movement is considered a reflection of class struggle. . . .

The awakened Islamic conscience of our society has induced it to search for Islamic values. This is the conscience of the cumulative enthusiasms of all classes of people, including perhaps some of the heretofore dissident groups, which has galvanized them into one concerted upsurge.

The roots of this movement shall have to be traced in the events that occurred during the last half century in our country [during the reign of the Pahlavi shahs, 1925–1979] and the way these events came into conflict with the Islamic spirit of our society.

It is evident that during the last half century, there have been events which adopted a diametrically opposite direction as far as the nobler objectives of Islam were concerned and which aimed at nullifying the aspirations of the well-meaning reformers for the last century. This state of affairs could not continue for long without reaction.

What happened in Iran during the last half century may be summed up as under:

1. Absolute and barbaric despotism.
2. Denial of freedom of every kind.
3. A new type of colonialism meaning an invisible and dangerous colonialism embracing political, economic and cultural aspects of life.
4. Maintaining distance between religion and politics. Rather, divorcing politics from religion.
5. An attempt at leading Iran back to the age of ignorance of pre-Islamic days. . . .
6. Effecting a change and corrupting the rich Islamic culture and replacing it with the ambiguous Iranian culture.
7. Gruesome killing of Iranian Muslims, imprisonment and torture of the alleged political prisoners.
8. Ever increasing discrimination and cleavage among the classes of society despite so-called reforms.
9. Domination of non-Muslim elements over the Muslim elements in the government and other institutions.
10. Flagrant violation of Islamic laws either directly or by perpetrating corruption in the cultural and social life of the people.
11. Propaganda against Persian literature (which has always been the protector and upholder of Islamic spirit) under the pretext of purifying the Persian language of foreign terminology.
12. Severing relations with Islamic countries and flirting with non-Islamic and obviously with anti-Islamic countries like Israel.

. . .

What is the objective pursued by the [Islamic] movement and what does it want? Does it aim at democracy? Does it want to liquidate colonialism from our country? Does it rise to defend what is called in modern terminology human rights? Does it want to do away with discrimination, inequality? Does it want to uproot oppression? Does it want to undo materialism and so forth and so on?

In view of the nature of the movement and its roots as already brought under consideration and also in view of the statements and announcements given out by the leaders of the movement, what one may gather as an answer to these questions is "Yes" as well as "No."

"Yes" because all the objectives mentioned above form the very crux of it. And "No" because the movement is not limited to only these or any one of these objectives. An Islamic movement cannot, from the point of its objective, remain a restricted affair, because Islam, in its very nature, is "an indivisible whole" and with the realization of any of the objectives set before it, its role does not cease to be.

. . .

No movement can be led successfully without leadership. But who should be the leader or the group of leaders when the movement is an Islamic one in its nature and when its objective is exclusively Islam?

Evidently the leadership should, in the first place, fulfill the general conditions of the task before it. Then the leaders must be deeply Islamic, fully conversant with the ethical, social, political and spiritual philosophy of Islam. They must have the knowledge of Islam's universal vision, its insight about empirical matters like the creation, the origin, the creator of the universe, the need for creation of the universe, etc. They must have the deep knowledge of Islam's views and stipulations on man and his society. It is of great importance that the leaders must have a clear picture of the Islamic ideology of man's relations with his society; his manner and method of framing the social order; his abilities of defending and pursuing certain things and resisting others; his ultimate objectives and the means of attaining those objectives, etc.

It is obvious that only such persons can lead as have been brought up under the pure Islamic culture having perfectly mastered the branches of religious learning and Islamic sciences, the Qur'an, tradition, jurisprudence, etc. It is, therefore, only ecclesiastics who qualify for the leadership of such a movement.

III. TALIBAN DECREES (1996)

[In 1994 the Taliban emerged suddenly out of the bitter conflicts that gripped Afghanistan following the Soviet invasion of 1979. For many Afghans, nearly all of whom are Muslim, resistance to the Soviets in the 1980s was a holy war (jihad)*. However, when the Soviets withdrew in defeat in 1989, ethnic and tribal differences among the Afghans quickly surfaced. Fierce fighting between the Pashtuns, the dominant group in the south, and an unstable coalition of northern groups—Uzbeks, Tajiks, and Hazaras— rent the country for several years. It was this Afghan crucible of violence in the 1980s and early 1990s that gave rise to the Taliban, a movement of mostly young and impoverished Pashtun males. Many of the Taliban grew up in refugee camps in northern Pakistan where they obtained only the most rudimentary education in fundamentalist Muslim schools* (madrasas)*. As they fought their way to power in 1994–1996, large numbers of Afghans, especially Pashtuns, welcomed the Taliban both for their promise to restore social order and for their Muslim piety. The three decrees are reproduced as translated by the Taliban.]*

TALIBAN DECREES

1.

Decree announced by the General Presidency of Amr Bil Maruf and Nai Az Munkar (Religious Police.)
Kabul, November 1996.

Women you should not step outside your residence. If you go outside the house you should not be like women who used to go with fashionable clothes wearing much cosmetics and appearing in front of every men before the coming of Islam.

Islam as a rescuing religion has determined specific dignity for women, Islam has valuable instructions for women. Women should not create such opportunity to attract the attention of useless people who will not look at them with a good eye. Women have the responisbility as a teacher or coordinator for her family.

Husband, brother, father have the responsibilty for providing the family with the necessary life requirements (food, clothes, etc). In case women are required to go outside the residence for the purposes of education, social needs or social services they should cover themselves in accordance with Islamic Sharia regulation. If women are going outside with fashionable, ornamental, tight and charming clothes to show themselves, they will be cursed by the Islamic Sharia and should never expect to go to heaven.

All family elders and every Muslim have responsibility in this respect. We request all family elders to keep tight control over their families and avoid these social problems. Otherwise these women will be threatened, investigated and severely punished as well as the family elders by the forces of the Religious Police (*Munkrat*).

The Religious Police (*Munkrat*) have the responsibility and duty to struggle against these social problems and will continue their effort until evil is finished.

2.

Rules of work for the State Hospitals and private clinics based on Islamic Sharia principles. Ministry of Health, on behalf of Amiz ul Momineen Mullah Mohammed Omar. Kabul, November 1996.

1. Female patients should go to female physicians. In case a male physician is needed, the female patient should be accompanied by her close relative.
2. During examination, the female patients and male physicians both should be dressed with Islamic *hijab* (veil).
3. Male physicians should not touch or see the other parts of female patients except for the affected part.
4. Waiting room for female patients should be safely covered.
5. The person who regulates turn for female patients should be a female.
6. During the night duty, in what rooms which female patients are hospitalized, the male doctor without the call of the patient is not allowed to enter the room.
7. Sitting and speaking between male and female doctors are not allowed, if there be need for discussion, it should be done with *hijab*.
8. Female doctors should wear simple clothes; they are not allowed to wear stylish clothes or use cosmetics or make-up.
9. Female doctors and nurses are not allowed to enter the rooms where male patients are hospitalized.
10. Hospital staff should pray in mosques on time.
11. The Religious Police are allowed to go for control at any time and nobody can prevent them.

Anybody who violates the order will be punished as per Islamic regulations.

3.

General Presidency of Amr Bil Maruf. Kabul, December 1996.

1. To prevent sedition and female uncovers (Be Hejabi). No drivers are allowed to pick up women who are using Iranian *burqa*. In case of violation the driver will be imprisoned. If such kind of female are observed in the

street their house will be found and their husband punished. If the women use stimulating and attractive cloth and there is no accompany of close male relative with them, the drivers should not pick them up.

2. To prevent music. To be broadcasted by the public information resources. In shops, hotels, vehicles and rickshaws cassettes and music are prohibited. This matter should be monitored within five days. If any music cassette found in a shop, the shopkeeper should be imprisoned and the shop locked. If five people guarantee the shop should be opened the criminal released later. If cassette found in the vehicle, the vehicle and driver will be imprisoned. If five people guarantee the vehicle will be released and the criminal released later.

3. To prevent beard shaving and its cutting. After one and a half months if anyone observed who has shaved and/or cut his beard, they should be arrested and imprisoned until their beard gets bushy.

4. To prevent keeping pigeons and playing with birds. Within ten days this habit/hobby should stop. After ten days this should be monitored and pigeons and any other playing birds should be killed.

5. To prevent kite-flying. The kite shops in the city should be abolished.

6. To prevent idolatory. In vehicles, shops, hotels, room and any other place pictures/portraits should be abolished. The monitors should tear up all pictures in the above places.

7. To prevent gambling. In collaboration with the security police the main centres should be found and the gamblers imprisoned for one month.

8. To eradicate the use of addiction. Addicts should be imprisoned and investigation made to find the supplier and the shop. The shop should be locked and the owner and user should be imprisoned and punished.

9. To prevent the British and American hairstyle. People with long hair should be arrested and taked to the Religious Police department to shave their hair. The criminal has to pay the barber.

10. To prevent interest on loans, charge on changing small denomination notes and charge on money orders. All money exchangers should be informed that the above three types of exchanging the money should be prohibited. In case of violation criminals will be imprisoned for a long time.

11. To prevent washing cloth by young ladies along the water streams in the city. Violator ladies should be picked up with respectful Islamic manner, taken to their houses and their husbands severely punished.

12. To prevent music and dances in wedding parties. In case of violation the head of the family will be arrested and punished.

13. To prevent the playing of music drum. The prohibition of this should be announced. If anybody does this then religious elders can decide about it.

14. To prevent sewing ladies cloth and taking female body measures by tailor. If women or fashion magazines are seen in the shop the tailor should be imprisoned.

15. To prevent sorcery. All the related books should be burnt and the magician should be imprisoned until his repentance.

16. To prevent not praying and order gathering pray at the bazaar. Prayer should be done on their due times in all districts. Transportation should

be strictly prohibited and all people are obliged to go to the mosque. If young people are seen in the shops they will be immediately imprisoned.

STUDY QUESTIONS

1. How did Banna explain the resurgence of Islam? What aspects of the Western way of life did he oppose? What did he see as the strengths of Islam? What was his view of Nazism, Fascism, and Communism?

2. According to Mutahhari, how was the Iranian revolution different from other revolutions?

3. How does Mutahhari explain the causes of the Iranian revolution? Did he see the causes as basically political, economic, or religious? How did he describe the revolution's goals? Do you see a tension between Mutahhari's Iranian nationalism and his Muslim piety?

4. What goals are stated or implied in the Taliban decrees? How do the decrees suggest the social and cultural background of the Taliban? What fears are implied in the decrees? What groups would benefit from their implementation? Who would lose?

5. How do the ideas of Banna, Mutahhari, and the Taliban compare with the thinking of Ziya Gokalp? (See Chapter 44) How do you explain the differences?

6. What political, military, economic, and social changes in recent decades have contributed to the renewed appeal of Islam? Are there similar tendencies in other religions, such as Christianity and Hinduism?

7. What are the advantages and disadvantages of separating political authority from religious authority? Is Islam compatible with democracy?

8. What are the similarities and differences between the Iranian revolution and the leftist revolutions in Russia and China and Cuba? Are any of these revolutions likely to be emulated in the future?

9. Why is there so much diversity within the great world religions?

VISUAL SOURCE

A PILGRIM'S PRIDE

Islam is the one world religion that requires its members to go on pilgrimage. In traveling to the holy city of Mecca to visit *Ka'bah* and other holy sites, Muslims follow the example set by Muhammad and also re-enact events in the lives of Abraham, his wife Hagar, and their son Ishmael.

One indication of the resurgence of Islam in recent decades is the sharp increase in the number of Muslim pilgrims. In 1940 about 100,000 pilgrims from outside of Saudi Arabia journeyed to Mecca for the annual holy rites. Since that time the number has steadily increased. In 2000 the number of pilgrims to Mecca from foreign countries was approximately 1 million. Another 1 million came from within Saudi Arabia.

Although the Koran urges pilgrimage on all the faithful, only about 10 percent of Muslims ever make the sacred journey. Many of those who do so require subventions from family members and neighbors in order to pay the costs of the trip. Thus, when pilgrims return home, their pride is genuine and their standing among their coreligionists is much enhanced. In Egypt many pilgrims have murals painted on the walls of their houses commemorating their visit to the holy places. The Arabic calligraphy on the Egyptian house here quotes a key verse from the Koran: "Pilgrimage to the House [the *Ka'bah* in Mecca] is a duty to Allah for all who can make the journey" (3:97).

Mural on the Side of the House of an Egyptian Pilgrim to Mecca, ca. 1980. (Photo by Graham Harrison)

STUDY QUESTIONS

1. What features of Muslim pilgrimage are illustrated in the mural?
2. How does the photo suggest aspects of the Islamic resurgence?

47

Chinese Revolutionaries: Sun Yatsen and Mao Zedong

The twentieth century was one of the most tumultuous in the history of China. Buffeted by the shocks from Western and Japanese imperialism and unable to deal effectively with China's many internal problems, the Qing dynasty finally collapsed in 1912. A republic was immediately declared, but a protracted period of instability and confusion ensued. For more than a decade warlords fought for control of the country. During this period Sun Yatsen (1866–1925) emerged as the leading advocate of a Western-style republic in China. Sun, who had been born near Hong Kong and educated in Western schools, founded China's first real political party, the Guomindang (National People's Party) and became enormously popular as its leader. But at the time of Sun's death China's crisis was far from resolved.

In 1927 Chiang Kaishek, Sun's successor as head of the Guomindang, was able to impose a kind of unity on China from his capital in Nanjing. Chiang was the nominal head of state in China until 1949, but his regime, while strongly nationalistic in rhetoric and gesture, was corrupt and ineffective. When Japan invaded eastern China in 1937 Chiang's government was unable to muster much of a defense. He moved his capital deep into the interior of the country and became increasingly dependent on aid from the British and the United States.

In contrast to Chiang's ineffectiveness, China's rural-based Communist Party, led by Mao Zedong (1891–1976), organized a strong and popular resistance movement against the Japanese. By the end of World War II in 1945 the Chinese Communist Party claimed millions of members, had its own large and battle-tested army, and governed much of northern China. Attempts to reconcile the Communists and the Nationalists in 1945 and 1946 quickly broke down. The result was full-scale civil war. In 1949 the Communists swept to power—moving from the countryside to the cities and from north to south—and they have governed the country ever since.

Selection I from *Sources of Chinese Tradition*, Vol. II, edited by Theodore de Bary, Wing-tsit Chan, and Burton Watson (New York: Columbia University Press, 1960), pp. 768–771; Selection II from *The People's Republic of China: A Documentary History of Revolutionary Change*, edited by Mark Selden (New York: Monthly Review Press, 1979), pp. 176–178.

The first selection is a series of passages taken from lectures that Sun Yatsen gave to Party members in 1924. Sun's discourse is followed by excerpts from a speech given by Mao Zedong in the summer of 1949. In the speech Mao discusses the policies that would guide the soon-to-be-founded People's Republic of China.

TWO REVOLUTIONARY LEADERS

I. SUN YATSEN: THE THREE PEOPLE'S PRINCIPLES

[*China as a Heap of Loose Sand*]. For the most part the four hundred million people of China can be spoken of as completely Han Chinese. With common customs and habits, we are completely of one race. But in the world today what position do we occupy? Compared to the other peoples of the world we have the greatest population and our civilization is four thousand years old; we should therefore be advancing in the front rank with the nations of Europe and America. But the Chinese people have only family and clan solidarity; they do not have national spirit. Therefore even though we have four hundred million people gathered together in one China, in reality they are just a heap of loose sand. Today we are the poorest and weakest nation in the world, and occupy the lowest position in international affairs. Other men are the carving knife and serving dish; we are the fish and the meat. Our position at this time is most perilous. If we do not earnestly espouse nationalism and weld together our four hundred million people into a strong nation, there is danger of China's being lost and our people being destroyed. If we wish to avert this catastrophe, we must espouse nationalism and bring this national spirit to the salvation of the country. . . .

[*China as a "Hypo-Colony"*]. Since the Chinese Revolution [of 1911], the foreign powers have found that it was much less easy to use political force in carving up China. A people who had experienced Manchu [Qing] oppression and learned to overthrow it, would now, if the powers used political force to oppress it, be certain to resist, and thus make things difficult for them. For this reason they are letting up in their efforts to control China by political force and instead are using economic pressure to keep us down. . . . As regards political oppression people are readily aware of their suffering, but when it comes to economic oppression most often they are hardly conscious of it. China has already experienced several decades of economic oppression by the foreign powers, and so far the nation has for the most part shown no sense of irritation. As a consequence China is being transformed everywhere into a colony of the foreign powers.

Our people keep thinking that China is only a "semi-colony"—a term by which they seek to comfort themselves. Yet in reality the economic oppression we have endured is not just that of a "semi-colony" but greater even than that of a full colony. . . . Of what nation then is China a colony? It is the colony of every nation with which it has concluded treaties; each of them is China's master. Therefore China is not just the colony of one country; it is the colony of many countries. We are not just the slaves of one country, but the slaves of many countries. In the event of natural disasters like flood and drought, a nation which is sole master appropriates funds for relief and distributes them, thinking this its own duty; and the people who are its slaves regard this relief work as something to which their masters are obligated. But when North China suffered drought several years ago, the foreign powers did not regard it as their responsibility to appropriate funds and distribute relief; only those foreigners resident in China raised funds for the drought victims, whereupon Chinese observers remarked on the great generosity of the foreigners who bore no responsibility to help. . . .

From this we can see that China is not so well off as Annam [under the French] and Korea [under the Japanese]. Being the slaves of one country represents a far higher status than being the slaves of many, and is far more advantageous. Therefore, to call China a "semi-colony" is quite incorrect. If I may coin a phrase, we should be called a "hypo-colony." This is a term that comes from chemistry, as in "hypo-phosphite." Among chemicals there are some belonging to the class of phosphorous compounds but of lower grade, which are called phosphites. Still another grade lower, and they are called hypo-phosphites. . . . The Chinese people, believing they were a semi-colony, thought it shame enough; they did not realize that they were lower even than Annam or Korea. Therefore we cannot call ourselves a "semi-colony" but only a "hypo-colony." . . .

[*Nationalism and Traditional Morality*]. If today we want to restore the standing of our people, we must first restore our national spirit. . . . If in the past our people have survived despite the fall of the state [to foreign conquerors], and not only survived themselves but been able to assimilate these foreign conquerors, it is because of the high level of our traditional morality. Therefore, if we go to the root of the matter, besides arousing a sense of national solidarity uniting all our people, we must recover and restore our characteristic, traditional morality. Only thus can we hope to attain again the distinctive position of our people.

This characteristic morality the Chinese people today have still not forgotten. First comes loyalty and filial piety, then humanity and love, faithfulness and duty, harmony and peace. Of these traditional virtues, the Chinese people still speak, but now, under foreign oppression, we have been invaded by a new culture, the force of which is felt all across the nation. Men wholly intoxicated by this new culture have thus begun to attack the traditional morality, saying that with the adoption of the new culture, we no longer have need of the old morality. . . . They say that when we formerly spoke of loyalty, it was loyalty to princes, but now in our democracy there are no princes, so loyalty is unnecessary and can be dispensed with. This kind of reasoning is certainly mistaken. In our country princes can be dispensed with, but not loyalty. If they say loyalty can be dispensed with, then I ask: "Do we, or do we not, have a nation? Can we, or can we not, make loyalty serve the nation? If indeed we can no longer speak of loyalty to princes, can we not, however, speak of loyalty to our people?"

II. MAO ZEDONG (1949)

Twenty-four years have passed since Sun Yatsen's death, and the Chinese Revolution, led by the Communist Party of China, has made tremendous advances both in theory and practice and has radically changed the face of China. Up to now the principal and fundamental experience the Chinese people have gained is twofold:

1. Internally, arouse the masses of the people. That is, unite the working class, the peasantry, the urban petty bourgeoisie and the national bourgeoisie, form a domestic united front under the leadership of the working class, and advance from this to the establishment of a state which is a people's democratic dictatorship under the leadership of the working class and based on the alliance of workers and peasants.

2. Externally, unite in a common struggle with those nations of the world which treat us as equals and with the peoples of all countries. That is, ally ourselves with the Soviet Union, with the people's democracies, and with the proletariat and the broad masses of the people in all other countries, and form an international united front.

"You are leaning to one side." Exactly. The forty years' experience of Sun Yat-sen and the twenty-eight years' experience of the Communist Party have taught us to lean to one side, and we are firmly convinced that in order to win victory and consolidate it we must lean to one side. In the light of the experiences accumulated in these forty years and these twenty-eight years, all Chinese without exception must lean either to the side of imperialism or to the side of socialism. Sitting on the fence will not do, nor is there a third road. . . .

"We want to do business." Quite right, business will be done. We are against no one except the domestic and foreign reactionaries who hinder us from doing business. Everybody should know that it is none other than the imperialists and their running dogs, the Chiang Kaishek reactionaries, who hinder us from doing business and also from establishing diplomatic relations with foreign countries. When we have beaten the internal and external reactionaries by uniting all domestic and international forces, we shall be able to do business and establish diplomatic relations with all foreign countries on the basis of equality, mutual benefit, and mutual respect for territorial integrity and sovereignty.

"Victory is possible even without international help." This is a mistaken idea. In the epoch in which imperialism exists, it is impossible for a genuine people's revolution to win victory in any country without various forms of help from the international revolutionary forces, and even if victory were won, it could not be consolidated. This was the case with the victory and consolidation of the great October Revolution, as Stalin told us long ago. This was also the case with the overthrow of the three imperialist powers in World War II and the establishment of the people's democracies. And this is also the case with the present and the future of People's China. . . .

"You are dictatorial." My dear sirs, you are right, that is just what we are. All the experience the Chinese people have accumulated through several decades teaches us to enforce the People's Democratic Dictatorship, that is, to deprive the reactionaries of the right to speak and let the people alone have that right.

Who are the people? At the present stage in China, they are the working class, the peasantry, the urban petty bourgeoisie, and the national bourgeoisie. These classes, led by the working class and the Communist Party, unite to form their own state and elect their own government; they enforce their dictatorship over the running dogs of imperialism—the landlord class and bureaucrat-bourgeoisie, as well as the representatives of those classes, the Kuomintang reactionaries and their accomplices—suppress them, allow them only to behave themselves and not to be unruly in word or deed. If they speak or act in an unruly way, they will be promptly stopped and punished. Democracy is practiced within the ranks of the people, who enjoy the rights of freedom of speech, assembly, association and so on. The right to vote belongs only to the people, not to the reactionaries. The combination of these two aspects, democracy for the people and dictatorship over the reactionaries, is the People's Democratic Dictatorship. . . .

The serious problem is the education of the peasantry. The peasant economy is scattered, and the socialization of agriculture, judging by the Soviet Union's experience, will require a long time and painstaking work. Without socialization of agriculture, there can be no complete, consolidated socialism. The steps to socialize agriculture must be coordinated with the development of a powerful industry having state enterprise as its backbone. The state of the People's Democratic Dictatorship must systematically solve the problems of industrialization. . . .

The People's Democratic Dictatorship is based on the alliance of the working class, the peasantry and the urban petty bourgeoisie, and mainly on the alliance of the workers and the peasants, because these two classes comprise 80 to 90 percent of China's population. These two classes are the main force in overthrowing imperialism and the Guomindang reactionaries. The transition from new democracy to socialism also depends mainly upon their alliance.

The People's Democratic Dictatorship needs the leadership of the working class. For it is only the working class that is most farsighted, most selfless and most thoroughly revolutionary. . . .

To sum up our experience and concentrate it into one point, it is: the People's Democratic Dictatorship under the leadership of the working class (through the Communist Party) and based upon the alliance of workers and peasants. This dictatorship must unite as one with the international revolutionary forces. This is our formula, our principal experience, and our main program.

STUDY QUESTIONS

1. Why did Sun Yatsen think the Chinese people must "espouse nationalism"?
2. According to Sun, how had China become stronger since the Revolution of 1911?
3. What did Sun mean by the term "hypo-colony"?
4. What was the Sun's attitude toward China's traditional Confucian culture?
5. According to Mao Zedong in 1949, what important changes had taken place in China since the death of Sun Yatsen?
6. What did Mao mean by "leaning to one side"?
7. How did Mao define "People's Democratic Dictatorship"?
8. What view of China's traditional Confucian culture was implied in Mao's address?
9. What similarities and differences do you see in the ideas of Sun Yatsen and Mao Zedong? In what sense were Sun and Mao ambivalent toward the West? How did their views compare with the ideas in the "self-strengthening" movement in nineteenth-century China? (See Chapter 27.)
10. Compare the ideas of Mao with those of Lenin and Stalin. (See Chapters 41 and 42.) What similarities and differences do you see?

48

China under Communist Rule: Peasants and Students

When the Qing dynasty collapsed in 1912 the great majority of the people of China—perhaps 80 percent of the population—lived in the countryside. Farms were quite small by Western standards, averaging from three to five acres (compared with about 150 acres in the United States). Perhaps a third of the rural population was landless; peasants without their own land were forced to rent plots from prosperous landowners, often at very high rates. Many other peasants owned plots that were too small for them to survive on; they too were compelled to rent land.

During the 1930s and 1940s conditions worsened for Chinese peasants in significant ways. The worldwide Great Depression of the 1930s hit the Chinese economy hard and drove down the living standards of both urban and rural dwellers. During World War II, which began for the Chinese with the Japanese invasion of 1937, much of the rural economy was devastated. Most of the 10 million Chinese who died in the fighting were peasants. In the subsequent Civil War of 1946 to 1949, between the Communists and the Nationalists the farming economy was battered once again, bringing the suffering of the peasants to a new low.

How have Chinese peasants—who remain today the majority of the population—fared under Communist rule? The memoir of Wang Xin, a peasant who was born near Beijing in 1941, helps us to answer this question. It is worth noting that Wang Xin's account of his life appeared in the *Bejing Review*, an official publication of the Chinese government. Thus, he underplays the hardships experienced by many peasants during the period of the Great Leap Forward (1958-1960), when Mao Zedong's policies to collectivize land immediately and move China quickly toward industrialization resulted in massive famine and economic chaos. Nonetheless, Wang's recollections are valuable for the light they shed on how life changed for hundreds of millions of Chinese peasants during the Mao period (1949–1976), and then changed again as a result of policies introduced by Mao's successor, Deng Xiaoping (1904-1997), during the 1980s.

From Wang Xin with Yang Xiaobing, "A Peasant Maps His Road to Wealth," *Beijing Review,* 27 (12 November 1984), pp. 28–30. Reprinted by permission.

The photo of students in Tiananmen Square that follows Wang's memoir draws our attention to major changes in Chinese urban life that date from the early 1980s.

THE MEMOIR OF WANG XIN (1984)

There is a long story behind my family's prosperity. My family's history is closely linked with the history of the Chinese society. So let me start my story with the rise and fall of the country.

In 1941, I was born to a poor peasant family in Pinggu County. At the time, my family had 10 members from three generations, but we had no farmland at all. My grandpa and his brother had to work for the landlord. My father and his brother wove at home and traded their coarse cloth at the market for some food. While peddling their handmade cloth, they had to be alert and evasive to avoid being forced to bribe the police.

One winter day, my grandpa's brother had two fingers bit off while feeding cattle for the landlord. The landlord simply dismissed him when he saw he was no longer useful. This made our lives even worse. My grandma had no other way to earn money but to pick wild jujubes in the mountains, which were ground up and mixed with wild herbs to make something like a bun.

At the time, my grandparents and parents wanted to work hard and get rich. Their desire, however, was merely a dream.

Bright Dawn

In 1949 New China was founded and we peasants became masters of the country. Land reform was carried out, the feudalist land ownership abolished and farmland returned to the tillers. All the 300 peasant families in my village got shares of farmland, averaging 0.2 hectare per person [approximately one-half acre]. For us peasants, this really meant something to live on.

During the land reform, the landlords' surplus rooms were confiscated and the extra rooms distributed among the poor. My family moved from a three-room thatched house into a tile-roofed house with seven rooms. Though only a small child at the time, I clearly remember how happy the peasants were.

In 1951 the agricultural collectivization movement got underway in my village. We first got organized into mutual-aid production teams and then into elementary agricultural co-operatives, pooling our land and sharing the dividends. In 1956 we switched to the advanced agricultural co-operatives and put our farmland into public ownership. The principle of "to each according to his work" was followed. The removal of land boundary stakes made it possible to develop a unified farming plan on a larger scale and created favourable conditions for water conservatation projects and agricultural mechanization.

With the land under public ownership, all the villagers met to discuss how to use their farmland and how to distribute the income. This was completely different from preliberation days when we had no land at all.

During those years, since everyone worked hard and the government provided the co-operative with preferential loans and farm tools, production grew rapidly. The grain output, for instance, grew from 2,250 kg per hectare [2.5 acres] before 1949 to 4,225 kg in 1956. I remember my family got more than enough wheat that year. We lived quite well during those years.

In July of 1957, our village was hit by a hailstorm. With crops ruined, old people worried that they would have to go begging as they had in the past when natural disasters struck. But when the government heard about our problems, it exempted us from agricultural taxes for that whole year, shipped in grain seeds and potato seedlings and urged us to tide over the difficulty while developing production. By relying on the collective strength of the village and everybody's hard work, no one ran short of food.

In 1957 something important happened to me. I was enrolled in the county's middle school after I graduated from the primary school in my village. Before me, for generations all my family had been illiterate.

Twists and Turns

In 1958 we got organized into the people's commune, which brought about some desirable changes, but also resulted in some baffling developments.

A people's commune usually consisted of several villages (a village was usually an advanced co-operative). To see many people working on a vast expanse of land was really a spectacular view. Soon after the founding of the people's commune, a tractor station was set up to oversee ploughing and sowing.

The year of 1959, however, was chaotic. Some people said we had arrived at real communism. All the people in my village ate at the same canteen, free of charge. We produced hundreds of thousands of kilogrammes of sweet potatoes. But nobody wanted them. The result was that all the potatoes rotted in the field. Some people were prone to boasting and exaggeration. There was a 0.13 hectare plot of farmland by my middle school. About 2,500 kg of wheat seeds were sown and people said it would yield 100,000 kg. But, in reality, it produced only 250 kg (because far too many seeds were sown). Though the Central Committee of the Chinese Communist Party later criticized this mistake of being boastful and exaggerating, much of wealth had already been wasted. The negative impacts of such actions were felt for years.

The people's commune authorities also gave some arbitrary and impractical orders. Our village had a piece of land which should have been planted with soybeans. Some cadres of the people's commune, however, ordered us to grow carrots. Another piece of land which had already been planted with sweet potatoes was designated for soybeans. All these illogical orders resulted in sizable losses.

It now becomes clear that the inclination to boast and give arbitrary orders came from "Leftist" thinking.

Of course, the people's commune did some good. The most visible improvements were the water conservation projects. I myself took part in building several big projects.

In 1960 I came back home after graduation from junior middle school. My family of 10 members was then broken up into several small ones. I moved in with my uncle and his wife. Peasants from surrounding villages were then building the Haizi Reservoir, which would irrigate almost 10,000 hectares, one-third of the county's total farmland. The builders, in addition to getting subsidies from the state, were paid in cash by the people's commune and received food rations.

This made it attractive work and made it possible for the people's commune to mobilize enough people to build the big projects. The water conservation projects on which I worked are still benefiting the people.

I got married in 1962 and later had two sons and one daughter. More mouths need more money. I managed to increase the income for my family. The next year, I spent my spare time collecting firewood in the winter and growing melons on my family's private plot in the summer. The extra work brought in more than 400 yuan. Our life was pretty good.

In 1966, the chaotic "cultural revolution" began. I could no longer collect firewood or grow melons because these were seen as capitalist undertakings. We peasants, unlike workers who have regular wages, had to work in the fields or we would have had nothing to eat. So our agricultural production continued as usual.

In retrospect, my life improved steadily after I began working. But I always thought I could have done much better. I was held back. In 1969, I was elected deputy leader of the brigade in charge of sideline production. One day I bought some eggs from a state chicken farm in order to hatch chickens for the brigade. I sold some the surplus eggs and made 100 yuan for the brigade. I was shocked when I was criticized for selling the eggs. I was labelled a capitalist speculator.

Affluence Begins

It is only in recent years that I have been able to work hard and grow prosperous without restrictions.

In 1979 I learnt from newspapers and broadcasts that the Party had adopted flexible policies in the countryside. The contract responsibility system, which guaranteed more pay for more work, became popular in my village. The new policies allowed us peasants to become the real masters of agriculture and set us free to work hard and make more money. I wondered what I could do to get wealthy.

In 1981, I chose to raise chickens. I spent 380 yuan to buy 500 chicks. I was then a Communist Party member and the brigade's deputy leader. What I did raised some eyebrows in the village, but it didn't affect my job. The policy supported me. I got rich by working hard. Nothing wrong. I earned 850 yuan that year.

I then expanded the scope of my chicken business. The state credit co-operative offered me loans and encouraged me to forge ahead. I read books and studied to learn how to raise chickens scientifically. I also learnt how to treat chicken diseases such as diarrhoea and typhoid fever. In 1982, I sold the state 6,000 chickens for 9,000 yuan. With my income from the brigade and other household sidelines, I earned a total of more than 10,000 yuan, a figure larger than my combined income for the previous 10 years. The county recognized my achievements and rewarded me.

The Party policy is to bring into full play everyone's enthusiasm for production. It creates more wealth for the country and provides a good life for the peasants. Being among the first in my county to get rich, I'd like to lead others to prosperity.

Wang Shuchen has eight family members, but only two are able men. They have had a hard time. I explained the Party's policy to him and asked if he would like to raise chickens, too. I lent him 580 yuan, saying, "Please use this money to raise chickens. If the chickens die, I won't ask for the money back." Because he was less experienced in raising chickens, I went to his home several times every day to help him write observation notes, make plans for buying chicken feed, keep balance sheets and cure chicken diseases. Last year Wang earned more than 5,000 yuan from his chicken business alone.

So far, I have encouraged 80 families to raise chickens. Last year alone, I lent the families 5,800 yuan free of interest. In addition, I took time to help them treat chicken diseases and teach them how to raise chickens. I was always available whenever I was asked.

My family's life has improved very much in recent years. However, I spent only 400 yuan buying a radio cassette recorder for my daughter to study a foreign language for her college examinations. Other than that, I have spent not a single penny for other electric appliances for my family. I'd rather spend my money expanding production. I bought a walking tractor that cost more than 3,000 yuan.

Not long ago, I was elected secretary of the village Party branch. Since the Party job took much of my time, my chicken business suffered. But it is worth it, because we are helping more people become prosperous.

I am now wondering how to boost enthusiasm even more so that we can turn our village into a village which specializes in chicken raising. We also want to develop other sideline business and to raise other livestock in order to make our village more competitive in commodity production. Our village cadres have decided that whoever comes up with a practical plan to make more than 10,000 yuan next year will be the first to get material assistance from the village.

STUDY QUESTIONS

1. How did Wang Xin and his family benefit from policies introduced by the communists after 1949?
2. What evidence is there in Wang's memoir of problems in China during the period of communist rule?
3. How did Chinese agricultural policies of the 1980s differ from those of the Mao Zedong period?
4. What hints does Wang's memoir contain regarding the continuing importance of Confucian values in China?
5. Is Wang Xin a Communist or a capitalist?
6. How successful have China's Communists been in their attempts to solve the problems pointed to by the Confucian reformers at the end of the nineteenth century and later by Sun Yatsen? Is China still a "heap of loose sand"?
7. Why did Communism collapse in Russia but not in China?

VISUAL SOURCE

THE DEMOCRACY MOVEMENT OF 1989

In the spring of 1989 China's university students organized and led a powerful movement for democratic reform. Born too late to have suffered during the chaos of the Mao Ze-dong years, the students had grown up in the period of economic growth and expanding educational opportunities sponsored by Deng Xiaoping in the 1980s. Although their numbers were tiny when compared to the size of the overall population, many of the students were the sons and daughters of Communist Party officials. In addition, student activism in China had been important at various times in the past.

The movement was triggered by the death in April of a leading Party official, Hu Yaobang, who had been sympathetic to the cause of democratic reform. Students from leading universities immediately organized large demonstrations in honor of Hu. Confused

Pro-Democracy Students in Tiananmen Square, May 22, 1989.
(AP/World Wide Press)

327

by the demonstrations and frightened by possibility that the students might find allies among the workers, Party leaders dithered for several weeks. In May thousands of students occupied Tiananmen (Heavenly Peace) Square, the vast space that symbolized political authority in China and the site of famous student protests on May 4, 1919.

This photo was taken at the peak of the student demonstrations, just after the authorities proclaimed martial law and shortly before the bloody repression of June 3-4. Behind the students (but not visible in this photo) a portrait of Mao Zedong hangs from the massive Tiananmen Gate, the place where he stood as he proclaimed the establishment of the People's Republic of China on October 1, 1949.

STUDY QUESTIONS

1. What does the photo suggest about the complexity of the changes underway in modern China?
2. Would Wang Xin have been a likely supporter of the students in Tiananmen Square?

49

World War II: Memories of the Atomic Bomb

Present-day Hiroshima is a bustling and attractive city of approximately 1 million people located on Japan's southeast coast, about 500 miles from Tokyo. The city sits on a cluster of islands (Hiroshima means "broad island") and first became important at the end of the sixteenth century when Mori Terumoto, a member of the *daimyo* class, built his castle there. By 1945 Hiroshima was home to about 350,000 people.

In the center of the city, a short walk from Mori's castle, stands the stark remains of a domed structure that was, until 8:15 a.m. on August 6, 1945, the Hiroshima Industrial Promotion Hall. Across the Motoyasu River from the dome there is a lovely park filled with some of Japan's most beautiful flowers and shrubs. Established at the point where two of the many streams that flow through the city converge, the park has the shape of a triangle and is somewhat smaller than a football field. Within its boundaries are several memorials to the victims of the atom bomb and a museum, the Peace Memorial Museum, dedicated to preserving the memory of August 6, 1945.

The bomb that was dropped on Hiroshima was about nine feet long and weighed about four tons. It was detonated about 600 feet above the center of the city, which had no air defense system, and struck with the force of about 13,000 tons of dynamite. Huge fires spread immediately. Powerful winds fanned the flames and flattened structures up to 2 miles from ground zero (but not, improbably, the Industrial Promotion Hall). Massive amounts of radiation given off by the blast killed many thousands of people. Although there will always be uncertainty over the number of people killed by the bomb at Hiroshima, it is likely that by the end of the year more than 140,000 Hiroshima residents were dead. Later, many more died from burns, from radiation poisoning, and from various other bomb-related causes.

In the selections that follow Yamaoka Michiko and Kimura Yasuko, both of whom were school children in Hiroshima in 1945, recall their experiences during and after the blast. Their memories were recorded by two American researchers around

From Haruko Taya Cook and Theodore F. Cook, eds., *Japan at War: An Oral History* (New York: New Press, 1992), pp. 384–387, 395–399.

1990. How do these recollections help us to understand the larger meaning of World War II?

MEMORIES OF THE BLAST

I. YAMAOKA MICHIKO

That year, on August 6, I was in the third year of girls' high school, fifteen years old. I was an operator at the telephone exchange. We had been mobilized from school for various work assignments for more than a year. My assigned place of duty was civilian, but we, too, were expected to protect the nation. We were tied by strong bonds to the country. We'd heard the news about the Tokyo and Osaka bombings, but nothing had dropped on Hiroshima. Japan was winning. So we still believed. We only had to endure. I wasn't particularly afraid when B-29s flew overhead.

That morning I left the house at about seven forty-five. I heard that the B-29s had already gone home. Mom told me, "Watch out, the B-29s might come again." My house was one point three kilometers from the hypocenter. My place of work was five hundred meters from the hypocenter. I walked toward the hypocenter in an area where all the houses and buildings had been deliberately demolished for fire breaks. There was no shade. I had on a white shirt and *monpe* [trousers]. As I walked there, I noticed middle-school students pulling down houses at a point about eight hundred meters away from the hypocenter. I heard the faint sound of planes as I approached the river. The planes were tricky. Sometimes they only pretended to leave. I could still hear the very faint sound of planes. Today, I have no hearing in my left ear because of damage from the blast. I thought, how strange, so I put my right hand above my eyes and looked up to see if I could spot them. The sun was dazzling. That was the moment.

There was no sound. I felt something strong. It was terribly intense. I felt colors. It wasn't heat. You can't really say it was yellow, and it wasn't blue. At that moment I thought I would be the only one who would die. I said to myself, "Goodbye, Mom."

They say temperatures of seven thousand degrees centigrade hit me. You can't really say it washed over me. It's hard to describe. I simply fainted. I remember my body floating in the air. That was probably the blast, but I don't know how far I was blown. When I came to my senses, my surroundings were silent. There was no wind. I saw a slight threadlike light, so I felt I must be alive. I was under stones. I couldn't move my body. I heard voices crying, "Help! Water!" It was then I realized I wasn't the only one. I couldn't really see around me. I tried to say something, but my voice wouldn't come out.

"Fire! Run away! Help! Hurry Up!" They weren't voices but moans of agony and despair. "I have to get help and shout," I thought. The person who rescued me was Mom, although she herself had been buried under our collapsed house. Mom knew the route I'd been taking. She came, calling out to me. I heard her voice and cried for help. Our surroundings were already starting to burn. Fires burst out from just the light itself. It didn't really drop. It just flashed.

It was beyond my mother's ability. She pleaded, "My daughter's buried here, she's been helping you, working for the military." She convinced soldiers nearby to help her and they started to dig me out. The fire was now blazing. "Woman, hurry up, run away from here," soldiers called. From underneath the stones I heard the crackling of flames. I called to her, "It's all right. Don't worry about me. Run away." I really didn't mind dying for the sake of the nation. Then they pulled me out by my legs.

Nobody there looked like human beings. Until that moment I thought incendiary bombs had fallen. Everyone was stupefied. Humans had lost the ability to speak. People couldn't scream, "It hurts!" even when they were on fire. People didn't say, "It's hot!" They just sat catching fire.

My clothes were burnt and so was my skin. I was in rags. I had braided my hair, but now it was like a lion's mane. There were people, barely breathing, trying to push their intestines back in. People with their legs wrenched off. Without heads. Or with faces burned and swollen out of shape. The scene I saw was a living hell.

Mom didn't say anything when she saw my face and I didn't feel any pain. She just squeezed my hand and told me to run. She was going to go rescue my aunt. Large numbers of people were moving away from the flames. My eyes were still able to see, so I made my way towards the mountain, where there was no fire, toward Hijiyama. On this flight I saw a friend of mine from the phone exchange. She'd been inside her house and wasn't burned. I called her name, but she didn't respond. My face was so swollen she couldn't tell who I was. Finally, she recognized my voice. She said, "Miss Yamaoka, you look like a monster!" That's the first time I heard that word. I looked at my hands and saw my own skin hanging down and the red flesh exposed. I didn't realize my face was swollen up because I was unable to see it.

The only medicine was *tempura* oil. I put it on my body myself. I lay on the concrete for hours. My skin was now flat, not puffed up anymore. One or two layers had peeled off. Only now did it become painful. A scorching sky was overhead. The flies swarmed over me and covered my wounds, which were already festering. People were simply left lying around. When their faint breathing became silent, they'd say, "This one's dead," and put the body in a pile of corpses. Some called for water, and if they got it, they died immediately.

Mom came looking for me again. That's why I'm alive today. I couldn't walk anymore. I couldn't see anymore. I was carried on a stretcher as far as Ujina, and then from there to an island where evacuees were taken. On the boat there I heard voices saying, "Let them drink water if they want. They'll die either way." I drank a lot of water.

I spent the next year bedridden. All my hair fell out. When we went to relatives' houses later they wouldn't even let me in because they feared they'd catch the disease. There was neither treatment nor assistance for me. Those people who had money, people who had both parents, people who had houses, they could go to the Red Cross Hospital or the Hiroshima City Hospital. They could get operations. But we didn't have any money. It was just my Mom and I. Keloids covered my face, my neck. I couldn't even move my neck. One eye was hanging down. I was unable to control my drooling because my lip had been burned off. I couldn't get any treatments at a hospital, so my mother gave me massages. Because she did that for me, my keloids aren't as bad as they would have been. My fingers were all stuck together. I couldn't move them. The only thing I could do was sew shorts, since I only needed to sew a straight line. I had to do something to earn money.

The Japanese government just told us we weren't the only victims of the war. There was no support or treatment. It was probably harder for my Mom. Once she told me she tried to choke me to death. If a girl has terrible scars, a face you couldn't be born with, I understand that even a mother could want to kill her child. People threw stones at me and called me Monster. That was before I had my many operations. I only showed this side of my face, the right hand side, when I had to face someone. Like I'm sitting now.

A decade after the bomb, we went to America. I was one of the twenty-five selected by Norman Cousins to be brought to America for treatment and plastic surgery. We were called the Hiroshima Maidens. The American government opposed us, arguing that it would be acknowledging a mistake if they admitted us to America, but we were supported by many civilian groups. We went to Mount Sinai Hospital in New York and spent about a year and a half undergoing treatment. I improved tremendously. I've now had thirty-seven operations, including efforts at skin grafts.

When I went to America I had a deep hatred toward America. I asked myself why they ended the war by a means which destroyed human beings. When I talked about how I suffered, I was often told, "Well, you attacked Pearl Harbor!" I didn't understand much English then, and it's probably just as well. From the American point of view, they dropped that bomb in order to end the war faster, in order to create more damage faster. But it's inexcusable to harm human beings in this way. I wonder what kind of education there is now in America about atomic bombs. They're still making them, aren't they?

II. KIMURA YASUKO

Hiroshima was a military capital, full of army and navy facilities. Children in that town were all like minisoldiers. Everything was done to orders. We never doubted Japan would win. We were truly little patriots! When my mother wrote to me at where I'd been evacuated with my school, that I would be able to return home when the war was over, I was unable to forgive her. I was nine years old then. The teachers at the temple to which we were evacuated were very strict. We weren't allowed to take even one step outside the temple grounds except to go to school. Yet, the house mothers were very kind and gentle. That was our salvation. They were local village people, nineteen or twenty years old.

The temple was located on a high hill between Shimane and Hiroshima prefectures. From there we could look out and see the people coming along the road. Following that day in August, we saw many injured fleeing Hiroshima on the road. Somebody said, "Hiroshima's been attacked with a new type of bomb." Our teacher went there and brought back the news that all of Hiroshima had been destroyed.

The three hundred children of Noborichō National School at the evacuation point were all from families who'd lived within eight hundred meters of where the bomb was dropped, the hypocenter. We were part of a group evacuation, kids who had no other place to go. Only the children could be evacuated, so our families had all stayed in Hiroshima. Now we waited at the temple for some word from them. Somehow, some families managed to send messages like "Elder sister lived," or "Father is alive."

On August 15, the war ended. Group evacuation was officially suspended all over Japan, but the children of Hiroshima had no place to go. It was finally decided that they would send back any children who had received word from surviving family members. I remained where I was.

Children boast among themselves about anything. They say, "My grade's better than yours!" At the temple, we boasted about the numbers who had been killed. Those who had lost the most family members were the biggest braggarts. We were called forward by the teachers and told who in our family had died. We'd then go back and say, "I had three." A person who'd lost more could say, "I lost five," and they were superior. I thought, "three, just three." I was somehow envious. I even thought, "Five's better." We didn't know what dying meant. But when our evacuation ended, those who'd been belittled—"Only one of yours died"—well, they had someone to come and take them back early. That's when we learned what it meant to have five family members die. It meant nobody would come for you.

When they could assemble a group of thirty or forty children who had received word, they sent them back by truck and handed them over to relatives who met them in the burned-out ruins of Hiroshima. I got word that my father had survived. Finally it was my turn to go home.

We arrived in the early evening. The reddish setting sun hung in the sky. The ruins from an ordinary fire are burned black, aren't they? But the ruins of Hiroshima were brown, the color of unfired pottery. The glaze of the roof tiles was completely gone and they were spotted and mottled, all reddish brown. The city didn't look as if it had been burned. Yet it was flattened. In the middle of the ruins two buildings, a department store and the newspaper, stood alone. There, my father met me. He couldn't stand waiting at the assigned meeting place any longer, so he walked part of the way to meet my truck. I remember his figure standing there. Behind him was the stone wall of Hiroshima Castle. I remember the tears in his eyes when I met him.

I knew that Mother had died. When I was taken to a relative's house, there was a round flower vase with a piece of writing paper tied with packing twine. "This is Mother," Grandmother told me. It was eerie. Even with all the roof tiles knocked off and broken into bits, there was this completely unbroken vase. Its glaze had been burnt off. Its surface was rough. That, they told me, was her. I was frightened. I couldn't believe it. I drew back instinctively.

Mother must have died instantly, we think. I was told she was standing in the hall along the back of the house. Her ashes were found there. I was told that only bones were left. In an ordinary fire the body is burned black. You can tell that from the pictures of the Tokyo air raids. But here, only bones were left. White bones, lots of them.

That day, my elder sister, in her first year of girls' school, had been mobilized to clear the remains of demolished houses to make firebreaks. Almost all the schoolgirls and boys of the same age as my sister were killed. Perhaps ten thousand. My father searched and searched on the sixth, the day the bomb fell. And all day the next day, too. On the eighth he found her name at a hospital. He was told she'd died the previous day and had already been cremated. They piled all the bodies up, soaked them in gasoline, and then burned them. There really weren't any bones left. According to a nurse, she reached the hospital completely burned and called out, "Mother! Mother!" until the moment she died.

We don't know anything about my younger brother. He was six years old. Later, one of our neighbors told us that he was playing with his children, that he heard their voices until that moment. Even when people were burned to death you could usually find the bones and at least say, this is my house, so this must be them, but we found nothing. They must have been blown away somewhere.

That morning, Father and Grandmother were on the outskirts of the city, moving our luggage from temporary storage. Father entered the city immediately to search for the family, so he was exposed to radiation. My elder brother, who was in the second year of middle school and had been mobilized for factory work, also came into Hiroshima that day.

After I returned, I refused to let myself be separated from my grandmother. Wherever she went, I followed her. I didn't want to be alone. Whenever Granny bumped into someone she knew, before saying hello, they'd ask each other, "What were you doing when the flash came?" That was the greeting in Hiroshima. "How did you survive? How did your family members die?" That's what she asked everyone she met, and that's what they talked about again and again.

Wherever you went, you could see tiny bones. That was horrible. I couldn't stand those bones. The whole area had been burned down. No matter where you went you didn't bother to take the roads. Everything was flat, nothing was standing, no gates, pillars, walls, or fences. You just walked in a straight line to where you wanted to go. Practically everywhere you came across small bones that had been left behind. There just were too many to collect them all.

We moved to Tokyo when I was in the second year of high school. For the first time I wondered what Hiroshima had been all about. I had thought the whole of Japan was like that, but it was only Hiroshima. From then on, I wanted to forget. I was now far away from Hiroshima and in a sense I had nothing to do with it. I never really signed any petitions calling for the prohibition of atomic or hydrogen bombs. I thought it had nothing to do with me. A friend once asked, "Don't you think your mother was murdered?" "No, not particularly. It's the same as dying any other way, isn't it?" That was the way I answered. If you try hard to forget you can forget. If you have thirty years it's possible. I abhorred the word *Hiroshima*. If it came up, I wouldn't mention that I had family members who'd died there. On August 6 I refused to watch television and never read the newspapers.

I did feel some desire to see the place where as a schoolgirl I had been evacuated before the bomb. My life had been saved there. But I didn't make the trip until many years had passed. I couldn't remember anything about that time until I stepped from the car that took me there. It was the season when the rice was in flower, early August, and that fragrance brought everything back to me. In the midst of the rice fields, I had been told that my mother had died. I couldn't help crying. I didn't know why I was crying, but then the memories came pouring out. I began reading books and asking questions of my one surviving brother.

A number of years ago, a group of about a hundred of us went back again to our evacuation site in two buses. But we never asked each other what happened to our families. Nobody volunteered information about themselves and nobody asked. Not asking was the most considerate thing to do. There was no real need to ask. Everyone had someone killed.

That's one of the things about Hiroshima. You can talk about your own experience, but you can't speak for others. When you're able to sort out in your own mind what happened, only then are you at last able to speak of your own experiences. I only lost three. As many as three survived. I was one of the truly lucky ones. My father survived and was able to return and function in society. He brought me up properly before he died of cancer. Only three were killed, but it took me thirty years to reconcile myself to that.

My sister's classmates seem to feel differently from me. They were all mobilized from school and all were supposed to be there. I recently spoke with some of the girls who survived. They apologized to me for surviving. By chance, only those who played hooky and skipped labor service that day lived. I told them to please go on living. To live life for my sister, too.

My brother is alive, but he was exposed to secondary radiation. It causes terrible pain. He lives in agony. He's a member of a *hibakusha* [one who was exposed to the atomic bomb] group. Members younger than he die one by one, and he thinks he'll be next. He takes sleeping pills. Even during the day he gets drunk from them. He's become that kind of drop-out. Even those who survive have their minds torn apart.

I'm sorry I fled from it for thirty years. I was the only one in the family who wasn't exposed to the atomic bomb. Had I actually been exposed, I would have thought about how my family suffered, or how they died. Instead, I simply ran away.

STUDY QUESTIONS

1. What memories of August 6 are most important to Yamaoka and Kimura?
2. How does their testimony reveal important aspects of life in wartime Japan?
3. What do their statements suggest about the importance of Buddhism and Confucianism in Japanese culture?
4. Was there a relationship between the Meiji Restoration and Pearl Harbor? (See Chapter 25.)
5. Did the Japanese attack on Pearl Harbor justify the dropping of the atomic bomb on Hiroshima?
6. Should nuclear weapons be outlawed? What can be done to prevent the use of nuclear weapons in the future?
7. What are the strengths and possible weaknesses of oral history?

VISUAL SOURCE

THE ARCHITECTURE OF COMMEMORATION

Six weeks after the atomic blast a severe typhoon struck Hiroshima, inflicting additional damage on the already devastated city. Soon afterward, however, green weeds began to sprout in some of the neighborhoods, makeshift markets opened, and many schools resumed classes (often in the open air). The city's residents, now known as *hibakusha* (survivors of the atomic bomb), began to put their lives back together.

Beginning in 1946 the people of Hiroshima turned to the issue of how to commemorate August 6. Local officials convened meetings to solicit suggestions. Much discussion ensued. In August a Peace Restoration Festival market the first anniversary of the blast. At 8:15 a.m. on August 6 sirens sounded throughout the city and people stood in silence for 1 minute. Since that time, a Peace Memorial Ceremony on August 6 has become an annual event in the city. In 1949 the Japanese Diet, responding to a petition from the city's citizens, enacted the "Hiroshima Peace Memorial City Reconstruction Law," for the purpose of reconstructing Hiroshima as a "Peace Memorial City, a symbol of the ideal of making peace a lasting reality."

Remains of the Industrial Promotion Hall, Hiroshima, 1985. (Photos by Stephen S. Gosch)

STUDY QUESTIONS

1. How would the reactions of Japanese and American visitors to this site likely differ? What might their responses have in common?
2. How would Chinese and Korean visitors to the site be likely to react to it?
3. What is the difference between a peace memorial and a war memorial?

50

Changing Gender Relations in Modern Japan

Japan's emergence as a modern industrial society was one of the most important developments in world history during the second half of the twentieth century. At the end of World War II the country lay in ruins. However, postwar economic growth—the Japanese "miracle"—quickly overcame both the cost of the war and the destruction from U.S. air raids in 1944 and 1945. By 1965 the Japanese economy was nearly four times as productive as it had been in the 1930s. In the late 1990s the Japanese gross national product was one of the largest in the world and Japanese living standards were also among the highest worldwide.

The dynamic growth of Japanese industry and agriculture was accompanied by the rapid urbanization of the country. These long-term processes had major implications for gender relations. The extended family of the countryside was replaced by the urban nuclear family. Life expectancy for both men and women increased significantly (making for much longer marriages), while the number of children born to the average woman fell sharply. New educational and occupational opportunities opened up for both men and women.

There were also major political and legal reforms during the postwar period that affected gender relations. During the period of the U.S. occupation (1945 to 1952) a new constitution and a series of additional legal reforms extended full political rights to women and established the principle of equality before the law for men and women.

Despite the foregoing changes, in Japan, as elsewhere, many men (and women) held fast to the view that women should be subordinate to men. Japanese women who sought careers in business, government, and academia faced obstacles more formidable than those faced by their Western counterparts.

This selection is from an article written in the 1980s by the feminist and social critic Higuchi Keiko; it illustrates many of the changes in Japanese gender relations that have been under way since World War II.

From Higuchi Keiko, "Japanese Women in Transition," *Japan Quarterly,* 29 (July–September 1982), pp. 311, 313–318.

HIGUCHI KEIKO (1982)

"The Age of Women"—so ran the catch-phrase adorning a Japanese newspaper advertisement on New Year's Day 1979, the eve of the 80s. The ad went on in part to say: "Dazzling—simply dazzling, the women of today. Mothers and daughters taking off suddenly on trips abroad, or giving up their diets and going in for yoga instead. Expressing themselves freely, without fear or hesitation, these are women who know the art of enjoying life to the full. . . . Today's women are off the sidelines to stay."

The slogan notwithstanding, this message is probably best understood as a gift of flattery from male salesmen to female buyers. Beginning with this advertisement, the decade of the 80s has come with increasing frequency to be called "the age of women." And yet one has the distinct sense that before yielding any substantial results, the term was quickly taken over by the advertising industry as a piece of "fashion." In any case, the emergence of language such as this in newspaper advertising is surely a sign of change in the situation of Japanese women. . . .

The consciousness of Japanese women is now in a state of transition. Their attitude toward the idea that "men should work outside the home, women inside" has changed greatly in the last 10 years. In a 1972 survey of attitudes on women's issues undertaken by the Prime Minister's Office, over 80 percent of women respondents agreed with the idea as stated above. But in a similar survey conducted in 1976, the year after International Women's Year, those concurring that "men work, and women stay home" were 49 percent, while 40 percent disagreed and 11 percent were undecided. The wording of the question as well as the range of possible answers vary, making simple comparisons difficult, but it would seem clear at any rate that doubts regarding the traditional idea of sex-differentiated work roles are rapidly growing. In 1979 the Prime Minister's Office conducted another survey posing the same questions as in 1976, but this time, in response to the assertion that "men work and women stay home," pollees were evenly divided among "agree," "disagree" and "don't know," with each answer drawing a response in the 30th percentile. When the question pertains to "men" and "women," people are somewhat likely to go against the traditional view, but when the words "husbands" and "wives" are substituted, resistance declines. Acceptance of sex-differentiated work roles is still deep-rooted in Japan.

Among the younger generation, however, there is possibility for more rapid change. In the 1979 survey by the Prime Minister's Office, the assertion by 25 percent of unmarried women that they had "no wish to marry" attracted wide notice. Japanese have a high marriage rate, so much so that they have been called a people "fond of marrying": by age 50, 97 percent of both men and women have been married at least once. The Prime Minister's Office asked the same question in 1972, but at that time only 14 percent of women declared themselves uninterested in marrying. In the 1979 survey, a mere 12 percent of men selected the same response, thus revealing a gap in attitudes toward marriage between the sexes. Moreover, women responding that "a woman's happiness lies in marriage" went down from 40 percent to 32 percent.

Yearly surveys by Nippon Recruit Center, an employment agency, on "attitudes of female university students toward employment" shows that until the late 70s, even among graduates of four-year colleges, those desiring to work "until retirement age" amounted to scarcely 20 percent. In the 1981 survey, however, 41 percent of respondents (19 percent for junior college graduates) gave that answer.

The most frequently given answer was to work "until a child is born, then again after the child is older" (58.7 percent). Significantly, those who said simply "until marrying" or "until a child is born" —thus relegating work to a brief period early in their lifetimes—were in the minority for the first time at 25.3 percent or one quarter of the sample. For Japan, where women are held to be at a particular disadvantage in combining marriage and a career, and where long-term female employment is much rarer than in Europe and America, such a shift in attitudes is truly remarkable. . . .

In the Tokyo residential area where I live, around 10 every morning housewives clad in short, above-the-knee outfits get on their bikes, tennis rackets in baskets, and pedal off in a row for the local tennis court. A conspicuous change in the last 10 years has been the phenomenal growth in large cities nationwide of housewives' hobby and culture centers, sponsored by newspapers, broadcasting companies, department stores and even big businesses. Women in their 30s and 40s, freed from the burden of caring for small children, flock to tennis courts and culture centers out of a desire to be with others like themselves—a hunger, perhaps, for companionship—as they seek the pattern for the latter half of their lives. In the past, Japanese women were referred to by their husbands as *kanai,* meaning literally "inside the house"—and that is exactly where they stayed. Today, as women step out more and more in search of entertainment, education and a wide variety of activities, one sometimes hears a man say of his wife, "She's no *kanai;* she's my *kagai* ('outside the house')."

But housewives commuting to tennis courts and cultural enrichment centers are, after all, outnumbered by those commuting to work. The number of female employees is steadily increasing, and at present nearly 70 percent are married. In addition, more than half of all unemployed housewives aged 40 and above "would like to work." By far their biggest motivation is to bring the family budget out of the red. Although real earnings of household heads have declined in the last few years, the standard of living has held its own, thanks largely to increases in wives' earnings.

Not long ago, when I was in a department store, two clerks called out to me one after the other. They told me they had heard me speak at a lecture meeting sponsored by a grade-school PTA. Both of them are active as PTA members while holding down part-time jobs in a department store. The day of the lecture meeting, they said, they had taken off work to attend. I could not help feeling struck by this clear example of change. It wasn't many years ago that at PTA meetings one frequently heard the complaint that "so many women have jobs nowadays, there's nobody to work for the PTA." Some ladies even went so far as to take part-time jobs only when officers' elections came around, then plead work as an excuse to decline. Now many women manage successfully to juggle work outside the home with active participation in community affairs. Working housewives have become so commonplace that it can no longer be said that "PTA is for mothers who don't work."

Toward the end of April 1982, the Ministry of Labor published results of a "Basic survey on Wage Structure in 1981." According to these results, although until recently male workers attained their top earning power in their 50s, now male wages have begun to peak earlier, in the 45–50 age bracket. "My husband's earnings will peak when he's in his 40s—so I'd better go to work to help out the budget." This sort of determination appears to be spreading rapidly among Japanese women.

Women in Japan are stepping out of the house in ever-swelling numbers. Yet men persist in clinging to the notion that "women's work is in the home." Those most critical of sex-differentiated labor roles are not men, but women. It appears inevitable, therefore, that discord will arise between the sexes.

Conflict between husband and wife is apt to arise from the work overload of working wives. The belief that household affairs are the wife's exclusive responsibility is deeply ingrained in Japanese society, and many women would in fact regard their husband's entrance into the kitchen as an unwelcome intrusion. According to a 1976 research survey by the Prime Minister's Office on "Lifestyles in Society," unemployed housewives spend an average of five hours and 54 minutes each day on housework and childcare, compared to three hours and 29 minutes for those with outside jobs. Husbands of unemployed wives, for their part, contribute an average of seven minutes daily to the same tasks, while for husbands of working women the figure is an astounding six minutes. Thus, utterly betraying the expectation that "it is only natural for the husband to help around the house if the wife works too," Japanese married men reign as *shujin* ("husband"; literally, "master") in their homes, and whether or not the wife has an outside job they do virtually no housework.

The husband expects his wife to look after the home, and in the home he seeks a place of recreation and relaxation in which to garner strength for the coming day's work. This is the view of the wife's role, and of the function of the home, given often in Japanese textbooks for the lower, compulsory levels of school. The husband, behaving exactly as the textbooks predict he will, hands over his pay envelope to his wife without even looking inside. Most big corporations nowadays transfer paychecks directly to employees' bank accounts, but the wife remains firmly in charge of home finances. The husband sees the act of turning over his entire salary to his wife simultaneously as an expression of love and a fulfillment of obligation. The wife, however, has begun to entertain misgivings about an existence spent for the most part waiting passively at home for her husband's return.

The profound changes in the lifestyles of Japanese women surely have few precedents anywhere in the world. It is well known that Japanese women expend more love and energy on their children than on their husbands. But the children who are objects of so much maternal devotion have decreased drastically in number per family while average life expectancies have continued to rise. In 1940, a woman whose youngest child had just entered school had only 7.6 years of life remaining; in 1978, the number of years she could count on had jumped to 44. After the youngest child marries, moreover, she and her husband can still look forward to nearly a score of years of married life. . . .

The new women's liberation movement which spread to Japan in the early 70s brought pressure for change in the lives of both men and women. And the U.N.'s Decade for Women forced the Japanese government to face up to many of the issues involved. At the same time, the extremely rapid aging of Japanese society—a phenomenon without precedent or equal in the world—is forcing upon us, willy-nilly, a reevaluation of relationships between the sexes, married and unmarried alike.

Aged people (those 65 years old and above) now comprise a mere 9 percent of the population of Japan, but in the coming 30 to 40 years it is anticipated that their numbers will swell to more than 23 percent. No advanced nation has yet experienced a society in which one out of every four people is elderly.

The life span of Japanese women is approaching 80 years. The question of how middle-aged Japanese women are to spend the latter half of this extended lifetime is one that must be asked. With marriage as the single-minded goal of their youth, followed by harried years of caring for husband and children, they have had little time for self-reflection; now, realizing after their children are grown or their husband retires that without a personal goal they will be unable to face the loneliness of widowhood, these women are full of consternation. Among Japanese aged 65 and over, those whose spouse is living account for 80 percent of the men, but only one in three of the women. Soon there will be one million old people living alone in Japan, 80 percent of them female. Their income, moreover, is less than half that of men. And of those looking after elderly invalids in their own homes, as many as 90 percent are women. Lately the idea that "the problems of old age are women's problems" is voiced more and more often at women's gatherings. . . .

The traditional life-patterns for Japanese men and women—until very recently thought natural and common-sensical—are now, under the pressures of a highly developed, rapidly aging industrial society, in a period of transition, as people seek to put them in a new frame of reference.

STUDY QUESTIONS

1. In what ways did attitudes toward gender relations and work begin to change in Japan during the 1970s? How did differences in attitudes vary by age and sex?
2. How are leisure-time activities and employment patterns changing for Japanese women?
3. What do you learn from the article about family life in Japan? What hints about the continuing influence of Confucian values on the Japanese family does the article contain? What changes seem to be underway?
4. How do demographic changes in Japan since the 1940s help to explain the recent changes in gender relationships?
5. Compare the ideas of Higuchi Keiko with those of Madhu Kishwar. (See Chapter 52.) What similarities and differences do you see?
6. Does the process of industrialization inevitably move societies in the direction of gender equality?

South Asia

51

Gandhi and Modern India

No individual has been more important to the history of modern India than Mohandas K. Gandhi (1869–1948). Descended from a prosperous Hindu family of merchants and public officials in western India, Gandhi studied law in London during the late 1880s. He then spent 20 years in South Africa, where he led the Indian minority community in a struggle against discrimination by the British and the Boers. Returning to India in 1915. Gandhi plunged into the nationalist movement. From the end of World War I to his assassination three decades later, Gandhi was the most popular and most effective leader of the Indian struggle for freedom from British colonial rule.

Gandhi's legacy is both rich and ambiguous. For many Indian patriots Gandhi's greatest achievement was his leadership in transforming the leading nationalist organization, the Indian National Congress, into a genuine mass movement. There is general agreement among scholars that it was the Mahatma (Great Soul) who won the peasants of India to the national cause after World War I and that this development was decisive in compelling the British to withdraw from India following World War II. In addition, many of his contemporaries in India and around the world admired Gandhi's commitment to *satyagraya* (nonviolent resistance), as well as his vigorous efforts on behalf of India's untouchables, and his desire for harmony between Hindus and Muslims (called "communal unity" in India). On the other hand, some Hindus—including Gandhi's assassin—and most Muslims saw him as too favorable to their religious adversaries. Other critics of Gandhi think that his opposition to both modern technology and the kind of mass insurrection the Communists led in China contributed to the survival of poverty and inequality in independent India.

The following selection comes from a speech given by Gandhi in 1936.

From The Moral and Political Writings of Mahatma Gandhi, Volume III, pp. 370–374, edited by Raghaven Iyer (1987). Reprinted by permission of Oxford Univerisity Press.

SPEECH BY MAHATMA GANDHI (1936)

. . . I am going to say nothing new today. The cult of the spinning-wheel is 18 years old. I said in 1918 that we could win *swaraj* through the spinning-wheel. My faith in the ability of the spinning-wheel is as bright today as when I first declared it in 1918. It has become richer for the experience and experiment of all these years.

But you should know the implications of the wheel or *khadi* [hand-spun cloth], its product. It is not enough that one wears *khadi* on ceremonial occasions or even wears it to the exclusion of all other cloth if he surrounds himself with *videshi* [foreign goods] in everything else. *Khadi* means the truest *swadeshi* [self-reliant] spirit, identification with the starving millions.

Let there be no mistake about my conception of *swaraj*. It is complete independence of alien control and complete economic independence. So at one end you have political independence, at the other the economic. It has two other ends. One of them is moral and social, the corresponding end is *dharma*, i.e., religion in the highest sense of the term. It includes Hinduism, Islam, Christianity, etc., but is superior to them all. You may recognize it by the name of Truth, not the honesty of expedience but the living Truth that pervades everything and will survive all destruction and all transformation. Moral and social uplift may be recognized by the term we are used to, i.e., non-violence. Let us call this the square of *swaraj*, which will be out of shape if any of its angles is untrue. In the language of the Congress we cannot achieve this political and economic freedom without truth and non-violence, in concrete terms without a living faith in God and hence moral and social elevation.

By political independence I do not mean an imitation of the British House of Commons, or the Soviet rule of Russia or the Fascist rule of Italy or the Nazi rule of Germany. They have systems suited to their genius. We must have ours suited to ours. What that can be is more than I can tell. I have described it as *Ramarajya*, i.e., sovereignty of the people based on pure moral authority. The Congress constitutions of Nagpur and Bombay for which I am mainly responsible are an attempt to achieve this type of *swaraj*.

Then take economic independence. It is not a product of industrialization of the modern or the Western type. Indian economic independence means to me the economic uplift of every individual, male and female, by his or her own conscious effort. Under that system all men and women will have enough clothing—not the mere loin-cloth, but what we understand by the term necessary articles of clothing and enough food including milk and butter which are today denied to millions.

This brings me to socialism. Real socialism has been handed down to us by our ancestors who taught: 'All land belongs to Gopal, where then is the boundary line? Man is the maker of the line and he can therefore unmake it.' Gopal literally means shepherd; it also means God. In modern language it means the State, i.e., the people. That the land today does not belong to the people is too true. But the fault is not in the teaching. It is in us who have not lived up to it.

I have no doubt that we can make as good an approach to it as is possible for any nation, not including Russia, and that without violence. The most effective substitute for violent dispossession is the wheel with all its implications. Land and all property is his who will work it. Unfortunately the workers are or have been kept ignorant of this simple fact.

Let us now see how India came to be utterly impoverished. History tells us that the East India Company ruined the cotton manufacture and by all kinds of means made her dependent upon Lancashire for her cloth, the next great necessity of man. It is still the largest item of import. It thus created a huge army of partially unemployed men and women counted in millions and gave them no other employment in return. With the destruction of hand-ginning, carding, spinning and weaving to a certain extent, perished the other industries of India's villages. Continuous unemployment has induced in the people a kind of laziness which is most depressing. Thus whilst the alien rule is undoubtedly responsible for the growing pauperism of the people, we are more responsible for it. If the middle-class people, who betrayed their trust and bartered away the economic independence of India for a mess of pottage, would now realize their error and take the message of the wheel to the villagers and induce them to shed their laziness and work at the wheel, we can ameliorate the condition of the people to a great extent. It would be a terrible thing if laziness replaces industry and despair triumphs over hope.

The parliamentary programme is in the air. It has come to stay and rightly. But it cannot bring us independence. Its function is strictly limited though quite necessary. Its success will prevent the Government from claiming that Ordinance rule or any measure restricting our progress to the goal was sanctioned by popular representatives. Hence the necessity for voters voting for the Congress candidates who dare not vote for unpopular measures without being liable to Congress discipline. The success of that programme may also bring some relief in individual cases such as the release of Shri Subhas Bose or the detenus. But that is not independence, political or economic.

Then look at it in another way. Only a limited number of men and women can become members of legislatures, say 1,500. How many from this audience can become legislators? And just now no more than $3\frac{1}{2}$ crores [upper income groups, about 35 million people] can vote for these 1,500 members. What about the remaining $3\frac{1}{2}$] crores? In our conception of *swaraj* they are the real masters and the $3\frac{1}{2}$ crores are the former's servants who in their turn are masters of the 1,500. Thus the latter are doubly servants, if they will be true to their trust.

But the $3\frac{1}{2}$ crores have also a trust to discharge towards themselves and the nation of which they as individuals are but tiny parts. And if they remain lazy, know nothing of *swaraj* and how to win it, they will themselves become slaves of the 1,500 legislators. For my argument the $3\frac{1}{2}$ crores of voters here belong to the same category as the $3\frac{1}{2}$ crores. For if they do not become industrious and wise, they will be so many pawns in the hands of 1,500 players, it is of little consequence whether they are Congressmen or otherwise. If the voters wake up only to register their votes every three years or more and then go off to sleep, their servants will become their masters.

The only way I know to prevent such a catastrophe is for the 35 crores to be industrious and wise. This they can only be if they will take up the spinning-wheel and the other village industries. They will not take to them unintelligently. I can tell you from experience that the effort means adult education of the correct type and requires possession of patience, moral fibre and a scientific and practical knowledge of the industry the worker seeks to introduce in the village of his choice.

In such a scheme the spinning-wheel becomes its centre. If you call it the solar system, the wheel becomes the golden disc and the industries the planets revolving round it in obedience to the inviolable law of the system. When the sun lost its illuminating power by the action of the East India Company, the planets lost their power and became invisible or almost so. The sun is being reinstated in his past status now and the planets are regaining their motion in exact proportion to the strength of the sun.

Now perhaps you will understand the meaning and the message of the *charkha* [spinning wheel]. I said in 1920 that if the Congress truly and successfully worked the programme laid down in 1920 including the fourfold Constructive Programme of *khadi*, communal unity, prohibition of intoxicants and removal by Hindus of untouchability, the attainment of *swaraj* within a year was a certainty. I am neither sorry for nor ashamed of having made that declaration. I would like to repeat that declaration before you today. Whenever the fourfold programme is achieved in its fulness, you can have *swaraj* for the asking. For you will then have attained the power to take it. Just think for a moment where the *charkha* stands today in your faith or action. Is the mutual secret assassination of Bombay a sign of communal unity? Where is total prohibition? Have the Hindus rid themselves of untouchability root and branch? One swallow does not make a summer. Travancore's great Proclamation [ending certain kinds of discrimination against untouchables] may be the beginning of the end, but it is not the end. If we remove the untouchability of *Harijans* [literally, "children of God," Gandhi's name for the untouchables], but treat Mussalmans or others as such, we have not removed the blot. 'All land belongs to God' has a deeper meaning. Like the earth we, of it, also belong to God, and hence we must all feel like one and not erect boundary walls and issue prohibition decrees against one another.

This is the non-violent way in action. If we could fulfil this programme, there would be no need to offer disobedience, there would certainly be no need to do violence. Thirty-five crores of people conscious of their numerical strength as one man would be ashamed of doing violence to 70,000 white men in India, no matter how capable they are of dealing destruction and administering poison gas to millions in a moment. The *charkha* understood intelligently can spin not only economic salvation but can also revolutionize our minds and hearts and demonstrate to us that the non-violent approach to *swaraj* is the safest and the easiest. Though the progress may seem slow, it will prove quickest in the long run.

Believe me if Jawaharlal [Nehru, independent India's first Prime Minister, 1947–1964] is not in jail today, it is not because he is afraid of it. He is quite capable of walking into prison doors as of mounting the gallows with a smile on his lips. I do not think I have lost the power or faith in the efficacy of such suffering. But there is no issue for it today as far as I can see. But what I feel is that all that suffering can be avoided if by united faith and will we achieve the Constructive Programme. If we can, I promise that we won't need to struggle with or against the British nation, but Lord Linlithgow will come to us and own that he was mistaken in his disbelief of our nonviolence and truth and will undertake on behalf of his nation to abide by our decisions. Whether he does or not, I am working towards that and no other. 'All belong to God.'

STUDY QUESTIONS

1. What did Gandhi mean by the "square of *swaraj*"?
2. What was Gandhi's attitude toward Western-style capitalist industrialization?
3. Was Gandhi a socialist?
4. According to Gandhi, how had British rule harmed India? How would the use of the spinning wheel help to counteract the problems created by the British?
5. What was Gandhi's attitude toward parliamentary government?
6. What was Gandhi's "Constructive Programme" of 1920?
7. Was Gandhi opposed to modernization?
8. In what ways was this speech an attempt by Gandhi to shift his listeners' sense of identify from caste, region, and religion to a sense of membership in the Indian nation? Does he include everyone?
9. Compare Gandhi's ideas with those of Rammohun Roy (See Chapter 26).
10. Gandhi, Ziya Gokalp (see Chapter 44), and Sun Yatsen (see Chapter 47) were all born within a few years of 1870. What similarities and differences do you see in their ideas? What sets Gandhi apart from the others?

VISUAL SOURCE

THE SPINNING WHEEL AND INDIAN NATIONALISM

For Gandhi the spinning wheel (*charkha*) had both economic and political significance. He thought that if the people of India would devote part of each day to spinning cotton yarn by hand (as Gandhi did from the 1920s to the end of his life), they would take an important step toward restoring their country's economic well-being. Because spinning, unlike weaving, had never been associated with a particular caste, Gandhi also believed that the spinning wheel could serve as the icon of the Indian national movement.

In 1921 the Indian National Congress accepted Gandhi's view of the importance of hand spinning. The Congress announced a boycott of foreign cloth and adopted a flag that featured the *charkha*. Also important was Congress's decision to require its leaders to engage in daily spinning and to wear clothing made from hand-spun and hand-woven cloth (*khadi*).

One additional feature of Gandhi's campaign on behalf of the *charkha* is worthy of note: Spinning was traditionally "women's work" in India, as it was in many other countries. In present-day India, spinning continues to be a daily activity for the women in India's villages, where about 60 percent of the population resides.

***Charkha* at Fatehpur Sikri, Northern India, 2000.** (Photos by Stephen S. Gosch)

STUDY QUESTIONS

1. In what ways did Gandhi's advocacy of the spinning wheel and the wearing of *khadi* represent attempts to reduce caste differences and class divisions in India?
2. What was the likely impact of Gandhi's advocacy of the *charkha* on gender relations?
3. What were the benefits and possible drawbacks of choosing the spinning wheel as the symbol of the Indian national movement?

52

Love and Marriage in Modern India

The establishment of Indian independence in 1947 led to important legal reforms in gender relations. Voting rights were extended to women by the Constitution of 1950, which also outlawed discrimination by sex. Laws adopted somewhat later provided for divorce by mutual consent, banned polygamy (except among Indian Muslims), and established the right of women to have abortions.

The new laws benefited upper-class, well-educated women who took advantage of increased opportunities for careers in politics, business, and education. However, regardless of the law and their abilities, career women in India were often unable to win acceptance as equals by their male colleagues and associates. Circumstances were far worse for the hundreds of millions of poor women, most of whom lived in India's 560,000 rural villages. For these women, issues such as access to the most minimal level of education, obtaining adequate nutrition and basic health care (especially relating to childbirth), and opportunities for paid work of any kind remained major concerns.

In the 1970s the continuing obstacles Indian women faced led to the emergence of a feminist movement. As their counterparts did in other countries, Indian feminists founded organizations and journals, conducted research on gender issues, lobbied governmental officials, became active in the labor movement, ran for public office, and organized protest demonstrations. The striking achievements in recent decades of female Indian writers such as Anita Desai, Ruth Prawer Jhabvala, Gita Mehta, and Arundhati Roy gave literary expression to the new feminist activism.

Indian feminists have had to face more difficult challenges compared to their counterparts in the West. The tradition of *purdah* (the physical exclusion of women) continues to be significant in India's rural villages. In addition, owing to widespread poverty and the social pressure on families to provide dowries for their daughters, female infanticide in some rural regions is still a serious problem. Finally, there is widespread prejudice in India against widows, a lingering legacy of the once-significant practice of widow-suicide (*sati*).

As the product of Indian realities (as well as contacts with feminists in the West and elsewhere), the views of Indian feminists have their own distinctiveness. The selection by Madhu Kishwar, one of India's leading feminists, provides us with an interesting illustration of this point. Kishwar's essay, which appeared in the journal *Manushi* (Woman), argues in favor of what she calls "family-arranged" marriage (which is still the way most

From Madhu Kishwar, "Love and Marriage," *Manushi,* 80 (1994): 11–14, 17–19.

marriages come about in India), as opposed to Western-style "self-arranged" marriage. The article led to much debate in the pages of *Manushi* and should not be understood as *the* authoritative view of India's feminists on the issue of marriage. It is, nonetheless, an important statement and is included here because of the window it opens on important aspects of Indian society and culture in the late twentieth century.

"LOVE AND MARRIAGE" FROM *MANUSHI* MAGAZINE

Feminists, socialists and other radicals often project the system of arranged marriages as one of the key factors leading to women's oppression in India. This view derives from the West, which recognises two supposedly polar opposite forms of marriage—"love marriage" versus arranged marriage. "Love marriages" are assumed to be superior because they are supposedly based on romance, understanding, and mutual love—they are said to facilitate compatibility. In "love marriages" the persons concerned are supposed to have married out of idealistic considerations while arranged marriages are assumed to be based on materialistic considerations, where parents and family dominate and deny individual choice to the young people. Consequently, family arranged marriages are believed to be lacklustre and loveless. It is assumed that in arranged marriages compatibility rarely exists because the couple are denied the opportunity to discover areas of common interests and base their life together on mutual understanding. Moving away from family arranged marriages towards love marriages is seen as an essential step towards building a better life for women. To it the social reformers add another favourite *mantra*—dowryless marriages as proof that money and status considerations play no role in determining the choice of one's life partner. The two together—that is, a dowryless love marriage—[are] projected as the route to a happy married life.

Does experience bear this out? From what I have seen of them, "love marriages" compel me to conclude that most of them are not based on love and often end up being as big a bore or fiasco as many arranged marriages. Among the numerous cases I know I have found that often there is nothing more than a fleeting sexual attraction which does not last beyond the honeymoon period. And then the marriage is as loveless or even worse than a bad arranged marriage. Nor have I found any evidence that material considerations do not play as important a role in people's choice when they decide to "fall in love" with someone with a view to matrimony. . . .

My colleague Giri Deshingkar tells me an amusing story of the time he worked as a pool typist in England. Like most Indian men, he never wore a wedding ring. Mistaking him as an eligible bachelor, his female colleagues showered him with attention and competed with each other in wooing him. However, as soon as they got to know through a chance remark that he was already married, they dropped him like a hot brick. No more teas and coffees and other gestures of attention. Suddenly he became invisible for them. They would not hesitate to discuss their boyfriends and love affairs in his presence. He found them absolutely cynical in their calculation of who they were going to select as a target for loving attention. The experience cured him of all naive notions about love and romance.

This does not surprise me because I have seen these calculations at work at close quarters. For instance, during my university days, I found most of my fellow Mirandians from an English speaking elite background determined to "fall in love" with a Stephanian and would not "stoop" to have a relationship with a man from Khalsa or Rao Tula Ram College, because those were considered low status institutions, where people from ordinary middle class backgrounds went to study. The additional qualification they looked for was that the man's family own a house in one of South Delhi's posh colonies. Thus men from colonies such as Jor Bagh, Golf Links or Sundar Nagar were much sought after. Likewise, sons of senior bureaucrats, ambassadors, and top industrialists could have the choicest pick among the beauties and cuties of Miranda House. But a man whose father was a small shopkeeper in Kamla Nagar or a clerk in a government office stood no chance, no matter how bright or decent he might be. I witnessed several instances of my fellow students ditching a man they had been having an affair with for years as soon as someone from a wealthier background appeared on the scene. Often they would not even bother to hide the crassness of their calculations; a friend conveniently "fell out of love" with her boyfriend who owned a motorbike in favour of someone who had a car to take her out on dates.

While many of my friends would have scoffed at the idea of their parents "arranging" for them to meet a man with a view to matrimony, they were only too eager to go to parties arranged by Stephanians so that they could pick girl friends. In western campuses young people eagerly read notices of "Mixers" in order to find future mates.

Men do precisely what women do about "falling in love." They take family status, who among her family are "green card" holders, and other such material considerations into account before they take the plunge.

While men and women may be somewhat more adventurous when choosing someone for a mere sexual affair, the same people tend to become far more "rational" in their calculations when "falling in love" is meant to be a prelude to marriage.

In the 1950s a study which is considered a classic on factors that determine love and marriage in America showed that it was easy to statistically predict the characteristics of the person a man or a woman is likely to fall in love with and marry. Three major factors that have a great influence on who a person falls in love with are: proximity, opportunity, and similarity. Thus it is no coincidence that most whites marry whites and rich people marry among themselves even in a "free" society like America where marriages are self contracted. Why then are we surprised if most Brahmins marry within the Brahmin fold or Jats and Mahars do likewise in family contracted marriages?

Whatever the form of marriage, the motivations and calculations that go into it are fairly simple. Desire for regular sex, economic security, enhancement of one's social status and the desire to have children all play a role in both kinds of marriages. Therefore, instead of describing them as "love" marriages, it is more appropriate to call them self arranged marriages. Love, in the sense of caring for another person, may even be altogether absent in these marriages. Therefore, I feel the term love marriage needs to be restricted to those marriages where people actually have a loving respect for each other and where there is continuing satisfaction in togetherness.

Self Arranged Marriages

Critics of the family arranged marriage system in India have rightly focused on how prospective brides are humiliated by being endlessly displayed for approval when marriages are being negotiated by families. The ritual of *ladki dikhana,* with the inevitable rejections women (now even men) often undergo before being selected, does indeed make the whole process extremely stressful.

However, women do not really escape the pressures of displaying and parading themselves in cultures where they are expected to have self arranged marriages. Witness the amount of effort a young woman in western societies has to put in to look attractive enough to hook eligible young men. One gets the feeling they are on constant self display as opposed to the periodic displays in family arranged marriages. Western women have to diet to stay trim since it is not fashionable nowadays to be fat, get artificial padding for their breasts (1.5 million American women are reported to have gone through silicon surgery to get their breasts reshaped or enlarged), try to get their complexion to glow, if not with real health, at least with a cosmetic blush. They must also learn how to be viewed as "attractive" and seductive to men, how to be a witty conversationalist as well as an ego booster—in short, to become the kind of appendage a man would feel proud to have around him. Needless to say, not all women manage to do all the above, though most drive themselves crazy trying. Western women have to compete hard with each other in order to hook a partner. And once having found him, they have to be alert to prevent other women from snatching him. So fierce is the pressure to keep off other grabbing females that in many cases if a woman is divorced or single she is unlikely to be invited over to a married friend's house at a gathering of couples lest she try to grab someone else's husband.

The humiliations western women have to go through, having first to grab a man, and then to devise strategies to keep other women off him, is in many ways much worse than what a woman in parent arranged marriages has to go through. She does not have to chase and hook men all by herself. Her father, her brother, her uncles and aunts and the entire *kunba* join together to hunt for a man. In that sense the woman concerned does not have to carry the burden of finding a husband all alone. And given the relative stability of marriage among communities where families take a lot of interest in keeping the marriage going, a woman is not so paranoid about her husband abandoning her in favour of a more attractive woman. Consequently, Indian women are not as desperate as their western counterparts to look for ever youthful, trim and sexually attractive marriage partners. . . .

Family Pressures

My impression is that it takes much more than two people to make a good marriage. Overbearing parents on either side can indeed make married life difficult for a young couple and often women have to put up with a great deal of maltreatment at the hands of their in-laws. But more solidly enduring and happy marriages are almost always those where the families on both sides genuinely join together to celebrate their coming together and invest a lot of effort and emotion in making the marriage work. Very few people have the emotional and other resources required to make a happy marriage all on their own. Two people locked up with each other in a nuclear family having to meet with varied expectations inevitably generate too much heat and soon tend to suffocate each other. The proximity of other family members takes a lot of the load off. They can act as a glue, especially during times of crisis. In cultures where marriage is considered an internal affair of the couple with no responsibility taken by families on either side for the continuation and well being of the marriage, breakdown in marriages is more frequent.

There is also the negative side. In communities where families consider it their responsibility to prevent divorce as far as possible women do very often get to be victims of vicious pressures against breaking out of abusive marriages. Among several communities in India a divorced woman is viewed with contempt and parents often force their daughters to keep their marriages going no matter what the cost. Consequently, many end up committing suicide or getting murdered because they are unable to walk out of abusive marriages. Many more have to learn to live a life of humiliation and even suffer routine beatings and other forms of torture. However, in such cultures, divorced men get to be viewed with some suspicion and are somewhat stigmatised. . . .

In family arranged marriages, few parents are interested in marrying their young daughter to a divorced man, unless he is willing to marry a woman from a much poorer family (so that the family escapes having to pay dowry) or marry a divorced woman or widow. In India, relatively few men resort to divorce even when they are unhappy in marriage. The sigma attached to divorce for men, if not as great as for women, is at least substantial enough to get them to try somewhat to control themselves. They know that they cannot get away with having a series of divorces, as they do in the West, and yet find a young, beautiful bride 30 years their junior. But this is only true for marriage within tight knit communities where the two families have effective ways of checking on each other's background. There is no dearth of instances nowadays in which parents fail to investigate the groom's background and end up marrying their daughters to men who have beaten or even murdered the first wife. My impression is that this is happening more among groups who are marrying beyond their kinship groups through matrimonial advertisement or professional marriage brokers.

Inter Community Marriages

Hollywood, Bollywood propaganda tells us that passionate romance is the foundation of a real marriage; according to these myth makers marriage is and ought to be an affair between two individuals. Marriages between people who defy caste, class, community and other prevalent norms are seen as demonstrating thereby their true love for each other and are glorified. This is not only over simplistic but highly erroneous.

Our crusades against social inequality and communal prejudices [are] one thing. The ingredients that make for a good marriage are quite another. A married couple is more likely to have a stable marriage if the spouses can take 90 per cent of things for granted and have to work at adjustment in no more than 10 per cent of the areas of mutual living. The film *Ek Duje ke Liye* type of situation is very likely to spell disaster in real life. The hero and the heroine come from very different regional and linguistic groups. They don't even understand each other's languages and communicate mostly through sign or body language—yet are shown as willing to die for each other. In real life this may make for a brief sexual affair, but not a good marriage. The latter depends more on how well people understand and appreciate each other's language, culture, food habits, personal nuances and quirks, and get along [with] and win respect from each other's family. If the income gap is too large and the standards of living of the two families are dramatically different, the couple are likely to find it much harder to adjust to each other.

The willing participation of the groom's family is very often crucial to the well being of a marriage especially if the couple lives in a joint family with the groom's parents. But even if the couple is to live in a nuclear family after marriage, the support of her in-laws will help a woman keep her husband disciplined and domesticated. Most of my friends who have happy and secure marriages get along with their in-laws so well that they are confident that if their husbands were to behave irresponsibly or start extra marital affairs, their in-laws would not only side with the daughter in-law but go as far as to ask the son to quit the house.

Safety Measures for Women

I am not against self arranged marriages but I feel they have a poor track record despite pompous claims about their superiority. A self arranged marriage cannot arrogate to itself the nomenclature of a love marriage unless it endures with love. My own experience of the world tells me that marriages in which the two people concerned genuinely love and respect each other, marriages which slowly grow in the direction of mutual understanding, are very rare even among groups and cultures who believe in the superiority of self arranged marriages.

The outcome of marriage depends on how realistic the calculations have been. For instance, a family may arrange the marriage of their daughter with a man settled in the USA in the hope of providing better life opportunities to the daughter. But if they have not been responsible enough to inquire carefully into the family, personal and professional history of the man, they could end up seriously jeopardising their daughter's well being. He may have boasted of being a computer scientist but could turn out to be a low paid cab driver or a guard in New York. He could well be living with or married to an American woman and take the Indian wife to be no more than a domestic servant or a camouflage to please his parents. He could in addition be a drunkard given to violent bouts of temper. His being so far away from India would isolate the young wife from all sources of support and thus make her far more vulnerable than if she were married in the same city as her parents.

Another case at the other end of the spectrum could end up just as disastrously if the woman concerned makes wrong calculations. Let's say a young student in an American University decides to arrange her marriage with a fellow student setting out to be a doctor. Through the years that her husband is studying to become a doctor, she works hard at a low or moderately paying job to support the family. When he becomes a doctor she decides to leave her job and have a baby. In a few years he becomes successful whereas she has become economically dependent on him. At this point he finds a lot of young and attractive women willing to fall at his feet and he decides to "fall in love" with one of them, divorces his wife and remarries a much younger woman. The wife is left at a time when she needs a marriage partner most.

All she can hope to do is to get some kind of a financial settlement after lengthy legal proceedings. But that is not a substitute for a secure family.

The factors that decide the fate of women in marriage are:

- Whether the woman has independent means of survival. If she is absolutely dependent on her husband's goodwill for survival, she is more likely to have to lead a submissive life than if she is economically self sufficient.
- Whether or not her husband is willing and equipped to take on the responsibility that goes with having a family.
- Whether or not a woman's in-laws welcome her coming into the family and how eager they are to make it work.
- How well the two families get along with and respect each other.
- Whether or not there are social restraints through family and community control on men's behaviour. In societies where men can get away with beating wives or abandoning them in favour of younger women, women tend to live in insecurity. However, in communities where a man who treats his wife badly is looked down upon and finds it harder to find another wife because of social stigma, men are more likely to behave with a measure of responsibility.
- The ready availability of other women even after a man is known to have maltreated his wife tilts the balance against women. If men can easily find younger women as they grow older while women cannot as readily find marriage partners when they are older or divorced, the balance will inevitably tilt in favour of men irrespective of whether marriages in that culture are self arranged or parent arranged.
- Whether or not her parents are willing to support her emotionally and financially if she is facing an abusive marriage. Most important of all is whether her parents are willing to give her the share due to her in their property and in the parental home. In communities where parents' expectation concerning a daughter is that only her *arthi* (funeral pyre) should come out of her husband's house, family pressure can prove really disastrous.

Undoubtedly, there are numerous situations whereby family elders do take an altogether unreasonable position; defiance of their tyranny then becomes inevitable, even desirable. Parents can often go wrong in their judgments. Parents must take into account their children's best interests and preferences if they are to play a positive role.

We have to devise ways to tilt family support more in favour of women rather than seeking "freedom" by alienating oneself from this crucial source of support over romanticising self arranged marriages and insisting on individual choice in marriage as an end in itself rather than as one means to more stable, dignified and egalitarian marriages.

STUDY QUESTIONS

1. According to Madhu Kishwar, what is wrong with the idea of "love marriage"? Why does she believe that "self-arranged" marriage is a more useful term than "love marriage"?

2. What advantages does Kishwar see in "family-arranged" marriages? What problems does she acknowledge in family-arranged marriages?

3. Is there a contradiction between family-arranged marriages and love between spouses?

4. What does this article suggest about the emotional life of Indian married couples? About the importance of individualism in India?

5. Is Kishwar's portrait of marriage in the West accurate?

6. How do the views of Madhu Kishwar compare with those of Higuchi Keiko in Chapter 50, and the African women in Chapter 47?

53

Twentieth-Century Latin American Politics: The Revolutionary Challenge

Since their independence from Spain and Portugal (1810–1825), Latin American republics have experienced periods of severe political instability. From the 1830s to the 1860s *caudillos,* local military leaders left over from the wars of independence, often seized national office, pillaged the treasury, and were in turn deposed by others. During the late nineteenth century, when Latin America began exporting raw materials (metals, fertilizers) and food (sugar, coffee, wheat, bananas), oligarchical elites closely linked to the export economy consolidated stable political regimes. This stability was purchased by limiting the exercise of political power to a narrow few and excluding commoners through voting restrictions. At the beginning of the twentieth century, population growth plus immigration from Europe greatly swelled the ranks of laborers, professionals, clerical people, and the urban poor. Most remained apolitical, but key groups such as railroad workers, dockworkers, and meatpackers formed unions, while professionals, small property owners, and clerical people formed middle-class political parties.

Social unrest along with often inflexible political regimes has led to a series of revolutions and other upheavals in twentieth-century Latin America. The following selections deal with three of the major episodes. All express some of the basic social grievances that have created unrest, thus suggesting answers to the question of why Latin America has been so productive of political turmoil in the twentieth century and beyond.

Selection I from Emiliano Zapata, *The Plan of Ayala* (29 November 1911), translated by Erick D. Langer. Reprinted by permission. Selection II from Angel Perelman, *Como Hicimos el 17 de Octobre* (Buenos Aires: Editorial Coyoacan, 1961), pp. 44–46, translated in *Why Peron Came to Power. The Background to Peronism in Argentine,* edited by Joseph R. Barager (New York: Alfred A. Knopf, 1968), pp. 200–202. Copyright © 1968, Alfred A. Knopf. Reprinted by permission. Selection III from Fidel Castro, *History Will Absolve Me. Moncada Trial Defence Speech Santiago de Cuba, October, 16, 1953* (London: Jonathan Cape, 1958), pp. 40–45. First published in Cuba in 1967, and published in Great Britain in 1968 by Jonathan Cape Limited. Reprinted by permission.

The first selection comes from the Mexican Revolution of 1910. It was issued by the most radical peasant leader, Emiliano Zapata. Zapata never seized control of the Mexican Revolution, but the radical economic demands of his Plan of Ayala influenced the course of Mexican social development for the next 30 years.

The second selection reflects a new kind of strongman rule that characterized several major Latin states during the twentieth century. In Argentina, Juan Perón resembled revolutionaries in seeking to avoid foreign (in this case almost entirely economic) domination. Perón, a middle-class military man, appealed to working people neglected by earlier civilian governments. The passage shows how union leaders—in this case the head of the metalworkers' union—had become disenchanted with communist control and preferred a military ruler who could get things done for the workers. This decision resulted in state control of unions after Perón became president, from 1946 to 1955, and an enduring attachment of many Argentine workers to an authoritarian, but populist, government.

A new round of revolutionary activity emerged during the 1950s, building on social and economic problems similar to those in Mexico earlier on. The lone successful change came in 1959 with Fidel Castro in Cuba, but his example then spurred other guerrilla movements that, particularly in Central America, have continued to the present day. Later on it also helped inspire outright revolution in Nicaragua.

Although he became a symbol of communist insurrection, Castro viewed his revolution as authentically Cuban. Looking back into Cuba's past, Castro saw a deformed nation. At each moment when a true nationalist sought political power, either he was blocked by foreign intervention, or he betrayed the cause. José Marti, the intellectual spirit of the Cuban independence movement against Spain in 1895, was an authentic Cuban hero. Yet his political program was never realized because of the intervention of the United States during the Spanish-American War of 1898. From that year until Castro seized power in 1959, the United States dominated Cuba politically and economically, despite Cuba's nominal independence. Presidents of Cuba, such as Batista (1940–1944, 1952–1958), talked of reform but used their office to become wealthy, especially by diverting U.S. loans into their own pockets. Meanwhile, the majority of the Cuban people—the poor—were neglected. For Cuba to take control of its destiny, Castro saw the necessity of revolution. After the failure of his first military operation on July 26, 1953, Castro—while in jail—described why the revolution was being fought and what he would do once in power. In Selection III, one can see that the spirit that animates his program is the same spirit that guides revolutionaries in other parts of Latin America.

LATIN AMERICAN REVOLUTIONARY DOCUMENTS

I. THE PLAN OF AYALA

The liberating Plan of the sons of the State of Morelos, affiliated with the Insurgent Army which defends the fulfillment of the Plan of San Luis Potosí, with the reforms which they have believed necessary to add for the benefit of the Mexican Fatherland.

We, the subscribers [to this Plan], constituted in a Revolutionary Council . . . declare solemnly before the countenance of the civilized world which judges us and before the Nation to which we belong and love, the principles which we have formulated to terminate the tyranny which oppresses us and redeem the Fatherland from the dictatorships which are imposed on us, which are determined in the following Plan:

1. [Accuses Francisco I. Madero, the leader of the 1910 revolution and President of Mexico, of betraying the Revolution and allying himself with the oppressive old guard in the State of Morelos.]

2. Francisco I. Madero is disavowed as Chief of the Revolution and as President of the Republic, for the above reasons, [and we will] endeavor to overthrow this official.

3. The illustrious General Pascual Orozco, second of the *caudillo* Don Francisco I. Madero, is recognized as Chief of the Liberating Revolution, and in case he does not accept this delicate post, General Emiliano Zapata is recognized as Chief of the Revolution.

4. The Revolutionary Junta of the State of Morelos manifests the following formal points . . . and will make itself the defender of the principles that it will defend until victory or death.

5. The Revolutionary Junta of the State of Morelos will not admit transactions or political compromises until the overthrow of the dictatorial elements of Porfirio Díaz and Francisco I. Madero, since the Nation is tired of false men and traitors who make promises as liberators but once in power, forget them and become tyrants.

6. As an additional part of the Plan which we invoke, we assert that: the fields, woodland, and water which the haciendados [landlords], *científicos* or bosses in the shadow of tyranny and venal justice have usurped, will revert to the possession of the towns or citizens who have their corresponding titles to these properties. [These properties] have been usurped through the bad faith of our oppressors, who maintained all along with arms in hand the above mentioned possession. The usurpers who feel they have the right [to ownership], will demonstrate this before special tribunals which will be established when the Revolution triumphs.

7. In virtue of the fact that the immense majority of the towns and Mexican citizens are not masters of the soil they step upon, suffering horrors of misery without being able to better their social condition at all nor dedicate themselves to industry or agriculture because of the monopoly in a few hands of the land, woodlands, and waters, for this reason [the lands] will be expropriated, with indemnity of the third part of these monopolies to their powerful owners, so that the towns and citizens of Mexico can obtain common lands [*ejidos*], colonies, and legitimate resources for towns or agricultural fields and that above all the lack of prosperity and wellbeing of the Mexican people is improved.

8. The haciendados, *científicos* or bosses who oppose directly or indirectly the present plan, will have their possessions nationalized and two thirds of what they own will be destined for war indemnities, [and] pensions for the widows and orphans of the victims who succumb in the fight for this Plan.

9. To regulate the procedures in regard to the items mentioned above, the laws of disentailment and nationalization will be applied as is appropriate. [The laws] put into effect by the immortal Juarez regarding Church lands will serve as a guide and example, which set a severe example to the despots and conservatives who at all times have tried to impose the ignominious yoke of oppression and backwardness.

10. The insurgent military chiefs of the Republic, who rose up in armed revolt at the behest of Francisco I. Madero to defend the Plan of San Luis Potosí and who now oppose by force the present Plan, are to be judged traitors to the cause they defended and to the Fatherland, given the fact that in actuality many of them to please the tyrants for a handful of coins, or for bribes, are spilling the blood of their brethren who demand the fulfillment of the promises which don Francisco I. Madero made to the Nation.

11–14. [Details the payment of the expenses of war, the administration of the country after the Plan's success, and bids Madero to step down voluntarily.]

15. Mexicans: Consider that the cleverness and the bad faith of one man is spilling blood in a scandalous manner because of his inability to govern; consider that his system of government is putting the Fatherland in chains and by brute force of bayonets trampling under foot our institutions; and as we raised our arms to elevate him to power, today we turn them against him for having gone back on his agreements with the Mexican people and having betrayed the Revolution he initiated; we are not personalists, we are believers in principles, not in men.

People of Mexico: Support with your arms in hand this Plan and you will create prosperity and happiness for the Fatherland.

Justicia y ley. [Justice and Law.]
Ayala, 28 of November, 1911.

II. PERONISM (METAL WORKERS MEETING WITH PERÓN MID-1944)

Once the resistance of the [Communist] directors was overcome, we arranged with the Secretariat of Labor to convoke a meeting at which Perón would speak to the metal workers. The date fixed, we calculated that we could fill the assembly hall of the Deliberating Council, where the Secretariat of Labor and Social Welfare was located.

We had no resources for publicizing this meeting. Until noon of the day of the gathering, we were still sticking together some posters announcing the convocation. It was a great surprise when, by the time of the meeting, the meeting hall was completely filled, and an enormous multitude of nearly 20,000 metal workers was concentrated outside in the Diagonal Roca. The shops they came from were identified by improvised placards and reflected the enormous repercussion the growth of industry was having on the working class at that time. . . .

Colonel Perón, in one of the salient parts of his discourse, told us that he was gratified to see the metal workers enter the house of the workers and that he had assumed that, since they were one of the last unions to come together there, they must be very well paid. But he added that, as a result of the remarks of the comrade who had preceded him on the platform, it appeared that this was not so, and consequently he was urging the metal workers to form a powerful union to defend their rights and the country's sovereignty. At this moment a metal worker interrupted to shout: "Thus speaks a *criollo!*" [true Argentine] Banners and posters fluttered approval of the metal worker's remark. We went out of that meeting with the conviction that the metal workers' union would soon be transformed into a very powerful labor organization. And in effect it was; from a membership of 1,500 we transformed that union "of form" into the present Union of Metal Workers (UOM) with 300,000 workers in the fold. So profound was the need for the country to defend its political independence and economic sovereignty, and for the working class to organize at last its unions on a grade scale, that, faced by the treason of the parties of the left, this need had to be embodied in a military man who had come from the ranks of the Army.

And we came to constitute then that ideological tendency known by many people as the "national left." In our union activities at the end of 1944 we witnessed unbelievable happenings: labor laws neglected in another era were being carried out; one did not need recourse to the courts for the granting of vacations; such other labor dispensations as the recognition of factory delegates, guarantees against being discharged, etc., were immediately and rigorously enforced. The nature of internal relations between the owners and the workers in the factories was completely changed. The internal democratization imposed by the metal workers' union resulted in factory delegates constituting the axis of the entire organization and in the direct expression of the will of the workers in each establishment. The owners were as disconcerted as the workers were astounded and happy. The Secretariat of Labor and Social Welfare was converted into an agency for the organization, development, and support of the workers. It did not function as a state regulator for the top level of the unions; it acted as a state ally of the working class. Such were the practical results that constituted the basis for the political shift of the Argentine masses and that were manifested in the streets on October 17, 1945. [Date when a massive demonstration took place that secured Perón's release from prison.]

III. CASTRO'S PROGRAM (OCTOBER 16, 1953)

When we speak of the people we do not mean the comfortable ones, the conservative elements of the nation, who welcome any regime of oppression, any dictatorship, any despotism, prostrating themselves before the master of the moment until they grind their foreheads into the ground. When we speak of struggle, the people means the vast unredeemed masses to whom all make promises and whom all deceive; we mean the people who yearn for a better, more dignified and more just nation; who are moved by ancestral aspirations of justice, for they have suffered injustice and mockery generation after generation; who long for great and wise changes in all aspects of their life; people who, to attain the changes, are ready to give even the very last breath of their lives, when they believe in something or in someone, especially when they believe in themselves. . . . The people we counted on in our struggle were these:

Seven hundred thousand Cubans without work, who desire to earn their daily bread honestly without having to emigrate in search of a livelihood.

Five hundred thousand farm labourers inhabiting miserable shacks (*bohíos*), who work four months of the year and starve during the rest, sharing their misery with their children; who have not an inch of land to till, and whose existence would move any heart not made of stone.

Four hundred thousand industrial labourers and stevedores [workers who load and unload ships] whose retirement funds have been embezzled, whose benefits are being taken away, whose homes are wretched quarters, whose salaries pass from the hands of the boss to those of the money-lender (*garrotero*), whose future is a pay reduction and dismissal, whose life is eternal work and whose only rest is in the tomb.

One hundred thousand small farmers who live and die working on land that is not theirs, looking at it with sadness as Moses looked at the promised land, to die without ever owning it; who, like feudal serfs, have to pay for the use of their parcel of land by giving up a portion of its products: who cannot love it, improve it, beautify it, nor plant a lemon or an orange tree on it, because they never know when a sheriff will come with the rural guard to evict them from it.

Thirty thousand teachers and professors who are so devoted, dedicated and necessary to the better destiny of future generations and who are so badly treated and paid.

Twenty thousand small business men, weighted down by debts, ruined by the crisis and harangued by a plague of grafting and venal officials.

Ten thousand young professionals: doctors, engineers, lawyers, veterinarians, school teachers, dentists, pharmacists, newspapermen, painters, sculptors, etc., who come forth from school with their degrees, anxious to work and full of hope, only to find themselves at a dead end with all doors closed, and where no ear hears their clamour or supplication.

These are the people, the ones who know misfortune and, therefore, are capable of fighting with limitless courage!

To the people whose desperate roads through life have been paved with the bricks of betrayals and false promises, we were not going to say: "We will eventually give you what you need," but rather—"Here you have it, fight for it with all your might, so that liberty and happiness may be yours!"

In the brief of this case, the five revolutionary laws that would have been proclaimed immediately after the capture of the Moncada Barracks and would have been broadcasted to the nation by radio should be recorded. It is possible that Colonel Chaviano may deliberately have destroyed these documents, but even if he has done so I remember them.

The First Revolutionary Law would have returned power to the people and proclaimed the Constitution of 1940 the supreme Law of the State, until such time as the people should decide to modify or change it. And, in order to effect its implementation and punish those who had violated it, there being no organization for holding elections to accomplish this, the revolutionary movement, as the momentous incarnation of this sovereignty, the only source of legitimate power, would have assumed all the faculties inherent in it, except that of modifying the Constitution itself: in other words, it would have assumed the legislative, executive and judicial powers. . . .

The Second Revolutionary Law would have granted property, non-mortgageable and non-transferable, to all planters, non-quota planters, lessees, share-croppers, and squatters who hold parcels of five *caballerí as* of land or less, and the State would indemnify the former owners on the basis of the rental which they would have received for these parcels over a period of ten years.

The Third Revolutionary Law would have granted workers and employees the right to share thirty per cent of the profits of all the large industrial, mercantile and mining enterprises, including the sugar mills. The strictly agricultural enterprises would be exempt in consideration of other agrarian laws which would be implemented.

The Fourth Revolutionary Law would have granted all planters the right to share fifty-five per cent of the sugar production and a minimum quota of forty thousand *arrobas* for all small planters who have been established for three or more years.

The Fifth Revolutionary Law would have ordered the confiscation of all holdings and ill-gotten gains of those who had committed frauds during previous regimes, as well as the holdings and ill-gotten gains of all their legatees and heirs. To implement this, special courts with full powers would gain access to all records of all corporations registered or operating in this country, in order to investigate concealed funds of illegal origin, and to request that foreign governments extradite persons and attach holdings rightfully belonging to the Cuban people. Half of the property recovered would be used to subsidize retirement funds for workers and the other half would be used for hospitals, asylums and charitable organizations.

STUDY QUESTIONS

1. The documents offer a comparison with earlier grievances, when Latin American nations struggled for political independence (see Chapter 30). What has changed among the goals and actors on center stage?
2. What are the goals of Zapata's revolution? How much change would take place if they were implemented?
3. How do the goals of Peronist workers resemble as well as differ from more explicitly revolutionary currents in Latin America?
4. How radical were Castro's goals? What were the political implications of implementing them? Who would have been harmed by their implementation? Who would have benefited? How do they compare with Zapata's goals?

VISUAL SOURCE

By courting labor and nationalist voters, army officer Juan Perón (1895–1974) was elected president of Argentina in 1946. Although driven from office in 1955 by a military coup, his program of social justice (*Justicialismo*) became the foundation of the Peronist Party. Disenchantment with military rule and persistent popularity of the Peronist Party led to Perón's return from exile in Spain and reelection in 1973. His wife, Eva Duarte de Perón (1919–1952), a struggling, ambitious, young actress whom he married in 1945, aided his rise to power. Because she had been poor and illegitimate, "Evita" identified with the downtrodden in Argentina. During Juan Perón's first period in office, she organized and administered the nation's welfare agencies. Her death from cancer at age 32 led to a public outpouring of grief.

Juan Perón and his wife Eva leave the presidential palace on their way to the Teatro Colon on Argentina's Independence Day in 1950. (AP/World Wide Press)

STUDY QUESTIONS

1. How do you expect your politicians to dress? Do Juan and Evita Perón meet your expectations?
2. How might Juan and Evita Perón reconcile their public display of wealth, elegance, and splendor with their identification with the poor?

54

Searching for the Soul of the Latin American Experience

Essayists and novelists have struggled to capture the uniqueness of Latin America. Although their descriptions are set in specific countries and locations, they tend toward common themes. For example, the Mexican essayist Octavio Paz, in search of his identity as well as that of his nation, wrote about the "labyrinth of solitude." The Colombian novelist Gabriel García Márquez examined the experiences of a family and a town through "one hundred years of solitude." The common theme of solitude becomes for these two men the chief vehicle for understanding Latin American civilization.

Gabriel García Márquez was awarded the Nobel Prize for literature in 1982. In his acceptance speech, "The Solitude of Latin America," he explained the source of that solitude. To García Márquez, Latin Americans lacked a conventional means of believing their past. Rather, they lived in a world of illusion that produced separation and solitude. This "fantasy reality" could not be understood by outsiders, who were equipped only with their own cultural tools. Europeans, for example, accepted Latin American literature. They, however, ridiculed the Latin Americans' attempts at social change. Latin Americans were accepted not as a distinct whole, but as an incomplete Western form. García Márquez asserts that Latin America is distinct. Latin Americans will invent their own solutions and utopias. They will affirm their own reality, illusory or not.

The concern about identity in Latin America reflects an important facet of Latin American culture, but this is not unique. Other twentieth-century civilizations worry about identity issues; these Latin American reflections can thus be compared with the issues of identity in societies such as sub-Saharan Africa.

LATIN AMERICAN IDENTITY

Antonio Pigafetta, a Florentine navigator who went with Magellan on the first voyage around the world, wrote, upon his passage through our southern lands of America, a strictly accurate account that nonetheless resembles a venture into

From Gabriel García Márquez, "The Solitude of Latin America" (Nobel Lecture, 1982), translated from the Spanish by Mariana Castaneda in Julio Ortega, *Gabriel García Márquez and the Powers of Fiction* (Austin: University of Texas Press, 1988), pp. 87–91. Reprinted by permission of The Nobel Foundation.

fantasy. In it he recorded that he had seen hogs with navels on their haunches, clawless birds whose hens laid eggs on the backs of their mates, and others still, resembling tongueless pelicans, with beaks like spoons. He wrote of having seen a misbegotten creature with the head and ears of a mule, a camel's body, the legs of a deer and the whinny of a horse. He described how the first native encountered in Patagonia was confronted with a mirror, whereupon that impassioned giant lost his senses to the terror of his own image.

This short and fascinating book, which even then contained the seeds of our present-day novels, is by no means the most staggering account of our reality in that age. The Chroniclers of the Indies left us countless others. Eldorado, our so avidly sought and illusory land, appeared on numerous maps for many a long year, shifting its place and form to suit the fantasy of cartographers. In his search for the fountain of eternal youth, the mythical Alvar Núñez Cabeza de Vaca explored the north of Mexico for eight years, in a deluded expedition whose members devoured each other and only five of whom returned, of the six hundred who had undertaken it. One of the many unfathomed mysteries of that age is that of the eleven thousand mules, each loaded with one hundred pounds of gold, that left Cuzco one day to pay the ransom of Atahualpa and never reached their destination. Subsequently, in colonial times, hens were sold in Cartagena de Indias, that had been raised on alluvial land and whose gizzards contained tiny lumps of gold. The founders' lust for gold beset us until recently. As late as the last century, a German mission appointed to study the construction of an interoceanic railroad across the Isthmus of Panama concluded that the project was feasible on one condition: that the rails not be made of iron, which was scarce in the region, but of gold.

Our independence from Spanish domination did not put us beyond the reach of madness. General Antonio López de Santa Anna, three times dictator of Mexico, held a magnificent funeral for the right leg he had lost in the so-called Pastry War. General Gabriel García Moreno ruled Ecuador for sixteen years as an absolute monarch; at his wake, the corpse was seated on the presidential chair, decked out in full-dress uniform and a protective layer of medals. General Maximiliano Hernández Martínez, the theosophical despot of El Salvador who had thirty thousand peasants slaughtered in a savage massacre, invented a pendulum to detect poison in his food, and had street lamps draped in red paper to defeat an epidemic of scarlet fever. The statue to General Francisco Morazán erected in the main square of Tegucigalpa is actually one of Marshal Ney, purchased at a Paris warehouse of second-hand sculptures.

Eleven years ago, the Chilean Pablo Neruda, one of the outstanding poets of our time, enlightened the audience with his word. Since then, the Europeans of good will—and sometimes those of bad, as well—have been struck, with ever greater force, by the unearthly tidings of Latin America, that boundless realm of haunted men and historic women, whose unending obstinacy blurs into legend. We have not had a moment's rest. A promethean president, entrenched in his burning palace, died fighting an entire army, alone; and two suspicious airplane accidents, yet to be explained, cut short the life of another great-hearted president and that of a democratic soldier who had revived the dignity of his people. There have been five wars and seventeen military coups; there emerged a diabolic dictator who is carrying out, in God's name, the first Latin American ethnocide of our time. In the meantime, twenty million Latin American children died before the age of one—more than have been born in Europe since 1970. Those missing because of repression number nearly one hundred and twenty thousand, which is as if no one could account for all the inhabitants of Upsala. Numerous women arrested while pregnant have given birth in Argentina prisons, yet nobody knows the whereabouts and identity of their children, who were furtively adopted or sent to an orphanage by order of the military authorities. Because they tried to change this state of things, nearly two hundred thousand men and women have died throughout the continent, and over one hundred thousand have lost their lives in three small and ill-fated countries of Central America: Nicaragua, El Salvador, and Guatemala. If this had happened in the United States, the corresponding figure would be that of one million six hundred thousand violent deaths in four years.

One million people have fled Chile, a country with a tradition of hospitality—that is, ten percent of its population. Uruguay, a tiny nation of two and a half million inhabitants which considered itself the continent's most civilized country, has lost to exile one out of every five citizens. Since 1979, the civil war in El Salvador has produced almost one refugee every twenty minutes. The country that could be formed of all the exiles and forced emigrants of Latin America would have a population larger than that of Norway.

I dare to think that it is this outsized reality, and not just its literary expression, that has deserved the attention of the Swedish Academy of Letters. A reality not of paper, but one that lives within us and determines each instant of our countless daily deaths, and that nourishes a source of insatiable creativity, full of sorrow and beauty, of which this roving and nostalgic Colombian is but one cipher more, singled out by fortune. Poets and beggars, musicians and prophets, warriors and scoundrels, all creatures of that unbridled reality, we have had to ask but little of imagination, for our crucial problem has been a lack of conventional means to render our lives believable. This, my friends, is the crux of our solitude.

And if these difficulties, whose essence we share, hinder us, it is understandable that the rational talents on this side of the world, exalted in the contemplation of their own cultures, should have found themselves without a valid means to interpret us. It is only natural that they insist on measuring us with the yardstick that they use for themselves, forgetting that the ravages of life are not the same for all, and that the quest of our own identity is just as arduous and bloody for us as it was for them. The interpretation of our reality through patterns not our own serves only to make us ever more unknown, ever less free, ever more solitary. Venerable Europe would perhaps be more perceptive if it tried to see us in its own past. If only it recalled that London took three hundred years to build its first city wall, and three hundred years more to acquire a bishop; that Rome labored in a gloom of uncertainty for twenty centuries, until an Etruscan king anchored it in history; and that the peaceful Swiss of today, who feast us with their mild cheeses and apathetic watches, bloodied Europe as soldiers of fortune, as late as the sixteenth century. Even at the height of the Renaissance, twelve thousand lansquenets in the pay of the imperial armies sacked and devastated Rome and put eight thousand of its inhabitants to the sword.

I do not mean to embody the illusions of Tonio Krüger, whose dreams of uniting a chaste north to a passionate south were exalted here, fifty-three years ago, by Thomas Mann. But I do believe that those clear-sighted Europeans who struggle, here as well, for a more just and humane homeland, could help us far better if they reconsidered their way of seeing us. Solidarity with our dreams will not make us feel less alone, as long as it is not translated into concrete acts of legitimate support for all the peoples that assume the illusion of having a life of their own in the distribution of the world.

Latin America neither wants, nor has any reason, to be a pawn without a will of its own; nor is it merely wishful thinking that its quest for independence and originality should become a Western aspiration. However, the navigational advances that have narrowed such distances between our Americas and Europe seem, conversely, to have accentuated our cultural remoteness. Why is the originality so readily granted us in literature so mistrustfully denied us in our difficult attempts at social change? Why think that the social justice sought by progressive Europeans for their own countries cannot also be a goal for Latin America, with different methods for dissimilar conditions? No: the immeasurable violence and pain of our history are the result of age-old inequities and untold bitterness, and not a conspiracy plotted three thousand leagues from our home. But many European leaders and thinkers have thought so, with the childishness of old-timers who have forgotten the fruitful excesses of their youth as if it were impossible to find another destiny than to live at the mercy of the two great masters of the world. This, my friends, is the very scale of our solitude.

In spite of this, to oppression, plundering, and abandonment, we respond with life. Neither floods nor plagues, famines nor cataclysms, not even the eternal wars of century upon century have been able to subdue the persistent advantage of life over death. An advantage that grows and quickens: every year, there are seventy-four million more births than deaths, a sufficient number of new lives to multiply, each year, the population of New York sevenfold. Most of these births occur in the countries of least resources—including, of course, those of Latin America. Conversely, the most prosperous countries have succeeded in accumulating powers of destruction such as to annihilate, a hundred times over, not only all the human beings that have existed to this day, but also the totality of all living beings that have ever drawn breath on this planet of misfortune.

On a day like today, my master William Faulker said, "I decline to accept the end of man." I would feel unworthy of standing in this place that was his, if I were not fully aware that the colossal tragedy he refused to recognize thirty-two years ago is now, for the first time since the beginning of humanity, nothing more than a simple scientific possibility. Faced with this awesome reality that must have seemed a mere utopia through all of human time, we, the inventors of tales, who will believe anything, feel entitled to believe that it is not yet too late to engage in the creation of the opposite utopia. A new and sweeping utopia of life, where no one will be able to decide for others how they die, where love will prove true and happiness be possible, and where the races condemned to one hundred years of solitude will have, at last and forever, a second opportunity on earth.

STUDY QUESTIONS

1. What occurrences in Latin American history led García Márquez to conclude that the reality of Latin America was "unearthly," "outsized," and "unbridled"?
2. What is the source of "solitude" in Latin America?
3. According to García Márquez, in what ways should Europeans view Latin America?
4. Compare the cultural values expressed in this selection with the cultural values expressed in Sarmiento's "Civilization and Barbarism" in Chapter 32.
5. Just like the Latin Americans, sub-Saharan Africans also worry about identity issues. Why does the theme of defining identity echo in both African and Latin American civilizations? Is it in effect the same theme?

55

Latin America's Social Crisis in the Twentieth Century

Latin America is presently undergoing a social crisis of vast proportions. Population has increased dramatically during the twentieth century. For example, Mexico's population has increased from 13.6 million in 1900 to 94.3 million in 1997; Brazil's from 18 million to 163.7 million; and Peru's from 3 million to 24.4 million over the same period. Cities have grown disproportionately faster than rural areas, resulting in the appearance of mega-cities such as Mexico City with 20 million residents and São Paulo, Brazil with 15 million. Poverty, landlessness, and lack of jobs have driven the rural poor to the cities. But job creation in Latin America's industrial cities has not nearly kept pace with population growth. Industrial development has led to the expansion of an urban middle class, but these same zones attracted million of slum dwellers. They live a precarious, insecure life, surviving in the "informal economy." Many of the poor either pick up odd jobs day by day, or sell small items or beg. They have no security; no access to a system of social services. Although population growth rates have declined in the 1990s because of birth control campaigns, problems of poverty, insecurity, and sporadic bouts of despair persist. They are encountered both in the city and the countryside. The first selection describes the lives of struggling workers in the urban slum of Chorillos in Lima, Peru. The second is an oral history of a mother in the impoverished rural sugar-producing zone of Pernambuco in Northeastern Brazil.

LATIN AMERICAN STRUGGLES

I. CHORILLOS, LIMA, PERU, 1967

Jacinta Vegas "I come from the district of Piura in northern Peru, and I have lived in Lima for sixteen years, almost half my life. It is difficult living here, but I have got used to it and my children, after all, were born here. I have no money in Lima, but then I wouldn't have any money in Piura either.

Selection I from Sven Lindqvist, *The Shadow: Latin America Faces the Seventies,* translated by Keith Bradfield (Harmondworth, England: Penguin, 1972), pp. 19–22. Selection II from Nancy Scheper-Hughes, *Death Without Weeping: The Violence of Everyday Life in Brazil,* (Berkeley, University of California Press, 1992), pp. 348–351.

"The father of my eldest boy was a good-for-nothing, he denied paternity. But the boy bears my present man's name. We aren't married. We met here in Lima, but he is also from Piura.

"My eldest boy wants to be an engineer or doctor. He'll go to night school, he says. He is twelve years old now, and in the fifth grade. The eldest girl is five, and she goes to kindergarten for a dollar 20 cents a month. She gets food there and they look after her while I work. The two youngest I take with me.

"I work at the Regatta Club down by the beach. It's a very exclusive club. I clean the toilets and work as a cloakroom attendant, looking after people's cases and clothes while they bathe. I work for two days a week, and make two dollars a day. For three months during the summer I have work every day, and on top of that I get an annual bonus of twelve dollars. That's when I buy school things for the boy, he gets a big writing book with over 100 pages.

"We moved to this shed four years ago, and we own the site, it's a good shed, very solid, fresh bamboo mats in the walls. And two rooms! Everything looked fine, but two years ago I got a sore on my foot, and had to stay in bed for a month. Then my man fell sick, and was in bed for six months. And then the boy got appendicitis. The operation cost 120 dollars. We took the money we had saved to build a proper house, and borrowed the rest.

"Three months ago it happened. My man is a driver, he got mixed up in a traffic accident, hit someone in the dark and the police took his papers away. He was supposed to pay 200 dollars in damages, so he had to go underground. He ran away, and I haven't heard from him since. I have to manage on my own. We spend about twenty or forty cents a day. We eat porridge made from pea-meal or oatmeal. On Sundays, we eat porridge made with flour. Sometimes we manage rice and stewed vegetables. Never meat.

"I've never voted. I don't have a birth certificate. I went to the authorities, and asked for dispensation. It cost twelve dollars, I took my annual bonus and paid. But I got a paper that was no good, the signature was wrong and the stamp. My employer went back with me, and the man was sent to prison. But I never got my money back, and I still have no birth certificate. So I've never voted.

Rinaldo Rivas Loude   I work for Manufactura de Calzado [shoe factory] Glenny, España 211, Chorrillos. I'm the one who sews on the uppers. I get a dollar 30 per dozen and I do a dozen to a dozen and a half a day. I don't get more work than that until Christmas, then I get as much as I want and can work all round the clock.

"I support a wife and four children, and my two brothers, aged fifteen and eight, all with this machine. I had a bit of luck when I picked it up second-hand eight years ago. Then it cost 72 dollars. Today a new one would cost 480 dollars. I also work as guard for the Leasehold Association, which means that I can live in this house for two dollars a month. Of course, this means that one of us—my wife or I—must always be at home. But I sit here all day in any case, at the machine.

"There are fifteen guards here altogether. We have to sound the alarm if there is an invasion. Yes, you see, those who have leases here don't want other people to come and settle and build huts. Four years ago, this was one great rubbish heap. The Association, they say, paid 4,000 dollars to get the rubbish away, and in the end the members had to come and move it out themselves. Now everything has been cleaned up, and they don't want anyone else moving in.

"I was born in Lima, just near here in Barranco, in 1933. My parents rented a room in a *barriada* [slum town]. I started early as an apprentice, and I have worked for six years since my training ended.

"Better pay? Well, I could take an extra job. Or look for some other job. More than a dollar 30 per dozen? I never thought of it. No, I'm not a union member. It's just not worth it. The factory is owned by Juan García and Victor Glenny. They decide. There are ten of us working for them. The factory provides the leather, I buy my own thread, needles, whetstone and other bits and pieces. It makes a bit of a change to go into Lima on business.

"My eldest brother is in the *primaria,* in fifth grade. I think he can go on to the first or second year of the *secundaria.* I can't support him any longer than that, the secondary school is more expensive. Then he can start in the police school or join the army if he wants to go on studying. But my brothers are not big enough yet to understand what a burden they are to me.

"When did I last eat meat? On Sunday. We have meat on Sundays. Otherwise we have soups and porridge. The worst thing is that the children never get milk. The cinema? I get round to it every other week, I suppose. And every other week some friends come over, and we have a few drinks. Otherwise, I have the transistor here on the machine.

"Yes, I've voted. I voted for the present mayor. I believed in him, he grew up in a *barriada* himself. He has promised water, street lights, sewerage, pavements, everything. So far there's only lighting on the main road over there, it's still a long way to us. But he's got two years to do the job.

"Fidel? I've read the newspapers. He's done some good things. But here in Peru, well, we have Hugo Blanco [Peruvian revolutionary], of course, but I don't think he's the sort of man who could fight a guerrilla war in the hills, like they're doing in Bolivia.

"What I fear most is eviction. What I want most of all is a safe site, where no one can put us out, and a house of sun-dried brick. Also, of course, I can fall sick. I have no insurance, and the factory doesn't do anything for you if you are ill. It should, of course. I must try to find out a bit more about it."

The whole time we are talking, I can hear a whining sound as if from a dog that has been shut in. It comes from a little cubicle by the door. A small boy is lying there, in the rags of the family bed. Lying absolutely silent in the darkness, perfectly still, with fright in his eyes. The new baby is on the earthen floor, smeared with feces. Flies are crawling round his eyes. The whining is from him.

II. A MOTHER'S LIFE IN PERNAMBUCO, BRAZIL: BOM JESUS DE MATA, 1966

"I never learned to read or write, although Mama and Auntie tried to make me go to school. It was no use. I learned to sign my name, but not very well, because it is a complicated name and it has a lot of parts to it. When I was about five years old Mãe [mother] took me away from Tia [aunt] and gave me to another woman, a woman who lived next to us on the plantation. It was during this time that my aunt found a job as a maid in Recife, and she could take only one child with her. So we got divided up. Mama took Biu, Tia took Antonieta, and I stayed at Bela Vista with my godmother, Dona Graças.

"My *madrinha* was a real mother to me. Dona Graças raised me with care and great sacrifice. In those days food was scarce, and some days all we had to eat was the coarsest manioc flour, *farinha de roça*. I found it hard to swallow because of a sickness that injured my throat when I was a small baby. It made my godmother sad to see me getting skinny, so she begged a few spoonfuls of the finest whitest *farinha* every day from her *patroa* [female landowner] so that she could make me a smooth custard. When there was no other food, Madrinha would take an ear of hard Indian corn, and she would roast it and coax me into eating the dried kernels one by one. I was close to dying more than once, but my godmother fought with me to stay alive. And she won!

"When I was fifteen I married for the first time. I became the legitimate wife of Severino José da Silva. But it was a marriage that wasn't worth much, and it soon fell apart. We lived in a tiny room built onto the side of Tia's house on the Alto do Cruzeiro, so small you could only lie down in it. Severino was miserable the whole time we were together. He never wanted to marry me; it was Mama and Auntie who forced him into it. In those days when a boy ruined a virgin, he was made to marry the girl, and if he refused, the judge could put him behind bars. So when it happened like that to me, Mãe and Tia went to the judge and made a formal complaint against Severino. When he heard what my family was up to, he ran away. But a boy of fifteen doesn't have too many places to hide, and within a week he was back on the Alto staying with friends. José Leiteiro, the old *pai dos santos* (Xangô master), spotted Severino, and he ran down the path, grabbed him, and tied him up good. Then José called Mãe and Tia, and the three of them carried Severino to the judge. Severino refused to have me, and so the judge locked him up. Severino stayed in jail for two weeks until he gave in. When they let him out, I was standing right there in my best dress, and they married us on the spot with two police for witnesses. It was a real *casamento matuto,* a shotgun wedding!

"Even though we didn't have a good start to our marriage, I was determined to make it turn out all right. I worked myself sick. I did everything I could to put food on the table, but all Severino did was lie around and mope. He was lovesick, but not for his bride! You see, all along Severino had promised himself to another woman, and during the time that he was living with me, he was always thinking about *her*. That's why he had put up such a fight not to marry me. Finally, he left me to live with his other woman. By then I was almost glad to be rid of him.

"Well, once Severino was gone, I had to figure out what to do. First I lived with Mãe, then Auntie, and then with our neighbor Beatrice. Bea found me a live-in job as an assistant to a shoemaker and his wife in town. I lived with them for two years, and then I outgrew it. So I left to work outside of town in a ceramic factory, and that's where I met my second husband, Nelson. Nelson's job was firing roof tiles, and he was very skilled at this. I can't really say that Nelson was my 'husband,' though, because I was still legally married to Severino. And I can't even say that we 'lived together' because Nelson was very attached to his old grandmother, and he never stopped living with her the whole time we were together.

"At first Nelson was good to me. Every Saturday he would climb the Alto to visit, and he always brought a basket of groceries for the week. He never once came empty-handed. And so everyone really thought of him as my husband. But after I got pregnant, everything changed. Nelson began to abuse me. It looked like I was going to follow in my mother's footsteps. I was actually glad that my firstborn died right away. Things got better for a little bit, and then I was pregnant again. After Zezinho was born, things went from bad to worse. I was living in a hovel without even a roof over my head. It was worse than living in an outhouse. Virgin Mary, goats on the Alto lived better than me! But I clung to Nelson thinking he would change. I had it in my head that he mistreated me only because he was so young and still very attached to his grandmother. But finally I began to see that Nelson was abusing me for the fun of it. It was a kind of sport. He wanted to keep making me pregnant just so he could threaten to leave me again and again. I was young and emotional and so I cried a lot, but once I saw what he was up to, I got stronger, and I put him out for good.

"That was all well and good, but there I was still living in my stick house with my stick baby, Zezinho. What a mess, and I was only eighteen years old! I was my mother's daughter for sure. That's when I decided to go to Ferreiras to find work picking vegetables. I spent three months working in the tomato fields, and that's where I met Milton, my third husband, the one you liked so well and whose tongue was so tied up in his mouth that no one could understand him. They put us working together on the same *quadro,* and he looked over at me, and I looked over at him, and before long nature had its way. I was too afraid to say anything when I got pregnant again because Mama and Tia were losing patience with me. So I tried to hide it, and I never told anyone at all about Milton.

"I was low and dispirited during this time. It was the only time in my life that I didn't have energy for anything. I didn't have any interest in Zezinho, and I never did anything to prepare for the birth of Wagner. That's how it happened that I had to call on you at the last minute to cut the cord. I didn't care about anything. I *wanted* that baby to die and Zezinho, too. But it turned out to be a pretty baby. Still, they were the cause of my misery! I was so unhappy that I didn't pay any attention when you took Zé away to raise him in the creche. You could have taken him and never brought him back, for all it mattered to me then. *Oxente* [expression of surprise], and today that boy is my arms and legs, more than a husband, better than any husband could ever be!

"After Wagner was born there was no reason to hide what was going on. So finally Milton came to visit, carrying a big sack of fresh corn on his head to give as a present to Mãe. He told both Mãe and Tia that he was responsible for the baby. And that's how he became my third husband. Well, with Milton I finally had some luck. It worked out, and I wound up living with him for fourteen years. I was pregnant ten more times with him. I had three miscarriages and seven live births, and of those I managed to raise four. So we didn't do badly. The three of his that died all died quickly. The first one died in his hammock while I was away working. One of the older children killed him. He got too close and yelled in his ear. He just frightened that baby to death. He died of *susto* [fright] in less than a day, and I didn't suffer very much. The other two were weak and sickly from birth. They had no 'knack' for life. The other four came into the world ready to confront [*enfrentar*] hardship and suffering, and so naturally they lived.

"Although things were going along well enough with Milton, I took a fancy to leave him and take up with Seu Jaime, the old widower I live with now. What can I say? First you love one, and then another one comes along, and your heart goes out to him. Isn't it Jesus that made us this way? Didn't he put these feelings into our hearts? If it is wrong, then we will be punished. That I know. Milton accepted it without much of a fuss. He went back to live in the *mata*, [woods] and people say that he has found himself another wife on the Engenho Votas and that he has a new family already. I'll say one thing about Milton: he has never forgotten his own children, and he always sends us produce from his *roçado* [garden plot].

"I have been living with my old man for almost four years now, and it hasn't been easy. Because of our sin, violence entered our lives. The first real trouble came from Jaime's side. A group of his first wife's relatives stoned him one night as he was coming home from work. They left him bleeding and unconscious on the sidewalk. 'My poor old man,' I said, 'what have they done to you all because of me?' How was it their business anyway? Jaime's first wife was dead, and he was free to do what he wanted with the rest of his life, even throw it away on a woman such as me! Jaime's old in-laws were Protestants, and they didn't want to see their family tainted by association with the likes of me. By bringing Seu Jaime down, I was bringing shame on them as well.

"Seu Jaime was so injured that he couldn't go back to work for a long time. I thought that we might have to move back to a shanty on the Alto. But then as luck would have it, my first husband, Severino, died suddenly, and as I was still his legal wife and not the other woman he'd lived with all these years, I was entitled to the widow's pension. So in the end it paid off, and Severino's pension brought a little bit of comfort into our lives. Now I hope that we are entering a period of calm and tranquility and that God has finally forgiven us."

STUDY QUESTIONS

1. What was the slum dweller's relationship to the state?
2. What types of events produced insecurity?
3. What was the purpose of the Leasehold Association? What was the attitude of the Leasehold Association toward people outside its area?
4. Describe the political attitudes of the poor in Chorillos. What did they expect from politicians?
5. What were the mother's attitudes toward marriage, childbearing, and death of children in Bom Jesus da Mata?
6. Identify the coping mechanisms of the poor. What do these mechanisms suggest about the political culture of the poor?

56

African Nationalism

Nationalism was one of the crucial, though unintended, products of European imperialism. Local leaders—particularly aspiring newcomers often exposed to European education—saw the importance of nationalism in Western society and used it as a vehicle for protesting colonial controls and demanding independence. Nationalism could also be mobilized to elicit loyalty to a newly free state, especially when appeals to tradition could not suffice because the nation combined different cultural groups. Thus nationalism had the merit of appealing both to past values and to the idea of progress, although the combination could sometimes be uncomfortable.

Nationalism began to blossom in Africa between the world wars. It had several facets, as indicated in the three selections that follow. One nationalist source stemmed from black leaders in the United States and West Indies sincerely concerned about Africa but also eager for the liberation of their own people. Marcus Garvey's black nationalist movement won loyalty on both sides of the Atlantic in the 1920s and helped define a positive African spirit. Jomo Kenyatta, a British-educated Kenyan—ultimately the first president of Kenya after many jail terms as a nationalist agitator under the colonial government—represents African nationalism directly. Writing in 1938, Kenyatta used traditional kinds of allegory to blast European greed and also defined a special African agenda of combining tradition with change plus very selective borrowing from the West.

The final selection is postcolonial and invites comparison with the earlier nationalist expression: How was nationalism maintained once independence had been achieved, and what changes resulted in tone and purpose? Written by Kwame Nkrumah, an American-educated leader and the first president of Ghana, this nationalist statement reflects a turn

Selection I from Marcus Garvey, "Redeeming the African Motherland," in *Philosophy and Opinions of Marcus Garvey*, Vol. 1, edited by Amy Jacques Garvey (New York: University Publishing House, 1923), pp. 71–74. Reprinted with the permission of Scribner, a division of Simon & Schuster Inc. Copyright 1923, 1925 by Amy Jacques-Garvey. Selection II from Jomo Kenyatta, *Facing Mt. Kenya* (New York: Random House, Inc., 1962). Copyright © 1962 by Random House, Inc. Reprinted by permission. Selection III from Kwame Nkrumah, *Revolutionary Path* (London: Panaf Books Limited, 1973). Copyright © 1973 Panaf Books Limited. Reprinted by permission of Zed Books Ltd.

away from Africa-in-general to a specific new nation. It also shows some shifts in goals. Once independence was achieved, what targets did African nationalists have? Nkrumah's own career illustrates some of the nationalist dilemma. A brilliant agitator, he proved less successful in running an independent Ghana. The economic problems he defined as next on the nationalist agenda proved more elusive than earlier goals of independence. Yet nationalism remained a factor in Africa, a guide to policy and a popular rallying point in the new nations. These three selections, from different decades as well as different inspirations, give a flavor of African nationalism and some indication of its power. They also permit comparison of African with Indian or Arab nationalism. Is nationalism always the same movement?

AFRICAN NATIONALISM DOCUMENTS

I. MARCUS GARVEY PREACHES AFRICAN REVOLUTION

George Washington was not God Almighty. He was a man like any Negro in this building, and if he and his associates were able to make a free America, we too can make a free Africa. Hampden, Gladstone, Pitt and Disraeli were not the representatives of God in the person of Jesus Christ. They were but men, but in their time they worked for the expansion of the British Empire, and today they boast of a British Empire upon which "the sun never sets." As Pitt and Gladstone were able to work for the expansion of the British Empire, so you and I can work for the expansion of a great African Empire. Voltaire and Mirabeau were not Jesus Christs, they were but men like ourselves. They worked and overturned the French Monarchy. They worked for the Democracy which France now enjoys, and if they were able to do that, we are able to work for a democracy in Africa. Lenin and Trotsky were not Jesus Christs, but they were able to overthrow the despotism of Russia, and today they have given to the world a Social Republic, the first of its kind. If Lenin and Trotsky were able to do that for Russia, you and I can do that for Africa. Therefore, let not man, let no power on earth, turn you from this sacred cause of liberty. I prefer to die at this moment rather than not to work for the freedom of Africa. If liberty is good for certain sets of humanity it is good for all. Black men, Colored men, Negroes have as much right to be free as any other race that God Almighty ever created, and we desire freedom that is unfettered, freedom that is unlimited, freedom that will give us a chance and opportunity to rise to the fullest of our ambition and that we cannot get in countries where other men rule and dominate.

We have reached the time when every minute, every second must count for something done, something achieved in the cause of Africa. We need the freedom of Africa now, therefore, we desire the kind of leadership that will give it to us as quickly as possible. You will realize that not only individuals, but governments are using their influence against us. But what do we care about the unrighteous influence of any government? Our cause is based upon righteousness. And anything that is not righteous we have no respect for, because God Almighty is our leader and Jesus Christ our standard bearer. We rely on them for that kind of leadership that will make us free, for it is the same God who inspired the Psalmist to write "Princes shall come out of Egypt and Ethiopia shall stretch out her hands unto God." At this moment methinks I see Ethiopia stretching forth her hands unto God and methinks I see the Angel of God taking up the standard of the Red, the Black and the Green, and saying "Men of the Negro Race, Men of Ethiopia, follow me." Tonight we are following. We are following 400,000,000 strong. We are following with a determination that we must be free before the wreck of matter, before the crash of worlds.

It falls to our lot to tear off the shackles that bind Mother Africa. Can you do it? You did it in the Revolutionary War. You did it in the Civil War; You did it at the Battles of the Marne and Verdun; You did it in Mesopotamia. You can do it marching up the battle heights of Africa. Let the world know that 400,000,000 Negroes are prepared to die or live as free men. Despise us as much as you care. Ignore us as much as you care. We are coming 400,000,000 strong. We are coming with our woes behind us, with the memory of suffering behind us—woes and suffering of three hundred years—they shall be our inspiration. My bulwark of strength in the conflict of freedom in Africa, will be the three hundred years of persecution and hardship left behind in this Western Hemisphere. The more I remember the suffering of my fore-fathers, the more I remember the lynchings and burnings in the Southern States of America, the more I will fight on even though the battle seems doubtful. Tell me that I must turn back, and I laugh you to scorn. Go on! Go on! Climb ye the heights of liberty and cease not in well doing until you have planted the banner of the Red, the Black and the Green on the hilltops of Africa.

II. JOMO KENYATTA DEFINES AMERICAN NATIONALISM

Once upon a time an elephant made a friendship with a man. One day a heavy thunderstorm broke out, the elephant went to his friend, who had a little hut at the edge of the forest, and said to him: "My dear good man, will you please let me put my trunk inside your hut to keep it out of this torrential rain?" The man, seeing what situation his friend was in, replied: "My dear good elephant, my hut is very small, but there is room for your trunk and myself. Please put your trunk in gently." The elephant thanked his friend, saying: "You have done me a good deed and one day I shall return your kindness." But what followed? As soon as the elephant put his trunk inside the hut, slowly he pushed his head inside, and finally flung the man out in the rain, and then lay down comfortably inside his friend's hut, saying: "My dear good friend, your skin is harder than mine, and as there is not enough room for both of us, you can afford to remain in the rain while I am protecting my delicate skin from the hailstorm."

The man, seeing what his friend had done to him, started to grumble; the animals in the nearby forest heard the noise and came to see what was the matter. All stood around listening to the heated argument between the man and his friend the elephant. In this turmoil the lion came along roaring, and said in a loud voice: "Don't you know that I am the King of the Jungle! How dare anyone disturb the peace of my kingdom?" On hearing this the elephant, who was one of the high ministers in the jungle kingdom, replied in a soothing voice, and said: "My Lord, there is no disturbance of the peace in your kingdom. I have only been having a little discussion with my friend here as to the possession of this little hut which your lordship sees me occupying." The lion, who wanted to have "peace and tranquillity" in his kingdom, replied in a noble voice, saying: "I command my ministers to appoint a Commission of Enquiry to go thoroughly into this matter and report accordingly." He then turned to the man and said: "You have done well by establishing friendship with my people, especially with the elephant who is one of my honourable ministers of state. Do not grumble any more, your hut is not lost to you. Wait until the sitting of my Imperial Commission, and there you will be given plenty of opportunity to state your case. I am sure that you will be pleased with the findings of the Commission." The man was very pleased by these sweet words from the King of the Jungle, and innocently waited for his opportunity, in the belief that naturally the hut would be returned to him.

The elephant, obeying the command of his master, got busy with other ministers to appoint the Commission of Enquiry. The following elders of the jungle were appointed to sit in the Commission: (1) Mr. Rhinoceros; (2) Mr. Buffalo; (3) Mr. Alligator; (4) The Rt. Hon. [Right Honorable] Mr. Fox to act as chairman; and (5) Mr. Leopard to act as Secretary to the Commission. On seeing the personnel, the man protested and asked if it was not necessary to include in this Commission a member from his side. But he was told that it was impossible, since no one from his side was well enough educated to understand the intricacy of jungle law. Further, that there was nothing to fear, for the members of the Commission were all men of repute for their impartiality in justice, and as they were gentlemen chosen by God to look after the interest of races less adequately endowed with teeth and claws, he might rest assured that they would investigate the matter with the greatest care and report impartially. . . .

Then the man decided that he must adopt an effective method of protection, since Commissions of Enquiry did not seem to be of any use to him. He sat down and said: "Ng'enda thi ndeagaga motegi," which literally means, "there is nothing that treads on the earth that cannot be trapped," or in other words, you can fool people for a time, but not forever.

Early one morning, when the huts already occupied by the jungle lords were all beginning to decay and fall to pieces, he went out and built a bigger and better hut a little distance away. No sooner had Mr. Rhinoceros seen it than he came rushing in, only to find that Mr. Elephant was already inside, sound asleep. Mr. Leopard next came in at the window, Mr. Lion, Mr. Fox, and Mr. Buffalo entered the doors, while Mr. Hyena howled for a place in the shade and Mr. Alligator basked on the roof. Presently they all began disputing about their rights of penetration, and from disputing they came to fighting, and while they were embroiled together the man set the hut on fire and burnt it to the ground, jungle lords and all. Then he went home, saying "Peace is costly, but it's worth the expense," and lived happily ever after. . . .

There certainly are some progressive ideas among the Europeans. They include the ideas of material prosperity, of medicine, and hygiene, and literacy which enables people to take part in world culture. But so far the Europeans who visit Africa have not been conspicuously zealous in imparting these parts of their inheritance to the Africans, and seem to think that the only way to do it is by police discipline and armed force. They speak as if it was somehow beneficial to an African to work for them instead of for himself, and to make sure that he will receive this benefit they do their best to take away his land and leave him with no alternative. Along with his land they rob him of his government, condemn his religious ideas, and ignore his fundamental conceptions of justice and morals, all in the name of civilisation and progress.

If Africans were left in peace on their own lands, Europeans would have to offer them the benefits of white civilisation in real earnest before they could obtain
the African labour which they want so much. They would have to offer the African a
way of life which was really superior to the one his fathers lived before him, and a
share in the prosperity given them by their command of science. They would have to
let the African choose what parts of European culture could be beneficially transplanted, and how they could be adapted. He would probably not choose the gas
bomb or the armed police force, but he might ask for some other things of which he
does not get so much today. As it is, by driving him off his ancestral lands, the Europeans have robbed him of the material foundations of his culture, and reduced him
to a state of serfdom incompatible with human happiness. The African is condi-
tioned, by the cultural and social institutions of centuries, to a freedom of which Europe has little conception, and it is not in his nature to accept serfdom for ever. He
realises that he must fight unceasingly for his own complete emancipation; for without this he is doomed to remain the prey of rival imperialisms, which in every successive year will drive their fangs more deeply into his vitality and strength.

III. ECONOMIC NATIONALISM: KWAME NKRUMAH

Organization presupposes planning, and planning demands a programme for its
basis. The Government proposes to launch a Seven-Year Development Plan in January, 1963. The Party, therefore, has a pressing obligation to provide a programme
upon which this plan could be formulated.

We must develop Ghana economically, socially, culturally, spiritually, educa-
tionally, technologically and otherwise, and produce it as a finished product of a
fully integrated life, both exemplary and inspiring.

This programme, which we call a programme for "Work and Happiness," has
been drawn up in regard to all our circumstances and conditions, our hopes and
aspirations, our advantages and disadvantages and our opportunities or lack of
them. Indeed, the programme is drawn up with an eye on reality and provides the
building ground for our immediate scientific, technical and industrial progress.

We have embarked upon an intensive socialist reconstruction of our country.
Ghana inherited a colonial economy and similar disabilities in most other directions. We cannot rest content until we have demolished this miserable structure
and raised in its place an edifice of economic stability, thus creating for ourselves a
veritable paradise of abundance and satisfaction. Despite the ideological bankruptcy and moral collapse of a civilization in despair, we must go forward with our
preparations for planned economic growth to supplant the poverty, ignorance, disease, illiteracy and degradation left in their wake by discredited colonialism and decaying imperialism.

In the programme which I am today introducing to the country through this
broadcast, the Party has put forward many proposals. I want all of you to get copies
of this programme, to read and discuss it and to send us any observations or suggestions you may have about it.

Tomorrow, the National Executive Committee of the Party will meet to discuss the Party programme and officially present it to the nation. I feel sure that it

will decide in favour of an immediate release of this programme to the people. The Party, however, will take no action on the programme until the masses of the people have had the fullest opportunity of reviewing it.

This programme for "Work and Happiness" is an expression of the evidence of the nation's creative ability, the certainty of the correctness of our Party line and action and the greatest single piece of testimony [to] our national confidence in the future.

Ghana is our country which we must all help to build. This programme gives us the opportunity to make our contributions towards the fulfillment of our national purposes.

As I look at the content of the programme and the matters it covers, such as Tax Reform, Animal Husbandry and Poultry Production, Forest Husbandry, Industrialization, Handicrafts, Banking and Insurance, Foreign Enterprise, Culture and Leisure, I am convinced beyond all doubt that Ghana and Ghanians will travel full steam ahead, conscious of their great responsibilities and fully aware that the materialization of this bright picture of the future is entirely dependent on their active and energetic industry. Remember that it is at the moment merely a draft programme and only your approval will finalize it.

At this present moment, all over Africa, dark clouds of neocolonialism are fast gathering. African States are becoming debtor-nations and client States day in and day out, owing to their adoption of unreal attitudes to world problems, saying "no" when they should have said "yes," and "yes" when they should have said "no." They are seeking economic shelter under colonialist wings, instead of accepting the truth—that their survival lies in the political unification of Africa.

Countrymen, we must draw up a programme of action and later plan details of this programme for the benefit of the whole people. Such a programme is the one that the Party now brings to you, the people of Ghana, in the hope that you will approve it critically and help to make it a success.

We have a rich heritage. Our natural resources are abundant and varied. We have mineral and agricultural wealth and, above all, we have the will to find the means whereby these possessions can be put to the greatest use and advantage. The Party's programme for work and happiness is a pointer to the way ahead, the way leading to a healthier, happier and more prosperous life for us all. When you have examined and accepted this programme, the Government and the people will base on it and initiate our Seven-Year Development Plan, which will guide our action to prosperity.

STUDY QUESTIONS

1. What are Marcus Garvey's goals for Africa? How does he justify them? Does he identify crucial African values? Does he suggest what Africa will be once it is free?
2. How does Kenyatta describe European imperialism—and is it a fair characterization (see Chapters 33 and 35)? What does he see as the goals of African nationalism? What methods does he suggest?
3. What is Kenyatta's attitude to Western achievements? What aspects of African tradition does he seek to protect or restore?

4. How do Nkrumah's concerns as a nationalist compare with those of preindependence leaders like Kenyatta? What problems is he referring to under the heading of neocolonialism? What are his main solutions? Do they fit under the heading of nationalism?

5. What are the similarities and differences between African and Turkish nationalism? (See Chapter 44.) Between African and Gandhi's Indian nationalism? (See Chapter 51.)

57

Changes in African Culture and Society

New forces continued to have an impact on the traditional culture of sub-Saharan Africa throughout the twentieth century. Conversions both to Islam and to Christianity gained ground, although a polytheist minority remained. Whereas in 1900 80 percent of all sub-Saharan Africans adhered to traditional religions, by 1990 80 percent were either Muslim or Christian. Conversion brought more than new beliefs about the deity; it also attacked family traditions (such as polygamy, for Christians) and traditional ideas of harmony with nature. Some African conservatives blamed the new religions for Africans' willingness to attack animals and forests with a new vigor that threatened ecological balance, for the monotheistic religions held humans to be above nature. Education spread, and with it not only literacy but, often, knowledge of a European language—another force for change.

The selections that follow deal with missionary activity, urbanization, and changes in family roles as sources of change and tension in twentieth-century African society. European missionary activity, both Catholic and Protestant, increased rapidly from 1890 onward, as various Western teachers and medical personnel worked hard to modify or undermine traditional African religious values, property concepts, and family practices. African reactions to missionary efforts ranged from stark rejection to a combination effort to outright acceptance. (It is important to remember that Islam was also spreading rapidly in the nineteenth and twentieth centuries; Christians were not the only missionaries, and Muslims might be preferred precisely because they were not European.)

Urban growth was another framework for cultural change. African cities, once small, grew rapidly both under colonial administration and with independence. About a quarter of all sub-Saharan Africans lived in cities by the 1970s, and the rate increases steadily. Urban Africans, though often poor, were more often educated than their rural

Selection I from Chinua Achebe, *Things Fall Apart* (London: William Heinemann Ltd., 1959), pp. 138–141, 162, 163, 166–167, 186–188. Copyright © 1959 by Chinua Achebe. Reprinted by permission of William Heinemann Limited. Selection II from Chinua Achebe, *No Longer at Ease* (London: William Heinemann, Ltd., 1960), pp. 19–22, 149–150. Copyright © 1960 by Chinua Achebe. Reprinted by permission of William Heinemann Limited. Selection III from Perdita Huston, *Third World Women Speak out* (New York: Praeger Publishers, 1979), pp. 21, 22–23, 42–43. Copyright © 1979 by Praeger Publishers. Reprinted by permission. Selection IV from Ifi Amadiume, *Male Daughters, Female Husbands: Gender and Sex in an African Society* (London: Zed Books, 1987), pp. 3–4, 15, 89–90, 91, 132, 141. Reprinted by permission of the publisher.

counterparts, and they enjoyed the excitement of city life. But they were also confusingly torn from traditional community customs.

The selections in this chapter are divided into two parts: the first two selections deal with successive waves of cultural change affecting parts of Nigeria; they are drawn from the work of a perceptive Nigerian novelist who chronicled what he saw as major and in some ways tragic cultural disruption. The third and fourth selections involve reactions of African women, drawn to change themselves but with various specific qualifications and hesitations.

The first selection, by Chinua Achebe, reflects deep awareness of the complex balance of gain and loss brought by changes away from tradition. Discussing British missionary activity around 1900, Achebe conveys the different types of Africans and different kinds of motives involved in at least partial religious conversion, and at the same time the reasons for resistance (and its failure). The selection is fictional and written after the fact, but it conveys ongoing intellectual issues in Africa. The passage ends with a resistance meeting, centered on the strong traditionalist figure of Okonkwo (whose son had converted) and the arrival and death of a messenger sent by the British colonial administration to prevent disorder.

The second selection comes from another Achebe novel, this one involving Okonkwo's grandson, now an urbanite, after World War II but before independence. Obi Okonkwo is the first village member to receive higher education in British-run schools. He goes to Lagos, the growing Nigerian capital, to take a civil-service job. He finds the glitter of city life there, but also a consumerist culture and a pleasure-seeking sexual ethic both influenced by Western standards. These at first shock and then beguile him so that he cannot respond to village customs in the old way, for example, to a tragedy such as his mother's death. The combination of stimulation and confusion gives this Achebe novel its title, *No Longer at Ease.*

The third selection focuses less on confusion, more on new aspirations and opportunities. Many African women found new roles as they moved to cities and gained education. Even rural women had new power when their men left to take urban jobs; willy-nilly, they had to run their families and often support themselves. Thus African family bonds, which once gave women security while holding them subordinate, loosened rapidly. The passages come from a series of interviews done by a Western anthropologist with women in Kenya, including one group organized in a cooperative to try to compensate for new uncertainties about family ties and support from men.

Cultural change, including some expressions striking for their resemblance to modern Western movements such as feminism, is clearly a major factor in contemporary Africa. In the fourth selection, the African feminist Ifi Amadiume discusses gender relations between African men and women, although in terms that challenge Western feminism as well as current African realities.

All these cultural changes and reactions express Africa's growing international contacts, but also new uncertainties as older institutions unravel. As in the West in previous periods, greater individualism can be both exhilarating and damaging. Africans themselves disagree over whether new opportunity or the erosion of vital traditions should receive the main emphasis. Not surprisingly, important traditional emphases, such as family solidarity, persist as well, as Africans create their own cultural amalgams.

AFRICAN VOICES

I. THINGS FALL APART

The missionaries spent their first four or five nights in the marketplace, and went into the village in the morning to preach the gospel. They asked me who the king of the village was, but the villagers told them that there was no king. "We have men of high title and the chief priests and the elders," they said.

It was not very easy getting the men of high title and the elders together after the excitement of the first day. But the missionaries persevered, and in the end they were received by the rulers of Mbanta. They asked for a plot of land to build their church.

Every clan and village had its "evil forest." In it were buried all those who died of the really evil diseases, like leprosy and smallpox. It was also the dumping ground for the potent fetishes of great medicine men when they died. An "evil forest" was, therefore, alive with sinister forces and powers of darkness. It was such a forest that the rulers of Mbanta gave to the missionaries. They did not really want them in their clan, and so they made them that offer which nobody in his right senses would accept.

"They want a piece of land to build their shrine," said Uchendu to his peers when they consulted among themselves. "We shall give them a piece of land." He paused, and there was a murmur of surprise and disagreement. "Let us give them a portion of the Evil Forest. They boast about victory over death. Let us give them a real battlefield in which to show their victory." They laughed and agreed, and sent for the missionaries, whom they had asked to leave them for a while so that they might "whisper together." They offered them as much [of] the Evil Forest as they cared to take. And to their greatest amazement the missionaries thanked them and burst into song.

"They do not understand," said some of the elders. "But they will understand when they go to their plot of land tomorrow morning." And they dispersed.

The next morning the crazy men actually began to clear a part of the forest and to build their house. The inhabitants of Mbanta expected them all to be dead within four days. The first day passed and the second and third and fourth, and none of them died. Everyone was puzzled. And then it became known that the white man's fetish had unbelievable power. It was said that he wore glasses on his eyes so that he could see and talk to evil spirits. Not long after, he won his first three converts.

Although Nwoye had been attracted to the new faith from the very first day, he kept it secret. He dared not go too near the missionaries for fear of his father. But whenever they came to preach in the open marketplace or the village playground, Nwoye was there. And he was already beginning to know some of the simple stories they told.

"We have now built a church," said Mr. Kiaga, the interpreter, who was now in charge of the infant congregation. The white man had gone back to Umuofia, where he built his headquarters and from where he paid regular visits to Mr. Kiaga's congregation at Mbanta.

"We have now built a church," said Mr. Kiaga, "and we want you all to come in every seventh day to worship the true God."

On the following Sunday, Nwoye passed and repassed the little red-earth and thatch building without summoning enough courage to enter. He heard the voice of singing and although it came from a handful of men it was loud and confident. Their church stood on a circular clearing that looked like the open mouth of the Evil Forest. Was it waiting to snap its teeth together? After passing and re-passing by the church, Nwoye returned home.

It was well known among the people of Mbanta that their gods and ancestors were sometimes long-suffering and would deliberately allow a man to go on defying them. But even in such cases they set their limit at seven market weeks or twenty-eight days. Beyond that limit no man was suffered to go. And so excitement mounted in the village as the seventh week approached since the impudent missionaries built their church in the Evil Forest. The villagers were so certain about the doom that awaited these men that one or two converts thought it wise to suspend their allegiance to the new faith.

At last the day came by which all the missionaries should have died. But they were still alive, building a new red-earth and thatch house for their teacher, Mr. Kiaga. That week they won a handful more converts. And for the first time they had a woman. Her name was Nneka, the wife of Amadi, who was a prosperous farmer. She was very heavy with child.

Nneka had had four previous pregnancies and childbirths. But each time she had borne twins, and they had been immediately thrown away. Her husband and his family were already becoming highly critical of such a woman and were not unduly perturbed when they found she had fled to join the Christians. It was a good riddance. . . .

"Does the white man understand our custom about land?"

"How can he when he does not even speak our tongue? But he says that our customs are bad; and our own brothers who have taken up his religion also say that our customs are bad. How do you think we can fight when our own brothers have turned against us? The white man is very clever. He came quietly and peaceably with his religion. We were amused at his foolishness and allowed him to stay. Now he has won our brothers, and our clan can no longer act like one. He has put a knife on the things that held us together and we have fallen apart." . . .

There were many men and women in Umuofia who did not feel as strongly as Okonkwo about the new dispensation. The white man had indeed brought a lunatic religion, but he had also built a trading store and for the first time palm-oil and kernel became things of great price, and much money flowed into Umuofia. . . .

Mr. Brown [the missionary to the Ibo village] learned a good deal about the religion of the clan and he came to the conclusion that a frontal attack on it would not succeed. And so he built a school and a little hospital in Umuofia. He went from family to family begging people to send their children to his school. But at first they only sent their slaves or sometimes their lazy children. Mr. Brown begged and argued and prophesied. He said that the leaders of the land in the future would be men and women who had learned to read and write. If Umuofia failed to send her children to the school, strangers would come from other places to rule them. They could already see that happening in the Native Court, where the D.C. [District Commision] was surrounded by strangers who spoke his tongue. Most of these strangers came from the distant town of Umuru on the bank of the Great River where the white man first went.

In the end Mr. Brown's arguments began to have an effect. More people came to learn in his school, and he encouraged them with gifts of singlets and towels. They were not all young, these people who came to learn. Some of them were thirty years old or more. They worked on their farms in the morning and went to school in the afternoon. And it was not long before the people began to say that the white man's medicine was quick in working. Mr. Brown's school produced quick results. A few months in it were enough to make one a court messenger or even a court clerk. Those who stayed longer became teachers; and from Umuofia laborers went forth into the Lord's vineyard. New churches were established in the surrounding villages and a few schools with them. From the very beginning religion and education went hand in hand. . . .

"You all know why we are here, when we ought to be building our barns or mending our huts, when we should be putting our compounds in order. My father used to say to me: 'Whenever you see a toad jumping in broad daylight, then you know that something is after its life.' When I saw you all pouring into this meeting from all the quarters of our clan so early in the morning, I knew that something was after our life." He paused for a brief moment and then began again:

"All our gods are weeping. Idemili is weeping, Ogwugwu is weeping, Agbala is weeping, and all the others. Our dead fathers are weeping because of the shameful sacrilege they are suffering and the abomination we have all seen with our eyes." He stopped again to steady his trembling voice.

"This is a great gathering. No clan can boast of greater numbers or greater valor. But are we all here? I ask you: Are all the sons of Umuofia with us here?" A deep murmur swept through the crowd.

"They are not," he said "They have broken the clan and gone their several ways. We who are here this morning have remained true to our fathers, but our brothers have deserted us and joined a stranger to soil their fatherland. If we fight the stranger we shall hit our brothers and perhaps shed the blood of a clansman. But we must do it. Our fathers never dreamed of such a thing, they never killed their brothers. But a white man never came to them. So we must do what our fathers would never have done. Eneke the bird was asked why he was always on the wing and he replied: 'Men have learned to shoot without missing their mark and I have learned to fly without perching on a twig.' We must root out this evil. And if our brothers take the side of evil we must root them out too. And we must do it *now*. We must bale this water now that it is only ankle-deep. . . ."

At this point there was a sudden stir in the crowd and every eye was turned in one direction. There was a sharp bend in the road that led from the marketplace to the white man's court, and to the stream beyond it. And so no one had seen the approach of the five court messengers until they had come round the bend, a few paces from the edge of the crowd. Okonkwo was sitting at the edge. . . .

"What do you want here?"

"The white man whose power you know too well has ordered this meeting to stop."

In a flash Okonkwo drew his machete. The messenger crouched to avoid the blow. It was useless. Okonkwo's machete descended twice and the man's head lay beside his uniformed body.

The waiting backcloth jumped into tumultuous life and the meeting was stopped. Okonkwo stood looking at the dead man. He knew that Umuofia would not go to war. He knew because they had let the other messengers escape. They had broken into tumult instead of action. He discerned fright in that tumult. He heard voices asking: "Why did he do it?"

He wiped his machete on the sand and went away.

II. NO LONGER AT EASE

As a boy in the village of Umuofia he had heard his first stories about Lagos from a soldier home on leave from the war. Those soldiers were heroes who had seen the great world. They spoke of Abyssinia, Egypt, Palestine, Burma and so on. Some of them had been village ne'er-do-wells, but now they were heroes. They had bags and bags of money, and the villagers sat at their feet to listen to their stories. One of them went regularly to a market in the neighboring village and helped himself to whatever he liked. He went in full uniform, breaking the earth with his boots, and no one dared touch him. It was said that if you touched a soldier, Government would deal with you. Besides, soldiers were as strong as lions because of the injections they were given in the army. It was from one of these soldiers that Obi had his first picture of Lagos.

"There is no darkness there," he told his admiring listeners, "because at night the electric shines like the sun, and people are always walking about, that is, those who want to walk. If you don't want to walk you only have to wave your hand and a pleasure car stops for you." His audience made sounds of wonderment. Then by way of digression he said: "If you see a white man, take off your hat for him. The only thing he cannot do is mold a human being."

For many years afterwards, Lagos was always associated with electric lights and motorcars in Obi's mind. Even after he had at last visited the city and spent a few days there before flying to the United Kingdom his views did not change very much. Of course, he did not really see much of Lagos then. His mind was, as it were, on higher things. He spent the few days with his "countryman," Joseph Okeke, a clerk in the Survey Department. Obi and Joseph had been classmates at the Umuofia C.M.S. Central School. But Joseph had not gone on to a secondary school because he was too old and his parents were poor. He had joined the Education Corps of the 82nd Division and, when the war ended, the clerical service of the Nigerian Government.

Joseph was at Lagos Motor Park to meet his lucky friend who was passing through Lagos to the United Kingdom. He took him to his lodgings in Obalende. It was only one room. A curtain of light-blue cloth ran the full breadth of the room separating the Holy of Holies (as he called his double spring bed) from the sitting area. His cooking utensils, boxes, and other personal effects were hidden away under the Holy of Holies. The sitting area was taken up with two armchairs, a settee (otherwise called "me and my girl"), and a round table on which he displayed his photo album. At night, his houseboy moved away the round table and spread his mat on the floor.

Joseph had so much to tell Obi on his first night in Lagos that it was past three when they slept. He told him about the cinema and the dance halls and about political meetings.

"Dancing is very important nowadays. No girl will look at you if you can't dance. I first met Joy at the dancing school." "Who is Joy?" asked Obi, who was fascinated by what he was learning of this strange and sinful new world. "She was my girl friend for—let's see . . . "—he counted off his fingers—" . . . March, April, May, June, July—for five months. She made these pillowcases for me."

Obi raised himself instinctively to look at the pillow he was lying on. He had taken particular notice of it earlier in the day. It had the strange word *osculate* sewn on it, each letter in a different color.

"She was a nice girl but sometimes very foolish. Sometimes, though, I wish we hadn't broken up. She was simply mad about me; and she was a virgin when I met her, which is very rare here."

Joseph talked and talked and finally became less and less coherent. Then without any pause at all his talk was transformed into a deep snore, which continued until the morning.

The very next day Obi found himself taking a compulsory walk down Lewis Street. Joseph had brought a woman home and it was quite clear that Obi's presence in the room was not desirable; so he went out to have a look round. The girl was one of Joseph's new finds, as he told him later. She was dark and tall with an enormous pneumatic bosom under a tight-fitting red and yellow dress. Her lips and long fingernails were a brilliant red, and her eyebrows were fine black lines. She looked not unlike those wooden masks made in Ikot Ekpene. Altogether she left a nasty taste in Obi's mouth, like the multicolored word *osculate* on the pillowcase. . . .

On top of it all came his mother's death. He sent all he could find for her funeral, but it was already being said to his eternal shame that a woman who had borne so many children, one of whom was in a European post, deserved a better funeral than she got. One Umuofia man who had been on leave at home when she died brought the news to Lagos to the meeting of the Umuofia Progressive Union.

"It was a thing of shame," he said. Someone else wanted to know, by the way, why that beast [meaning Obi] had not obtained permission to go home. "That is what Lagos can do to a young man. He runs after sweet things, dances breast to breast with women and forgets his home and his people. Do you know what medicine that *osu* woman may have put into his soup to turn his eyes and ears away from his people?" . . .

"Everything you have said is true. But there is one thing I want you to learn. Whatever happens in this world has a meaning. As our people say: 'Wherever something stands, another things stands beside it.' You see this thing called blood. There is nothing like it. That is why when you plant a yam it produces another yam, and if you plant an orange it bears oranges. I have seen many things in my life, but I have never yet seen a banana tree yield a coco yam. Why do I say this? You young men here, I want you to listen because it is from listening to old men that you learn wisdom. I know that when I return to Umuofia I cannot claim to be an old man. But here in this Lagos I am an old man to the rest of you." He paused for effect. "This boy that we are all talking about, what has he done? He was told that his mother died and he did not care. It is a strange and surprising thing."

III. KENYAN WOMEN SPEAK OUT

What we need in this village is teachers to teach women handicrafts and sewing and agricultural skills. We have organized a women's group. I am one of the leaders. We are saving up for a building to meet in. All women are trying to earn money, and we want to have a building for our meetings. It will be called the "adult education building" —with rooms for handicrafts, literacy, and other things.

We also want our children to be educated—so we can have good leaders to keep our country good. I think now it is best to have only four children—so you can take care of them.

It is better to educate a girl than a boy, although one should educate both. Girls are better. They help a lot. See this house? My daughters built it for me. If you don't have any daughters, who will build for you? The boys will marry and take care of their wives—that's all. They don't care about mothers. For example, if my son gets married, the daughter-in-law will say, "Let's take our mothers to live with us." The son will say, "No, we will just have our own family and do our own things." So you are left alone. What do you do? . . .

My mother has eleven children. She is my father's only wife. She works in the fields and grows the food we eat. She plants cabbage, spinach, and corn. She works very hard, but with so many children it is difficult to get enough food or money. All of my sisters and brothers go to school. One is already a teacher, and that is why I am trying to learn a profession. If I can get enough schooling, I can serve the country and my own family. I can also manage to have a life for myself. That is why I came to this school. We have a big family, and I have to help.

My life is very different from my mother's. She just stayed in the family until she married. Life is much more difficult now because everybody is dependent on money. Long ago, money was unheard of. No one needed money. But now you can't even get food without cash. Times are very difficult. That is why the towns are creating day-care centers—so women can work and have their own lives. I have to work, for without it I will not have enough money for today's life.

These are the problems I face and try to think about. How shall I manage to pick up this life so that I can live a better one? You know, we people of Kenya like to serve our parents when they are still alive—to help the family. But first, women have to get an education. Then if you get a large family and don't know how to feed it—if you don't have enough money for food—you can find work and get some cash. That's what I will teach my children: "Get an education first."

If I had a chance to go to the university, I would learn more about health education. I could help women that way. If I were in a position of authority, I would really try to educate women. Right now, girls are left behind in education. It costs money, and parents think it is more important to educate boys. But I think that if people are intelligent, there is no difference. Girls and boys should be educated the same. I would make rules and teach women who are not educated and who have never been to school. They, too, much understand what today's problems are. If I have any spare time, I want to learn new things. I would like to learn how to manage my life, my future life, and have enough say in things so that my husband and I could understand each other and share life with our family. And I would change the laws so that men would understand women and their needs and not beat them as they do.

I only hope that I will have a mature husband who will understand and discuss things with me. . . .

Most women don't rely on their husbands now. If they get some money, well and good; and if they don't, they just try to get money for themselves—selling vegetables or making and selling handicrafts.

Life is very difficult these days, and men are paying less attention to their wives. You see, men have wrongly just taken advantage of having more money. Instead of using money properly, to improve the lives of their families, they spend it on all the "facilities" available at hotels. Instead of spending nights in their own homes, they fight at home and seek women outside—in the hotels. Many men cheat on their wives now because they are employed and have money. A husband can say, "I have been sent as a driver to Nairobi" (or elsewhere), when he actually spends the money on girls.

So women are fed up. They think now that relying on a man can be a problem. They say, "We should try to do something ourselves. Then, whether we get something from our men or not, we still will be able to raise our children properly." The problem that many women face is that they must become self-supporting. They either have no support from their husbands at all, or very little. And there is no law to protect them.

But women *are* trying to do something for themselves, and if they had the capital they could establish businesses to help them make money. The main problem here is the money problem. Many women are alone. They need to earn for their families.

Women feel very hurt because they think their men don't recognize them as human brings. They are unhappy because of this inequality. I am lucky; my husband is good. He never took another wife. We are still together. . . . My wish would be that men and women could live as two equal people.

IV. IFI AMADIUME

When the 1960s and 1970s female academics and Western feminists began to attack social anthropology, riding on the crest of the new wave of women's studies, the issues they took on were androcentrism and sexism. . . . The methods they adopted indicated to Black women that White feminists were no less racist than the patriarchs of social anthropology whom they were busy condemning for male bias. They fantasized a measure of superiority over African and other Third World women. Black women's critique could not therefore be restricted to the male bias of social anthropology and not challenge White women. Drawing their data from the Third World, especially Africa, works on women produced in Europe and America have shown White women's unquestioning acceptance of anthropology's racist division of the world. In the debates in the West, the Third World supplied the 'raw data' for random sampling, citation and illustration of points. It baffles African women that Western academics and feminists feel no apprehension or disrespectful trivialization in taking on all of Africa or, indeed, all the Third World in one book. It is revealing that most such works have not been written by women from Third World nations; they, instead, tend to write about their particular ethnic group, their country or surrounding region. . . .

Igbo women were clearly unlike European women. . . . In their system, male attributes and male status referred to the biologically male sex—man—as female attributes and female status referred to the biologically female sex—woman. To break this rigid gender construction carried a stigma. Consequently, it was not usual to separate sex from gender, as there was no status ambiguity in relation to gender.

The flexibility of Igbo gender construction meant that gender was separate from biological sex. Daughters could become sons and consequently male. Daughters and women in general could be husbands to wives and consequently males in relation to their wives, etc. . . .

An insight into this remarkable gender system is crucial to the understanding and appreciation of the political status women had in traditional Igbo societies and the political choices open to them. . . .

It can, therefore, be claimed that the Igbo language, in comparison with English for example, has not built up rigid associations between certain adjectives or attributes and gender subjects, nor certain objects and gender possessive pronouns. The genderless word *mmadu,* humankind, applies to both sexes. There is no usage, as there is in English, of the word 'man' to represent both sexes, neither is there the cumbersome option of saying 'he or she,' 'his or her,' 'him or her.' In Igbo, *O* stands for he, she and even it, *a* stands for the impersonal one, and *nya* for the imperative, let him or her.

This linguistic system of few gender distinctions makes it possible to conceptualize certain social roles as separate from sex and gender, hence the possibility for either sex to fill the role. This, of course, does not rule out competition between the sexes, and situations in which a particular sex tends to monopolize roles and positions, and generates and stresses anti-opposite sex gender ideologies in order to maintain its own interests.

The two examples of situations in which women played roles ideally or normally occupied by men—what I have called male roles—in indigenous Nnobi society . . . were as 'male daughters' and 'female husbands'; in either role, women acted as family head. The Igbo word for family head is the genderless expression *di-bu-no.* The genderless *di* is a prefix word which means specialist in, or expert at, or master of something. Therefore, *di-bu-no* means one in a master relationship to a family and household, and a person, woman or man, in this position is simply referred to as *di-bu-no.* In indigenous Nnobi society and culture, there was one head or master of a family at a time, and 'male daughters' and 'female husbands' were called by the same term, which translated into English would be 'master.' Some women were therefore masters to other people, both men and women.

The reverse applied to those in a wife relationship to others. The Igbo word for wife, *onye be,* is a genderless expression meaning a person who belongs to the home of the master of the home. The other words for wife, *nwunye* or *nwanyi,* female or woman, also denote one in a subordinate, service or domestic relationship to one in a master position. It was therefore possible for some men to be addressed by the term 'wife,' as they were in service or domestic relationship to a master. . . . There is a series of contradictions here; . . . there were, for example, women in master or husband roles and men in wifely or domestic roles. . . .

The use of these weapons of war must be understood in the context of polygynous marriage and compound structure. Of course it was possible for a man to turn to another wife when one wife refused to have sexual relations with him. The important point here is that women lived separately. The fact that a wife did not spend the night with her husband made it possible for her to use sexual refusal as a weapon of war without running the risk of marital rape. This is not the case for women in monogamous marriages who cling to the Christian idea of the sanctity and sexual exclusiveness of their matrimonial beds. Western feminists are still finding it difficult to have rape in marriage recognized as a legal offence.

Refusal of sexual compliance by a wife still proved effective even when a man had sexual access to other wives. Such refusal implied defiance and denial of rights, and was ultimately a challenge to a husband's authority over his wife. The customary solution was not for the man to take the law into his own hands; he had the option of calling in other members of the family or appealing to the formal patrilineage organizations. . . . Obviously the weapon of sexual denial was most effective when used collectively, either by all the wives of a man, all the wives of a patrilineage, or better still, all the women of Nnobi.

Indeed the earliest recorded mass protest movement by Igbo women was the Nwaobiala—the dancing women's movement of 1925. The basic demand of the movement, which was dominated by elderly women, was the rejection of Christianity and a return to traditional customs. Nnobi is mentioned as one of the three towns where a military escort was sent to restore order, as women there burnt the market, blocked the main road and piled refuse in the court house. Children were withdrawn from school and the market was boycotted. . . .

This resistance to conversion has been sustained by a few people in Nnobi. Eze Agba, the present priest of Idemili, does not go to church, nor does Nwajiuba, the 'male daughter,' who is head of the first and most senior *obi* in Nnobi. Together with a few other elderly people, they practise the indigenous religion—the worship of the goddess. The Christians refer to them as 'pagans' or 'heathens,' but they call themselves *ndi odinani,* the custodians of the indigenous culture. The youngest of them are middle-aged. All their children and grandchildren are Christians. Ironically, a new resistance against Christianity now springs from the Western-educated élite, who were in fact brought up in the church and educated in mission schools. They are now strong supporters and admirers of the indigenous religionists and preach the doctrine of cultural revival while condemning aspects of Western culture and dominance. . . .

Overwhelming evidence shows that women in Nnobi and in Igboland in general were neither more comfortable nor more advantaged from an economic point of view under colonialism. They had lost their grip on the control of liquid cash; men had invaded the general market, and women were becoming helpless in their personal relations with husbands. But, most important of all, pro-female institutions were being eroded both by the church and the colonial administration. . . .

. . .[W]omen's centrality in the production and sale of palm-oil and kernels in traditional Nnobi society gave them a considerable advantage over their husbands. The introduction of pioneer oil mills mechanized the whole process of extracting the palm-oil and cracking the kernels. This, of course, meant a much higher oil yield which necessitated bulk buying by the agents of the mills and the channelling of most of the village's palm fruit to the mills. The main centre of production was therefore shifted from the family to the mills. At the same time, wives lost the near monopoly they enjoyed in the traditional method of production and the independent income they derived from it. . . . Instead of wives selling the palm-oil and keeping some of the profits, husbands now sold direct to the oil mills or their agents, and collected the money.

STUDY QUESTIONS

1. What were the main disputes over Christianity in the Nigerian region Achebe describes? What kinds of people were most drawn to this religion? Why? What kinds of people most resisted?

2. Given the novel's title, *Things Fall Apart,* does Achebe suggest that it would be best to go back to the traditional values?

3. What are the value dilemmas in the excerpt from *No Longer at Ease*? What are the dominant features of the urban culture of Lagos? How do they relate to traditional culture?

4. What are the main aspirations of the Kenyan women interviewed in the third selection? What is new about them? In what ways do they clearly seek to defend older cultural and social traditions?

5. What problems of interpretation do novels raise in trying to get at historical conditions? What kinds of problems do interviews raise, even one conducted by a skilled Western scholar?

6. On what bases does Ifi Amadiume criticize the evaluations of African women by Western feminists and anthropologists?

7. What, in her view, were the three main strengths, for women, of traditional Igbo language, family structure, and economy? By implication, what goals should modern Igbo women have?

8. Would the Kenyan women interviewed in the third selection agree or disagree with Amadiume's prescriptions for the most part? Are they reacting to changes in ways Amadiume would approve of?

9. Do Achebe and Amadiume agree on the nature of African gender traditions? Do they agree on what combination of change and tradition is desirable for contemporary Africa?

10. How do the cultural changes discussed in this chapter compare with African nationalist goals and reactions? Would nationalism help deal with some of the cultural issues raised by Achebe, Amadiume, and the Kenyan women?

VISUAL SOURCE

This picture portrays economic activities far different from those of industrial societies in the late twentieth century. The focus is on village agriculture and the production of grain. Women and boys are involved, rather than the men who traditionally participated in agricultural work. The picture, in other words, shows both highly traditional and dramatically new characteristics, and both invite analysis.

Pictures like this were common parts of magazine articles about African life. This raises questions about the kind of audience the picture was intended for, and what impact it was supposed to have. It was not a picture intended as a keepsake for the people involved, who probably would never see it.

African Women's Work. From Kenya, in the late 1990s. (Betty Press/Woodfin Camp & Associates)

STUDY QUESTIONS

1. What kind of work was being done here?
2. What does this type of work say about women's conditions in contemporary Africa? What relationship is suggested between family and work?
3. Why were adult men not pictured here?
4. How do these women's work patterns compare with those in more industrial societies? Aside from the obvious technological differences, are there any similarities?
5. What audience was this picture intended for? What impact was it meant to have?
6. How does this kind of evidence about African women compare to anthropologist interviews? to statements by African women intellectuals?

58

The Environment in the Twentieth Century: A Disaster Story

One of the key issues of twentieth-century world history involves changes in and anxieties about the natural environment. Human impact on the environment goes far back in world history, and the precedents are important. Agriculture, both in its settled and its slash-and-burn varieties, early involved deforestation and impacts on riverways. Several agricultural societies markedly altered their environments, and some may have perished as a result. Excessive grain growing reduced soil quality in part of the Middle East and North Africa, in some cases expanding desert conditions.

Modern environmental history adds three new factors to the old story of human impact and its frequent heedlessness. The first factor involves the massive increase in population. Handling human wastes, long a problem for some cities, takes on more general proportions. Efforts to expand the food supply, which so far, against some dire expectations, have been largely successful, involve use of chemical fertilizers and additional deforestation. The second new factor is the intensification and expansion of modern industry. Chemical pollutants jeopardize air as well as water quality, affecting rivers, lakes, and soils in many areas. Societies that have pressed for rapid industrialization as a means of catching up with the West have sometimes suffered particular problems, although the United States remains the world air pollution leader. By the 1990s one quarter of Russia was judged environmentally degraded. China, with its growing manufacturing as well as its vast population, was moving into the number two spot in generating air pollutants that cause global warming.

The third novel factor involves the international scale, as well as the extent, of environmental problems. Industry in the American Midwest affects trees in Canada, thanks to high smokestacks that spread chemical pollutants; the Ruhr mining and metallurgical center in western Germany has a similar impact on Scandinavia. International

From Grigorii Medvedev, *The Truth about Chernobyl,* translated by Evelyn Rossiter (New York: Basic Books, 1991), pp. 86–87, 238–242.

oil shipments recurrently generate ocean spills that affect many shorelines. The general increase in the international production of hydrocarbons is widely seen as raising temperatures worldwide, while global markets for certain minerals and agricultural products, inducing clearance of tropical rain forests, eliminate certain animal and vegetable species while reducing the production of oxygen. By the 1970s, international conferences began to take the global dimensions of the environment into account, and many countries pledged controls. But the tension between local economic expansion and more amorphous environmental criteria promised a long struggle to achieve effective implementation.

The following document deals with the most famous among several disastrous environmental "events" of the late twentieth century: The explosions on April 25, 1986, that destroyed a nuclear reactor at the Chernobyl power plant in the Soviet Union (in the region that is now part of Ukraine). The result was an unprecedented meltdown that spread radiation over the whole region, with measurable increases in nations to the west and north. Twenty-six people died immediately; many others were injured and probably still more genetically damaged. Some who died from the explosion had to be buried in lead coffins, lest irradiated bodies further contaminate the soil. The account comes from Grigorii Medvedev, a nuclear expert who had held a high position at Chernobyl in the 1970s. He was assigned to report, and later wrote a book about, the whole catastrophe. In the first passage, he sketches some eyewitness accounts, and in the second he describes his own visit, with a driver, Volodya, two weeks after the explosions.

It is important to note that this is only one of many examples of environmental "events." An American chemical company operating in Bhopal, India, suffered an explosion that killed and injured far more people. A Japanese village experienced a series of deaths in the 1970s from chemical poisoning. An obvious question is: What general conclusions can be drawn from these recurrent if scattered events?

CHERNOBYL

I. EYEWITNESS

On hearing the explosions and seeing the fire, most of the people out fishing stayed there until morning, while others, vaguely alarmed by these events, returned to Pripyat, with dry throats and smarting eyes. The booming that normally accompanied the opening of relief valves sounded just like an explosion, so people had grown accustomed to ignoring such loud noises. As for the fire, someone would doubtless extinguish it. It was really nothing! Hadn't there been fires at the Armyanskaya and Byeloyarsk nuclear power stations?

At the time of the explosion, there were two more fishermen sitting on the bank of the feeder channel, trying to catch young fish, 260 yards (240 m) directly across from the turbine hall. Serious fishermen dream about catching fry like this. And without fry as bait it's better not to try for perch. Here the fry, especially in spring, manage to come closer and closer to the reactor unit, straight for the pump station, where they mass in great numbers. One of the two fishermen, by the name of Pustovoit, had no particular occupation. The second, Protasov, was a maintenance man who had been brought in from Kharkov. He thought very highly of Chernobyl; it had such clean air and wonderful fishing. He had even thought of taking up residence there permanently—if it could be arranged. It was, after all, in the Kiev region, where residence permits were hard to come by; it would be no easy matter moving there. He was catching plenty of fish fry that night and was in a good mood. It was a warm, starry Ukrainian night. It was hard to believe that it was still April, as it felt more like July. No. 4 reactor unit, a handsome snowy-white building, lay straight ahead. The unexpected combination of magnificent, dazzling nuclear power and the tender young fish wriggling in the net was a most pleasant surprise.

First they heard two dull explosions within the unit, which sounded as if they had come from underground. The fishermen could feel the ground shake. Then came a powerful steam explosion; and only after that did the reactor explode, with a blinding flash of flame and a firework display consisting of fragments of red-hot fuel and graphite. Pieces of reinforced concrete and steel beams went cascading through the air, blasted in all directions.

The fishermen's figures were, unknown to them, illuminated by nuclear light. Thinking that something had burst inside the plant, perhaps a gasoline tank, the two men went on fishing, not suspecting that they, just like the fry they hoped to catch, had themselves been caught in the powerful trap of a nuclear disaster. They watched with some curiosity as events unfolded. They could see with their own eyes as Pravik and Kibenok deployed their teams of firefighters, who then climbed up nearly 100 feet and attacked the fire.

"See that? One of them has got up on top of V block, more than 200 feet up! He's taken his helmet off! Fantastic! He's a real hero! You can see how hot it is over there."

A few hours later, as dawn approached, the two fishermen, each of whom had received a dose of 400 roentgens, became severely nauseated and both felt extremely ill. They had a burning sensation inside their chests, their eyelids smarted, and their heads felt as if they had just been on a wild drinking spree. And nonstop vomiting left them totally exhausted. By morning their skin had turned black, as if they had been roasting in the sun at Sochi, on the Black Sea coast, for a month. They now had a nuclear tan, but still had not the faintest idea what was happening to them.

At daybreak they noticed that the men who had been up on the roof seemed also extremely sluggish and disoriented. That made them feel slightly better, as they were clearly not the only ones. But what had hit them all of a sudden? What could it be?

They made their way somehow to the medical center, and eventually were sent to the Moscow clinic.

Much later, one of them tried to make light of it, saying: "If you're ignorant, being curious can only get you into trouble, especially if your sense of responsibility is atrophied."

In the summer of 1986, Pustovoit, the man with no particular occupation, appeared on the cover of a foreign magazine and became famous in Europe. Misfortune can befall any living creature, but nuclear misfortune is all the more profound in that it runs counter to life itself.

Even next morning, on 26 April, more and more fishermen arrived at the same spot. The fact that they did shows how ignorant and careless people can be, how they had come to take emergencies for granted throughout all the years when news of such events was suppressed, and when those responsible were never punished. . . .

II. THE LATER REPORT

A Moskvich drove up from the direction of Pripyat and was stopped. The wheels and underside of the car, and the top of the trunk, were checked with a sensor. The passengers and driver were asked to get out; then the car was washed with desorbent solutions. The soldiers were wearing respirators, and tight cloth hoods covered their head and ears, with a large flap descending over their shoulders.

One of the soldiers, with a radiometer on his chest and a long stick-sensor, waved to us to stop. He checked our pass, which Volodya had stuck on the windscreen, and found it in order. The sensor, when passed over our Niva, showed background levels.

"You can go," he said. "But remember, your car will get contaminated where you're going. That Moskvich over there has 3 roentgens per hour, and washing won't get it off. Take pity on your car!"

"We have a radiometer," said I, pointing to the instrument. "And we'll be careful."

The soldier stared at me with his piercing blue eyes and seemed to be shaking his head uncertainly, as if doubting my word. He then slammed the door and waved us on.

Volodya accelerated, and the car shot forward with a whistling noise. I looked at the asphalt roadway bordered by pink concrete shoulders, and thought that we had rejoiced too soon, back in the days when the concrete had just been added, at not having to repair cracked asphalt any more. Now everything—including the asphalt and the concrete—was severely contaminated.

Thinking it might be interesting to see how fast the radioactivity increased as we approached Pripyat, I rolled down the window and held the sensor outside. On the right and straight ahead, beyond the radioactive vegetation flashing past, I could see the buildings of the Chernobyl nuclear power station, a bright white in the May sunlight, and the latticework structures of the high tension power masts of the 330- and 750-kilovolt switching stations.

I already knew that the explosion had ejected fragments of fuel onto the ground around the 750-kilovolt switching stations, where they continued to emit large amounts of radiation.

The pile of blackened wreckage visible outside No. 4 unit made a stark, painful contrast with all that elegant whiteness and latticework.

To begin with, the needle on the radiometer showed 100 milliroentgens per hour, and then steadily crept to the right—200, 300, 500 milliroentgens per hour. Suddenly it shot off the scale. I switched through the ranges. What could that mean? Probably a nuclear gust from the damaged reactor building. A mile or so farther on, the needle dropped again, this time to 700 milliroentgens per hour.

The familiar old sign was now plainly visible in the distance: "Lenin Nuclear Power Station, Chernobyl" with a concrete torch. Beyond that, a concrete sign: "Pripyat, 1970."

We turned right, past the construction offices and the cement plant, toward the reactor unit straight ahead and then slightly to the left, in the direction indicated by the concrete arrow, the bridge over the railroad, with Yanov station on the left, and then into the town of Pripyat, where only recently 50,000 people used to live. But now . . .

"Volodya, let's go into Pripyat first."

He veered off to the left, accelerated, and soon we were crossing the bridge. Soon the snow-white town came into view, in the bright sunlight. As the needle on the radiometer had swung right on the bridge, I began to switch through the ranges.

"Let's get out of here—fast," I said. "The radioactive cloud passed this way and did some real damage. Faster!"

We shot over the hump of the bridge and raced into the streets of the dead town. A painful sight met our eyes immediately: the bodies of cats and dogs, everywhere, on the roads, in the yards, on the squares—white, brown, black, and spotted corpses of shot animals.

These sinister sights reminded us that this was an empty, abandoned town, to which normal times would never return. I wondered, nonetheless, why someone did not clean up. After all . . .

"Drive along Lenin Street," I said to Volodya. "It's easier to go by the house where I lived when I worked here."

It was number 9, I remembered.

Down the middle of Lenin Street there were young poplars, already quite tall, and on either side of the street, paths with benches and thick bushes. The imposing building of the Party Committee of Pripyat could be seen at the end of the street. To the right of that was the ten-story Pripyat Hotel, and farther to the right, the jetty on the Pripyat River. Beyond that was a restaurant, and the road to the Lastochka Hotel, where visiting high officials used to stay.

The town looked really strange, as if it was quite early in the morning; but, in fact, it was bright daylight, with the sun high in the sky. Everything was in a deep sleep, from which it could not be awakened. There were household objects and laundry on the balconies and wilted flowers on the window sills. The sun's reflections in some of the windows had an unreal quality; one window had been left open, its curtain hanging out like a dead man's tongue.

"Stop, Volodya. Here, on the right. Slow down."

The needle of the radiometer crept in either direction, from 1 roentgen per hour to 700 milliroentgens per hour.

"Go slow," I asked. "There's my house. That's where I lived, on the second floor. Look how high that mountain ash has grown. Its blossom is all radioactive now. When I was here, it hadn't reached the second floor, but now it's up to the fourth."

The place was empty. The windows were all shuttered, but you could sense that there was no life behind the shutters. They were painfully still. There were some bicycles on the balcony, some boxes, an old refrigerator, skis with red poles. And no sign of life anywhere.

The body of a large black Great Dane with white spots lay across the narrow concrete path across the yard. I asked Volodya to stop nearby so that I could check the radiation level on its coat. He turned so that the left wheels went over a flower bed and stopped. Radiation had darkened the green leaves and made the flowers wilt. The ground and the concrete on the road measured 60 roentgens per hour.

"Look!" said Volodya, pointing to the three-story school building and the large windows of the gymnasium. "My son went there. I remember going to the school hall for special occasions, and all the kids and teachers looking so happy."

Two large but emaciated pigs were running toward us along a narrow path from the school, along the wall of a five-story building. They rushed toward the car and, whimpering, rubbed their snouts against the wheels and the radiator. They had a plaintive, hunted look in their bloodshot eyes, and their movements were shaky and ill coordinated. They were obviously extremely weak.

I held my sensor close to the side of one of the pigs—50 roentgens per hour; and then to the body of the Great Dane—110 roentgens per hour. The pig tried to catch the sensor in its teeth, but I pulled it away in time. The radioactive pigs started to devour the Great Dane. They easily tore off chunks of the partially decomposed flesh, shaking the body and dragging it along the concrete. A swarm of alarmed blue flies flew out of the open mouth and the decaying eyes.

"Just look at those flies! Aren't they something? Radiation has no effect on them! Let's go back, Volodya."

"Where to?"

"To the bridge and then on to the damaged reactor building."

"What if we stall?" said Volodya a second time, with a sly smile.

"If it stalls, you'll start it again," I said, with exactly the same tone. "Let's go."

Once we had turned onto Lenin Street, Volodya asked, "Shall we go in the wrong lane. Or what? We should be over there. Shall we drive round the square?"

"There's no need."

"It feels really funny. People get tickets for things like that."

"See any traffic anywhere?"

Volodya smiled grimly, and we drove quickly past the corpses of cats and dogs, on the wrong side of the road, toward the damaged reactor building. We went really fast over the railroad bridge. The radiometer reading was suddenly very high and then fell again.

We drove along the old road which runs past the power station construction offices, the residential construction plant, the Lisova Peniya restaurant, and the cement works.

On the right we could see the horrendous destruction that had occurred at the No. 4 reactor building. The smashed masonry and the pile of rubble were all severely charred. Streams of gas ionized by radiation were surging upward above the floor of what had once been the central hall, where the reactor was located. Amid the blackened wreckage, the drum-separators, which had been wrenched from their moorings and lifted sideways, looked curiously new and sinister as they reflected the bright rays of the sun.

STUDY QUESTIONS

1. What happened at Chernobyl? What were the immediate environmental consequences?
2. Why were initial reactions often casual?
3. How does an event like Chernobyl fit into twentieth-century Soviet history? How does it fit into world history?
4. Did the Soviet government seem to react vigorously to the disaster? Can and should governments be responsible for preventing such crises?

VISUAL SOURCE

The picture shows a Russian helicopter taking radiation measurements. The picture was published in newspapers as part of the follow-up stories about the disaster. The picture invites comparison with other kinds of disasters, some of which have more dramatic visual potential.

The Ruins of the Chernobyl Nuclear Plant, April, 1986.
(Corbis/Bettmann)

STUDY QUESTIONS

1. What, if anything, in this picture suggests disaster? How would this picture fit in Medvedev's account of Chernobyl?
2. Where was the photographer taking the picture from? What were the constraints in providing visual evidence about Chernobyl?
3. Can you think of other kinds of photographs that would represent Chernobyl's impact?
4. What does this photo suggest about the visual impact of environmental issues, compared with more traditional kinds of disasters?

59

Global Contacts: The Emergence of Multinational Companies

Commercial companies with international activities have been a factor in world history for many centuries. In the postclassical period, Arab merchants knew how to use banks to transfer money from one region of trade to another, and they also used local representatives in their extensive shipping operations. In the early modern period, European companies established representatives in many regions, again to facilitate trade. Thus English merchants might have "factors" stationed in Russia, the Ottoman Empire, or India to arrange the transfer of goods and funds. Industrialization added new dimensions to international companies. With more goods to trade and larger ships to send them in, international commercial ventures proliferated. But many factory centers also found it profitable to set up branch production operations abroad, using their special techniques and know-how to earn profits in several national markets. Even some middle-sized textile firms in northern France, for example, set up operations in Rhode Island and in South America in 1850. Branch operations proliferated after 1870 in industries such as chemicals, agricultural equipment, and, soon, automobiles. By this point, U.S. companies were becoming aggressive, along with British, German, Belgian, and other European ventures, in setting up international trade and production branches.

The post-World War II multinational company was an outgrowth of this historical context, but it had some additional features. In the first place, Japanese and Pacific Rim companies, as well as European and American concerns, were now actively in the game, adding to the complexity of international contacts. In the second place, international connections now meant even more than commercial representation and branch production: They meant relatively easy acquisitions of established companies across national boundaries and setting up specialized manufacturing centers wherever labor conditions and laws provided a particular advantage. Increasingly, products like automobiles were composed of parts made in nine or ten different countries, each division located for best advantage. These developments meant that multinational companies now wielded huge

Selection I from "Sony and CBS Records: What a Romance!" *the New York Times,* September 18, 1988, pp. 35–36, 38, 40, 42, 44, 46–47. Selection II from Norma Prieto, *Beautiful Flowers of the Maquiladora: Life Histories of Women Workers in Tijuana,* translated by Michael Stone and Gabriella Winkler (Austin: University of Texas Press, 1997), pp. 2–3, 4–5, 11, 16–17, 19–20, 48, 52–53, 91, 95. Reprinted by permission.

power, often greater than that of many national governments. Their capacity to influence labor conditions, the environment, and even politics grew immensely.

The first of the two selections in this chapter, from a journalistic account, outlines how multinational companies like Japan-based Sony now operate in the international arena. It shows how setbacks in one region—in this case, a "Black Monday" stock market collapse in the United States—can work to the advantage of alert multinationals elsewhere. It shows how easily huge international deals can be made, thanks to modern technology and a clearly international business culture. And it shows how multinationals affect culture as well as the economy.

The second selection involves the other side of the multinational company phenomenon: the worker's side. The passages come from interviews with women Mexican workers, done by a Mexican social scientist whose work was first published in 1985. Her focus was on the type of work situation fostered by United States- and Japanese-based multinationals, as they spread operations to Mexico from the 1970s onward.

Multinationals deliberately seek cheap labor (and sometimes limitations on trade unions and lax environmental laws) to manufacture parts for products that may be assembled elsewhere and certainly will be sold in various markets, including those of industrial societies like the United States. The results bring lower prices for consumers and/or larger profits for the companies. They also bring into factory work large numbers of Mexicans, Chinese, Filipinos, and others in societies where manufacturing has advanced but remains less fully developed than in the multinationals' home base. In this passage, dealing with what is called the *maquiladora* industry sponsored by foreign, mainly U.S., multinationals (the term *maquiladora* is often not translated, but it has come to mean border factory), Mexican women workers in Tijuana (just south of San Diego, and convenient for reshipping back to the United States) describe their conditions. What is the impact of multinationals on them? Debate rages over precisely this interpretive issue, with some arguing that experience and regular (if low) wages will help places like Mexico set a basis for further development, others arguing that sheer exploitation only holds the society back. Workers themselves report important pluses and minuses and find it difficult to protest, as the passage from the end of the interview suggests. Debate rages also over the resultant impact on places like the United States: Are *maquiladora* workers taking jobs away from Americans, or do lower prices and greater purchasing power enhance the United States' opportunities?

Finally, the two sides of the multinationals—the tycoon side and the worker side—need to be combined into a judgment about what multinationals are and what impact they have on all societies concerned.

CORPORATIONS AND WORKERS

I. SONY AND CBS RECORDS

On the morning of last Oct. 20, Laurence A. Tisch, the president and chief executive officer of CBS, Inc., sat in his office on the 35th floor of Black Rock thinking pessimistic thoughts. In the background, a single television set was tuned to the Financial News Network, which was airing a Wall Street report. Tisch was meeting with a business associate that morning, and their conversation was the conversation that businessmen across the country were having that day, the day after Black Monday, when the stock market collapsed: What could it mean?

Mr. Tisch believed he knew its meaning, and it was bleak. It meant a whole new ball game, he said: investors' attitudes would be changed forever. "Business in the United States," Tisch darkly concluded, "will never be the same again."

Six thousand miles away, in a corporate office in Tokyo, where it was late evening, a starkly different mood prevailed. At the headquarters of Sony, the giant international electronics firm, there was an air of excitement and anticipation, and for Sony executives, a feeling approaching triumph. To them, as a senior Sony official later put it, "Black Monday was a very fortunate day." After 13 months of frustration, Sony's quest to acquire CBS Records, the largest record company in the world, was near fruition. Sony's man in America was on the phone, telling them that Tisch had decided, finally and firmly, to sell.

For more than a month, Sony's latest offer to meet Tisch's price—a staggering $2 billion, fattened from an original bid of $1.25 billion—had sat on the table, sniffed over and pondered by a CBS board of directors that was reluctant to part with a cherished piece of CBS's legacy nearly as old as the company itself. The hesitancy largely reflected the ambivalence of William S. Paley, the CBS founder who bought Columbia Records, the flagship label of what became CBS Records, in 1938, and had spoken of it, even half a century later, as "my baby." But this was business, and $2 billion was a rich price. Tisch, the tough-minded investor who was running CBS now, wanted the deal; Black Monday was the convincer.

And so, the deal was done, and CBS Records—pioneer of the LP, repository of the great Broadway musical recordings from "My Fair Lady" to "A Chorus Line," recording home of Michael Jackson and Billy Joel, Barbra Streisand and Bruce Springsteen and Cyndi Lauper—passed into Japanese hands. It was the first Japanese jumbo acquisition of an American company, and the transaction made headlines. But the story of Sony's acquisition of CBS Records is much more than that.

It is a story of Larry Tisch's drastic transformation of Bill Paley's CBS, and of a bitter personality clash, between the colorful, free-wheeling head of CBS Records, Walter R. Yetnikoff, and Tisch, the cost-conscious corporate president. And, in the end, it is a story of two profoundly different business and cultural philosophies—the investor orientation of Tisch, with its focus on stock price and earnings (familiar thinking in American business culture in the 1980's), and the longer-term strategy of Sony, which hoped for a deal that history, if not Wall Street, would admire. Tisch was selling off pieces of CBS, and building a pile of cash; Sony wanted a marriage of hardware and software that would still be paying off in the next century. Stock management on one side, company management on the other.

A year later, both sides are delighted with the deal. Tisch is happy because the sale brought CBS "increased earnings per share, and at the same time removed the risk in a business that is both cyclical and can be hazardous." Akio Morita, the 67-year-old co-founder and chairman of Sony, on the other hand, looks past the short-term risks and stock values to the day that Sony's ownership of the world's biggest record company will give its hardware innovations an irresistible edge in the marketplace. "Twenty years from now," Morita says, "history will prove us right." . . .

[In November 1986], Michael P. Schulhof, vice chairman of Sony's American operations and a pilot, landed the Sony jet at Teterboro Airport in New Jersey after a flight from California. At the airport, he telephoned his office for messages and was told that he'd received an urgent call from Walter Yetnikoff. He called Yetnikoff, and the record executive told him that he'd been authorized by Tisch to find a buyer for CBS Records. Yetnikoff said that he'd tried to work out a leveraged buyout on his own and was ready to give up on that. Would Sony be interested? "The deal is $1.25 billion for CBS Records," Yetnikoff told Schulhof, plus a side deal that would keep Yetnikoff and his management team in place. As Yetnikoff put it that day: "Fifty million dollars for me and the *mishpocheh*"—the family. There was some urgency, Yetnikoff said; the CBS board was meeting in two days.

The phone call didn't totally surprise Schulhof. He'd known Yetnikoff for several years and had heard him complain about Tisch's style of management—that no one on the corporate side of CBS cared about the records division, that CBS in the Tisch era was obsessed with costs and indifferent to "managing creative talent," as Yetnikoff put it. Yetnikoff wanted out from under his new boss, and if his own leveraged buyout wasn't workable, then Sony was the natural buyer; the electronics giant could easily come up with the cash, and besides, it had the inside track on CBS Records. For 20 years, CBS/Sony, a joint venture between the two companies, had operated in Tokyo. Walter Yetnikoff, then a young CBS lawyer, had drafted that deal in 1967. He knew the Sony people and liked them, and the sentiment appeared to be mutual.

Schulhof recalls standing at the Teterboro Airport and thinking, "This is a once-in-a-lifetime opportunity, and we ought to make a quick decision, which is not something the Japanese companies are known for. . . ." He was certain, however, that Sony wanted the deal. For one thing, there was the joint venture, which was far more than just a corporate backwater to Sony. Beginning in 1968 with $1 million from each company, it had, without any further capital investment, grown to produce sales of $730 million and more than $100 million in pretax profits last year. The value of the property owned by CBS/Sony in land-squeezed Tokyo was incalculable. If CBS Records were going to get a new corporate parent, Sony had more than a passing interest.

But more compellingly, there was Sony's dream for the future: the marriage of software—the records, tapes and compact disks that are the business of CBS Records—and hardware—the equipment that consumers play them on, which is Sony's core business. Sony had learned a hard lesson in the 1970's with Betamax, its videotape player, which lost its war with the "other" format, VCR. Although Beta was widely deemed a superior product, it turned out that consumers didn't much care; the VCR, marketed by a group of other companies, was cheaper, and viewers were interested in seeing programs, not technology. Had Sony owned a movie studio, it could have fed the marketplace movies in the Beta format exclusively, and the result might have been different. (With an eye toward future technologies, Sony is, in fact, reportedly contemplating a studio purchase).

In the consumer electronics business, the fundamental imperative is to keep coming up with new technology—the Sony "Walkman" portable stereo, for example. Now, with several other companies, Sony is developing the digital audio tape recorder. The D.A.T., as it is called, is a computerized recording system capable of rendering near-perfect sound. In late 1986, Sony began to envision how much easier it would be to sell the new system if it were linked to the catalogue of music belonging to the world's largest record company. "Software and hardware," says Norio Ohga, Sony's president and C.E.O., "are two wheels of the same cart."

So Sony was definitely interested, but Schulhof would have to act quickly. Still at Teterboro Airport, where it was 7 P.M., Schulhof called Tokyo, where the work day was beginning, and told Morita and Ohga of the development. Twenty minutes later, he called Yetnikoff back: CBS had a deal if it wanted it.

Sony, innocent in the ways of big-time mergers and acquisitions, knew that it would need help. Schulhof called on a new "boutique" merchant banking firm, The Blackstone Group, headed by a former co-C.E.O. of the Lehman Brothers investment banking firm and United States Secretary of Commerce, Peter G. Peterson, and Stephan A. Schwarzman, an acquaintance of Schulhof's. The next morning, the two dealmakers met with Schulhof and Sony's lawyer, Paul Burak, at the Mayfair Regent hotel on Park Avenue. They discussed the ramifications of the acquisition, and concluded that the first order of business was to make a deal with Yetnikoff. It was by then 9:30 A.M., but Schulhof knew that Yetnikoff, a late riser, would still be at home, so the four men got in their cars and were driven the few blocks to Yetnikoff's home on East 56th Street. After an hour, they had their deal with management.

It was all new and strange for Sony, both because of the size of the transaction and the haste that it required. Even Yetnikoff was startled by how fast things were moving—"I thought maybe I didn't ask for enough money," he later joked. But what happened next seemed little short of bizarre. The management deal set, Yetnikoff, still in his bathrobe, called Tisch. The others in the room watched as a look of concern came over his face; something was clearly wrong. Peterson, who knew Tisch, asked to speak with him, but it was too late; Tisch had hung up. Yetnikoff then broke the bad news. Tisch had spoken to board members, but was hesitant to say anything until the board met formally the next day.

The following afternoon, Tisch called Morita, who by pure coincidence was in New York City at the time. Tisch wanted the deal, but Paley didn't; some on the board had been shocked when Tisch presented the idea in an informal meeting the night before.

The Sony brass was dumbfounded. Was this the way Americans did big deals? "I was so surprised," says Norio Ohga. "The head of the company said they would sell to us. Then we start to negotiate, and the board of the company said, 'No-no-no, this is just Mr. Tisch's idea.' It was a very unusual circumstance. We have never seen such a thing. The president wanted to sell, but not the board. . . . Such a headache!" . . .

In the meantime, Sony remained patient. In New York, Schulhof, with Tisch's approval, quietly went to work on Paley, arranging a series of private meetings. . . . Tisch was once again ready to push for a sale.

Schulhof got Tisch's call on a Monday morning, as he was preparing to fly to Tokyo for routine Sony meetings. Tisch said it was important, so Schulhof found Peter Peterson and went to see Tisch, who told the two that he'd decided on a new price. "If you're willing to offer $2 billion for this company, I'll sell it to you," Schulhof quotes Tisch as saying. Schulhof says that he expressed reservations about Paley's willingness, and Tisch answered, "Don't worry, I'll talk to Bill. I'll convince him this is in the interest of the shareholders." The CBS financial officer, Fred Meyer, came up with the record division's profits and loss statements and projections, and Schulhof had them sent to Japan by satellite facsimile, then boarded a plane for Tokyo. Again, haste was of the essence; the CBS board was to meet two days later.

When Schulhof arrived in Tokyo, it was the evening of the next day, a holiday in Japan. Still, he found Morita, Ohga and several members of the board awaiting him at Sony headquarters. Yetnikoff, who was in Japan for Michael Jackson's tour, also stopped by. They discussed Tisch's new price, a hefty jump from Sony's last offer. Yetnikoff thought it was too much money. But the yen was by then worth significantly more dollars, and Morita, sensing that Tisch's price was not negotiable, finally gave the approval. Schulhof telephoned Tisch in New York, where it was by now the morning of the CBS board meeting, and said, "O.K., we'll meet your price."

This time, the Japanese were confident that they had a deal. Still, Schulhof suggested it would be a good idea for Morita to make a personal call to Paley, one pioneer to another. Morita made the call, telling his old acquaintance that he understood how hard this must be for him, but that Sony was in the best position to care for the company Paley had nurtured. Morita offered Paley a place in the new company, as honorary chairman, and he said that Sony would make a contribution in Paley's name to his pet project, the Museum of Broadcasting. Then, the Sony group retired for the night.

The next morning, they reassembled, eager to hear the results of the CBS board meeting. Yetnikoff was designated to make the call to Tisch.

Again, Sony was in for a shock. Tisch said the board hadn't made up its mind on a sale, and what's more, it wanted to commission an outside consulting firm to assess the future of the record business. The decision had been postponed for at least another month. . . .

Then, five days after the CBS board had for the third time refused Sony's offer, Sony got lucky: the stock market crashed. Suddenly, Tisch's spinoff idea didn't look very good; who would buy the stock? For that matter, it occurred to him that maybe Sony would no longer be willing to pay the $2 billion. . . .

In Tokyo, Morita made the decision to go ahead with the deal. While Black Monday may have been significant to Tisch, the investor, Morita was unmoved. "If it was worth $2 billion to us a week ago," he told his associates, "it is worth $2 billion now."

The deal was done.

With the announcement of Sony's purchase of CBS Records, some in the record industry lamented the selling of a part of American culture to the Japanese. "We're obviously very disappointed that a great American record company with a very strong history in the business has been sold to a foreign company," a Warner's executive told The Wall Street Journal. One columnist wrote of the Japanese, "They make good cars, TV sets, tractors. But will they, or the executives they hire, know another Duke Ellington when they hear one?"

Some inside CBS feared a dramatic culture change at the company, an invasion of Japanese executives sent from the home base. But so far, there has been virtually no change at CBS Records. The only Japanese have been Sony accountants, acquainting themselves with the record company's accounting system.

Indeed, by most accounts, life at CBS Records has improved under Sony's hand. For example, now that the company is a tenant in the CBS building, the floors are cleaned regularly (the janitorial staff had been pared on one of Tisch's cutbacks, but if you lease, you get special services). As for Yetnikoff, he is the happiest of all, and understandably so. One of his first acts under Sony was to replace the president of CBS Records, Alvin N. Teller, with one of his old pals, Tommy Mottola, who had headed a successful management office. Mottola and three other new senior executives were given a rich deal that Yetnikoff insists wouldn't have been possible under Tisch.

What's more, Yetnikoff is now personally secure. He has a multiyear deal with Sony that will pay him $20 million. Earlier this year, he went to a Jaguar dealership and ordered a 1988 Vanden Plas, the top of the line. When the salesman asked what options Yetnikoff wanted, he replied, "All of them." And, there is a new toy in his office—a model of the corporate jet, a Falcon 900, that Sony has agreed to buy for Yetnikoff.

On the other hand, there looms an issue that may bring the beneficence of Sony's stewardship into question: the matter of digital audio tape. Sony helped create the new, advanced sound system, but its marketing in the United States has been passionately opposed by record companies—with CBS Records leading the opposition. They argue that the near-perfect reproduction capability of D.A.T. will encourage pirating of tapes and disks, costing the industry (and recording artists) millions in lost royalties. Yetnikoff insists that he is not worried, and that now that Sony owns a record company, it would not do anything to hurt its interests.

But it is clear that Sony intends for D.A.T. to have its day. Morita, the engineer who built the giant hardware company, becomes nearly dreamy when discussing the new technology. "Digital sound," he says, "is the first innovation since Edison invented the phonograph." Schulhof, too, suggests its inevitability: "Eventually, there will be a digital replacement for compact cassettes."

Even Yetnikoff allows that there is a conflict between his view that Sony will protect CBS Records from the evils of D.A.T. and Sony's expressed strategy of teaming hardware with software. "Yes, it is somewhat inconsistent, yes, I acknowledge that," he says. "On the other hand, since they have spent a lot of money on this company, they're not going to do something to screw it up. Because we are so close, maybe we can find a common solution. I can use them to talk to the hardware people and they can use me to talk to the software people."

In the matter of D.A.T., as with the CBS Records deal itself, Sony seems prepared to wait for the proper moment. "I'm not in a rush," Morita says. "You know, sometimes American people are rushing. Always they say, 'We have no time.' But business has to continue a long, long time. So, it doesn't have to be this year. I'm very patient."

II. MAQUILADORA WORKERS

Angela, on Managers

Ángela paused for a breath: "Really, thank God he switched us back, because it was a killer to work all night and get home just in time to make breakfast and clean the house, before trying to get some sleep with all the daytime racket."

Ángela was grateful to the manager. She associated the North Americans with the good and the humane. At various times she has commented to me that they should replace all the Mexican supervisors with North Americans, because the latter are much better. Many female factory workers shared this notion. In their opinion, the Mexicans were tyrants, good-for-nothings. The women concurred in viewing the North Americans as more responsible, more considerate, and, above all, more appreciative and considerate of women. As one observed, "We have never had North American supervisors, but I know that they're better because those who have been to the factory, the engineers and the coordinators, are very nice people."

The workers at Ángela's plant once proposed to the manager that he replace all the Mexican supervisors with North Americans. He smiled at the flattery of his North American pride. "Let's see what we can do," he responded, but nothing changed. Clearly, the firm has no interest in changing supervisors. It is necessary to maintain the reputation of the considerate North American, but the supervisor, as an intermediary representing the owners' interests, can rarely afford to be considerate. Besides, a North American supervisor would earn a very high salary, paid in dollars. . . .

Angela, on Work and Pay

I lasted seven years assembling cassettes, and I was doing the same thing for hours, days, and years. I got so tired that I asked for a transfer. I was so exhausted that I felt like my lungs were collapsing. At times I arrived home crying from the pain. I went to a private doctor and he told me I was very tired, that the best thing would be to rest a bit, although he knew that I couldn't stop working. He said that if I continued working, my lungs were going to collapse. They ignored my complaints at Social Security. They said there was nothing wrong with me, and then sent me back home without doing anything. They never even took an X ray to see what was going on with me. . . .

In the factory's good times we were sixteen hundred women making cassettes. There was a lot of competition among us, and none of us wanted to let up. We ate in ten minutes instead of the fifty minutes the company allowed, because we were interested in making more cassettes than our counterparts. I had a very good record; they took all the women on our line out to eat a number of times as a prize for having been the most productive group. During that period I never felt any aches and pains, and I didn't feel exhausted. Initially, I earned $18.99 a week, then $26.50, $36.00, and $56.00. Then, after the devaluation, we began to be paid in pesos. We were all very angry because we preferred to be paid in dollars, but the company said it was not convenient.

Gabriela, on Health Conditions

The room still lacks good fans, and the ones they have often don't work at all. I don't know how the *muchachas* keep working there, because neither the general conditions nor the safety measures have been improved in the least. Surely, they are going to suffer the same problems that I did. That work with acids is very exacting and dangerous, because if you don't mix the chemicals properly, they can explode. Everything has to be done by the book, using precise measures. Despite the hazardous nature of the work, and the fact that you must be specially trained to do it, they pay the same as for any other job, and they fail to recognize its critical importance.

One time there was an explosion and two co-workers were burned. Fortunately, their clothing was stripped off right away and they were washed down, which kept them from being badly burned. If the chemicals had gotten on them, even one drop in the eyes, they would have been blinded. One of the safety measures that we did have was goggles, but we rarely used them because they made us so hot, as the room has no ventilation. . . .

Alma, on Pay and Product

I had been working for six years in a textile maquiladora, where I nearly destroyed my kidneys and my eyes. I never earned a fixed salary. They paid me by the job, on a piecework basis, as they also call it. In this maquiladora here, we work quite differently from the way they do in other textile plants. . . .

The dresses we make are beautiful, for very fashionable women. They're incredibly expensive! They sell them in the best stores in the United States and they cost $200 or $300. And what do we get? We make 45 pesos [about U.S. $1] per dress. Incredible, don't you think? We spend ten hours a day in front of a sewing machine to make a man rich and we don't even know him. And the worst of it is that we continue doing it, some not even making the minimum wage, without complaining, asleep at the wheel, watching time go by, years in front of the sewing machine. I recognize the glares, I know how we protest on the inside because we don't dare say anything to the bosses. We wait for the quitting bell to ring so we can hit the street, believing that it's all a bad dream, and that it's going to change. It's like we put these thoughts aside for a moment and go back to work, without doing anything more about it. At times we forget why the devil we're working, just waiting for a little bit of money so our kids can survive.

You get used to it all, or at least we pretend to. At times we let ourselves be carried away by the noise or the music of the radios we all carry. It helps us forget the fatigue and the back pain we all have working in front of the sewing machine. The moment came when I just couldn't take any more and I quit, knowing that the money my husband makes, together with what our oldest daughter gives us, wasn't going to be enough.

Elena and Gabriela, on Conditions

I was very apprehensive about going to work in a maquiladora. I preferred to find work as a domestic. I always thought that the plants could easily catch fire, because they're full of electric wires, machines, and other things. Still, I decided to go to work there because I needed the money.

At first when I arrived in Tijuana, the girls I knew told me about the maquiladoras and they urged me to go to work with them. They told me, "Here they pay you every week, you get health benefits, and you know lots of people; it's not like domestic work!" I had never been inside a factory, but I had an idea of what they were like, because I had seen some in the movies and on television.

The picture I had about the maquiladoras was pretty close to reality. When I went inside, I saw that the place was pretty old. It was like a refurbished warehouse with a tin roof. Oh, the dreams I have of that cursed tin roof. It's wretched! Here in Tijuana the climate is very extreme, so in winter the factory is freezing, and in summer it's an inferno. . . .

The plants don't have any windows. It's just walls on all sides, so the lights and ventilation are artificial. In winter it gets dark very early, so we enter and leave work in darkness; we go for days without seeing the sun. It's like another world. I know that working for so many hours under artificial light is bad for the eyes, most of all because the lights are so poor. At times everything looks yellow because the light is so low. It really irritates me! What would it cost them to put in some more lights? I don't get it. In the factory where my sister works everything is very clean and well lit. It's a new factory, really big, with a very nice atmosphere. What we would give to have such a nice place to work. If one is obliged to work, at least it could be nice and clean, with the best conditions.

Where I work, there's only one fan for the entire department of sixty workers. The environment is oppressive from bad ventilation; the air is full of gas from arsenic and other chemicals whose names I don't know, because we just distinguish them by the color keys they come marked with. . . .

Maria Luisa, on Urban Life

I didn't know anything about Tijuana. I had never been in a city. I had never left the village, and the village wasn't very big! So it was quite an experience to go to Mazatlán and take the train. Everything seemed beautiful to me.

I got to Tijuana and I couldn't pronounce a lot of words. I couldn't pronounce "carpet," or "linoleum," or "newspaper." I didn't even know these things existed. The old lady's niece told me, "You don't say it like that! You say it this way." She taught me how to pronounce the words correctly. I was really taken with TV because I had never seen it. I had seen movies, because there was a man who brought them to show in the village. I had only seen movies, that was it. But I had never imagined there could be this little box, you turn it on, and there are people talking. I really liked TV. It's very entertaining! . . .

Angela, on Factory Life Compared with Village Work and the Domination of an Abusive Husband

It might seem like I exaggerate, but it gave me a great sense of happiness to start working at the maquiladora; I thought I had overcome my past. It was the moment in which God heard my prayers and changed my life. I could forget what was behind me. That part of my life was so very difficult that on one occasion I threw myself in front of a car, and on another I took a bunch of pills. What I wanted was to die.

Obdulia, on Hopes

I hope that my son is successful in his studies and becomes a doctor. He's been at it for a year and a half, and I'm going to help him so he can continue. Being a doctor must be an excellent career; anyway it's better to work on your own account than to be under a supervisor's thumb all day long.

Gabriela, on a Plant Strike

We workers were affected by the devaluation, but for the owners it was a great deal. Here in Tijuana, and generally along the entire border, we have to buy a lot of American products—basic necessities—with prices marked in dollars. Every time there is a devaluation we buy fewer products; every time we poor people become poorer, and the rich become richer.

During the strike the manager tried to bribe the union membership, offering money and better salaries on the condition the people leave the union. After ten days of striking, the Board of Conciliation and Arbitration [Junta de Conciliación y Arbitraje] declared the strike null and void.

The first day of February 1983 they closed the plant permanently. They fooled us good. We were all demoralized: the state government, the American owners, and the Mexican manager had united to do us in. They stopped at nothing to destroy the union. We pressured the Board of Conciliation and Arbitration to secure compensation, and after fighting around the clock, they gave us only 70 percent of what we were owed.

STUDY QUESTIONS

1. Why did it make sense for a major Japanese company to buy CBS Records? Why did Sony think it needed an American, rather than another Japanese, company?
2. What were the potential bonds between the industry giants Morita and Paley? Why did the U.S. government help facilitate this deal?
3. How was a company like Sony able to be so adept in dealing with American concerns—in CBS, in the U.S. government—as part of its purchase campaign?
4. How do modern technologies facilitate deals like the Sony-CBS Records deal? How do modern cultural contacts, between countries like the United States and Japan, also facilitate deals in culturally dependent businesses like the record industry?
5. Were there any particular international impediments in the way of this deal? Was the deal much different from a major business purchase deal within a single country?
6. How do maquiladora workers and their conditions compare with those of workers in industrialized societies? Why do multinationals locate facilities in places like Tijuana?
7. What are the main advantages and disadvantages of working for a multinational in Mexico? Are most workers basically contented or discontented, and why?
8. What is the Mexican government's policy toward multinationals in Tijuana?
9. Are multinational business operations good, bad, or indifferent for individual nations such as the United States, Japan, and Mexico? Is the answer basically the same for each country? How might the answer vary, depending on the social group involved *within* each nation?

60

The Cold War

In 1946 the former prime minister of Britain, Winston Churchill, delivered a commencement speech at an American college in which he coined the term "iron curtain" to describe the barriers between communist societies in Europe and what would become known as the "free world." With this speech, the recognition of the emerging Cold War advanced. Joseph Stalin, leader of the Soviet Union, replied to the speech, making counteraccusations.

The Cold War had been building for some time. After the Russian revolution, countries like Britain and the United States attempted intervention, and long opposed the apparent threat of communism. Winston Churchill, as a conservative politician in Britain, was firm in his opposition to the revolutionary regime, though he also warned of the Nazi threat. Western hostility helped persuade Stalin, in 1939, briefly to join with Germany.

Then came Hitler's attack on Russia, and for several years the Soviets, British, and Americans were united against the Axis powers. Negotiations toward a postwar settlement, however, revealed increasing differences, with the Soviets eager to extend communism and set up a buffer zone in Eastern Europe, Churchill and the American leaders equally eager to resist. By 1946, Soviet actions to increase communist power in the East European countries it occupied, including its zone of Germany, seemed increasingly ominous. Soon, American-led responses, backed by Britain, would seek to bolster the rest of Europe against the Soviet threat. The Cold War was on.

The first two documents in this passage derive from the Churchill speech, entitled "The Sinews of Peace" and Stalin's reply (which among other things reminded Churchill that he had been voted out of office in Britain after his wartime leadership).

The second set of documents comes from a later crisis point in the Cold War, with Dwight Eisenhower as American President, Nikita Krushchev as Soviet leader. The Soviets had shot down a high-altitude American spy plane that was violating Soviet airspace. The Soviets and the American-led West were still at odds, the Cold War was in many ways as polarized and dangerous as before, but the rhetoric had evolved in interesting ways.

Historians have been debating the nature of the Cold War for several decades. At first, American scholars largely blamed Soviet aggression. But a revisionist school, emerging

Selection I from Robert Rhodes James, *Winston S. Churchill: His Complete Speeches* (New York and London: Chelsea House Publishers), Vol. VII, 1943–1949, pp. 7,285–7,293; Selection II from "Stalin's Reply to Churchill," March 14, 1946, interview with Pravda, *the New York Times*, p. 4.

in the 1960s, wondered if American actions had not been at least as significant, in drawing lines and mounting confrontations that were not necessary.

The Cold War divided much of the world for over 40 years. It led to a massive arms race, whose implications are still important in the world today. It fueled several regional wars, including Korea, Vietnam, and, for the Soviets, Afghanistan. It ultimately exhausted the Soviet economy and challenged American vitality, until, with the Soviet collapse in 1989–1991, it drew to a close.

COLD WAR DOCUMENTS

I. THE CHURCHILL SPEECH

I can . . . allow my mind, with the experience of a lifetime, to play over the problems which beset us on the morrow of our absolute victory in arms, and to try to make sure with what strength I have that what has been gained with so much sacrifice and suffering shall be preserved for the future glory and safety of mankind.

The United States stands at this time at the pinnacle of world power. It is a solemn moment for the American Democracy. For with primacy in power is also joined an awe-inspiring accountability to the future. If you look around you, you must feel not only the sense of duty done but also you must feel anxiety lest you fall below the level of achievement. Opportunity is here now, clear and shining for both our countries. To reject it or ignore it or fritter it away will bring upon us all the long reproaches of the after-time. It is necessary that constancy of mind, persistency of purpose, and the grand simplicity of decision shall guide and rule the conduct of the English-speaking peoples in peace as they did in war. We must, and I believe we shall, prove ourselves equal to this severe requirement.

When American military men approach some serious situation they are wont to write at the head of their directive the words "over-all strategic concept." There is wisdom in this, as it leads to clarity of thought. What then is the over-all strategic concept which we should inscribe today? It is nothing less than the safety and welfare, the freedom and progress, of all the homes and families of all the men and women in all the lands. And here I speak particularly of the myriad cottage or apartment homes where the wage-earner strives amid the accidents and difficulties of life to guard his wife and children from privation and bring the family up in the fear of the Lord, or upon ethical conceptions which often play their potent part.

To give security to these countless homes, they must be shielded from the two giant marauders, war and tyranny. We all know the frightful disturbances in which the ordinary family is plunged when the curse of war swoops down upon the breadwinner and those for whom he works and contrives. The awful ruin of Europe, with all its vanished glories, and of large parts of Asia glares us in the eyes. When the designs of wicked men or the aggressive urge of mighty States dissolve over large areas the frame of civilized society, humble folk are confronted with difficulties with which they cannot cope. For them all is distorted, all is broken, even ground to pulp.

When I stand here this quiet afternoon I shudder to visualize what is actually happening to millions now and what is going to happen in this period when famine stalks the earth. None can compute what has been called "the unestimated sum of human pain." Our supreme task and duty is to guard the homes of the common people from the horrors and miseries of another war. We are all agreed on that.

Our American military colleagues, after having proclaimed their "over-all strategic concept" and computed available resources, always proceed to the next step—namely, the method. Here again there is widespread agreement. A world organization has already been erected for the prime purpose of preventing war, UNO [United Nations], the successor of the League of Nations, with the decisive addition of the United States and all that means, is already at work. We must make sure that its work is fruitful, that it is a reality and not a sham, that it is a force for action, and not merely a frothing of words, that it is a true temple of peace in which the shields of many nations can some day be hung up, and not merely a cockpit in a Tower of Babel. Before we cast away the solid assurances of national armaments for self-preservation we must be certain that our temple is built, not upon shifting sands or quagmires, but upon the rock. Anyone can see with his eyes open that our path will be difficult and also long, but if we persevere together as we did in the two world wars—though not, alas, in the interval between them—I cannot doubt that we shall achieve our common purpose in the end. . . .

It would nevertheless be wrong and imprudent to entrust the secret knowledge or experience of the atomic bomb, which the United States, Great Britain, and Canada now share, to the world organization, while it is still in its infancy. It would be criminal madness to cast it adrift in this still agitated and un-united world. No one in any country has slept less well in their beds because this knowledge and the method and the raw materials to apply it, are at present largely retained in American hands. I do not believe we should all have slept so soundly had the positions been reversed and if some Communist or neo-Fascist State monopolized for the time being these dread agencies. The fear of them alone might easily have been used to enforce totalitarian systems upon the free democratic world, with consequences appalling to human imagination. God has willed that this shall not be and we have at least a breathing space to set our house in order before this peril has to be encountered: and even then, if no effort is spared, we should still possess so formidable a superiority as to impose effective deterrents upon its employment, or threat of employment, by others. Ultimately, when the essential brotherhood of man is truly embodied and expressed in a world organization with all the necessary practical safeguards to make it effective, these powers would naturally be confided to that world organization.

Now I come to the second danger of these two marauders which threatens the cottage, the home, and the ordinary people—namely, tyranny. We cannot be blind to the fact that the liberties enjoyed by individual citizens throughout the British Empire are not valid in a considerable number of countries, some of which are very powerful. In these States control is enforced upon the common people by various kinds of all-embracing police governments. The power of the State is exercised without restraint, either by dictators or by compact oligarchies operating through a privileged party and a political police. It is not our duty at this time when difficulties are so numerous to interfere forcibly in the internal affairs of countries which we have not conquered in war. But we must never cease to proclaim in fearless tones the great principles of freedom and the rights of man which are the joint inheritance of the English-speaking world and which through Magna Carta, the Bill of Rights, the Habeas Corpus, trial by jury, and the English common law find their most famous expression in the American Declaration of Independence.

All this means that the people of any country have the right, and should have the power by constitutional action, by free unfettered elections, with secret ballot, to choose or change the character or form of government under which they dwell; that freedom of speech and thought should reign; that courts of justice, independent of the executive, unbiased by any party, should administer laws which have received the broad assent of large majorities or are consecrated by time and custom. Here are the title deeds of freedom which should lie in every cottage home. Here is the message of the British and American peoples to mankind. Let us preach what we practice—let us practice—what we preach. . . .

A shadow has fallen upon the scenes so lately lighted by the Allied victory. Nobody knows what Soviet Russia and its Communist international organization intends to do in the immediate future, or what are the limits, if any, to their expansive and proselytizing tendencies. I have a strong admiration and regard for the valiant Russian people and for my wartime comrade, Marshal Stalin. There is deep sympathy and goodwill in Britain—and I doubt not here also—towards the peoples of all the Russias and a resolve to persevere through many differences and rebuffs in establishing lasting friendships. We understand the Russian need to be secure on her western frontiers by the removal of all possibility of German aggression. We welcome Russia to her rightful place among the leading nations of the world. We welcome her flag upon the seas. Above all, we welcome constant, frequent and growing contacts between the Russian people and our own people on both sides of the Atlantic. It is my duty however, for I am sure you would wish me to state the facts as I see them to you, to place before you certain facts about the present position in Europe.

From Stettin in the Baltic to Trieste in the Adriatic, an iron curtain has descended across the Continent. Behind that line lie all the capitals of the ancient states of Central and Eastern Europe. Warsaw, Berlin, Prague, Vienna, Budapest, Belgrade, Bucharest and Sofia, all these famous cities and the populations around them lie in what I must call the Soviet sphere, and all are subject in one form or another, not only to Soviet influence but to a very high and, in many cases, increasing measure of control from Moscow. Athens alone—Greece with its immortal glories—is free to decide its future at an election under British, American and French observation. The Russian-dominated Polish Government has been encouraged to make enormous and wrongful inroads upon Germany, and mass expulsions of millions of Germans on a scale grievous and undreamed—of are now taking place. The Communist parties, which were very small in all these Eastern States of Europe, have been raised to pre-eminence and power far beyond their numbers and are seeking everywhere to obtain totalitarian control. Police governments are prevailing in nearly every case, and so far, except in Czechoslovakia, there is no true democracy. Turkey and Persia are both profoundly alarmed and disturbed at the claims which are being made upon them and at the pressure being exerted by the Moscow Government. An attempt is being made by the Russians in Berlin to build up a quasi-Communist party in their zone of Occupied Germany by showing special favors to groups of left-wing German leaders. At the end of the fighting last June, the American and British Armies withdrew westwards, in accordance with an earlier agreement, to a depth at some points of 150 miles upon a front of nearly four hundred miles, in order to allow our Russian allies to occupy this vast expanse of territory which the Western Democracies had conquered.

If now the Soviet Government tries, by separate action, to build up a pro-Communist Germany in their areas, this will cause new serious difficulties in the British and American zones, and will give the defeated Germans the power of putting themselves up to auction between the Soviets and the Western Democracies. Whatever conclusions may be drawn from these facts—and facts they are—this is certainly not the Liberated Europe we fought to build up. Nor is it one which contains the essentials of permanent peace.

The safety of the world requires a new unity in Europe, from which no nation should be permanently outcast. It is from the quarrels of the strong parent races in Europe that the world wars we have witnessed, or which occurred in former times, have sprung. Twice in our own lifetime we have seen the United States, against their wishes and their traditions, against arguments, the force of which it is impossible not to comprehend, drawn by irresistible forces, into these wars in time to secure the victory of the good cause, but only after frightful slaughter and devastation had occurred. Twice the United States has had to send several millions of its young men across the Atlantic to find the war; but now war can find any nation, wherever it may dwell between dusk and dawn. Surely we should work with conscious purpose for a grand pacification of Europe, within the structure of the United Nations and in accordance with its Charter. That I feel is an open cause of policy of very great importance.

In front of the iron curtain which lies across Europe are other causes for anxiety. In Italy the Communist Party is seriously hampered by having to support the Communist-trained Marshal Tito's claims to former Italian territory at the head of the Adriatic. Nevertheless the future of Italy hangs in the balance. Again one cannot imagine a regenerated Europe without a strong France. All my public life I have worked for a strong France and I never lost faith in her destiny, even in the darkest hours. I will not lose faith now. However, in a great number of countries, far from the Russian frontiers and throughout the world, Communist fifth columns are established and work in complete unity and absolute obedience to the directions they receive from the Communist center. Except in the British Commonwealth and in the United States where Communism is in its infancy, the Communist parties or fifth columns constitute a growing challenge and peril to Christian civilization. These are somber facts for anyone to have to recite on the morrow of a victory gained by so much splendid comradeship in arms and in the cause of freedom and democracy; but we should be most unwise not to face them squarely while time remains. . . .

On the other hand I repulse the idea that a new war is inevitable; still more that it is imminent. It is because I am sure that our fortunes are still in our own hands and that we hold the power to save the future, that I feel the duty to speak out now that I have the occasion and the opportunity to do so. I do not believe that Soviet Russia desires war. What they desire is the fruits of war and the indefinite expansion of their power and doctrines. But what we have to consider here to-day while time remains, is the permanent prevention of war and the establishment of conditions of freedom and democracy as rapidly as possible in all countries. Our difficulties and dangers will not be removed by closing our eyes to them. They will not be removed by mere waiting to see what happens; nor will they be removed by a policy of appeasement. What is needed is a settlement, and the longer this is delayed, the more difficult it will be and the greater our dangers will become.

From what I have seen of our Russian friends and Allies during the war, I am convinced that there is nothing they admire so much as strength, and there is nothing for which they have less respect than for weakness, especially military weakness. For that reason the old doctrine of a balance of power is unsound. We cannot afford, if we can help it, to work on narrow margins, offering temptations to a trial of strength. If the Western Democracies stand together in strict adherence to the principles of the United Nations Charter, their influence for furthering those principles will be immense and no one is likely to molest them. If however they become divided or falter in their duty and if these all-important years are allowed to slip away then indeed the catastrophe may overwhelm us all.

Last time I saw it all coming and cried aloud to my own fellow-countrymen and to the world, but no one paid any attention. Up till the year 1933 or even 1935, Germany might have been saved from the awful fate which has overtaken her and we might all have been spared the miseries Hitler let loose upon mankind. There never was a war in all history easier to prevent by timely action than the one which has just desolated such great areas of the globe. It could have been prevented in my belief without the firing of a single shot, and Germany might be powerful, prosperous and honored to-day; but no one would listen and one by one we were all sucked into the awful whirlpool. We surely must not let that happen again. This can only be achieved by reaching now, in 1946, a good understanding on all points with Russia under the general authority of the United Nations Organization and by the maintenance of that good understanding through many peaceful years, by the world instrument, supported by the whole strength of the English-speaking world and all its connections. There is the solution which I respectfully offer to you in this Address to which I have given the title "The Sinews of Peace.". . .

II. JOSEPH STALIN'S REPLY

. . . In substance, Mr. Churchill now stands in the position of a firebrand of war. And Mr. Churchill is not alone here. He has friends not only in England but also in the United States of America.

In this respect, one is reminded remarkably of Hitler and his friends. Hitler began to set war loose by announcing his racial theory, declaring that only people speaking the German language represent a fully valuable nation. Mr. Churchill begins to set war loose, also by a racial theory, maintaining that only nations speaking the English language are fully valuable nations, called upon to decide the destinies of the entire world.

The German racial theory brought Hitler and his friends to the conclusion that the Germans, as the only fully valuable nation, must rule over other nations. The English racial theory brings Mr. Churchill and his friends to the conclusion that nations speaking the English language, being the only fully valuable nations, should rule over the remaining nations of the world. . . .

As a result of the German invasion, the Soviet Union has irrevocably lost in battles with the Germans, and also during the German occupation and through the expulsion of Soviet citizens to German slave labor camps, about 7,000,000 people. In other words, the Soviet Union has lost in men several times more than Britain and the United States together.

It may be that some quarters are trying to push into oblivion these sacrifices of the Soviet people which insured the liberation of Europe from the Hitlerite yoke.

But the Soviet Union cannot forget them. One can ask therefore, what can be surprising in the fact that the Soviet Union, in a desire to ensure its security for the future, tries to achieve that these countries should have governments whose relations to Soviet Union are loyal? How can one, without having lost one's reason, qualify these peaceful aspirations of the Soviet Union as "expansionist tendencies" of our Government? . . .

Mr. Churchill wanders around the truth when he speaks of the growth of the influence of the Communist parties in Eastern Europe. . . . The growth of the influence of communism cannot be considered accidental. It is a normal function. The influence of the Communists grew because during the hard years of the mastery of fascism in Europe, Communists showed themselves to be reliable, daring and self-sacrificing fighters against fascist regimes for the liberty of peoples.

Mr. Churchill sometimes recalls in his speeches the common people from small houses, patting them on the shoulder in a lordly manner and pretending to be their friend. But these people are not so simpleminded as it might appear at first sight. Common people, too, have their opinions and their own politics. And they know how to stand up for themselves.

It is they, millions of these common people, who voted Mr. Churchill and his party out in England, giving their votes to the Labor party. It is they, millions of these common people, who isolated reactionaries in Europe, collaborators with fascism, and gave preference to Left democratic parties. . . .

III. NIKITA KHRUSHCHEV: SUMMIT CONFERENCE STATEMENT, PARIS, MAY 16, 1960

As is generally known, a provocative act by the American air force against the Soviet Union has recently taken place. It consisted in the fact that on May 1 of this year a U.S. military reconnaissance plane intruded into the U.S.S.R. on a definite espionage mission of gathering intelligence about military and industrial installations on Soviet territory. After the aggressive purpose of the plane's flight became clear, it was shot down by a Soviet rocket unit. Unfortunately, this is not the only instance of aggressive and espionage actions by the U.S. air force against the Soviet Union.

Naturally, the Soviet government was obliged to describe these actions by their proper name and show their perfidious character, inconsistent with the elementary requirements of normal peacetime relations between states, to say nothing of their conflicting grossly with the aim of reducing international tension and creating the conditions needed for fruitful work at the Summit conference. This was done both in my speeches at the session of the U.S.S.R. Supreme Soviet and in a special protest note sent to the U.S. government. . . .

It is natural that under these conditions we are unable to work at the conference, unable to work at it because we see from what positions it is desired to talk to us—under threat of aggressive intelligence flights. Everyone knows that spying flights are undertaken for intelligence purposes with a view to starting war. Accordingly, we reject the conditions in which the United States is placing us. We cannot take part in any negotiations, not even in the settlement of questions which are already ripe, because we see that the U.S. has no desire to reach agreement. . . .

We wish to be rightly understood by the peoples of all countries of the globe, by public opinion. The Soviet Union is not abandoning its efforts for agreement, and we are sure that reasonable agreements are possible, but evidently at some other, not this particular time. . . .

The Soviet government is profoundly convinced that if not this U.S. government, then another, and if not another, then a third, will understand that there is no other solution than peaceful co-existence of the two systems, the capitalist and the socialist. It is either peaceful co-existence, or war, which would spell disaster for those now engaging in an aggressive policy. . . .

[W]e firmly believe in the necessity of peaceful co-existence, for to lose faith in peaceful co-existence would mean dooming humanity to war, it would mean accepting that war *IS* inevitable—and everyone knows what calamities war today would spell for all the peoples of the globe. . . .

We regret that this Meeting has been torpedoed by the reactionary element in the United States as the outcome of provocative flights by American military planes over the Soviet Union.

We regret that this meeting has not led to the results which all the peoples of the world expected to follow from it.

Let the shame and blame for it fall on those who have proclaimed a brigand policy in relation to the Soviet Union. . . .

I think that both Mr. Eisenhower and the American people will understand me rightly.

The Soviet government declares that it for its part will continue to do everything in its power to promote the relaxation of international tension and the solution of the problems which today still divide us; in this we shall be guided by the interests of furthering the great cause of peace on the basis of the peaceful co-existence of states with differing social systems.

IV. DWIGHT EISENHOWER: SUMMIT CONFERENCE STATEMENT, PARIS, MAY 16, 1960

In my statement of May 11th and in the statement of Secretary Herter of May 9th the position of the United States was made clear with respect to the distasteful necessity of espionage activities in a world where nations distrust each other's intentions. We pointed out that these activities had no aggressive intent but rather were to assure the safety of the United States and the free world against surprise attack by a power which boasts of its ability to devastate the United States and other countries by missiles armed with atomic warheads. . . .

There is in the Soviet statement an evident misapprehension on one key point. It alleges that the United States has, through official statements, threatened continued overflights. The importance of this alleged threat was emphasized and repeated by Mr. Khrushchev. The United States has made no such threat. Neither I nor my Government has intended any. The actual statements go no further than to say that the United States will not shirk its responsibility to safeguard against surprise attack.

In point of fact, these flights were suspended after the recent incident and are not to be resumed. Accordingly, this cannot be the issue.

I have come to Paris to seek agreements with the Soviet Union which would eliminate the necessity for all forms of espionage, including overflights. I see no reason to use this incident to disrupt the conference.

Should it prove impossible, because of the Soviet attitude, to come to grips here in Paris with this problem and the other vital issues threatening world peace, I am planning in the near future to submit to the United Nations a proposal for the creation of a United Nations aerial surveillance to detect preparations for attack. This plan I had intended to place before this conference. This surveillance system would operate in the territories of all nations prepared to accept such inspection. For its part, the United States is prepared not only to accept United Nations aerial surveillance but to do everything in its power to contribute to the rapid organization and successful operation of such international surveillance.

We of the United States are here to consider in good faith the important problems before this conference. We are prepared either to carry this point no further or to undertake bilateral conversations between the United States and the U.S.S.R. while the main conference proceeds.

Mr. Khrushchev brushed aside all arguments of reason and not only insisted upon this ultimatum but also insisted that he was going to publish his statement in full at the time of his own choosing. It was thus made apparent that he was determined to wreck the Paris conference. . . .

In spite of this serious and adverse development I have no intention whatsoever to diminish my continuing efforts to promote progress toward a peace with Justice. This applies to the remainder of my stay in Paris as well as thereafter.

STUDY QUESTIONS

1. How does Churchill define the Iron Curtain and the Soviet threat? What does he propose to resist this threat?
2. How did Stalin defend Soviet actions? How would he have explained the growing tension with the West?
3. Judging by the Churchill and Stalin speeches, who was responsible for the Cold War? Was one side more involved than the other?
4. What prompted the 1960 crisis? How did both American and Russian leaders avoid outright war?
5. How did Krushchev's rhetoric compare with that of Stalin? Eisenhower's with that of Churchill? What were the major Cold War issues by this point?

61

International Terrorism

The final decades of the twentieth century were filled by periodic encounters with terrorism. These spilled over, massively, to the twenty-first century when on September 11, 2001, 19 terrorists commandeered four commercial airplanes in the United States and flew three of them into landmark buildings, the World Trade Center in New York, and the Pentagon near Washington, D.C.

Terrorism is not easy to define or explain. It often involves discriminate use of violence by groups who believe their cause is just but who face opposition from a superior force. The violence often targets civilians, who are seen as legitimate victims as part of a larger effort to challenge and disrupt a society seen as oppressive. Terrorist methods often depend on relatively modern technologies such as car bombs or hijacking airplanes.

A large number of modern protest movements have used terrorism. A radical wing of the labor movement used methods that could be called terrorist early in the twentieth century. Various small nationalist groups, such as those associated with the struggle over Northern Ireland, used terrorism. Extreme Catholic nationalists used terrorism against England, while Protestant nationalists did much the same against Catholic neighborhoods. European student movements in the 1970s spawned extremist groups that employed terrorism against the established order.

The most widespread terrorism of the late twentieth century emanated from extremist Muslim groups, protesting Western activities in the Middle East and Israeli treatment of Palestinians in and around Israel. Pro-Western or simply repressive Middle Eastern governments were also targets. Attacks within Israel, killings of Western tourists, and acts of violence in Europe, Russia, and the United States made this wave of terrorism a truly international threat. Terrorist groups were typically small and loosely organized. Specific grievances varied widely. But there were some common elements. Use of a radical version of Islam was one, and many terrorists believed they were engaged in a holy war. A revulsion against Westernized international styles, including consumerism and new freedom for women, was another. While many individual terrorists came from educated backgrounds, they drew on the widespread poverty and sense of powerlessness of masses of people in and around the Middle East.

The methods terrorists used were scary and widely condemned. But many analysts urged that terrorist motives deserved attention nevertheless, as they reflected real griev-

Selection I from http://www.fas.org/irp/world/para/docus/980223-fatwa.htm. Selection II from http://politics.guardian.co.uk/labour2001/story/O.1414.562006.OO.html

ances about the power alignments in the Islamic world. It was not clear how terrorism could be dealt with, and some understanding of underlying issues might be crucial in that connection as well. Certainly, international terrorism is one of the leading issues on a global agenda early in the twenty-first century.

The two passages that follow offer starkly different views of radical terrorism. The first is a 1998 decree, or fatwa, issued by Osama bin Laden, widely regarded as the most significant terrorist leader by that date. Osama bin Laden was a member of a wealthy Saudi Arabian family, who had broken with his background to lead radical Muslim resistance. By 1998 he was based in Afghanistan, where a new regime, the Taliban, gave him shelter and support while pursuing an extremely intolerant version of Islam. The whole context built upon the disruption of Afghanistan by the failed Soviet invasion of the 1980s, by the ongoing attacks on Iraq and military presence in the Arabian Peninsula by the United States and Britain after the 1991 Gulf War, and by the longstanding tension between Israel and the Palestinians. The 1998 fatwa, a terrorist declaration of war, explains some of the thinking behind this new, unorthodox, and frightening military movement. The fatwa was widely publicized on the Internet, a tool that bin Laden's organization used adeptly, and clearly struck a chord among a minority of Muslims, particularly in the Middle East.

The second passage comes from an October 2, 2001, speech to the Labor Party Congress by Tony Blair, the British Prime Minister. In the wake of the September 11 terrorist attacks on New York and Washington, widely attributed to bin Laden's organization, Blair emerged as the West's most articulate spokesperson. [Note that casualty estimates at this point were higher than what turned out to be the case.] Blair explains a widespread reaction to mounting terror, and what might be done against it. As he anticipated, Britain and the United States launched a vigorous attack on terrorist activities in Afghanistan in early October. The war was initially backed by many nations around the world, including, though with a number of cautions, moderate Muslim leaders and most Muslim Americans.

The clash between terrorism and the West is an ongoing chapter in contemporary world history. What was the likely outcome? How much would understanding both sides help in containing this new threat to world peace? What did terrorism and Western response have to do with broader processes of globalization?

BIN-LADEN AND BLAIR

I. PRO-TERRORISM

Jihad Against Jews and Crusaders
World Islamic Front Statement

23 February 1998

Shaykh Usamah Bin-Muhammad Bin-Ladin
Ayman al-Zawahiri, amir of the Jihad Group in Egypt
Abu-Yasir Rifái Ahmad Taha, Egyptian Islamic Group
Shaykh Mir Hamzah, secretary of the Jamiat-ul-Ulema-e-Pakistan
Fazlur Rahman, amir of the Jihad Movement in Bangladesh

Praise be to God, who revealed the Book, controls the clouds, defeats faction-alism, and says in His Book: "But when the forbidden months are past, then fight and slay the pagans wherever ye find them, seize them, beleaguer them, and lie in wait for them in every stratagem (of war)"; and peace be upon our Prophet, Muhammad Bin-Ábdallah, who said: I have been sent with the sword between my hands to ensure that no one but God is worshipped, God who put my livelihood un-der the shadow of my spear and who inflicts humiliation and scorn on those who disobey my orders.

The Arabian Peninsula has never—since God made it flat, created its desert, and encircled it with seas—been stormed by any forces like the crusader armies spreading in it like locusts, eating its riches and wiping out its plantations. All this is happening at a time in which nations are attacking Muslims like people fighting over a plate of food. In the light of the grave situation and the lack of support, we and you are obliged to discuss current events, and we should all agree on how to settle the matter.

No one argues today about three facts that are known to everyone; we will list them, in order to remind everyone:

First, for over seven years the United States has been occupying the lands of Islam in the holiest of places, the Arabian Peninsula, plundering its riches, dictat-ing to its rulers, humiliating its people, terrorizing its neighbors, and turning its bases in the Peninsula into a spearhead through which to fight the neighboring Muslim peoples.

If some people have in the past argued about the fact of the occupation, all the people of the Peninsula have now acknowledged it. The best proof of this is the Americans' continuing aggression against the Iraqi people using the Peninsula as a staging post, even though all its rulers are against their territories being used to that end, but they are helpless.

Second, despite the great devastation inflicted on the Iraqi people by the crusader-Zionist alliance, and despite the huge number of those killed, which has exceeded 1 million . . . despite all this, the Americans are once again trying to re-peat the horrific massacres, as though they are not content with the protracted blockade imposed after the ferocious war or the fragmentation and devastation.

So here they come to annihilate what is left of this people and to humiliate their Muslim neighbors.

Third, if the Americans' aims behind these wars are religious and economic, the aim is also to serve the Jews' petty state and divert attention from its occupation of Jerusalem and the murder of Muslims there. The best proof of this is their ea-gerness to destroy Iraq, the strongest neighboring Arab state, and their endeavor to fragment all the states of the region such as Iraq, Saudi Arabia, Egypt, and Sudan into paper statelets and through their disunion and weakness to guarantee Israel's survival and the continuation of the brutal crusade occupation of the Peninsula.

All these crimes and sins committed by the Americans are a clear declaration of war on God, his messenger, and Muslims. And ulema have throughout Islamic history unanimously agreed that the jihad is an individual duty if the enemy de-stroys the Muslim countries. This was revealed by Imam Bin-Qadamah in "Al-Mughni," Imam al-Kisái in "Al-Badái," al-Qurtubi in his interpretation, and the shaykh of al-Islam in his books, where he said: "As for the fighting to repulse [an enemy], it is aimed at defending sanctity and religion, and it is a duty as agreed [by the ulema]. Nothing is more sacred than belief except repulsing an enemy who is attacking religion and life."

On that basis, and in compliance with God's order, we issue the following fatwa to all Muslims:

The ruling to kill the Americans and their allies—civilians and military—is an individual duty for every Muslim who can do it in any country in which it is possible to do it, in order to liberate the al-Aqsa Mosque and the holy mosque [Mecca] from their grip, and in order for their armies to move out of all the lands of Islam, defeated and unable to threaten any Muslim. This is in accordance with the words of Almighty God, "and fight the pagans all together as they fight you all together," and "fight them until there is no more tumult or oppression, and there prevail justice and faith in God."

This is in addition to the words of Almighty God: "And why should ye not fight in the cause of God and of those who, being weak, are ill-treated (and oppressed)?— women and children, whose cry is: 'Our Lord, rescue us from this town, whose people are oppressors; and raise for us from thee one who will help!'"

We—with God's help—call on every Muslim who believes in God and wishes to be rewarded to comply with God's order to kill the Americans and plunder their money wherever and whenever they find it. We also call on Muslim ulema [religious leaders], leaders, youths, and soldiers to launch the raid on Satan's U.S. troops and the devil's supporters allying with them, and to displace those who are behind them so that they may learn a lesson.

Almighty God said: "O ye who believe, give your response to God and His Apostle, when He calleth you to that which will give you life. And know that God cometh between a man and his heart, and that it is He to whom ye shall all be gathered."

Almighty God also says: "O ye who believe, what is the matter with you, that when ye are asked to go forth in the cause of God, ye cling so heavily to the earth! Do ye prefer the life of this world to the hereafter? But little is the comfort of this life, as compared with the hereafter. Unless ye go forth, He will punish you with a grievous penalty, and put others in your place; but Him ye would not harm in the least. For God hath power over all things."

Almighty God also says: "So lose no heart, nor fall into despair. For ye must gain mastery if ye are true in faith."

II. ANTI-TERRORISM

In retrospect, the Millennium marked only a moment in time. It was the events of September 11 that marked a turning point in history, where we confront the dangers of the future and assess the choices facing humankind.

It was a tragedy. An act of evil . . .

• • •

There is no justification for their [survivors of the victims] pain. Their son did nothing wrong. The woman, seven months pregnant, whose child will never know its father, did nothing wrong.

They don't want revenge. They want something better in memory of their loved ones.

I believe their memorial can and should be greater than simply the punishment of the guilty. It is that out of the shadow of this evil, should emerge lasting good: destruction of the machinery of terrorism wherever it is found; hope amongst all nations of a new beginning where we seek to resolve differences in a calm and ordered way; greater understanding between nations and between faiths; and above all justice and prosperity for the poor and dispossessed, so that people everywhere can see the chance of a better future through the hard work and creative power of the free citizen, not the violence and savagery of the fanatic.

I know that here in Britain people are anxious, even a little frightened. I understand that. People know we must act but they worry what might follow.

· · ·

And, of course there are dangers; it is a new situation.

· · ·

Every reasonable measure of internal security is being undertaken.

Our way of life is a great deal stronger and will last a great deal longer than the actions of fanatics, small in number and now facing a unified world against them.

People should have confidence.

This is a battle with only one outcome: our victory not theirs.

What happened on 11 September was without parallel in the bloody history of terrorism.

Within a few hours, up to 7000 people were annihilated, the commercial centre of New York was reduced to rubble and in Washington and Pennsylvania further death and horror on an unimaginable scale. Let no one say this was a blow for Islam when the blood of innocent Muslims was shed along with those of the Christian, Jewish, and other faiths around the world.

We know those responsible. In Afghanistan are scores of training camps for the export of terror. Chief amongst the sponsors and organisers is Usama Bin Laden.

He is supported, shielded and given succour by the Taliban regime.

Be in no doubt: Bin Laden and his people organised this atrocity. The Taliban aid and abet him. He will not desist from further acts of terror. They will not stop helping him.

Whatever the dangers of the action we take, the dangers of inaction are far, far greater.

Look for a moment at the Taliban regime. It is undemocratic. That goes without saying.

There is no sport allowed, or television or photography. No art or culture is permitted. All other faiths, all other interpretations of Islam are ruthlessly suppressed. Those who practice their faith are imprisoned. Women are treated in a way almost too revolting to be credible. First driven out of university; girls not allowed to go to school; no legal rights; unable to go out of doors without a man. Those that disobey are stoned.

There is now no contact permitted with western agencies, even those delivering food. The people live in abject poverty. It is a regime founded on fear and funded on the drugs trade. The biggest drugs hoard in the world is in Afghanistan, controlled by the Taliban. Ninety per cent of the heroin on British streets originates in Afghanistan.

The arms the Taliban are buying today are paid for with the lives of young British people buying their drugs on British streets.

. . .

So what do we do?

Don't overreact some say. We aren't.

We haven't lashed out. No missiles on the first night just for effect.

Don't kill innocent people. We are not the ones who waged war on the innocent. We seek the guilty.

Look for a diplomatic solution. There is no diplomacy with Bin Laden or the Taliban regime.

State an ultimatum and get their response. We stated the ultimatum; they haven't responded.

Understand the causes of terror. Yes, we should try, but let there be no moral ambiguity about this: nothing could ever justify the events of 11 September, and it is to turn justice on its head to pretend it could.

The action we take will be proportionate; targeted; we will do all we humanly can to avoid civilian casualties. But understand what we are dealing with. Listen to the calls of those passengers on the planes. Think of the children on them, told they were going to die.

Think of the cruelty beyond our comprehension as amongst the screams and the anguish of the innocent, those hijackers drove at full throttle planes laden with fuel into buildings where tens of thousands worked.

They have no moral inhibition on the slaughter of the innocent. If they could have murdered not 7,000 but 70,000 does anyone doubt they would have done so and rejoiced in it?

There is no compromise possible with such people, no meeting of minds, no point of understanding with such terror.

Just a choice: defeat it or be defeated by it. And defeat it we must.

Any action taken will be against the terrorist network of Bin Laden.

As for the Taliban, they can surrender the terrorists; or face the consequences and again in any action the aim will be to eliminate their military hardware, cut off their finances, disrupt their supplies, target their troops, not civilians. We will put a trap around the regime.

I say to the Taliban: surrender the terrorists; or surrender power. It's your choice. . . .

For the first time, the UN security council has imposed mandatory obligations on all UN members to cut off terrorist financing and end safe havens for terrorists.

Those that finance terror, those who launder their money, those that cover their tracks are every bit as guilty as the fanatic who commits the final act.

Round the world, 11 September is bringing Governments and people to reflect, consider and change. And in this process, amidst all the talk of war and action, there is another dimension appearing.

There is a coming together. The power of community is asserting itself. We are realising how fragile are our frontiers in the face of the world's new challenges.

When we act to bring to account those that committed the atrocity of September 11, we do so, not out of bloodlust.

We do so because it is just. We do not act against Islam. The true followers of Islam are our brothers and sisters in this struggle. Bin Laden is no more obedient to the proper teaching of the Koran than those Crusaders of the 12th century who pillaged and murdered, represented the teaching of the Gospel.

It is time the west confronted its ignorance of Islam. Jews, Muslims and Christians are all children of Abraham.

This is the moment to bring the faiths closer together in understanding of our common values and heritage, a source of unity and strength.

It is time also for parts of Islam to confront prejudice against America and not only Islam but parts of western societies too.

· · ·

So I believe this is a fight for freedom. And I want to make it a fight for justice too. Justice not only to punish the guilty. But justice to bring those same values of democracy and freedom to people round the world.

STUDY QUESTIONS

1. What was bin Laden's interpretation of Islam? How did it relate to basic Islamic principles?
2. How can international terrorism best be defined?
3. What results did bin Laden expect from terrorist methods? Why did he single out the United States?
4. How do bin Laden's views relate to the twentieth-century history of the Middle East? How do they relate to the wider processes of globalization?
5. How did Tony Blair define the West's position against terrorism?
6. What were Blair's views of Islam?
7. Can you think of reasonable alternatives to Blair's approach, in the wake of a truly unprecedented act of terrorist violence?
8. Was 2001 a turning point in world history, as Blair claimed? How does one assess claims like this concerning very recent developments?